Developing and Applying Biologically-Inspired Vision Systems:

Interdisciplinary Concepts

Marc Pomplun
University of Massachusetts Boston, USA

Junichi Suzuki
University of Massachusetts Boston, USA

Managing Director:	Lindsay Johnston
Editorial Director:	Joel Gamon
Book Production Manager:	Jennifer Romanchak
Publishing Systems Analyst:	Adrienne Freeland
Development Editor:	Austin DeMarco
Assistant Acquisitions Editor:	Kayla Wolfe
Typesetter:	Henry Ulrich
Cover Design:	Nick Newcomer

Published in the United States of America by
Information Science Reference (an imprint of IGI Global)
701 E. Chocolate Avenue
Hershey PA 17033
Tel: 717-533-8845
Fax: 717-533-8661
E-mail: cust@igi-global.com
Web site: http://www.igi-global.com

Library of Congress Cataloging-in-Publication Data

Developing and applying biologically-inspired vision systems: interdisciplinary concepts / Marc Pomplun and Junichi Suzuki, editors.
pages cm
Includes bibliographical references and index.
Summary: "This book provides interdisciplinary research that evaluates the performance of machine visual models and systems in comparison to biological systems, blending the ideas of current scientific knowledge and biological vision"--Provided by publisher.
ISBN 978-1-4666-2539-6 (hardcover) -- ISBN 978-1-4666-2541-9 (print & perpetual access) -- ISBN 978-1-4666-2540-2 (ebook) 1. Computer vision. 2. Bionics. I. Pomplun, Marc, 1969- II. Suzuki, Junichi, 1974-
TA1634.D48 2013
006.3'7--dc23

2012031910

British Cataloguing in Publication Data
A Cataloguing in Publication record for this book is available from the British Library.

Editorial Advisory Board

List of Reviewers

Table of Contents

Section 2
Binocular Vision

Section 3
Visual Cortical Structures

Detailed Table of Contents

Section 1
Visual Attention

Various computational models of visual attention rely on the extraction of salient points or proto-objects, i.e., discrete units of attention, computed from bottom-up image features. In recent years, different solutions integrating top-down mechanisms were implemented, as research has shown that although eye movements initially are solely influenced by bottom-up information, after some time goal driven (high-level) processes dominate the guidance of visual attention towards regions of interest (Hwang, Higgins & Pomplun, 2009). However, even these improved modeling approaches are unlikely to generalize to a broader range of application contexts, because basic principles of visual attention, such as cognitive control, learning and expertise, have thus far not sufficiently been taken into account (Tatler, Hayhoe, Land & Ballard, 2011). In some recent work, we showed the functional role and representational nature of long-term memory structures for human perceptual skills and motor control. Based on these findings, we extended a widely applied saliency-based model of visual attention (Walther & Koch, 2006) in two ways: first, we computed the saliency map using the cognitive visual attention approach (CVA) that shows a correspondence between regions of high saliency values and regions of visual interest indicated by participants' eye movements (Oyekoya & Stentiford, 2004). Second, we added an expertise-based component (Schack, 2012) to represent the influence of the quality of mental representation structures in long-term memory (LTM) and the roles of learning on the visual perception of objects, events and motor actions.

Alterations in gazing patterns and visual attention have often been noted among patients with intellectual and developmental disabilities (IDD) relative to neurotypical individuals. Here we discuss visual attention with a particular focus on attention overselectivity. Overselectivity is observed when a subject focuses on a limited subset of available stimuli, or attends to a limited spatial field of vision. It is a widely-observed problem among individuals with IDD, notably, children with autism spectrum disorders (ASD). In this chapter we survey computational and experimental approaches to analyze selective visual attention patterns, including overselectivity. These may provide useful computational frameworks for modeling visual attention in ASD patients and quantifying how it differs from neurotypical patterns. Computer-automated routines would be a boon for the field, distilling key dependent measures for aberrant attentional processes (a) for group studies of pathological processes and (b) on a single-subject basis for clinical description and possible remediation of attentional deficits.

Most biologically-inspired models of object recognition rely on a feed-forward architecture in which abstract representations are gradually built from simple representations, but recognition performance in such systems drops when multiple objects are present in the input. This paper puts forward the proposal that by using multiple passes of the visual processing hierarchy, both bottom-up and top-down, we can address the limitations of feed-forward architectures and explain the different recognition behaviors that primate vision exhibits. The model relies on the reentrant connections that are ubiquitous in the primate brain to recover spatial information, and thus allow for the selective processing of stimuli. The paper ends with a discussion of the implications of this work, its explanatory power and a number of predictions for future experimental work.

The stereo correspondence problem is a topic that has been the subject of considerable research effort. What has not yet been considered is an analogue of stereo correspondence in the domain of attention. In this chapter we bring this problem to light revealing important implications for computational models of attention and in particular how these implications constrain the problem of computational modeling of attention. A model is described which addresses attention in the stereo domain, and it is revealed that a variety of behaviors observed in binocular rivalry experiments are consistent with the model's behavior. Finally, we consider how constraints imposed by stereo vision may suggest analogous constraints in other non-stereo feature domains with significant consequence to computational models of attention.

Section 2
Binocular Vision

We discuss local constraints for the perception of three-dimensional (3D) binocular motion in a geometric-probabilistic framework. It is shown that Bayesian models of binocular 3D motion can explain perceptual bias under uncertainty and predict perceived velocity under ambiguity. The models exploit biologically plausible constraints of local motion and disparity processing in a binocular viewing geometry. Results from computer simulations and psychophysical experiments support the idea that local constraints of motion and disparity processing are combined late in the visual processing hierarchy to establish perceived 3D motion direction.

Binocular transparency is perceived if two surfaces are seen in the same spatial location, but at different depths. Similarly, motion transparency occurs if two surfaces move differently over the same spatial location. Most models of motion or stereo processing incorporate uniqueness assumptions to resolve ambiguities of disparity or motion estimates and, thus, can not represent multiple features at the same spatial location. Unlike these previous models, we suggest a model with local center-surround interaction that operates upon analogs of cell populations in velocity or disparity domain of the ventral second visual area (V2) and dorsal medial middle temporal area (MT) in primates, respectively. These modeled cell populations can encode motion and binocular transparency. Model simulations demonstrate the successful processing of scenes with opaque and transparent materials, not previously reported. Our results suggest that motion and stereo processing both employ local center-surround interactions to resolve noisy and ambiguous disparity or motion input from initial correlations.

recognition of the aperture's form, were localized along the ventral pathway. After the bars moved, the ECDs were localized along the dorsal pathway, presumably in response to motion of the bars. In addition, for the perception of grouped motion and not normal motion, ECDs were localized to the middle frontal gyrus and the inferior frontal gyrus.

Even though there are distinct areas for different functionalities in the mammalian neo-cortex, it seems to use the same algorithm to understand a large variety of input modalities. In addition, it appears that the neo-cortex effortlessly identifies the correlation among many sensor modalities and fuses information obtained from them. The question then is, can we discover the brain's learning algorithm and approximate it for problems such as computer vision and automatic speech recognition that the mammalian brain is so good at? The answer is: it is an orders of magnitude problem, i.e., not a simple task. However, we can attempt to develop mathematical foundations based on the understanding of how a human brain learns. This chapter is focused along that direction. In particular, it is focused on the ventral stream – the "what pathway" - and describes common algorithms that can be used for representation and classification of signals from different sensor modalities such as auditory and visual. These common algorithms are based on dictionary learning with a beta process, hierarchical graphical models and embedded hidden Markov models. In this chapter, we also provide the results of applicability of dictionary learning in processing images by filling in the missing pixels and enhancing noisy images. Some example applications of hierarchical graphical models are also provided. Moreover, we demonstrate that the same learning algorithm can be used in representing both visual and audio signals. This indicates that it is possible to approximate how the neo-cortex processes multi-sensory data. The results provided in this chapter are promising and the described algorithms may constitute a step in the right direction for approximating the brain's learning, understanding and inferring algorithms.

Section 4
Artificial Vision Systems

For long time, it was thought that the sensing of polarization by animals is invariably related to their behavior, such as navigation and orientation. Recently, it was found that polarization can be part of a high-level visual perception, permitting a wide area of vision applications. Polarization vision can be used for most tasks of color vision including object recognition, contrast enhancement, camouflage breaking, and signal detection and discrimination. The polarization based visual behavior found in the animal kingdom will be briefly covered. Then, we will go in depth with the bio-inspired applications based on polarization in computer vision and robotics. The aim is to have a comprehensive survey highlighting the key principles of polarization based techniques and how they are biologically inspired.

Foreword

This volume, "Developing and Applying Biologically-Inspired Vision Systems: Interdisciplinary Concepts," highlights many significant contributions to vision systems research that take an interdisciplinary approach, effectively using our knowledge of biological visual processing to build better computer vision systems. As such it represents one more important milestone on a path that was started quite some time ago. In 1962 Harry Blum wrote a report titled "An Associative Machine for Dealing with the Visual Field and Some of its Biological Implications." The title reveals that he was not only inspired by, but also attempted to have impact on, biological vision. Blum also received inspiration from the Gestalt psychologists in developing algorithms for extracting shape descriptors (1967) and even tried to map his algorithm onto the results of Hubel and Wiesel's (1962) study of visual cortical neurons. Reading what is widely acknowledged as the first PhD thesis in computer vision by Larry Roberts (1963), one sees a strong influence from J.J. Gibson, and to a lesser extent Attneave. As Roberts writes, the requirement that perceived shapes be invariant to perspective projection was derived from Gibson's work. Azriel Rosenfeld and John Pflatz (1966) certainly cared about computational operations on images that had perceptual relevance in defining algorithms for computing connected components and distance functions in digital images. The character of human vision played a huge role in the very important "General Purpose Models: Expectations about the Unexpected" paper by Steven Zucker, Azriel Rosenfeld, and Larry Davis (1975). There, they urged a broader view of the problem of computer vision using the generality of human vision as the guide. It was this paper, as I recall, that played a major role in my own formative years. Rosenfeld went on to found and organize a highly influential series of workshops on how human vision might inspire machine vision and Zucker continues to this day to inform his work on shape and curvature interpretation by the neurobiology of the early visual cortex and provide both effective new algorithms for computer vision as well as predictions for new human experimental work. Since those very early days of computer vision, several others have also carried the baton arguing for why the characteristics of biological vision must play a deeper role in the development of computational algorithms (David Marr, Olivier Faugeras, Jan Kooenderink, Dana Ballard, Jan-Olof Eklundh come to mind prominently, among others). If one carefully looks at the development of computer vision from those early years to the present, it is easy to see specific examples of how our knowledge of how to build effective computer vision systems has increased as a result.

It is important to note that this enterprise is not an easy one. It is not the case that we fully understand biological vision, and our task is to only determine how to best use that knowledge to further computer vision. Our knowledge of visual processes in the brain is evolving, quite extensive for some aspects (such as early processing) but quite inadequate for others (such as general object or event recognition, or attentional control). Many have even abandoned this connection saying that our understanding is too meager to enable its effective use. This point of view was common perhaps 20 years ago or so, and likely justifiably so. However, I would argue that the explosion of research on human and non-human primate visual systems in the past 20-30 years has been quite successful at filling in gaps and creating a body of knowledge that is far more appealing to computational researchers. As a result, one sees in recent years more and more papers in mainstream computer vision conferences and journals that reveal biological inspiration.

Consider only one example. Blum was influenced by the Gestalt studies of shape. He points out that the Gestaltists (citing Koffka, Deustch, Kazmierczak, and others) used field theoretic concepts and proposed diffusion/propagation models. These ideas motivated Blum, but he found them unsatisfactory as presented due to their lack of precision and detail. This is a characteristic of functional conceptualization that persists even in the best of current work. This is not a criticism; rather, it is a justification for interdisciplinary efforts where each discipline works on the areas of their expertise. Blum thus took those ideas and developed the now well-known Medial Axis Transform (MAT or 'grass fire' algorithm). This path, in its general sense, is the one followed by the authors represented in this book. One of the papers, by Rodriguez-Sanchez and myself (chosen only because I know it well and for its conceptual connection with Blum), looks at the detection and description of single object 2D silhouettes, the same kind of silhouettes on which MAT might operate. In this case however, the quest is to develop a formalization of the stages of processing the primate visual cortex uses for this task and to show the correspondence between the computational result and the responses of single neurons to the same stimuli.

This volume, well-organized and presented by Marc Pomplun and Jun Suzuki, gives us a detailed view of many current attempts to continue the interdisciplinary inspiration. Topics such as visual representations, visual attention, motion, robot behavior, shape and object recognition, and more are nicely represented, among others. I hope that both current and next generation of scientists and engineers receive the same inspiration for this research enterprise by reading the papers in this book as I did from those very early papers.

ABOUT THE FOREWORD AUTHOR

John K. Tsotsos
York University, Canada

John Tsotsos *is Distinguished Research Professor of Vision Science at York University and hold the Canada Research Chair in Computational Vision. He received York's Inaugural President's Research Excellence Award, is also a Fellow of the Royal Society of Canada, has been a Fellow of the Canadian Institute of Advanced Research and received several other awards. Born in Windsor, Ontario, he holds a doctoral degree from Computer Science at the University of Toronto where he is cross-appointed in Computer Science and Ophthalmology and Vision Sciences. His research spans computer science, psychology and neuroscience and is focused on visual attention and visual object recognition in both man and robots as well as mobile robotics and assistive technology.*

REFERENCES

Blum, H. (1962). *An associative machine for dealing with the visual field and some of its biological implications*. Air Force Cambridge Research Labs. doi:10.1007/978-1-4684-1716-6_34

Blum, H. (1967). A transformation for extracting descriptors of shape . In Wathen-Dunn, W. (Ed.), *Models for the perception of speech and visual forms* (pp. 362–380). MIT Press.

Roberts, L. G. (1963). *Machine perception of 3-dimensional solids.* Doctoral Dissertation, Dept. of Electrical Engineering, MIT.

Rosenfeld, A., & Pfaltz, J. L. (1966). Sequential operations in digital picture processing. *Journal of the ACM, 13*(4), 471–494. doi:10.1145/321356.321357

Zucker, S. W., Rosenfeld, A., & Davis, L. S. (1975). General-purpose models: Expectations about the unexpected. *ACM SIGART Bulletin, 54*, 7–11. doi:10.1145/1045247.1045249

Preface

While machine vision systems are becoming increasingly powerful, in most regards they are still far inferior to their biological counterparts. For instance, in terms of object segmentation, recognition of object categories, viewpoint and lighting invariance, or material recognition, much can be learned from the visual systems of humans and animals. Studying the biological systems and applying the findings to the construction of computational vision models and artificial vision systems is therefore a promising way of advancing the field of machine vision. Conversely, evaluating the performance of such models in comparison to the biological systems can provide important feedback for a better understanding of the brain mechanisms underlying natural vision. Bio-inspired machine vision is thus a truly interdisciplinary research endeavor that benefits all scientific disciplines involved.

The objective of this book is to present current scientific knowledge about vision from fields such as computer science, engineering, psychology, neuroscience, and biology to a similarly diverse audience interested in developing and applying biologically inspired technical vision systems. This interdisciplinary compilation of ideas is intended to inspire new approaches and initiate cross-disciplinary research partnerships that will lead to novel approaches and applications in machine vision as well as the study of biological vision. The book therefore primarily addresses both academic and industrial researchers in fields relevant to bio-inspired machine vision.

Section 1 of the book focuses on visual attention, a mechanism allowing organisms to flexibly align their visual processing resources with current task goals. It is crucial for extracting behaviorally relevant information from the vast stream of incoming visual data and for shaping our everyday conscious experience. Recently, visual attention has received an enormous surge in research interest not only from the fields of neuroscience, psychology, and biology, but also from computer science and engineering. Clearly, a better understanding of the biological attention processes could substantially improve the performance and efficiency of artificial vision systems. In Chapter 1, Kai Essig, Oleg Strogan, Helge Ritter, and Thomas Schack discuss their study titled "Influence of Movement Expertise on Visual Perception of Objects, Events and Motor Action: A Modeling Approach," which provides insight into attentional processes from an empirical perspective through the analysis of domain experts' eye movements and subsequent computational modeling. Nurit Haspel, Alison Shell, and Curt Deutsch also follow a mixed empirical and modeling approach in Chapter 2, titled "Computational Approaches to Measurement of Visual Attention: Modeling Overselectivity in Intellectual and Developmental Disabilities," while studying visual attention in the context of mental disability. In Chapter 3, Albert Rothenstein develops a framework for modeling object recognition using mechanisms of visual attention. His contribution is titled: "Task, Timing and Representation in Visual Object Recognition." Finally, in Chapter 4, "Attention in Stereo Vision: Implications for Computational Models of Attention," Neil Bruce and John Tsotsos propose a model of attention in binocular vision with relevance for both the understanding of biological systems and the construction of stereo computer vision systems.

Chapter 4 also provides a nice transition to Section 2, which is focused on binocular vision. For both empirical studies on biological vision and machine vision approaches, the inclusion of binocular aspects is not very common. While some fundamental aspects of vision can certainly be studied from a monocular perspective, binocular vision has to be considered for a comprehensive understanding of the natural functioning of our visual system. In Chapter 5, "Local Constraints for the Perception of Binocular 3D Motion," Martin Lages, Suzanne Heron, and Hongfang Wang present models of three-dimensional motion perception that could provide new clues to understanding the neurophysiology of this ecologically vital perceptual ability., In Chapter 6, "Modeling Binocular and Motion Transparency Processing by Local Center-Surround Interactions," Florian Raudies and Heiko Neumann specifically address the problem of resolving ambiguities created by binocular and motion transparency, which exceeds the capabilities of most current models of stereo vision and motion perception. Section 2 of the book concludes with Chapter 7, titled "Early Perception-Action Cycles in Binocular Vision: Visuomotor Paradigms and Cortical-Like Architectures" by Silvio Sabatini, Fabio Solari, Andrea Canessa, Manuela Chessa and Agostino Gibaldi. Their contribution closes the loop of vision and its ultimate purpose, the initiation and guidance of motor action, and develops the principles for its implementation in robotic stereo vision systems.

Section 3 of this book addresses the large-scale cortical structures of the visual system and how they provide specific functionality. Numerous pathways and hierarchical structures in the human visual system have been identified or hypothesized, but often the neural mechanisms underlying the coordinated performance of the involved brain areas are not well understood. Further study biological vision from this point of view can provide useful guidance for the overall physical and functional structure of efficient, bio-inspired artificial vision systems. In Chapter 8, titled "The Roles of Endstopped and Curvature Tuned Computations in a Hierarchical Representation of 2D Shape," Antonio Rodríguez-Sánchez and John Tsotsos propose a model of the object recognition pathway demonstrating the importance of intermediate shape representation layers. In the following chapter "A Measure of Localization of Brain Activity for the Motion Aperture Problem Using Electroencephalograms," Isao Hayashi reviews an EEG study investigating the contributions of the dorsal and ventral pathways in the visual cortex to the perception of motion direction. Based on known functional brain structures and mathematical considerations, in Chapter 10, titled "Mathematical Foundations Modeled after Neo-Cortex for Discovery and Understanding of Structures in Data," Shubha Kadambe presents a novel approach to modeling the brain's learning ability and demonstrates its applicability to problems in image processing.

The book concludes with Section 4, which is devoted to the application of bio-inspired technology to real-world machine vision problems. It can be argued that the greatest benefit to artificial vision systems by replicating their biological counterparts can be achieved if both its hardware and its software, i.e., both its physical structure and its mechanisms, are inspired by biological principles. Chapter 11 by Abd El Rahman Shabayek, Olivier Morel, and David Fofi, titled "Visual Behavior Based Bio-Inspired Polarization Techniques in Computer Vision and Robotics," surveys methods of exploiting the light polarization information to improve the capabilities of computer vision systems. In Chapter 12, titled "Implementation and Evaluation of a Computational Model of Attention for Computer Vision Applications," authors Matthieu Perreira Da Silva and Vincent Courboulay once again address the important topic of visual attention, with a focus on how to implement attention in artificial systems in order to maximize their efficiency. Christopher Wing Hong Ngau, Li-Minn Ang, and Kah Phooi Seng, in their

Chapter 13 titled "Implementation of Biologically Inspired Components in Embedded Vision Systems," present the hardware implementation and evaluation of an efficient visual attention model on a Field-Programmable Gate Array to test its feasibility for computer vision applications. In the final Chapter 14, Samuel Romero, Christian Morillas, Antonio Martínez, Begoña del Pino, Francisco Pelayo, and Eduardo Fernández report their study "Replicating the Role of the Human Retina for a Cortical Visual Neuroprosthesis" that is aimed at restoring vision in humans through artificial retinae. This is clearly a significant computer vision subject that inherently requires the integration of biological and technical principles.

We hope that you will find this selection of contributions from renowned researchers as inspiring and thought-provoking as we do. Perhaps some of the insight into their work can stimulate your own research or your interest in a particular field of study.

Marc Pomplun
University of Massachusetts Boston, USA

Junichi Suzuki
University of Massachusetts Boston, USA

Acknowledgment

We would like to sincerely thank all the chapter authors, without whom this book could not have been published, for their interest and significant contribution. We also appreciate the reviewers for their valuable comments and suggestions that helped improve the quality and presentation of this book. Special thanks go to the Editorial Advisory Board members for their help that made our job much easier and enjoyable. We also extend our deepest gratitude to Hannah Abelbeck of IGI Global for her professional assistance, guidance, and most importantly, patience in producing this book.

Marc Pomplun
University of Massachusetts Boston, USA

Junichi Suzuki
University of Massachusetts Boston, USA

Section 1
Visual Attention

Chapter 1
Influence of Movement Expertise on Visual Perception of Objects, Events and Motor Action: A Modeling Approach

Kai Essig
Bielefeld University, Germany

Helge Ritter
Bielefeld University, Germany

Oleg Strogan
Bielefeld University, Germany

Thomas Schack
Bielefeld University, Germany

ABSTRACT

Various computational models of visual attention rely on the extraction of salient points or proto-objects, i.e., discrete units of attention, computed from bottom-up image features. In recent years, different solutions integrating top-down mechanisms were implemented, as research has shown that although eye movements initially are solely influenced by bottom-up information, after some time goal driven (high-level) processes dominate the guidance of visual attention towards regions of interest (Hwang, Higgins & Pomplun, 2009). However, even these improved modeling approaches are unlikely to generalize to a broader range of application contexts, because basic principles of visual attention, such as cognitive control, learning and expertise, have thus far not sufficiently been taken into account (Tatler, Hayhoe, Land & Ballard, 2011). In some recent work, the authors showed the functional role and representational nature of long-term memory structures for human perceptual skills and motor control. Based on these findings, the chapter extends a widely applied saliency-based model of visual attention (Walther & Koch, 2006) in two ways: first, it computes the saliency map using the cognitive visual attention approach (CVA) that shows a correspondence between regions of high saliency values and regions of visual interest indicated by participants' eye movements (Oyekoya & Stentiford, 2004). Second, it adds an expertise-based component (Schack, 2012) to represent the influence of the quality of mental representation structures in long-term memory (LTM) and the roles of learning on the visual perception of objects, events, and motor actions.

DOI: 10.4018/978-1-4666-2539-6.ch001

INTRODUCTION

We evaluated our modeling approach by investigating a simple task, where participants had to look at and grasp 12 known and unknown objects. Unlike existing approaches our model can adapt to differences in participants' gaze behavior that results from better LTM created through a learning interactive phase. Knowledge about the cognitive and learning principles of action-based perception and the selection process of action relevant information from the steady flow of ongoing events is of great importance for the establishment of biologically inspired visual systems and the development of humanoid robots and intelligent systems.

We live in a dynamic environment and have multimodal information inflow in the form of seeing, hearing, and haptic contact. Since the human brain is too limited to process all this information, we have to focus our attention to scene relevant details – like the spotlight in a theatre (Posner, 1980). When reorienting the gaze to a new location, the focus of attention first has to be disengaged from the current location before it can be shifted towards the new location (Vickers, 2007). The scene is then explored by successively directing the focus to the relevant areas (Frintop, Rome & Christensen, 2010; Duchowski, 2007). Through eye movements, humans can control the duration and the temporal and spatial order of fixations and thus, which image regions fall into the foveal field. The order in which a scene is investigated is determined by the mechanisms of *selective attention* (Frintrop, Rome and Christensen, 2010). When perceiving static objects, horizontal and vertical eye movements have an amplitude between 1 and 60 minutes of arc. During a fixation the eye is not completely still - there are different types of micro movements to move the image on the retina by several receptors, providing the photoreceptive cells with a constant flow of new stimulus (Holmqvist et al., 2011; Martinez-Conde, Macknik, & Hubel, 2004; Rötting, 2001).

Although the main components of a scene can be relatively quickly processed and an object can also be recognized in the periphery, a close inspection of an object requires a shift of attention towards it: the focus of attention is directed toward the region of interest, followed by a gaze shift enabling the further perception at higher resolutions (Frintrop, Rome & Christensen, 2010). Deubel and Schneider (1996) argue for an obligatory and selective coupling of saccade programming and visual attention to one common target object. In this context it is worth mentioning that humans are able to attend simultaneously to multiple regions of interest, usually between 4 and 5 regions (McMains & Somers, 2004). When resources are shared, for example in mobile robots, focusing on the relevant data is even more important than scene viewing (Frintrop, Rome & Christensen, 2010). Different modules have to be flexibly prioritized and coordinated in order to fulfill the respective needs of the mobile robots. This fact becomes even more prominent considering the fact that nowadays many robots are expected to act in complex environments and have to interact with human partners. In order to cope with these requirements, computational systems have been developed over the past 5-10 years to investigate how the concepts of human selection mechanisms can be exploited for object recognition, robot localization, and human-machine interaction (Frintrop, Rome & Christensen, 2010).

In order to enhance our understanding of the complex visual processes, a quasi-formal *model* (i.e., algorithmic descriptions of the suggested interpretations of the experimental data) can be constructed that attempts to simulate the empirical observations and thus can help us to better understand the complex processes underlying human behavior. The comparison of the results given by the empirical data and the model reveals information about the adequacy of the computational simulation. Computer simulations can usually be parameterized in order to test the influence and the interactions of the different parameters on the model output. Thus, if there are discrepancies, the model parameters can be optimized to produce optimal results. Additionally, the initial premises and the suggested interpretations of the empirical data that led to the generation of the model can be verified. There exist several computational models of attention resulting from different schools of thought, as well as different modeling strategies. Computational models of visual attention have been applied in many different applications such as psychology (Heinke & Humphreys, 2004), neurobiology and psychophysics (Rothenstein & Tsotsos, 2006), computer vision, robotics, and for surveillance (Frintrop, Rome & Christensen, 2010). For a more thorough survey of different lines of computational models as well as their basic theories and hypotheses, the interested reader could look at Bundesen, Habekost and Kyllingsbaek (2005), Tsotsos and Rothenstein (2011) and Frintrop, Rome and Christensen (2010).

In recent years, different top-down mechanisms were integrated into modeling approaches, as research has shown that although eye movements are initially solely influenced by bottom-up information, after some time goal driven (top-down) processes dominate guidance of visual attention towards regions of interest (Hwang, Higgins & Pomplun, 2009). This top-down information consists of, among other things, world knowledge, information about the objects and task representations. However, these improved models are also unlikely to generalize across various application contexts and natural behavior. Basic principles of visual attention, such as cognitive control, behavioral relevance or reward, uncertainty about the state of the environment, learning and expertise, have thus far not been sufficiently taken into account in these modeling approaches (Tatler, Hayhoe, Land & Ballard, 2011). But how can these underlying principles of eye guidance be integrated into a model of visual attention? Recent research (Schack & Ritter, 2009) can provide valuable hints: It has been shown that the functional interplay between perceptual skills and mental representation plays a central role in the control and implementation of actions. In different fields of action, mental representation makes it possible to select and combine effective sources of information. Based on these findings, we extended a widely applied saliency-based model of visual attention (Walther & Koch, 2006) in two ways: first, we computed the saliency map using the *cognitive visual attention approach* (CVA) that shows a correspondence between regions of high saliency values and regions of visual interest indicated by participants' eye movements (Oyekoya & Stentiford, 2004). Second, we added an expertise-based component (called *Structural Dimensional Analysis of Mental Representation, SDA-M*) (Schack, 2012). This approach reflects the roles of cognitive control, expertise and learning on the visual perception of objects, events and motor actions by considering the influence of the quality of mental representation structures in long-term memory on the gaze allocation process. In an initial experiment we evaluated our modeling approach by comparing its results to empirical data of humans recorded during a natural everyday task, the most frequently used model of visual attention (Itti, Koch & Niebur, 1998; Walter & Koch, 2006) and the original CVA model (Barmidele, Stentiford & Morphett, 2004; Oyekoya & Stentiford, 2004). Developing models of visual attention that can generalize to gaze allocations in various situations are important to further understand any visually guided behavior (Tatler, Hayhoe, Land & Ballard, 2011). This knowledge is of great importance for the establishment of biologically inspired visual systems and the development of humanoid robots and intelligent systems. Before we motivate our modeling approach and describe the initial experiment in more detail, we first describe the saliency model (Walther & Koch, 2006) which we extended.

COMPUTATIONAL MODELING OF VISUAL ATTENTION

An important class of models that have addressed a great deal of research over the last few years are visual attention models. The motivation behind computational models of visual attention is to replicate the visual gaze behavior of humans (e.g., recorded in eye-tracking experiments) using different mathematical, algorithmic or computational techniques, and therefore predicting or explaining the principles behind human attention (Tsotsos & Rothenstein, 2011). They are used to understand the human perceptual capability to select, process and act upon certain parts of one's sensory input in a different way to the rest of the input. Additionally, they can be used to explain the data from visual search and object recognition techniques (Wischnewski, Belardinelli, Schneider & Steil, 2010). Understanding the principles that underlie the deployment of gaze in space and time is important for understanding any visually guided behavior (Tatler, Hayhoe, Land, & Ballard, 2011). Such models can be easily evaluated by comparing their outcome with that of participants' gaze allocations (recorded in an eye-tracking experiment) using a scan path comparison tool (Duchowski et al., 2010; Jarodzka, Holmqvist & Nyström, 2010). In this section we describe the saliency based model of visual attention by Walther and Koch (2006), a mostly pixel-wise feature and location-based approach, in detail. Later we describe how we extend it to create our novel expertise-based modeling approach to visual attention.

The Saliency-Based Model of Visual Attention

The saliency-based model of visual attention (Itti, Koch & Niebur, 1998) is widely used to detect the most salient, and thus, unique features in the environment, by simulating the ability of the visual system to detect salient regions of a scene at the expense of other regions. There exist real time implementations of the model (Ouerhani, Hügli, Burgi & Rüdi, 2002), which, because of the model's universality, are applied to many research fields, such as Computer Vision and Robotics. The basic idea behind the saliency-based model of visual attention by Itti and Koch (2001) is that uniform regions along some image dimensions are uninformative, whereas distinct ones are informative. Its implementation consists of three main steps (see Figure 1): the calculation of the single (bottom-up) *feature maps* and their transformation into corresponding *conspicuity maps*, which highlight areas of the images that strongly differ from their surrounding according to the applied image features. Finally, the conspicuity maps are linearly combined into an overall *saliency map*. Regions with high saliency values should indicate areas that attract attention.

The implementation steps are as follows: the first step is the pre-attentive calculation of primitive image features in a parallel manner over the entire visual field. In general n, the number of primitive features, is set to 3 (i.e., intensity, color and orientation). These are computed from the images resulting from 42 feature maps, representing different elementary features of a visual scene. Feature maps code the characteristics of the local *conspicuity* of the feature compared to the surrounding image regions. The intensity contrast models the centre-surround neurons sensitivity in primate visual cortex to either dark centers to bright surrounds or bright centers to dark surrounds. The calculation of the color saliency models the *color-opponent cells* in the visual cortex. Color-opponent cells have an antagonistic centre-surround receptive field. Their centre is excited by one color and inhibited by another and an opposite reaction is found in the area surrounding it. Such color opponencies exist for the red/green, green/red, blue/yellow and yellow/blue pairs in the primary visual cortex. The orientation saliencies are calculated from the intensity image (I) by applying *Gabor Pyramids* $O(\sigma,\theta)$, where $\sigma \in [0..8]$ is the scale and $\theta \in \{0°,45°,90°,135°\}$ are the orientations. Each feature map is first normalized. Then, the single feature maps are

Figure 1. General architecture of the saliency-based model of visual attention (from Itti, Koch & Niebur, 1998)

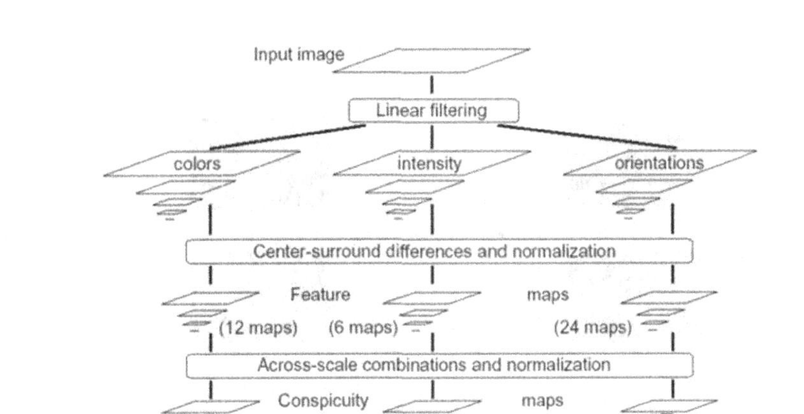

combined into three conspicuity maps for intensity ($\bar{I}$), color ($\bar{C}$) and orientation ($\bar{O}$) (see Figure 1). The three conspicuity maps are finally combined into the overall saliency map.

The combination of the single feature maps is implemented by across-scale addition (±) (Itti, Koch, & Niebur, 1998). Similar features compete for saliency, whereas different ones contribute independently to the overall saliency. This motivates the calculation of three separate conspicuity maps and their individual normalization. In the final step, the three conspicuity maps are normalized and linearily combined into the overall saliency map S (see Figure 1). Increased saliency in a single feature map leads automatically to an increase in the saliency in the overall map. The maximum in S defines the most salient image region, to which the focus of attention should be directed. The most salient regions are successively selected by a *winner-take-all network* (Koch and Ullmann, 1985; Itti, Koch, & Niebur, 1998; Walther & Koch, 2006).

Walther and Koch (2006) extended the saliency based model of visual attention to a biologically plausible model for generating and attending to proto-objects (i.e., a contiguous region of high activity in the feature map) (see Figure 2). In this approach, first the conspicuity map is chosen that contributes the most to the activity at the most salient location. Then a labeling procedure (4-connected neighborhood pixels of above-threshold activity) is applied to the winning conspicuity map to connect salient pixels to the resulting proto-object (see Figure 2, lower right). Then the shape of the proto-object is determined and mapped to the winning location in the image. The center of the proto-object serves as the landing point for the next saccade. This approach can be used to model the serialized object recognition processes for complex scenes in the visual cortex (Riesenhuber & Poggio, 1990).

Even though a weighted linear combination of three important features (i.e., spatial orientation, intensity and color) seems to be sufficient to

Figure 2. The saliency maps and resulting scan path generated using the latest MATLAB implementation of the saliency toolbox (downloaded from http://www.saliencytoolbox.net) using the default parameters (for details see Walther & Koch, 2006).

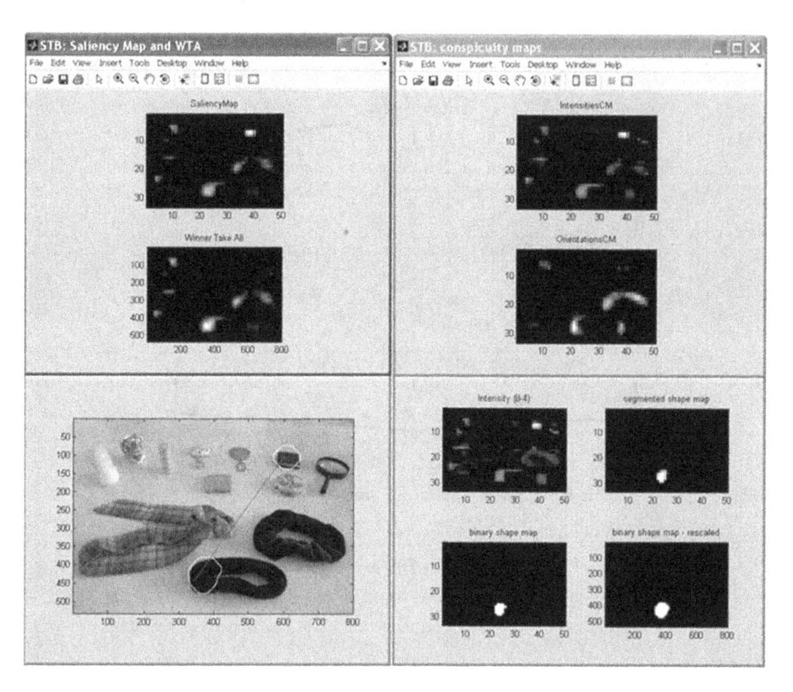

predict salient regions that correlate with human perception, complicated scenes or complete simulation of gaze patterns require more image features (Parkhurst et al., 2002). Furthermore, the quality of the saliency map can be improved by considering knowledge-based information, for example, visual properties of the objects in a scene (Rao et al., 2002). Even though saliency maps are a promising model for visual attention, it is still unclear whether the three chosen features (intensity, contrast and orientation) play a central role in the determination of fixation locations. Furthermore, top-down factors for fixation location are insufficiently incorporated into the model. Additionally, the direction of the initial saccade is influenced by scene information perceived during the first fixation (Henderson, Weeks & Hollingworth, 1999). Thus, recent work applies accumulated statistical knowledge of visual features (Navalpakkam & Itti, 2006) to tune bottom-up maps for optimal target detection. In another work, the influence of bottom-up cues, task knowledge and target influence on the guidance of attention have been modeled in a biologically plausible manner (Navalpakkam & Itti, 2005). Another approach to calculate a saliency map from an input image matching humans' gaze allocations (Oyekoya & Stentiford, 2004) is the cognitive visual attention approach (CVA), described in the following section.

The Cognitive Visual Attention Approach (CVA)

The cognitive visual attention approach (CVA) was suggested by Bamidele, Stentiford and Morphett (2004). CVA is based on the theory of surround suppression in primate V1, an area of the visual cortex (Nothdurft, Gallant & Van Essen, 1999). The core idea is that high values of visual attention is assigned to pixels at randomly selected neighboring pixel configurations when their feature vectors (e.g., RGB color values) do not match the feature vectors of identical positional configurations at other randomly selected pixels in the image (see Figure 3). The correspondence between image regions with high attention values predicted by the CVA model and regions of visual interest was given by participants' eye movements when looking at the images (Oyekoya & Stentiford, 2004). Even though the results varied considerably between participants, it was shown that participants' gaze within the first two seconds of image presentation was directed towards regions with high visual attention values. Additionally, frequent saccades occurred between highlighted areas. The implementation of the CVA approach is described in Bamidele, Stentiford and Morphett (2004).

The CVA approach assigns high values of visual attention to image pixels P that archive high mismatching scores over a range of t neighboring pixel sets S_P. This means pixels with features rarely present elsewhere in the image (e.g. anomalous objects, edges or boundaries), receive high attention scores, whereas those with common features get small values. The motivation behind keeping the mismatching neighborhood is that once such a configuration is generated, it is likely that it also mismatches identical neighborhoods in other areas of the image. Thus, the rise of the visual attention scores is accelerated if the process is not interrupted by a subsequent match. The value for the threshold δ, i.e., the RGB color differences between identical pixels in compared neighborhood configurations (see Figure 3), depends on the chosen image features. In the CVA implementation used to calculate the saliency map in our expertise-based modeling approach, only the RGB color information was used. The threshold δ was set to 80 in order to find high differences in RGB color values. It means that if the sum of the differences in the red, green and blue component between a pixel pair is above 80, then a mismatch is detected. Typical parameters for the algorithm are: $\varepsilon = 3$, $t = 100$ and $\delta = 8$, where ε is the size of the neighborhood and t the number of iterations (see Figure 3). These values provided good results for our test images. For images with different scales, other parameter values might have to be selected. Higher values for δ improve the level of confidence in the details of the visual attention map because only regions with high differences in the RGB color values (compared to identical neighborhoods in other areas of the image) receive salience. For lower δ, regions with smaller color differences are also extracted, i.e., the model outputs a higher number of salient regions. Having described two different models of visual attention, we now explain the motivation behind and the implementation of our approach to visual attention.

Figure 3. Neighborhood configuration for pixel P and pixel Q ($\varepsilon = 3$, $t = 100$ and $\delta = 80$), where ε is the size of the neighborhood, t the number of iterations, and δ the threshold for the RGB color difference between identical pixels in the compared pixel configurations . The neighborhood of pixel P is marked by the red square. The neighborhood configuration of pixel Q is indicated by grey squares.

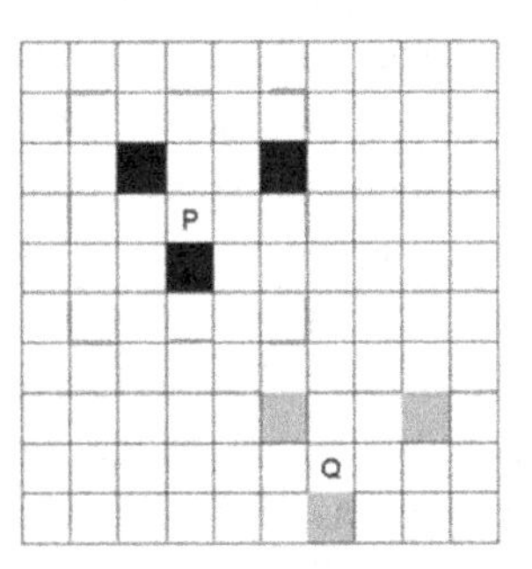

The Expertise-Based Model of Visual Attention (EBMS)

Motivation for an Expertise-Based Approach

Our recent research (Schack & Ritter, 2009) has shown that the functional interplay between perceptual skills and mental representation plays a central role in the control and implementation of actions. In different fields of action, mental representation makes it possible to select and combine effective sources of information. Regardless of whether a surgeon has to select the appropriate instrument for an operation; a mechanic, a suitable tool for repairing an engine; or a basketball player, which member of the team to pass the ball to, actors have to use their mental representation as a basis to identify possible and functionally relevant sensory inputs. Frequently, this identification has to be made under extreme time pressure. Many eye-tracking studies in the field of sports have revealed group specific differences (experts versus novices) in the visual perception strategy, as well as in various eye parameters, like number of fixations and fixation durations (Vickers, 2007; Williams & Ward, 2007). Furthermore, experts apply a more spatial gaze strategy, i.e., they focus on relevant image regions, whereas novices consider also task-irrelevant information and social cues in their decision processes (functional gaze strategy) (Raab & Johnson, 2007; Schack & Essig, 2011). Hence, mental representation has to be available quickly and provide clear criteria for selecting relevant information. At the same time, mental representation forms the functional basis for a meaningful and, thereby, task-related reduction in the large number of potential behaviors available to us and our social and technological systems. Mental representation does not just facilitate information selection, but also more generally permits a target-related and purposeful adaptation of behavioral potentials to conditions in the environment. In other words, mental representation helps to *shape interaction patterns* in purposeful ways. This also includes storing the cognitive perceptual outcomes of learning processes as items in long-term memory.

In a series of recent experiments, studies of soccer (instep kick) and handball (7-meter) actions, we were already able to show expertise dependent effects of perceptual resonance during the observation of complex motor actions. For example, when the visual attention of expert soccer players is drawn to the acting effector (i.e., foot kicking a ball [action-relevant information]) during the observation of a soccer kick, they demonstrate faster responses with the foot that is compatible with the observed kicking direction, whereas soccer novices pay more attention to the head of the player (i.e., gaze direction [action-irrelevant information]) (Weigelt, Bosbach, Schack & Kunde, 2006; Essig et al., 2010; Schack & Essig, 2011). Figure 4 shows a so called fixation map, where the gaze data from different participants (e.g. separately for experts and novices) can be aggregated, to provide a quick, intuitive and in some cases objective visual representation of eye-tracking data that can give users an understanding of the results (Holmqvist et al., 2011). Fixation maps are used to highlight image areas receiving high attention, whereas sparsely fixated areas are blurred (Pomplun, Ritter & Velichkovsky, 1996; Wooding, 2002). In an fixation map each pixel is assigned a value between 0 and 1 depending on how long the participants focused on a particular pixel (values closer to 1 indicate higher attention by the participant). Color-spots indicate which areas were attended and how intensively the participants looked at them. A detailed description of how the fixations maps are mathematically calculated from participants gaze data, can be found in Pomplun, Ritter and Velichkovsky (1996), Wooding (2002), and Holmqvist et al. (2011).

Raab and Johnson (2007) investigated expertise-based differences in search and game decision strategies in a 2-year longitudinal handball study. They found that experts applied more spatial gaze strategies, whereas near-experts use primarily functional gaze strategies, which may explain the expertise-based differences in the game decision strategies. Williams, Janelle, and Davids (2004) concluded that experts search their visual field more effectively than novices, i.e., their attention process is more refined and they possess more task specific knowledge. Vickers (2007) defines the quiet eye as the final fixation or tracking gaze that is located on a specific location or object in the visuo-motor workspace within 3° of visual angle for a minimum of 100 ms. Elite performer's quiet-eye onset is invariably earlier and longer

Figure 4. Visualization of the attention areas for experts and novices for cues at the head and on the ball. The numbers in the brackets represent the percentage of image pixels with a threshold above 0.2. Colors are used to visualize the extent to which image areas were fixated, where red means that the area is highly fixated, dark means that the area was not fixated at all.

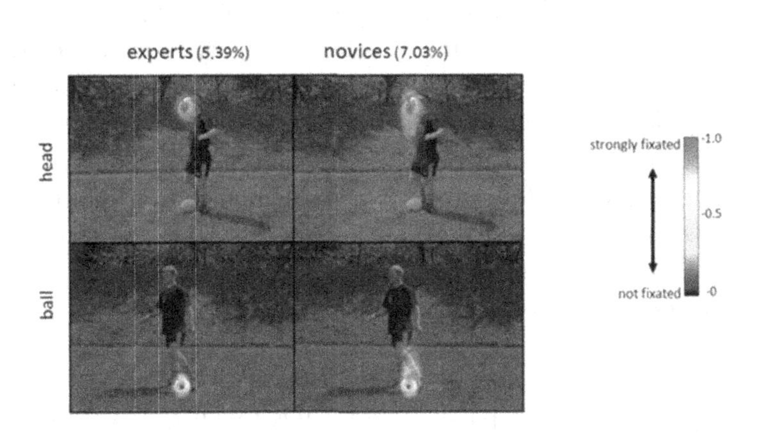

than that of near-elite or lower skilled performers, i.e., near-elite players see critical information earlier and process the visual information longer than less-skilled athletes.

These results show the functional interplay between perceptual skills and mental representation structures. In order to address the basic principles of visual attention, such as cognitive control, behavioral relevance, learning and expertise, we extended a saliency model of visual attention with an *expertise-based component* using the results of a hierarchical sorting paradigm, *SDA-M* (Schack, 2012), to integrate the influence of the structure of mental representations in long-term memory, as well as their changes over the learning process, on the visual perception of objects, events and motor actions. By extending a saliency-based model of visual attention by an expertise-based module, we can investigate the interplay between certain *eye-movement parameters* and the quality of *mental representation structures* during *selective perception* of *action–relevant information,* i.e., how do different levels of *expertise* affect the influence of *top-down* on *bottom-up* mechanism during the perception of *complex tasks*. By adding information about the units and the structure of the mental representation to the model, we are able to specify different levels of expertise as a top-down factor implemented in a visual attention model. Interesting lines of research addressed with this model are the identification of the specific sources of perceptual information that players use to identify patterns of play, as well as the differences in the gaze patterns over the learning process and under various scenarios (Williams & Ward, 2007; Essig & Schack, 2011). But how can we measure the mental representation structure and the structure formation in long-term memory over the learning process?

Structural Dimensional Analysis of Mental Representation (SDA-M)

We access the quality of mental representation structures in long-term memory in a *cognitive experimental task* by using the *structural dimensional analysis of mental representation* (*SDA-M)* method (Schack, 2012). In the cognitive architecture of human action, *basic action concepts* (BACs) are identified as the mental counterparts of functionally relevant elementary components or transitional states of complex movements. They are characterized by recognizable perceptual features and can be described verbally as well as pictorially and are often labeled with a linguistic marker. For example, "turning the head" or "bending the knees" could be BACs in the case of, say, a complex floor exercise. In order to determine subjective distances between the BACs, the participant performs the following split procedure in the SDA-M: In each round of decisions one selected BAC is presented constantly as an "anchoring unit" in red writing on the computer screen. The rest of the BACs are presented in yellow writing as a randomly ordered list. The participant judges whether each of these additional yellow-colored BACs are "functionally related" (associated) to the red anchor BAC while performing the movement or not. Here it is important to note that the SDA-M method does not ask participants to give explicit statements about their (inherent) long-term memory structure for a particular skill, but rather reveals this structure by means of knowledge-based decisions in an experimental setting. As an example, we consider the tennis serve. A tennis serve consists of three distinct phases, each fulfilling distinct functional and biomechanical demands. In a pre-activation phase, body and ball are brought into position, and tension energy is stored to prepare for the strike. The following BACs are identified for this phase: (1) ball throw, (2) forward movement of the pelvis, (3) bending the knees, and (4) bending the elbow. In the subsequent strike phase, energy is conveyed to the ball. The following BACs are identified: (5) frontal upper body rotation, (6) racket acceleration, (7) whole body stretch motion, and (8) hitting point. In the final swing phase, the balance is maintained and the racket movement is decelerated after the strike. The following BACs are identified: (9) wrist flap, (10) forward bending of the body, and (11) racket follow-through.

Using the splitting procedure for the tennis serve example, 11 decision trees per participant were created. First, the binary decisions generated by each participant were used to calculate a correlation matrix (*R*) that is a reflection matrix of the mental representation structure of the 11 BACs for the tennis serve in participants' long-term memory. Low values (close to -1) mean concepts (or in case of the tennis serve, BACs) are dissimilar and high values (close to 1) mean that concepts are similar. A distance matrix, *D,* is then computed from the correlation matrix:

$$D_{ik} = \sqrt{2N(m)} \cdot \sqrt{1 - R_{ik}}\,,$$

with N = number of concepts (11 in this case), i and k are the indices of the correlation matrix R, and m is usually equal to N (but is used as a correction factor if R is not square). The entries in the distance matrix reflect the Euclidean distances between individual concepts. Based on the distance matrix a greedy algorithm is used in a hierarchical cluster analysis with the distances based on the subjective distance judgments of all combinations of pairs of 11 BACs obtained in the previous step. As a result the individual partitioning of the 11 BACS were obtained (hierarchical tree-like structures), the so called *dendograms* (see Figure 5). Cluster solutions were calculated for all individual participants and for whole groups. Each cluster solution was established by determining a critical Euclidean distance d_{crit}, with all junctures lying below this value forming an individual concept cluster. The critical value d_{crit} depends on the number of concepts. The algorithm tries to calculate the optimal critical value d_{crit}, but in cases of sub-optimal d_{crit} calculation, some manual tuning is possible. For further details on the splitting procedure see (Schack, 2010; 2012).

If two BACs are often labeled as being "functionally related", they have a small Euclidean distance, and this results in a low projection of the BACs on the vertical line in the tree diagram (see BACs 1 and 2 in Figure 5 left). If two BACs are not judged to be "functionally related", and therefore not selected together during the splitting procedure, the Euclidean distance is big and the projection of the two BACs is high in the tree diagram (see BACs 1 and 3 in Figure 5 right).

The measure of similarity between two tree diagrams can be calculated and is expressed in λ, ranging from 0 (no similarity at all) to 1 (tree diagrams are identical). An alpha level of p=.05 was used in all analyses. This means that there was a significant difference between clusters when $\lambda < \lambda_{crit} = 0.68$. In high-level experts (see Figure 5 left) these representations are organized in a distinct hierarchical tree-like structure and are well matched with the functional and biomechanical demands of the task. In comparison, action representations in novices are organized less hierarchically and match poorly the functional and biomechanical demands (see Figure 5 right). These results support the hypothesis that voluntary movements are planned, executed, and stored in memory directly through representations of their anticipated perceptual effects (Schack, 2012; Schack & Mechsner, 2006; Bläsing, Tenenbaum & Schack, 2009). Thereby, the strength of motor resonance depends directly on the quality of the observer's own mental skill representation (Weigelt & Schack, 2007). The *SDA-M* (Schack, 2012) has been developed and implemented successfully for different sports such as volleyball, gymnastics, sky surfing, and dancing (Schack & Ritter, 2009; Bläsing, Tenenbaum & Schack, 2009). It has also already been applied to everyday scenarios, such as drinking from a cup, leisure time activities, using tools, and grasping objects of different sizes (Maycock, et al., 2010; Braun et al., 2007).

The Expertise-Based Component in the EBMS Model: Selection of the Salient Regions (Proto-Objects)

We implemented a novel computational approach to visual attention that applies the CVA algorithm to calculate the saliency map from the input image (see Figure 6(a)) and extended it by introducing an expertise-based component in order to model the role of cognitive control and the influences of learning and expertise on the visual perception

Figure 5. Representation structures for two chosen expertise groups (experts, non-players) based on the hierarchical cluster analysis of basic-action concepts (BACs) in the tennis serve. The horizontally aligned numbers denote the BACs (for the code, see text) the vertical numbers are the Euclidean distances. The lower the number, the lower the distances in long-term memory. Each cluster solution was established by determining a critical Euclidean distance d_{crit} (dotted line), with all junctures lying below this value forming an individual concept cluster. For every group it holds $n = 11$, $p = 0.05$, $d_{crit} = 3.46$ (Schack & Mechsner, 2006).

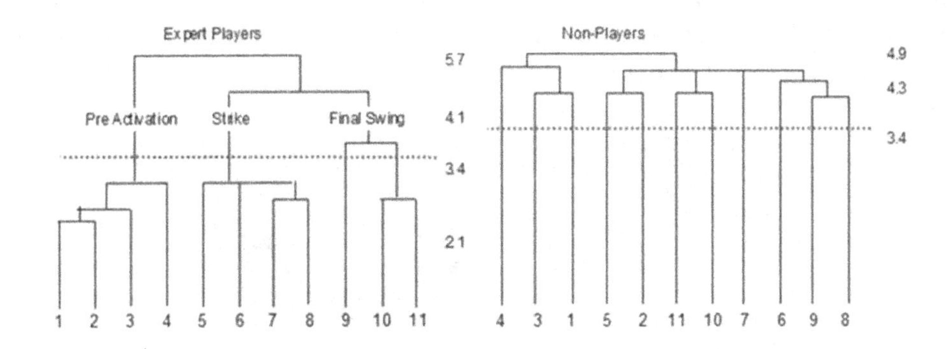

processes. We use the λ-value from the SDA-M method, which reflects the quality of the mental representation structure, i.e., how closely the participants' dendrogram structure matches that of an optimal cluster solution, as an input parameter for the EBMS model. Once the saliency map and λ have been computed, our approach follows that of Walther & Koch (2006): The winner-take-all algorithm successively finds the salient regions of decreasing importance in the saliency map. From the single winning locations (x_w, y_w), the activation spreads over the shape of the proto-object at this location, which is defined by a contiguous 4-connected neighborhood of above-threshold activity that depends on the quality of the mental representation structures, i.e., the λ value. We used an image processing algorithm that labels the resulting image according to:

$$P(x,y) = \begin{cases} 1, & if\, F(x,y) \geq \lambda \\ 0, & otherwise \end{cases},$$

where $F(x,y)$ is the saliency value (between 0 and 1) at pixel position (x,y) calculated by the CVA approach (see Figure 6(a)). By adding information about the units and the structure of the mental representation to the model, we are able to specify different levels of movement expertise as a top-down factor implemented in a visual attention model. If the mental representation is hierarchically structured, i.e., close to the optimal structure of representation (λ > 0.68), the model extracts more proto-objects of smaller size depicting finer scene details in order to reflect the spatial perception processes of experts (see Figure 7(b)). If the mental-representation structure is less structured (λ < 0.68), fewer proto-objects of a larger size are extracted in order to reflect the functional gaze strategy of novices (see Figure 7(a)). This coherence also applies for the weight assignment for the single proto-objects: For experts, proto-objects located close to the saccade landing points are weighted higher, whereas for novices, proto-objects in the periphery gets higher weights and therefore influences the direction of the next saccade. This reflects the different search behavior as a function of the quality of the mental representation structures.

Experimental Validation

In order to evaluate our EBMS model, an initial experiment was designed in which the task was to look at and to cluster twelve (mostly unknown) objects (see Figure 8). Finally, we compare the scan path recorded from the participants in the empirical experiments with the output of our EBMS approach, the model described in Walther & Koch (2006) (in the following referred to as the Walther & Koch model) and the original cognitive visual attention approach (referred to as CVA).

Figure 6. (a): Saliency map resulting from the CVA-algorithm (ε = 3, t= 200 and δ = 80). The brighter the color, the closer the similarity value is to the maximum value (i.e., 1). (b): Fixation Map calculated from (a) by starting with the most salient image pixel and successively taking those pixels with decreasing saliency values as the location of the next fixation.

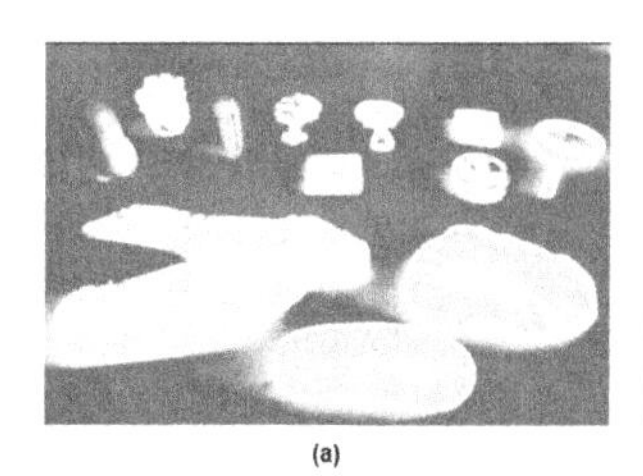

(a)

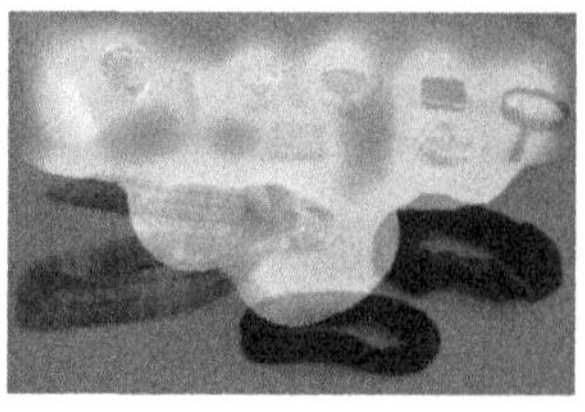

(b)

Figure 7. Results of the EBMS model after 30 iterations using different λ values. (a) λ = 0.6, (b) λ=0.98.

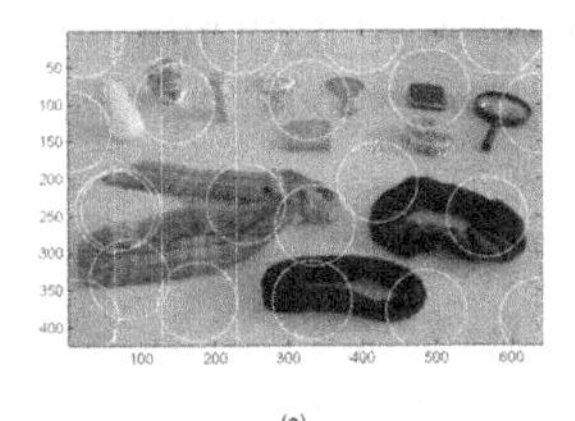

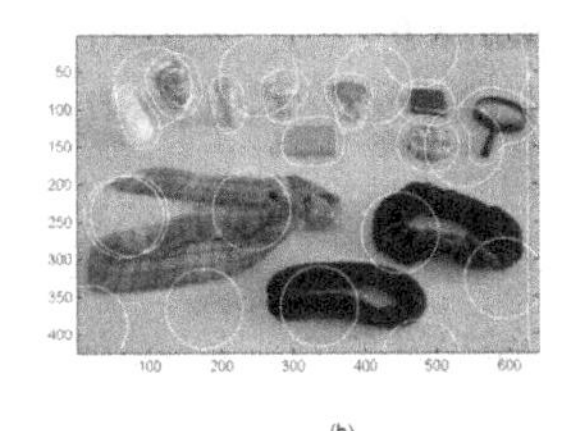

Material

For the experiment, an SR Research Eyelink II head-mounted eye tracker was used to record participants' eye movements (see Figure 9). This system employs a headset with two cameras to enable recording of binocular eye movements. Further features of the EyeLink II system are a high sampling rate of 500 Hz and an average on-screen gaze position error between 0.5° and 1.0°. The experiment was designed with the experimental software package V-Designer (Koesling & Ritter, 2001). The EyeDataAnalyser (EDA) software package provided the analysis of the eye-tracking parameters and created the fixation maps (Essig, Pohl & Ritter, 2005). Mental representation structures of the objects were analyzed using the SDA-M method (Schack, 2012), once before and then after participants had grasped the objects.

Experimental Procedure

To test our model extension, a simple five-stage experiment was designed. Six participants (3 male and 3 female adults, age between 25-52 years) were shown twelve objects from four different classes: toothpick holders, magnifying glasses, hair bands and mirrors (see Figure 8). Each cluster consists

Figure 8. All 12 objects used in the experiment. There are 4 clusters (hair bands, toothpick holders, magnifying glasses and mirrors), each consisting of 3 objects: 0. red hair band, 1. black hair band, 2. blue hair band, 4. foldable magnifier, 5. magnifying glass, 6. (Chinese style) magnifying glass, 7. normal mirror, 8. decorated mirror, 9. make-up mirror, 10. toothpick holder, 11. (plastic) toothpick holder, 12. (Chinese style) toothpick holder.

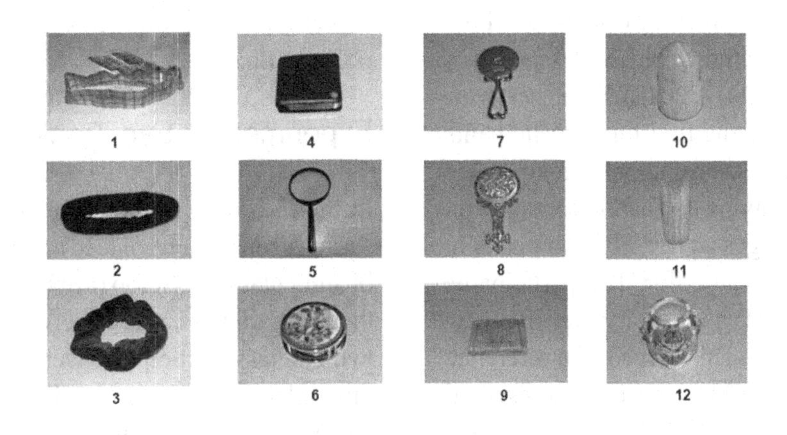

Figure 9. The three stages of the experiment. In the hierarchical sorting procedure (SDA-M) participants should cluster the objects according to if they are "functionally related in everyday use". In the eye-tracking experiment participants looked for 30 seconds on the image while their gaze was recorded. In the interaction phase the participants grasped each object in order to identify them (no data was recorded).

I. SDA-M / Eye Tracking

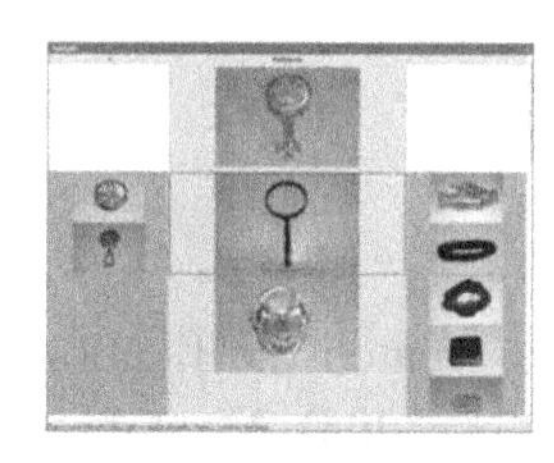

II. Interaction Phase

III. SDA-M / Eye Tracking

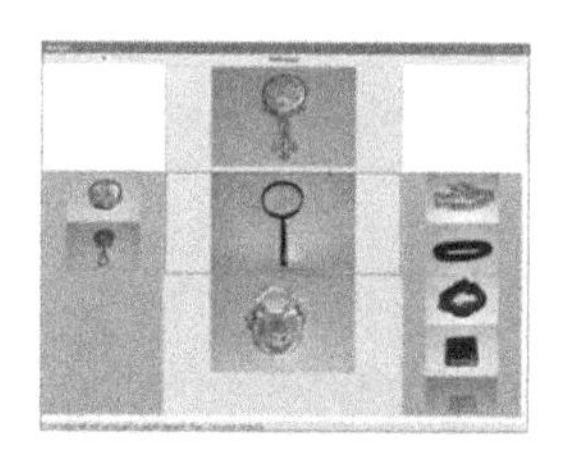

of three objects. The majority of these objects had not been previously seen by participants and are therefore classed as unknown objects for this study. The experiments took place in the Eye-Tracking Laboratory at Bielefeld University. The experiment was carried out according to the principles laid out in the 1964 Declaration of Helsinki.

Experiment 1: Hierarchical Sorting Procedure (SDA-M)

During the first experiment we analyzed how participants clustered the 12 objects by means of the SDA-M (Schack, 2010; 2012). When performing Experiment 1 for the first time, participants had to cluster the objects using only pictures (see Figure 9), without having had haptic contact with the objects. The images were *380* x *253* pixels in size and were shown in color. The participants were seated in front of a laptop on which they saw one of the 12 objects. This served as a reference object. The remaining 11 objects were presented underneath the reference object in a column. Each object was presented and participants had to judge whether they were "functionally related" to the reference object in terms of everyday use (see Figure 10). If the participants thought that objects were functionally related, they pressed the right arrow key and the current object shifted to the right side of the screen (positive list). Otherwise, participants pressed the left arrow key and the object was shifted to the left side of the screen (negative list). This procedure was repeated until all 11 objects were compared to the reference object and every object occupied the reference position once.

Experiment 2: Eye-Tracking Experiment

In the eye-tracking experiment all objects were shown in one image, placed on a table and ordered by their class affiliation (see Figures 8 and 9). Although the objects were closely arranged according to their class, participants were not explicitly told this and therefore interaction with the objects was a necessary prerequisite to revealing the objects

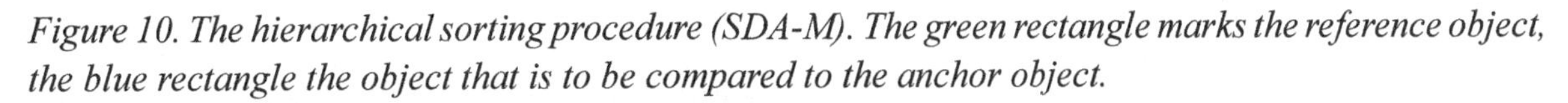

Figure 10. The hierarchical sorting procedure (SDA-M). The green rectangle marks the reference object, the blue rectangle the object that is to be compared to the anchor object.

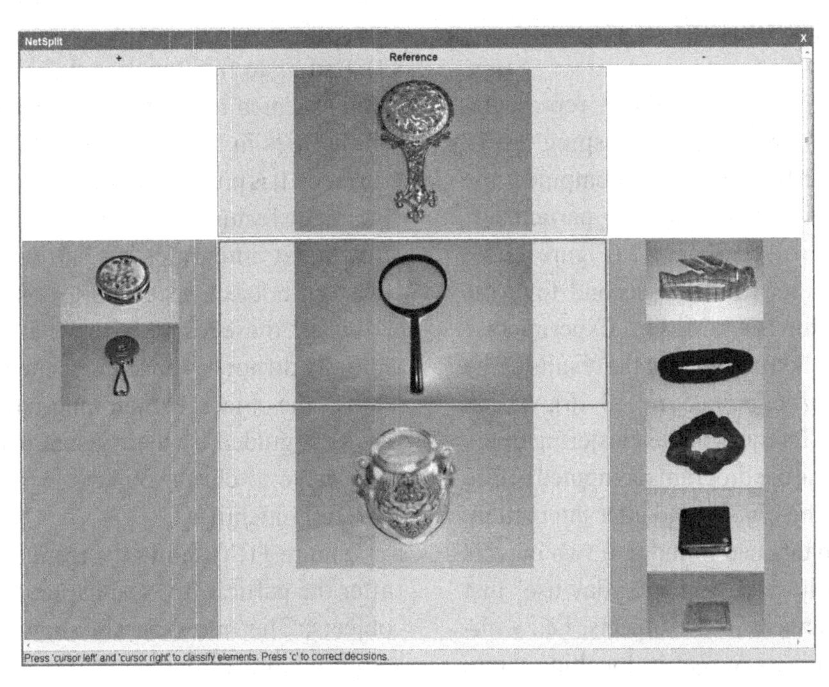

functionality. For example, participants had to push the magnifying glass out of the round case to identify the object (see Figure 8, object 6), which is a Chinese style magnifying glass. The participants were seated at a distance of 60cm in front of a 21.5 inch widescreen monitor (52.1cm x 32.5cm) with a resolution of *1280x1024* pixels (see Figure 9). The display was adjusted to the correct solution under Windows in order to show an undistorted image of the objects on the screen. All participants had normal or corrected-to-normal vision. The participants looked at the picture for 30 seconds while their eye-movements were recorded. Note, when performing the SDA-M and the eye-tracking experiment for the first time, the participants had to cluster the objects according to information they got from the pictures, without having had haptic contact with them.

Experiment 3: Interaction Phase

In this experiment participants were shown the real objects. They were instructed to grasp each object and to interact with it in order to try to figure out what its purpose was (see Figure 9). There was no time restriction, but most participants needed around 3-5 minutes for all objects. No data was recorded during this handling task. The aim of this task was to become familiar with the objects and to get an idea about their functionality.

Experiment 4 and 5: SDA-M and Eye Tracking

After the participants had haptic contact with the objects, they finally had to return to Experiment 1 and 2 (SDA-M and Eye Tracking) with the same stimuli. Finally, the participants were thanked and debriefed. The study (i.e., Experiment 1-5) took altogether around 30-40 minutes. The whole experimental structure is depicted in Figure 9.

RESULTS

Mental Representation of Objects

In order to compare the cognitive representation structures before and after grasping the 12 (mostly unknown) objects, we computed the average dendrograms over all the participants from the results of Experiment 1 (Figure 11(a)) and then the results from the second time the participants did the SDA-M, i.e., Experiment 4 (Figure 11(b)). When comparing the results of the cluster analysis (n=6, p=0.05, d_{crit}=3.46), we can clearly see the differences in the clustering of the objects between the dendrograms computed before interaction with the objects and after interaction. Initially, participants had to judge if two objects were "functionally related in everyday use" just by comparing pictures of the objects, i.e., without seeing the objects in real or touching them. Participants found it difficult to find objects with similar functionalities, and thus the Euclidean distance of objects within clusters is quite high. The resulting dendogram (see Figure 11(a)) reveals three clusters: cluster 1: red – blue - black hair band, cluster 2: (Chinese style) magnifying glass – decorated mirror, cluster 3: (plastic) toothpick holder – (Chinese style) toothpick holder. Except for the hair bands, the participants found it difficult to group the objects into suitable clusters. Cluster 2 reveals that the participants used bottom-up features (like color, shape and texture) to cluster the objects. Both objects have a round shape and they are colorful (see Figure 8, object 6 and 8). In the case of cluster 3, they assumed correctly that object 12 is a (Chinese style) toothpick holder and assigned it to the (plastic) toothpick holder (see Figure 8, object 11 and 12). Although, they could not identify the "closed" toothpick holder (see Figure 8, object 10), because this object does not have common bottom-up features with other objects: it is singled out, i.e. it does not form a cluster with another object in the dendrogram (see Figure 11(a)). As can also be seen from Figure 11(a), although its juncture is below the critical value to form an individual concept cluster, the participants try to cluster the make-up mirror and the foldable magnifier (see Figure 8, object 4 and 9). Failing to find functional similarities, participants seemed to cluster the objects according to similarities in shape and size (flat and rectangle surface). It is probable that they assumed that similar image features match function. Failing to find functional similarities, the participants seemed to cluster the objects according to bottom-up features. All in all, these results reveal that the participants initially do not have a suitable mental representation of the objects in their long-term memory and are first guided by their visual perception when they have to cluster objects, which they cannot correctly identify.

Figure 11(b) shows the results of the SDA-M after the participants had haptic contact with the objects. The tree diagram shows four clusters, representing the four object classes. The unknown objects were assigned to the correct groups: cluster 1: red – blue - black hair band, cluster 2: make-up mirror – decorated mirror – normal mirror, cluster 3: (Chinese style) magnifying glass – magnifying glass - foldable magnifier, cluster 4: (plastic) toothpick bin – (Chinese style) toothpick bin – toothpick bin. After having used the objects, participants grouped them according to their functionality and not according to similarities in their shape and size features. Now, the "closed" toothpick holder (see Figure 8, object 10) is correctly identified by the participants and assigned to the class of toothpick holders. Additionally, the participants do not cluster the make-up mirror and the foldable magnifier any more (see Figure 8, object 4 and 9). The make-up mirror is clustered into the mirror group, whereas the foldable magnifier is assigned to the group of the magnifying glasses. These results reveal that the participants were at first unfamiliar with the functionality of the unknown objects, but by interacting with them, their mental representation structures were updated and meaningful functional clusters could be formed – resulting in the four final clusters. As can be seen from Figures

Figure 11. Average cluster solutions of all participants before (a) and after (b) handling with the objects. On the horizontal line the numbers of the single objects are represented as corresponding with the list shown in Figure 8. The Euclidean distance between the single objects is depicted on the y-axis. The solid horizontal line marks d_{crit} ($n = 6$, $p = 0.05$, $d_{crit} = 3.46$).

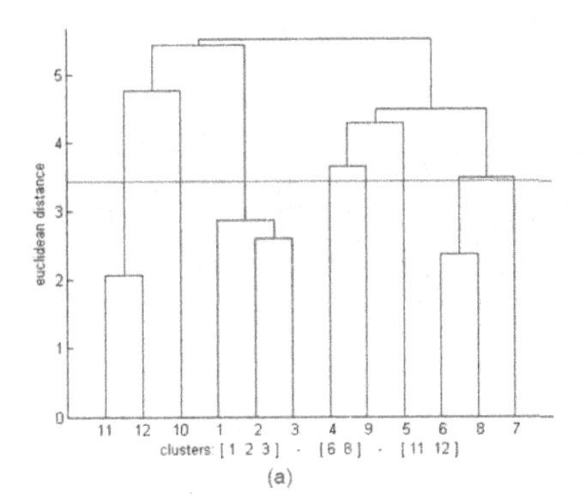

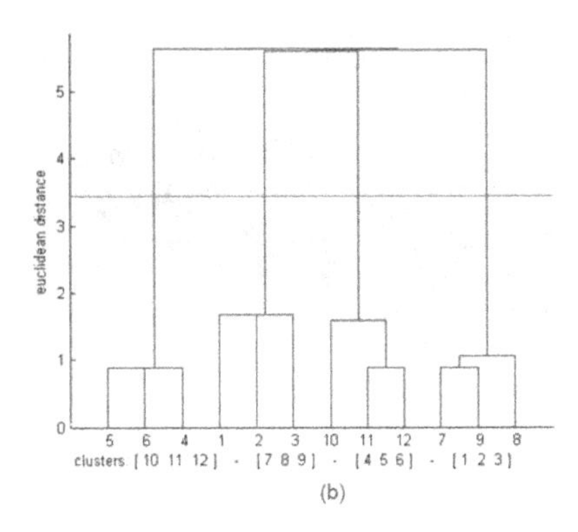

11(a) and (b), the known objects are clustered in the same way before and after participants had haptic contact with them. After the participants interacted with the objects, they were more familiar with all objects and managed to cluster the previously unknown objects also into adequate clusters (shown by the clear clustering of the objects into the four functionality classes).

Results for the Empirical Data

Figure 12 (a) and (b) shows the fixation maps for all participants before and after they had haptic contact with the objects. The analysis of the recorded gaze data before the interaction phase (see Figure 12(a)) revealed that the participants seem to focus more on single objects, because there are more separated attention areas when compared to the fixation map shown in Figure 12(b). The only exception is in the case of the foldable magnifier and the (Chinese style) magnifying glass (see Figure 8, objects 4 and 6), as there we see these spots are merged. It shows that at first the participants' gazes were directed towards the single objects in order to identify them (probably according to bottom-up features), whereas later, after performing a typical task with the objects, they focused more strongly on object groups (i.e., the attention spreads among the objects of a functional group).

It could be that they are trying to find similar features across objects of a particular functional group. After haptic contact with the objects, the participants clustered them according to their functionality. The fixation map also shows that the hair bands receive even less attention after haptic contact with the objects than before (see Figure 12 (a) and (b)). This is also reflected in the mental representation structures before participants had haptic contact with the objects (see Figure 11(a)): the hair bands form the only complete cluster in the dendogram. Attention on the hair bands is located around the knot. These areas give the participant hints about the flexibility along with information about the objects' purpose. Much more attention was directed towards unknown objects with inhomogeneous and colorful surfaces, e.g., the decorated mirror and the (Chinese style) toothpick holder (see Figure 8, objects 8 and 10). Both objects have several prominent features (color and shape) that attract participants' attention. Participants seem to concentrate on the objects indicated by the higher number of fixations in order to identify their prominent features and with it their functionality. This is in line with the findings in Pannasch, Helmert, Roth, Herbold and Walter (2008); Land & Tatler (2009): They support the existence of at least two qualitatively distinct modes of viewing scenes: global and local

Figure 12. Fixation map over all participants before (a) and after (b) they had haptic contact with the objects

(a)

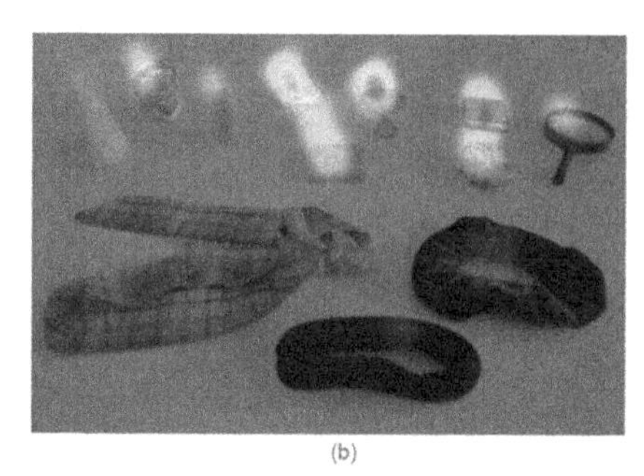
(b)

scanning. Global scanning periods, restricted to the first two seconds of viewing photographic scenes, are associated with large amplitude saccades and short duration fixations, whereas local scanning periods are associated with smaller amplitude saccades and longer fixations. There are also a lot of fixations on the make-up mirror and the foldable magnifier (see Figure 8, objects 4 and 9). These two objects have a square shape which is a common feature for many different objects. Thus, participants seem to spend a lot of time looking at the objects for a detailed inspection in order to find adequate features for object classification. This shows the specific interplay between eye movements and the quality of mental representation structures during the selective perception of (action-) relevant information: it can clearly be seen that the participants did not cluster the make-up mirror and the foldable magnifier (see Figure 8, objects 4 and 9) with other objects in the dendrogram before they had haptic contacts with the objects (see Figure 11(a)). Thus, they focused on these objects for a longer time in order to get hints about their functionality (see Figure 12(a)). Region analysis revealed that there are not many attention shifts between the make-up mirror and the foldable magnifier. Because both objects have quite similar shapes, it could have been expected that the participants switch their attention between the two objects for a closer inspection of their differences. The participants only glanced briefly at the plastic toothpick holder (see Figure 8, object 11). Maybe, even though the contrast to the background is quite low, they could quickly identify the toothpicks, and therefore recognize the object. More time was spent on the white (Chinese style) toothpick holder (see Figure 8, object 10), because it is homogeneously colored and the participants could not identify its content (because of the cover). Additionally, its shape can be easily mixed up with those of other objects, such as a deo roll-on.

After the participants had haptic contact with the objects, their fixation map changes (see Figure 12(b)). Now, they focused mainly on the make-up mirror, foldable loop, (Chinese style) magnifying glass, followed by the decorated mirror (see Figure 8, objects 4, 6, 8 and 9). There are less fixations on all the other objects compared to the gaze pattern before the participants had contact with the objects (see Figure 12(a)). Maybe, participants were sensitized to the functionality of the objects (after they had grasped them) and they tried to find object and group specific features in the picture.

Results of the Two Modeling Approaches

The models (EBMS and Walther & Koch) were executed with a number of iterations corresponding to the average number of fixations made by

Figure 13. The proto-objects generated (a) by the saliency model (Walther & Koch, 2006) and (b) by the EBMS model (with λ=0.98) after 90 iterations

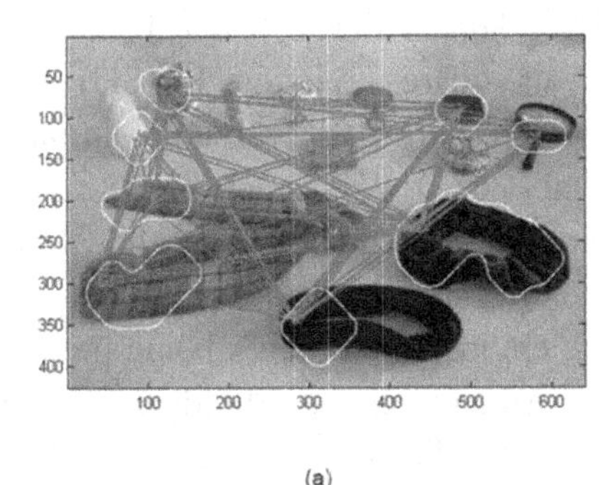

(a)

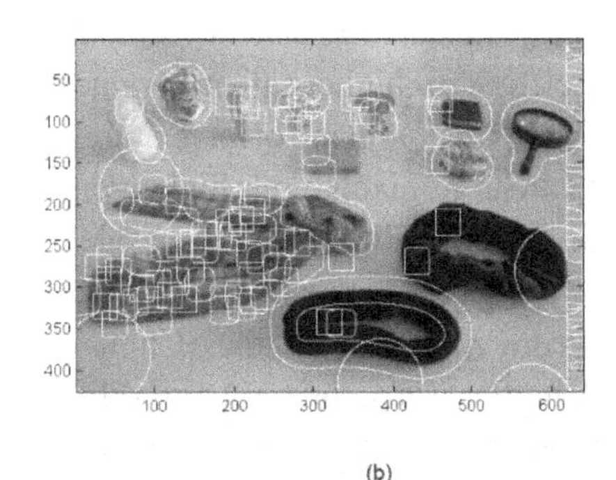

(b)

the participants when viewing the image during the eye-tracking experiment (N = 100). In each iteration, one proto-object and with it, one gaze position is generated (see Figure 13). The input to the model is a black-and white image with a size of *640 x 426* pixels. Computation time takes on average 5 minutes on a Intel Core™ 2 Quad CPU Q 9300 with 2.5 GHz with 4 GB DDR-RAM to produce a scan path of 100 fixations.

The output of the Walther & Koch model after 100 iterations can be seen in Figure 13 (a). The proto-objects are located on the most salient regions (see Figure 2 upper left). The salience points are those regions that have a prominent intensity and orientation contrast. These are the dark objects on the right hand side of the image which have a clear contrast against the wooden colored desk. Additionally, the edges of the red hair band and the colorful toothpick holder are areas of high saliency because of their high contrast against the background. The plastic toothstick holder, all mirrors and the (Chinese style) magnifying glass are not assigned high saliency values by the model (see Figure 13(a)), although participants did focus intensively on these objects (see Figure 12). This is in line with the findings in Tatler, Baddeley and Vincent (2006), who found less correspondence between saliency maps and empirical data when the observer has a cognitive, instead of a free-viewing, task. In our study, the task was to group the objects according to "their functionality in everyday use". Thus, because of the cognitive task there is a stronger focus on previously unknown and hard to identify objects, such as the make-up mirror and the foldable magnifier (see Figure 8, objects 4 and 9). Because of the inhibition of return mechanism and the relatively small number of salient regions, a cyclic behavior is found in the scan path resulting from the Walther & Koch model (see Figure 13(a)). This cyclic behavior is neither typical for the perception of complex scenes (see Figure 12), nor is there any empirical evidence for strict inhibition of return process when viewing complex scenes. Therefore, new approaches for driving attention through a scene, like the *Facilitation of Return,* allow the return of attention to previously attended location, which can be a potential source of information (Smith & Henderson, 2009; Tatler, Hayhoe, Land & Ballard, 2011). All in all, the scan path generated by the Walther & Koch model seems to be different from those of human participants when viewing the scene with the 12 objects. It seems that the participants attend to interesting objects suggesting that these objects better predict fixations and that early salience has only an indirect effect on attention (Einhäuser, Spain & Perona, 2008).

The EBMS model approach results in a completely different output with regard to the locations and shapes of the proto-objects, leading to a more distributed scan path (see Figure 13(b)).

There are no repeating cycles in the scan path as in the Walther & Koch model. Because the CVA approach, used to calculate the saliency map in the EBMS model, assigns higher saliency values to the regions with predominant color features, there are larger areas of pixels with high attention values than in the Walther &Koch m odel, especially for the objects with different colors, such as the decorated mirror or the (Chinese style) toothpick holder. Thus, the CVA algorithm shows a better separation of the objects from the background and the edges (and with it the shape) becomes more prominent (see Figure 6(a)). In the scan path produced by the EBMS model all objects receive attention, especially unknown ones (like in the human observers' case (see Figure 12 and 13(b))), in contrast to the Walther & Koch model, where the gaze positions are located on a relatively small number of salient points. Additionally, the clustering algorithm for the proto-objects using the threshold (λ) of the SDA-M method, leads to smaller proto-objects compared to the Walter & Koch model (see Figure 13(a) and (b)). In contrast to the Walter&Koch model, each object in the scene is associated with several proto-objects, like the mirrors (see Figure 13(b)). Thus, several fixations are located on one object which is also the case for the attention areas calculated from participants gaze data (see Figure 12). However, there are many fixations on the hair bands in the gaze allocations created by the EBMS model, which is not the case in the fixation maps generated from the empirical data. Here, the Walther & Koch model shows better results (see Figure 13(a)).

Comparison of the Empirical Results with the Model Outputs

We compare fixation maps computed from scan paths generated by the modeling approaches (Walther & Koch, CVA and EBMS) (see Figure 15) and the gaze patterns recorded in the experimental study (see Figure 12). Based on the dissimilarity between the attention distribution predicted by the model and that of the participants, we are able to ascertain the reliability of the model. The *Root Mean Square Error* (RMSE) (also called the root mean square deviation, RMSD) is a frequently used measure for the variability in data (Holmqvist et al., 2011). We use RMSD to calculate the difference between the gaze allocations predicted by the three models and those observed from the environment that is being modeled (i.e., the experiment). These individual differences are also called residuals, and the RMSE serves to aggregate them into a single measure of predictive power. The RMSE of a model prediction with respect to the estimated variable X_{mod} is defined as the square root of the mean squared error between the observed value ($X_{obs,i,j}$) and the predicted values from the different model approaches ($X_{mod,i,j}$) at image locations (i,j) in the corresponding fixation maps (see Figure 15):

$$RMSE = \sqrt{\frac{\sum_{i=1}^{n}\sum_{j=1}^{m}(X_{obs,i,j} - X_{\mathrm{mod},i,j})^2}{N}}.$$

The fixation map width and height is denoted by n and m, respectively. N is the total number of image pixels. In our approach, $X_{obs,i,j}$ and $X_{mod,i,j}$ are values between 0 and 1, and are the attention values at the corresponding pixel locations in the fixation maps.

We marked those regions in the images that received high attention by the participants with a region of interest (ROI) (see Figure 14). Those regions correspond to the clusters for the toothpick holders (region 1), the mirrors (regions 2), the magnifying glasses (region 3) and the knot in the red hair band (region 4). We calculate the RMSE between the fixation maps calculated from the empirical and model data for the whole image, as well as for the four ROIs. This allows us to calculate how closely the gaze allocations generated by the three models resemble the data recorded in the empirical experiments for the overall image, as looking separately at the four

Figure 14.Regions of high attention calculated from participants' eye movements recorded in the experimental study. Region 1 (white): toothpick holders, region 2 (green): mirrors, region 3 (blue): magnifying glasses, region 4 (yellow): knot in the red hair band

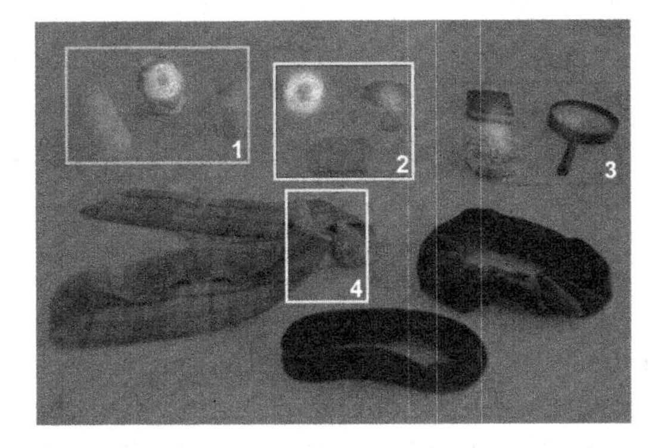

regions that received the highest attention. Small RSME dissimilarity values (close to 0) indicate that the scan paths generated by the models are close to the scan paths of the participants in the experiment. A value close to 1, on the other hand, indicates high differences between both gaze allocations.

Table 1 and Table 2 show the different RMSE dissimilarity values for the fixation maps calculated from the experimental data before and after the participants had haptic contact with the objects (see Figure 15 (a) and (b)), and the data generated by our EBMS approach (with different values for the parameter λ) and the Walther & Koch model, respectively. The entry EBMS_30 in the table means that λ is set to 0.30 (i.e., hierarchically less structured mental representation structures). Furthermore, we calculated the results for the "original CVA" approach (named CVA in Tables 1 and 2) to compare it to our EBMS model. Because there is no suggestion for the calculation of the scan path in the original literature (Bamidele, Stentiford & Morphett, 2004), we constructed a gaze allocation from the original CVA-saliency map (see Figure 6(a)) by starting with the most salient image pixel and successively taking those pixels with decreasing saliency values as the location of the next fixation. If several pixels have the same saliency value the pixel with the smallest index is taken. We selected the most salient points as fixation locations for the resulting scan path,

Figure 15. Fixation maps calculated from the empirical data (before (a) and after (b) participants had haptic contact with the objects) and from the gaze allocations generated by the Walther & Koch model (c) and the EBMS with different parameter λ ((d),with λ=0.3, (e),with λ=0.6, (f),with λ=0.98)

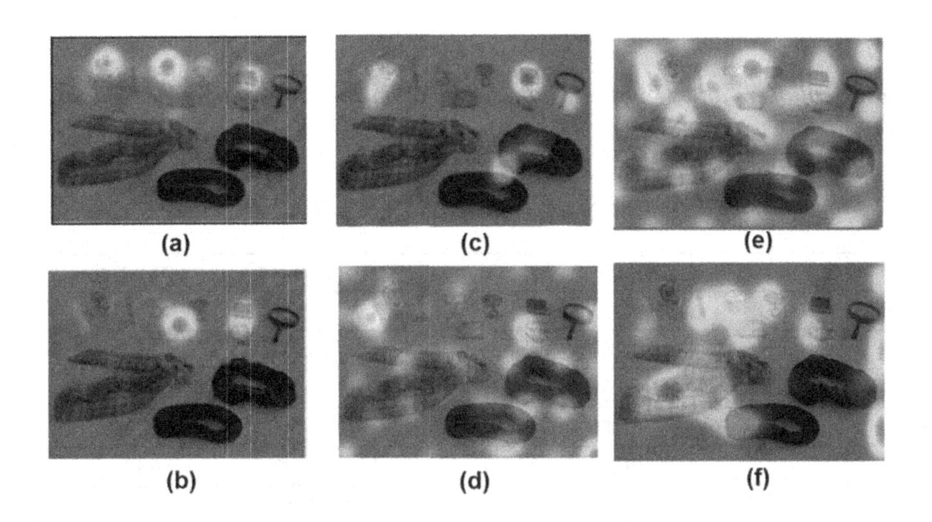

Table 1. RMSE dissimilarity values (for the whole image and the 4 sub-regions (see Figure 14)) between the fixation maps calculated from the empirical data and the data from the different model approaches (see Figure 15) before the participants had haptic with the objects (EBMS_30 means the EBMS model with λ=0.30). The last column depicts the sum over all RMSE values.

Model (Before)	RMSE	RMSE 1	RMSE 2	RMSE 3	RMSE 4	Σ
Walther & Koch	0.235	0.263	0.435	0.228	0.147	1.308
CVA	0.507	0.32	0.256	0.392	0.616	2.091
EBMS_30	0.277	0.278	0.248	0.253	0.208	1.264
EBMS_60	0.323	0.354	0.341	0.221	0.279	1.518
EBMS_70	0.222	0.241	0.306	0.27	0.151	1.190
EBMS_98	0.273	0.27	0.277	0.191	0.167	1.178

because Oyekoya and Stentiford (2004) found a correspondence between regions of high saliency values in the original CVA model and regions of visual interest indicated by participants' eye movements. The resulting fixation map is depicted in Figure 6(b).

The results (see Tables 1 and 2) show that the EBMS models reflect more closely participants' gaze behavior before and after they had haptic contact with the objects. Especially the EBMS models with the higher λ values perform better (see Figure 15 (e) and (f)). This threshold generates a higher number of focused attention areas, reflecting more closely human gaze allocations from the empirical study (see Figure 12 and 13(b)). Only for the hair band area (see Figure 14, region 4) the Walther & Koch model is superior. The participants needed only few fixations (i.e., they may use peripheral vision) to identify the regularly striped or homogeneously colored hair bands (see Figures 15 (a) and (b)). The Walther & Koch model detects 4 proto-object regions (see Figure 13 (a)). These regions, especially for the dark hair bands, cover the attention areas of the participants in the empirical study (see Figure 12). Because the hair bands cover the majority of the image size, the dissimilarity value for the whole image (RSME) is quite small for the Walther & Koch model compared to the other approaches (see Tables 1 and 2). The fixation map generated from the gaze allocation of the CVA model is quite distributed over the whole image and therefore

Table 2. RMSE dissimilarity values (for the whole image and the 4 sub-regions (see Figure 14)) between the fixation maps calculated from the empirical data and the data from the different model approaches (see Figure 15) after the participants had haptic with the objects (EBMS_30 means the EBMS model with λ=0.30). The last column depicts the sum over all RMSE values.

Model (After)	RMSE	RMSE 1	RMSE 2	RMSE 3	RMSE 4	Σ
Walther & Koch	0.222	0.235	0.436	0.207	0.07	1.170
CVA	0.526	0.303	0.269	0.442	0.67	2.210
EBMS_30	0.283	0.278	0.248	0.244	0.254	1.307
EBMS_60	0.339	0.401	0.346	0.241	0.332	1.659
EBMS_70	0.220	0.265	0.21	0.247	0.184	1.126
EBMS_98	0.265	0.171	0.290	0.165	0.194	1.085

does not adequately model the participants' attention distribution (see Figure 6(b)). Only in case of the mirrors (see Figure 14, region 2), the CVA model outperforms the Walther & Koch model (i.e., the RSME 2 values of the CVA model are smaller in Tables 1 and 2). The reason is that the features used in the Walther & Koch model do not adequately find salient regions for the mirrors (see Figure 13 (a)). Therefore, the model does not assign proto-objects to this region. No saliency area is assigned to this area (see Figure 13 (a)) and therefore there is no attention spot in the fixation map (see Figure 15 (c)) leading to high dissimilarity values. The CVA approach, on the other hand, assigns high saliency values to the hair bands (see Figure 14, region 4), because their color features are different from the rest of the image, leading to a high number of gaze positions. That is the reason why the CVA approach performs worse. This is also the problem for the EBMS models with lower λ thresholds. They generate larger regions of high importance on the salient points calculated from the CVA approach. This means that they also put attention on salient areas that are not focused on by the participants. The EBMS approaches with higher λ values can compensate for this behavior by extracting smaller regions, i.e., generation less gaze allocations on salient areas not focused on in the empirical study. This is less pronounced in case of the mirrors (see Figure 14, region 2), where the CVA model already show a low dissimilarity value (RMSE 2).

After participants had haptic contact with the objects, the RSME values for the EBMS models with lower λ value increase (except for the magnifying glasses for the EBMS_30 model– region 3 in Figure 14). The two EBMS models with higher λ values show better RSME dissimilarity values for the whole image and the magnifying glasses (see Figure 14, region 3). Additionally, the EBMS_70 model performs better for the mirrors (see Figure 14, region 2) and the EBMS_98 model for the toothpick holders (see Figure 14, region 1). The Walter&Koch has better results with regard to the overall RSME value and the $\sum$ value (see Tables 1 and 2). But this is mainly due to lower dissimilarity values (RMSE 4) for the hair bands (see Figure 14, region 4). A calculation of $\sum$ (without RSME 4) reveals 1.161 (before) and 1.1 (after) for the Walter&Koch, and 1.011 (before) and 0.891 (after) for the EBMS_98 model. These results show that the EBMS_70 and EBMS_98 models adapt better to the learning process: the eye movements of the participants before and after handling with the objects are different and this should also be reflected in the model outcome. Furthermore, it can be seen from the fixation maps (see Figure 15 (d)–(f)) that the EBMS model outputs a higher number of focused gaze allocations with increasing value of λ, which goes along with the differences in the functional versus spatial gaze behavior between novices and experts found in various sport studies (Schack & Essig, 2011; Raab & Johnson, 2007; Williams, A.M. & Ward, P. 2007) (see Figure 4).

When compared to our model, the Walther & Koch model produces good overall results, particularly with respect to the hair bands, because it correctly does not assign high attention to these objects (see Figure 15). It also shows better (RSME 1) values for the toothpick objects (see Figure 14, region 1). Because of the intensity contrast, it produces a high salient region at the bottom of the (Chinese style) toothpick holder (see Figure 13 (a) and Figure 8, object 12). Before participants had haptic contact with the toothpick holders, there is an attention spot on the top of the (Chinese style) toothpick holder (see Figure 15 (a)). Since the location of the attention spot in the Walther & Koch model (see Figure 15 (c)) is different from the location of the area focused by the participants (see Figure 15(a)), the RSME 1 dissimilarity value before the contact with the objects is higher. After the contact, participants focused less on the (Chinese style) toothpick holder (see Figure 15 (b)). Therefore, the RSME 1 value slightly decreases. For the case of the magnifying glasses attention is directed more toward the foldable magnifier and the (Chinese style) magnifying glass (see Figure 8, objects 4 and 6) after participants had haptic contact with them. This attention distribution is better reflected in the EBMS_98 model, because its RSME 3 value shows the highest decrease. Again, the Walter&Koch model performs best for the hairbands (see Figure 14, region 4). It extracts just two large salient regions on the hairbands (see Figure 13 (a)), whereas all the EBMS models place more attention on them. Participants do not focus on the black hairbands after grasping the objects (see Figure 15 (b)). This explains the highest decrease in the dissimilarity value for the hair bands (RMSE 4) for the Walther & Koch model.

Regarding the learning process, the Walter&Koch model does not reflect the changes in gaze behavior as adequately as the EBMS models with a higher λ threshold. Except for the hair band area, the EBMS models show the lowest RMSE dissimilarity values (see Table 2). The reason is that the Walther & Koch model always produces the same gaze allocations, because it only considers bottom-up information (see Figure 13 (a)). The region-selection algorithm of the Walther & Koch does not change its output and thus cannot adapt to the differences in participants' gaze behavior resulting from a better mental object representation in long-term memory. It provides a first rough guess (based on purely bottom-up, stimuli driven features) of the extent of salient regions, without image segmentation and what describes an object (Walther & Koch, 2006). The EMBS models can adapt their output by changing the λ threshold. The higher values of λ result in a gaze allocation that more adequately reflects the different gaze behavior resulting from the structuring process in the mental representations as a learning process through the interaction with the objects.

All in all, the results of the EBMS models with higher λ thresholds better reflect the gaze patterns of the participants when viewing the objects than the Walther & Koch model (see Tables 1 and 2), whereas the other two EBMS models show an increase in the dissimilarity values after the participants had haptic contact with the objects. Thus, the expertise-based component of the EBMs model, reflected by the λ value, better adapts to the differences in participants' gaze behavior resulting from hierarchically structured mental object representations in long-term memory after contact with the objects. There is no cyclic behavior in the gaze pattern generated by the EBMS models when compared to the Walther & Koch model. The EBMS_98 model represents participants' gaze behavior by assigning higher saliency values and smaller proto-objects to the single objects. The disadvantage of the Walther & Koch model is that the applied features do not find adequate salient regions in the image, resulting in an inadequate number and size of proto-objects that leads to a cyclic behavior. The participants do not give much attention to the hair bands. This is in contrast to the results of the EBMS approach. Therefore, the Walther & Koch model provides quite good RSME values for the whole image, although the EBMS models better describe the gaze pattern of participants for the single objects groups especially, after the participants had haptic contact with the objects. The fixation map generated from the gaze allocation of the CVA model is quite distributed over the whole image and therefore does not adequately model participants' attention distribution.

CONCLUSION AND FUTURE RESEARCH DIRECTIONS

Until now, the basic principles of visual attention, such as cognitive control, learning and expertise, have not received a lot of attention in modeling approaches for visual attention (Tatler, Hayhoe, Land & Ballard, 2011). Therefore, we implemented a novel computational approach to visual attention that applies the CVA algorithm to calculate the saliency map from the input image (see Figure 6(a)) and extended it by introducing an expertise-based component in order to model the role of cognitive control and the influences of learning and expertise on the visual perception processes. We evaluated our modeling approach by investigating a simple task, where participants had to look at and grasp 12 known and unknown objects and compared the output of our model to the results of the original saliency-map based model of visual attention (Itti, Koch, & Niebur, 1998; Itti & Koch, 2001; Walther & Koch, 2006) and the original cognitive visual attention (CVA) approach (Barmidele, Stentiford & Morphett, 2004).

Our results clearly revealed differences in the mental representation structures for the 12 objects in the long-term memory before and after participants had haptic contact with them. First, the participants were not familiar with all the objects and clustered them according to shape and size features, i.e., they do not have an adequate mental representation of the objects in their long-term memory. Participants found it difficult to find objects with similar functionalities, and thus the Euclidean distance of objects within clusters is quite high. Later, after they had haptic contact with them, the mental representations of the objects were updated – resulting in a higher number of objects clustered according to their functionality. The analysis of the gaze data shows more attention areas of smaller sizes at the beginning. It seems that the participants first focused on individual objects in order to identify characteristic features necessary to classify them according to their functionality in everyday use. Unknown objects are analyzed using local scanning periods associated with smaller amplitude saccades and longer fixations (Pannasch, Helmert, Roth, Herbold and Walter, 2008; Land & Tatler, 2009) - revealing a higher cognitive load needed to perform an adequate analysis of the object features. After the interaction phase, participants' attention seems to be more linked among particular objects belonging to the same functional group. There were less large attention areas in the fixation map. This may indicate that the participants were trying to find cluster features instead of individual object characteristics. A comparison of the scan paths generated by our model, the widely applied Walther & Koch model (Walther & Koch, 2006) and the CVA approach revealed that our approach better approximates the gaze allocation processes. Regarding the learning process, the Walther & Koch and CVS models do not reflect the changes in gaze behavior as adequately as the EBMS models with a higher λ threshold.

There is much further room for modeling the close interaction between visual attention, cognitive control, learning and expertise for optimal (individualistic) search strategies to perceive the relevant information. First of all, we will test our approach in a much wider area of applications fields where expertise and learning play a significant role, such as sports, assembling, human-human and human-machine interaction. In order to get a better understanding, we will also compare the results of our approach to further widely applied models of visual attention (Frintop, Rome, & Christensen, 2010; Tsotsos & Rothenstein, 2011). An important aspect could be to define a standard test set that may serve as a benchmark to evaluate different approaches of visual attention models. We believe that our suggested model to extend a saliency-based model of visual attention with an expertise based component to reflect the (individualistic) influence of the quality of mental representation structures in long-term memory and the roles of cognitive control, expertise and learning, is a promising approach to reflect sets of observed principles underlying eye guidance on the visual perception of objects, events and motor actions (Schack & Essig, 2011; Land & Tatler, 2009; Williams, A.M. & Ward, P. 2007).

Developing models of gaze allocations that generalize across many instances of natural behavior is a difficult task (Tatler, Hayhoe, Land, & Ballard, 2011). The computation of object semantics beyond the pure saliency, i.e., the assignment of feature points to particular objects in the individual images, is a promising approach to increase the robustness of the model (Walther & Koch, 2006). We are currently working on the integration of biologically motivated techniques for object recognition and the extraction of image semantics, because gaze allocations depend on task demands (Tatler, Hayhoe, Land & Ballard, 2011). The classification and recognition of particular objects in the scene, e.g., the position of a goal-keeper or an opponent in a soccer game, influences people's perception and reaction behavior (Essig et al, 2010). In these situations the learning aspect plays a functional role: experts have a different perceptual and motor behavior than novices. We can use this knowledge to improve the subsequent selection process for salient image regions while considering the quality of the mental representation structures, for example by the spatial inhomogeneous feature processing in the human retina (Wischnewsky, Schneider, Bellardinelli & Steil, 2009) and different weighting schemes for features in the eccentricity along the degree of expertise. This research addresses the complex interplay between information extraction (via the fovea, parafoveal, and visual periphery) and the identification of specific sources of perceptual information that humans use in interaction scenarios. Although participants were not explicitly told, the arrangement of the objects according to their classes may have primed them. It could be expected that a random arrangement of objects would have resulted in quite different scan paths, i.e., much more forward and backward saccades between the different objects. The implemented inhibition of return in the models does not consider these jumps. Recent research revealed that there is not any empirical evidence for a strict inhibition of return process when viewing complex scenes (Smith & Henderson, 2009; Tatler, Hayhoe, Land & Ballard, 2011). Therefore, new approaches for driving attention through a scene, like the *Facilitation of Return* (Smith & Henderson, 2009), allow the return of attention to the previously attended location, which is a potential source of information. We plan to integrate this feature together with statistical dependencies between successive eye movements (i.e., what the eyes have just done strongly influences the characteristics of each new fixation and saccade) (Land & Tatler, 2009) into our model in future work.

Predicting where a user might look next opens up new possibilities in diverse areas, such as augmented reality, interactive advertisement, and human-machine interaction (e.g. in intelligent systems with smart user interfaces). Knowledge about the cognitive and learning principles of action-based perception and the selection process of action relevant information from the steady flow of ongoing events is of great importance for the establishment of biologically inspired human-machine interfaces and the development of humanoid robots and intelligent systems. We build on the theory that the development of cognition is closely linked with the capability of acting and perceiving one's environment and causing changes to it (Schack & Ritter, 2009). These insights into the human learning and perceptual processes when encountering unknown situations are of importance for the field of cognitive neuroscience robotics in order to build artificial cognitive systems that can interact with a human in an intuitive way. By measuring the cognitive architecture of motor actions/object relations and attention processes, robotic systems can get insights into the level of expertise and visual interests of interaction partners. From this data a cognitive neuroscience robot could possibly select and adjust its actions flexibly in a given situation, e.g., while assisting an older or handicapped person.

ACKNOWLEDGMENT

We thank Dirk Bernhardt Walther from the Beckman Institute of Advanced Science Technology, University of Illinois at Urbana-Champaign, for providing the MATLAB source code of his saliency toolbox (downloaded from http://www.saliencytoolbox.net). Finally, we wish to thank

Jonathan Maycock for his helpful comments and suggestions.

REFERENCES

Bamidele, A., Stentiford, F. W. M., & Morphett, J. (2004). An attention based approach to content based image retrieval. *BT Technology Journal*, *22*, 151–160. doi:10.1023/B:BTTJ.0000047129.83260.79

Bläsing, B., Tenenbaum, G., & Schack, T. (2009). The cognitive structure of movements in classical dance. *Psychology of Sport and Exercise*, *10*, 350–360. doi:10.1016/j.psychsport.2008.10.001

Braun, S. M., Beurskens, A. J., Schack, T., Marcellis, R. G., Oti, K. C., Schols, J. M., & Wade, D. T. (2007). It is possible to use the structural dimension analysis of motor memory (SDA-M) to investigate representations of motor actions in stroke patients? *Clinical Rehabilitation*, *21*, 822–832. doi:10.1177/0269215507078303

Bundesen, C., Habekost, T., & Kyllingsbaek, S. (2005). A neural theory of visual attention: Bridging cognition and neurophysiology. *Psychological Review*, *112*, 291–328. doi:10.1037/0033-295X.112.2.291

Deubel, H., & Schneider, W. X. (1996). Saccade target selection and object recognition: Evidence for a common attentional mechanism. *Vision Research*, *36*, 1812–1837. doi:10.1016/0042-6989(95)00294-4

Duchowski, A. T. (2007). *Eye tracking methodology: Theory and practice*. New York, NY: Springer Verlag.

Duchowski, A. T., et al. (2010). Scanpath comparison revisited. *Eye Tracking Research & Applications (ETRA 2010)* Austin, USA.

Einhäuser, W., Spain, M., & Perona, P. (2008). Objects predict fixations better than early saliency. *Journal of Vision (Charlottesville, Va.)*, *8*, 1–26. doi:10.1167/8.14.18

Essig, K., Berger, A., Hoffmeister, M., Koesling, H., Weigelt, M., & Schack, T. (2010). Der Einflusses der Torwartposition beim 7-Meter im Handball auf das Blick- und Entscheidungsverhalten von Handball-Experten und -Laien. In Mattes, K., & Wollesen, B. (Eds.), *Bewegung und Leistung - Sport, Gesundheit & Alter* (p. 23). Hamburg, Germany: Czwalina.

Essig, K., Pohl, S., & Ritter, H. (2005). EyeDataAnalyser – A general and flexible visualization and analysation tool for eye tracking data-files. *Proceedings 13th European Conference on Eye Movements (ECEM 13)*, Bern, Switzerland.

Frintop, S., Rome, E., & Christensen, H. I. (2010). Computational visual attention systems and their cognitive foundation: A survey. [TAP]. *ACM Transactions on Applied Perception*, *7*, 1–39. doi:10.1145/1658349.1658355

Heinke, D., & Humphreys, G. W. (2004). *Computational models of visual selective attention. A review. Connectionist models in psychology* (pp. 273–312). London, UK: Psychology Press.

Henderson, J. M., Weeks, P. A., & Hollingworth, A. (1999). Effects of a semantic consistency on eye movements during scene viewing. *Journal of Experimental Psychology. Human Perception and Performance*, *25*, 210–228. doi:10.1037/0096-1523.25.1.210

Holmqvist, K., Nyström, M., Andersson, R., Dewhurst, R., Jarodzka, H., & van de Weijer, J. (2011). *Eye tracking – A comprehensive guide to methods and measures*. New York, NY: Oxford University Press.

Hwang, A. D., Higgins, E. C., & Pomplun, M. (2009). A model of top-down attentional control during visual search in complex scenes. *Journal of Vision (Charlottesville, Va.)*, *9*(5), 1–18. doi:10.1167/9.5.25

Itti, L., & Koch, C. (2001). Computational modeling of visual attention. *Nature Neuroscience Review*, *2*, 194–204. doi:10.1038/35058500

Itti, L., Koch, C., & Niebur, E. (1998). A model of saliency-based visual attention for rapid scene analysis. *IEEE Transactions on Pattern Analysis and Machine Intelligence*, *20*, 1254–1259. doi:10.1109/34.730558

Jarodzka, H., Holmqvist, K., & Nyström, M. (2010). A vector-based, multidimensional scanpath similarity measure. In C. Morimoto, & H. Instance (Eds.), *Proceedings of the 2010 Symposium on Eye Tracking Research & Applications ETRA '10* (pp. 211-218). New York, NY: ACM.

Koch, C., & Ullman, S. (1985). Shifts in selective visual attention – towards the underlying neural circuity. *Human Neurobiology*, *4*, 219–227.

Koesling, H., & Ritter, H. (2001). VDesigner – A visual programming environment for eye-tracking experiments. *Proceedings 11th European Conference on Eye Movements ECEM11*, Turku, Finland.

Land, M. F., & Tatler, B. W. (2009). *Looking and acting. Vision and eye movements in natural behavior*. New York, NY: Oxford University Press. doi:10.1093/acprof:oso/9780198570943.001.0001

Land, M. F., & Tatler, B. W. (2009). *Looking and acting – Vision and eye movements in natural behavior*. New York, NY: Oxford University Press. doi:10.1093/acprof:oso/9780198570943.001.0001

Martinez-Conde, S., Macknik, S. L., & Hubel, D. H. (2004). The role of fixational eye movements in visual perception. *Nature Reviews. Neuroscience*, *5*, 229–240. doi:10.1038/nrn1348

Maycock, J., Bläsing, B., Bockemühl, T., Ritter, H., & Schack, T. (2010). Motor synergies and object representation in virtual and real grasping. *Conference Record of the 1st International Conference on Applied Bionics and Biomechanics (ICABB)*, Venice, Italy.

Mc Mains, S. A., & Somers, D. C. (2004). Multiple spotlights of attentional selection in human visual cortex. *Neuron*, *42*, 677–686. doi:10.1016/S0896-6273(04)00263-6

Navalpakkam, V., & Itti, L. (2005). Modeling the influence of task on attention. *Vision Research*, *45*(2), 205–231. doi:10.1016/j.visres.2004.07.042

Navalpakkam, V., & Itti, L. (2006). An integrated model of top-down and bottom-up attention for optimal object detection. *Proceedings IEEE Conference on Computer Vision and Pattern Recognition (CVPR)*, (pp. 2049-2056).

Nothdurft, H.-C., Gallant, J. L., & van Essen, D. C. (1999). Response modulation by texture surround in primate area V1: Correlates of popout under anasthesia. *Visual Neuroscience*, *16*, 15–34. doi:10.1017/S0952523899156189

Ouerhani, N., Hügli, H., Burgi, P.-Y., & Rüdi, P.-F. (2002). A real time implementation of the saliency-based model of visual attention on a SIMD architecture. *Proceedings of the 24th DAGM Symposium on Pattern Recognition, Lecture Notes in Computer Science, 2449*, (pp. 282-289). Springer Verlag.

Oyekoya, O., & Stentiford, F. W. M. (2004). Exploring human eye behaviour using a model of visual attention. *International Conference on Pattern Recognition,* Vol. 4, (pp. 945-948).

Pannasch, S., Helmert, J. R., Roth, K., Herbold, A.-K., & Walter, H. (2008). Visual fixation durations and saccade amplitudes: Shifting relationship in a variety of conditions. *Journal of Eye Movement Research*, *2*(2), 1–19.

Parkhurst, D., Law, K., & Niebur, E. (2002). Modeling the role of salience in the allocation of overt visual attention. *Vision Research*, *42*, 107–123. doi:10.1016/S0042-6989(01)00250-4

Pomplun, M., Ritter, H., & Velichkovsky, B. M. (1996). Disambiguating complex visual information: Towards communication of personal views of a scene. *Perception*, *25*, 931–948. doi:10.1068/p250931

Posner, M. I. (1980). Orienting of attention. *The Quarterly Journal of Experimental Psychology*, *32*, 3–25. doi:10.1080/00335558008248231

Raab, M., & Johnson, J. G. (2007). Expertise-based differences in search and option- generation strategies. *Journal of Experimental Psychology. Applied*, *13*, 158–170. doi:10.1037/1076-898X.13.3.158

Rao, R. P. N., Zelinsky, G. J., Hayhoe, M. M., & Ballard, D. H. (2002). Eye movements in iconic visual search. *Vision Research*, *42*, 1447–1463. doi:10.1016/S0042-6989(02)00040-8

Riesenhuber, M., & Poggio, T. (1999). Hierarchical models of object recognition in cortex. *Nature Neuroscience*, *2*, 1019–1025. doi:10.1038/14819

Rothenstein, A., & Tsotsos, J. (2006). Attention links sensing to recognition. *Image & Vision Computing Journal. Special Issue on Cognitive Vision Systems*, *26*, 114–126.

Rötting, M. (2001). *Parametersystematik der Augen- und Blickbewegungen. Für Arbeitswissenschaftliche Untersuchungen*. Aachen, Germany: Shaker Verlag.

Schack, T. (2012). A method for measuring mental representation. IN G. Tenenbaum, R. C. Eklund, & A. Kamata (Eds.), *Handbook of measurement in sport,* (pp. 203-214). Human Kinetics.

Schack, T., & Essig, K. (2011). Perceptual motor skills and the cognitive architecture of action - Methods and perspectives in motor control research. In Columbus, A. M. (Ed.), *Advances in psychology research* (*Vol. 81*, pp. 35–73). New York, NY: Nova Science Publishers.

Schack, T., & Mechsner, F. (2006). Representation of motor skills in human long-term memory. *Neuroscience Letters*, *391*, 77–81. doi:10.1016/j.neulet.2005.10.009

Schack, T., & Ritter, H. (2009). The cognitive nature of action – functional links between cognitive psychology, movement science, and robotics. *Progress in Brain Research*, *174*, 231–251. doi:10.1016/S0079-6123(09)01319-3

Smith, T. J., & Henderson, J. M. (2009). Facilitation of return during scene viewing. *Visual Cognition*, *17*, 1083–1108. doi:10.1080/13506280802678557

Tatler, B. W., Baddeley, R. J., & Vincent, B. T. (2006). The long and the short of it: Spatial statistics at fixation vary with saccade amplitude and task. *Vision Research*, *46*, 1857–1862. doi:10.1016/j.visres.2005.12.005

Tatler, B. W., Hayhoe, M. M., Land, M. F., & Ballard, D. H. (2011). Eye guidance in natural vision: Reinterpreting salience. *Journal of Vision (Charlottesville, Va.)*, *11*(5), 1–23. doi:10.1167/11.5.5

Tsotsos, J. K., & Rothenstein, A. (2011). Computation models of visual attention. *Scholarpedia*, *6*(1), 6201. doi:10.4249/scholarpedia.6201

Vickers, J. N. (2007). *Perception, cognition and decision training: The quiet eye in action*. Champaign, IL: Human Kinetics.

Walther, D., & Koch, C. (2006). Modeling attention to salient proto-objects. *Neural Networks*, *19*, 1395–1407. doi:10.1016/j.neunet.2006.10.001

Weigelt, M., Bosbach, S., Schack, T., & Kunde, W. (2006). Wenn wir anderen Menschen beim Handeln zusehen, interpretieren wir gleichzeitig auch deren Intention. In Raab, M., Arnold, A., & Gärtner, K. (Eds.), *Zukunft der Sportspiele: Fördern, fordern, forschen* (pp. 49–52). Flensburg, Germany: University Press.

Weigelt, M., & Schack, T. (2007). Selektive Effekte unbewusster Handlungsbahnung beim Beobachter anderer Fußballspieler. In *Abstract-Band, Congress of the DVS-Committee Soccer in the Sport Center* Kamen-Kaiserau (pp. 9-10).

Williams, A. M., & Ward, P. (2007). Perceptual-cognitive expertise in sport: Exploring new horizons. In Tenenbaum, G., & Eklund, R. C. (Eds.), *Handbook of sport psychology* (pp. 203–223). Hoboken, NJ: John Wiley & Sons.

Wischnewski, M., Belardinelli, A., Schneider, W. X., & Steil, J. J. (2010). Where to look next? Combining static and dynamic proto-objects in a TVA-based model of visual attention. *Cognitive Computation*, *2*, 326–343. doi:10.1007/s12559-010-9080-1

Wooding, D. S. (2002). Eye movements of large populations: II. Deriving regions of interest, coverage, and similarity using fixation maps. *Behavior Research Methods, Instruments, & Computers*, *34*, 518–528. doi:10.3758/BF03195481

KEY TERMS AND DEFINITIONS

Attentional Landscapes: A visualization technique for the gaze data recorded from several participants: Image regions receiving much attention are highlighted, whereas sparsely fixated areas are blurred/darkened.

Computational Modelling: Implemented algorithmic descriptions of the suggested interpretations of the experimental data that attempts to simulate the empirical observations.

Expertise: Great skill or knowledge in a particular field or hobby. Experts are characterized by having more than 10000 hours experiences on their field.

Eye Tracking: The spatio-temporal recording of participants' eye movements when viewing 2D or 3D stimuli.

Hierarchical Sorting Paradigm (SDA-M): With the Structural Dimensional Analysis of Mental Representation is a method to access the quality of mental representation structures in long-term memory in a *cognitive experimental task*.

Mental Representation Structures: Results from different lines of research addressing the mental representation level showed that not only the structure formation of representations in long-term memory, but also that chunk formations in working memory are built upon motor primitives and relate systematically to movement structures. Experiments show that representational frameworks are organized in a hierarchical tree-like structure and revealed a good match with the bio-mechanical demands of the task.

Visual Attention: A cognitive process to allocate the processing resources to selectively concentration on one aspect of environment while ignoring other things.

Chapter 2
Computational Approaches to Measurement of Visual Attention:
Modeling Overselectivity in Intellectual and Developmental Disabilities

Nurit Haspel
University of Massachusetts Boston, USA

Alison Shell
University of Massachusetts Medical School, USA

Curtis K. Deutsch
University of Massachusetts Medical School, USA

ABSTRACT

Alterations in gazing patterns and visual attention have often been noted among patients with intellectual and developmental disabilities (IDD) relative to neurotypical individuals. Here, the authors discuss visual attention with a particular focus on attention overselectivity. Overselectivity is observed when a subject focuses on a limited subset of available stimuli, or attends to a limited spatial field of vision. It is a widely-observed problem among individuals with IDD, notably, children with autism spectrum disorders (ASD). In this chapter, the authors survey computational and experimental approaches to analyze selective visual attention patterns, including overselectivity. These may provide useful computational frameworks for modeling visual attention in ASD patients and quantifying how it differs from neurotypical patterns. Computer-automated routines would be a boon for the field, distilling key dependent measures for aberrant attentional processes (a) for group studies of pathological processes and (b) on a single-subject basis for clinical description and possible remediation of attentional deficits.

DOI: 10.4018/978-1-4666-2539-6.ch002

INTRODUCTION

There are limits to the ability to process information, and what is commonly referred to as "attention" provides one means of winnowing down available data for more efficient management. Perhaps no one has captured the essence of selective attention as succinctly as William James, over 120 years ago:

Everyone knows what attention is. It is the taking possession by the mind, in clear and vivid form, of one out of what seem several simultaneously possible objects or trains of thought.

W James (1890). *The Principles of Psychology*

Over recent decades, psychologists have subdivided attention itself into a variety of forms. One category, that of visual selective attention, can be parsed into several sub-categories, including attention to regions of space, stimulus features, and whole objects (Freiwald & Kanwisher, 2004).

Computational and experimental approaches have been widely used to investigate patterns of human visual attention. In this chapter we review computational approaches designed to characterize selective attention, with a worked example on attention to facial patterns. We also discuss the potential application of computational methods to quantitatively analyze the gazing patterns of patients with IDD.

Selective attention has been classified in psychology using different organizational principles. In this discussion, we will refer to visual selective attention to specific stimuli and areas of a visual array. Posner (1987) also discusses selective attention, focusing on the process of attentional engagement and subsequent disengagement from visual stimuli. Specifically, the inability to disengage from a stimulus, which could be seen as overselectivity, has been observed in some IDD including ADHD and Schizophrenia (see for example (Butler and Javitt, 2005, Elahipanath et al., 2007, Laprevote et al., 2010, Le et al., 2003, Nestor et al., 2009, Tseng et al., 2010)).

Attentional Overselectivity in IDD Patients

In this chapter we discuss one aspect of visual selective attention and its variant, stimulus overselectivity. In overselectivity (*restricted stimulus control*), a subject focuses on only limited elements of a complex configuration (for example, in scanning an image of a face, attention to only a narrow array of features) or a limited spatial area in a visual display (Lovaas et al., 1979, Dube, 2009, Jemel et al, 2006). Further, we discuss visual data processing methodologies developed in other areas of computer science that may be applied to the phenomenon of attentional overselectivity; conceivably, these may contribute to understanding and quantifying abnormalities of visual attention among diagnostic subgroups of IDD patients.

Dube and McIlvane (1997) have shown that specific stimuli attended to overselectively could be systematically influenced by adjusting the schedules of reinforcement for attending. They have developed methodologies for more informative assessments and effective remediation of overselective attending (e.g., (Dube and McIlvane, 1999); (Dube et al, 1999); (Dickson et al., 2006a,b); (Dube et al., 2010)).

The phenomenology of overselectivity has also been observed in attention to facial patterns among subjects with autism. Recent studies have pointed to selective attending in autism to facial pattern arrays, notably, to the mouth and relatively less so to the eyes (the converse of typically-developing individuals' attention) (Klin and Jones, 2008); (Jones et al, 2008).

Overselective attention has been observed in a spectrum of IDD conditions, and is not isolated to autism spectrum disorders or specific intellectual levels. Studies by Dickson et al (2006a,b) investigated a sample of IDD subjects at a residential school. Though they found that overselective attention tended to be associated with lower Mental Age Equivalent scores (Dickson et al, 2006b), it was observed across a wide range of mental age-equivalent scores, and not limited to only the lower scorers. Additionally, overselectivity was more likely to occur among subjects with higher autism symptom severity, based on an observational scale ((Dickson et al, 2006a). It is worth noting that overselectivity has also been observed among individuals who do not have IDD. For example, it has been seen among subjects who have sustained traumatic brain injury and no diagnosis of IDD ((Wayland and Taplin, 1985).

Eye-tracking methodology that follows eye movement and points-of-fixation is a useful tool in the study of overselective attending. For example, one can observe meandering visual attention in a subject whose attention appears to be drawn to a restricted area of a display (see Figure 1). This figure is an illustration of visual attention integrated over time, and is drawn from a case documented by the laboratory of Dr William Dube (personal communication). Starting from a point of central fixation on a CRT, the subject's attention wanders widely but is drawn to an increasingly narrow region (the lower left corner). One can also configure an analysis of visual inspection of a face, presented on a CRT. An example is given in Figure 2, in which a time-series - reading from left to right - demonstrates that attention is focused increasingly over time. In this case, attention is directed to the mouth area (consistent with visual gaze patterns often observed for ASD); with each successive frame, one sees that the area of visual fixation gravitates more tightly to the mouth.

Figure 1. Spatial overselectivity. In this simulation, the point of gaze is tracked on a CRT using an eye tracking device. Starting at a point of central fixation, the point of gaze meanders initially then gravitates to the lower left corner of the display.

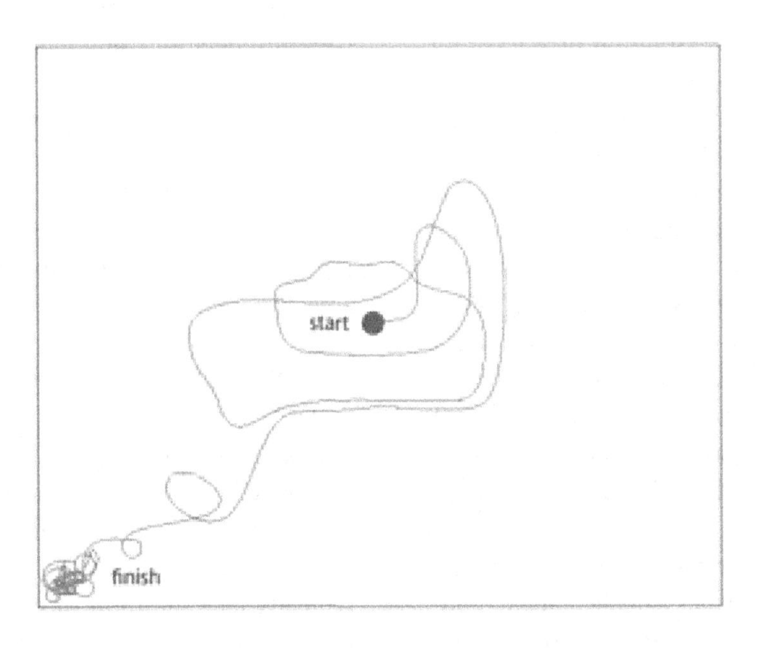

Figure 2. Narrowing of attentional field in facial scan. This figure illustrates a sequence of frames in which attention is focused on one delineated region (in red). This region narrows over time and in this illustration attention does not diverge from the area circumscribing the mouth.

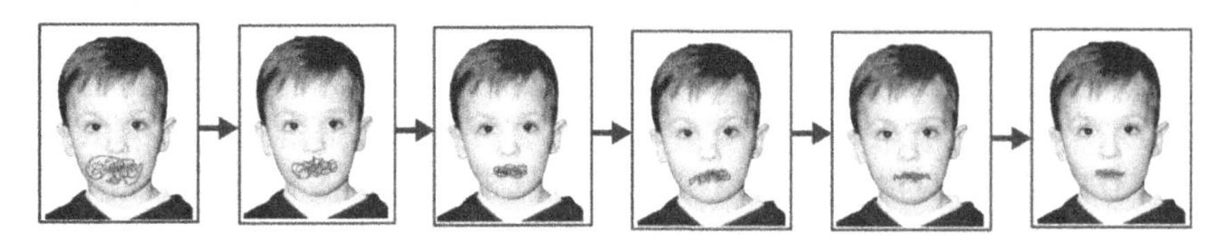

COMPUTATIONAL METHODOLOGIES TO ANALYZE VISUAL DATA

Computational methods have been used extensively to model the human visual system and gain insight into the perceptual and cognitive process underlying the processing of visual data and visual attention (Le Meur et al., 2006). A number of these methods are surveyed below. While even advanced computational methods cannot fully take into account cognitive mechanisms that underlie visual attention, the quantitative measurement of gazing patterns can be used to extract valuable information about the sequence in which the subjects inspect the target image and to what regions in the image they give the most attention. Computational models of visual attention may be divided into bottom-up (stimulus driven) or top down (goal-driven). Such models have been used for analyzing visual attention in complex images and real-world scenes (Henderson, 2003, Hwang et al., 2009), for example, for investigating the sex differences in acquiring skills such as hand movement following viewing and imitation of a sequence of movements (Cohen et al., 2009), saccadic selectivity in complex visual search display (Pomplun, 2006), understanding contextual ambiguity while reading (Sheridan et al., 2009) and more. Bottom-up (stimulus driven) methods are further reviewed by Itti and Koch (Itti and Koch, 2001).

A computational framework for gaze pattern analysis methods includes a mathematical representation of the scene as a function of temporal and spatial parameters, feature extraction and mapping, generation of a saliency map. A gaze policy (a function which takes the saliency map as input and derives the location where attention should be next directed) is then applied to the map to extract points of increased attention (Shic et al. 2006, Shic et al. 2007).

The study of visual attention may also profitably draw upon allied areas of computer science such as data mining, bioinformatics, computational geometry, computer vision, image analysis, and dynamical systems to (a) analyze and quantify the distribution of the gazing patterns and (b) locate high-density regions in visual attention. Below, we survey some of these methods that can potentially be applied to the problem of analyzing the gazing pattern of patients with overselectivity.

We focus here on methods to analyze the gazing pattern trajectory using eye tracking methodology. The eye-scan data can be referred to as a set of points in space. These can be analyzed using various image analysis and informational theoretic techniques, especially with respect to the time- or space-dependent trajectory of the gaze and to the density distribution of the dots, reflecting the areas where the tested subjects focus their gaze.

Attentional Landscapes

Pomplun and his colleagues (Pomplun et al., 1996) introduced the concept of the 3D *fixation map*, a record of the locations of the viewers' points of fixation when regarding an image. These maps typically take the form of either individual eye movement tracing or a selection of traces. By way of illustration, we describe an approach to the fixation map created by Wooding (Wooding, 2002). In addition to the two dimensions of the visual scanning of the image, there is a third dimension, which in this 2002 paper constituted the cumulative frequency of fixations. An example can be seen in Figure 3, which illustrates how this attentional landscape can shift and grow over time.

In Wooding's study, an automated eye tracker was left running in a room of the National Gallery in London. Over a million samples were collected from over 5000 visitors to the museum. The resulting 3D maps were comprised of peaks representing the areas of increased attention across the image viewed. The fixation map is initially blank, in this case using the same dimensions in pixels as the original stimulus, an artwork. For each location of fixation, a 3D Gaussian of unit height is recorded on the map (Figure 3A). If this fixation overlaps with an existing fixation, the height at that location is added to the existing height at that point. Thus, the landscape over time is redrawn, highlighting the areas that have attracted more attention. (Figure 3B).

Pomplun and his colleagues (Pomplun et al., 1996) constructed attentional landscapes which measured attention to views of ambiguous images, introducing a continuous "attention function" based on fixations. They adjusting the height of the 3D Gaussian in proportion to the duration of fixation; in this way, the fixation landscape took the form of a *dwell map*.

How might the peaks of these attentional landscapes be quantified? Morphometry of focused attention over time may find application here. We propose comparing properties of volumes derived by integrating across areas of gaze of the type, as in the peaks of the "mountainous" terrains seen in Figure 3. One metric that may be derived is the size and/or shape (ratio of principal axes) of these volumes. The principal axes can be readily obtained using principal component analysis (PCA) on feature points representing high-density areas in the geometric shape. For example, a long, narrow geometric shape would yield one long and two relatively short principal axes. The volume can be modeled using geometric approaches (Tang et al, 2007) reducing the complexity of the derived geometry. For example, due to the narrowing gaze as illustrated in Figures 1 and 2, we anticipate that the volume of shape patterns would be significantly smaller than the shape generated by typically-developing subjects.

Figure 3. An illustration of a 3D attentional landscape with peaks representing areas of increased attention. (A) shows a contour plot of the fixation map for three individual fixations, and which over time is transformed to a more varied terrain after 17 fixations (B). Adapted with permission from (Wooding et al., 2002)

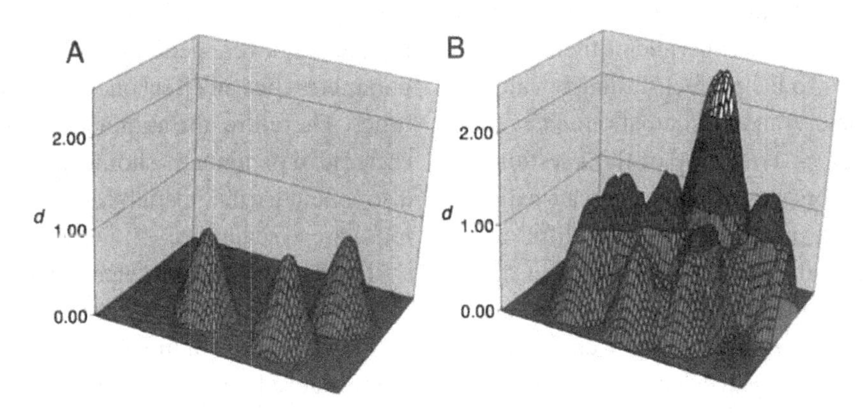

Scan-Paths

In order to perform a temporal and spatial analysis of the gazing pattern an alternative approach can be used. The set of points can be referred to as a scan-path. An illustration of a hypothetical scan-path is seen in Figure 4. The dots represent areas of gaze fixation and the lines connecting them represent consecutive areas of attention. Therefore, using models suggested in this chapter to analyze the scan-path we expect the scan-path of attention over-selectivity patients to lead to specific areas in the tested scene – for example the mouth area, rather than ending at any random locations, and the area of their attention narrows over time. Conceivably, the dots that result from the eye scan tracking tend to be denser in regions where the tested subjects focus their gaze. Such an approach was employed by Pomplun and colleagues (Pomplun et al., 2006), who used several computational path analysis methods to analyze the scan-paths formed by participants asked to look at a random distribution of identical dots or items of varying colors and form attributes. The scan-path was modeled as a graph with fixations as nodes and transitions between them as edges. They investigated the geometrical regularities of the path using five computationally simulated models which were compared to the empirical ones. The authors used a similarity value to evaluate the performance of each of the simulated models. The value of similarity between two paths, A and B, was obtained by comparing the number of edges between dots that appeared in path A as well as in path B. In these experiments there were 29 possible edges so the perfect similarity value was 29. A completely random simulation achieved a similarity value of 1.75. One of the questions asked by the authors was whether the scan-paths had any preferred direction. The five different strategies used by the authors to reconstruct the scan-path or the temporal order of attended dots from the recorded gaze trajectories were – 1) A "greedy" heuristic: out of all the unvisited dots, the algorithm jumps to the nearest one to the current gaze position. 2) A Traveling salesman strategy (TSS), in which the algorithm tries to minimize the length of the entire path and not only the nearest jump. 3) A clustering method which is a variant of the TSS algorithm that calculates local paths of minimal length connecting dots within each cluster as well as a minimum cost global path connecting clusters. It relies on the assumption that human scan-paths are generated by clustering items. 4) A self organizing map approach, based on a neural network approach, and 5) A receptive field simulation which uses neurons with a particular type of receptive fields. The authors found that the TSS based approach is the most effective in reproducing human scan-paths, especially the clustered variant (see method 3 above). Even the simple "greedy" approach performed much better than a random simulation.

It should be noted that there are several algorithms to analyze fixation patterns arising from scan-paths, many of them measure the dispersion of the points with respect to other points in that fixation or with respect to the centroid of the set of points. These algorithms are summarized in (Salvucci and Goldberg, 2000) and (Duchowski, 2003). A number of studies tried to assess the effect of the parameters used by these algorithms on the measured fixation time and scanning patterns of the tested population. One study that examined the scanning patterns of typically developing toddlers, that of (Shic et al., 2008a), used a variety of algorithms. They found that, while the algorithms behaved inherently in a similar manner, and were generally robust, changing the parameters had an effect on the measured fixation times. Therefore, the authors suggested that several sets of parameters should be evaluated. They also concluded that spatial scanning, at least among toddlers, is scale-free.

In this context, overselective attention can be expressed by a trajectory scan-path leading to a particular area in an image and getting more and more focused with time. Therefore, dots may be

Figure 4. An illustration of a scan-path generated by connecting dots representing gaze fixations. The edges connecting the dots represent transition between regions.

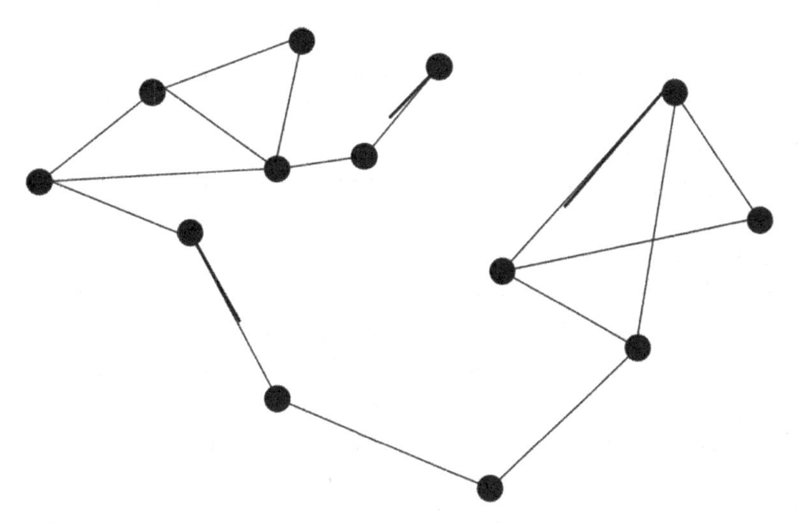

clustered more densely in regions corresponding to the mouth area and this clustered region of dots is expected to become narrower with time. Trajectory analysis methods are therefore needed to characterize the various properties of the scan-path.

Other Trajectory analysis methods have been used in various areas of science where time related behavior of dynamic objects is being tested. One of the most common uses for trajectory analysis methods is analyzing physical systems, such as robotic systems, whose motion needs to be planned carefully using dynamics and physical constraints (Niku, 2001). Another widely used application is molecular systems. Dynamic simulation methods produce a trajectory of structures, energies, velocities and other properties of the simulated molecular systems and analysis methods can be used to extract important information about the system such as interaction and potential energies, structural changes and more (Case et al., 2005, Haspel et al., 2006, Haspel et al., 2008). Trajectory analysis methods are also used in computer vision, for example to build semantic scene models for observation of moving objects in a scene (Wang et al., 2006).

Density of Points in Various Regions of the Bounding Box

In addition to temporal and spatial analysis of the eye-tracking data that employ trajectory analysis methodologies, described above, there is also interest in analyzing the distribution of attentional patterns that result from the eye-scan. To gain insight into the points at which subjects tend to fixate their gaze, we can estimate the density of the points inside various regions in the image; this is quantified by entropy measurement methods which were originally developed to analyze the distribution of information in some domain represented by a probability distribution.

An entropy function is a measure that quantifies the uncertainty associated with a value of some discrete random variable X. Given a partition function of the values of X in the measured domain, high entropy is associated with a more uniform distribution of the variable values in the measured space, whereas low entropy indicates the existence of regions with high density.

Several methods from computer vision, image processing, data mining and information theory have been suggested to estimate the entropy of a set of data points or an image for the purpose of, for example, image annotation (Yanai and Barnard, 2005), medical imaging data (Studholme et al., 1999), semantic ambiguity in written text using data and text mining methods (Melamed, 1997), or molecular biology to measure the conformational entropy of molecules as part of their free energy calculations (Adami 2004).

Entropy measures have been used in the past to measure the difference in gazing pattern among toddlers with autism versus typically developing toddlers (Shic 2008a). The authors showed face images to the tested population. Face stimuli were broken into seven basic regions: the left eye, right eye, mouth, facial areas (face skin areas including the nose), outer features (hair and body), background, and non-stimulus (including blinks and periods where the child looked away from the eye-tracker). The authors conducted a dynamic analysis of the gazing pattern, where the entropy represents the uniformity of transition between different regions in the image. The entropy function used for this purpose was

$$H(R) = -\sum_{r_i \in R} p(r_i) \log_2 p(r_i)$$

where R is the set of transitions from inner (informative) to outer (less informative) areas and $p(r_i)$ is the probability of looking at a particular transition r_i in R. The authors also used a Markov chain entropy analysis of the scanning patterns of the three stage outer-inner-subregions circuit. The approximate Markov matrix M was calculated for the sampling and the entropy of the matrix was calculated using the following formula:

$$H(M) = \sum_{X \in X'} P(X) H(X)$$

$$H(X') = -\sum_{r_i \in R} m_{X'_i} \log m_{X'_i}$$

where each $m_{X'_i}$ is a transition probability in a kth order Markov matrix, X is the set of all possible histories, X' is a kth order history of past states (i.e., - the last k places the tested patient looked at in the image) and H(X') is the entropy of X'.

Utilizing the dynamic analysis, the authors found that children with autism tend to look towards non-stimulus areas, but counter-intuitively, no significant difference in the time spent at the eyes and mouth areas was found between typically-developing children and children with autism.

Yet another entropy-related approach has been taken by Vetro et al (2010), addressing the question of characterizing high complexity regions in images. This question is related to estimating the entropy of the data in the image. In that work the authors present two algorithms for the mining of high complexity regions or sub-domains in images represented as sets of pixels with values of gray. The work uses a quad-tree, a structure defined on a finite set of nodes that either contains no nodes or is comprised of a root node and 4 quad-subtrees. In a full quad-tree, each node is either a leaf or has a degree of exactly 4. The algorithms output a quad-tree showing the feature concentration along the whole image area. In this representation, leaves are assigned a shade of gray, based on their location on the tree level. Leaves located closer to the root correspond to areas of the image assigned with darker shades of gray whereas leaves located further from the root correspond to areas of the image assigned with lighter shades of gray. The entire image area is the root of the quad-tree. The algorithm also highlights the leaves at the highest tree level with highest feature value. In most cases, those leaves correspond to high complexity regions of the image. The first method presented in the paper performs an information theoretic analysis based on entropy to find diverse areas. The Shannon entropy evaluates the uniformity of a finite set S containing the possible value of a random variable X. Let $p = B_1 \ldots B_n$ be the partition of S, the Shannon entropy of p is given by:

$$H = -\sum_{i=1}^{n} \frac{|B_i|}{|S|} \log \frac{|B_i|}{|S|}$$

Here, entropy increases as the uniformity of the distribution of elements in S increases. The algorithm evaluates the Shannon entropy on sub-areas of the image, where the partition is given by blocks of a node which consist of pixels of the same shade of gray. The algorithm uses the entropy evaluation to split nodes where the entropy is above a pre-defined threshold.

The second method described in that paper applies the concept of box-counting dimension related to fractal geometry. The box-counting dimension is used to determine the fractal dimension of a set S in a metric space. It reflects the variation of the results of measuring a set at a diminishing scale, which allows the observation of smaller and smaller details. The box-counting dimension of a sub-area is defined as the number of intercepting boxes in the sub-area. A box is a sub-area in an image whose size is equal to a predefined minimum. An intercepting box is a box where the number of different shades of gray is greater or equal to a threshold. The method presented in the paper computes the box-counting dimension associated with the gray level histogram of the boxes in a node's area. If a node corresponds to a box area, the number of intercepting boxes in a box area is the number of different shades of gray in the histogram. Otherwise, the number of intercepting boxes is the number of boxes with histogram values that has a number of gray shades greater or equal to some threshold. A node is split according to a threshold related to the fraction of intercepting boxes found in it. The authors conducted experiments on decompressed gray scale jpeg images where a gray shade in the image is corresponding to a level in the final tree is assigned to every leaf node.

Leaves at highest tree level with highest feature values correspond to high complexity regions. The authors found that in both methods the resulting quad-trees are rather similar and leaves with higher entropy correspond to regions with high complexity in the image.

The methods described in detail above (Vetro et al., 2010) can also be adapted for the analysis of the pattern generated from the eye scan of subjects with ASD and comparison to the patterns generated from typically developing subjects. The eye scan pattern can be represented as an image with black dots while entropy measurement methods can help estimate high complexity regions in the pattern, as well as the distribution of dots. We expect the input density of dots representing gaze fixation areas to be denser around certain areas representing the lower part of the face for patients with attention overselectivity with little density of data points elsewhere.

An Alternative Model: Dynamical Systems Theory

Yet another way to model selective attention is to consider it as a continuously integrated flow, and use applied mathematical models to determine regions that affect this flow. Here, the flow can be visualized using the tracking of the subject's gaze. This approach (termed *continuous dynamical systems*) is used to describe the behavior of dynamical systems by using the metrics of differential equations (Abraham, 1990).

One feature of dynamical systems models is the modeling of a landscape, with regions of "attraction", in this case the attraction of attention. Conversely, there may be regions that could be classified as "repellers". This classification provides nomenclature for selective attention, including overselectivity. For example, a complex, dynamical system can converge on a fixed location. This location is a terminal attractor, and has been employed in models for associative memory (review by Ben-Hur et al, 2002). This attraction of attention to a specific locus, after initial meandering, is of the type illustrated in Figure 1. Overselective attention in this case may be thought of as an emergent state of a complex dynamic system (Deutsch, 1998) in which attention is drawn to a specific region of an image or to facial features.

DISCUSSION

Analysis of visual selective attention would benefit from the use of computational approaches of the types reviewed here. Several of these approaches have already been applied to various problems in visual attention, notably the analysis of attentional landscapes, scan-paths, and trajectory. It is likely that computer-automated methods to quantify attentional pathology would spur research in this area of investigation, since individual differences and variability of attentional performance is complex and analysis of attending over time is compute-intensive. Quantitative dependent measures are likely to find application in group studies of ASD, to determine which aspects of deficits cohere in the presence of heterogeneity (Deutsch et al., 2008).

A remarkable number of identified etiologic conditions are associated with autism (Deutsch et al., 2012, in press). Indeed, a key question is how such a miscellany of conditions could converge on a simple neuropsychiatric phenotype. There are broad individual differences in autistic behavior, even for variables that are considered to cardinal features of the disorder, and for this reason it is important to come to grips with heterogeneous behavioral phenotypes. Quantitative measures of attentional pathology of the types reviewed here may provide the means of discriminating among subtypes, and studying genotype-phenotype relationships. Other clinical benefits of these computational approaches may accrue, as well, including the provision of metrics for the evaluation of treatment of attentional pathology in IDD in general and ASD in particular.

REFERENCES

Abraham, F. D. (1990). *A visual introduction to dynamical systems theory for psychology*. Santa Cruz, CA: Aerial Press.

Adami, C. (2004). Information theory in molecular biology. *Physics of Life Reviews*, *1*(1), 3–22. doi:10.1016/j.plrev.2004.01.002

Ben-Hur, A., Siegelmann, H. T., & Fishman, S. (2002). A theory of complexity for continuous time systems. *Journal of Complexity*, *18*, 51–86. doi:10.1006/jcom.2001.0581

Butler, P., & Javitt, D. (2005). Early-stage visual processing deficits in schizophrenia. *Current Opinion in Psychiatry*, *18*, 151–157. doi:10.1097/00001504-200503000-00008

Case, D. A., Cheatham, T., Darden, T., Gohlke, H., Luo, R., & Merz, K. M. Jr (2005). The Amber biomolecular simulation programs. *Journal of Computational Chemistry*, *26*, 1668–1688. doi:10.1002/jcc.20290

Cohen, N. R., Pomplun, M., Gold, B. J., & Sekuler, R. (2009). Sex differences in acquisition of complex skilled movements. *Experimental Brain Research*, *205*, 183–193. doi:10.1007/s00221-010-2351-y

Deutsch, C. K. (1998). Emergent properties of brain function and development. In S. Soraci & W. J. McIlvane Jr. (Eds.), Perspectives on fundamental processes in intellectual functioning, Vol. 1, (pp. 169-188; 1-86).

Deutsch, C. K., Ludwig, W. W., & McIlvane, W. J. (2008). Heterogeneity and hypothesis testing in neuropsychiatric illness. *The Behavioral and Brain Sciences*, *31*, 266–267. doi:10.1017/S0140525X08004275

Deutsch, C. K., & McIlvane, W. J. (2012. (in press). Non-Mendelian etiologic factors in neuropsychiatric illness: Pleiotropy, epigenetics, and convergence. [in press]. *The Behavioral and Brain Sciences*.

Dickson, C. A., Deutsch, C. K., Wang, S. S., & Dube, W. V. (2006b). Matching-to-sample assessment of stimulus overselectivity in students with intellectual disabilities. *American Journal of Mental Retardation*, *111*, 447–453. doi:10.1352/0895-8017(2006)111[447:MAOSOI]2.0.CO;2

Dickson, C. A., Wang, S. S., Lombard, K. M., & Dube, W. V. (2006a). Overselective stimulus control in residential school students with intellectual disabilities. *Research in Developmental Disabilities*, *27*, 618–631. doi:10.1016/j.ridd.2005.07.004

Dube, W. (2009). Stimulus overselectivity in autism: A review of research. In Reed, P. (Ed.), *Behavioural theories and interventions for autism* (pp. 23–46). New York, NY: Nova Science Publishers.

Dube, W. V., Dickson, C. A., Balsamo, L. M., Lombard O'Donnell, K., Tomanari, G. Y., & Farken, K. M. (2010). Observing behavioral and atypically restricted stimulus control. *Journal of the Experimental Analysis of Behavior*, *94*, 297–313. doi:10.1901/jeab.2010.94-297

Dube, W. V., Lombard, K. M., Farren, K. M., Flusser, D., Balsamo, L. M., & Fowler, T. R. (1999). Eye tracking assessment of stimulus overselectivity in individuals with mental retardation. *Experimental Analysis of Human Behaviour Bulletin*, *13*, 267–271.

Dube, W. V., & McIlvane, W. J. (1997). Reinforcer frequency and restricted stimulus control. *Journal of the Experimental Analysis of Behavior*, *68*, 303–316. doi:10.1901/jeab.1997.68-303

Duchowski, A. (2003). *Eye tracking methodology: Theory AND Practice*. Springer.

Elahipanah, A., Christensen, B. K., & Reingold, E. M. (2007). Do patients with schizophrenia have a smaller visual span? *Schizophrenia Bulletin*, *33*(2), 517.

Freiwald, W. A., & Kanwisher, N. (2004). Visual selective attention: Insights from brain imaging and neurophysiology. In Gazzaniga, M. S. (Ed.), *The cognitive neurosciences* (3rd ed.). Cambridge, MA: MIT Press.

Haspel, N., Ricklin, D., Geisbrecht, B., Lambris, J., & Kavraki, L. (2008). Electrostatic contributions drive the interaction between staphylococcus aureus protein efb-c and its complement target c3d. *Protein Science*, *17*(11), 1894–1906. doi:10.1110/ps.036624.108

Haspel, N., Zanuy, D., Aleman, C., Wolfson, H., & Nussinov, R. (2006). De-novo tubular nanostructure design based on self-assembly of beta-helical protein motifs. *Structure (London, England)*, *14*, 1137–1148. doi:10.1016/j.str.2006.05.016

Henderson, J. M. (2003). Human gaze control during real-world scene perception. *Trends in Cognitive Sciences*, *7*(11), 498–504. doi:10.1016/j.tics.2003.09.006

Hwang, A. D., Higgins, E., & Pomplun, M. (2009). A model of top-down attentional control during visual search in complex scenes. *Journal of Vision (Charlottesville, Va.)*, *9*(5), 1–18. doi:10.1167/9.5.25

Itti, L., & Koch, C. (2001). Computational modelling of visual attention. *Nature Reviews. Neuroscience*, *2*, 194–203. doi:10.1038/35058500

James, W. (1890). *The principles of psychology* (*Vol. 1*, pp. 403–404). New York, NY: Henry Holt. doi:10.1037/11059-000

Jemel, B., Mottron, L., & Dawson, M. (2006). Impaired face processing in autism: Fact or artifact? [Springer Netherlands.]. *Journal of Autism and Developmental Disorders*, *36*(1), 91–106. doi:10.1007/s10803-005-0050-5

Kaplan, D., & Glass, L. (1995). *Understanding nonlinear dynamics*. Springer Verlag. doi:10.1007/978-1-4612-0823-5

Klin, A., Jones, W., Schultz, R., Volkmar, F., & Cohen, D. (2002). Visual fixation patterns during viewing of naturalistic social situations as predictors of social competence in individuals with autism. *Archives of General Psychiatry*, *59*(9), 809–816. doi:10.1001/archpsyc.59.9.809

Laprevote, V., Oliva, A., Delerue, C., Thomas, P., & Boucart, M. (2010). Patients with schizophrenia are biased towards low spatial frequency to decode facial expression at a glance. *Neuropsychologia*, *48*, 4164–4168. doi:10.1016/j.neuropsychologia.2010.10.017

Le, S., Raufaste, E., & Demonet, J. (2003). Processing of normal, inverted and scrambled faces in a patient with prosopagnosia: Behavioural and eye tracking data. *Brain Research. Cognitive Brain Research*, *17*, 26–35. doi:10.1016/S0926-6410(03)00077-6

Le Meur, O., Le Callet, P., Barba, D., & Thoreau, D. (2006). A coherent computational approach to model bottom-up visual attention. *Pattern Analysis and Machine Intelligence*, *28*(5), 802–817. doi:10.1109/TPAMI.2006.86

Lovaas, O., Koegel, R., & Schreibman, L. (1979). Stimulus overselectivity in autism: A review of research. *Psychological Bulletin*, *86*(6), 1236–1254. doi:10.1037/0033-2909.86.6.1236

Melamed, I. D. (1997). *Measuring semantic entropy*. SIGLEX Workshop on Tagging Text with Lexical Semantics, Washington DC.

Nestor, P., Klein, K., Pomplun, M., Mizkikiewicz, M., & McCarley, R. (2009). Gaze cueing of attention in schizophrenia: Individual differences in neuropsychological functioning and symptoms. *Journal of Clinical and Experimental Neuropsychology*, *32*(3), 281–288. doi:10.1080/13803390902984472

Niku, S. B. (2001). *Introduction to robotics: Analysis, systems, applications*. Prentice Hall.

Pomplun, M. (2006). Saccadic selectivity in complex visual search display. *Vision Research*, *46*, 1886–1900. doi:10.1016/j.visres.2005.12.003

Pomplun, M., Carbone, E., Koesling, H., Sichelschmidt, L., & Ritter, H. (2006). Computational models of visual tagging. In Rickheit, G., & Wachsmuth, I. (Eds.), *Situated communication* (pp. 213–246). Berlin, Germany: Mouton de Gruyter.

Pomplun, M., Ritter, H., & Velichkovsky, B. (1996). Disambiguating complex visual information: Towards communication of personal views of a scene. *Perception*, *25*(8), 931–948. doi:10.1068/p250931

Posner, M. I. (1987). Cognitive neuropsychology and the problem of selective attention. *Electroencephalography and Clinical Neurophysiology. Supplement*, *39*, 313–316.

Salvucci, D., & Goldberg, J. (2000). Identifying fixations and saccades in eye tracking protocols. *Proceedings of the Symposium on Eye Tracking Research and Applications*, (pp. 71–78).

Sheridan, H., Reingold, E. M., & Daneman, M. (2009). Using puns to study contextual influences on lexical ambiguity resolution: Evidence from eye movements. *Psychonomic Bulletin & Review*, *16*(5), 875–881. doi:10.3758/PBR.16.5.875

Shic, F., Chawarska, K., Bradshaw, J., & Scassellati, B. (2008) Autism, eye-tracking, entropy. In *Proceedings of the 7th IEEE International Conference on Development and Learning,* Monterrey, California, August 2008.

Shic, F., Chawarska, K., & Scassellati, B. (2008). The incomplete fixation measure. *Proceedings of the 2008 Symposium on Eye Tracking Research and Applications*, (pp. 111-114). Savannah, GA: ACM.

Shic, F., Jones, W., Klin, A., & Scassellati, B. (2006). *Swimming in the underlying stream: Computational models of gaze in a comparative behavioral analysis of autism*. 28th Annual Conference of the Cognitive Science Society, 2006.

Shic, F., & Scassellati, B. (2007). Pitfalls in the modeling of developmental systems. *International Journal of Humanoid Robotics*, *4*, 435–454. doi:10.1142/S0219843607001084

Shin, D., Lee, S., Kim, B., Park, Y., & Lim, S. (2008). Visual attention deficits contribute to impaired facial emotion recognition in boys with attention-deficit/hyperactivity disorder. *Neuropediatrics*, *39*(6), 323–327. doi:10.1055/s-0029-1202286

Studholme, C., Hill, D. L. G., & Hawkes, D. J. (1999). An overlap invariant entropy measure of 3D medical image alignment. *Pattern Recognition*, *32*, 71–86. doi:10.1016/S0031-3203(98)00091-0

Tang, G., Peng, L., Baldwin, P. R., Mann, D. S., Jiang, W., Rees, I., & Ludtke, S. J. (2007). EMAN2: An extensible image processing suite for electron microscopy. *Journal of Structural Biology*, *157*, 38–46. doi:10.1016/j.jsb.2006.05.009

Tseng, P., Cameron, I., Munoz, D., & Itti, L. (2010). Differentiating patients from controls by gazing patterns. *Journal of Vision (Charlottesville, Va.)*, *10*(7), 277. doi:10.1167/10.7.277

Vetro, R., Ding, W., & Simovici, D. (2010). Mining for high complexity regions using entropy and box counting dimension quad-trees. In *Proceedings of the 9th IEEE International Conference on Cognitive Informatics,* Beijing, China.

Wang, X., Kinh, T., & Grimson, E. (2006). Learning semantic scene models by trajectory analysis. *Computer Vision – ECCV 2006. Lecture Notes in Computer Science*, *3956*, 110–123. doi:10.1007/11744078_9

Wayland, S., & Taplin, J. E. (1985). Feature-processing deficits following brain injury, part I - Overselectivity in recognition memory for compound stimuli. *Brain and Cognition*, *4*, 338–355. doi:10.1016/0278-2626(85)90026-0

Wooding, D. S. (2002). Eye movements of large populations, part II - Deriving regions of interest, coverage and similarity using fixation maps. *Behavior Research Methods, Instruments, & Computers*, *34*(4), 518–528. doi:10.3758/BF03195481

Yanai, K., & Barnard, K. (2005). Image region entropy: A measure of "Visualness" in web images associated with one concept. *Proceedings of ACM Multimedia*, Singapore.

Chapter 3
Task, Timing, and Representation in Visual Object Recognition

Albert L. Rothenstein
York University, Canada

ABSTRACT

Most biologically-inspired models of object recognition rely on a feed-forward architecture in which abstract representations are gradually built from simple representations, but recognition performance in such systems drops when multiple objects are present in the input. This chapter puts forward the proposal that by using multiple passes of the visual processing hierarchy, both bottom-up and top-down, it is possible to address the limitations of feed-forward architectures and explain the different recognition behaviors that primate vision exhibits. The model relies on the reentrant connections that are ubiquitous in the primate brain to recover spatial information, and thus allow for the selective processing of stimuli. The chapter ends with a discussion of the implications of this work, its explanatory power, and a number of predictions for future experimental work.

INTRODUCTION

The study of visual perception abounds with examples of surprising results, and perhaps none of these has generated more controversy than the speed of object recognition. Some complex objects can be recognized with amazing speed even while attention is engaged on a different task. Some simple objects need lengthy attentional scrutiny, and performance breaks down in dual-task experiments (Koch & Tsuchiya, 2007). These results are fundamental to our understanding of the visual cortex, as they clearly show that not all stimuli are represented in the same way in the brain, and not all visual recognition tasks are the same.

DOI: 10.4018/978-1-4666-2539-6.ch003

Most if not all biologically-inspired models of object recognition rely on a feed-forward architecture in which abstract representations are gradually built from simple representations, e.g. (Hummel & Stankiewicz, 1996; Riesenhuber & Poggio, 1999b; Hummel, 2001; Serre et al., 2007), but recognition performance in feed-forward systems drops when multiple objects are present in the input. This has been demonstrated mathematically (Tsotsos, 1987, 1988; Rensink, 1989; Tsotsos, 1990; Grimson, 1990) by showing that pure data-directed approaches to vision (and in fact to perception in any sensory modality) are computationally intractable. Computational modeling studies (Walther et al., 2002; Kreiman et al., 2007) support this conclusion. Behavioral studies also confirm this, e.g. (Duncan, 1984; Behrmann et al., 1998; VanRullen et al., 2004), and extensive experimental evidence has been presented that neural responses in the inferior temporal (IT) visual area to an object are typically reduced when additional objects are presented in the neuron's receptive field, e.g. (Sato, 1989; Miller et al., 1993; Rolls & Tovee, 1995; Missal et al., 1999; Zoccolan et al., 2005; Meyers et al., 2010).

Initial work on the HMAX (also called the "standard") model of object recognition (Riesenhuber & Poggio, 1999a) claims no need for attention and binding, and, in fact, the feed-forward max-like mechanism prevents any effective top-down traversal since decisions regarding relevance for elements of a neuron's receptive field are made early. A later extension shows that such a model can recognize objects with limited clutter but performance decreases rapidly when clutter is increased. This has led others to analyze the multi-stimulus performance of the HMAX model (Walther et al., 2002; Walther, 2006), showing that, despite the initial optimism, the model suffers from the same limitations as other purely feed-forward object recognition models. In order to solve this problem, saliency-based spatial visual attention (Koch & Ullman, 1985; Itti et al., 1998) is added to the HMAX system, with some limited feature-sharing implemented in order to match the size of the selected area to that of the selected object (Walther et al., 2002).

Extensive evidence has been presented in the literature that neural responses to objects are typically reduced when additional objects are presented (Moran & Desimone, 1985; Sato, 1989; Miller et al., 1993; Rolls & Tovee, 1995; Missal et al., 1999; Zoccolan et al., 2005). One of the classic experiments of Moran & Desimone (1985) explores the response of neurons to one and two stimuli present in their receptive field in the absence of attention. One of the stimuli is preferred (i.e., generating a high response), while the other is not (i.e., generating a low response). The main observation of this experiment is that responses to the preferred stimulus are reduced when a non-preferred stimulus is added in the receptive field. More recently, a systematic examination of IT responses to pairs and triplets of objects (Zoccolan et al., 2005) found that a large fraction of the response of each IT neuron to multiple objects is reliably predicted as the average of its responses to the constituent objects in isolation, regardless of object identity. This average effect is shown to be a primarily feed-forward response property, consistent with mechanistic models in which IT neuronal outputs are normalized by summed synaptic drive into IT or spiking activity within IT.

These results show that feed-forward processing is insufficient for object recognition in clutter or in the presence of distracters, both in the brain and in computational models, and additional mechanisms are needed. This paper starts with a critical evaluation of theoretical and experimental results in human object recognition. Based on these results, we propose a framework for object recognition that moves past these limitations by making explicit different visual tasks that the system must accomplish. The paper concludes with an overview of the explanatory power of the model and a number of predictions.

EXPERIMENTAL GUIDANCE

Efforts to develop computational models of human object recognition must be informed by experimental observations of human (and other primate) visual performance. In particular, here we will look at the different kinds of visual tasks that are collectively referred to as "recognition," their timing, and their performance with multi-stimulus images.

Categorization vs. Identification

While terminology is often misleading and not used consistently, we distinguish between a number of modes of "recognition," inspired by the experimental taxonomy of Macmillan & Creelman (2004), that can be summarized as:

1. Detection tasks include a null (noise) stimulus and the subject needs to choose between noise and noise+signal.
2. Categorization tasks require the subject to connect each stimulus to a prototype, or class of similar stimuli (cars with cars, houses with houses).
3. Identification tasks have the requirement that a stimulus is associated with a particular sub-category or individual from a class (bungalows, split-level, and other such house types, for example).
4. Hard identification tasks involve identification in difficult circumstances, such as in the presence of extensive clutter, transparency, etc.

A more detailed discussion of visual tasks and their computational requirements can be found in (Tsotsos et al., 2008), but this subset is sufficient for the present discussion. The fact that recognition as defined above is not a monolithic process, but rather a collection of different tasks is the crucial observation that drives the rest of this research.

Timing of Object Recognition

Experiments show that detecting and categorizing an object seem to take about 150ms, while identification always requires longer processing time (on average, 215ms) for similar performance (Grill-Spector & Kanwisher, 2005). The median time required for visual information to propagate through the visual system (retina to orbito-frontal) has been measured at 150ms (Bullier, 2001), which is consistent with the hypothesis that detection and categorization are achieved through a single feed-forward pass.

Various experimental paradigms demonstrate that in object-based attention experiments the latency of attentional modulations decreases from lower to higher visual areas, e.g. (Mehta et al., 2000). We hypothesize that the first feed-forward pass through the visual system produces a representation of the input image that is sufficient for certain tasks, but limited in its descriptive power and lacking precise spatial information, and attentional feedback produces the detailed representations needed for identification and for localizing the stimuli.

Based on these results regarding the time course and processing sequence in the primate visual system, and using the number of processing steps (i.e. layers evaluated, both feed-forward and feedback) as a first approximation for processing time, we propose the following sequence of processing stages in visual recognition tasks. Upon presentation of stimuli, a feed-forward, diverging, cone of neural pathways is activated within the visual hierarchy. At the end of this feed-forward traversal, sufficient processing has been completed for detection and categorization tasks. The identification task, i.e. providing details about an object, such as identity (within-category identification) or type, requires additional processing time. We hypothesize that the additional time is needed by top-down attentional feedback to localize the stimulus in the input image and generate the detailed representation needed for identification.

Representation

How visual information is represented in the brain is the crucial question that drives most research in the field, and answering it will mean significant theoretical and practical advances in the understanding of the brain (Kreiman, 2004).

Proponents of sparse representations suggest that highly selective, specialized neurons, introduced as cardinal cells by Barlow (Barlow, 1972), explicitly code each percept. Energy minimization and information theoretic arguments have been used to justify relatively sparse representations (Foldiak & Young, 1995). The main problem with this solution is the combinatorial explosion in the number of units needed to represent all the different possible stimuli. At the same time, due to the fact that different neurons encode different stimuli, one distinct advantage of sparse codes is their capacity to encode multiple stimuli simultaneously.

Others have suggested distributed/population codes, either by using a variety of combinations of active and inactive columns for individual features, somewhat indicative of parts based representation (Tsunoda et al., 2001), or by suggesting that neural computation is akin to a Bayesian inference process, with population activity patterns representing uncertainty about stimuli in the form of probability distributions (Pouget et al., 2003). These representations have high encoding capacity, but due to the fact that the same neurons are used to encode different stimuli, they suffer from the source separation problem.

While different engineering solutions for the source separation problem have been proposed, see (Jadhav & Bhalchandra, 2008) for a review, the brain seems to have opted for sequential processing of the stimuli based on visual attention mechanisms. The simultaneous vs. sequential signature of these different coding schemes can be seen in the observed characteristics of the different tasks that the visual system can accomplish. Experiments show that detection and classification can be performed in parallel (McElree & Carrasco, 1999; Rousselet et al., 2002), indicating that the brain is using a sparse code for these tasks. At the same time detailed identification with multiple stimuli is serial (Grill-Spector & Kanwisher, 2005; Evans & Treisman, 2005), indicative of a population code.

As these terms have been used to mean different things by different authors, and due to the fact that even the simplest of visual stimuli trigger the activation of many neurons, it is important to clarify what is meant by sparse vs. population codes. In this paper, "sparse code" will be used to denote the situation in which the stimulus is represented in such a way that a particular task involving a single stimulus (e.g. categorization) can be performed by using the activation of a single neuron (or a localized groups of neurons), while a decision regarding two stimuli (e.g. discrimination) can be performed by using the activation of two neurons (or two localized groups of neurons). "Population code" will be used to denote the situation in which the stimulus is represented in such a way that a particular task can only be performed by using the activation of a collection that is formed of multiple distributed neurons. The representation used in this research is closer to the combination of active and inactive features interpretation of (Tsunoda et al., 2001), rather than the probabilistic view.

Discussion

One characteristic of vision is that not all stimuli in the visual field can and need to be represented at the same time to a high degree of accuracy (Tsotsos, 1990). This implies that some selection needs to be made, constrained by the experimental observations presented above. To summarize, focusing on categorization and identification tasks: categorization is fast, consistent with feed-forward processing through the visual system, and multiple stimuli can be categorized simultaneously, consistent with a sparse code representation. Identification is slower, consistent with processing beyond one feed-forward pass, and serial, consistent with a population code representation.

These results will be used in the following sections to propose an object recognition framework that has visual attention at its centre, forming a bridge between a sparse, fast, and parallel initial representation that supports categorization and a slow, serial, and detailed population representation needed for identification.

SELECTIVE TUNING

The primate visual system consists of a multi-layer hierarchy with pyramidal abstraction, a structure that makes computations tractable, but characterized by a loss of spatial information (Tsotsos, 1987). As information progresses up the hierarchical structure, neurons represent more and more abstract information, but with less and less spatial accuracy. Due to the nature of the pyramidal structure, a neuron activated at the highest level of the pyramid corresponds to a whole sub-region in the first layer of the pyramid. In an extreme situation, the top layer can consist of a single neuron that is only active if a particular item exists in the input image. A mechanism is needed to be able to go down the pyramidal structure and locate the detected item at high spatial resolution, a mechanism provided by the Selective Tuning (ST) model of visual attention (Tsotsos et al. 1995, 2005). This is performed in practice via a Winner-Take-All (WTA) mechanism that will select the most activated region at the highest level. Results are propagated down the pyramidal structure through winner-take-all competitions within the winning receptive fields, until the first layer is reached. Regions that do not contribute to the high level decision are inhibited, thus eliminating distracters and improving the signal-to-noise ratio. This process effectively segments out the detected structure in the input layer, as demonstrated in a variety of visual domains, including shape, motion and color, results summarized by Tsotsos (2011). A second feed-forward pass through the pyramidal structure will allow only the signals corresponding to the selected stimulus to propagate upwards. This second feed-forward pass will provide representations free from interference, since features from the input layer that do not correspond to the selected stimulus and that would normally propagate up the pyramid are now blocked.

OBJECT RECOGNITION FRAMEWORK

Taking cues from the behavioral and physiological studies presented above, we propose that the categoric level information can be represented sparsely due to the fact that the number of biologically relevant categories is relatively small. The Stoddart Visual Dictionary (Corbeil, 1986) proposes 25,000 visual categories - is this number "relatively small?" It is worth remembering that 100, 000 is on the order of magnitude of the number of neurons in a hypercolumn (Kandel et al., 2000), while temporal cortex neuron densities in humans are estimated at 125−130,000 under $1mm^2$ of cortical surface (Witelson et al., 1995), and total inferior temporal surface area is estimated at $29.6cm^2$ (Tramo et al., 1995), so indeed, relative to the number of neurons in the whole visual cortex, or even the total number of inferior temporal neurons, this is a very small number, that can conceivably be represented by a sparse code. On the other hand, not only can the number of exemplars in each category be very large, but information about pose, illumination and any number of other attributes ensure that a sparse representation is not sufficient for the detailed recognition of individual stimuli. In this case a population code is required, but such a code is susceptible to much greater interference from distracters, so in the presence of clutter, recognition performance will decrease, and additional processing is needed to isolate the stimulus response from the clutter response.

The hypothesis that drives our object recognition framework is that after a first feed-forward pass through an object recognition system a sparse representation can be used for detection and categorization tasks even in the presence of distracters. Due to the fact that the classification code is sparse, it is less affected by the presence of multiple stimuli in the receptive fields of the neurons. This is in general agreement with experimental results that show primates are able to detect and classify multiple stimuli in parallel (McElree & Carrasco, 1999; Rousselet et al., 2002).

Following this, the ST model of visual attention (Tsotsos et al., 1995) is used to recover the spatial location and extent of the visual information that has contributed to a categoric decision and inhibit the contribution of the distracters. ST attentional selection proceeds in two main stages: a top-level WTA selects an overall winner between the output neurons of the classification network, and a feedback stage traces activations down to the input through a series of local WTA competitions. This process is described in detail by Tsotsos et al. (1995, 2005) and Tsotsos (2011). The attentional selection triggers a feedback cascade of modulations, moving back towards early visual areas (Mehta et al., 2000; O'Connor et al., 2002) and inhibiting distracters (Desimone & Duncan, 1995; Kastner et al., 1998; Caputo & Guerra, 1998; Reynolds et al., 1999; Vanduffel et al., 2000; Cutzu & Tsotsos, 2003).

This allows for the detailed processing of the selected information at the expense of other stimuli present in the image. The feedback and selective processing create the detailed population code corresponding to the attended stimulus. The expectation is that in a sufficiently complex network, ST feedback will be able to accurately localize and segment the recognized objects in the input. The "sufficiently complex" qualifier applies to both the network and the set of stimuli used, and is necessary to ensure that the classification network does not simply exploit local regularities or diagnostic features in the input, but rather has to create holistic representations based on most of the pixels that define the recognized object.

Counting the evaluation of each hierarchical level in the system, both feed-forward and feedback, as one processing step, stimulus classification is achieved at the end of the first feed-forward pass, localization of the stimulus in the input after the feedback steps, and identification even later, after the second feed-forward evaluation of the identification network. While significantly more detail needs to be fleshed out before exact processing times can be described, at a qualitative level the biological pattern of fast classification and slower identification is matched.

OBJECT RECOGNITION

While the proposal presented in this paper is theoretical in nature, to make the discussion concrete a system implementing these ideas is presented. It is important to note that the system as presented is only an illustration of the principles presented above, and not a fully-fledged object recognition system. The implementation is intentionally kept very simple, and no claims are made about the biological plausibility and performance of the system beyond its ability to solve the multi-object problem presented above with a sequence of processing and timing consistent with primate vision.

Stimulus Set

The stimulus set used in this set of experiments and illustrated in Figure 1 consists of 200 images grouped in 5 classes: four-legged animals, birds, human faces, non-human primate faces, and fruits and vegetables. This is a subset of the stimulus set used in (Kiani et al., 2007) to investigate the representation of object classes and its hierarchical organization in the macaque monkey.

Figure 1. Sample images from the stimulus set used in the classification and identification examples

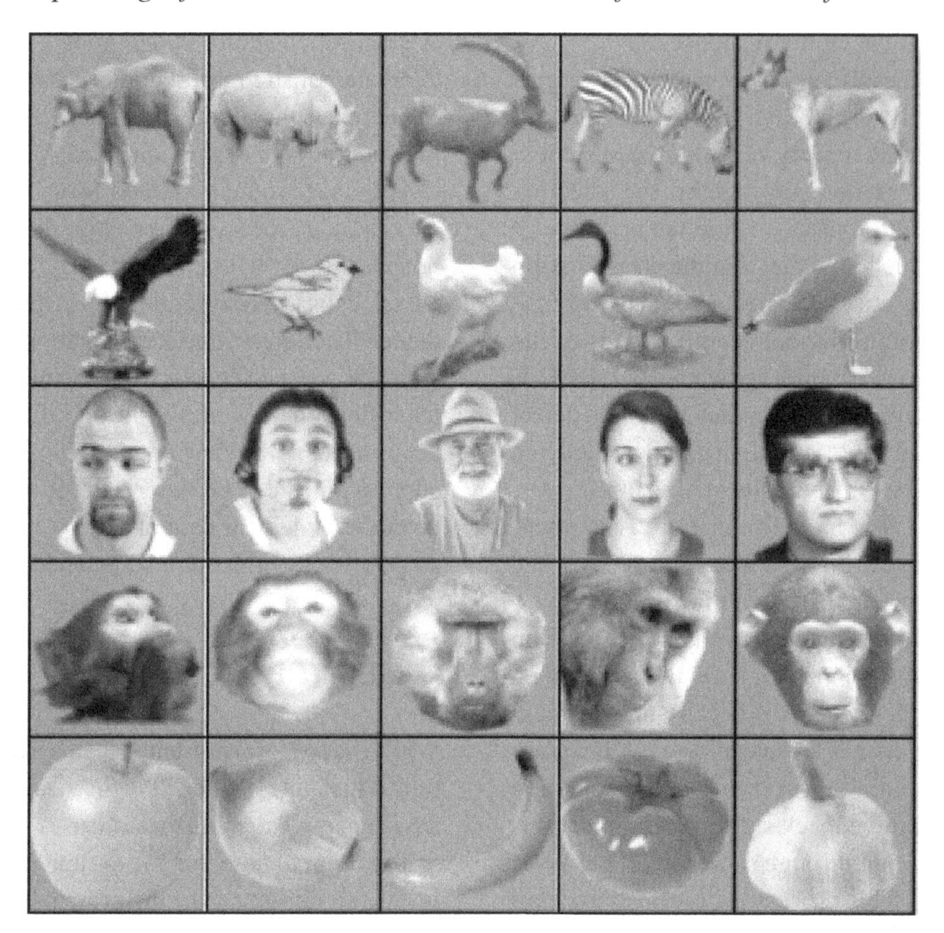

The original color images have been converted to gray scale, reduced in size to 30x30 pixels and placed on the left and/or right side of 60x30 images that are used as input to the system. The training of the system has been done with single-stimulus images, and testing with dual-stimulus images. Example images in Figure 2 are used to illustrate the process and discuss the results.

Implementation

Neural representations for categorization and identification are present in the same areas of the primate brain, but for clarity of the explanation, these functions are presented as separate processing pathways in the model.

In order to illustrate the two-step approach to object recognition described above, we propose a system of two parallel pathways, one detecting and classifying objects in input images, while the second pathway implements an object identification system. The pathways are trained using standard backpropagation, on input images containing a single stimulus. The TarzaNN neural network simulator (Rothenstein et al., 2005) has been extended to include supervised learning layers. After the training stage, ST was integrated into the network and the performance of the system evaluated on input images with two stimuli. The network, shown schematically in Figure 3, consists of an object classification pathway that produces as output a sparse code identifying the class of the stimulus, and an object identification pathway that

Figure 2. Dual stimulus input image examples. (a) consists of a camel on the left (class 0, four-legged animals, stimulus 9) and a human face on the right (class 2, human faces, stimulus 105). (b) consists of a chicken on the left (class 1, birds, stimulus 44) and a monkey face on the right (class 3, monkey faces, stimulus 125)

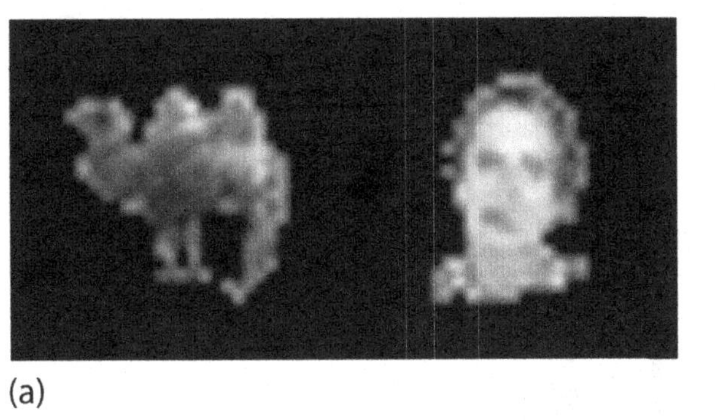

(a)

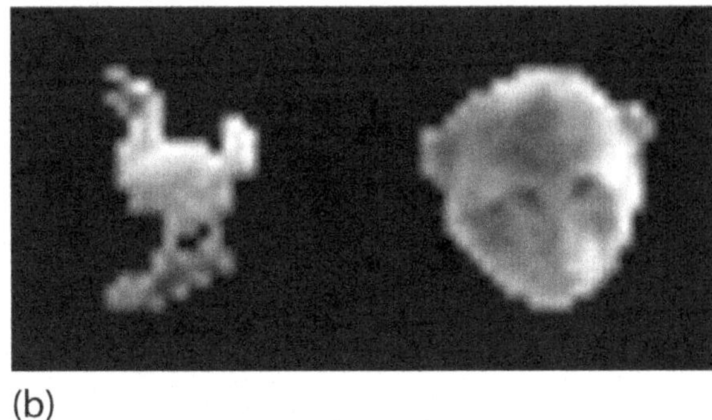

(b)

produces as output a population code identifying the specific stimulus, both in a location-invariant manner. Here again sparse and population code are used in the sense defined above. This coding allows detection and classification to be performed in parallel, similar to primate visual performance (McElree & Carrasco, 1999; Rousselet et al., 2002), while detailed identification with multiple stimuli must be serial (Grill-Spector & Kanwisher, 2005; Evans & Treisman, 2005).

For simplicity the position of the objects was limited to two locations. Training was performed with single stimulus images, with stimuli placed in one of the two positions, stimuli and positions being selected randomly for each learning step. Testing and the attention experiments were performed on images containing two stimuli chosen randomly.

The output of the classification network consists of five neurons that are activated when a stimulus is presented in the field of view, each neuron being trained to preferentially be activated by stimuli of one class, while the output of the identification network is a population code described below. In order to avoid any bias in the generation of the population code, 200 unique 16-bit codes were generated using a uniform random distribution (i.e., on average, for each stimulus 50% of the neurons fire, and 50% are silent). Table 1 presents the target identification codes used for the first 10 stimuli.

While the learning targets are binary, neuron activations are continuous, and the following convention will be used for the graphical representation of the network activity: activations will be represented by gray levels, bright for high activation, dark for low; in figures illustrating attentional selection, the selected activations will be shown in light gray and indicated by a white arrow, while the inhibited activations will be

Table 1. Target values used for the coding of the first 10 stimuli

Stimulus	Code
00	1 0 1 0 1 1 1 1 1 1 1 1 1 1 1 1
01	1 0 1 1 1 0 1 1 0 1 0 0 1 0 1 1
02	1 0 1 1 1 0 0 1 0 1 1 1 0 0 1 1
03	1 1 1 0 0 0 1 1 0 0 0 0 1 0 1 0
04	0 0 0 1 1 1 0 1 0 1 1 0 0 1 0 1
05	0 1 1 0 0 0 0 1 1 1 1 1 1 1 1 1
06	1 1 0 1 0 1 1 1 1 1 0 0 0 1 1 1
07	1 0 0 0 1 1 1 0 1 0 1 1 1 1 0 0
08	1 1 0 1 0 1 0 1 1 1 0 1 1 0 0 1
09	1 0 1 1 1 0 1 0 0 1 1 1 1 0 1 0

Figure 3. Forward pass 1. The classifier is on the left, the object identification network on the right. The classifier detects the two input classes. Identification network presents combined code.

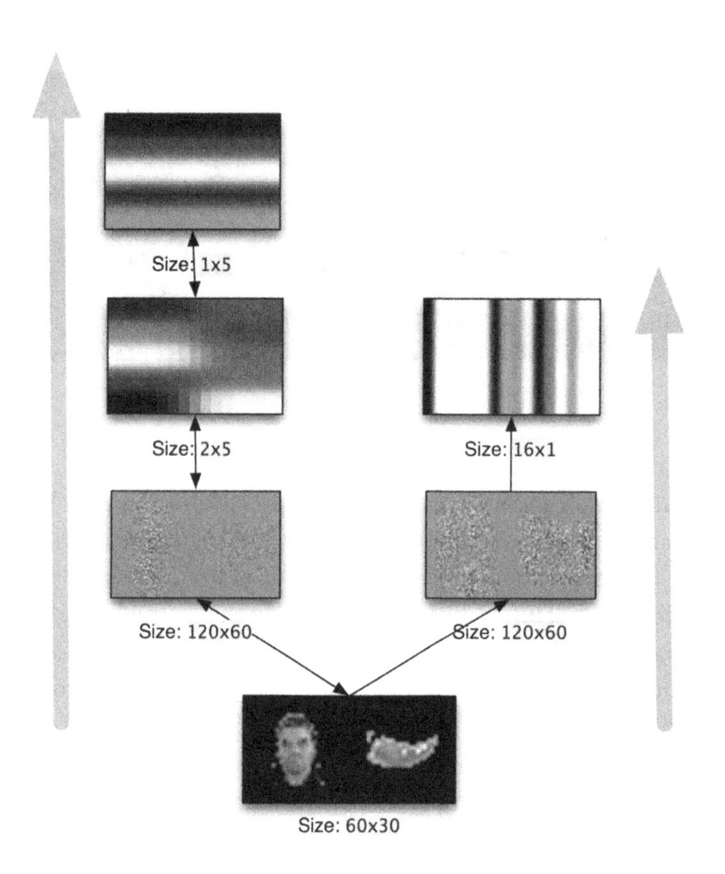

shown in darker gray; large gray arrows indicate the main flow of information through the network for the stage of processing described in the figure.

Figure 4 shows a few example learned codes for the stimuli in the middle column. On the left, the activation of the five neurons that represent the classification are shown. Indexes run left to right. As the four example images belong to the 0, 2, 4, and 3 classes, respectively, high activation can be observed in neurons with the corresponding index. The right side of the image shows the unique output codes corresponding to each stimulus.

For each neuron, activation is calculated as a logistic sigmoid function $A(x) = \frac{1}{1+e^{-x}}$ applied to the weighted sum of its inputs. The object classification pathway is a four layer neural network (60×30, 120×60, 2×5 and 1×5 neurons, respectively). Receptive field sizes for the successive layers are 7×7, 59×59 and 2×1, i.e. the network is not fully connected, as is customary with backpropagation networks. The first three layers effectively implement two parallel classification networks for the left and right stimuli, while the last layer combines the activations in the third layer into a single location-independent code. The first three layers were trained to classify the 200 individual input stimuli by indicating the class of the stimulus as output for each image. Training was performed using backpropagation on single-stimulus images, and was stopped when a plateau performance was reached (41,500 training steps).

Figure 4. Coding examples. Stimuli in the middle column, learned 5 neuron classification code on the left, learned 16 neuron identification code on the right. In the classification code a single neuron has high activation (white) for each stimulus class. In the identification code, each individual stimulus is represented by a unique code of 16 neurons, on average 8 of which are active.

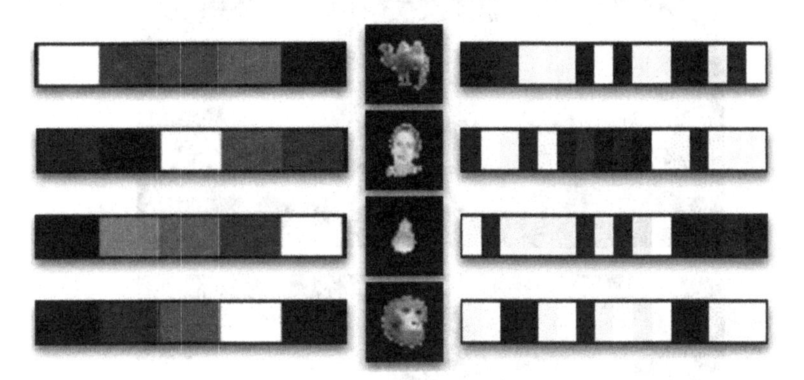

The object identification pathway is a three layer neural network (60×30, 120×60 and 16×1 neurons, respectively). Receptive field sizes for the successive layers are 7×7 and 119×59. The network was trained to recognize the 200 individual input stimuli by producing the desired 16-bit code as output for each image. Training was performed using backpropagation on single-stimulus images, and was stopped when a plateau performance was reached (60,000 training steps).

Classification with Two Stimuli in the Field of View

The sparse nature of the classifier output is illustrated in Figure 5 for two sample images. In Figure 5(c) high activation of neurons 0 and 2 corresponds to the classes of the input stimuli (class 0, four-legged animals, and class 2, human faces). Similarly, in Figure 5(e) high activation of neurons 1 and 3 corresponds to the classes of the input stimuli (class 1, birds, and class 4, monkey faces).

Identification with Two Stimuli in the Field of View

Experimental results indicate that the responses of neurons to pairs of stimuli tend towards the average of the individual stimulus responses (Reynolds et al., 1999). Furthermore, it has been shown that the average effect is a primarily feed-forward response property (Zoccolan et al., 2005). The population code in our simulation is affected by the presence of multiple stimuli in the receptive field of the neuron in a manner similar to its biological counterpart – in all cases both the activation of the individual neurons and the activation corresponding to the entire code is closer to the average of the activations, and the difference is highly significant, having an average p-value under 0.0001. This is a purely feed-forward effect, that doesn't rely on the notion of stimulus competition through lateral connection, in concordance with experimental results (Zoccolan et al., 2005).

The effect of multiple stimuli in the receptive fields of the top-level identification neurons is

Figure 5. Classification with dual stimulus images: (a,b) – input images, (c,e) – output activations for the classification network, (d,f) – WTA winners

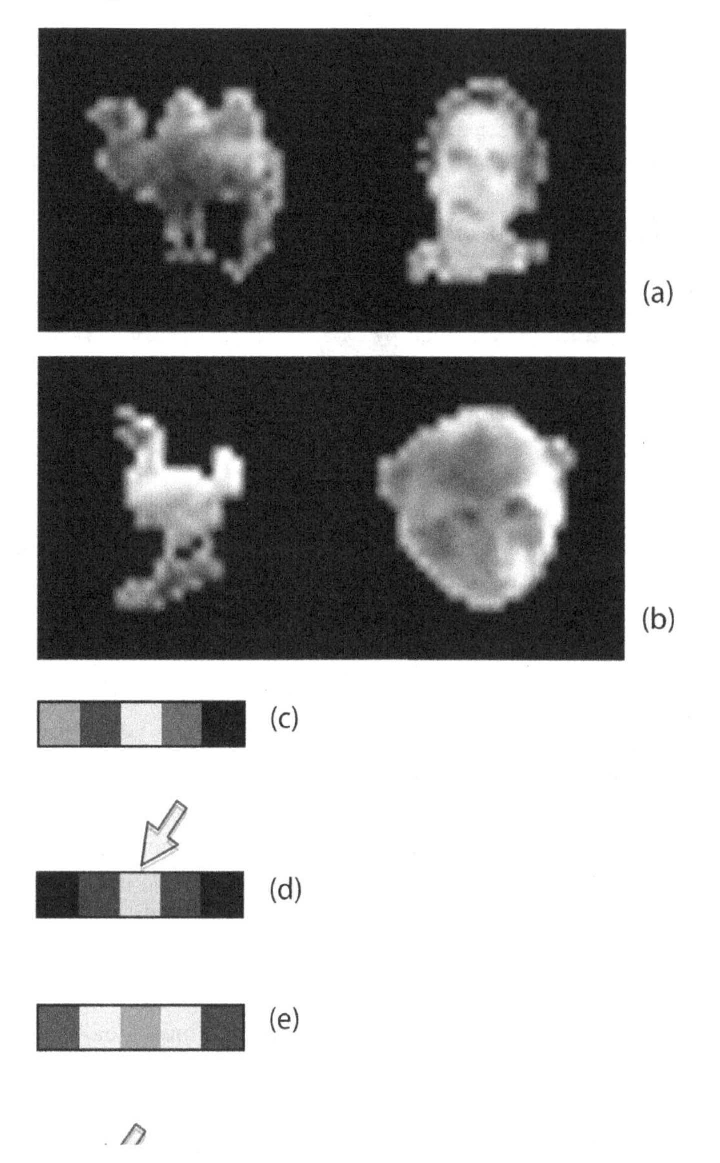

illustrated in Figure 6. The top two rows show the output of the identification network for the individual stimuli, while the bottom row corresponds to the dual-stimulus input images. It can be observed that the latter is a combination of the two codes in both examples of Figure 6(a) and Figure 6(b).

Attentional Selection

The attentional selection triggers a feedback cascade of attentional modulations, illustrated in Figure 7, moving back towards early visual areas and inhibiting distracters.

Attentional selection and the inhibition of distracters allow the system to reevaluate the stimuli present in the input image, but due to the

Figure 6. The identification code is affected by the presence of multiple stimuli in the input. Top two rows – identification network output for individual stimuli, bottom row – identification network output for dual stimulus input images. The output at the bottom shows the effect of the interference between the two stimuli, in both examples.

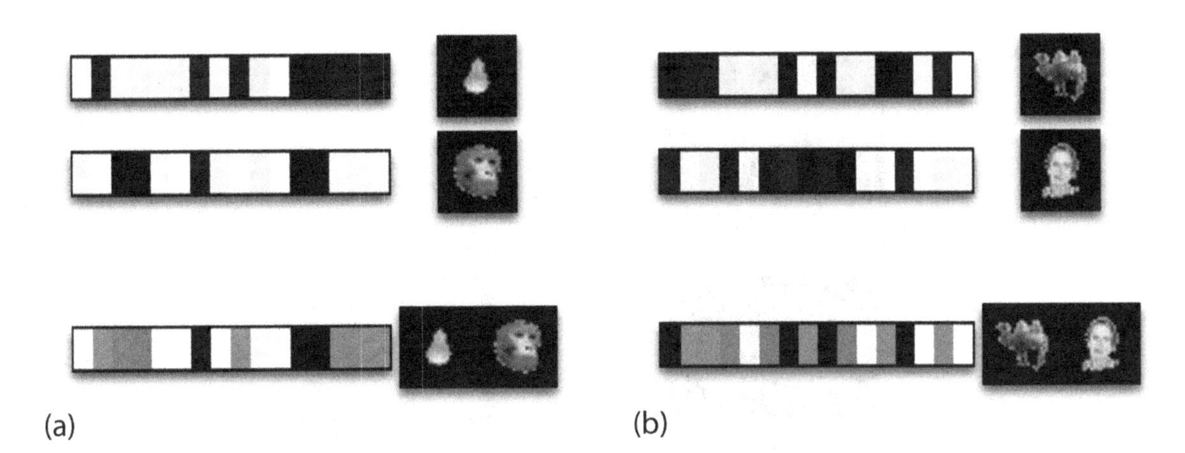

need to eliminate interference, this process is sequential. Inhibition is implemented by reducing the input activations corresponding to the distracter. The second feed-forward pass is illustrated in Figure 8. While not shown here, processing continues with the selection of the next-highest output, so that all stimuli in the input image are processed in sequence.

The top-level selection is illustrated in Figure 5 for the two sample stimuli. In Figure 5(d) the higher activation of neuron 2 (class 2, human faces) leads the ST WTA process to select it. Similarly, in Figure 5(f) the higher activation of neuron 1 (class 1, birds) is selected by the ST WTA process, and the feedback process traces the activations back to the input image. As illustrated in Figure 9, the feedback process is able to perform the localization for the two sample stimuli, corresponding to the detection presented in Figure 5.

Timing

Counting the evaluation of each hierarchical level in the system, both feed-forward and feedback, as one processing step, stimulus classification is achieved in 3 steps (shown in Figure 3), localization of the stimulus in the input in 6 steps (3 additional steps shown Figure 7), and identification in 8 steps (2 additional steps shown in Figure 8). While a significantly more realistic implementation of the proposed framework would be needed to evaluate exact processing times, at a qualitative level the biological pattern of fast classification and slower identification is matched.

Modulation

Depending on visual area investigated and experimental paradigm used, attentional modulation of neuronal firing rates in primates has been reported in the range of 10% (McAdams & Maunsell, 1999) to 63% (Chelazzi et al., 2001), see (Walther, 2006) for a summary of experimental results. To investigate the influence of the level of attentional modulation on identification performance, the amount of inhibition applied to the distracter was varied between 0 and 100%, and performance was evaluated in terms of absolute error, determined by taking the sum of the absolute difference between the output of the identification neurons and the desired output for the selected stimulus in isolation. Inhibition was implemented as a reduction of the luminance of the distracter by the given

Figure 7. Feedback pass. Attentional competition selects one class representation. Feedback localizes the corresponding input stimulus and inhibits the distracter.

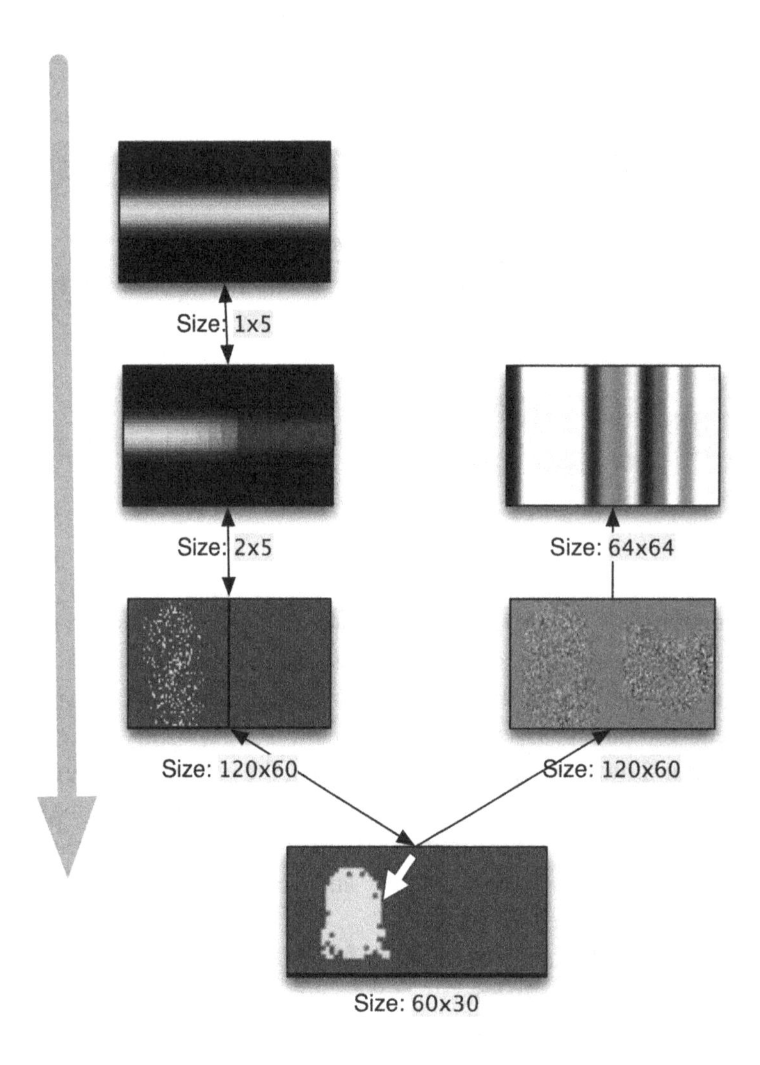

percentage (i.e. 0% means no inhibition, 100% means the distracter is invisible). Figure 10 shows the dependence of absolute error on the degree of inhibition for the data set.

Predictions and the Explanatory Power of the Model

This paper presents a novel approach to object recognition that forms a powerful framework for understanding primate vision, whose broad explanatory power allows it to tackle a wide range of experimental results, including some long-standing controversies in the field.

Various paradigms including visual backward masking (Enns & Di Lollo, 2000) and trans-cranial magnetic stimulation (Barker et al., 1985) of early visual areas show that when processing beyond the first feed-forward pass is disrupted, recognition performance is seriously degraded. In visual backward masking experiments, a target stimulus is briefly presented, followed by a second stimulus called a "mask." The task of the subject is to report some property of the target stimulus. Even though

Figure 8. Second forward pass. Representation for identification corresponds to selected stimulus.

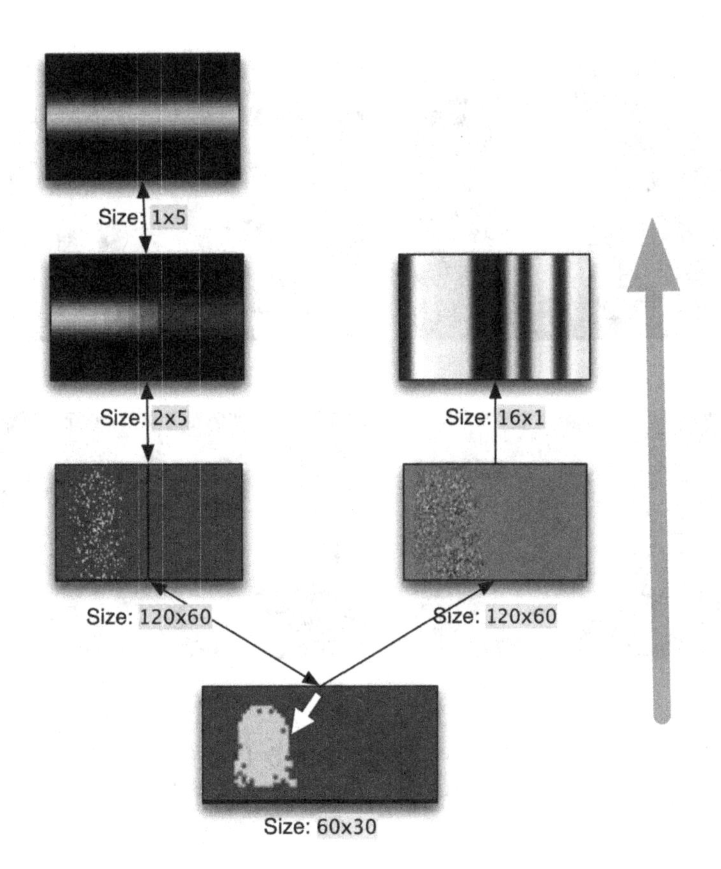

the target stimulus is highly visible when presented by itself, it can be rendered invisible by the mask. Based on the spatial relationship between the target and the mask, two types of backward masking are usually identified. In pattern masking, the mask is spatially superimposed over the target, while in metacontrast masking the mask closely fits the contour of the target, but does not overlap it. As the framework presented here relies on competition within the receptive fields of the top level winning units, spatial overlap between the mask and the stimulus is not needed, all that is required is that the mask falls within the area of competition (i.e. the receptive fields). Feedback will select the mask and the second pass will process it, producing a representation for recognition of the mask rather than the target. A similar phenomenon was described as "the four-dot mask" effect (Enns & Di Lollo, 2000), accompanied by the comment that "there are no standard theories that predict that masking will occur with the four-dot mask."

Based on the observation that learning improves the ability to process learned stimuli in parallel (Schneider & Shiffrin, 1977), the representation used in this paper suggest a powerful new way of investigating the nature of cortical representations and their evolution through learning. As has been previously hypothesized and demonstrated for early cortical areas, e.g. (Olshausen & Field, 1997), it is quite conceivable that learning spar-

Figure 9. Feedback selection for the sample stimuli. Left - dual stimulus input images, right - selected input stimulus is indicated by the white arrow..

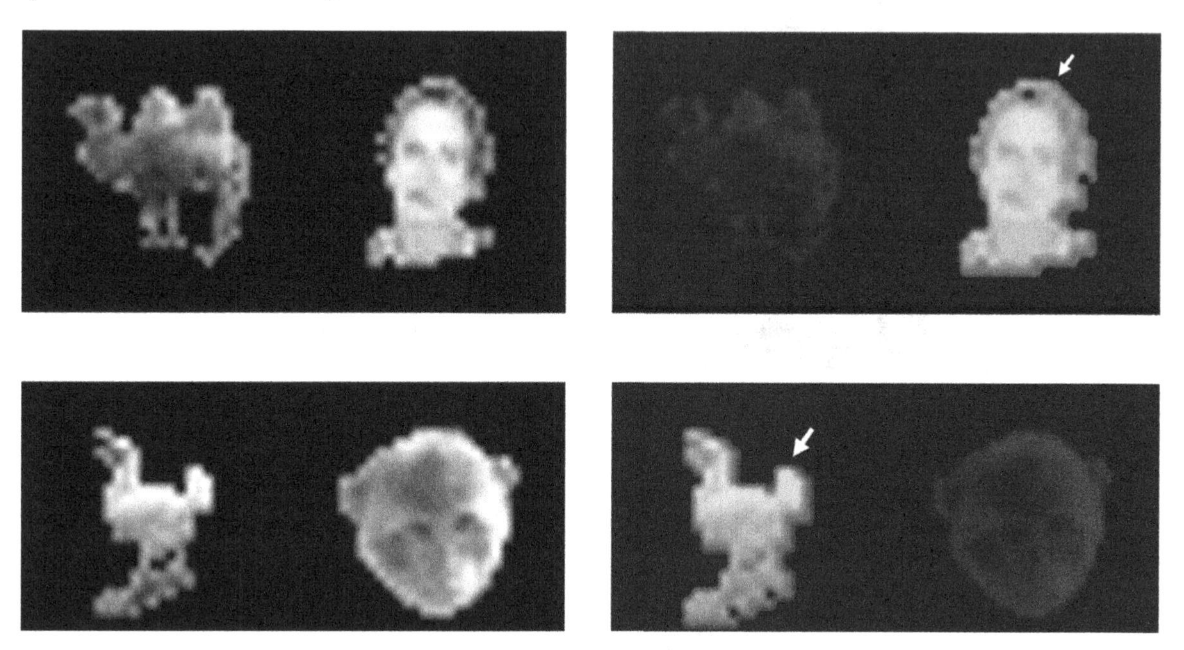

sifies high level identification representations. This process has to happen under the control of attentional processes, as they have been shown to not only play an important role in learning, and more specifically they seem to tune population codes (Saproo & Serences, 2010).

Figure 10. Absolute error of the identification representation vs. percent inhibition discussion

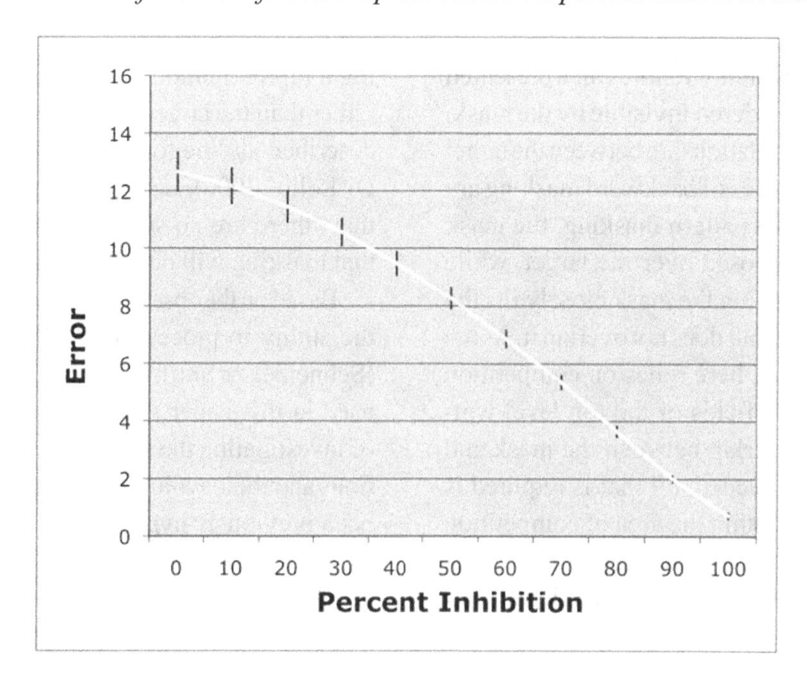

This paper demonstrated the effect of multiple stimuli on the population code used for recognition. The main observation is that the representation for pairs of stimuli is closer to the average between the two individual representations than each of the representations individually. In contrast to the Biased Competition model, which predicts response increases with attention (Reynolds et al., 1999), this model predicts the temporal evolution of the responses from the code for pairs of stimuli in the direction of the responses to the attended stimulus. Thus, each neuron taking part in the population code is predicted to have its activation modulated in the direction of its activation corresponding to the attended stimulus.

How can the results presented in this paper be reconciled with the results that indicate that even the first few spikes to arrive in high-level visual recognition areas contain most of the information needed to perform object recognition, e.g. (Hung et al., 2005)? A careful analysis shows that these experiments are performed with single target images, which, as predicted, will not suffer from interference. This decoding breaks down in the presence of multiple stimuli (Meyers et al., 2010), and especially when stimuli are in close proximity to the target (Tsotsos et al., 1995), and when they are similar (Tombu & Tsotsos, 2008).

The proposed representation model makes the predictions of sparse coding and population coding theories concrete, by specifying under what conditions each will be observed. The predictions of sparse coding theories will manifest themselves in detection tasks, with categoric decisions, or with over-learned stimuli, while population code behavior will be observed in detailed recognition tasks. Through this, the proposed binding and representation model makes a connection between observed performance in object recognition tasks, and the internal representation of the stimulus.

CONCLUSION

A novel view of how task, timing and representation are inter-related and contribute to object recognition has been presented. The main point of originality of the computational framework is the task-driven architecture obtained through a tight integration of attention and recognition sub-tasks. The result is a proposed architecture for object recognition that matches the temporal characteristics of the primate visual system, can solve a particular class of vision tasks quickly and in parallel, can solve other tasks at the expense of longer processing time, and can generate testable predictions.

We view this as a first version of such a framework, and a significant amount of work still needs to be done to demonstrate a system that exhibits the full characteristics of human vision. In particular the set of tasks considered is very limited; see (Tsotsos et al., 2008) for a more detailed discussion of visual tasks and their computational requirements. Using the fact that recognition is not a monolithic process and analyzing the different characteristics of the sub-tasks provides us with a divide and conquer strategy that has been missing in the computational object recognition literature.

A number of facets of vision share similar characteristics, as reviewed in this paper. First, attention has been described along an axis from preattentive (fast, simultaneous processing of certain stimuli) to attentive (slow, serial) processing. Similarly, tasks like detection and classification can be performed in parallel for some stimuli, while slow, serial identification can be performed on any stimulus. Yet another dichotomy, different experiments have demonstrated the presence of both sparse and population representations in the brain.

These seemingly distinct characteristics of vision and their time course suggest a theory of vision that has attention at its centre, forming a bridge between a sparse, fast, and parallel initial representation that supports object detection and a slow, serial, and detailed population representation needed for full identification. While this paper proposes a possible mechanism by which this link is accomplished in the context of Selective Tuning, and shows how this solution can account for diverse existing experimental results, developing these ideas into a full-fledged and cohesive theory will take significant additional work.

REFERENCES

Barker, A. T., Jalinous, R., & Freeston, I. L. (1985). Non-invasive magnetic stimulation of human motor cortex. *Lancet*, *1*(8437), 1106–1107. doi:10.1016/S0140-6736(85)92413-4

Barlow, H. B. (1972). Single units and sensation: A neuron doctrine for perceptual psychology? *Perception*, *1*(4), 371–394. doi:10.1068/p010371

Behrmann, M., Zemel, R. S., & Mozer, M. C. (1998). Object-based attention and occlusion: Evidence from normal participants and a computational model. *Journal of Experimental Psychology. Human Perception and Performance*, *24*(4), 1011–1036. doi:10.1037/0096-1523.24.4.1011

Bullier, J. (2001). Integrated model of visual processing. *Brain Research. Brain Research Reviews*, *36*(2-3), 96–107. doi:10.1016/S0165-0173(01)00085-6

Caputo, G., & Guerra, S. (1998). Attentional selection by distractor suppression. *Vision Research*, *38*(5), 669–689. doi:10.1016/S0042-6989(97)00189-2

Chelazzi, L., Miller, E. K., Duncan, J., & Desimone, R. (2001). Responses of neurons in macaque area V4 during memory-guided visual search. *Cerebral Cortex*, *11*(8), 761–772. doi:10.1093/cercor/11.8.761

Corbeil, J.-C. (1986). *The Stoddart visual dictionary*. Toronto, Canada: Stoddart Publishing.

Cutzu, F., & Tsotsos, J. K. (2003). The selective tuning model of attention: Psychophysical evidence for a suppressive annulus around an attended item. *Vision Research*, *43*(2), 205–219. doi:10.1016/S0042-6989(02)00491-1

Desimone, R., & Duncan, J. (1995). Neural mechanisms of selective visual attention. *Annual Review of Neuroscience*, *18*, 193–222. doi:10.1146/annurev.ne.18.030195.001205

Duncan, J. (1984). Selective attention and the organization of visual information. *Journal of Experimental Psychology. General*, *113*(4), 501–517. doi:10.1037/0096-3445.113.4.501

Enns, J. T., & Di Lollo, V. (2000). What's new in visual masking? *Trends in Cognitive Sciences*, *4*(9), 345–352. doi:10.1016/S1364-6613(00)01520-5

Evans, K. K., & Treisman, A. M. (2005). Perception of objects in natural scenes: Is it really attention free? *Journal of Experimental Psychology. Human Perception and Performance*, *31*(6), 1476–1492. doi:10.1037/0096-1523.31.6.1476

Foldiak, P., & Young, M. (1995). Sparse coding in the primate cortex. In Arbib, M. A. (Ed.), *The handbook of brain theory and neural networks* (pp. 895–898). MIT Press.

Grill-Spector, K., & Kanwisher, N. (2005). Visual recognition: As soon as you see it, you know what it is. *Psychological Science*, *16*(2), 152–160. doi:10.1111/j.0956-7976.2005.00796.x

Grimson, W. E. L. (1990). *Object recognition by computer-The role of geometric constraints*. Cambridge, MA: MIT Press.

Hummel, J. E. (2001). Complementary solutions to the binding problem in vision: Implications for shape perception and object recognition. *Visual Cognition*, *8*, 489–517. doi:10.1080/13506280143000214

Hummel, J. E., & Stankiewicz, B. J. (1996). An architecture for rapid, hierarchical structural description. In Inui, T., & McClelland, J. (Eds.), *Attention and Performance XVI: Information Integration in Perception and Communication* (pp. 93–121). MIT Press.

Hung, K. P., Kreiman, G., Poggio, T., & DiCarlo, J. J. (2005). Fast readout of object identity from macaque inferior temporal cortex. *Science*, *301*, 863–866. doi:10.1126/science.1117593

Itti, L., Koch, C., & Niebur, E. (1998). A model of saliency-based visual attention for rapid scene analysis. *IEEE Transactions on Pattern Analysis and Machine Intelligence*, *20*(11), 1254–1259. doi:10.1109/34.730558

Jadhav, S., & Bhalchandra, A. (2008). Blind source separation: Trends of new age - A review. In *IET International Conference on Wireless, Mobile and Multimedia Networks, 2008,* (pp. 251 –254).

Kandel, E. R., Schwartz, J. H., & Jessell, T. M. (2000). *Principles of neural science* (4th ed.). New York, NY: McGraw-Hill.

Kastner, S., De Weerd, P., Desimone, R., & Ungerleider, L. G. (1998). Mechanisms of directed attention in the human extrastriate cortex as revealed by functional MRI. *Science*, *282*(5386), 108–111. doi:10.1126/science.282.5386.108

Kiani, R., Esteky, H., Mirpour, K., & Tanaka, K. (2007). Object category structure in response patterns of neuronal population in monkey inferior temporal cortex. *Journal of Neurophysiology*, *97*, 4296–4309. doi:10.1152/jn.00024.2007

Koch, C., & Tsuchiya, N. (2007). Attention and consciousness: Two distinct brain processes. *Trends in Cognitive Sciences*, *11*(1), 16–22. doi:10.1016/j.tics.2006.10.012

Koch, C., & Ullman, S. (1985). Shifts in selective visual attention: Towards the underlying neural circuitry. *Human Neurobiology*, *4*(4), 219–227.

Kreiman, G. (2004). Neural coding: Computational and biophysical perspectives. *Physics of Life Reviews*, *2*, 71–102. doi:10.1016/j.plrev.2004.06.001

Kreiman, G., Serre, T., & Poggio, T. (2007). On the limits of feed-forward processing in visual object recognition. *Journal of Vision (Charlottesville, Va.)*, *9*(7).

Macmillan, N. A., & Creelman, C. D. (2004). *Detection theory: A user's guide*. Routledge.

McAdams, C. J., & Maunsell, J. H. (1999). Effects of attention on orientation-tuning functions of single neurons in macaque cortical area V4. *The Journal of Neuroscience*, *19*(1), 431–441.

McElree, B., & Carrasco, M. (1999). The temporal dynamics of visual search: Evidence for parallel processing in feature and conjunction searches. *Journal of Experimental Psychology. Human Perception and Performance*, *25*(6), 1517–1539. doi:10.1037/0096-1523.25.6.1517

Mehta, A. D., Ulbert, I., & Schroeder, C. E. (2000). Intermodal selective attention in monkeys, I: distribution and timing of effects across visual areas. *Cerebral Cortex*, *10*(4), 343–358. doi:10.1093/cercor/10.4.343

Meyers, E., Embark, H., Freiwald, W., Serre, T., Kreiman, G., & Poggio, T. (2010). *Examining high level neural representations of cluttered scenes*. Tech. Rep. MIT-CSAIL-TR-2010-034, Massachusetts Institute of Technology.

Miller, E. K., Gochin, P. M., & Gross, C. G. (1993). Suppression of visual responses of neurons in inferior temporal cortex of the awake macaque by addition of a second stimulus. *Brain Research*, *616*(1-2), 25–29. doi:10.1016/0006-8993(93)90187-R

Missal, M., Vogels, R., Li, C. Y., & Orban, G. (1999). Shape interactions in macaque inferior temporal neurons. *Journal of Neurophysiology*, *82*(1), 131–142.

Moran, J., & Desimone, R. (1985). Selective attention gates visual processing in the extrastriate cortex. *Science*, *229*(4715), 782–784. doi:10.1126/science.4023713

O'Connor, D., Fukui, M., Pinsk, M., & Kastner, S. (2002). Attention modulates responses in the human lateral geniculate nucleus. *Nature Neuroscience*, *5*(11), 1203–1209. doi:10.1038/nn957

Olshausen, B. A., & Field, D. J. (1997). Sparse coding with an overcomplete basis set: A strategy employed by V1? *Vision Research*, *37*, 3311–3325. doi:10.1016/S0042-6989(97)00169-7

Pouget, A., Dayan, P., & Zemel, R. (2003). Inference and computation with population codes. *Annual Review of Neuroscience*, *26*, 381–410. doi:10.1146/annurev.neuro.26.041002.131112

Rensink, R. (1989). *A new proof of the NP-Completeness of visual match. Tech. Rep. TR 89-22*. Dept. of Computer Science, University of British Columbia.

Reynolds, J. H., Chelazzi, L., & Desimone, R. (1999). Competitive mechanisms subserve attention in macaque areas V2 and V4. *The Journal of Neuroscience*, *19*(5), 1736–1753.

Riesenhuber, M., & Poggio, T. (1999a). Are cortical models really bound by the "binding problem"? *Neuron*, *24*(1), 87–93. doi:10.1016/S0896-6273(00)80824-7

Riesenhuber, M., & Poggio, T. (1999b). Hierarchical models of object recognition in cortex. *Nature Neuroscience*, *2*(11), 1019–1025. doi:10.1038/14819

Rolls, E. T., & Tovee, M. J. (1995). The responses of single neurons in the temporal visual cortical areas of the macaque when more than one stimulus is present in the receptive field. *Experimental Brain Research*, *103*(3), 409–420. doi:10.1007/BF00241500

Rothenstein, A., & Tsotsos, J. K. (2008). Attention links sensing with perception. *Image & Vision Computing Journal. Special Issue on Cognitive Vision Systems*, *26*(1), 114–126.

Rothenstein, A. L., Zaharescu, A., & Tsotsos, J. K. (2005). In Paletta, L., Tsotsos, J. K., Rome, E., & Humphreys, G. (Eds.), *TarzaNN: A general purpose neural network simulator for visual attention modeling* (*Vol. 3368*, pp. 159–167). Lecture Notes in Computer Science Springer Verlag. doi:10.1007/978-3-540-30572-9_12

Rousselet, G., Fabre-Thorpe, M., & Thorpe, S. J. (2002). Parallel processing in high level categorization of natural images. *Nature Neuroscience*, *5*, 629–630.

Saproo, S., & Serences, J. T. (2010). Spatial attention improves the quality of population codes in human visual cortex spatial attention improves the quality of population codes in human visual cortex. *Journal of Neurophysiology*, *104*, 885–895. doi:10.1152/jn.00369.2010

Sato, T. (1989). Interactions of visual stimuli in the receptive fields of inferior temporal neurons in awake macaques. *Experimental Brain Research*, *77*, 23–30. doi:10.1007/BF00250563

Schneider, W., & Shiffrin, R. (1977). Controlled and automatic human information processing, I- Detection, search, and attention. *Psychological Review*, *84*(1), 1–66. doi:10.1037/0033-295X.84.1.1

Serre, T., Wolf, L., Bileschi, S., Riesenhuber, M., & Poggio, T. (2007). Object recognition with cortex-like mechanism. *IEEE Transactions on Pattern Analysis and Machine Intelligence*, *29*(3), 411–426. doi:10.1109/TPAMI.2007.56

Tombu, M., & Tsotsos, J. K. (2008). Attending to orientation results in an inhibitory surround in orientation space. *Perception & Psychophysics*, *70*(1), 30–35. doi:10.3758/PP.70.1.30

Tramo, M. J., Loftus, W. C., Thomas, C. E., Green, R. L., Mott, L. A., & Gazzaniga, M. S. (1995). Surface area of human cerebral cortex and its gross morphological subdivisions: In vivo measurements in monozygotic twins suggest differential hemisphere effects of genetic factors. *Journal of Cognitive Neuroscience*, *7*(2), 292–302. doi:10.1162/jocn.1995.7.2.292

Tsotsos, J. K. (1987). *A 'complexity level' analysis of vision*. In International Conference on Computer Vision: Human and Machine Vision Workshop, London, England.

Tsotsos, J. K. (1988). A 'complexity level' analysis of immediate vision. *International Journal of Computer Vision*, *2*(1), 303–320. doi:10.1007/BF00133569

Tsotsos, J. K. (1990). Analyzing vision at the complexity level. *The Behavioral and Brain Sciences*, *13*(3), 423–445. doi:10.1017/S0140525X00079577

Tsotsos, J. K. (2011). *A computational perspective on visual attention*. The MIT Press.

Tsotsos, J. K., Culhane, S. M., Wai, W. Y. K., Lai, Y. H., Davis, N., & Nuflo, F. (1995). Modeling visual-attention via selective tuning. *Artificial Intelligence*, *78*(1-2), 507–545. doi:10.1016/0004-3702(95)00025-9

Tsotsos, J. K., Liu, Y., Martinez-Trujillo, J.-C., Pomplun, M., Simine, E., & Zhou, K. (2005). Attending to visual motion. *Computer Vision and Image Understanding*, *100*(1-2), 3–40. doi:10.1016/j.cviu.2004.10.011

Tsotsos, J. K., Rodriguez-Sanchez, A.-J., Rothenstein, A. L., & Simine, E. (2008). The different stages of visual recognition need different attentional binding strategies. *Brain Research*, *1225*, 119–132. doi:10.1016/j.brainres.2008.05.038

Tsunoda, K., Yamane, Y., Nishizaki, M., & Tanifuji, M. (2001). Complex objects are represented in macaque inferotemporal cortex by the combination of feature columns. *Nature Neuroscience*, *4*, 832–838. doi:10.1038/90547

Vanduffel, W., Tootell, R. B. H., & Orban, G. A. (2000). Attention-dependent suppression of metabolic activity in the early stages of the macaque visual system. *Cerebral Cortex*, *10*(2), 109–126. doi:10.1093/cercor/10.2.109

VanRullen, R., Reddy, L., & Koch, C. (2004). Visual search and dual tasks reveal two distinct attentional resources. *Journal of Cognitive Neuroscience*, *16*(1), 4–14. doi:10.1162/089892904322755502

Walther, D. (2006). *Interactions of visual attention and object recognition: Computational modeling, algorithms, and psychophysics*. Ph.D. thesis, California Institute of Technology.

Walther, D., Itti, L., Riesenhuber, M., Poggio, T., & Koch, C. (2002). Attentional selection for object recognition - A gentle way. *Proceedings Biologically Motivated Computer Vision, LNCS*, *2525*, 472–479. doi:10.1007/3-540-36181-2_47

Witelson, S. F., Glezer, I. I., & Kigar, D. L. (1995). Women have greater density of neurons in posterior temporal cortex. *The Journal of Neuroscience*, *15*, 3418–3428.

Wolfe, J. M. (1998). Visual search. In Pashler, H. (Ed.), *Attention*. Taylor & Francis.

Wolfe, J. M., & Horowitz, T. S. (2004). What attributes guide the deployment of visual attention and how do they do it? *Nature Reviews. Neuroscience*, *5*(6), 495–501. doi:10.1038/nrn1411

Zoccolan, D., Cox, D. D., & DiCarlo, J. J. (2005). Multiple object response normalization in monkey inferotemporal cortex. *The Journal of Neuroscience*, *25*(36), 8150–8164. doi:10.1523/JNEUROSCI.2058-05.2005

Chapter 4
Attention in Stereo Vision:
Implications for Computational Models of Attention

Neil D. B. Bruce
University of Manitoba, Canada

John K. Tsotsos
York University, Canada

ABSTRACT

The stereo correspondence problem is a topic that has been the subject of considerable research effort. What has not yet been considered is an analogue of stereo correspondence in the domain of attention. In this chapter, the authors bring this problem to light, revealing important implications for computational models of attention, and in particular, how these implications constrain the problem of computational modeling of attention. A model is described which addresses attention in the stereo domain, and it is revealed that a variety of behaviors observed in binocular rivalry experiments are consistent with the model's behavior. Finally, the authors consider how constraints imposed by stereo vision may suggest analogous constraints in other non-stereo feature domains with significant consequence to computational models of attention.

1. INTRODUCTION

An important problem faced by the primate brain, is that of understanding the 3D structure of one's environment based on the two dimensional view received by each eye. Having two slightly different perspectives of the scene allows the possibility of estimating scene structure based on small differences between the images captured by the left and right eyes. Differences between the location of points appearing in the left and right eye are referred to as stereo disparities, and the perception of depth based on such disparities is referred to as stereopsis. An important problem then becomes

DOI: 10.4018/978-1-4666-2539-6.ch004

that of deciding which features observed in one eye correspond to features observed in the other; this is referred to in the literature as the stereo correspondence problem.

In light of the problems posed by stereo vision in the domain of attention modeling, we demonstrate that the Selective Tuning model is able to accommodate for stereo vision with no additional assumptions or requirements imposed on the model. This is in contrast to other classes of models for which we highlight the pitfalls posed by stereo correspondence in the attention domain.

An additional consideration is the relationship between binocular rivalry and attention. In recent years it has become increasingly evident that attention plays a significant role in the perceptual alternation observed when viewing a rivalry stimulus. In Section 7, we reveal that when applied to stereo vision, behavior consistent with psychophysical results in this domain emerge from the Selective Tuning model (Tsotsos et al., 1995).

As a whole, the body of work demonstrates that stereo vision in itself imposes strict requirements on computational models of attention, Selective Tuning is able to accommodate for stereo vision with a variety of rivalry behaviors emerging directly from the model, and some of the problems posed by stereo vision may have non-stereo analogues.

The balance of this chapter is structured as follows: In Section 2, we motivate the need for attention in biological systems, appealing to issues tied to interference among competing signals within a neural representation, and also to the inherent complexity of visual search. In Section 3, we summarize evidence tied to the relationship between attention, and deployment in 3D space. In particular, we show that while this relationship is complicated, there does appear to be the basic ability to attend in depth. We further introduce a novel constraint on systems that achieve attention in depth deemed the Attentional Stereo Correspondence Problem (ASCP) in this work. In Section 4, we describe a basic hierarchical computational model that realizes stereo correspondence, inspired by energy models in visual computation. This is followed in Section 5 by a more generic description of a mechanism of attentional selection that acts upon the interpretive network that simulates stereo computation. Section 6 describes how the attentional computation outlined in section 5 acts upon the putative visual representation in Section 4 towards allowing attention to be deployed within 3-dimensional space. This is followed in Section 7 by considering some of the possible implications of such a marriage including possible explanations for observed binocular and pattern rivalry behavior. In Section 8, we comment on the manner in which the ASCP constrains models of attention as a whole, and highlight certain classes of models for which this domain may pose a challenge. Finally, we close the chapter by summarizing some of the important points, and highlight the elements most relevant as a guide to computational modeling within this area.

2. THE NEED FOR ATTENTION

Attention provides a mechanism for selection of particular aspects of a scene for subsequent processing while eliminating interference from competing visual events. A common misperception is that attention and fixation are one and the same phenomenon. Attention focuses processing on a selected region of the visual field that needn't coincide with the centre of fixation. This is perhaps exemplified by the perceived ability to look out of the corner of one's eye. There exist numerous formal arguments demonstrating the necessity of attention to solve the visual search problem (Tsotsos, 1988; Burt, 1988). In lieu of exhaustively describing each of these arguments, we instead summarize some of the more important elements and comment specifically on implications in the domain of stereo vision.

A question that frequently arises with regards to attention, is that of why attention is necessary. Many arguments for attention appeal to reducing the complexity of visual search. The intention of this section is to motivate why this is not the entire story, since the issue at hand is greater in scope than simply reducing computational complexity. One of the primary goals of attention, unrelated to complexity, concerns interference between signals generated by unrelated visual events: In a feedforward network, crossover between signals and blurring may result in a response at the output level that is highly confused.

Tsotsos examined the problem of visual search as derived from first principles (Tsotsos, 1988) within a well-defined framework including images, a model base of objects and events, and an objective function that affords a metric of closeness between an image subset and an element of the model base. On the basis of this formulation, it may be shown that visual search in the general case (i.e. when no explicit target is given) is NP-complete. One conclusion that emerges on the basis of this analysis and other complexity arguments (Uhr, 1972; Burt, 1988; Anderson and Essen, 1987; Nakayama and Silverman, 1991), is that the computational complexity of vision demands a pyramidal processing architecture. Such an architecture is observed in the primate brain on the basis of increasing receptive field size and the observed connectivity between neurons as one ascends visual pathways (Palmer, 1999). Pyramidal processing may greatly reduce the computation required to accomplish a particular task by reducing the size of instances to be processed. Tsotsos et al. outline four major issues that arise in a pyramid processing architecture, all of which result in corruption of information as input flows from the earliest to later layers (Tsotsos et al., 1995). The four cases are depicted in Figure 1. The pyramid depicted in the top left (Fig. 1a) demonstrates the context effect. The response of any given unit at the top of the pyramid results from input from a very large portion of the input image. As such, the response of a given unit at the top of the pyramid may result from a variety of different objects or events in the image. On the basis of this observation, it is clear that the response at the output layer with regards to a particular event depends significantly on the context of that event. The top right pyramid (Fig. 1b) demonstrates the blurring effect. A small localized event in the input layer eventually impacts on the response of a large number of neurons at the output layer. This may result in issues in localizing the source of the response at the output layer, as a localized event may be represented by a large portion of the highest layer. In the stereo domain this also implies the inability to determine which eye the winning activation derives from. The pyramid on the bottom left (Fig. 1c) displays the cross-talk effect. Cross-talk refers to the overlap of two image events in the pyramid which results in interference between signals in higher layers of the pyramid. This issue is of particular importance in the context of stereo vision since there exist many neurons in the human visual system that respond to input from the two eyes. Often the input from each eye is in agreement in which case interference is not an issue. However, in the event that the two eyes receive disparate input, an appropriate mechanism is required to resolve such interference. Finally, the pyramid on the bottom right (Fig. 1d) displays the boundary effect. Units at the outer edges connect to fewer units in higher layers of the pyramid. As a result, a significantly stronger response may result from the same stimulus centered in the visual field relative to near the boundaries. Means of overcoming this difficulty are discussed in detail in (Tsotsos et al., 1995; Culhane, 1992).

At this point, the rationale of the preceding discussion may not yet be apparent. The motive for addressing such issues is that an appropriate attentional mechanism may overcome the aforementioned interference issues inherent in pyramid processing. In particular, the Selective Tuning Model (Tsotsos et al., 1995) was designed with these issues in mind. Attenuation of appropriate connections in the network allows each of the aforesaid issues to be overcome. The exact mechanism by which such issues are handled becomes evident in the description of the Selective Tuning Model presented in Section 5.

Figure 1. Four major issues in pyramid information flow: a) The context effect, b) The blurring effect, c) The cross-talk effect, d) The boundary-effect; Adapted from (Tsotsos, 2003)

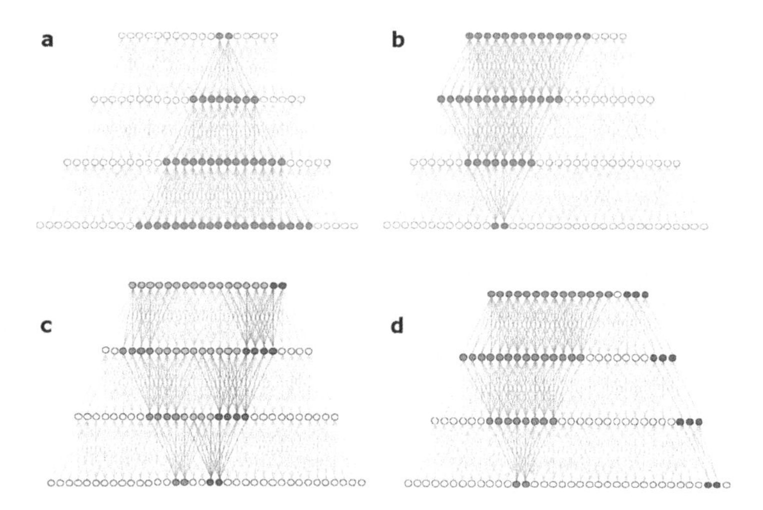

3. ATTENTION AND DEPTH

Perhaps the most crucial question in this discussion is that of whether attention operates in three-dimensional space. Discussion of attention in depth may become very convoluted owing to apparent differences between viewer centred, object centred, or action centred frames of reference in the context of allocating attention in three dimensions. The following section intentionally avoids this distinction, instead presenting evidence in favour of and against a three-dimensional focus of attention. This basic element is the sole consideration that has any bearing on the discussion presented in the sections that follow. In contrast to results on 2D deployment of attention, the literature involving 3D attention is far more contemporary. There is a great deal of conflicting results found in the current literature, but the following establishes that the proverbial spotlight of attention appears to reside in 3D space.

In a three-dimensional analogue of the Posner paradigm, Hoffman and Mueller show that a cue (brightening a dot) can produce cueing effects associated with a 3D location (Hoffman and Mueller, 1994).

In a pair of studies investigating the role of interference from distractors, it was observed that attending to a specific location defined by disparity, eliminated interference from distractors in other depth planes (Arnott and Shedden, 2000; Theeuwes et al., 1986).

Atchley et al. conducted a set of experiments in which observers were cued to one of four positions (left-right and near-far) in a stereoscopic display (Atchley et al., 1997). They found a larger reaction time in shifting attention in x,y and depth than switching attention in the frontoparallel plane alone suggesting a "depth-aware" spotlight.

The results of Atchley and colleagues receive support from the Event-Related-Potential (ERP) study of Kasai et al (Kasai et al., 2003). Kasai et al. observed ERP responses when subjects directed attention to locations appearing on the left and right of the display and either near or far relative to fixation. A response to a target at the attended location was required. Previous findings observed that attending to a location modulates incoming sensory signals, reflected by P1 and N1

ERP components. Kasai et al. observed a greater effect of P1 amplitude for left- right selection in the near condition, and an N1 amplitude increase for the combination of location-and depth.

Viswanathan and Mingolla considered the allocation of attention in depth in a multi-element tracking paradigm (Viswanathan and Mingolla, 2002). The task required tracking a subset of 2-8 elements moving around the display. They demonstrated that depth cues improve performance in a multi-element tracking task and establish through control experiments that such improvement derives from the spatial separation in three dimensions.

Theeuwes and Pratt consider inhibition of return in the stereo domain. Their results suggest that attentional cueing happens in three-dimensional space while inhibition of return appears to spread across depth planes (Theeuwes and Pratt, 2003). The authors suggest that this result may be explained by an inhibition of return (IOR) mechanism that avoids returning to any part of a previously attended object. While this result begs additional questions about the role of IOR in stereo attention, it further supports the notion that attention operates in three-dimensional space.

Andersen and Kramer carried out an experiment involving a response compatibility task. Subjects were instructed to respond to a central target while ignoring distractors (Andersen and Kramer, 1993). Flanking distractors were presented at 7 different depths as well as 3 different horizontal and vertical distances. The findings were that response-compatibility varied in x-y directions as well as in depth. Interestingly, the effect was stronger for horizontal shifts than for vertical shifts and stronger for crossed versus uncrossed disparities.

Marrara and Moore describe a set of experiments aimed at discerning specific conditions on observing attention in depth (Marrara and Moore, 2000). They demonstrate that some previous failures to observe attention in depth relate to issues of timing. Their results as a whole strongly suggest a 3D focus of attention, for which perceptual organization is an important influence.

There also exist a handful of studies that fail to find any effect of cueing in depth (Ghirardelli and Folk, 1996; Iavecchia and Folk, 1995; Theeuwes et al., 1998). Most authors seem to attribute inconsistencies in results to either the attentional requirements of the tasks involved, or issues pertaining to frame of reference. While these failures to observe attention in depth do not invalidate the body of literature as a whole, they do highlight the apparent complexity of the mechanisms involved.

It seems fair to conclude that the bulk of the literature is in favor of a representation of attention that resides in three-dimensional space. We will demonstrate that this consideration has important implications when cast into the domain of attention modeling in the sections that follow.

The Attentional Stereo Correspondence Problem (ASCP)

In Section 1, the stereo correspondence problem was briefly described. In this section, we will establish why stereo correspondence presents an additional problem in the domain of attention. Recall that the stereo correspondence problem refers to matching points appearing in the left eye to the same visual stimuli appearing in the right eye. The additional problem posed by attention, is that the locus of attention need not correspond to the locus of fixation. Therefore in addition to determining which points in the two eyes correspond for the purpose of inferring depth, one must also ascertain that the locus of attention falls on a single visual event, even in the case that this event falls on different coordinates in the left and right eye. Although the geometry of stereo correspondence may be rather involved in the general case, which may involve vertical disparities and torsional eye movements, for the purposes of exposition the discussion in this chapter considers the simpler case of horizontal disparities such that a stimulus to be attended falls on coordinates (x, y) in the left eye and (x + δ, y) in the right eye.

Consider the situation presented in Figure 2. While the eyes are fixated on the background target, the focus of attention as indicated by the highlighted area falls on the closer hexahedron. This requires that the system that deploys attention holds some knowledge of which points in the left eye correspond to the same item or visual event in the right eye. If this constraint is not satisfied, one might imagine undesirable movements of the two eyes, or a signal that is comprised of interference between two unrelated items in an image as activation corresponding to the two attended items converges on binocular neurons later on in the visual system. In the later sections, we further discuss how this problem constrains the type of model that might achieve intuitively appropriate deployment of attention.

4. A SUFFICIENT MODEL

In this section we present a model of stereo computation in primates with specificity sufficient to demonstrate constraints on achieving attentional selection in depth. The proposed framework is based largely on the Ohzawa and colleagues model of early primate stereo vision (Ohzawa, 1998). Properties of the model include disparity selective monocular neurons at early layers, binocular neurons at higher layers, pooling across orientation, and spatial frequency, and increasing

Figure 2. An illustration of the attentional stereo correspondence problem. The two eyes fixate on the red cross located on the background target. Attention is deployed covertly to the yellow region residing on the hexahedron, which requires knowledge of stereo correspondence to deploy attention appropriately.

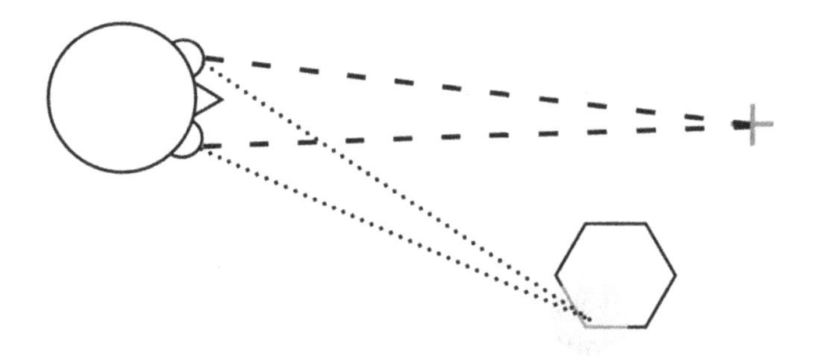

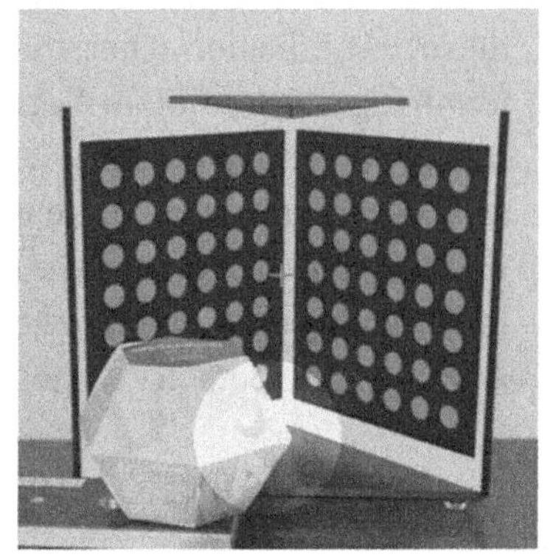

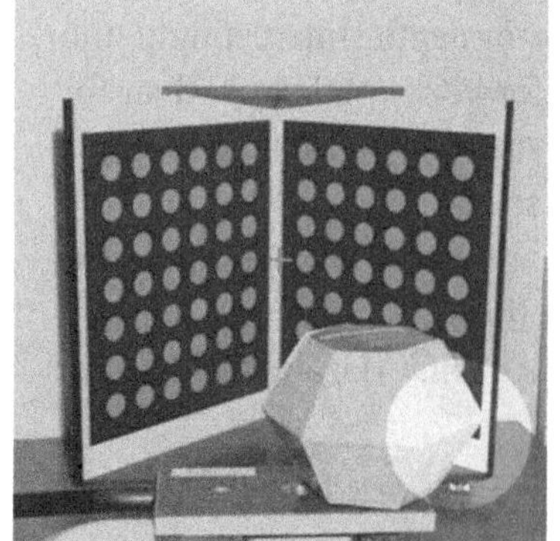

receptive field size as once ascends the visual hierarchy. All of these elements are consistent with the organization of the primate visual system and also consistent with more general properties of neural organization. The organization of the stereo framework is as follows:

Layer 1: Gabor maps of the form:

$$G_{\beta}(x,y,\theta,\sigma,\phi,\psi) = \psi \exp\left(-\frac{x'^2+\gamma^2 y'^2}{2\sigma^2}\right)\cos\left(2\pi\frac{x'}{\lambda}+\phi\right)$$

with $x' = x\cos\theta + y\sin\theta$ and $y' = -x\sin\theta + y\cos\theta$. $\beta \in \{l,r\}$ indicates the eye from which input to G is derived (left or right). Four different orientations were included in the implementation corresponding to $\theta \in \{0, \pi/4, \pi/2, 3\pi/4\}$. γ is fixed at 1 yielding a circular region of support for all feature maps, and feature maps include values for σ corresponding to 23 by 4 to 39 cycles per 100 pixels. $\phi \in \{0, \pi/2\}$ and $\psi \in \{-1,1\}$ yielding 0 or $\pi/2$ radians phase positive and negative filters. These are depicted in layer 1 of Figure 3. As a whole, this results in 2*4*5*2*2=160 feature maps at layer 1 corresponding to 2 eyes, 4 orientations, 5 spatial frequencies and 4 combinations of phase and sign.

Layer 2: Binocular simple cells tuned to various disparities (ä = 0 to 12 pixels in increments of 2) are derived by summing the output of a Gabor filter at a particular spatial frequency, and orientation acting on each of the left and right eye input, and shifted by the degree of disparity δ:

$$s_{\delta}(x,y,\theta,\sigma,\phi,\psi) = G_l(x,y,\theta,\sigma,\phi,\psi) + G_r(x+\delta,y,\theta,\sigma,\phi,\psi)$$

This gives rise to 560 feature maps (160*7/2) corresponding to 7 disparities ä for each feature set in layer 1 and combined across the two eyes. Binocular simple cells of this type are found among early visual areas, and often involve a differential contribution from each of the two eyes according to variation in ocular dominance along neural columns. In the context of our implementation, including this consideration would give rise to an appreciably larger number of feature maps and no generality is lost in our argument in assuming equal weighted inputs from each eye.

Layer 3: Complex binocular cells are produced by summing the squared output of 4 simple binocular neurons corresponding to the 4 different Gabor filter types for a particular orientation, spatial frequency and disparity.

$$C_{\delta}(x,y,\theta,\sigma) = \sum_{\phi\in\{0,\pi/2\}}\sum_{\psi\in\{-1,1\}} s_{\delta}(x,y,\theta,\sigma,\phi,\psi)^2$$

The choice of this operation is biologically motivated and means that output is not sensitive to contrast polarity, and disparity sensitivity is constant for all stimulus positions in the receptive field. The output of the above operation to compute C_{δ} is convolved with a gaussian with ó =5 pixels to simulate the pooling of simple cell responses by complex cells as in (Chen and Qian, 2004).

Layer 4: Responses are combined across orientation, and spatial frequency giving rise to 9 feature maps corresponding to the 9 disparities considered.

$$D_{\delta} = \sum_{\theta}\sum_{\alpha} C(\theta,\alpha)$$

This operation is suggested in the stereo model of Fleet et al. (Fleet et al., 1996) which is also inspired by the energy model of Ohzawa (Ohzawa, 1998). Combining across orientation and spatial frequency reduces false peaks inherent in narrow band signals. This operation is also appropriate since most

Figure 3. The computational architecture underlying disparity based computation

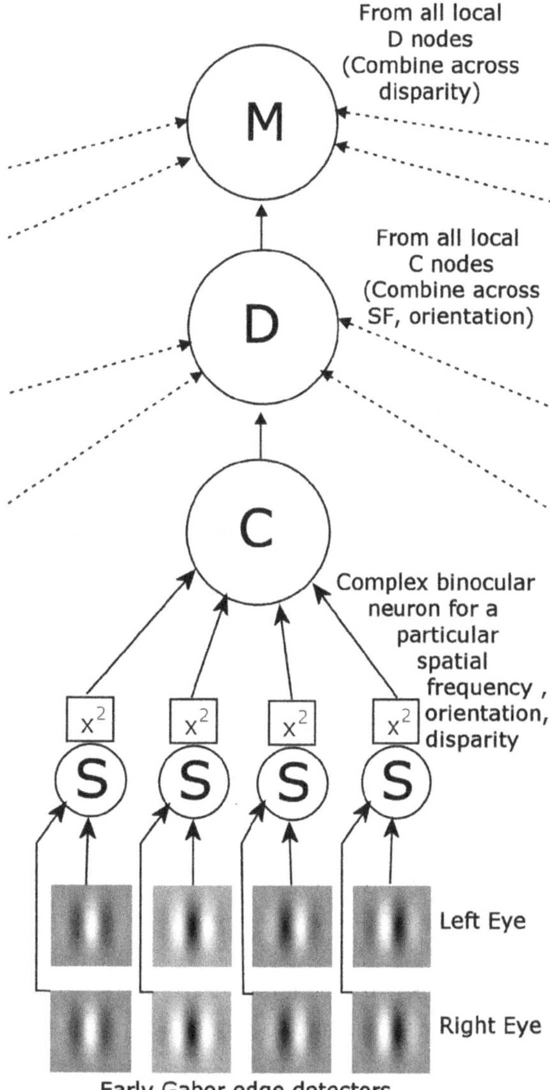

models of stereo vision will presumably rely on some form of pooling at a later stage of processing.

Layer 5: The 7 disparity maps are averaged to produce a single representation of disparity related activity:

$$M = \sum_{\delta} D_{\delta}^{2}$$

M is convolved with a Gaussian of $\sigma = 5$ pixels to produce a smooth master activation map at the highest layer. The overall architecture is depicted in Figure 3.

5. THE SELECTIVE TUNING (ST) MODEL

In this paper, selective attention in depth is achieved in the context of the Selective Tuning model. In the later discussion, it should become clear that this model is consistent with a broad range of psychophysical results pertaining to attention in depth, while other efforts encounter difficulties when tested on the same conditions.

Many design choices in the Selective Tuning Model are formed on the basis of overcoming the issues of complexity and problems inherent in pyramid processing discussed earlier. Selective Tuning simultaneously handles the issues of spatial selection of relevant stimulus and features. Spatial selection is accomplished by way of inhibition of appropriate connections in the network. Feature selection is accomplished through bias units which allow inhibition of responses to irrelevant features. The Selective Tuning Model is characterized by a multi-scale pyramid architecture with feedforward and feedback connections between units of each layer. A high level schematic of the model is depicted in Figure 4. Details concerning the connectivity between adjacent layers are displayed in Figure 5.

Variables shown in Figure 5 are as follows (also refer to Tsotsos et al. (1995) for a more detailed description):

- $\hat{I}_{l,k}$: interpretive unit in layer l and assembly k

Figure 4. A high-level schematic of the selective tuning model. a. Bottom up feedforward computation. Stimulus at the input level (green) causes a spread in activity in successively higher layers. Winner selected at the highest layer is shown by the orange oval. b. Top-down WTA selection. WTA selection happens in a top-down– manner with the winning unit at each level indicated by the orange region. A suppressive annulus around the attended item caused by inhibition of connections is depicted by the greyed region.

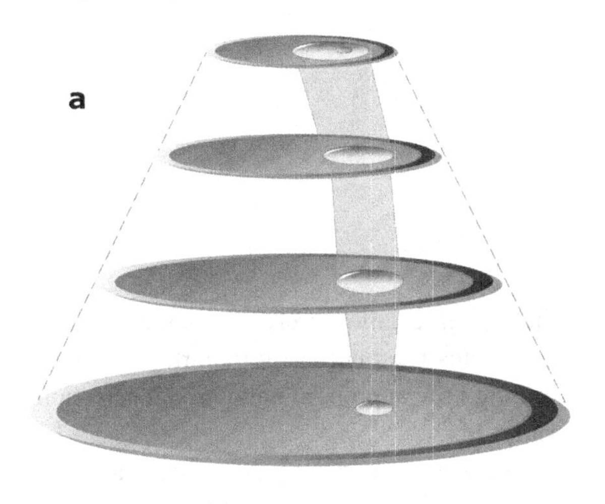

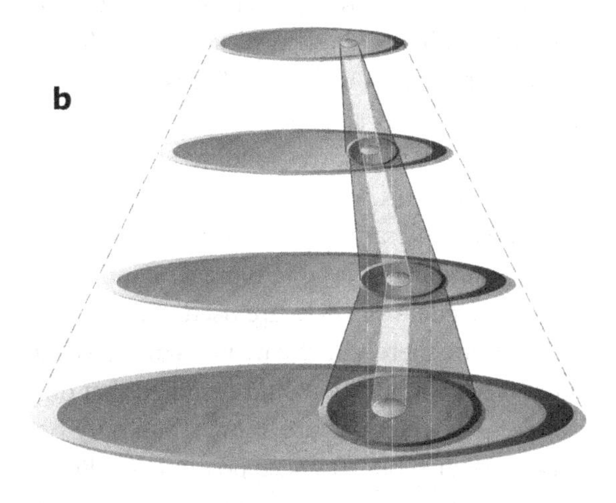

- $\hat{G}_l, k, j$: jth gating unit in the Winner-Take-All (WTA) network in layer l, assembly k which links $\hat{I}_{l,k}$ to $\hat{I}_{l-1,j}$
- $\hat{g}_{l,k}$: gating control unit for the WTA over inputs to $\hat{I}_{l,k}$
- $\hat{b}_{l,k}$: bias unit for $\hat{I}_{l,k}$
- $q_{l,j,i}$: weight corresponding to $\hat{I}_{l-1,i}$ in computing $\hat{I}_{l,j}$
- $n_{l,x}$: scale normalization factor
- $M_{l,k}$: set of gating units corresponding to $\hat{I}_{l,k}$

Selection is accomplished through two traversals of the pyramid. First, the responses of interpretive units are computed from the lowest level to the highest level of the pyramid in a feedforward manner. Next, WTA competition takes place between all units at the highest layer to select a single winning unit. In subsequent layers, units in layer *l* that connect to the winning unit in layer *l* +*1* compete for selection. This ultimately leads to selection of a localized response in the input layer. Note that interference between competing elements is eliminated by way of selection. Bias is handled through a connected network of bias units that impact on the response of interpretive units they are tied to in a multiplicative manner. Bias units may be used to modify the response of interpretive units that correspond to a particular stimulus type, such as bright items, horizontal edges, or blue objects. Bias values less than one might be assigned to the response of non-blue units to bias selection in favor of blue pixels. The exact circuitry for initiating bias is left unspecified in this implementation except to assume that there is some circuitry that allows the response of units of any type and at any layer to be modulated. The WTA process employed in Selective Tuning differs from that of Koch and Ullman (Koch and Ullman, 1985) in a number of aspects. The effect of unit i in the WTA network on unit j is quantified by the following expression:

$$y = \begin{cases} q_{l,k,i} G^{l-1}_{l,k,i} - q_{l,k,j} G^{l-1}_{l,k,j}, if & 0 < \zeta < q_{l,k,i} G^{l-1}_{l,k,i} - q_{l,k,j} G^{l-1}_{l,k,j} \\ 0, & otherwise \end{cases} \quad (1)$$

Figure 5. A detailed depiction of connectivity between units and layers in the selective tuning model; Tsotsos et al., 1995

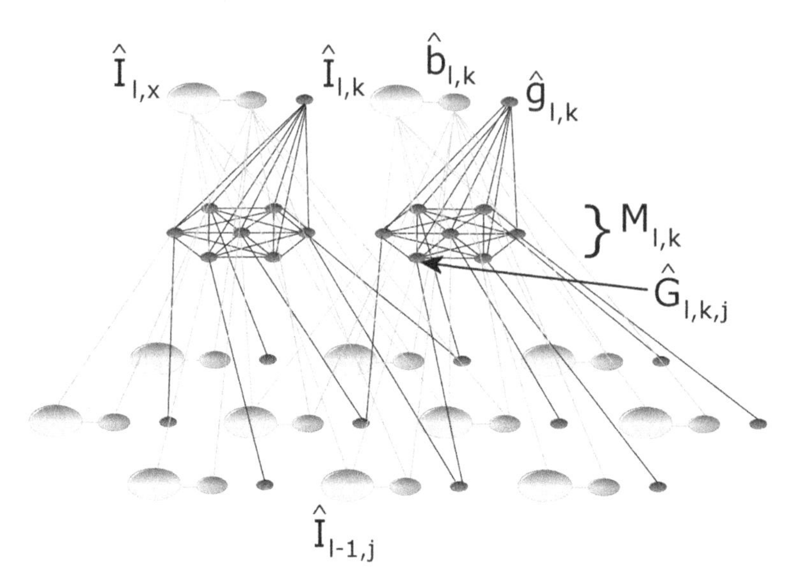

with $\zeta = \dfrac{Z}{2^{\gamma}+1}$, γ a parameter that controls the convergence rate of the WTA network (converges within γ iterations) and $G^{t_0}_{l,k,j} = b_{l-1} n_{l-1} I_{l-1,j}$. The choice of this particular scheme is tied to provable guarantees associated with convergence, and the desire to preserve the nature of the winning signal. A more detailed version of the preceding description concerning the WTA scheme, and in particular parameters tied to the interpretive network, may be found in (Tsotsos et al., 1995). Appropriate deployment of attention in 3D space is achieved via Selective Tuning combined with the interpretive network comprised of the basic biologically inspired model of primate binocular vision described in Section 4.

6. SHIFTING ATTENTION IN DEPTH

It is straightforward to describe the manner in which selection of appropriate units in each eye is achieved given the principles of Selective Tuning, and the computational circuitry involved in the implementation presented here. Figure 6 demonstrates 4 distinct stages important for demonstrating how appropriate attentional selection is achieved.

In Figure 6 i, A vertically oriented bar appears in front of the background surface. The receptive fields of a unit at a single position responding to vertical and horizontal stimuli respectively is shown for stimuli appearing in the left eye for position (x, y), and corresponding to three positions $(x - \delta, y)$, (x, y), $(x + \delta, y)$ in the right eye. The network hierarchy above this is shown in a manner similar to that of Figure 3. Each of the lowercase letters s/c, d, m are used to emphasize that these are merely single neurons of thousands in the feature maps. It should be noted that only 2 of the 4 orientations are shown, and only one of the 4 filter types (0 phase positive) is shown. The computation which takes place from the inputs to the binocular simple cells, to the output of the binocular complex cells is compressed into a single operation shown as (s/c) for the purpose of exposition.

In Figure 6 ii, activation flows upwards through the hierarchy. The saturation of green indicates

Figure 6. Four stages in the feedforward interpretive computation, and feedback selection that achieves appropriate deployment of attention in depth. Refer to the text for further details.

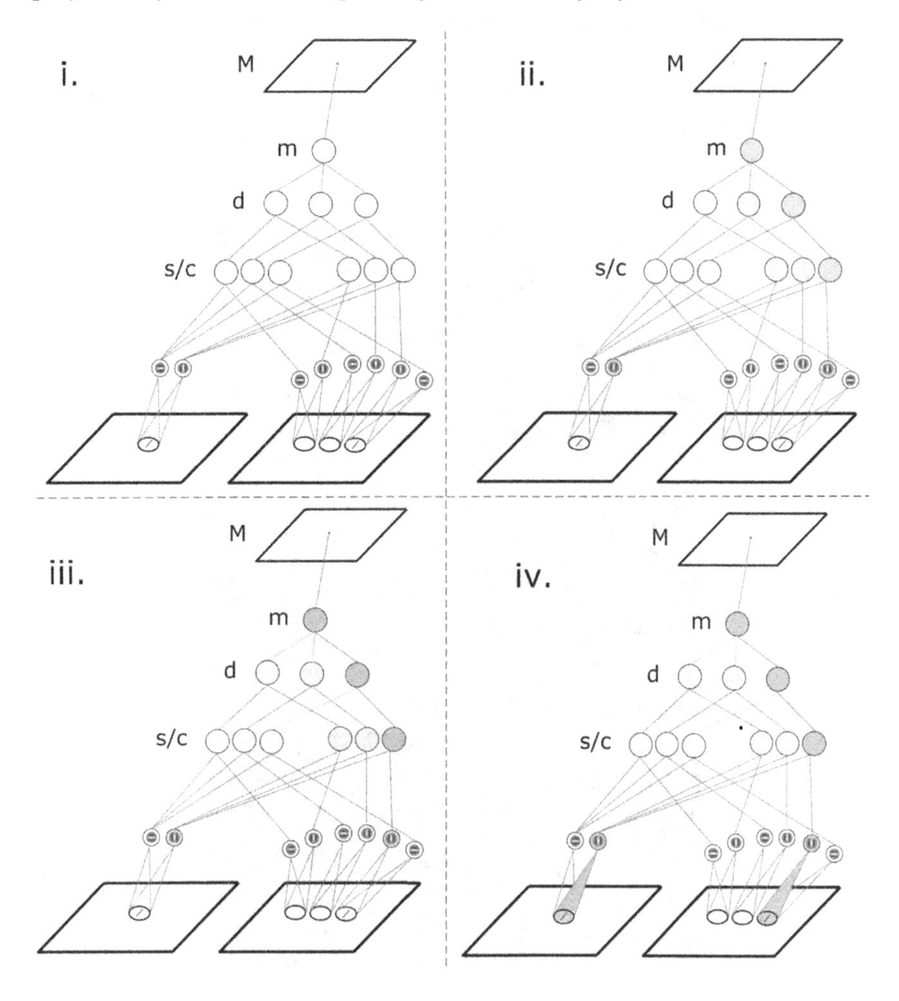

the intensity of firing of the neurons involved. Note that some of the binocular cells are weakly activated by a stimulus appearing in only one of the two eyes, but the strongest response derives from a true correspondence.

In Figure 6 iii, winner-take-all competition selects the winning units at the highest layer which includes the single neuron belonging to layer M shown in the diagram. Subsequently, WTA competition is initiated at the next layer down for units that contribute to the winner selected at layer M. This process propagates down the pyramid with flow along connections that do not contribute appreciably to the winning response attenuated (selected units appear as orange). The cascade of WTA activation is shown up to the point where monocular units from the two eyes converge on a binocular unit.

In Figure 6 iv, a variety of outcomes may arise at this stage. In most cases, the winning binocular unit will elicit a strong response which derives from a stimulus of appropriate disparity appearing in both eyes. This is the case in the example shown, and the focus of attention is directed to region (x, y) in the left eye, and $(x + \delta, y)$ in the right eye. An alternative possibility is that the winning binocular response derives from a very strong stimulus appearing in only one of the two eyes. This case is considered in later sections.

Figure 7. Selection results based on a letter C that appears in front of the background. (From left to right) Top row: View given as input to right eye and left eye respectively. A central "C"-shaped region containing random dots is offset horizontally from one eye to the other, yielding a stereo view when each image is presented to one of the two eyes. This can also be observed using the cross-eyed, or parallel viewing techniques for stereo image pairs. 2nd row: Region selected by algorithm for right and left eyes respectively superimposed on original image at half contrast. Bottom row: Ground truth, and selection superimposed on ground truth aligned with right eye view.

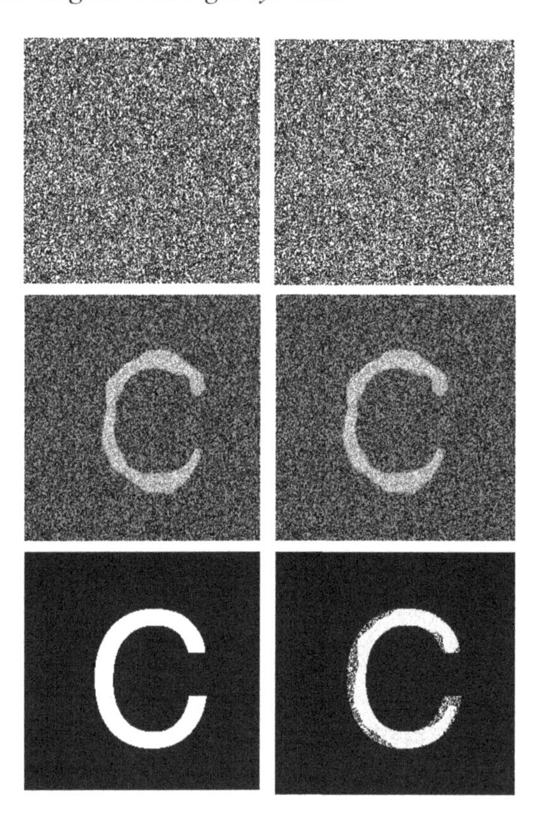

At this stage, we have shown that a selection mechanism that acts on the same interpretive network that realizes stereo correspondence is a sufficient condition on achieving appropriate deployment of attention in three dimensions. The simulation results produced by the model also demonstrate that top-down selection on such a hierarchy provides sufficient conditions for appropriate attentional selection. In Figure 7: Top row: A pair of random dot stereograms is presented to the two eyes (right eye on left for cross fusing). Middle Row: The resulting selected regions in the right and left eye respectively. Bottom row: Ground truth and selected regions superimposed on ground truth, white corresponds to 12 pixels and black to 0.

Figure 8 demonstrates the result of two successive runs of Selective Tuning. Top Row: The random dot stereogram on which results in Figure 8 is based. Second Row: Bias is initiated in favor of near disparity with the bias values corresponding to disparities of 0,2,4,6,8,10, and 12 pixels given by multiplicative modulation by the square root of 0, 1, 2, 4, 8, 16 and 32 respectively. Third Row: Bias is initiated in favor of far disparity (non-zero) with bias values of the square root of 0, 32, 16, 8, 4, and 2 respectively. Fourth Row:

Figure 8. Selection results for a random dot stereogram containing three boxes at different depths. (From left to right) Top row: View given as input to right and left eyes respectively. Three box shaped regions containing random dots are offset by a different horizontal extent yielding a stereo view when each image is presented to one of the two eyes. This can also be observed using the cross-eyed, or parallel viewing techniques for stereo image pairs. from 2nd row: Regions selected for right and left eyes in the attend near condition. 3rd row: Regions selected for right and left eyes in the "attend far" condition. Bottom row: Ground truth and selected regions superimposed on ground truth aligned with right eye view.

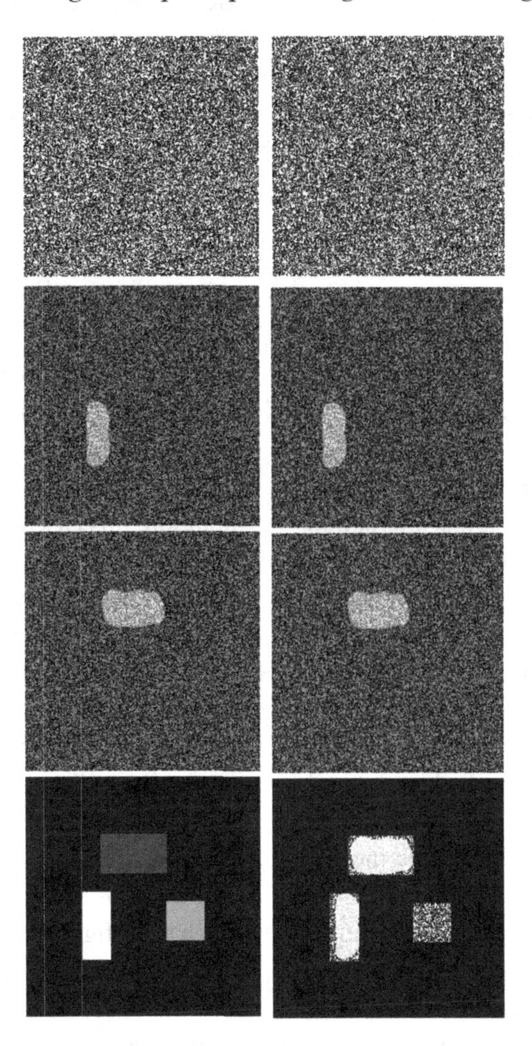

The ground truth disparity map is shown for comparison.

It is perhaps worth emphasizing again that fixation and attention are not the same. This point is sometimes overlooked in work that deals with 2D attention because changes in image correspond to changes in fixation. In human vision, there is variable spatial resolution and so the distinction is important. In three-dimensions, the problem becomes even larger as fixation introduces an additional dimension of complexity corresponding to the additional geometric constraints.

This section established that Selective Tuning is capable of attentional deployment in three dimensions. The implementation results are included largely for proof of concept from a practical standpoint. In the sections that follow, less common cases than the standard stereo correspondence problem are considered, with implications of such cases discussed.

7. ATTENTION AND BINOCULAR RIVALRY

Binocular rivalry is a phenomenon that occurs when the two eyes are presented with very different images. The resulting percept involves one of the images appearing for a brief period of time, then the other, then the first and so on. The following section considers the role of attention in binocular rivalry with specific reference to the model we have described. Attention has recently been shown to play an important role in determining the nature of perceptual alternation observed during binocular rivalry. The following section establishes that: (i) Perceptual alternation of the kind observed during binocular rivalry is predicted by the model proposed in section 4. (ii) The behavior is consistent with a wide array of psychophysical data with regard to the role of top-down attention and saliency in the perceptual alternation that is observed. (iii) The psychophysical literature is suggestive of a hierarchical structure underlying binocular rivalry, consistent with the representation assumed by the model. As a whole, this section provides insight into the computational architecture underlying binocular rivalry and additionally, further establishes the plausibility of Selective Tuning as an accurate account of attentional function in primates.

Rivalry and Winner-Take-All Competition

One existing effort at modeling binocular rivalry is complementary to our proposal (Wilson, 1999). In (Wilson, 1999) it is revealed that perceptual reversals of the form observed in binocular rivalry paradigms may be achieved via the combination of WTA behavior of the form assumed by ST in combination with neural decay in the form of spike frequency adaptation. Selection of one of the rivalry patterns causes spike frequency adaptation to the extent that WTA competition eventually selects the competing rivalry stimulus once sufficient adaptation has transpired. A hypothetical example of this appears in Figure 9: Feedforward activation leads to selection of a unit at the highest layer of the processing hierarchy by ST. Subsequently, a cascade of winner-take-all competitions proceeds downward from the highest layer to the lowest, selecting units that contribute strongly to observed activation, while attenuating pathways that do not contribute appreciably to the observed activation at each layer. At the level of binocular complex cells, one of the alternatives among the 2 competing stimuli is selected, with the input from the competing stimulus suppressed by virtue of gating. Subsequently, following a period of adaptation, this cascade of competition switches to selecting the alternative rivalrous stimulus. Both are not selected simultaneously owing to the fact that there are no units higher up in the pyramid that respond to orthogonal orientations in the two eyes (i.e., a horizontal stimulus in one eye along with a vertical stimulus in the other).

Additionally, units driven by different patterns exert mutually inhibitory influence, while collinear facilitation is driven by recurrent excitation among units attuned to the same pattern type. Such a configuration is easily realized within the proposed model by adding appropriate local lateral inhibitory connections between neurons that respond to different features, and excitatory connections within feature. The effect of such connections, is nonlinear wave propagation resulting in a percept that changes in sweeping waves from one rivalry stimulus to the other. It is important to note that at the core of this behavior, is the presence of WTA competition on units at multiple levels of a hierarchical visual processing framework (see Figure 9).

Figure 9. A demonstration of network behavior for the rivalry stimuli. Four stages in the feedforward interpretive computation, and feedback selection that achieves appropriate deployment of attention in depth. Refer to the text for further details.

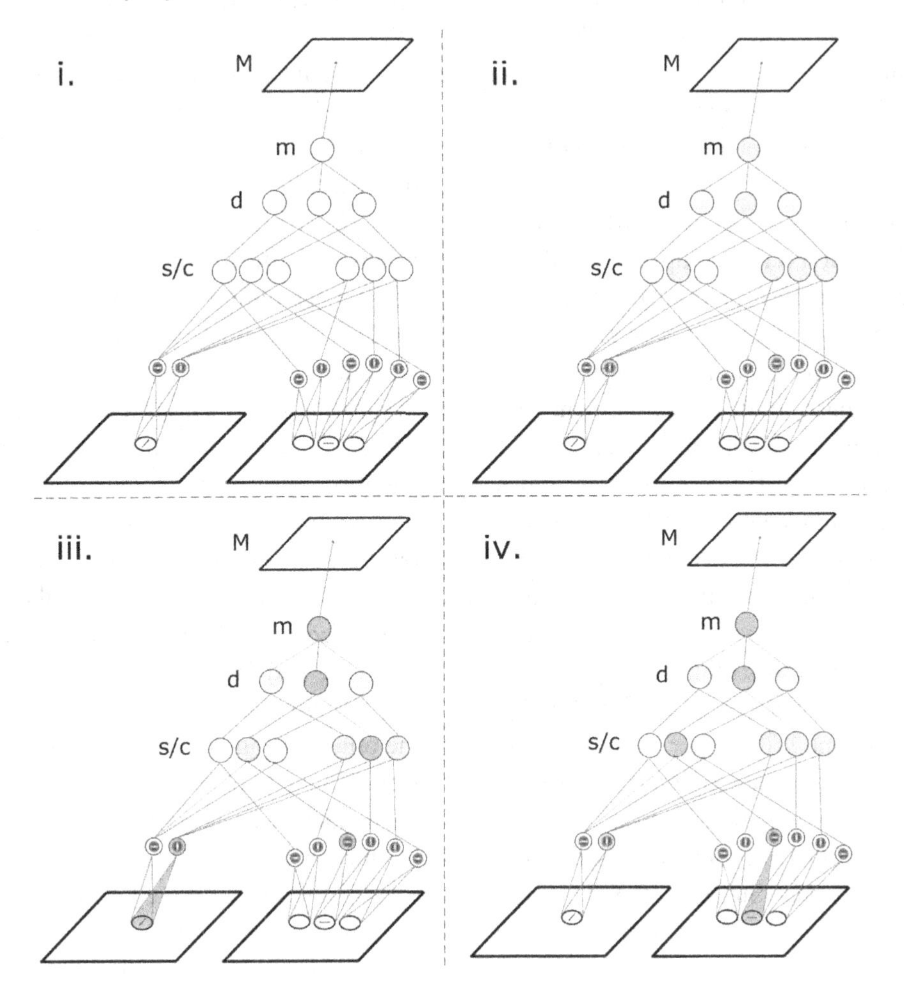

The Role of Saliency

It has long been debated whether rivalry happens by virtue of direct interocular competition, or competition between high-level pattern representations. The latter would be suggestive of a greater role of attention in determining dominance. A natural question to begin with is: What is the role of saliency in determining pattern dominance? One might expect that if a pop-out cue accompanies the rivalry stimulus appearing in one eye, this may bias the dominant image in favor of the eye containing the popout stimulus.

There are a few studies that shed some light on this consideration. Kanai et al. investigated the effect of visual transients on four types of perceptual alternation, including binocular rivalry (Kanai et al., 2005). A variety of experiments were performed each of which included a bistable stimulus followed by a flash. In each case, the influence of the flash on perceptual dominance was observed. As a whole the experiments establish that a flash may trigger perceptual reversals for all cases provided the flash is in the vicinity of the bistable stimulus.

Ooi and He carried out a study involving rivalry stimuli, with the image appearing in one of the eyes accompanied by a pop-out cue in some cases (Ooi and He, 1999). They found that there is a greater likelihood of a rivalry stimulus becoming dominant in the event that it is accompanied by a pop-out cue provided the cue is proximal to the rivalry stimulus.

The main conclusion that may be drawn from the above discussion is that it appears possible to selectively bias bistable perception in favor of one eye via exogenous cues provided such cues are proximal to the rivalry stimulus appearing in one eye. It is interesting to note that the aforementioned considerations agree with the expected behaviour of ST as is established in the example that follows.

A pop-out or transient cue in the vicinity of the rivalry stimulus in one eye tends to result in the dominance of that eye. Intuitively, we would expect that the cue will result in an increase in activation associated with stimulus appearing in one of the two eyes increasing its likelihood of becoming dominant. With respect to the behavior of the model, a salient cue proximal to the rivalry stimulus in one eye will elicit a strong response from neurons within the vicinity of the salient cue in one of the two eyes. Subsequent WTA selection is likely to then select the stimulus in this eye, which should then trigger nonlinear wave propagation associated with the stimulus properties appearing in the target eye via inter-feature inhibition and intra-feature facilitation (e.g. collinear facilitation for simple edges and inhibition among orthogonal orientations).

Top-Down Influences on Bistable Perception

The preceding section establishes that there exist bottom-up influences on dominance in binocular rivalry. Another important consideration is the extent to which top-down influences play a role in binocular rivalry. In this case, it is perhaps worthwhile to consider predictions of the model in this context. One might posit that as it is possible to attend to a particular feature type (e.g., a red circle) and effectively modulate the response of neurons associated with this feature, the same kind of volitional control should allow the extension of the time taken for a dominant image to be suppressed as activation associated with the dominant image decays. One might also expect that selective attention to the suppressed stimulus might lower the required threshold sufficiently to cause a perceptual reversal.

The psychophysical literature concerning volitional control in binocular rivalry is largely in agreement with the aforementioned prediction. Mitchell et al. carried out an experiment in which attention was directed to one of two overlapping transparent surfaces and subsequently the image of one surface was deleted from each eye (Mitchell et al., 2004). In most cases, only the cued surface was perceived following deletion.

Meng and Tong presented a rivalry stimulus consisting of a face in one eye and a house in the other (Meng and Tong, 2004). They found a significant effect on time of exclusive dominance of the face or house when attention was cued to the face or the house respectively.

Ooi and He employed a covert attention cueing paradigm to consider the effect of voluntary attention to a rivalry stimulus (Ooi and He, 1999). They found that voluntary attention to a grating appearing in one eye decreased the incidence of suppression of the grating by a moving target appearing in the other eye. This was only true if the attended patch was in the proximity of the moving target. In cases where the moving target passed over a non-attended patch, the patch was suppressed with the same incidence as the control case. The conclusion drawn by the authors is that voluntary attention may extend perception of the dominant image in a rivalry stimulus. An important companion question is that of whether the dominant percept may be suppressed by selectively attending to the non-dominant stimulus. Ooi and He claim that this is probably not the case as attention is directed to the grating in cases that it is suppressed and should revert to dominance if such reversal is possible. This explanation is hardly satisfactory since their paradigm precludes considering this possibility on account of the short time course involved.

The claim of Ooi and He concerning perceptual reversal is in conflict with the predicted behavior of our model. As noted, one would expect that lowering the threshold associated with the suppressed stimulus might allow it to regain dominance. It is worth noting that the model predicts that this result should be more difficult to observe than that of whether or not it is possible to extend the period of the dominant percept. Since driving the neurons associated with the dominant percept or attenuating the response of the non-dominant units is guaranteed to extend the period of dominance assuming decay of the signal, the result that Ooi and He have demonstrated should be observed without fail. However, there is no guarantee that voluntary attention may allow the attenuation of the dominant percept to the extent that the suppressed stimulus regains dominance. That said, we predict there should be instances where voluntary attention expedites perceptual reversal such that a suppressed stimulus regains dominance. Verification of this claim would prove invaluable in validating the model, and might be realized in an experimental design that looks specifically at triggering perceptual reversal and allows a longer time course for such reversal to occur.

Hierarchical Organization and Dynamics

The preceding sections assume the notion of competition within a hierarchical neural framework. There are a variety of issues related to this assumption as follows: (i) To what extent is there support for top down hierarchical cortical competition as opposed to direct competition of inputs at a low level? (ii) What implications does a hierarchical organization hold with respect to binocular rivalry and other forms of pattern rivalry? (iii) Do imaging studies support hierarchical competition in binocular rivalry? (iv) What are the dynamics associated with binocular rivalry and are such dynamics consistent with the proposed model?

It is reasonable to assume that competition associated with rivalry might take place prior to the convergence of visual pathways that are purely monocular. There are a variety of models that make this assumption, most of which assume competition at the level of the LGN or within layer IV of V1 (Matsuoka, 1984; Lehky and Maunsell, 1996; Blake, 1989; Mueller, 1990).

More recent evidence suggests that rivalry has no impact on LGN neurons (Lehky and Maunsell, 1996). Further, there now exist some rather convincing arguments against such simple competitive models and in favor of a hierarchical configuration. In one of the more prominent studies, Logothetis and colleagues performed single cell recordings in trained monkeys while the rivalry stimulus was rapidly swapped between the two eyes (Logothetis et al., 1996). This study reveals a number of surprising results: (i) The majority of neurons whose activity correlates with perceptual alternation are binocular and are found in higher visual areas. (ii) Perceptual alternation in this paradigm exhibits dynamics identical to the static (non-swapping) stimulus case under certain conditions. (iii) Competition reflects a high-level representation of the stimulus and is eye independent. (iv) The perceptual alternation observed in binocular rivalry is much closer to other forms of bistable perception than previously thought.

An even stronger result appears in (Wilson et al., 2001) demonstrating that a hierarchical model consisting of at least two layers is necessary to account for rivalry data. Wilson presents a two-stage model in which orthogonal gratings compete via strong reciprocal inhibition at both monocular and binocular levels of processing.

There also exists rivalry of a slightly different nature termed pattern rivalry (or monocular rivalry). Pattern rivalry refers to the wavering percept which results from superimposing two transparent patterns and results in periods of exclusive visibility of each pattern. Maier et al. demonstrate that multistable perception in pattern rivalry appears to be driven by a global holistic interpretation of the stimuli (Maier et al., 2005). Typically when a stimulus of sufficient contrast appears in one eye, with no superimposed stimulus in the other eye, the monocular stimulus is perceived with little or no suppression. Such a configuration is oft referred to as a rivalry-free region. Maier et al. demonstrated that the stimulus in a rivalry-free region may be suppressed on the basis of properties shared with the more global surround. This result indicates that competition relies on resolution of a more global representation of the scene rather than merely local spatial or ocular conflict.

The above discussion supports a variety of important considerations from a modeling perspective: (i) Rivalry exists within a hierarchy and is present at several levels of representation. (ii) There is a significant role of saliency in determining perceptual dominance. (iii) Primates may exert some degree of volitional control on the rate of perceptual alternation. (iv) There is significant similarity between binocular rivalry and other forms of perceptual rivalry. This type of configuration may also account for the behavior described by Maier et al. Global selection of a pattern that is distinct from the pattern constituting the rivalry-free region might prompt its suppression via lateral inhibitory interaction.

Discussion

Binocular rivalry is a useful domain to consider owing to its apparent ties to attention, allowing the relationship between attention and binocular vision to be examined. It is interesting to note that Selective Tuning in conjunction with the simplistic model of primate binocular vision is able to account for a wide array of behavior associated with binocular rivalry.

Overall, the discussion included in this section provides a strong case for selection in the binocular domain within a hierarchical configuration of the form that Selective Tuning assumes. A variety of aspects of the model are in strong agreement with the psychophysical literature including competition within a hierarchy, competition at every level of the hierarchy, a role of attention (bottom-up and top-down) in all forms of pattern rivalry, and with more global competition mediating local suppression. Further, the dynamics associated with rivalrous perception may be produced through the addition of simple lateral connections. Each of these elements provides a case not only for Selective Tuning, but additionally implies a set of constraints on how attentive behavior is achieved. What is not yet apparent is how such behavior might be achieved in the context of other classes of models. This consideration is dealt with in some detail in the section that follows.

8. ATTENTIONAL STEREO CORRESPONDENCE REVISITED

In the preceding section, the discussion of binocular rivalry in the context of attention alluded to a variety of issues that may deny explanation by particular types of attention models. In this section, we further explore this notion by considering conditions on achieving appropriate attentive behavior under the assumption of binocularity. For the sake of discussion, let us begin by assuming that the sole constraint that stereo attention need satisfy is the selection of a region, feature, or object that corresponds to a true stereo correspondence. We will refer to this as the attentional stereo correspondence problem (ASCP).

The ASCP evidently poses a challenge for computational models of attention. The Selective Tuning model might be described as a model that includes top-down selection on a feedforward interpretive network. Other models fall predominantly in one of two categories: (i) Saliency-based models, a category of models that derive from Treisman's feature integration theory (Treisman and Gelade, 1980). (ii) Models with feedforward selection mechanisms wherein flow through the network is gated as it proceeds up the feedforward interpretive network. Each of these classes encounters problems when faced with the issue of stereo vision and requires further thought in light of the observations presented in this paper.

Let us first consider implications of stereo vision for models based on the notion of a saliency map; a ubiquitous element of attention models in the literature (Treisman and Gelade, 1980; Koch and Ullman, 1985; Sandon, 1989; Wolfe and Cave, 1989; Mozer, 1991; Itti et al., 1998; Bruce and Tsotsos, 2006, 2009). There appear to be inherent limitations to such a representation which preclude the ability to localize a corresponding region, feature or object in the binocular domain.

Consider the saliency map in its current form. A variety of feature maps are derived from the retinal input, and subsequently converge on a single unique topographical representation of saliency. A selection mechanism then acts on this representation to select an attended location. The problem with such a representation is that the saliency map retains no memory of what gave rise to the observed activation. Although the selection mechanism knows where to attend, it has no knowledge of what is being attended.

The most obvious issue with this kind of representation is that each eye has a slightly different view, and a feature may fall on different retinal coordinates in each eye. Consequently, binocular attention could require the selection of two locations from a single saliency map. Since no knowledge of what gives rise to the resulting activation is maintained, there is no hope of selecting a true stereo correspondence on this basis. It would in principle be possible to have disparity selective neurons project onto the saliency map with attention acting in a cyclopean reference frame. This however is in disagreement with the psychophysical data summarized in section 3.

A second possibility that proponents of a saliency-based architecture might suggest is that each eye may have its own saliency map. This claim is also inherently flawed in that it would require solving the correspondence problem on a representation devoid of information concerning local structures or features. Although it is conceivable that matching could proceed on the basis of the saliency landscapes, there are also additional complications inherent in making this assumption. For example, there exist neurons tuned to near, far and at fixation binocular disparity. Amalgamating the representation carried by these different units into a saliency map would imply blurring in depth. It would seem that such a configuration would be prone to errors in attending in 3D. As a whole, a computational saliency based mechanism based on a pair of saliency maps invites numerous problems when attending in depth is considered.

As a whole, the issue at hand is that a saliency map does not retain the information required to solve the stereo correspondence problem. In the section that follows, we consider the possibility that this is simply a special case of a more general problem. The issue of what information is available, and when, is important in understanding attention. In the section that follows, we explore how such a consideration constrains computational models of attention.

On the basis of the basic problem posed by ASCP, one might also challenge the possibility that selection proceeds as activation ascends a feedforward hierarchical interpretive network. In this case, selection at the monocular level would occur first, and may preclude attending to true correspondences. That said, the section that follows considers the possibility that the ASCP simply serves to highlight a more general problem in the domain of attentional selection which raises questions for models that assume feedforward interpretive computation.

A More General Problem?

The preceding section is suggestive of a more general problem with how saliency based models operate. In the case of stereo vision, it is evident that a saliency map lacks the information necessary to attend to a true stereo correspondence. This case is especially convincing since it relies on spatial coordinates but hints at a much more important issue: that of how non-spatial content is selected. A saliency map includes no memory of which features gave rise to the winning activation in the same manner that the information necessary to establish stereo correspondence is lacking. A consequence of this consideration is that selection in space must precede selection of features in an exogenous cueing paradigm for any model based on a saliency map.

This last consideration runs contrary to the experimental literature on the subject. In perhaps the strongest result in opposition to the possibility that spatial attention may precede feature based attention, Hopf et al. demonstrate that attention to features precedes attention to locations (Hopf et al., 2004) in an ERP/ERMF paradigm. In the experiment of Hopf et al. a red and green C were presented to left and right visual field with the position of each determined randomly. In half the blocks the subjects responded to the red C and in the other half, responded to the green C. The response required indicating the orientation of the target C. The red and green C's appearing in each visual field were both flanked by six distracting blue C's on all trials. Four conditions included distractors in both visual fields sharing the same orientation as the target C, distractors in neither visual field sharing the same orientation as the target C, or target compatible C's appearing in only the target or non-target hemifield with non-compatible oriented C's appearing in the non-target or target hemifield. Their chief finding was that modulation occurred primarily within the hemisphere contralateral to distractors sharing the same orientation as the target, independent of the hemifield in which the target letter appeared. Approximately 30 ms following such modulation, the neural response reflecting focused attention on the target began (N2pc component). This strongly suggests that knowledge of the target properties is present prior to localization, a consideration strongly inconsistent with saliency based models. It is also shown in (Grill-Spector and Kanwisher, 2005) that the categorization of a presented object happens with a time course at least as short as detection of the object.

These studies raise questions for models that assume feedforward WTA selection. Given a feedforward WTA configuration, one might expect activity corresponding to localization to precede or at least coincide with activity pertaining to target features. This is a consideration inconsistent with the experimental literature.

Rivalry Revisited

In addition to the issues highlighted earlier in this section, saliency based models hold little hope for explaining any of the considerations pertaining to binocular rivalry as discussed in Section 7. Consideration in regard to specific issues would require making brazen assumptions on how saliency maps might be extended to handle binocular vision.

There is however one fundamental issue which is worth discussing. Rivalry is clearly cortical and not eye-based. Rivalry happens at every layer of the visual cortex. It is distributed and with global competition directing local suppression (Maier et al., 2005). These considerations paint a picture that bears little if any connection to a model based on a unique topographical feature blind saliency map.

With respect to feedforward WTA models, the assumption of feedforward gating is inconsistent with experiments indicating that perceptual alternation observed during binocular rivalry appears to be based on a global interpretation of the scene which presumably requires first the involvement of higher visual areas. This consideration holds even stronger when one considers that the same argument may be made of pattern rivalry in general. Monocular rivalry may be observed when pairs of transparent stimuli are presented overlapping, with temporal windows of exclusive visibility corresponding to one pattern or the other. Such alternation has little to do with local competition among competing stimuli, but rather the entire scene alternates on the basis of global competition (Maier et al., 2005). Attention is undeniably involved in the perceptual alternation observed during monocular rivalry and should provide an additional constraint on attention modeling at large.

9. GENERAL DISCUSSION

The problem of visual attention within a stereo framework has received relatively little consideration. This is especially true on the modeling side with few efforts considering how stereo vision informs the problem of visual attention. Previous computational efforts that give any consideration to binocularity generally treat stereo as a feature that contributes to some representation of global saliency in a cyclopean frame of reference (see Itti and Koch, 2001). As we have pointed out, this is a consideration that runs contrary to contemporary psychophysics literature.

In this paper, we argue that the ASCP is an important consideration for attention models to address, and highlighted difficulties for certain classes of models when faced with the ASCP. This hints at some potential problems that are more general, and in particular, the necessity to consider what kinds of information are available at different levels of visual processing including the relative order of distractor suppression, detection, localization and recognition. A few recent imaging studies shed some light on some of these details, and provide greater insight on the order and timing of these various attention related events.

We also argue, that the problem of binocular rivalry is one that cannot be disentangled from binocular vision, and the presence of rivalry behaviors that may be explained by a model based on top-down gating is encouraging. The last ten years has provided mounting evidence that attention plays an important role in binocular rivalry and also pattern rivalry, and one might argue that these are serious considerations for any computational proposal relating to attention to address. The fact that a global interpretation of a scene appears to factor appreciably in the type of modulation that takes place makes the distinction between models that assume feedforward gating versus top-down gating an important one.

It has been stressed that an important role of attention is in resolving interference within a hierarchical network. Resolution of cross-talk, and precise localization are important elements of an attention model, and we have established additional situations in the domain of stereo vision for which these issues are important.

We have put forth a proposal for attentional selection that appears to afford intuitively appropriate behavior with respect to simple selection in depth and various forms of rivalry. The significant agreement between Selective Tuning and behavioral observations associated with stereo attention provides a strong case for ST as a description of the computational hierarchy underlying visual attention. It is our hope that the variety of issues highlighted in this paper will provoke useful discussion on the strengths and shortcomings of existing models in the hope that an understanding closer to a consensus might be reached.

Consideration of stereo vision poses questions for any model of attention that does not include selection on the same interpretive network that resolves stereo correspondence, or, does not first factor in more global attributes of the scene to implement more local modulation. This consideration poses a challenge for the attention community at large, and should invoke important discussion on elements that constrain the space of possible models of attention drawing knowledge from connectionist arguments, known neurophysiology, timing, and the body of imaging data that will emerge in the next several decades.

REFERENCES

Andersen, G. J., & Kramer, A. F. (1993). Limits of focused attention in three-dimensional space. *Perception & Psychophysics*, *53*(6), 658–667. doi:10.3758/BF03211742

Anderson, C., & Essen, D. V. (1987). Shifter circuits: A computational strategy for dynamic aspects of visual processing. *Proceedings of the National Academy of Sciences of the United States of America*, *84*, 6297–6301. doi:10.1073/pnas.84.17.6297

Arnott, S. R., & Shedden, J. M. (2000). Attention switching in depth using random-dot autostereograms: Attention gradient asymmetries. *Perception & Psychophysics*, *62*(7), 1459–1473. doi:10.3758/BF03212146

Atchley, P., Kramer, A. F., Andersen, G. J., & Theeuwes, J. (1997). Spatial cuing in a stereoscopic display: Evidence for a depth-aware attentional focus. *Psychonomic Bulletin & Review*, *4*(4), 524–529. doi:10.3758/BF03214343

Blake, R. (1989). A neural theory of binocular rivalry. *Psychological Review*, *96*, 145–167. doi:10.1037/0033-295X.96.1.145

Bruce, N. D. B., & Tsotsos, J. K. (2006). Saliency based on information maximization. *Advances in Neural Information Processing Systems*, *18*, 155–162.

Bruce, N. D. B., & Tsotsos, J. K. (2009). Saliency, attention and visual search: An information theoretic approach. *Journal of Vision (Charlottesville, Va.)*, *9*(3), 1–24. doi:10.1167/9.3.5

Burt, P. (1988). Attention mechanisms for vision in a dynamic world. *Proceedings Ninth International Conference on Pattern Recognition*, (pp. 977–987).

Chen, Y., & Qian, N. (2004). A coarse-to-fine disparity energy model with both phase-shift and position-shift receptive field mechanisms. *Neural Computation*, *16*, 1545–1577. doi:10.1162/089976604774201596

Culhane, S. (1992). *Implementation of an attentional prototype for early vision*. University of Toronto, M.Sc. Thesis.

Fleet, D., Wagner, H., & Heeger, D. (1996). Neural encoding of binocular disparity: Energy models. *Vision Research*, *36*(12), 1839–1857. doi:10.1016/0042-6989(95)00313-4

Ghirardelli, T. G., & Folk, C. L. (1996). Spatial cueing in a stereoscopic display: Evidence for a depth-blind attentional spotlight. *Psychonomic Bulletin & Review*, *3*, 81–86. doi:10.3758/BF03210744

Grill-Spector, K., & Kanwisher, N. (2005). As soon as you know it is there, you know what it is. *Psychological Science*, *16*(2), 152–160. doi:10.1111/j.0956-7976.2005.00796.x

Hoffman, J., & Mueller, S. (1994). *An in depth look at attention*. Annual Meeting of the Psychonomic Society, St. Louis, MO.

Hopf, J. M., Boelmans, K., Schoenfeld, M. A., Luck, S. J., & Heinze, H. J. (2004). Attention to features precedes attention to locations in visual search: Evidence from electromagnetic brain responses in humans. *The Journal of Neuroscience*, *24*(8), 1822–1832. doi:10.1523/JNEUROSCI.3564-03.2004

Iavecchia, H. P., & Folk, C. L. (1995). Shifting visual attention stereographic displays: A time course analysis. *Human Factors*, *36*, 606–618.

Itti, L., & Koch, C. (2001). Computational modeling of visual attention. *Nature Reviews. Neuroscience, 2*(3), 194–203. doi:10.1038/35058500

Itti, L., Koch, C., & Niebur, E. (1998). A model of saliency-based visual attention for rapid scene analysis. *IEEE Transactions on Pattern Analysis and Machine Intelligence, 20*(11), 1254–1259. doi:10.1109/34.730558

Kanai, R., Moradi, F., Shimojo, S., & Verstraten, F. A. J. (2005). Perceptual alternation induced by visual transients. *Perception, 34*, 803–822. doi:10.1068/p5245

Kasai, T., Morotomi, T., Katayama, J., & Kumada, T. (2003). Attending to a location in three-dimensional space modulates early ERPs. *Brain Research. Cognitive Brain Research, 17*, 273–285. doi:10.1016/S0926-6410(03)00115-0

Koch, C., & Ullman, S. (1985). Shifts in selective visual attention: Towards the underlying neural circuitry. *Human Neurobiology, 4*, 219–227.

Lehky, S. R., & Maunsell, J. H. (1996). No binocular rivalry in the LGN of alert macaque monkeys. *Vision Research, 36*, 1225–1234. doi:10.1016/0042-6989(95)00232-4

Logothetis, N. K., Leopold, D. A., & Sheinberg, D. L. (1996). What is rivaling during binocular rivalry? *Nature, 380*, 621–624. doi:10.1038/380621a0

Maier, A., Logothetis, N. K., & Leopold, D. A. (2005). Global competition dictates local suppression in pattern rivalry. *Journal of Vision (Charlottesville, Va.), 5*, 668–677. doi:10.1167/5.9.2

Marrara, M. T., & Moore, C. M. (2000). Role of perceptual organization while attending in depth. *Perception & Psychophysics, 62*(4), 786–799. doi:10.3758/BF03206923

Matsuoka, K. (1984). The dynamic model of binocular rivalry. *Biological Cybernetics, 49*, 201–208. doi:10.1007/BF00334466

Meng, M., & Tong, F. (2004). Can attention selectively bias bistable perception? Differences between binocular rivalry and ambiguous figures. *Journal of Vision (Charlottesville, Va.), 4*, 539–551. doi:10.1167/4.7.2

Mitchell, J. F., Stoner, G. R., & Reynolds, J. H. (2004). Object-based attention determines dominance in binocular rivalry. *Nature, 429*, 410–413. doi:10.1038/nature02584

Mozer, M. (1991). *The perception of multiple objects*. MIT Press.

Mueller, T. J. (1990). A physiological model of binocular rivalry. *Visual Neuroscience, 4*, 63–73. doi:10.1017/S0952523800002777

Nakayama, K., & Silverman, G. (1991). Serial and parallel processing of visual feature conjunctions. *Nature, 320*, 264–265. doi:10.1038/320264a0

Ohzawa, I. (1998). Mechanisms of stereoscopic vision: the disparity energy model. *Current Opinion in Biology, 8*, 509–515.

Ooi, T. L., & He, Z. J. (1999). Binocular rivalry and visual awareness. *Perception, 28*, 551–574. doi:10.1068/p2923

Palmer, D. (1999). *Vision science: Photons to phenomenology*. Cambridge, MA: MIT Press.

Sandon, P. (1989). Simulating visual attention. *Journal of Cognitive Neuroscience, 2*(3), 213–231. doi:10.1162/jocn.1990.2.3.213

Theeuwes, J., Atchley, P., & Kramer, A. F. (1986). Serial and parallel processing of visual feature conjunctions. *Nature, 320*, 264–265. doi:10.1038/320264a0

Theeuwes, J., Atchley, P., & Kramer, A. F. (1998). Attentional control within 3-d space. *Journal of Experimental Psychology. Human Perception and Performance, 24*(5), 1476–1485. doi:10.1037/0096-1523.24.5.1476

Theeuwes, J., & Pratt, J. (2003). Inhibition of return spreads across 3-d space. *Psychonomic Bulletin & Review*, *10*(3), 616–620. doi:10.3758/BF03196523

Treisman, A., & Gelade, G. (1980). A feature integration theory of attention. *Cognitive Psychology*, *12*, 97–136. doi:10.1016/0010-0285(80)90005-5

Tsotsos, J. (1988). A complexity level analysis of immediate vision. *International Journal of Computer Vision*, *2*, 303–320. doi:10.1007/BF00133569

Tsotsos, J. (2003). *Visual attention mechanisms: The selective tuning model*. Kluwer Academic.

Tsotsos, J., Culhane, S., Wai, W., Lai, Y., Davis, N., & Nuflo, N. (1995). Modeling visual attention via selective tuning. *Artificial Intelligence*, *1-2*, 507–547. doi:10.1016/0004-3702(95)00025-9

Uhr, L. (1972). Layered recognition cone networks that preprocess, classify, and describe. *IEEE Transactions on Computers*, *21*, 758–768. doi:10.1109/T-C.1972.223579

Viswanathan, L., & Mingolla, E. (2002). Dynamics of attention in depth: Evidence from multi-element tracking. *Perception*, *31*, 1415–1437. doi:10.1068/p3432

Wilson, H. R. (1999). *Spikes, decisions and actions*. Oxford University Press.

Wilson, H. R., Blake, R., & Lee, S. (2001). Dynamics of travelling waves in visual perception. *Nature*, *412*, 907–910. doi:10.1038/35091066

Wolfe, J., & Cave, R. (1989). Guided search: An alternative to feature integration theory for visual search. *Journal of Experimental Psychology. Human Perception and Performance*, *15*, 419–443. doi:10.1037/0096-1523.15.3.419

Section 2
Binocular Vision

Chapter 5
Local Constraints for the Perception of Binocular 3D Motion

Martin Lages
University of Glasgow, UK

Suzanne Heron
University of Glasgow, UK

Hongfang Wang
University of Glasgow, UK

ABSTRACT

The authors discuss local constraints for the perception of three-dimensional (3D) binocular motion in a geometric-probabilistic framework. It is shown that Bayesian models of binocular 3D motion can explain perceptual bias under uncertainty and predict perceived velocity under ambiguity. The models exploit biologically plausible constraints of local motion and disparity processing in a binocular viewing geometry. Results from computer simulations and psychophysical experiments support the idea that local constraints of motion and disparity processing are combined late in the visual processing hierarchy to establish perceived 3D motion direction.

1. INTRODUCTION

The perceptual inference of the three-dimensional (3D) external world from two-dimensional (2D) retinal input is a fundamental problem (Berkeley, 1709/1975; von Helmholtz, 1910/1962) that the visual system has to solve through neural computation (Poggio,Torre, & Koch, 1985; Pizlo, 2001). This is true for static scenes as well as for dynamic events. For dynamic events the inverse problem implies that the visual system estimates motion in 3D space from local encoding and spatio-temporal processing.

Velocity in 3D space is described by motion direction and speed. Motion direction can be measured in terms of azimuth and elevation angle, and motion direction together with speed is conveniently expressed as a vector in a 3D Cartesian

DOI: 10.4018/978-1-4666-2539-6.ch005

coordinate system. Estimating local motion vectors is highly desirable for a visual system because local estimates in a dense vector field provide the basis for the perception of 3D object motion - that is direction and speed of a moving object. This information is essential for segmenting objects from the background, for interpreting objects as well as for planning and executing actions in a dynamic environment.

If a single moving point, corner, or other unique feature serves as binocular input then intersection of constraint lines or triangulation in a binocular viewing geometry provides a straightforward and unique geometrical solution to the inverse problem. If, however, the moving stimulus has spatial extent, such as an oriented line or contour inside a circular aperture or receptive field then local motion direction of corresponding receptive fields in the left and right eye remains ambiguous, and additional constraints are needed to solve the inverse problem in 3D (Lages & Heron, 2010).

The inverse optics and the aperture problem are well-known problems in computational vision, especially in the context of stereo processing (Poggio, Torre, & Koch, 1985; Mayhew & Longuet-Higgins, 1982), structure from motion (Koenderink & van Doorn, 1991), and optic flow (Hildreth, 1984). Gradient constraint and related methods (e.g., Johnston et al., 1999) belong to the most widely used techniques of optic-flow computation based on image intensities. They can be divided into local area-based (Lucas & Kanade, 1981) and into more global optic flow methods (Horn & Schunck, 1981). Both techniques usually employ brightness constancy and smoothness constraints in the image to estimate velocity in an over-determined equation system. It is important to note that optical flow only provides a constraint in the direction of the image gradient, the normal component of the optical flow. As a consequence some form of regularization or smoothing is needed. Various algorithms have been developed implementing error minimization and regularization for 3D stereo-motion detection (e.g., Bruhn, Weickert & Schnörr, (2005); Spies, Jähne & Barron, 2002; Min & Sohn, 2006; Scharr & Küsters, 2002). These algorithms effectively extend processing principles of 2D optical flow to 3D scene flow (Vedula, et al., 2005; Carceroni & Kutulakos, 2002).

However, computational studies on 3D motion are usually concerned with fast and efficient encoding. Here we are less concerned with the efficiency or robustness of a particular algorithm and implementation. Instead we want to understand local and binocular constraints in order to explain characteristics of human 3D motion perception such as perceptual bias under uncertainty and motion estimation under ambiguity. Ambiguity of 2D motion direction is an important aspect of biologically plausible processing and has been extensively researched in the context of the 2D aperture problem (Wallach, 1935; Adelson & Movshon, 1982; Sung, Wojtach, & Purves, 2009) but there is a surprising lack of studies on the 3D aperture problem (Morgan & Castet, 1997) and perceived 3D motion.

The entire perceptual process may be understood as a form of statistical inference (Knill, Kersten & Yuille, 1996) and motion perception has been modeled as an inferential process for 2D object motion (Weiss, Simoncelli & Adelson, 2002) and 3D surfaces (Ji & Fermüller, 2006). Models of binocular 3D motion perception however are typically deterministic and predict only azimuth or change in depth (Regan & Gray, 2009). In the following we discuss probabilistic models of 3D motion perception that are based on velocity constraints and can explain perceptual bias under uncertainty as well as motion estimation under ambiguity.

The purpose of this chapter is to introduce and promote Bayesian models of binocular 3D motion perception because they provide local estimates of 3D velocity under uncertainty and ambiguity. We will focus on local constraints of motion perception using basic features such as single dots, lines or edges moving in 3D space because these features are regarded as primitives of local encoding in the early stages of visual processing.

For the sake of simplicity we exclude eye, head and body movements of the observer and consider only passively observed, local motion. Smooth motion pursuit of the eyes and self-motion of the observer during object motion are beyond the scope of this chapter and have been considered elsewhere (Harris, 2006; Rushton & Warren, 2005; Miles, 1998).

2. BACKGROUND

Like many other predators in the animal kingdom humans have two eyes that are set a short distance apart so that an extensive region of the world is seen simultaneously by both eyes from slightly different points of view. Vision in this region of binocular overlap has a special quality that has intrigued artists, philosophers, and scientists (Figure 1).

Under natural viewing conditions the human visual system seems to effortlessly establish a 3D motion percept from local inputs to the left and right eye. The instantaneous integration of binocular input is essential for object recognition, navigation, action planning and execution. It appears obvious that many depth cues help to establish 3D motion perception under natural viewing conditions but local motion and disparity input features prominently in the early processing stages of the visual system (Howard & Rogers, 2002).

Any biologically plausible solution to the inverse 3D motion problem has to rely on binocular sampling of local spatio-temporal information (Beverley & Regan, 1973; 1974; 1975). There are at least three known cell types in primary visual cortex V1 that may be involved in local encoding of 3D motion: simple and complex motion detecting cells (Hubel & Wiesel, 1962; 1968; DeAngelis, Ohzawa, & Freeman, 1993; Maunsell & van Essen, 1983), binocular disparity detecting cells (Hubel & Wiesel, 1970; Ohzawa, DeAngelis & Freeman, 1990), and joint motion and disparity detecting cells (Anzai, Ohzawa & Freeman, 2001; Bradley, Qian & Andersen, 1995; DeAngelis & Newsome, 1999).

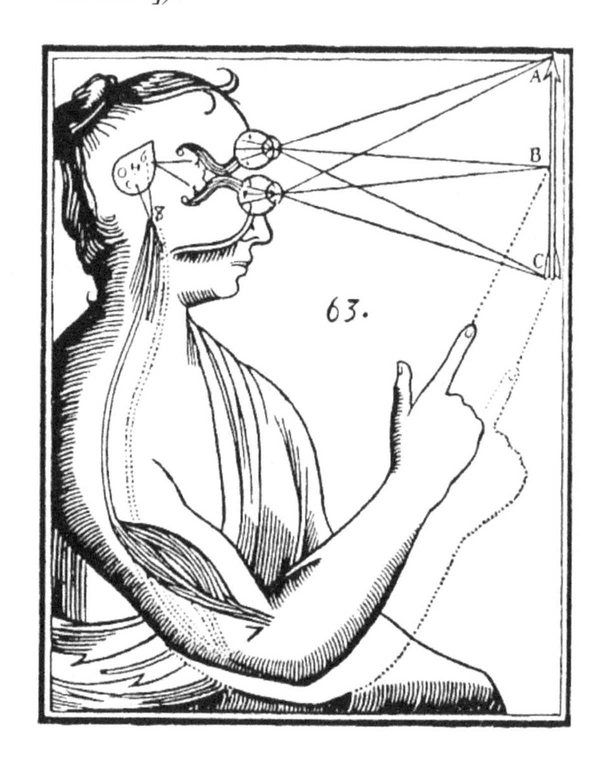

Figure 1. An early illustration of the binocular perceptual system after René Descartes (woodcut in Traité de l'Homme, 1664 [De Homine, 1633/1662]).

It is therefore not surprising that three approaches to binocular 3D motion perception emerged in the literature: (1) interocular velocity difference (IOVD) is based on monocular motion detectors, (2) changing disparity over time (CDOT) monitors output of binocular disparity detectors, and (3) joint encoding of motion and disparity (JEMD) relies on binocular motion detectors also tuned to disparity.

1. The *motion-first* model postulates monocular motion processing followed by stereo processing (Lu & Sperling, 1995; Regan & Beverley, 1973; Regan, et al., 1979). In this

model monocular motion is independently detected in the left and right eye before interocular velocity difference (IOVD) establishes motion in depth.

2. The *stereo-first* model assumes disparity encoding followed by binocular motion processing (Cumming & Parker, 1994; Peng & Shi, 2010). This model first extracts binocular disparities and then computes change of disparity over time (CDOT). Note that tracking of spatial position is also required to recover a 3D motion trajectory.
3. Finally, the *stereo-motion* model suggests joint encoding of motion and disparity (JEMD) or binocular disparity and interocular delay (Carney, Paradiso, & Freeman, 1989; Morgan & Fahle, 2000; Qian, 1994; Qian & Andersen, 1997). In neurophysiological studies it was shown that a number of binocular complex cells in cats (Anzai, Ohzawa, & Freeman, 2001) and cells in V1 and MT of monkey (Pack, Born, & Livingstone, 2003) are tuned to interocular spatial-temporal shifts but the significance of these findings has been questioned (Read & Cumming, 2005a,b).

These three approaches have generated an impressive body of results but psychophysical experiments have been inconclusive and the nature of 3D motion processing remains an unresolved issue (Regan & Gray, 2009; Harris, Nefs, & Grafton, 2008). Despite the wealth of empirical studies on 2D motion (*x-y* motion) and motion in depth (*x-z* motion) there is a lack of research on true 3D motion perception (*x-y-z* motion).

In psychophysical studies vision researchers have tried to isolate motion and disparity input by creating specific motion stimuli. These stimuli are rendered in stereoscopic view and typically consist of many random dots in so-called random dot kinematograms (RDKs) that give rise to the perception of a moving surface, defined by motion, disparity or both. However, psychophysical evidence based on detection and discrimination thresholds using these stimuli has been inconclusive, supporting interocular velocity difference (Brooks, 2002; Fernandez & Farrell, 2005; Portfors-Yeomans & Regan, 1996; Shioiri, Saisho, & Yaguchi, 2000; Rokers, et al., 2008), changing disparity (Cumming & Parker, 1994; Tyler, 1971) or both (Brooks & Stone, 2004; Lages, Graf, & Mamassian, 2003; Rokers et al., 2009) as possible inputs to 3D motion perception.

Another limitation of random-dot stimuli is that random dots moving in depth may invoke intermediate and higher processing stages similar to structure from motion and global object motion. A surface defined by dots can invoke mid-level surface and high-level object processing and therefore may not reflect characteristics of local motion encoding. Although the involvement of higher-level processing has always been an issue in psychophysical studies it is of particular concern when researchers relate behavioral measures of surface and object motion to characteristics of early motion processing.

In addition, detection and discrimination thresholds for RDKs often do not reveal biased 3D motion perception. Accuracy rather than precision of observers' perceptual performance needs to be measured to establish characteristics of motion and disparity processing in psychophysical studies (Harris & Dean, 2003; Welchman, Tuck & Harris, 2004; Rushton & Duke, 2007). Using the method of adjustment observers reported the perceived trajectory angle of a previously seen stimulus moving in depth. The results indicated overestimation of trajectory angle for a range of trajectories approaching the observer. To explain this perceptual bias it was suggested that observers exploit the cyclopean average by using the angle relative to the direction straight ahead along the line of sight (Harris & Drga, 2005). Although appealing in its simplicity this strategy only constrains perceived motion direction in *x-z* but does not solve the inverse problem of binocular 3D motion.

3. PERCEPTUAL BIAS UNDER UNCERTAINTY

The binocular viewing geometry imposes obvious constraints for stimulus trajectory and velocity. For a moving dot for example the intersection of constraint lines in *x-z* space determines trajectory angle and speed of the target moving in depth as illustrated in Figure 2.

If we assume that the eyes remain accommodated and verged at angle β_0 on a fixation point *F* straight ahead then motion information is projected onto the retina of the left and right eye as illustrated in Figure 2. The projection angles onto the retinae depend on the azimuth β and speed r of the motion stimulus, as well as viewing distance *D* and interpupillary distance *i*. The average of the left and right projection angle approximates the visual angle α in cyclopean view through point *C* and the difference defines binocular horizontal disparity δ. If the projection angles are interpreted as angular velocities then their difference also describes interocular velocity difference.

Motion and disparity constraint lines intersect at the same point in space, regardless of whether they are based on the computation of angular velocities or binocular disparities. Although binocular motion and changing disparity input share the same geometry and are mathematically equivalent, different neural encoding and processing of these inputs may be subject to noise resulting in characteristic perceptual bias. If however noise or uncertainty is introduced together with a motion or disparity prior then the intersection of constraint lines generates different predictions as illustrated in Figure 3. We will exploit these characteristics when modeling data from a psychophysical experiment.

Figure 2. Binocular viewing geometry in top view. If the two eyes are verged on a fixation point at viewing distance D with angle β_0 then projections of a moving target (arrow) with angle α_L in the left eye and α_R in the right eye constrain motion of the target in x-z space. The intersection of constraints (IOC) determines stimulus trajectory β and radius r. A Gaussian motion prior is indicated by the gray circle around the fixation point that is also the start point of motion.

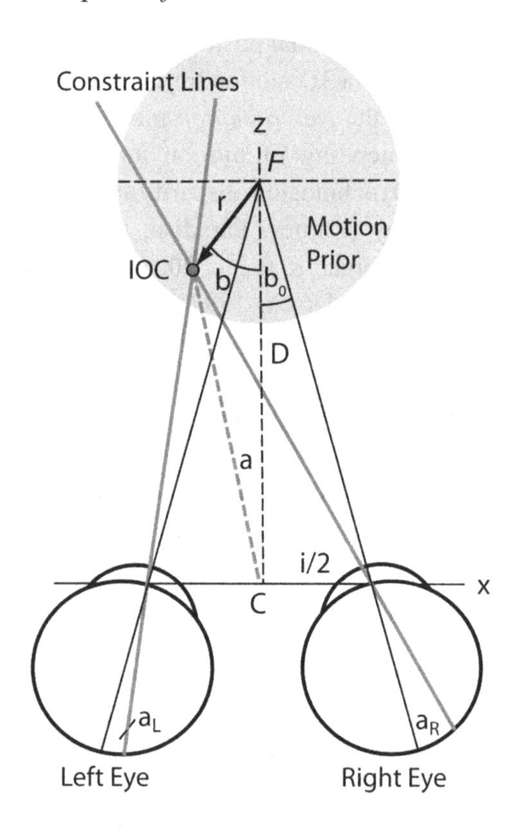

3.1 Bayesian Models of Motion Perception

Some promising Bayesian models have been developed in vision (Knill & Richards, 1996). Following Baye's Rule the likelihoods and priors of a scene S and image I are combined to produce a non-normalized posterior:

Figure 3. Illustration of predicted azimuth and speed for motion-first (BIOVD) and stereo-first (BCDOT) Bayesian model in top view. The veridical constraint lines and IOC (gray) shift as a consequence of biased velocity (solid) or disparity (dashed) processing.

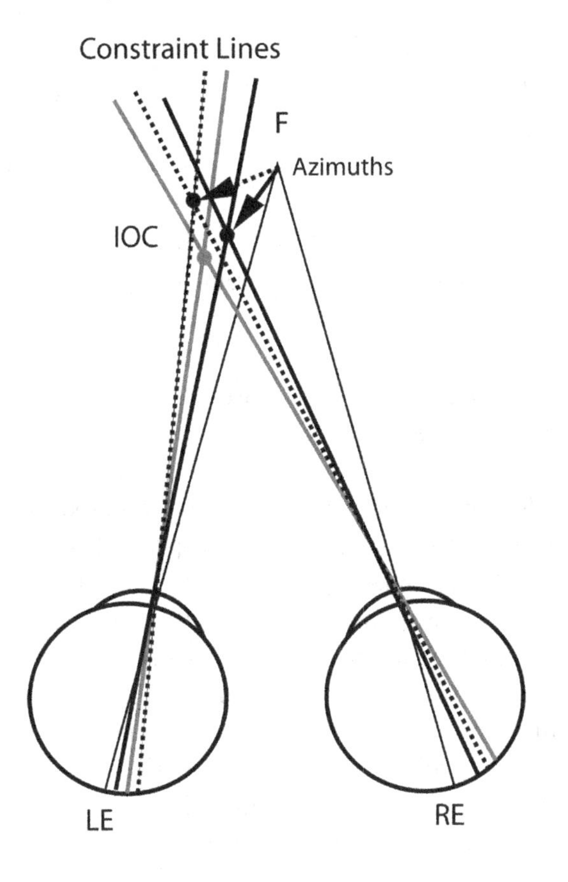

$$p(S \mid I) \propto p(I \mid S)p(S) \quad (1)$$

Various quantities given in the images, such as motion and disparity, can be used to infer aspects of a scene. Weiss, Simoncelli, and Adelson (2002), for example, combined motion constraints of local motion detectors with a Gaussian prior for slow motion to predict perceived motion direction and velocity of luminance-defined objects in 2D space. With this elegant approach they could explain a range of 2D motion illusions.

Most objects in natural scenes are stationary. If we assume that objects tend to move slowly on an arbitrary trajectory in *x-z* space then a bivariate Gaussian probability distribution centered on the starting point of a stimulus provides a plausible prior for 3D motion perception in *x-z* space. Symmetric perspective projections of this world prior into the left and right eye give rise to marginal Gaussian distributions defining motion priors centered on zero velocity. Similarly, the difference of the marginal distributions in the left and right eye defines a prior for disparity (change) centered on zero disparity. Thus, the same 3D motion prior in the world results in a Gaussian velocity and disparity prior on the retinae.

There are several potential sources for uncertainty and noise in binocular motion processing. For example, local moving targets in a sparse 3D environment offer limited motion and disparity input and other depth cues thereby introducing different degrees of uncertainty in the observer. Mini-saccades during fixation, or early noise in the encoding system are possible sources of uncertainty (Hogervorst & Eagle, 1998). In the following we extend the motion-first (IOVD) and stereo-first (CDOT) processing models to probabilistic models by adding Gaussian noise to the input and postulating a plausible prior for each processing scheme.

3.1.1 Bayesian Motion-First Model (BIOVD)

First assume that noise is present in the activation of monocular motion detectors optimally tuned to velocities in the left and right eye. The representation of angular velocity in each eye is therefore not exact but subject to noise (Ascher & Grzywacz, 2000). The corresponding likelihood distributions for angular velocity in the left and right eye are conveniently expressed as Gaussian distributions with equal variance centered on the true angular velocity of the stimulus in each eye. Each likelihood distribution is then combined with the motion prior. Motion priors favoring slow motion have been suggested in the context of 2D motion (Ascher & Yuille, 2000; Ullman & Yuille, 1989; Weiss et al., 2002).

In this framework perceived angular velocity of motion-first processing may be described as a product of likelihood and prior for the left and right eye

$$p(v_L \mid \beta) \propto p(\beta \mid v_L)p(v_L);$$
$$p(v_R \mid \beta) \propto p(\beta \mid v_R)p(v_R) \qquad (2)$$

using the same prior $p(v_L) = p(v_R) = p(v)$.

The likelihood for the left eye is modelled as a Gaussian distribution of angular velocities centered on the true angular velocity with $d\alpha_L(t) / dt$ abbreviated as $\dot{\alpha}_L$. The standard deviation σ_v of the likelihood distribution is left as a free parameter.

$$p(\beta \mid v_L;\sigma_v) = \frac{1}{\sqrt{2\pi}\sigma_v} \exp\left(\frac{-(v_L - \dot{\alpha}_L)^2}{2\sigma_v^2}\right) \qquad (3)$$

The likelihood for the right eye is modelled accordingly. The preference or prior for slow motion is described by a Gaussian distribution centered on zero velocity with unknown but fixed standard deviation σ.

$$p(v\ ;\sigma) = \frac{1}{\sqrt{2\pi}\sigma} \exp\left(\frac{-(v)^2}{2\sigma^2}\right) \qquad (4)$$

The product of the Gaussian likelihood distribution with such a conjugate prior $\mathcal{N}(0,\sigma)$ defines a posterior distribution, that is the probability of each possible angular velocity taking into account both prior and likelihood of the trajectory. Through differentiation the *maximum a posteriori* (MAP) estimates of angular velocity are found for the left eye and right eye, respectively.

$$\hat{\alpha}_L = \frac{1 / \sigma_v^2 \dot{\alpha}_L}{1 / \sigma_v^2 + 1 / \sigma^2} = \frac{\dot{\alpha}_L}{1 + (\sigma_v / \sigma)^2};$$
$$\hat{\alpha}_R = \frac{1 / \sigma_v^2 \dot{\alpha}_R}{1 / \sigma_v^2 + 1 / \sigma^2} = \frac{\dot{\alpha}_R}{1 + (\sigma_v / \sigma)^2} \qquad (5)$$

The noise ratio between likelihood and prior σ_v / σ is the only free parameter (Hürlimann, Kiper & Carandini, 2002).

3.1.2 Bayesian Disparity-First Model (BCDOT)

Alternatively, internal noise may be introduced by the activation of binocular disparity detectors tuned to different disparities. The likelihood distribution for disparity (change) is also conveniently expressed as a Gaussian distribution centered on the true disparity (change) of the stimulus. The disparity likelihood is then combined with the disparity prior favoring zero disparity. A similar disparity prior has been suggested in the context of sustained and transient stereo images (Read, 2002a,b).

The Bayesian stereo-first model describes perceived binocular disparity (change) as the product of likelihood and prior:

$$p(d \mid \beta) \propto p(\beta \mid d)p(d) \qquad (6)$$

The likelihood for binocular disparity (change) is modeled as a Gaussian distribution centered on the true disparity δ (or disparity change) measured at the endpoint of stimulus motion. The standard deviation σ_d of the distribution is left as a free parameter:

$$p(\beta \mid d; \sigma_d) = \frac{1}{\sqrt{2\pi}\sigma_d} \exp\left(\frac{-\left(d-\delta\right)^2}{2\sigma_d^2}\right) \quad (7)$$

The preference or prior for small disparity (change) is modeled as a Gaussian distribution centered on zero disparity:

$$p(d; \sigma) = \frac{1}{\sqrt{2\pi}\sigma} \exp\left(\frac{-\left(d\right)^2}{2\sigma^2}\right) \quad (8)$$

The MAP estimate for disparity is given by

$$\hat{\delta} = \frac{1/\sigma_d^2\,\delta}{1/\sigma_d^2 + 1/\sigma^2} = \frac{\delta}{1+\left(\sigma_d/\sigma\right)^2} \quad (9)$$

Changing disparity information needs to be coupled with spatial position to recover 3-D motion. The cyclopean azimuth $\dot{\alpha}$ is approximated by $(\dot{\alpha}_L + \dot{\alpha}_R)/2$ and disparity constraints are therefore given relative to angle $\dot{\alpha}$:

$$\hat{\alpha}_L = \dot{\alpha} - \hat{\delta}/2, \hat{\alpha}_R = \dot{\alpha} + \hat{\delta}/2 \quad (10)$$

3.1.3 Bayesian Stereo-Motion Model (BJEMD)

In the present framework velocity and disparity input can be combined in a Bayesian model with different noise ratios for motion and disparity processing. Uncertainty in velocity and disparity processing are combined and both uncertainty parameters are estimated together.

If we estimate cyclopean azimuth $\hat{\alpha}$ by $(\hat{\alpha}_L + \hat{\alpha}_R)/2$ and insert the velocity estimates from Eq (5) into Eq (10) then velocity and disparity input can be combined in a single Bayesian model

$$\hat{\alpha}_L = \hat{\alpha} - \hat{\delta}/2, \quad \hat{\alpha}_R = \hat{\alpha} + \hat{\delta}/2 \quad (11)$$

with estimates $(\hat{\alpha}_L, \hat{\alpha}_R, \hat{\delta})$ based on noise parameters for velocity σ_v and disparity σ_d processing.

Following Baye's rule, likelihoods and priors are combined to establish a posterior distribution for each model and trajectory. Applying a simple decision rule, such as the *maximum a posteriori* rule, provides *a posteriori* estimates of angular velocity and disparity. The estimates describe biased constraint lines and their intersection determines an azimuth angle and radial distance in *x-z*.

3.2 Simulating Perceived Velocity under Uncertainty

In this Bayesian framework uncertainty is modeled by the ratio of standard deviations between likelihood and prior. If uncertainty is negligible model predictions of azimuth angle are veridical but with increasing uncertainty model predictions approximate a shrinking circle for the motion-first and a compressed ellipse for the stereo-first Bayesian model. In Figure 4 predictions over the full range of 360° of stimulus azimuths are plotted for the two Bayesian models.

The unbiased prediction of azimuth angles, its circular shape, is the result of multiplying left and right angular velocity by the same factor. The increasingly flat elliptical shape is the consequence of a stronger bias for larger disparities near the *z*-axis or azimuths of 0° and 180° and weaker bias for smaller disparities near the *x*-axis or azimuths of 90° and 270°.

3.3 A Psychophysical Experiment on Perceived Horizontal Trajectory

Under natural viewing conditions there are many monocular cues to 3D motion but in a sparse environment only binocular motion and disparity cues may be available. In a psychophysical experiment Lages (2006) investigated perceived

Figure 4. Simulation results for (A) motion-first Bayesian IOVD and (B) stereo-first Bayesian CDOT and Bayesian JEMD. Plots show model predictions of trajectory angle and velocity in polar co-ordinates for azimuth angles of 10 to 350 deg in steps of 20 deg at a viewing distance of 114 cm. Uncertainty is modeled by the ratio of likelihood and prior ranging from 0.1 to 3.0 in steps of 0.2.

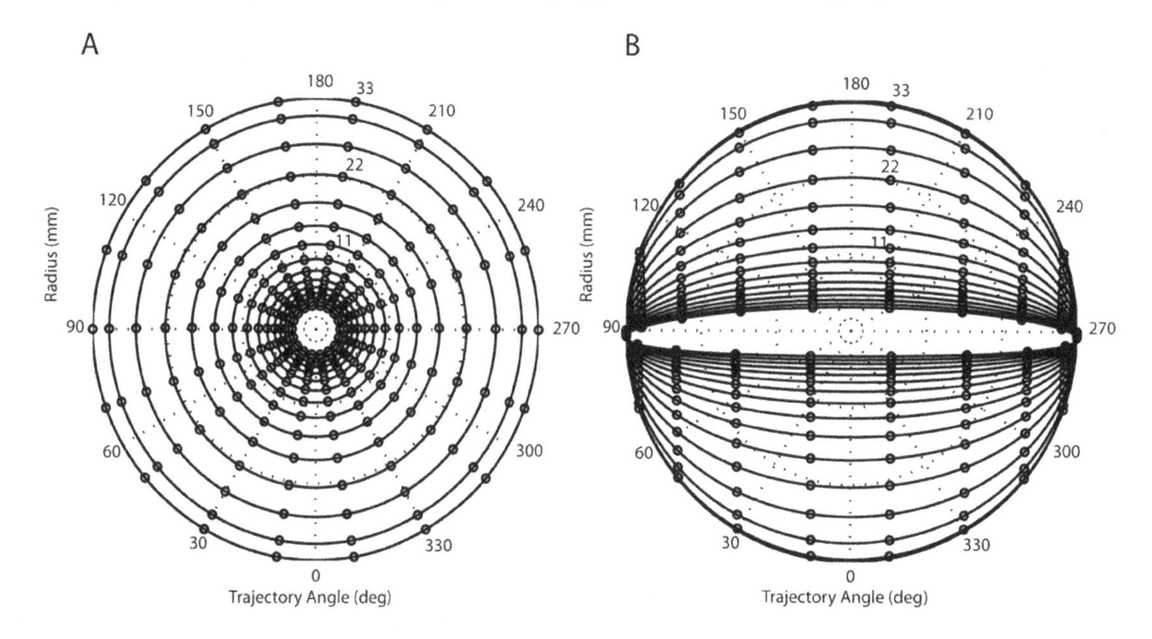

bias of motion trajectories of small target dots and used the Bayesian models of interocular velocity difference (BIOVD) and disparity change (BCDOT) as well as joined encoding (BJEMD) to explain the results.

Stimuli were presented to the left and right eye using a split-screen Wheatstone configuration. The observer viewed three anti-aliased dots presented above and below a fixation cross, surrounded by a rectangular fusion lock, at a viewing distance of 114 cm. Each dot subtended less than 4.4 arcmin at 27.7, 38.8 and 50 arcmin above and below fixation. In randomly intermixed trials the dots moved 16.6, 25, or 33.3 mm on the horizontal *x-z* plane for 833 ms (0.02, 0.03 and 0.04 m/s) on 36 different trajectories.

On each trial the observer verged on the fixation cross before they initiated motion of target dots by key-press. Azimuth angle of the target ranged between 0° and 350° in steps of 10°. Each observer attended a total of eight separate blocks (2 tasks x 4 repetitions) each comprising 108 trials (3 velocities x 36 trajectories). In each block of trials observers judged either motion azimuth or radial distance. Adjustments to 36 trajectories and 3 velocities were repeated four times in randomly intermixed trials.

In maximum likelihood (ML) fits individual adjustments of azimuth and radial distance were averaged across trials with the same stimulus velocity. Bayesian models with one free parameter (noise ratio between likelihood and prior determines perceived speed) for the motion-first model and two free parameters (perceived speed and noise ratio between likelihood and prior) for the stereo first model were fitted to data of each observer and three stimulus speeds and results are summarized in Table 1. The stereo-first Bayesian model gives better fits (one significant violation out of 16) and parameter values assume more plausible values than the motion-first model (four significant violations).

ML fits and parameters for the stereo-motion Bayesian model (BJEMD) are not reported be-

Table 1. Individual results from four observers and three stimulus speeds (radius in mm) from Lages (2006) Exp. 2. Parameter estimates and goodness-of-fit for motion-first and stereo-first Bayesian model.

Obs.	Radius	Motion-first Model			Stereo-first Model		
	r	$\sigma_v{:}\sigma$	r_v	$\chi^2(1)$	$\sigma_d{:}\sigma$	r_d	$\chi^2(1)$
A.G.	16.6	0.0	17.6	2.40	0.32	17.7	2.29
	25.0	0.0	20.6	6.63*	0.81	27.7	2.12
	33.3	0.0	25.2	17.2***	1.01	32.9	5.79*
M.L.	16.6	0.0	26.3	2.89	0.56	28.2	1.92
	25.0	0.0	30.8	4.07	0.49	34.3	3.09
	33.3	0.0	34.4	9.24**	0.77	39.5	3.00
R.G.	16.6	1.83	113	1.40	0.48	28.8	1.32
	25.0	2.84	274	3.40	0.87	35.4	0.58
	33.3	2.22	213	8.97**	1.00	43.2	1.45
S.S.	16.6	0.0	22.2	2.31	0.0	22.2	2.31
	25.0	0.0	36.1	1.45	0.58	39.3	1.14
	33.3	0.82	64.5	1.74	0.64	44.5	1.35

*p<.05;**p<.01;***p<0.001;

cause fits were almost identical to the stereo-first Bayesian model with no significant improvement for any of the individual data sets. As illustrated in Figure 5 fits of the stereo-first Bayesian model for each stimulus velocity suggest that an increase in stimulus velocity systematically raised uncertainty in the noise ratio. This trend appears in all observers except for Observer M.L. in the 16.6 mm condition.

A standard log-likelihood test (see -2log(Λ) in Table 2), approximated by a χ^2-distribution did not indicate any significant differences between BCDOT and BIOVD model fits. Bayes Information Content (BIC), however, as an approximation of the Bayes Factor (BF) suggests weak to positive evidence in favor of the stereo-first model (Raftery, 1995). The probability associated with BF_{BIC} indicates that given the empirical data the stereo-first model is on average 3 times more probable than the motion-first model.

Rendering 3D motion in a stereoscopic set-up is difficult and can introduce various artifacts and cue conflicts. In this experiment constant size and blur of the target stimuli moving in depth may have influenced perceived depth (Watt, Akeley, Ernst, & Banks, 2005). On the other hand, cue conflicts due to looming and accommodative cues are probably too small to account for the substantial and systematic bias found for small blurred targets that move maximally ±3.3 cm in depth at a viewing distance of 114 cm. Using LEDs moving in depth Harris and Dean (2003), as well as Welchman et al. (2004) reported systematic overestimation of perceived azimuths near the fronto-parallel plane, confirming that perceptual bias also exists for real-world stimuli at various trajectory angles.

Bayesian model fits for perceived azimuth angle and speed (radial distance) and Bayesian model selection promotes the idea that bias in 3D motion perception is introduced by disparity processing. This confirms previous findings in psychophysical studies that used different stimuli and methods (e.g., Cumming & Parker, 1994; Lages, Mamassian, & Graf, 2003). It is possible, however, that interocular velocity difference or optical flow contributes to 3D motion perception, especially when stimuli define surfaces that move on a trajectory near the observer's line of sight (Brooks & Stone, 2004).

In the stereo-first Bayesian model disparity estimates are derived from the endpoint of stimulus motion rather than integrated over time. As a consequence the stereo-first Bayesian model may be interpreted as (i) temporal integration of biased disparities or (ii) biased temporal integration of disparity. The latter interpretation appears more plausible since uncertainty estimates increased systematically with stimulus velocity as reported in Table 1 and Figure 5.

If 3D motion perception is based on velocity-tuned processing the relatively small change of stimulus velocity in our experiment should have very little effect on uncertainty. Disparity-tuned

Figure 5. Illustration of empirical results for four observers (adapted from Lages 2006, Figure 8). Polar plots for perceived azimuth and radial distance (speed) for stimulus velocities of 0.02 m/s (16.6 mm), 0.03 m/s (25.0 mm) and 0.04 m/s (33.3 mm) and best model fits of the stereo-first Bayesian model (BCDOT). Filled data points correspond to cardinal stimulus trajectories (0, 90, 180, 270 deg). With increasing stimulus speed estimates of radius and uncertainty increase and model fits and data assume a more compressed elliptical shape.

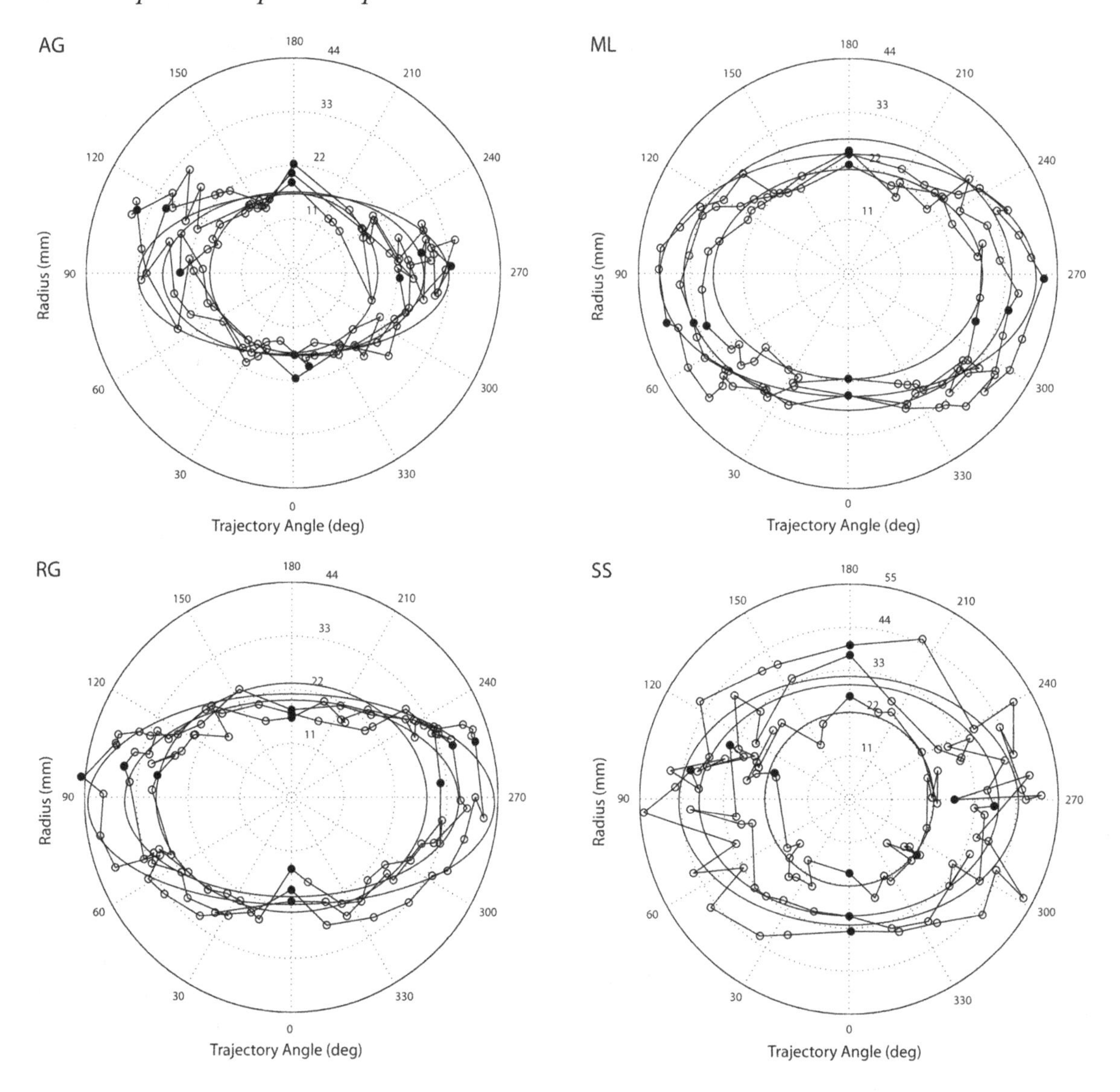

processing on the other hand may increase uncertainty levels for faster stimuli due to the temporal limits of disparity integration (Read & Cumming, 2005b; Tyler, 1971) in a transient stereo-system (Edwards & Schor, 1999).

One of the main goals of visual processing is to segregate and identify objects in space and time. With increasing proximity or size of a moving object local motion detectors signal a wider range of velocities. As a consequence a system that processes motion input first needs to establish

Table 2. Model selection for Bayesian motion-first and disparity-first model based on log-likelihood ratio test -2log(Λ) and BIC approximation of Bayes Factor BF_{BIC} with corresponding probability. Individual tests from four observers and three stimulus speeds (radius in mm; Lages, 2006, Exp. 2).

Obs.	Radius	Model Selection		
	r	-2log(Λ)	BF_{BIC}	Pr_{BIC}
A.G.	16.6	0.04	2.22	0.69
	25.0	0.99	3.57	0.78
	33.3	0.95	3.49	0.78
M.L.	16.6	0.36	2.60	0.72
	25.0	0.24	2.45	0.71
	33.3	0.98	3.55	0.78
R.G.	16.6	0.05	2.23	0.69
	25.0	1.54	4.69	0.82
	33.3	1.58	4.80	0.83
S.S.	16.6	0.0	2.18	0.69
	25.0	0.21	2.42	0.71
	33.3	0.22	2.43	0.71

correspondence between rather different monocular motions before it can build a percept of 3D object motion. Computationally it appears more parsimonious to solve the stereo correspondence problem before deriving a 3D motion percept. This argument also applies to joint encoding of motion and disparity (JEMD) because early encoding of true 3D motion would require a large number of detectors specifically tuned to all combinations of spatial frequency, orientation, and interocular spatio-temporal offsets to capture all possible local 3D motions.

It is concluded that under the present experimental conditions perceptual bias in 3D velocity is most likely the result of limited temporal integration when processing disparity change. This conclusion points to stereo-first or stereo-motion processing but rules out a motion-first mechanism that relies on interocular velocity difference only.

4. THE APERTURE PROBLEM IN 3D

So far models and experiments on 3D motion perception have only considered horizontal 3D motion trajectories of dots or unambiguous features that are confined to the *x-z* plane. In the following we investigate velocity estimates in the context of the 3D aperture problem. The 3D aperture problem arises when a line or edge moves in a circular aperture while endpoints of the moving stimulus remain occluded. Such a motion stimulus closely resembles local motion encoding in receptive fields of V1 (Hubel & Wiesel, 1968) but disambiguating motion direction and speed may reflect characteristics of motion and disparity integration in area V5/MT and possibly beyond (DeAngelis & Newsome, 2004). Similar to the 2D aperture problem (Adelson & Movshon, 1982; Wallach, 1935) the 3D aperture problem requires that the visual system resolves motion correspondence but at the same time it needs to establish stereo correspondence between binocular receptive fields.

Lines and edges of various orientations are elementary for image processing because they signify either a change in the reflectance of the surface, a change in the amount of light falling on it, or a change in surface orientation relative to the light source. For these and other reasons, lines and edges are universally regarded as important image-based features or primitives (Marr, 1982). The departure from random-dot kinematograms (RDKs), typically used in stereo research and binocular motion in depth (Julesz, 1971), may be significant because a line in a circular aperture effectively mimics the receptive field of a local motion detector. Local motion and disparity of a line, where endpoints are occluded behind a circular aperture, is highly ambiguous in terms of 3D motion direction and speed but it is interesting to know how the visual system resolves this ambiguity and which constraints are employed to achieve local and global scene flow estimates.

Figure 6. Illustration of the inverse problem for binocular 3D motion perception. Note that left and right eye velocity constraints of a line derived from vector normals in 2D, depicted here on a common fronto-parallel screen rather than the left and right retina, do not necessarily intersect in 3D space. If the constraint lines are skew the inverse problem remains ill-posed (adapted from Lages & Heron, 2010).

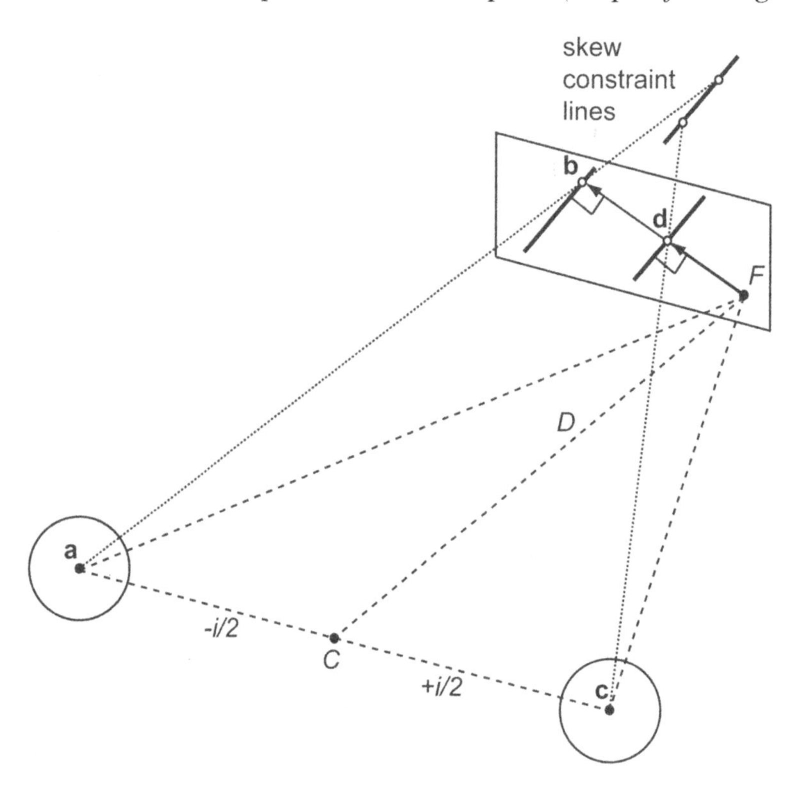

Consider, for example, a local feature with spatial extent such as an oriented line inside a circular aperture so that the endpoints of the line are occluded. Stereo correspondence between oriented lines or edges remains ambiguous (Morgan & Castet, 1997; van Ee & Schor, 2000). If an observer maintains fixation at a close or moderate viewing distance then the oriented line stimulus may project differently onto the left and right retina (see Figure 6 for an illustration with projections onto a single fronto-parallel screen). When an oriented line stimulus moves in depth at a given azimuth angle then local motion detectors tuned to different speeds may respond optimally to motion normal or perpendicular to the orientation of the line. If the intensity gradient or normal in 3D from the left and right eye serves as a default strategy, similar to the 2D aperture problem (Adelson & Movshon, 1982; Sung, Wojtach & Purves, 2009), then the resulting vectors in each eye may have different lengths. Inverse perspective projection of the retinal motion vectors reveals that monocular velocity constraint lines are usually skew so that an intersection of line constraints (IOC) does not exist (Lages & Heron, 2010).

Another violation occurs when the line is slanted in depth and projects with different orientations into the left and right eye. The resulting misalignment on the y-axis between motion vectors in the left and right eye is reminiscent of vertical disparity and the induced effect (Ogle, 1940; Banks & Backus, 1998). However, an initially small vertical disparity between motion gradients would increase over time. The stereo system can extract depth from input with vertical disparity (Hinkle & Connor, 2002) and possibly

Figure 7. Illustration of vector normal (VN, shortest distance in 3D) and cyclopean average (CA, shortest distances in 2D) as possible default strategies for local velocity estimation in the context of the 3D aperture problem (adapted from Lages & Heron, 2010).

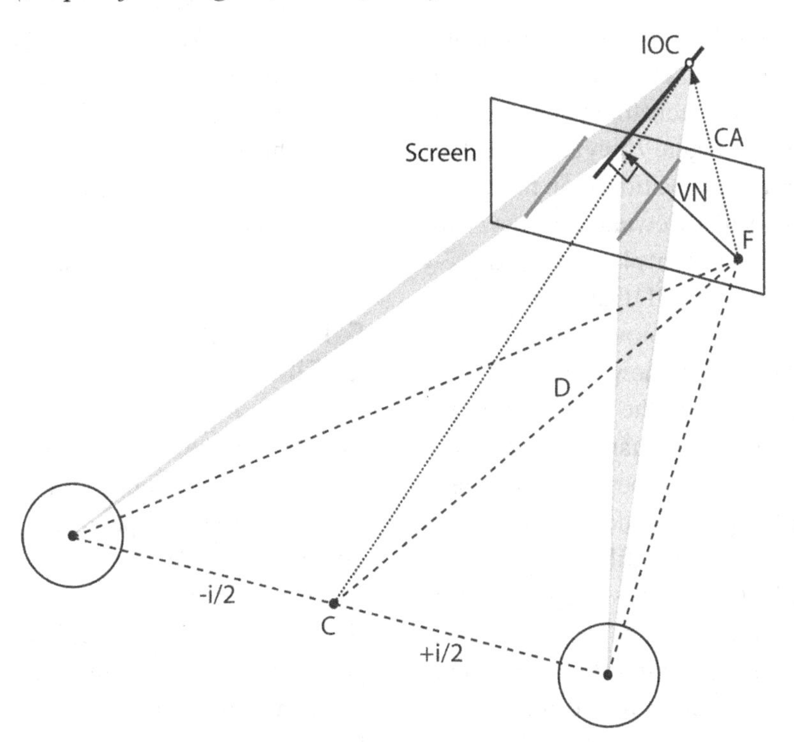

orientation disparity (Greenwald & Knill, 2009) but it seems unlikely that the motion system is based on monocular motion detectors tuned to different orientations and speeds. Since adaptive convergence of skew constraint lines is computationally expensive, it seems plausible that the visual system uses a different strategy to solve the aperture problem in 3D.

4.1 Velocity Constraints and Two Default Strategies

Which constraints does the visual system use to solve the inverse problem for local 3D line motion where endpoints are invisible or occluded? This is a critical question because it is linked to local motion encoding and possible contributions from depth processing.

The 3D motion system may establish constraint planes rather than constraint lines to capture all possible motion directions of a line or edge in 3D space - including motion in the direction of the orientation of the line or edge. The intersection of two constraint planes in a binocular viewing geometry specifies a constraint line oriented in 3D space (see Figure 7). We suggest that in analogy to 2D motion perception (Adelson & Movshon, 1982; Weiss et al., 2002) tracking of features in depth coupled with binocular velocity constraints from motion processing provides a flexible strategy to disambiguate 3D motion direction and to solve the inverse problem of 3D motion perception.

But which principles or local constraints are used under uncertainty and ambiguity? Does the binocular motion system prefer slow motion in 3D or slow retinal motion in 2D and the cyclopean average? Does it solve stereo correspondence before establishing binocular velocity constraints or does it average 2D velocity constraints from the left and right eye before stereo correspondence is established? We suggest two plausible default strategies to address these questions.

1. **Vector Normal (VN):** Velocity constraints of lines and edges in the left and right eye give rise to velocity constraint planes in 3D velocity space. In Figure 7 they are illustrated as shaded triangles positioned on the nodal points in a binocular viewing geometry. The intersection of constraint planes defines a velocity constraint line in 3D that also describes an end-position of the moving line or edge in space (black line). The vector normal of constraint line through the start point gives a default 3D motion estimate (black arrow). It is the shortest distance between start point and IOC in 3D space and denotes the slowest motion vector that fulfills both velocity constraints. Note that this strategy requires that the 3D motion system has established stereo correspondence so that the intersection of constraints as well as the vector normal can be found in 3D velocity space. The VN strategy is a generalization of the vector normal and IOC in 2D motion perception. It is related to area-based regression and gradient constraint models (Lucas & Kanade, 1981) where the local brightness constancy constraint ensures a default solution that is normal to the orientation of image intensity.
2. **Cyclopean Average (CA):** If the motion system computes retinal 2D motion independently in the left and right eye then their cyclopean average provides an alternative velocity constraint (Harris & Drga, 2005; Harris & Rushton, 2003). Averaging of monocular constraints increases robustness of the motion signal at the expense of binocular disparity information. Thus, a cyclopean average constrains velocity but does not provide a velocity estimate. However, if we attach (changing) disparity to the cyclopean average or use the IOC then the CA gives a default estimate of 3D velocity (see Figure 7).

   The CA strategy may be seen as a generalized version of the vector average (VA) strategy for 2D motion (Wilson, Ferrera, & Yo, 1992) and is linked to computational models of 3D motion that use global gradient and smoothness constraints (Horn & Schunck, 1981). These global models compute the average flow in the neighborhood of each point and refine the scene flow by the residual of the average flow vectors.

5. BAYESIAN 3D VELOCITY ESTIMATION

In the following we extend the geometric considerations for line stimuli moving in 3D space. Lines and contours have spatial extent and orientation reflecting properties of local encoding in receptive fields (Hubel & Wiesel, 1962; 1968; 1970). We suggest a generalized Bayesian model that provides velocity estimates for arbitrary azimuth and elevation angles. Again, this model requires knowledge about eye positions in a binocular viewing geometry together with 2D intensity gradients to establish velocity constraint planes for each eye. The velocity constraints are then combined with a 3D motion prior to estimate local 3D velocity. In the absence of 1D features such as points, corners, and T-junctions and no noise in the likelihoods, this approach approximates the VN strategy and can provide a dense array of local velocity estimates. A dense array of local estimates is a desirable feature of any 3D motion model because it captures scene flow. The present approach is also flexible because additional constraints or cues from moving features can be integrated to further disambiguate motion direction of objects under uncertainty or ambiguity (Weiss et al., 2002).

5.1 The Generalized Bayesian Model

Following Weiss and Fleet (2001), we incorporate intensity constraints into a Bayesian model of 3D

Figure 8. Illustration of the generalized Bayesian model. The left and right eye velocity constraint planes for an oriented line moving in 3D are indicated by triangles positioned on the nodal point of the left and right eye. The intersection of constraints (IOC) describes the end position of the line after movement in 3D space. A 3D motion prior for slow motion is illustrated as a translucent sphere centered on the start point that is also the fixation point F. The Bayesian MAP estimate for velocity approximates the vector normal **v** *of the IOC through F.*

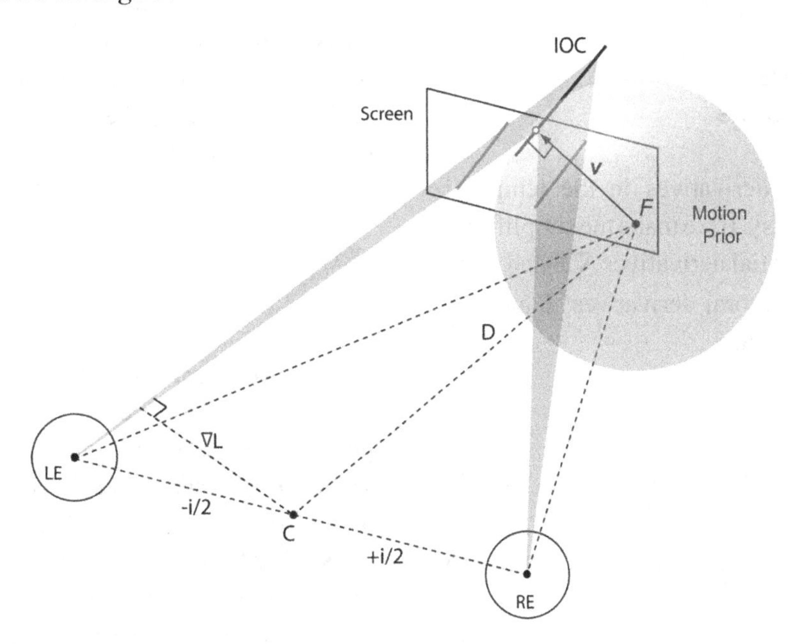

motion perception. However, the present approach extends Bayesian models of *x-y* (Weiss et al., 2002) and *x-z* motion (Lages, 2006; Welchman, et al., 2008) to true 3D motion in *x-y-z* thereby providing default estimates for the 3D aperture problem (Lages & Heron, 2010).

Local 2D motion constraints from the left and right eye in a binocular viewing geometry are sufficient to establish two velocity constraint planes or hyperplanes in 3D space: the moving line projects on the left and right retina. The projected lines together with each nodal point establish velocity constraint planes or hyperplanes for the left and right eye (see Figure 8). The left and right constraint plane are determined by a 3D gradient through the cyclopean point C or the fixation point F. Note that stereo correspondence in a 3D binocular viewing geometry needs to be established before velocity constraint planes can be defined. It seems plausible that vergence, accommodation and disparity cues as well as other depth cues help to establish stereo correspondence between images in the left and right eye.

Similar to 2D motion, intensity gradients in 3D may be approximated by first-order Taylor series expansion using brightness constraints. For corresponding receptive fields in the left and right eye we assume that

$$\mathbf{v}^T \nabla L + L_t = 0, \quad \mathbf{v}^T \nabla R + R_t = 0 \qquad (12)$$

where $\nabla L = (L_x, L_y, L_z)$ and $\nabla R = (R_x, R_y, R_z)$ denote the spatial gradients corresponding to constraint planes derived from local receptive fields in the left and right eye, respectively. For the sake of simplicity, we assume a binocular viewing geometry where the position of the projected fixation point F on the retina and the nodal points of the eyes (and therefore the cyclopean point) are known and only velocity of a local line or edge needs to be estimated. Since the visual system continuously monitors accommodation and vergence of both eyes it is reasonable to assume that local velocity constraints are available in form of intensity gradients.

5.1.1 Likelihoods and Velocity Constraints

Measurements of derivatives in the temporal domain, may be noisy. If we make the simplifying assumption that spatial derivatives ∇L and ∇R are precise but temporal derivatives L_t and R_t have additive noise then

$$L_t = L_t(x,y,z,t) + \eta(x,y,z,t), \quad R_t = R_t(x,y,z,t) + \eta(x,y,z,t) \tag{13}$$

where $\eta(x,y,z,t)$ has Gaussian density with zero mean and variance $\sigma_v^2 \mathrm{I}$, or $\mathcal{N}(0,\sigma_v^2\mathrm{I})$ for short where $\mathbf{I}$ is the 3 x 3 identity matrix. Given the gradient constraint equation holds, it follows that

$$\tilde{L}_t \sim \mathcal{N}(-\mathbf{v}^T\nabla L, \sigma_v^2\mathrm{I}), \quad \tilde{R}_t \sim \mathcal{N}(-\mathbf{v}^T\nabla R, \sigma_v^2\mathrm{I}) \tag{14}$$

If 3D velocity $\mathbf{v}$ is known then the probability of observing $(\nabla L, \tilde{L}_t)$ for the left and $(\nabla R, \tilde{R}_t)$ for the right eye can be expressed as

$$p(\nabla L, \tilde{L}_t \mid \mathbf{v}) = \frac{1}{\sqrt{2\pi}\sigma_v} \exp\left(\frac{-(\mathbf{v}^T\nabla L + \tilde{L}_t)^T(\mathbf{v}^T\nabla L + \tilde{L}_t)}{2\sigma_v^2}\right), \quad p(\nabla R, \tilde{R}_t \mid \mathbf{v}) = \frac{1}{\sqrt{2\pi}\sigma_v} \exp\left(\frac{-(\mathbf{v}^T\nabla R + \tilde{R}_t)^T(\mathbf{v}^T\nabla R + \tilde{R}_t)}{2\sigma_v^2}\right) \tag{15}$$

If the constraint planes through the left and right eye are not coincident or parallel their intersection constrains 3D velocities but does not provide a unique solution or local velocity estimate. As a consequence additional constraints are needed to disambiguate local velocity estimates. It seems plausible that disparity information from feature tracking, together with other depth cues, helps to disambiguate 3D motion perception (Lages & Heron, 2008; 2010). However, if disparity features and similar depth information is unavailable a weak prior for 3D motion resolves ambiguity and provides a local default estimate.

Here we propose the 3D Gaussian as a conjugate motion prior:

$$p(\mathbf{v}) = \frac{1}{\sqrt{2\pi}\sigma} \exp\left(\frac{-\mathbf{v}^T\mathbf{v}}{2\sigma^2}\right) \tag{16}$$

This world prior simply reflects a preference for slow motion in every direction. This is a plausible assumption as most features in natural scenes remain static and moving objects tend to move slowly.

Similar to Section 3.1, the posterior distribution is the result of combining likelihood constraints and prior using Baye's Rule where $L(\mathbf{x},t)$ and $R(\mathbf{x},t)$ describe intensities in world co-ordinates associated with the left and right eye. The denominator can be dropped because the expression is independent of $\mathbf{v}$ and scales the posterior by a constant factor.

$$p(\mathbf{v} \mid L(\mathbf{x},t), R(\mathbf{x},t)) \propto p(L(\mathbf{x},t) \mid \mathbf{v})\, p(R(\mathbf{x},t) \mid \mathbf{v})\, p(\mathbf{v}) \tag{17}$$

We can then approximate the posterior by replacing the intensities through gradients.

$$p(\mathbf{v} \mid (\nabla L, \tilde{L}_t), (\nabla R, \tilde{R}_t)) \propto p(\nabla L, \tilde{L}_t \mid \mathbf{v})\, p(\nabla R, \tilde{R}_t \mid \mathbf{v})\, p(\mathbf{v}) \tag{18}$$

The posterior distribution gives a random variable as an estimate. In order to find the most probable velocity or MAP estimate, we take the negative logarithm of the posterior, differentiate it with respect to $\mathbf{v}$ and set the derivative equal to zero.

Figure 9. Simulation results for the generalized 3D Bayesian model: 3D view in left plot and top view in right plot. Predicted velocity of a vertical line moving on horizontal azimuths ranging from 0° to 360° in steps of 10° are shown. Bayesian estimates (MAP) of predicted trajectories are shown as thick lines with open circles attached for a noise ratio between likelihood and prior of 1:32. Endpoints of geometric vector normal (VN) predictions are indicated by filled circles.

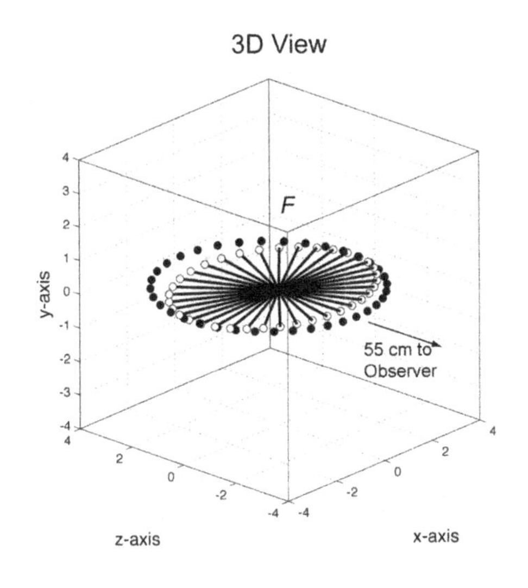

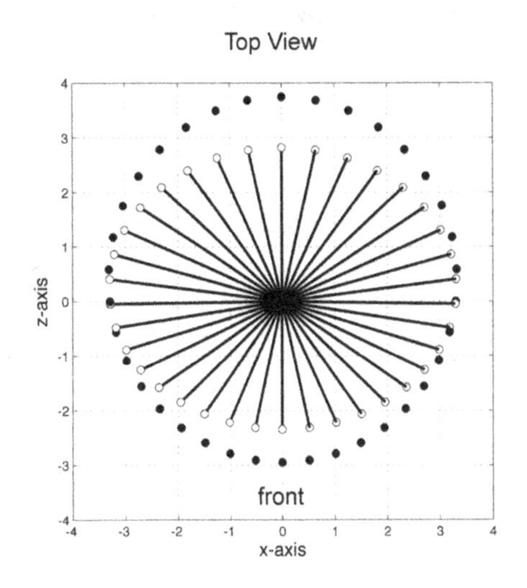

The logarithm of the posterior is quadratic in **v** so that the solution can be written in closed form using standard linear algebra.

$$-\hat{\mathbf{v}} = \left(\mathbf{M} + \frac{1}{\sigma^2}\mathbf{I}\right)^{-1} \mathbf{b} \tag{19}$$

where **I** is the 3 x 3 identity matrix, $\mathbf{M} = 1/\sigma_v^{\,2}\left(\nabla L \nabla L^T + \nabla R \nabla R^T\right)$, and $\mathbf{b} = 1/\sigma_v^{\,2}\left(\nabla L \tilde{L}_t + \nabla R \tilde{R}_t\right)$.

If the matrix in Equation (19) has full rank and is invertible then the solution is unique and a velocity estimate can be determined.

5.1.2 Simulating Perceptual Bias under Uncertainty

The previously-discussed bias in binocular 3D motion perception describes a perceptual bias in azimuth and speed. More specifically, as noise or uncertainty in the likelihoods increases perceived azimuth is biased towards the fronto-parallel fixation plane and perceived speed is reduced (see Figure 5). We implemented the General Bayesian model in MatLab (Mathworks) to simulate velocity estimation under uncertainty. We compared the Bayesian MAP estimates with the vector normal (VN), which is equivalent to the shortest distance between starting point *F* and IOC line in 3D space.

The line stimulus was vertical and moved on horizontal trajectories with azimuth ranging between 10° to 360° in steps of 10°. Viewing distance *D* was set to 55 cm and interocular distance *i* to 6.5 cm. In the degenerate case of a moving vertical line the elevation angle of motion direction remains at 0°. In this case predictions are equivalent to a single dot moving in the horizontal *x-z* plane as discussed in the previous section (see Figure 4 and 9).

The MAP estimates approximate VN predictions if likelihoods have very little noise compared to the prior (noise ratio $\sigma_v : \sigma$ <1:100). For a noise ratio of 1:32 MAP estimates are compressed in depth leading to trajectories that are biased towards

Figure 10. Simulation results for generalized 3D Bayesian model: 3D view in left plot and top view in right plot. Predicted trajectories to front (+iovd) and back (-iovd) as a function of orientation disparity (slant in depth varied between ±6° in steps of 2°) of a moving oblique stimulus line (thin line). Noise ratio between likelihood and prior is set to 1:100 and Bayesian estimates (MAP) are shown as thick lines, originating from fixation point F with open circles attached. Endpoints of geometric vector normal (VN) predictions are indicated by filled circles.

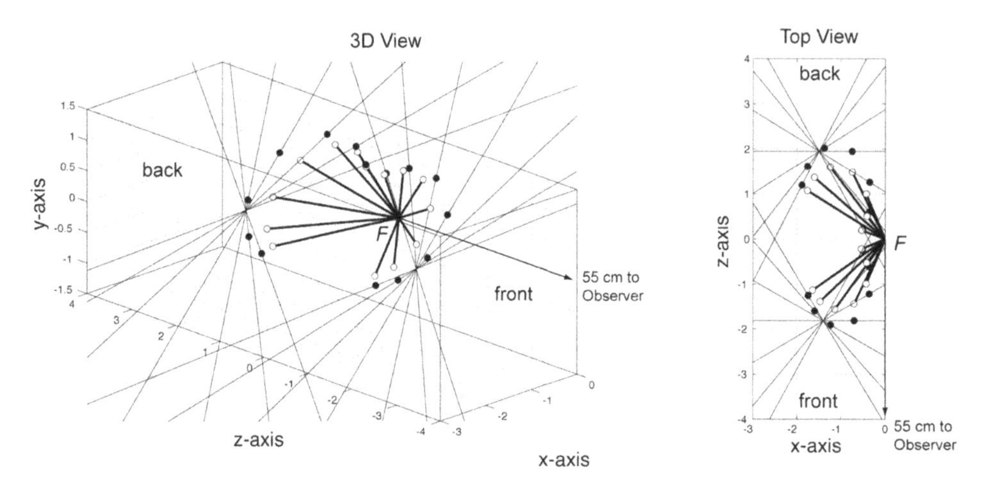

the fronto-parallel fixation plane. If trajectories point away from the fixation plane then speed is increasingly underestimated. These model characteristics match empirical results on perceived azimuth and speed of stimulus dots under uncertainty (see Figure 5 and Table 1 in Section 3.2).

5.1.3 Simulating the 3D Aperture Problem

We computed Bayesian MAP estimates for the 3D aperture problem at different noise ratios and compared the velocity estimates with vector normal (VN) predictions as a plausible default. The moving line stimuli were oblique or vertical (45 and 90 deg). In addition the line stimuli were slanted in depth due to systematic manipulation of orientation disparity between the projections into the left and right eye. Orientation disparity in the stimulus display ranged from -6° to +6°. As in the first simulation, viewing distance D was set to 55 cm and interocular distance i to 6.5 cm. At 0° elevation the line stimulus moved on a fixed azimuth of +52.5° (37.5°) to the front and -52.5° (142.5°) to the back. Note that an azimuth of 0° denotes motion frontoparallel to the observer (directly towards the observer).

We varied variability or noise of the likelihood σ_v while keeping the prior σ constant; the resulting ratio $\sigma_v : \sigma$ assumed values of 1:10, 1:32, and 1:100.

As in the first simulation MAP estimates approximate the VN solution if the noise ratio is less than 1:100. MAP estimates are only slightly biased away from the vector normal if the likelihoods have little noise compared to the prior (see Figure 10). As noise in the likelihoods increases MAP estimates shorten and move away from the IOC line towards the surface normal of the right or left eye constraint plane, whichever is closer to the starting point F. These results may approximate more local and instantaneous velocity estimates in the absence of any other disambiguating cues.

One of the strengths of the Bayesian approach is that it can incorporate multiple cues at the same or neighboring locations. For example, local velocity constraints for the left and right eye can be stabilized in an area-based approach (Lucas & Kanade, 1981) by using multiple overlapping apertures and likelihoods tuned to different spatial frequencies. In addition, the model can be extended to the perception of 3D object motion using a sufficiently dense array of local estimates to capture features such as endpoints, junctions, and corners. Constraints from depth processing can therefore disambiguate object motion direction similar to the Bayesian approach to 2D motion in Weiss et al. (2002).

In the present model intensity gradients, likelihood constraints, and motion prior are expressed in world co-ordinates. Transformations from image or retinal gradients into world co-ordinates may be achieved using the epipolar constraint (Hansard & Haroud, 2008) and the fundamental matrix (Faugeras, 1992; Hartley & Zisserman, 2004).

It is tempting to assume that intensity gradients, velocity constraints, and motion prior are exclusively the result of motion encoding and processing. However, solving the aperture problem locally requires stereo correspondence that suggests significant contributions from depth processing. Consider for example a moving line or edge that also changes size and orientation over time. If tilt, slant and size of the line changes over time then velocity constraint planes and their intersection are no longer sufficient. They need to be updated frequently. Estimating motion direction and speed of such a stimulus is only possible if stereo correspondence and depth is resolved with sufficient temporal resolution. Sampling of IOC constraints over time is equivalent to transient (orientation) disparity processing. A system that can encode rotational as well as translational line motion locally is also capable of capturing non-rigid object motion. Therefore, it seems likely that the visual system employs parallel processing of motion and disparity and late integration (DeAngelis & Newsome, 2004; Ponce et al., 2008) to overcome the inverse problem of 3D motion perception (Lages & Heron, 2010).

In summary, the present Bayesian model extends existing models of 3D motion perception. It captures bias in 3D motion perception and provides testable predictions in the context of the 3D aperture problem. In addition, however, it requires frequent inputs from depth processing to capture true 3D motion and to model behavioral data.

5.2 A Psychophysical Experiment on the 3D Aperture Problem

As discussed in Section 3.2 large and persistent perceptual bias was found for isolated dot stimuli with uncertain but unambiguous motion direction (Harris & Dean, 2003; Lages, 2006; Welchman et al., 2008). These results suggest processing strategies that introduce perceptual bias (Ji & Fermüller, 2006; Weiss et al., 2002) and are therefore different from standard approaches in computer vision. It seems promising to also investigate local motion with ambiguous motion direction, such as a line or edge moving inside a circular aperture (Heron & Lages, 2009) because this motion directly relates to local encoding (Hubel & Wiesel, 1962; 1968; 1970; DeAngelis, Ohzawa, & Freeman, 1993; Maunsell & van Essen, 1983; Anzai, Ohzawa, & Freeman, 2001; Bradley, Qian, & Andersen, 1995; DeAngelis, & Newsome, 1999) and may reveal basic principles of 3D motion processing in the visual system.

In a psychophysical experiment four observers matched perceived 3D motion direction of an oblique (tilted by 45° from vertical) line moving on a trajectory behind a circular aperture. In addition orientation disparity in the line stimulus was varied ranging from -6° to +6° in steps of 2°. The moving line appeared slanted in depth due to the orientation disparity between the projected lines in the left and right eye. Viewing distance was set to 55 cm. For horizontal motion at 0° elevation the line stimulus moved on a fixed azimuth of +52.5° (37.5°) to the front and -52.5° (142.5°) to the back. Note that an azimuth of 0° denotes motion frontoparallel to the observer (directly towards the observer).

First, we fitted the data of each observer to the geometric CA and VN model (Lages & Heron, 2010) and achieved relatively poor fits (not shown). The data suggest some characteristics of the VN strategy but on a very much reduced scale. Next, we applied the generalized Bayesian model as described in Section 5.1 with a free parameter for noise in the likelihood constraints and an additional parameter for noise in orientation disparity.

The first parameter captures deviations from VN as a consequence of noise in motion processing. This affects perceived trajectory as illustrated in Sections 5.1.2 and 5.1.3. The second parameter describes the possible influence of orientation disparity on perceived trajectory. If the second parameter has little noise perceived trajectories approximate the VN solution with relatively large changes in perceived trajectory as illustrated in Section 5.1.3. If however orientation disparity carries a lot of noise then the influence of orientation disparity is diminished leading to smaller changes in perceived trajectory.

The results of best-fitting model parameters across orientation disparities and motion to the front and back (see Figure 11) are summarized in Table 3 for the oblique (45°) and vertical line stimulus (90°). The model gives a reasonable fit with comparable estimates across observers. Uncertainty or noise estimates for motion are low whereas estimates for noise in orientation disparity are mostly greater than 1. The data fits suggest that orientation disparity of the stimulus within the probabilistic VN model has a small effect on perceived motion direction, possibly due to additional stimulus constraints.

Due to the size of the aperture and stimulus line it seems unlikely that processing in this task occurs only locally within a single receptive field. The stimulus size suggests that multiple receptive fields and higher-order features and their "readout" at intermediate and higher processing levels contribute to perceived motion direction. For example, the moving line stimulus in our experiment creates a moving lower and upper T-junction with the aperture. As the line moves away from the center the two T-junctions describe arcs that converge towards a single point on the aperture. If the visual system tracks both T-junctions and simply computes their average then this strategy coincides with the CA constraint in Section 4.1. It seems plausible that this cyclopean average constraint from feature tracking reduced the range of perceived motion trajectories as observed in the adjustment task. If the moving line is slanted in depth, one T-junction is always nearer whereas the other is further away from the aperture. Since features closer to an occluder are less extrinsic they influence perceived motion direction more than more extrinsic features further away from the occluder (Shimojo, Silverman, & Nakayama, 1989; Graf, Adams & Lages, 2004). As a consequence perceived motion direction of the line may be biased away from the nearer T-junction in the slanted line. Indeed, tracking T-junctions would also explain the limited range of adjustments and the effect of less-extrinsic T-junctions is compatible with the empirical data presented in Figure 11. In any case, orientation disparity of the stimulus line and/or their extrinsic T-junctions with the aperture highlight that disparity rather than motion processing disambiguate perceived 3D motion direction.

6. GENERAL DISCUSSION

Motion-first (IOVD) and stereo-first (CDOT) are extreme models because they only consider motion or disparity input, respectively. IOVD excludes contributions from binocular disparity processing but requires early stereo correspondence. It does not solve the inverse problem for local 3D line motion because it is usually confined to 3D motion in the x- or z-plane. CDOT on the other hand excludes contributions from motion processing

Figure 11. Results from binocular 3D motion direction matching experiment for lines with oblique orientation (45 deg) and systematically varied orientation disparity (between ±6° in steps of 2°). Data points averaged across four repeated trials are shown as black circles with horizontal and vertical error bars (±1SEM) for azimuth and elevation, respectively. Data for four observers are plotted in rows and for two motion trajectories (-iovd/to back and +iovd/to front) in columns. Individual fits of the generalized Bayesian model with two parameters (triangles) provide a reasonable fit (see Table 3).

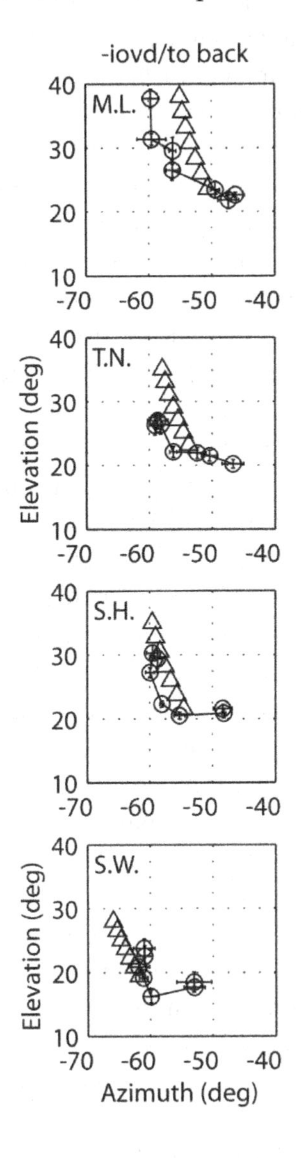

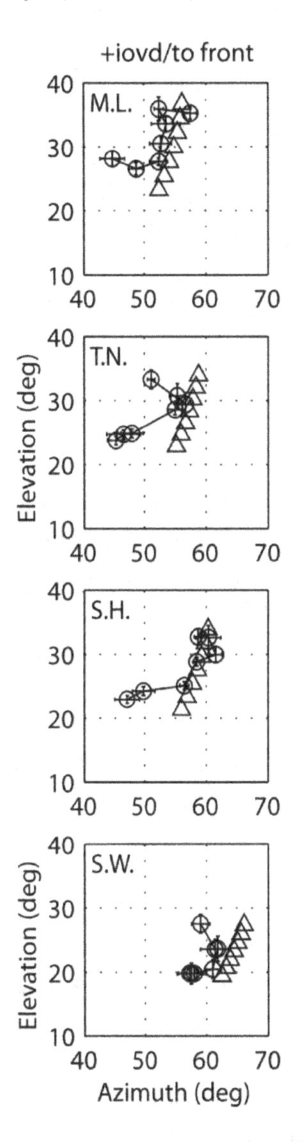

and therefore has problems to establish motion correspondence and direction. Without further assumptions it is confined to motion in depth along the line of sight.

If motion-only or disparity-only input determines 3D motion perception as suggested by IOVD and CDOT then processing of other input needs to be silenced or disengaged. This requires top-down interference rather than bottom-up processing by the visual system. Instead, we suggest that the visual system takes advantage of motion and disparity input (Bradshaw & Cumming, 1997;

Table 3. Individual model fits from four observers and two line orientations (oblique 45 and vertical 90). Parameter estimates of motion constraint noise and disparity noise as well as goodness-of-fit for the generalized Bayesian model.

Obs.	Ori	Velo	Ori Disp	Fit
		$\sigma_v{:}\sigma$	$\sigma_d{:}\sigma$	$\chi^2(11)$
S.H.	45	0.05	2.76	8.71
	90	0.06	1.44	30.5**
M.L.	45	0.05	2.58	8.26
	90	0.07	0.79	27.8*
T.N.	45	0.05	2.95	15.4
	90	0.06	1.98	10.8
S.W.	45	0.03	3.66	12.5
	90	0.06	1.00	40.1**

*p<.05;**p<.01

Lages & Heron, 2008) as well as additional cues. We favor parallel over serial processing and late integration over early joint encoding (Lages, Dolia, & Graf, 2007). The inverse problem of local 3D motion remains ill posed for joint early encoding and JEMD needs a population read-out at some later stage to approximate 3D motion.

Combining disparity or depth information with velocity constraints at a later stage solves the inverse problem of local 3D motion and provides a flexible scheme that can exploit intermediate depth processing such as relative and orientation disparity in V2 and V4 (Hinkle & Connor, 2002; Thomas, Cumming, & Parker, 2002). Velocity constraints may be processed in the ventral stream and binocular disparity together with other depth cues in the dorsal stream (Ponce et al., 2008). It seems anatomically and neurophysiologically plausible that integration of motion and disparity occurs late in subregions of human V5/MT (DeAngelis & Newsone, 2004; Orban, 2008; Majaj, Carandini, & Movshon, 2007; Rokers et al., 2009) if not in areas beyond V5/MT (Likova & Tyler, 2007).

What enables the visual system to instantaneously perceive 3D motion and to infer direction and speed of a moving object? It seems likely that the visual system exploits many cues in concert to make this difficult inference as reliable and veridical as possible. The diverse set of effective local and global cues in psychophysical studies (Bradshaw & Cumming, 1997; van Ee & Anderson, 2001) points at late integration within the visual processing hierarchy.

More specifically, we suggest that binocular 3D motion perception is based on parallel streams of motion and disparity processing. Thereby motion processing captures coarse spatio-temporal constraints in the scene whereas disparity processing provides a fine and frequently updated depth map that helps to disambiguate motion direction and to maintain a detailed spatial representation of the scene. Late integration of local motion and disparity constraints in combination with other cues solves the inverse problem of local 3D motion and allows the visual system to remain flexible when binding and segmenting local inputs from different processing stages into a global 3D motion percept. Parallel processing and late integration may explain why, compared to 2D motion perception, 3D motion perception shows reduced spatio-temporal tuning characteristics (Lages, Mamassian, & Graf, 2003; Tyler, 1971) and why motion perception can retain relatively fine spatial detail at slow speeds. The combination of local motion constraints with a more global dynamic depth map from higher-order features may even explain the perception of different types of non-linear motion, such as non-rigid and 2nd order motion.

The notion of parallel pathways feeding functionally different aspects of motion perception into a later stage is not new and has been advanced in the context of 2D speed perception (Braddick, 1974;1980), 2D pattern motion (Adelson & Movshon, 1982; Weiss et al., 2002; Wilson, Ferrera, Yo, 1992), eye movements (Rashbass & Westheimer, 1961; Masson & Castet, 2002), and the processing of higher order motion (Ledgeway & Smith, 1994; Lu & Sperling, 2001). Surprisingly however, it has not sufficiently been addressed in the context of binocular 3D motion perception (Lu & Sperling, 2001; Regan, Beverley, Cynader, & Lennie, 1979).

Considering the ill-posed inverse problem of existing approaches and the underdetermined characteristics of local binocular motion constraints, parallel processing and late integration of motion and disparity as well as other cues appears promising. Solving the inverse problem for local 3D motion adds a functional significant aspect to the notion of parallel streams of dynamic disparity and motion processing. It will require considerable efforts to unravel the entire process but geometric-probabilistic models can achieve motion and disparity integration under uncertainty and ambiguity (Wang & Lages, 2011).

7. FUTURE RESEARCH DIRECTIONS

How the visual system establishes binocular 3D motion perception from image-based local motion and disparity input remains a difficult and unresolved issue. It is hoped, however, that the present line of research improves understanding of local constraints in binocular 3D motion perception. The results should be of interest to researchers in computer vision, neuroscience, and psychology and may inform developments of 3D technology in applied areas.

Our results suggest that a geometric-statistical approach as exemplified by the Bayesian models provides a powerful framework to model binocular 3D motion perception. However, more empirical data are needed to evaluate perceived 3D trajectories and systematic distortions. More specifically, in order to validate the Bayesian approach it would be important to verify the motion prior for slow motion through real-world measurements of scene flow as well as experimental data from discrimination tasks adapted to binocular 3D motion. Note that due to environmental constraints the motion prior may not be isotropic and Gaussian. There is empirical evidence that the motion prior in 2D velocity space has heavier tails than a Gaussian (Stocker & Simoncelli, 2006). Also, if experience shapes the motion prior it may not only reflect slow motion but also horizontal motion along a ground plane and possibly downward motion aligned with the pull of gravity. As a consequence, the motion prior may not be entirely isotropic. On the other hand, any of these effects is likely to depend on multisensory integration and top-down processing, mainly affecting global object rather than local motion perception (Lages, Jenkins & Hillis, 2008).

We have only considered translation in 3D space but a moving line or edge may also change orientation over time. It is immediately clear that the present approach, which relies on translational motion, has a difficulty with encoding rotational movement of a stimulus. It seems likely that encoding of rotation of a local line stimulus requires tracking of features together with frequent updates of binocular depth, whereas translational motion is the result of instantaneous spatio-temporal encoding by local motion filters. According to recent neuroscientific evidence (Ponce et al. 2008; Rokers, et al., 2009) local input from motion and disparity processing is integrated late and disparity of features may be used to disambiguate velocity constraints. It seems possible that integration of velocity constraints and features in depth follows a characteristic time course similar to 2D motion perception (Osborn et al., 2004; Treue, Hol & Rauber, 2000; Montagnini et al., 2007).

8. CONCLUSION

Bayesian models of binocular motion perception for dots or local features moving on a horizontal depth plane (Lages, 2006) can be extended to 3D motion perception of lines or edges, predicting perceived azimuth and elevation under ambiguity (Lages & Heron, 2010; Heron & Lages, 2009).

Using a generalized Bayesian motion model (Lages & Heron, 2009; Wang & Lages, 2011), noisy velocity constraint planes define velocity likelihoods that, combined with a 3D motion prior, can explain perceptual bias under uncertainty and motion perception under ambiguity. It is suggested that the visual system integrates velocity constraints with feature tracking from disparity processing to arrive at velocity estimates of moving features and objects.

REFERENCES

Adelson, E. H., & Movshon, J. A. (1982). Phenomenal coherence of moving visual patterns. *Nature*, *300*, 523–525. doi:10.1038/300523a0

Anzai, A., Ohzawa, I., & Freeman, R. D. (2001). Joint encoding of motion and depth by visual cortical neurons: Neural basis of the Pulfrich effect. *Nature Reviews. Neuroscience*, *4*, 513–518.

Ascher, D., & Grzywacz, N. N. (2000). A Bayesian model for the measurement of visual velocity. *Vision Research*, *40*(24), 3427–3434. doi:10.1016/S0042-6989(00)00176-0

Banks, M. S., & Backus, B. T. (1998). Extra-retinal and perspective cues cause the small range of the induced effect. *Vision Research*, *38*, 187–194. doi:10.1016/S0042-6989(97)00179-X

Berkeley, G. (1975). *Philosophical works; Including the works on vision* (Ayers, M., Ed.). London, UK: Dent. (Original work published 1709)

Beverley, K. I., & Regan, D. (1973). Evidence for the existence of neural mechanisms selectively sensitive to the direction of movement in space. *The Journal of Physiology*, *235*, 17–29.

Beverley, K. I., & Regan, D. (1974). Temporal integration of disparity information in stereoscopic perception. *Experimental Brain Research*, *19*, 228–232. doi:10.1007/BF00238537

Beverley, K. I., & Regan, D. (1975). The relation between discrimination and sensitivity in the perception of motion in depth. *The Journal of Physiology*, *249*, 387–398.

Braddick, O. J. (1974). A short-range process in apparent motion. *Vision Research*, *14*, 519–527. doi:10.1016/0042-6989(74)90041-8

Braddick, O. J. (1980). Low-level and high-level processes in apparent motion. *Philosophical Transactions of the Royal Society of London*, *290B*, 137–151. doi:10.1098/rstb.1980.0087

Bradley, D. C., Qian, N., & Andersen, R. A. (1995). Integration of motion and stereopsis in middle temporal cortical area of macaques. *Nature*, *373*, 609–611. doi:10.1038/373609a0

Bradshaw, M. F., & Cumming, B. G. (1997). The direction of retinal motion facilitates binocular stereopsis. *Proceedings. Biological Sciences*, *264*, 1421–1427. doi:10.1098/rspb.1997.0198

Brooks, K. R. (2002). Interocular velocity difference contributes to stereomotion speed perception. *Journal of Vision (Charlottesville, Va.)*, *2*, 218–231. doi:10.1167/2.3.2

Brooks, K. R., & Stone, L. S. (2004). Stereomotion speed perception: Contributions from both changing disparity and interocular velocity difference over a range of relative disparities. *Journal of Vision (Charlottesville, Va.)*, *4*, 1061–1079. doi:10.1167/4.12.6

Bruhn, A., Weickert, J., & Schnörr, C. (2005). Lucas/Kanade meets Horn/Schunck: Combining local and global optic flow methods. *International Journal of Computer Vision*, *61*(3), 211–231. doi:10.1023/B:VISI.0000045324.43199.43

Carceroni, R. L., & Kutulakos, K. N. (2002). Multi-view scene capture by surfel sampling: From video streams to non-rigid 3D motion, shape and reflectance. *International Journal of Computer Vision*, *49*(2), 175–214. doi:10.1023/A:1020145606604

Carney, T., Paradiso, M. A., & Freeman, R. D. (1989). A physiological correlate of the Pulfrich effect in cortical neurons of the cat. *Vision Research, 29*, 155–165. doi:10.1016/0042-6989(89)90121-1

Cumming, B. G., & Parker, A. J. (1994). Binocular mechanisms for detecting motion in depth. *Vision Research, 34*, 483–495. doi:10.1016/0042-6989(94)90162-7

DeAngelis, G. C., & Newsome, W. T. (1999). Organization of disparity-selective neurons in macaque area MT. *The Journal of Neuroscience, 19*, 1398–1415.

DeAngelis, G. C., & Newsome, W. T. (2004). Perceptual "read-out" of conjoined direction and disparity maps in extrastriate area MT. *PLoS Biology, 2*, e0394. doi:10.1371/journal.pbio.0020077

DeAngelis, G. C., Ohzawa, I., & Freeman, R. D. (1993). Spatiotemporal organization of simple-cell receptive fields in the cat's striate cortex. 1. General characteristics and postnatal development. *Journal of Neurophysiology, 69*, 1091–1117.

Decartes, R. (1633/1664). *Traité de l'Homme (De Homine, 1662).*

Edwards, M., & Schor, C. M. (1999). Depth aliasing by the transient stereo-system. *Vision Research, 39*, 4333–4340. doi:10.1016/S0042-6989(99)00149-2

Faugeras, O. D. (1992). What can be seen in three dimensions with an uncalibrated stereo rig? In *Proceedings of ECCV 1992*, (pp. 563-578).

Fernandez, J. M., & Farell, B. (2005). Seeing motion-in-depth using inter-ocular velocity differences. *Vision Research, 45*, 2786–2798. doi:10.1016/j.visres.2005.05.021

Graf, E. W., Adams, W. J., & Lages, M. (2004). Prior monocular information can bias motion perception. *Journal of Vision (Charlottesville, Va.), 4*, 427–433. doi:10.1167/4.6.2

Greenwald, H. S., & Knill, D. C. (2009). Orientation disparity: A cue for 3D orientation. *Neural Computation, 21*, 2581–2604. doi:10.1162/neco.2009.08-08-848

Hansard, M., & Haroud, R. (2008). Cyclopean geometry of binocular vision. *Journal of the Optical Society of America. A, Optics, Image Science, and Vision, 25*(9), 2357–2369. doi:10.1364/JOSAA.25.002357

Harris, J. M. (2006). The interaction of eye movements and retinal signals during the perception of 3-D motion direction. *Journal of Vision (Charlottesville, Va.), 6*, 777–790. doi:10.1167/6.8.2

Harris, J. M., & Dean, P. J. A. (2003). Accuracy and precision of binocular 3-D motion perception. *Journal of Experimental Psychology: HPP, 29*(5), 869–881. doi:10.1037/0096-1523.29.5.869

Harris, J. M., & Drga, V. F. (2005). Using visual direction in three-dimensional motion perception. *Nature Reviews. Neuroscience, 8*, 229–233. doi:10.1038/nn1389

Harris, J. M., Nefs, H. T., & Grafton, C. E. (2008). Binocular vision and motion-in-depth. *Spatial Vision, 21*, 531–547. doi:10.1163/156856808786451462

Harris, J. M., & Rushton, S. K. (2003). Poor visibility of motion-in-depth is due to early motion averaging. *Vision Research, 43*, 385–392. doi:10.1016/S0042-6989(02)00570-9

Hartley, R., & Zisserman, A. (2004). *Multiple view geometry in computer vision* (2nd ed.). Cambridge University Press. doi:10.1017/CBO9780511811685

Heron, S., & Lages, M. (2009). Measuring azimuth and elevation of binocular 3D motion direction. *Journal of Vision (Charlottesville, Va.), 9*(8), 637a. doi:10.1167/9.8.637

Hildreth, E. C. (1984). The computation of the velocity field. *Proceedings of the Royal Society of London. Series B, Biological Sciences*, *221*, 189–220. doi:10.1098/rspb.1984.0030

Hinkle, D. A., & Connor, C. E. (2002). Three-dimensional orientation tuning in macaque area V4. *Nature Reviews. Neuroscience*, *5*, 665–670. doi:10.1038/nn875

Hogervorst, M. A., & Eagle, R. A. (1998). Biases in three-dimensional structure-from-motion arise from noise in the early visual system. *Proceedings. Biological Sciences*, *265*, 1587–1593. doi:10.1098/rspb.1998.0476

Horn, B. K. P., & Schunck, B. G. (1981). Determining optical flow. *Artificial. Intelligence*, *17*, 185–203.

Howard, I. P., & Rogers, B. J. (2002). Seeing in depth: *Vol. 2. Depth perception*. Ontario, Canada: I. Porteous.

Hubel, D. H., & Wiesel, T. N. (1962). Receptive fields, binocular interaction and functional architecture in the cat's visual cortex. *The Journal of Physiology*, *160*, 106–154.

Hubel, D. H., & Wiesel, T. N. (1968). Receptive fields and functional architecture of monkey striate cortex. *The Journal of Physiology*, *195*, 215–243.

Hubel, D. H., & Wiesel, T. N. (1970). Stereoscopic vision in macaque monkey. Cells sensitive to binocular depth in area 18 of the macaque monkey cortex. *Nature*, *225*, 41–42. doi:10.1038/225041a0

Hürlimann, F., Kiper, D. C., & Carandini, M. (2002). Testing the Bayesian model of perceived speed. *Vision Research*, *42*, 2253–2257. doi:10.1016/S0042-6989(02)00119-0

Ji, H., & Fermüller, C. (2006). Noise causes slant underestimation in stereo and motion. *Vision Research*, *46*, 3105–3120. doi:10.1016/j.visres.2006.04.010

Johnstone, A., McOwan, P. W., & Benton, C. (1999). Robust velocity computation from a biologically motivated model of motion perception. *Proceedings. Biological Sciences*, *266*, 509–518. doi:10.1098/rspb.1999.0666

Julesz, B. (1971). *Foundations of Cyclopean perception*. Chicago, IL: University of Chicago Press.

Knill, D. C., Kersten, D., & Yuille, A. L. (1996). Introduction: A Bayesian formulation of visual perception. In Knill, D. C., & Richards, W. (Eds.), *Perception as Bayesian inference*. Cambridge, UK: Cambridge University Press. doi:10.1017/CBO9780511984037.009

Knill, D. C., & Richards, W. (1996). *Perception as Bayesian inference*. Cambridge, UK: Cambridge University Press. doi:10.1017/CBO9780511984037

Koenderink, J. J., & van Doorn, A. J. (1991). Affine structure from motion. *Journal of the Optical Society of America*, *8*, 377–385. doi:10.1364/JOSAA.8.000377

Lages, M. (2006). Bayesian models of binocular 3-D motion perception. *Journal of Vision (Charlottesville, Va.)*, *6*(4), 508–522. doi:10.1167/6.4.14

Lages, M., Dolia, A., & Graf, E. W. (2007). Dichoptic motion perception limited to depth of fixation? *Vision Research*, *47*, 244–252. doi:10.1016/j.visres.2006.10.001

Lages, M., & Heron, S. (2008). Motion and disparity processing informs Bayesian 3D motion estimation. *Proceedings of the National Academy of Sciences of the United States of America*, *105*, E117. doi:10.1073/pnas.0809829105

Lages, M., & Heron, S. (2009). Testing generalized models of binocular 3D motion perception. *Journal of Vision (Charlottesville, Va.)*, *9*, 636a. doi:10.1167/9.8.636

Lages, M., & Heron, S. (2010). On the inverse problem of local binocular 3D motion perception. *PLoS Computational Biology*, *6*(11), e1000999. doi:10.1371/journal.pcbi.1000999

Lages, M., Jenkins, R., & Hillis, J. M. (2008). Anticipation of gravity alters perception of average speed. *Perception*, *37*(Supplement), 28.

Lages, M., Mamassian, P., & Graf, E. W. (2003). Spatial and temporal tuning of motion in depth. *Vision Research*, *43*(27), 2861–2873. doi:10.1016/j.visres.2003.08.006

Ledgeway, T., & Smith, A. T. (1994). Evidence for separate motion-detecting mechanisms for first-order and 2nd-order motion in human vision. *Vision Research*, *34*, 2727–2740. doi:10.1016/0042-6989(94)90229-1

Likova, L. T., & Tyler, C. W. (2007). Stereomotion processing in the human occipital cortex. *NeuroImage*, *38*, 293–305. doi:10.1016/j.neuroimage.2007.06.039

Lu, Z.-L., & Sperling, G. (1995). The functional architecture of human visual motion perception. *Vision Research*, *35*, 2697–2722. doi:10.1016/0042-6989(95)00025-U

Lu, Z.-L., & Sperling, G. (2001). Three systems theory of human visual motion perception: Review and update. *Journal of the Optical Society of America. A, Optics, Image Science, and Vision*, *18*, 2331–2370. doi:10.1364/JOSAA.18.002331

Lucas, B. D., & Kanade, T. (1981). An iterative image registration technique with an application to stereo vision. *DARPA Image Understanding Workshop*, (pp. 121–130).

Majaj, N., Carandini, M., & Movshon, J. A. (2007). Motion integration by neurons in macaque MT is local not global. *The Journal of Neuroscience*, *27*, 366–370. doi:10.1523/JNEUROSCI.3183-06.2007

Marr, D. (1982). *Vision*. New York, NY: W.H. Freeman & Co.

Masson, G. S., & Castet, E. (2002). Parallel motion processing for the intiation of short-latency ocular following in humans. *The Journal of Neuroscience*, *22*, 5149–5163.

Maunsell, J. H., & van Essen, D. C. (1983). Functional properties of neurons in middle temporal visual area of the macaque monkey, part I- Selectivity for stimulus direction, speed, and orientation. *Journal of Neurophysiology*, *49*, 1127–1147.

Mayhew, J. E. W., & Longuet-Higgins, H. C. (1982). A computational model of binocular depth perception. *Nature*, *297*, 376–378. doi:10.1038/297376a0

Miles, F. A. (1998). The neural processing of 3-D visual information: Evidence from eye movements. *The European Journal of Neuroscience*, *10*, 811–822. doi:10.1046/j.1460-9568.1998.00112.x

Min, D., & Sohn, K. (2006). Edge-preserving simultaneous joint motion-disparity estimation. *Proceedings of the 18th International Conference on Pattern Recognition* (ICPR'06) Vol. 2, (pp. 74-77).

Montagnini, A., Mamassian, P., Perrinet, L., Castet, E., & Masson, G. S. (2007)... *The Journal of Physiology*, *101*, 64–77.

Morgan, M. J., & Castet, E. (1997). The aperture problem in stereopsis. *Vision Research*, *37*, 2737–2744. doi:10.1016/S0042-6989(97)00074-6

Morgan, M. J., & Fahle, M. (2000). Motion-stereo mechanisms sensitive to interocular phase. *Vision Research, 40*, 1667–1675. doi:10.1016/S0042-6989(00)00016-X

Ogle, K. N. (1940). Induced size effect with the eyes in asymmetric convergence. *Archives of Ophthalmology, 23*, 1023–1028. doi:10.1001/archopht.1940.00860131147008

Ohzawa, I., DeAngelis, G. C., & Freeman, R. D. (1990). Stereoscopic depth discrimination in the visual cortex: Neurons ideally suited as disparity detectors. *Science, 249*, 1037–1041. doi:10.1126/science.2396096

Orban, G. A. (2008). Higher order visual processing in macaque extrastriate cortex. *Physiological Reviews, 88*, 59–89. doi:10.1152/physrev.00008.2007

Osborne, L. C., Bialek, W., & Lisberger, S. G. (2004). Time course of information about motion direction in visual area MT of macaque monkeys. *The Journal of Neuroscience, 24*(13), 3210–3222. doi:10.1523/JNEUROSCI.5305-03.2004

Pack, C. C., Born, R. T., & Livingstone, M. S. (2003). Two-dimensional substructure of stereo and motion interactions in macaque visual cortex. *Neuron, 37*, 525–535. doi:10.1016/S0896-6273(02)01187-X

Peng, Q., & Shi, B. E. (2010). The changing disparity energy model. *Vision Research, 50*, 181–192. doi:10.1016/j.visres.2009.11.012

Pizlo, Z. (2001). Perception viewed as an inverse problem. *Vision Research, 41*, 3145–3161. doi:10.1016/S0042-6989(01)00173-0

Poggio, T., Torre, V., & Koch, C. (1985). Computational vision and regularization theory. *Nature, 317*, 314–319. doi:10.1038/317314a0

Ponce, C. R., Lomber, S. G., & Born, R. T. (2008). Integrating motion and depth via parallel pathways. *Nature Reviews. Neuroscience, 11*, 216–223. doi:10.1038/nn2039

Portfors-Yeomans, C. V., & Regan, D. (1996). Cyclopean discrimination thresholds for the direction and speed of motion in depth. *Vision Research, 36*, 3265–3279. doi:10.1016/0042-6989(96)00065-X

Qian, N. (1994). Computing stereo disparity and motion with known binocular cell properties. *Neural Computation, 6*, 390–404. doi:10.1162/neco.1994.6.3.390

Qian, N., & Andersen, R. A. (1997). A physiological model for motion-stereo integration and a uni□ed explanation of Pulfrich-like phenomena. *Vision Research, 37*, 1683–1698. doi:10.1016/S0042-6989(96)00164-2

Raftery, A. E. (1995). Baysian model selection in social research. *Sociological Methodology, 25*, 111–163. doi:10.2307/271063

Rashbass, C., & Westheimer, G. (1961). Disjunctive eye movements. *The Journal of Physiology, 159*, 339–360.

Read, J. C. A. (2002a). A Bayesian approach to the stereo correspondence problem. *Neural Computation, 14*, 1371–1392. doi:10.1162/089976602753712981

Read, J. C. A. (2002b). A Bayesian model of stereopsis depth and motion direction discrimination. *Biological Cybernetics, 86*(2), 117–136. doi:10.1007/s004220100280

Read, J. C. A., & Cumming, B. G. (2005a). Effect of interocular delay on disparity-selective V1 neurons: Relationship to stereoacuity and the Pulfrich effect. *Journal of Neurophysics, 94*, 1541–1553. doi:10.1152/jn.01177.2004

Read, J. C. A., & Cumming, B. G. (2005b). The stroboscopic Pulfrich effect is not evidence for the joint encoding of motion and depth. *Journal of Vision (Charlottesville, Va.), 5*, 417–434. doi:10.1167/5.5.3

Regan, D., & Beverley, K. I. (1973). Some dynamic features of depth perception. *Vision Research, 13*, 2369–2379. doi:10.1016/0042-6989(73)90236-8

Regan, D., Beverley, K. I., Cynader, M., & Lennie, P. (1979). Stereoscopic subsystems for position in depth and for motion in depth. *Proceedings of the Royal Society of London. Series B, Biological Sciences, 42*, 485–501. doi:10.1098/rspb.1979.0042

Regan, D., & Gray, R. (2009). Binocular processing of motion: Some unresolved problems. *Spatial Vision, 22*, 1–43. doi:10.1163/156856809786618501

Rokers, B., Cormack, L. K., & Huk, A. C. (2008). Strong percepts of motion through depth without strong percepts of position in depth. *Journal of Vision (Charlottesville, Va.), 8*, 1–10. doi:10.1167/8.4.6

Rokers, B., Cormack, L. K., & Huk, A. C. (2009). Disparity- and velocity-based signals for three-dimensional motion perception in human MT+. *Nature Reviews. Neuroscience, 12*, 1050–1055. doi:10.1038/nn.2343

Rushton, S. K., & Duke, P. A. (2007). The use of direction and distance information in the perception of approach trajectory. *Vision Research, 47*, 899–912. doi:10.1016/j.visres.2006.11.019

Rushton, S. K., & Warren, P. A. (2005). Moving observers, relative retinal motion, and the detection of object movement. *Current Biology, 15*(14), R542. doi:10.1016/j.cub.2005.07.020

Scharr, H., & Küsters, R. (2002). A linear model for simultaneous estimation of 3D motion and depth. *IEEE Workshop on Motion and Video Computing*, Orlando FL, (pp. 1-6).

Shimojo, S., Silverman, G., & Nakayama, K. (1989). Occlusion and the solution to the aperture problem for motion. *Vision Research, 29*, 619–626. doi:10.1016/0042-6989(89)90047-3

Shioiri, S., Saisho, H., & Yaguchi, H. (2000). Motion in depth based on inter-ocular velocity differences. *Vision Research, 40*, 2565–2572. doi:10.1016/S0042-6989(00)00130-9

Spies, H., Jähne, B. J., & Barron, J.L. (2002). Range flow estimation. *Computer Vision Image Understanding (CVIU2002), 85*, 209-231.

Stocker, A. A., & Simoncelli, E. P. (2006). Noise characteristics and prior expectations in human visual speed perception. *Nature Neuroscience, 9*(4), 578–585. doi:10.1038/nn1669

Sung, K., Wojtach, W. T., & Purves, D. (2009). An empirical explanation of aperture effects. *Proceedings of the National Academy of Sciences of the United States of America, 106*, 298–303. doi:10.1073/pnas.0811702106

Thomas, O. M., Cumming, B. G., & Parker, A. J. (2002). A specialization for relative disparity in V2. *Nature Reviews. Neuroscience, 5*, 472–478. doi:10.1038/nn837

Treue, S., Hol, K., & Rauber, H. J. (2000). Seeing multiple directions of motion – Physiology and psychophysics. *Nature Neuroscience, 3*, 270–276. doi:10.1038/72985

Tyler, C. W. (1971). Stereoscopic depth movement: Two eyes less sensitive than one. *Science, 174*, 958–961. doi:10.1126/science.174.4012.958

Ullman, S., & Yuille, A. (1989). Rigidity and smoothness of motion. In Ullman, S., & Richards, W. (Eds.), *Image understanding*. Norwood, NJ: Ablex Publishing Corporation.

van Ee, R., & Anderson, B. L. (2001). Motion direction, speed and orientation in binocular matching. *Nature, 410*, 690–694. doi:10.1038/35070569

van Ee, R., & Schor, C. M. (2000). Unconstrained stereoscopic matching of lines. *Vision Research, 40*, 151–162. doi:10.1016/S0042-6989(99)00174-1

Vedula, S., Baker, S., Rander, P., Collins, R., & Kanade, T. (2005). Three-dimensional scene-flow. *IEEE Transactions on Pattern Analysis and Machine Intelligence*, 475–480. doi:10.1109/TPAMI.2005.63

von Helmholtz, H. (1962). In Southall, J. P. (Ed.), *Helmholtz's treatise on physiological optics* (*Vol. 1*, pp. 312–313). New York, NY: Dover. (Original work published 1910)

Wallach, H. (1935). Über visuell wahrgenommene Bewegungsrichtung. *Psychologische Forschung*, *20*, 325–380. doi:10.1007/BF02409790

Wang, H., & Lages, M. (2011). *A biologically-inspired Bayesian model of 3D velocity estimation.* AVA Meeting, Cardiff.

Watt, S. J., Akeley, K., & Banks, M. S. (2005). Focus cues affect perceived depth. *Journal of Vision (Charlottesville, Va.)*, *5*(10), 834–862. doi:10.1167/5.10.7

Weiss, Y., & Fleet, D. J. (2001). Probabilistic models of the brain: perception and neural function. In Rao, R. P. N., Olshausen, B., & Lewicki, M. S. (Eds.), *Velocity likelihoods in biological and machine vision* (pp. 81–100). Cambridge, MA: MIT Press.

Weiss, Y., Simoncelli, E. P., & Adelson, E. H. (2002). Motion illusions as optimal percepts. *Nature Reviews. Neuroscience*, *5*, 598–604. doi:10.1038/nn0602-858

Welchman, A. E., Lam, J. M., & Bülthoff, H. H. (2008). Bayesian motion estimation accounts for a surprising bias in 3D vision. *Proceedings of the National Academy of Sciences of the United States of America*, *105*, 12087–12092. doi:10.1073/pnas.0804378105

Welchman, A. E., Tuck, V. L., & Harris, J. M. (2004). Human observers are biased in judging the angular approach of a projectile. *Vision Research*, *44*, 2027–2042. doi:10.1016/j.visres.2004.03.014

Wilson, H. R., Ferrera, V. P., & Yo, C. (1992). A psychophysically motivated model for two-dimensional motion perception. *Visual Neuroscience*, *9*(1), 79–97. doi:10.1017/S0952523800006386

Chapter 6
Modeling Binocular and Motion Transparency Processing by Local Center-Surround Interactions

Florian Raudies
Boston University, USA & Center of Excellence for Learning in Education, Science, and Technology (CELEST), USA & Center for Computational Neuroscience and Neural Technology (CompNet), USA

Heiko Neumann
Institute of Neural Information Processing, University of Ulm, Germany

ABSTRACT

Binocular transparency is perceived if two surfaces are seen in the same spatial location, but at different depths. Similarly, motion transparency occurs if two surfaces move differently over the same spatial location. Most models of motion or stereo processing incorporate uniqueness assumptions to resolve ambiguities of disparity or motion estimates and, thus, can not represent multiple features at the same spatial location. Unlike these previous models, the authors of this chapter suggest a model with local center-surround interaction that operates upon analogs of cell populations in velocity or disparity domain of the ventral second visual area (V2) and dorsal medial middle temporal area (MT) in primates, respectively. These modeled cell populations can encode motion and binocular transparency. Model simulations demonstrate the successful processing of scenes with opaque and transparent materials, not previously reported. Results suggest that motion and stereo processing both employ local center-surround interactions to resolve noisy and ambiguous disparity or motion input from initial correlations.

DOI: 10.4018/978-1-4666-2539-6.ch006

INTRODUCTION

In real world situations transparency and semi-transparency often occur as likely as opaque surfaces in different depths or moving differently. For instance, reflections in the window of a driving vehicle overlay with the background outside the car. Driving with a dirty windshield, where the dust on the windshield is moving independently from the outside world creates two layers of independent motion in the same region of the visual field. Also, semi-transparency occurs, for instance, when viewing crowds of people moving in stripes of opposite directions from an elevated position. Here, by spatial and temporal integration of motion signals in the visual system, two motions are perceived at the same spatial locations of the visual field.

Although transparency and semi-transparency configurations occur in real-world situations common models of stereo and motion processing typically do not support the processing of transparent surfaces. Instead, these models assume the existence of a single computational solution generating a single depth representation or motion quantity for each spatial location. Thus, the majority of neural models do not successfully explain the processing of transparent and opaque surfaces. This motivated the development of a new generalized model for binocular and motion transparency processing using essentially the same computational mechanisms operating upon different feature domains. These proposed mechanisms and their representations are inspired by recent reports of neural populations in different visual areas and their selectivity to orientation, spatial frequency, disparity, and visual motion. These neural populations can encode multiple stimulus disparities or motions (Treue et al., 2000). Our objectives for the newly proposed model are several fold. First, we suggest that the perception of transparent (as well as opaque) motion and stereo stimuli can be explained by the same mechanism of local center-surround interaction. Second, the suggested mechanisms of our model architecture are in accordance with the general physiology on disparity and motion processing and show coinciding tuning properties of the model's population with recorded data. Finally, the model is probed with realistic image sequences and results demonstrate its successful application for computational vision.

Our modeling effort is inspired by the functions and representations of various brain areas that mainly contribute to visual processing. For example, in the primary visual area (V1) simple cells are selective to the high-low and low-high intensity edges and complex cells are sensitive to oriented edges independent of the local contrast polarity (Hubel & Wiesel, 1962). The results of further investigations lead to a refinement of models by describing motion and disparity selectivity in primary visual cortex based in specific filtering mechanisms, such as, e.g., Gabor functions (Priebe et al., 2006; Prince et al., 2002; Ringach, 2002; Cumming & Parker, 1999). These Gabor functions characterize the selectivity of neurons by spatial frequencies, size, orientation, and temporal frequency. This selectivity forms the initial feature representation in the primary visual area upon which motion and disparity processing mechanisms – among others – can operate. The secondary visual area (V2) is known to encode binocular disparity (Hubel & Wiesel, 1970; Hubel & Livingstone, 1987; Thomas et al., 2002). The middle temporal area (MT) can be seen as major stage for integration and segregation of visual image motion, but also encodes binocular disparity (Rodman & Albright, 1987; Born & Bradley, 2005; Bradley et al., 1995; Maunsell & Van Essen, 1983; Nover et al., 2005; Treue & Andersen, 1996). Taken together, these evidences inspired the development of a biologically plausible model for the processing of binocular and motion transparency presented below.

BACKGROUND

Perception and Neurophysiology of Binocular and Motion Transparency

The conditions under which binocular and motion transparency occur have been extensively studied in psychophysics and neurophysiology. For instance, the number of planes in random dot stereograms (RDS) at different depths that could be perceived in parallel is reported to vary between three and six (Tsirlin et al., 2008; Reeves et al., 2010). A closer look into the arrangement of planes at different distances (measured in visual degrees) shows that for values below approximately three min arc the distance is underestimated, above three min arc the distance is overestimated for a wide range of angular separations (Stevenson et al., 1991). This deflection between estimated and veridical distance is known as the effect of attraction and repulsion in perception.

The processing of motion transparency shares several properties with that of binocular transparency. For instance, the angular difference between two motion components in a random dot kinematogram (RDK) is perceived as smaller when directions differ less than 25° (motion direction attraction). When directions differ by more than 40° the difference is perceived as larger (motion direction repulsion). Veridical motion is perceived when motion directions differ by more than 135° (Edwards & Nishida, 1999; Braddick et al., 2002). Two components of line gratings with different speed can be perceived as transparently overlaid (Meso & Zanker, 2009). Two to three motions of different direction in RDKs can be perceived as transparently overlaid (Mulligan, 1992; Felisberti & Zanker, 2005; Greenwood & Edwards, 2009). Neural responses for RDKs with two motion components of different angle have a single peak for small angular differences and multiple peaks for angles above ~60° (Treue et al., 2000). Cells in the primary visual cortex (area V1) can represent more than one motion direction, e.g. by using different subpopulations. Cells in middle temporal area (MT) strongly respond to the preferred motion direction and weakly to the anti-preferred motion direction, although both directions are equally present in the stimulus RDK (Snowden et al. 1991). In sum, these findings provide hints about the underlying neural representations and mechanism employed in motion and stereo perception. Furthermore, these findings suggest that the occurrence of binocular and motion transparency is based on similar neural mechanisms to achieve the similar effect of attraction and repulsion.

Methods for Binocular and Motion (Transparency) Processing

Methods of binocular or motion transparency processing have to solve three intertwined problems: the spatial and temporal integration, the segregation, and the clustering of different stimulus components into, e.g., separate depth planes or motions. Visual motion signals have to be spatio-temporally integrated. Binocular stereo signals are spatially integrated and can profit from a temporal integration as well. But while integrating components, those originating from different objects in depth or with different motions have to remain separate. For instance, two planes, one transparent and leftward moving at close distance, another opaque and rightward moving at far distance, have to be kept segregated while integrating their belonging motion and depth signals. Otherwise the overall motion would be zero, assuming the same motion speed for both planes, and the extracted depth would be the mean of near and far, assuming a 50% transparency for the near plane. In contrast to the segregation, the clustering refers to the estimation of the number of components, e.g. that two motions exist in the above example. In general, the estimate of surface properties from noisy and ambiguous input profits from a uniqueness constraint implementing the assumption about a single component in one spatial location. However, transparency requires the detection and representation of multiple components which contradicts the uniqueness assumption.

In the binocular stereo domain the correspondence problem has to be solved, that is the identification and matching of the same point location between left and right eye's image. An early model for matching is the disparity energy model, which was inspired by the complex cell responses in cat's visual cortex (Ohzawa et al., 1990). Disparity energy is detected by four simple cells, two for each dominant eye input, whereas the two cells receiving input from one eye have a 90° phase difference. Responses of single cells are modeled by Gabor filtering of the input image of a stereo pair. Responses of the same phase are summed and squared for both phase signals. Finally, the two squared signals for the different phases are summed and the square root is taken. These computational steps define the neural model circuit of a disparity detector. Note that this circuit is the same that has been used for the motion energy detector (Adelson & Bergen, 1985). The disparity detector used together with a phase-mechanism, varying the phase for the left and right eye's image, allows the computation of likelihood maps for different disparity values[1] (Qian, 1994). Due to the constraints set by the sampling theorem (Nyquist, 2002) phase-shift based disparity detectors are always limited to $\pm\lambda/2$ with λ denoting the wavelength of the Gabor filter. Thus, the detection of large disparities requires Gabor filters with large wavelengths and large standard deviation. Subsequently, their detection works only on a low spatial resolution. To overcome this limitation, a phase-shift mechanism can be combined with a position-shift mechanism (Chen & Qian, 2004). In principle, the disparity detector approach can detect multiple point-correspondences for a single spatial location and, thus, potentially support binocular transparency.

Besides the methods proposed for initial correspondence finding, different schemes of interaction between disparities and neighboring spatial locations have been proposed. The cooperative competitive scheme of Marr & Poggio enforces uniqueness for all possible point matches, namely the disparities at one location, and assumes a continuity constraint to support similar disparity values at spatially adjacent locations (Marr & Poggio, 1976). Both rules, uniqueness and continuity, are embedded in an iterative scheme of local competitive-cooperative interactions between nodes whose activities represent the likelihood of a match of neighboring locations and different disparities at one location. A balance between the forces generated by these two rules is achieved after a few iterations. However, the uniqueness constraint is criticized for not supporting multiple matches at a single location, namely to allow the representation of binocular transparency (Weinshall, 1989). Another scheme of interaction that relaxes the uniqueness constraint was suggested by Prazdny (1985). This interaction uses a Gaussian function with the disparity distance divided by the distance of the referring pixel locations as argument (see Equation 1 in Prazdny, 1985). For a fixed disparity difference this leads to increased support if the reference locations are farther apart. In general this relaxed interaction scheme allows the representation of multiple activations at the same location or binocular transparency. A network trained with a modified back-prop learning rule based on sparse compatibility maps (the correspondences of locations with an intensity value of one in the RDS) was able to infer the uniqueness and continuity constraints (Qian & Sejnowski, 1989). The trained network showed reasonable results also for sparse transparency stimuli. Furthermore, Pollard and Frisby demonstrated that RDSs with binocular transparency can be successfully processed by using a competitive scheme that includes a uniqueness constraint (Pollard & Frisby, 1990). *How could uniqueness rule out transparency and still give reasonable results for RDSs including transparency?* For Pollard and Frisby's simulations only the pooled response over all image rows was reported, essentially leaving open if multiple correspondences for single locations were existent. In order to account for the perceptual performance of humans it remains which spatial resolution or pooling size is required to distinguish between semi-transparency and transparency in the stereo or motion domain.

Another form of interaction is defined by a coarse-to-fine scheme which includes the detection of disparity shifts or visual motions at multiple spatial resolutions. One possible incorporation of a coarse-to-fine scheme into a phase-shift and position-shift based model is the estimation of phase-shifts at each scale, whereas the estimate from the coarsest scale is propagated to finer scales by using the position-shift mechanism (Chen & Qian, 2004). The disparity energy model with a phase-shift mechanism for multiple spatial resolutions along with a template matching for read-out can account for binocular transparency (Tsai & Victor, 2003; Watanabe, 2008).

Similar to the approaches in the stereo domain, motion models use different detectors for the initial estimation of motion signals and similar interaction schemes for the spatio-temporal integration. Initial motion is detected by the Hassenstein-Reichardt detectors (Hassenstein and Reichardt, 1956), motion energy filters (Adelson and Bergen, 1985), also applied in the frequency domain (Heeger, 1987), or multi-channel gradients (Johnston et al., 1999). Furthermore, motion transparency processing has been analyzed for the Hassenstein-Reichardt detector (Zanker, 2005), motion energy filtering (Qian et al., 1994; Simoncelli and Heeger, 1998, Watanabe and Kikuchi, 2005), and multi-channel gradients (Durant et al., 2006). A simple interaction scheme is the pooling of initial motion signals over the entire visual space (Zanker, 2005; Durant et al., 2006), while advanced schemes use competitive mechanisms between opponent motion-directions (Qian et al., 1994b) or cross-talk between segregated responses attached to stimulus parts / motions (Watanabe and Kikuchi, 2005). This shows the remarkable similarity between models of binocular stereo and motion processing, using comparable detectors and schemes of interaction for spatio-temporal integration.

Computer vision algorithms segregate motions using parametric motion models that are simultaneously fitted to the data in space. These models are spatially and piecewise fitted to deformations and motions of the incoming image sequence (Darrell and Pentland, 1991; Langley et al., 1992; Darrell and Simoncelli, 1993; Black and Anandan, 1993, 1996; Ju et al., 1996), multiple motion models are fitted to the image sequence by using variational approaches (Ramirez-Manzanares et al., 2006), or a set of spatio-temporal filters is applied to extract two motions for each pixel (Liu et al., 1995). Integration in the visual field is achieved by incorporating spatio-temporal smoothness constraints which assume that no strong changes in motions occur at nearby spatial locations through time (Horn and Schunk, 1981). To cluster motions *n*th-order derivatives are combined (Langley et al., 1992) by utilizing a generalized structure tensor defined as the covariance of spatio-temporal derivatives of the same order. The rank of this tensor matrix determines the number of motions (Mota et al., 2004).

In sum, we conclude that still there does not exist a coherent model that deals with motion and stereoscopic input data from (semi-) transparent as well as opaque surface configurations that can be processed in a coherent architecture of visual processing. Here, we propose common mechanisms for stereo and motion processing defined on the basis of findings about the structure and function of the primate visual system. In the next paragraphs we develop these common mechanisms for the detection and integration of binocular stereo and motion signals, starting with an overview, then presenting correlation detectors for disparity and motion signals, proposing a three-step-processing cascade of layered neural processing, that is replicated in all three model areas, and the incorporation of local center-surround interactions enabling and stabilizing multiple activations for transparency stimuli.

A CORTICAL MODEL FOR BINOCULAR AND MOTION TRANSPARENCY PROCESSING

Our model resembles the cortical mechanisms of V1, second visual area (V2), and MT for the processing of stereo and motion stimuli, see Figure 1a. Model area V1 includes correlation detectors for spatially offset locations as well as temporally delayed signals. Initial correlation results are linked into a three-step-processing cascade that is replicated in model areas V2 and MT. Model areas V1 and V2 define the stereo signal processing pathway, containing a population of model neurons sensitive to disparity. Model areas V1 and MT define the processing pathway for visual image motion. Although there is an overlap between both pathways in area V1, they are kept mutually exclusive and, thus, do not interact. Note that area MT neurons show sensitivity to stereo signals as well (Born & Bradley, 2005); however, we used the traditional view of V2 being pathway for stereo vision (e.g., Hubel & Wiesel, 1970; Hubel & Livingstone, 1987). Both modeled pathways incorporate bidirectional connections between areas V1 and V2 for stereo signaling and V1 and MT for motion signaling. Feedback (FB) signals as part of the bidirectional connectivity modulate ascending, driving signals. In all model areas disparity and motion signals are represented in populations of neurons, selective to disparity and motion, respectively. These populations can represent multiple activations at a single spatial location through the formation of multiple local peaks in the activity distribution. Thus, these codes provide a solution to the problem of clustering; the estimation of the number of motions or disparities at a single location. The next paragraphs contain a formal definition and explanation for the initial correlation mechanisms to derive estimates, and the three-stage processing cascades in model areas V1, V2, and MT.

Spatial and Spatio-Temporal Correlation for the Detection of Initial Stereo and Motion Signals

Assume that the image intensity signal for left and right image is given by the function $f^{L/R}(x,y)$ for the 2D image coordinates *(x, y)*. The superscripts *L* and *R* denote the left eye's image and right eye's image, respectively. The **stereo** correlation signal is computed in five steps. First, the direct current (DC) component of left and right eye's input image is removed, defining

$$\overline{f}^{L/R}(x,y) = f^{L/R}(x,y) - \frac{1}{\left|I_{x,y}\right|}\sum_{x,y\in I_{x,y}} f^{L/R}(x,y), \tag{1}$$

where the second term on the right hand side denotes the mean value computed over all spatial locations *x* and *y* of the image domain $I_{x,y}$. Second, orientation specific response maps

$$r^{L/R}(x,y,\psi_k) = \overline{f}^{L/R}(x,y) * f^{Gauss}(x,y;\psi_k) \tag{2}$$

are constructed by convolving the DC free input signal with the orientation specific Gaussian filter $f^{Gauss}(x,y;\psi_k) =$ $\sin(\psi_k)\cdot\partial_x f^{Gauss}(x,y) + \cos(\psi_k)\cdot\partial_y f^{Gauss}(x,y)$, using the steerable filter theorem (Freeman & Adelson, 1991). The symbol * in Equation (2) denotes the convolution operator. Partial derivatives are denoted by ∂_x and ∂_y for the *x* and *y* dimension, respectively. These derivatives are numerically approximated by applying Sobel operators (Danielson & Segera, 1990). This oriented Gaussian filter approximates a Gabor filter (Daugman, 1985) with unit wavelength. Note that the selectivity of area V1 neurons has been characterized by using Gabor filters as a parameterized model (Ringach, 2002). All parameters of our

Figure 1. Visual areas and mechanism in our model that support transparency processing: (a) The suggested model resembles functions of primate visual areas V1, V2, and MT. Local correspondences for stereo and motion are computed in area V1 resulting in disparity and motion direction selectivity analog to neurons in V1. Stereo signals are integrated in area V2 and motion signals in area MT. (b) Binocular transparency and (c) motion transparency are supported by local center-surround interactions for disparity and motion speeds / directions, respectively. Local competition is depicted by the light gray ellipse to denote excitatory connectivity and the dark gray ellipse to denote inhibitory connectivity with reference to the left eye's disparity or motion at the center of the ellipses.

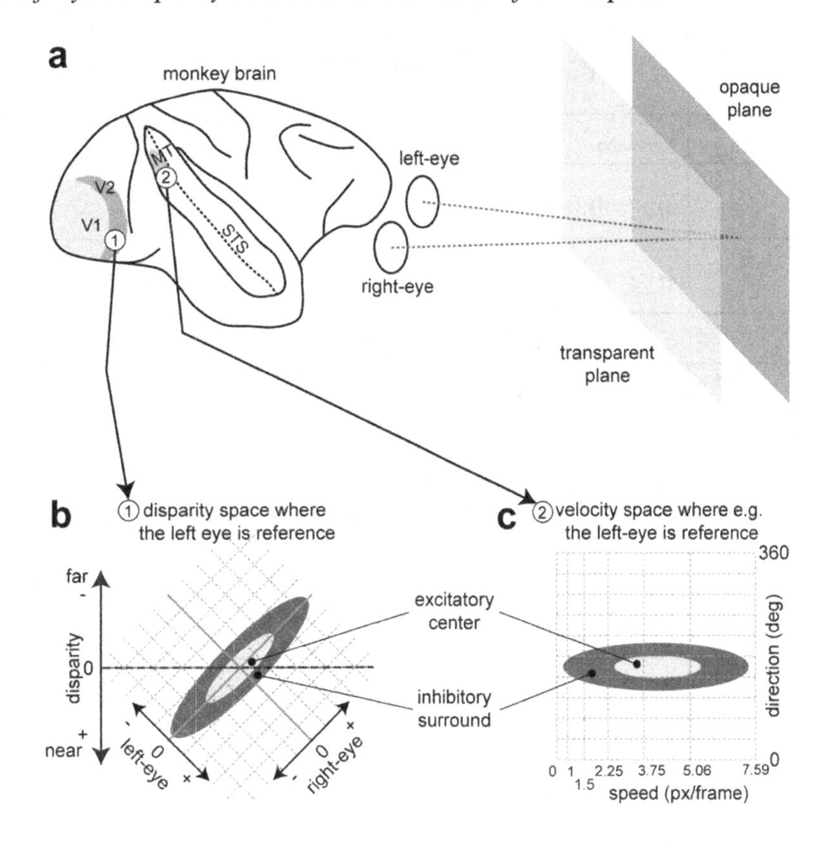

model are reported in Table 1. Third, the normalization over orientations

$$\bar{r}^{L/R}(x,y,\psi_k) = r^{L/R}(x,y,\psi_k) \,/\, (\eta_N + \frac{1}{N_{ori}} \sum_{k=1}^{N_{ori}} r^{L/R}(x,y,\psi_k)) \quad (3)$$

generates a signal that is independent of local brightness changes, which has been previously used in motion detectors (Heeger, 1987; Bayerl & Neumann, 2004). Fourth, these orientation maps are compared

$$c^L(x,y;\Delta x) = \frac{1}{N_{ori}} \cdot \sum_{k=1}^{N_{ori}} \exp(-\left[\bar{r}^L(x,y;\psi_k) - \bar{r}^R(x-\Delta x,y;\psi_k)\right]^2 / (2\cdot\sigma_c^2)) \quad (4)$$

for different horizontal disparities Δx between the left eye's (reference) and right eye's image by using a Gaussian function to rate pixel-similarity. Note that this similarity measure is inverse to the typically defined matching cost functions,

Table 1. Parameter values for initial signal detectors and three-step-processing cascades for signal integration in model areas V1, V2, and MT

Description	Parameter value		Eq.
Detection of initial disparity signals			
Description	**Parameter value**		**Eq.**
Orientations	$\psi_k = k \cdot \pi / N_{ori}$, $k = 1 \ldots N_{ori}$, $N_{ori} = 8$		2
Gaussian filter	$f^{Gauss}(x,y) = 1/(2 \cdot \pi \cdot \sigma^2) \cdot \exp(-(x^2 + y^2)/(2 \cdot \sigma^2))$ with $x, y \in \{-2, \ldots, +2\}$ pixel, and $\sigma = 0.75$ pixel		2
Boundary condition	Neumann		
Normalization	$\eta_N = 0.01$		3
Gaussian tuning	$\sigma_c = 0.5$		4
Detection of initial motion signals			
Orientations	$\psi_k = k \cdot \pi / N_{ori}$, $k = 1 \ldots N_{ori}$, $N_{ori} = 8$		6
Rings of the Gabor bank	$\omega_l = 2 \cdot \pi / (\eta \cdot s_1) \cdot \beta^{-(l-1)}$, $l = 1 \ldots N_{ring}$, $N_{ring} = 6$, $\beta = 1.5$		6
Overlap factors	$o^{\Psi} = 1.0$ and $o^{r} = 1.25$		6
Radial standard deviation	$\sigma_l^{\psi} = \omega_l \cdot \sin(\pi / N_{ori}) \cdot o^{\psi}$		6
Tangent standard deviation	$\sigma_l^{r} = \omega_l \cdot (\beta - 1)/(\beta + 1) \cdot o^{r}$		6
Speed to wavelength factor	$\eta = 2.5$ ($\eta \geq 2$ due to the sampling theorem)		6
Motion directions	$\varphi_m = m \cdot 2 \cdot \pi / N_{dir}$, $m = 1 \ldots N_{dir}$, $N_{dir} = 16$		8
Motion speeds	$s_l = s_1 \cdot \beta^{(l-1)}$, $l = 1 \ldots N_{ring}$, $s_1 = 1.0$ pixel/frame		8
Model area V1 parameters			
Description	**V1 (stereo domain)**	**V1 (motion domain)**	**Eq.**
Nonlinearity α	2	2	11a

continued on following page

Table 1. Continued

Gaussian filter $\Lambda_{disp/vel}$	Horizontal disparity: $\sigma_{disp} = 0.75$ pixel and $l_{disp} = 5$ pixel [a]	Motion speed: $\sigma_{speed} = 0.2$ pixel/frame and $l_{speed} = 5$ pixel/frame [a] Motion direction: $\sigma_{dir} = 0.75 \cdot 360 / 16^{\circ}$ and $l_{dir} = 5 \cdot 360 / 16^{\circ}$ [a]	11a
Boundary conditions	Zero padding	Motion speed: Neumann Motion direction: Circular	11a
Feedback constant γ	100	100	11b
Normalization A	0.01	0.01	11c
Normalization B	1	100/112	11c
Model area V2 and MT parameters			
Description	V2 (stereo domain)	MT (motion domain)	Eq.
Gaussian filter Λ_{space}	$\sigma_{space} = 2.5$ pixels and $l_{space} = 11$ pixels [a]	$\sigma_{space} = 5.0$ pixels and $l_{space} = 21$ pixels [a]	12a
Sampling rate f^{rate}_{sample}	2.5	5.0	12a
Nonlinearity α	2	2	12a
Gaussian filter $\Lambda_{disp/vel}$	Same as in V1	Same as in V1	12a
Gaussian filter Λ^{+}	Horizontal disparity: $\sigma_{disp} = 0.75$ pixel and $l_{disp} = 5$ pixels [a] Spatial domain: $\sigma_{space} = 1.5$ pixels and $l_{space} = 7$ pixels [a]	Motion speed: Dirac pulse, no kernel is applied. Motion direction: $\sigma_{dir} = 0.5 \cdot 360 / 16^{\circ}$ and $l_{dir} = 3 \cdot 360 / 16^{\circ}$ [a]	12c
Gaussian filter Λ^{-}	Horizontal disparity: $\sigma_{disp} = 2$ pixels and $l_{disp} = 9$ pixels [a]	Motion speed: $\sigma_{speed} = 0.5$ pixels/frame and $l_{speed} = 5$ pixels/frame [a] Motion direction: $\sigma_{dir} = 2 \cdot 360 / 16^{\circ}$ and $l_{dir} = 9 \cdot 360 / 16^{\circ}$ [a]	12c
Boundary conditions	Disparity: Zero padding Space: Neumann	Motion speed: Neumann Motion direction: Circular	12c
Normalization A	0.01	0.01	12c
Normalization B	2	10	12c

[a] The length specifies the size of the support for the filters.

such as squared difference, absolute difference, or wavelet phase (Scharstein & Szeliski, 2002). Individual pixel-similarities of each orientation are summed to improve the signal-to-noise ratio. For further improvement, the left eye's image is compared with the right eye's one in the same way, where the right eye's image serves as reference. Then pixel-similarity for the right eye's image are registered with those of the left eye's one by warping the pixel-similarity to the left according to the estimated horizontal disparity. Fifth, the left eye's and the registered right eye's pixel similarity are summed

$$\bar{c}^L(x, y; \Delta x) = 1/2 \cdot (c^L(x, y, \Delta x) + c^R(x - \Delta x, y, \Delta x)) \quad (5)$$

leading to the final correlation result with reference to the left image. Due to the missing pixel-correspondences at the left boundary, where no matching parts in the right image exist, these values in the non-match region are homogenously set to one. Later in the interaction scheme these values can be modulated by nearby spatial correlations.

Initial motion signals are detected by using a correlation mechanism of local image-phases. Motion sequences are defined as varying brightness changes by the function $f(x, y, t)$ with the spatial coordinates *x* and *y*, and the temporal coordinate *t*. Note that this image sequence refers to a generic image stream not directly bound to the left or right eye. However, in the simulations visual motions for stereo image sequences are computed with respect to the left eye's image. Input images of the sequence are convolved with Gabor filters of different spatial resolution according to the spatial shift values or visual motion speeds tested. These Gabor filters resemble the variety of neural selectivity of area V1 neurons better than the above oriented Gaussian filters (Ringach, 2002). The convolution of images from the motion sequence with Gabor filters is performed in the Fourier domain. Therefore, individual frames of the image sequence $f(x, y, t)$ are Fourier transformed into $\hat{f}(\omega_x, \omega_y, t)$ which is indicated by the hat-symbol and the change of arguments to angular frequencies ω_x and ω_y, corresponding to the spatial dimensions. The temporal dimension is not Fourier transformed. The Gabor filters for different spatial resolutions are defined in the Fourier domain as

$$\hat{f}^{Gabor}(\omega_x, \omega_y; \psi_k, \omega_l, \sigma_l^{\psi}, \sigma_l^r) = \frac{1}{2 \cdot \pi \cdot \sigma_l^{\psi} \cdot \sigma_l^r} \cdot \exp\left(-\frac{1}{2}\left[\left(\frac{\omega_r + \omega_l}{\sigma_l^r}\right)^2 + \left(\frac{\omega_\psi}{\sigma_l^\psi}\right)^2\right]\right) \quad (6)$$

by using Gaussians as window functions centered at the frequencies $\omega_r + \omega_l$ and ω_ψ given in angular coordinates. Spatial frequencies are defined in the Cartesian grid on 2D images. In order to use a reference frame that is invariant against any filter orientation, we utilize the local contrast orientation ψ_k as gauge for the filter kernel definition. Frequencies referring to a rotated axis (in Fourier space) are defined $\omega_r = \cos(\psi_k) \cdot \omega_x - \sin(\psi_k) \cdot \omega_y$ and $\omega_\psi = \sin(\psi_k) \cdot \omega_x + \cos(\psi_k) \cdot \omega_y$. We also account for representing different speeds s_l which are multiples of the minimal speed $s_1 = 1.0$ (pixel/frame) using a scaling scheme $s_l = s_1 \cdot \beta^{(l-1)}$ ($l = 1 \ldots N_{ring}$). The related frequencies ω_l can be expressed by using different speed ranges with their respective magnitudes, i.e. $\omega_l = 2 \cdot \pi / (\eta \cdot s_1) \cdot \beta^{-(l-1)}$ ($l = 1 \ldots N_{ring}$, $N_{ring} = 6$, $\beta = 1.5$). The factor $\eta = 2.5$ relates an angular frequency to a speed. Note, that due to the sampling theorem (Nyquist, 2002) only shifts smaller or equal to half of the wavelength of the angular frequency of the Gabor filter can be uniquely detected ($\eta \geq 2$). A normal flow detector computes correlation results only for an orientation orthogonal to the contrast orientation.

In our implementation we do not restrict the correlation to a specific orientation orthogonal to the motion direction, but rather test all orientations. Different orientations $\psi_k = k \cdot \pi / N_{ori}$ ($k = 1...N_{ori}$, $N_{ori} = 8$) are indexed by k. A filtering response for a Gabor filter is presented in Box 1 which uses the inverse Fourier transform F for the spatial dimension and the result are complex numbers. These complex numbers are used to define a local signal amplitude and local signal phase $\Phi_{k,l,t} = \arg\left\{r(x, y; \psi_k, \omega_l, \sigma_l^{\psi}, \sigma_l^{r})\right\}$. In our correlation detector only the local image phase is further used, because it is largely independent of local brightness variations and, thus, provides a signature of a local image region mainly independent of the overall brightness level. Therefore, a local normalization like for the disparity detector in Equation (3) is not required. Neurons in area V1 exist that encode local image phase (Mechler et al., 2002). Motion signals are calculated by using the extended Hassenstein-Reichardt detector (Hassenstein & Reichardt, 1956) estimating spatio-temporal correlations of local image phase. A local image phase

$$\Phi_{k,l,t}^{\Delta m,l} = \arg\left\{r(x - \Delta x_{l,m}, y - \Delta y_{l,m}; \psi_k, \omega_l, \sigma_l^{\psi}, \sigma_l^{r})\right\} \quad (8)$$

is spatially shifted by the horizontal and vertical offsets $\Delta x_{l,m} = s_l \cdot \cos(\varphi_m)$ and $\Delta y_{l,m} = s_l \cdot \sin(\varphi_m)$ and compared against the non-shifted but temporally delayed phase. For the forwards correlation from time t_0 to t_1 the detection is given by

$$c_{l,m}^{t_0 \to t_1} = \frac{1}{N_{ori}} \sum_{k=1}^{N_{ori}} \left[\cos(\Phi_{k,l,t_1}^{\Delta m,l} - \Phi_{k,l,t_0})\right]^{+}, \quad (9)$$

with $\left[\,\cdot\,\right]^{+} = \max(\,\cdot\,, 0)$ denoting a half-wave rectification operation and the correlation results for all orientations is summed[2]. The rectified cosine-function defines the tuning between phase differences. The backwards correlation $c_{l,m}^{L,t_1 \to t_0}$ is analogously defined. Forwards and backwards correlation are combined by subtracting the backwards correlation from the forwards correlation,

$$c(x, y, \varphi_m, s_l) = \left[c_{l,m}^{t_1 \to t_0} - c_{l,m}^{t_0 \to t_1}\right]^{+}, \quad (10)$$

because they appear in common only for flicker motion which should not be detected.

Different Speed and Disparity Ranges

The proposed disparity and motion correlation detectors use different filters due to the difference in the range of detected disparities and motion speeds. Typical benchmarks use disparity values between zero and 60 pixels; however, motion speeds rarely are above six pixels per frame. As we use a logarithmic scale to sample motion speeds (see Table 1), large disparities could be only sparsely sampled by utilizing the same filtering mechanisms in the disparity domain. Although selectivity for disparity values in areas V1 and V2 might be logarithmically sampled in cortex, benchmark sequences require a dense sampling of disparities over a wide range. Thus, instead

Box 1.

$$r(x, y, t; \psi_k, \omega_l, \sigma_l^{\psi}, \sigma_l^{r}) \quad \circ\!-\!F\left\{f\left(x, y\right)\right\}\!-\!\bullet \quad \hat{f}(\omega_x, \omega_y, t) \cdot \hat{f}^{Gabor}(\omega_x, \omega_y; \psi_k, \omega_l, \sigma_l^{\psi}, \sigma_l^{r}) \quad (7)$$

of applying a Gabor filter bank with various spatial resolutions for the detection of horizontal disparities based on local image phase as we did for the motion detector, disparity is detected by using a pixel-wise similarity measure defined in Equation 4.

In the visual cortex the same mechanism could be employed for detecting displacements caused either by stereo disparity or visual motion. For instance, the same energy models have been suggested to detect stereo disparity (Ohzawa et al., 1990) and visual motion (Adelson & Bergen, 1985), respectively. The sensitivity for displacements that is caused by stereo disparity ranges within ±0.4° of visual angle (Cumming & DeAngelis, 2001; their "Figure 5") while that of displacements caused by visual motion within 6...20 min arc or 0.1°...0.3° of visual angle (Kiorpes & Movshon, 2004; their Figure 1). Thus, in cortex, sensitivity ranges for displacement are similar, although sensitivity for motion displacements is slightly smaller than that of disparity displacements taking the above studies as example.

Model mechanisms in our initial detection stages reflect this small difference in the sensitivity between stereo disparity and visual motion. Initial detection stages of disparity and motion signals use a modified correlation-based scheme using a Gaussian function to measure similarity for disparity signals (Equation 4) or a rectified cosine function for motion signals (Equation 9). The intervals of tested disparities and velocities or speeds are adapted to the data used for in the model simulation.

Neurons in area V1 show a phase and shift selectivity (Prince et al., 2002) for different disparities capturing a spatial shift either by a shift of the entire Gabor filter or only by shifting its phase while the Gaussian support of the Gabor filter remains at the same location. Our model only includes shift selective neurons. Furthermore, only absolute disparity signals are encoded in our model area V2, excluding the encoding of relative disparity as found in V2 neurons (Thomas et al., 2002). Absolute disparity signals are encoded in model V1 as well as in V1 of macaque monkeys (Cumming & Parker, 1999).

Visual motion speeds and motion directions are encoded in areas V1 and MT of macaque monkey (Priebe et al., 2006; Cheng et al., 1994; Orban et al., 1986; Rodman & Albright, 1987). Motion speed and direction selectivity in our model are generated by spatio-temporally correlating local image phases extracted by Gabor filters of different orientation and spatial resolution. The relationship between the wavelength of the Gabor filter (spatial frequency) and the different spatial shifts to be tested are crucial mechanisms for our detector model. Spatial shifts have to be below half of the wavelength in accordance to the sampling theorem (Nyquist, 2002).

Due to the two frame correlation employed for simplicity, the motion detector does not detect different temporal frequencies. Instead spatio-temporal selectivity is generated by detecting different spatial frequencies for one temporal frequency. The corresponding image velocity is computed as $v = f(t) \,/\, f(x)$ where *f(t)* denotes the temporal frequency and *f(x)* denotes the spatial frequency. Measured cells and model cells both have a Gaussian-shaped tuning curve in the velocity domain (motion directions and speeds), where speeds are encoded on a logarithmic scale in area MT (Maunsell and Essen, 1983, compare with their "Figure 6-A"; Nover et al., 2005).

Three-Step Processing Cascade for Model Area V1

The three-stage processing cascade is motivated by the layered cortical processing within visual cortex. The *first processing step includes a spatial integration and nonlinear signal enhancement*, which takes place through signal processing in synapses and dendrites by the integration of incoming signals and is defined by the ordinary differential equation (ODE) [3]

Figure 2. Population response and perceived distance for planes at different depths and for motion components with different directions. (a) The angular separation is defined as the distance in depth between two planes with a dot texture (RDS) and this distance varies in the experiment. (b) Shows the activation of disparity selective neurons for different angular separations. The activation is computed from model area V2 and pooled over the entire visual space. Dashed lines indicate the veridical depth of planes. Note that these veridical depths do not correspond with the peak locations of the activation profile in all cases. (c) As a consequence, the read out angular distance does not coincide with the veridical one; underestimation (attraction) and overestimation (repulsion) of the angular distance or depth separation occurs. (d) Comparable effects are observed for humans reporting angular distance for the same display type (Redrawn based on Figure 2 in Stevenson et al. (1991) Depth attraction and repulsion in random dot stereograms. Vision Research 31 on page 807). (e) The angular difference is defined as the difference in motion direction between two randomly selected subsets of dots from a RDK. (f) Shows the population response of motion direction selective neurons from model area MT for varying angular differences. This population response is pooled over the entire visual space and motion speeds. Again, dashed lines indicate motion directions of the stimulus and these are not always coincident with the peak locations in the activation profile. (g) A read-out method interpreting the entire activation profile from (f) calculates the motion directions. Angular differences between these directions are underestimated (attraction) for small differences or overestimated (repulsion) for larger differences. Mean and standard deviation are computed for 50 trials. (h) Humans show the same effects of attraction and repulsion (Redrawn based on Figure 3c in Braddick et al. (2002) Directional performance in motion transparency. Vision Research 42 on page 1243). Note that the population responses in (b) and (d) are normalized across conditions.

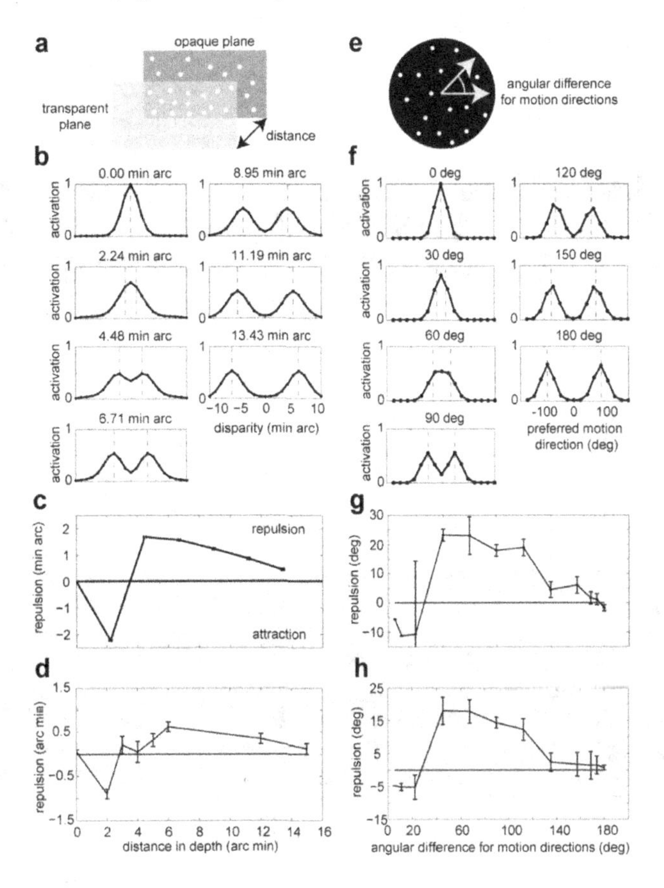

Figure 3. Representation of multiple transparently overlaid layers in depth or motions. (a) Shows a stereo image pair with two layers in depth. Note due to sampling for print the original resolution and arrangement of dots is not preserved and, thus, image fusion into stereo correspondence might not directly be possible. (b) Depicts the first two frames of the motion stimulus with two different motion components. (c) Shows the population response of spatially pooled V2 signals for a RDS with the entitled number of layers in depth. Dashed lines show the horizontal disparity values of each single layer. (d) Activity maps encode the likelihood value for a disparity indicated by the axis at the bottom of the four prints. Each activity map (tile) has entries that correspond to the spatial location in the stimulus. All 25 activity maps together show the activation of all model V2 neurons of the "output layer" – after the computation of the third processing step. (e) The depicted population responses of area MT direction selectivity are pooled by summing responses over visual space and motion speeds. (f) Shows activity maps for different motion directions (columns) and an increasing number of motion components (rows) present in the stimulus. Note that the activity profiles in (c) and (e) are normalized across conditions; in contrast, intensities in (d) and (f) are individually scaled for each row.

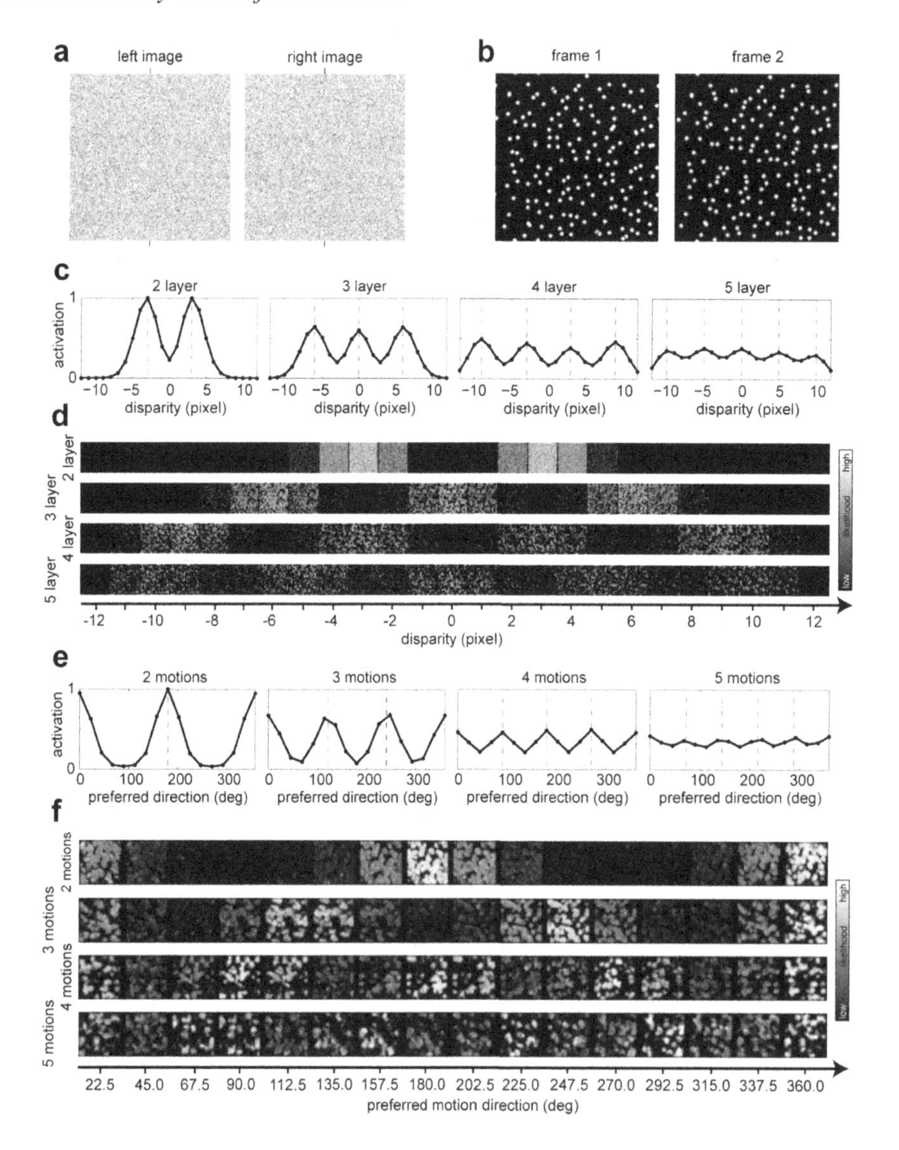

Figure 4. Disparity and motion speed gradients are processed for two moving tilted planes given a stereo observer. (a) Shows the configuration for the scenario: The inter-camera distance is one centimeter, the transparent front plane is six meters away (translating two centimeter per frame to the left) from the cameras (40° vertical field of view), and the opaque back plane is 10 meters away (translating one centimeter per frame to the right). (b) Shows the left and right camera's image for the 9th frame of the motion sequence. (c) Activity maps (explained in Figure 3's caption) from model area V2. Zoomed-in versions are indicated by frames in dashed lines. High likelihood values (activities) are present for stereo correspondences, first at the far back plane (left group of plots) and, then, at the close front plane (right group of plots). For both groups of the three plots (left and right) there is a transition of activity from left to right that indicates the encoding of a disparity gradient generated by the tilted planes. (d) Shows activity maps in model area MT for motion directions whereby activity is pooled over motion speeds. Again, groups of zoomed-in versions are indicated by the two dashed frames. High likelihood values occur for leftward motion (180°) of the transparent front plane (first group) and at the same time for rightward motion (360°) of the opaque back plane (second group). (e) Pooling of area MT activity over motion directions shows likelihoods for motion speeds. Motion speeds at the location of the closer foreground plane are higher than those of the farther background plane. High likelihoods shift from left to right of the activity maps as encoded motion speeds increase. This spatial shift of high likelihoods represents a motion speed gradient that corresponds to the decrease of distance from left to right as both planes are tilted by 45° with respect to the optical axes. All activity maps depict the model's state at the 9th frame of processing the (binocular) image sequence reporting the activity after the third-processing step.

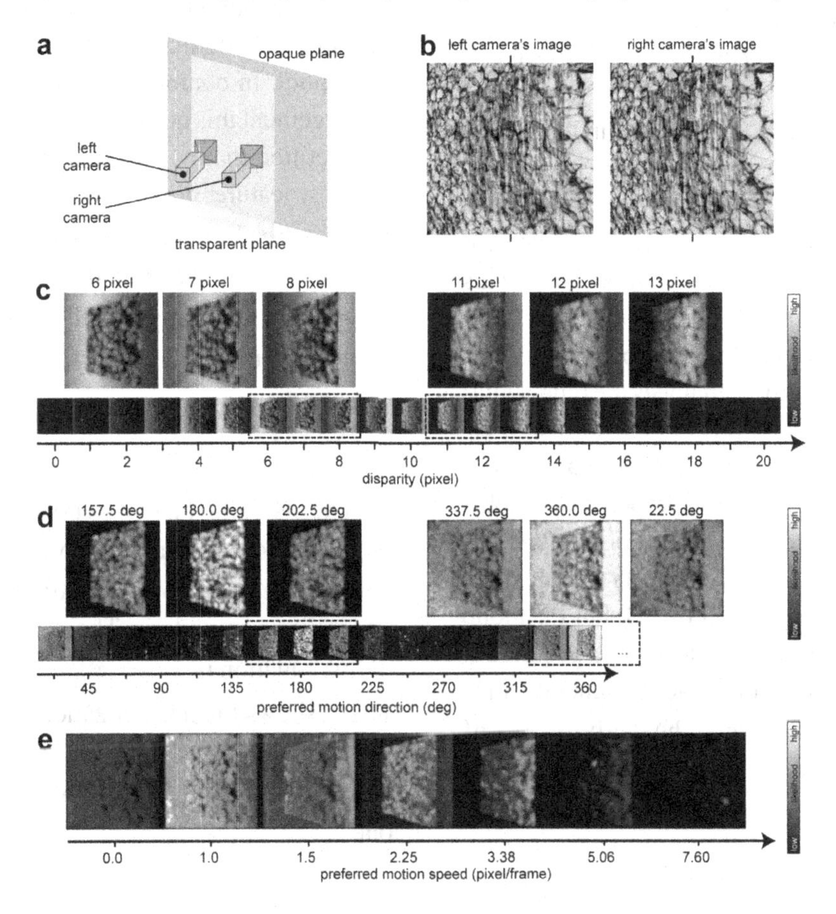

$$\dot{x}_{V1}^{(1)} = -x_{V1}^{(1)} + (x_{V1}^{FF})^{\alpha} * \Lambda_{disp/mot} \,. \quad (11a)$$

The signals $x_{V1}^{(1)}$ and x_{V1}^{FF} model the membrane potential, or more generally the activity, of a cell or firing rate (Stafstrom et al., 1984). This activation encodes the likelihood for a disparity or motion in the stimulus input. The signals x_{V1}^{FF} from the initial correlation, $x_{V1}^{FF} = \overline{c}^{L}$ from Equation 5 for the stereo signaling pathway or $x_{V1}^{FF} = c$ from Equation 10 for the motion signaling pathway, are first transformed by a non-linear function to model the nonlinearities of dendrites and synapses in signal processing. Here, we employ an exponential nonlinearity with $\alpha > 1$ as exponent. The signal is then convolved with the Gaussian filter $\Lambda_{disp/mot}$, where convolution takes place over either the disparity or motion domain. Note that these convolutions define an interaction between point processes of model cells.

In the *second processing step FB signals modulate driving forward signals*, where FB originates from visual areas higher in the hierarchy than the considered target area. By integrating over larger spatial regions of visual space in higher visual areas, FB provides disambiguated signals from a larger spatial neighborhood. This FB signal shapes the neural activity of early visual areas through the modulation of cell activities whose feature selectivity matches the representation built at the higher level in the cortical hierarchy of visual processing (Bullier et al., 2001). A modeling study details the properties of such a modulation, defined as the linking principle (Eckhorn et al., 1990). Linking suggests that the driving signal can be enhanced by FB, but FB alone can not generate activity, it always requires a driving forward signal in order to generate a response. In formal terms the activity $x_{V1}^{(2)}$ of model cells in the second processing step is formed by a non-linear combination of the FB signal x_{V1}^{FB} and the driving forward signal $x_{V1}^{(1)}$ from the first processing step

$$\dot{x}_{V1}^{(2)} = -x_{V1}^{(2)} + x_{V1}^{(1)} \cdot (1 + \gamma \cdot x_{V1}^{FB}), \quad (11b)$$

where γ is a parameter, typically in the range of 10 to 100, to amplify the FB signal and $x_{V1}^{(2)}$ typically ranges between zero and one. All equations and parameters appear without dimensions as we did not model the exact biophysical processes of synapses or neurons. Any paired occurrence of forward signal $x_{V1}^{(1)}$ and FB signal x_{V1}^{FB} leads to an amplification of $x_{V1}^{(2)}$ by an amount proportional to the product of both.

In the *third processing step signals are normalized by dividing activity of a target cell by the activation summed over encoded disparities or motions*. This division operation keeps activity in the system bounded and, thus, achieves an approximate normalization of the activities in a local pool. In combination with the modulatory enhancement this normalization realizes a biased competition that in turn deemphasizes activities for those features that did not receive any enhancement by FB. Formally, the activity $x_{V1}^{(3)}$ of model cells integrates those of the second processing step $x_{V1}^{(2)}$ by summing over all encoded disparities or motions, respectively, for each spatial location,

$$\dot{x}_{V1}^{(3)} = -A \cdot x_{V1}^{(3)} + x_{V1}^{(2)} - B \cdot x_{V1}^{(3)} \cdot \sum x_{V1}^{(2)} \,. \quad (11c)$$

The symbols A and B denote parameters. The parameter A is typically 0.1, whereas $x_{V1}^{(3)}$ ranges between zero and one. Values for parameter B typically are around one. The steady-state solution of this equation is $x_{V1}^{(3)} = x_{V1}^{(2)} \,/\, (A + B \cdot \sum x_{V1}^{(2)})$ which shows the normalization property. Due to the division by the sum and assuming $B \geq 1$, the values for $x_{V1}^{(3)}$ will not exceed the upper limit of one.

Figure 5. Crowded motion generates semi-transparency. Two cuts, each four frames long, of a movie from the Tokyo Shibuya crossing in Japan, provided at http://www.youtube.com/watch?v=Zrrm3zzIq3s have been analyzed. (a) Shows frame 4903 of the video sequence, where persons carrying umbrellas move to the left and right and their motion is organized in stripes. This juxtaposed movement leads to patches of opponent motion overlay in local regions of the visual field. The activity distribution for motion directions (activity for speeds summed) are analyzed by pooling over the area indicated by the circles of 100 pixels radius in dashed line 1, 2, and 3 with the (x, y) pixel coordinates (188, 129), (237, 347), and (349, 414), respectively with the upper left corner defined by pixel coordinates (1,1). (b) Regions with zero motion (black), a single motion (gray), and multiple motions (white) are depicted for frames 4703 to 4706. Regions of motion transparency occur at the boundary between different motions and are further spatio-temporally integrated, e.g. for the region 2. In region 1 there is no motion signal and in region 3 a single motion. (c) In the same movie at frame 1821, persons move partially toward and away from the camera, again organized in lines of similar motion. Pixel coordinates for local regions 1, 2, and 3, are (89, 85), (271, 353), and (437, 342), respectively. (d) Motion semi-transparency occurs at the boundary of different motions (white regions). The distribution of activity for motion directions is shown in circular histograms, in region 1 with no motion, in region 2 with transparent motion, and in region 3 with a single motion. For both cuts motion occurs only in the lower half of images where crowds move and the camera is stationary. Note that circular histograms in b and d have been individually scaled and, thus, can not be directly compared.

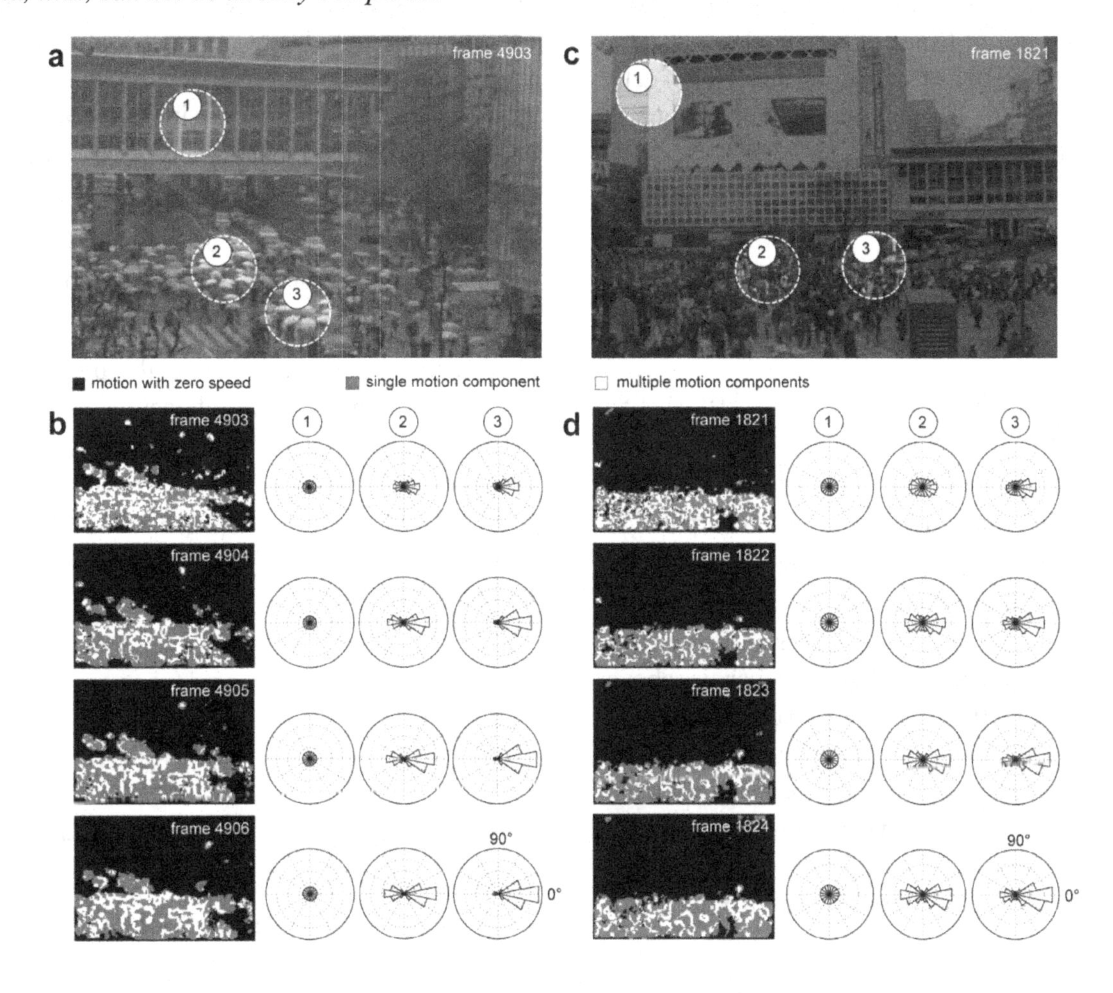

Three-Step-Processing Cascade for Model Areas V2 and MT

In the *first step we use an isotropic integration* from model area V1 to model area V2 or MT. During integration the spatial resolution is reduced by the factor 2.5 for V2 and by the factor five for MT. Note that the RF sizes in MT are about ten times larger than those of V1 [4] (Angelucci et al., 2002). This reduction in resolution is achieved by convolving the input velocity space in its spatial dimensions with a Gaussian filter of appropriate size (sampling theorem) (Nyquist, 2002). Samples for every 2.5th value for the disparity signal or every fifth value for the motion signal are taken from this Gaussian filtered signal. In cortex signal integration in MT leads to an increase in the direction tuning bandwidth (mean value 95°) compared to that of V1 (mean value 68°) (Albright, 1984). This increase of bandwidth is another indicator for the integrative or smoothing behavior of cells in area MT. In formal terms this integration is denoted by

$$\dot{x}^{(1)}_{V2/MT} = -x^{(1)}_{V2/MT} + f^{rate}_{sample}((x^{FF}_{V2/MT} * \Lambda_{space})^{\alpha}) * \Lambda_{disp/mot} \quad (12a)$$

For inter-area signal processing between area V1 and V2 or MT the input signal $x^{FF}_{V2/MT} = x^{(3)}_{V1}$ is spatially integrated by utilizing the function f^{rate}_{sample}. This function denotes a linear interpolation for the above rates. Before applying the linear interpolation, the signal is convolved by an appropriately parameterized Gaussian kernel that reduces the power of all signal frequencies above the maximum frequency divided by the sampling rate to ~1% [5]. This integration reflects the difference between receptive field sizes in area V1 and V2 or MT (Albright and Desimone, 1987). Next, activities are smoothed over the domain of disparities or velocities by convolving with $\Lambda_{disp/vel}$. Furthermore, a nonlinear transformation of the signal is incorporated with the exponent α, as in the Equation 11a.

In the *second step of the three-stage processing* cascade, FB from other model areas or an attention signal (Raudies & Neumann, 2010) could be included in principle. However, in the current model, areas V2 or MT are the highest areas in the model and do not receive any modulating input, nor do they incorporate any attention signal. Thus,

$$\dot{x}^{(2)}_{V2/MT} = -x^{(2)}_{V2/MT} + x^{(1)}_{V2/MT} \cdot (1 + \gamma \cdot x^{FB}_{V2/MT}) \quad (12b)$$

simply becomes the identity $x^{(2)}_{V2/MT} = x^{(1)}_{V2/MT}$ in its steady state.

In the *third step of the processing cascade*, a local center-surround interaction between different disparities or velocities is computed. For this interaction similar motions or depths support each other, whereas dissimilar ones inhibit each other. More formally, the input activity $x^{(2)}_{V2/MT}$ is convolved with Λ^{+}, a Gaussian filter in spatial, disparity, motion direction, or log-speed domain defining the field of local support. The inhibitory field is defined by convolution of $x^{(2)}_{V2/MT}$ with Λ^{-}, again a Gaussian filter in the previously mentioned domains. The interaction for these filters is depicted in Figure 1b for the disparity domain and in Figure 1c for the motion domain. Both, supporting and inhibiting, signals are combined in a competitive scheme by using divisive inhibition

$$\dot{x}^{(3)}_{V2/MT} = -A \cdot x^{(3)}_{V2/MT} + x^{(2)}_{V2/MT} * \Lambda^{+} - B \cdot x^{(3)}_{V2/MT} \cdot (x^{(2)}_{V2/MT} * \Lambda^{-}) \quad (12c)$$

The symbols A and B denote parameters. The parameter A is typically set to 0.1, whereas $x^{(3)}_{V2/MT}$ ranges between zero and one. Values for param-

Figure 6. Estimation of horizontal disparity for image pairs depicting objects with opaque material properties, and no clutter of objects occurs. All image pairs are from the Middlebury benchmark for stereo computation (http://vision.middlebury.edu/stereo/data/; 2003 and 2005 data sets). Names of the stereo image pairs are written atop. A ground truth and simulated disparity map read-out from model area V1 follows. At the bottom of each test case the interval of disparities used in each simulation is given. All disparity maps are computed with respect to the left image. Horizontal disparity is encoded by the gray-value code on the right.

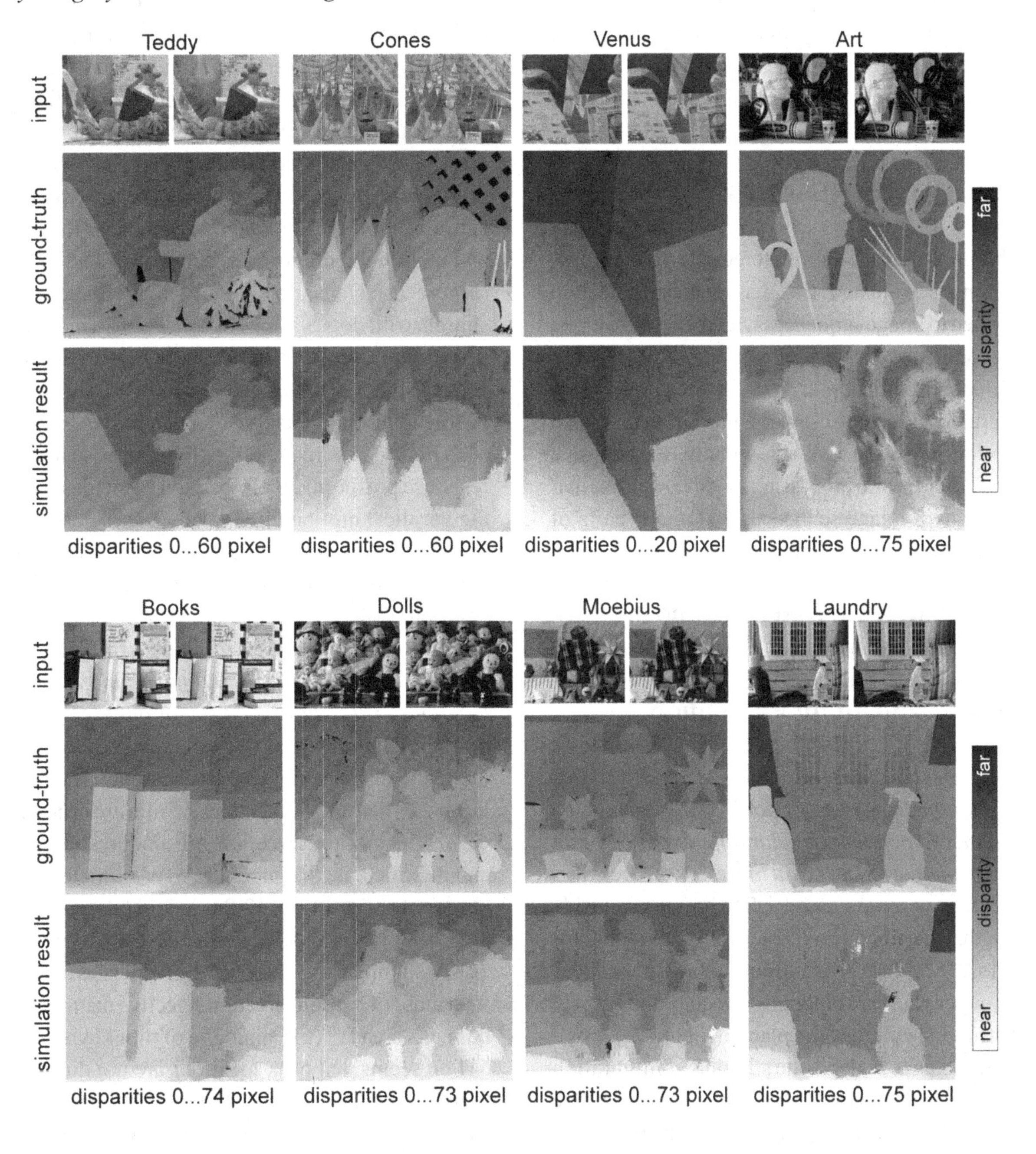

eter *B* typically range between 1 and 10. Because of the 'soft' competition between activities representing different disparities or motions, the representation of multiple activations is possible. This center-surround interaction is the main difference to previous models of stereo (Prazdny, 1985; Pollard & Frisby, 1990; Chen & Qian, 2004) or motion processing (Bayerl & Neumann, 2004; Zanker, 2005; Durant et al., 2006; Qian et al., 1994; Simoncelli and Heeger, 1998).

SIMULATION RESULTS

The proposed model of stereo and motion processing is evaluated, first, based on data and then applied to image sequences with realistic features, e.g. realistic textures and scene geometries that include tilts in depth. We test the model with captured videos of crowded motion that lead to motion semi-transparency. Finally, we simulate motion and stereo processing by using well-known benchmark image sequences and image pairs of opaque motion and stereo setups.

Encoding a Varying Distance in Depth or an Angular Difference by Multiple Activations and their Read-Out for Perception

What does the neural representation for binocular or motion transparency look like, varying the distance in depth or angular difference of motion directions for independent layers? To address this question we setup square RDS[6] with 256 pixels side length, where correspondences are given either for a closer or a distant plane, point-correspondences for either plane are randomly selected, and equally distributed amongst the planes (Figure 2a). For a large distance in depth the stimulus configuration leads to the percept of two planes, the closer one being transparent. For the model we analyzed the spatially pooled responses of area V2's disparity selective neurons. Distances smaller than or equal to 2.24 min arc show a single peak response in the population of disparity selective neurons (Figure 2b). The distance in depth is measured by angles of visual degrees in min arc, the idealized stimulus size is 256 pixels or 5 cm and the display distance is 60 cm; the disparity in pixels equals tan((angle in min arc)/60/180·π/2)·2·60 cm · 256/5 pixels/cm (2.24 min arc $\approx$ 2 pixels). Above 2.24 min arc two peaks of different overlap exist, and the location of each peak corresponds to the stimulus defined depth values of the surface planes. In all cases only a horizontal disparity has been simulated.

A second experiment investigates the differences in motion direction. Here we use RDKs[7] and motion direction varies between 0° and 180° (Figure 2e). Dots are randomly divided into two subsets with dots of each set consistently moving in different directions. Up to 60° of angular difference a single, but broad, peak exists in the response profile of motion sensitive model neurons in area MT (Figure 2f). Above 60° two peaks arise in the response profile and their location coincides with the veridical motion directions, as in the case of disparity. These simulated response profiles for varying angular differences are in agreement with neurophysiology (Treue et al., 2000).

What is the perceived difference in depth or motion direction and does it differ from the peak locations in the neural representations of area V2 and MT? Humans show two effects when asked to judge the distance in these transparency stimuli. Distances that are smaller than 2.5 min arc in depth or 25° in motion direction are underestimated and intermediate distances are overestimated for ranges of [2.5 min arc, 12.0 min arc] (stereo) and [25°, 135°] (motion), respectively (Figure 2c and 2g). Assuming that the population responses match with those of motion direction selective neurons in human's area V5 (the analogue of monkey's area MT) it seems that peak locations are not directly transformed into perceived motion direction, instead the entire activation profile is involved in the read-out mechanism to interpret a particular motion stimulus (Treue et al., 2000). This difference in peak location and perceived disparity or motion motivated to model an elaborated mechanism for the read-out of the population code. Peak locations are read-out iteratively; however, previous read-outs influence succeeding ones by applying an inhibitory field (Gaussian blob) at the read-out location before the next maximum location is detected. For single narrow peaked responses this inhibition leads mostly to a read-out of a single peak – the effect of attraction – depending on its width. If the single peak is broader, after the first read-out there is enough activation left for a successive read-out; however, the maximum location has been shifted away from the previous read-out location – the effect of repulsion. The perceived or interpreted disparities and motion directions are computed by applying this iterative read-out method with local inhibition to the individual responses which had been spatially pooled for profiles of Figure 2b and 2e. Mean and standard deviation for 50 trials are depicted in Figure 2d and 2h. Simulations match well with data.

Effects of attraction and repulsion might be a general perceptual phenomenon not only limited to the domain of stereo and motion processing (Rauber & Treue, 1999; Stevenson, 1991; Braddick et al., 2002). These effects occur also in ocular stimuli constructed by line parings (Westheimer, 1986). The perceived verticality of lines as well as the offset between two line segments is influence by a superimposed line grating mask. Alignment tasks for the two line segments show effects of attraction and repulsion (Tzvetanov et al., 2007). This suggests attraction and repulsion to be a general effect that happens to occur on the basis of population responses in various feature domains in vision.

What is the Maximum Number of Depth Layers or Motion Directions that Could Be Processed in Parallel?

In the previous simulation the question about the encoding between two different layers of different depth separation or angular difference in motion directions has been studied. *But, when does the representation of multiple activations for depth or motion directions deteriorate?* To study this case we arranged multiple layers in depth or motion. RDSs are 768 x 768 pixels in size and are constructed with depth layers at horizontal disparities ±3 pixels (two layers); 0 and ±6 pixels (three layers); ±3 and ±9 pixels (four layers); 0, ±5, and ±10 pixels (five layers) (see Figure 3a). Pixel positions were assigned to different depth layers by taking the linear index of a pixel modulus the layer number. Unlike the randomly assignment in the previous experiment this interleaved assignment of pixels allowed to create stereograms with multiple layers avoiding the formation of local clustering or cloud structures. RDKs are constructed in the same manner as in the previous simulation for varying angular difference between motion directions (see Figure 3b). In this simulation the angular difference between motions is defined as the fraction 360°/n where n is the number of motions. Activation profiles for both domains, stereo and motion directions look similar comparing Figure 3c for stereo with Figure 3e for motion directions. Peak signals increase as the number of encoded depth layers or motion directions decreases from two to five. Most importantly, these multiple activations are not only accomplished by integrating over the entire visual field, but also by integrating over a local neighborhood region of the visual field. This can be observed by looking at model V2 and MT neuron's responses. Figure 3d shows the activation of each model V2 neuron for its spatial location and horizontal disparity where all spatial locations are in a tile and tiles next to each other show different disparities. Responses for motion directions (pooled over speeds) are shown in Figure 3f by using the same tile organization. For two to three layers the activation in a small region of the visual space is relatively dense and is thinned out as more layers are represented (four or five in our case). Interestingly, psychophysical experiments show a 75% detection threshold for around three to four motion directions (Felisberti & Zanker, 2005) and the same number of different separable depth layers (Tsirlin et al., 2008). Furthermore, the perceivable number of depth layers can be improved by training (Reeves et al., 2010).

Processing of Stimuli with Realistic Textures, Disparity, and Speed Gradients

So far, the processed stimuli for binocular and motion transparency did not include gradients; neither did the stimuli have realistic textures. In the next simulation these two issues are addressed. The scene consists of two planes; both tilted 45° against the optical axes of the cameras (see Figure 4a). This tilt in depth leads to disparity gradients and if these planes move speed gradients occur as well. For the background plane a gravel-like texture and for the foreground plane a marble-like texture has been chosen. However, in the model the planes' texture is not used to separate them. Figure 4b shows the left and right camera's image. The model's simulation results are reported in Figure 4c for the disparity selective area V2 and in Figure 4d and 4e for the motion selective area MT. Each image tile shows the spatial activation for a disparity, motion direction (pooled over speeds), or motion speed (pooled over directions). Zoomed-in versions for tiles with 6, 7, 8, 11, 12, and 13 pixels disparity in Figure 3c show a transition of a maximum activity from the left to the right in visual space. This transition represents a disparity gradient caused by the tilt of planes. A similar transition occurs for motion speeds of 1.0, 1.5, 2.25, 3.38 pixels per frame in Figure 4e representing a speed gradient, again caused by the tilt of the planes. Motion directions show high activities for 180° and 360° at the location of the front plane, encoding the motion transparency. Note that the representation of disparity and speed gradients in the model does not require any specific mechanism; instead the used population code can represent gradients in the distribution of activation across disparity or motion and spatial position. However, this does not exclude that the visual cortex has a specific representation for gradients, e.g. in the lower bank of the superior temporal sulcus for disparity gradients (Jenssen et al., 2001) or area MT (Treue & Andersen, 1996) and higher visual brain areas for motion gradients (Sereno et al., 2002).

Crowded Motion Generates Semi-Transparency in Motion Displays

In video surveillance applications crowded motion makes it difficult to detect anomalous human behavior. We argue that an analysis on a large scale of motion crowds is related to the problem of detecting semi-transparent motion. Normal behavior of human motion in crowds includes walking in a single direction or, in terms of a crossing, in opposite direction organized in different stripes. Abnormal behavior includes crowds not moving, or single persons moving in a zigzag path through people moving in streams. Thus, normal behavioral motion leads to homogenous motion of a single component or of multiple components. If these multiple motion components are integrated over a local region of the visual field, semi-transparent motion occurs. For a model simulation we analyzed two cuts of a publicly available video from the Tokyo Shibuya crossing, see Figure 5a and 5c. Based on the motion signals in area MT we segmented each frame of the two sequences into the categories no motion, single motion, or multiple motions, depicted in Figure 5b and 5d. In addition, we show the activity of direction selective model area MT neurons pooled over three different local regions of visual space, indicated by the circles with the numbers 1, 2, and 3 in Figure 5a and 5c. For the region with no motion, in the upper half of the video cuts, all direction selective neurons weakly respond (region 1). Multiple motions (two in our case study) are represented in the lower half of the visual field where crowds of people form stripes of different motion directions (region 2). Sometimes people cluster into groups of similar motion (region 3). The activity in the polar histograms in Figure 5b and 5d builds up gradually over the time course of four simulated frames. The difference between the distributions of model MT neuron's activation for regions 1, 2, and 3 becomes more prominent, or in general the signal-to-noise ratio is increased over the time course of four iterations. This increase in signal-to-noise ratio is caused by the spatio-temporal integration of motion signals in the model, especially its FB signaling from model area MT to V1 that leads to a disambiguation of local motion signals (Bayerl & Neumann, 2004). A segmentation of video sequences into stationary, single, and multiple motion components is possible either by reading-out or directly analyzing the activity distributions of motion selective neurons of model area MT. This segmentation might help to detect regions of interest in video surveillance systems monitoring public places.

Scenarios with Opaque Materials Are Processed with the Same Model

How does the model perform for stereo image pairs and image sequences with only opaque materials and non-crowded objects? For stereo and visual motion processing a large body of test cases is provided at http://vision.middlebury.edu (Baker et al., 2011; Scharstein & Szeliski, 2003; Scharstein & Pal, 2007). Model simulations for these tests cases have been performed with the same parameter values as in the above simulations, with exception of the possible disparity or speed ranges that vary for these test cases. To compare simulation results in full resolution, activities of model area V1 have been read-out after the third processing step. For our stereo model 20 iterations have been applied feeding the model with the same input in each step, instead of an input from temporally successive frames. For the stereo and motion domain we use a weighted vector summation to interpret the population of disparity or motion selective neurons. This summation uses the disparity or motion as a vector and the activity as weights which are normalized by the sum of all activities for a given spatial location. The resulting disparity maps are depicted in Figure 6. All maps look like a smoothed version of the ground-truth. This is explained by the model's spatial integration and FB loop between model areas V1 and V2. So far, neither the model nor the read-out method include an explicit mechanism to preserve depth or motion defined boundaries while integrating spatial or spatio-temporal coherent stimulus components, a mechanism that is used in various grouping schemes for contour segments (Grossberg and Mingolla, 1985; Franken et al., 2006; Brox et al., 2006) and in computer vision algorithms for flow-gradient preserving integration (Horn & Schunck, 1981; Bruhn et al., 2006). In the estimated disparity maps the left side is partly missing or blurred out. For these locations on the left side no stereo correspondences are given, as they fall into a region of the left image where the right one has no corresponding parts. Therefore, these regions are propagated from spatial locations in the left image where stereo correspondences still exist. Similarly, occluded parts, the black regions in the ground-truth disparity maps, are 'filled-in' by the model from neighboring regions with stereo-correspondences using the spatial interaction between model areas V1 and V2. In these simulations disparity ranges have been adjusted to the interval of horizontal disparity in the stereo image pairs. The used interval of disparity values is denoted below each column of the test cases shown in Figure 6.

Simulation results for optic flow are evaluated by comparison against ground-truth in terms of angular error (AE) and endpoint error (EE), see Table 2. Errors for image sequences with low speeds are small, especially the EE (e.g. 'Army', 'Yosemite', or 'Mequon') because low speeds can be accurately represented in the model; in contras, larger speeds are sparsely represented,

Table 2. Error statistics for optic flow estimation. Motion has been computed for the 10th frame of the Middlebury benchmark image sequences (http://vision.middlebury.edu/flow/data/) from the 7th frame on, except for the 'Teddy' frame pair. Thus, motion is integrated over four frames. Estimated optic flow is calculated by the average vector sum based on model area V1 activity. Due to higher motion speeds in some sequences the range of speeds has been extended to eight ($N_{ring} = 7$ not counting the zero speed). Angular error (AE) is defined as the angular difference of the estimated flow vector and ground-truth flow vector, whereas a third component of value one has been added to the 2D vectors. The endpoint error (EE) is defined as the Euclidian norm of the difference vector between estimate and ground-truth. Mean value and standard deviation (SD) are computed for these errors over the entire image region, including the boundary.

Error	Army	Mequon	Schefflera	Wooden	Grove	Urban	Yosemite	Teddy [a]
Mean AE (deg)	14.5	11.4	16.8	11.7	16.6	27.3	9.77	37.9
SD AE (deg)	12.0	16.9	21.0	19.4	24.2	33.4	7.38	41.0
Mean EE (deg)	0.45	1.07	1.55	0.97	**3.23**	**3.44**	0.43	**5.63**
SD EE (deg)	0.34	1.08	1.77	1.24	3.45	7.34	0.29	3.92

[a] The 'Teddy' sequence provides only two images, thus, motion integration across three frames is not possible and estimates of the model are very poor.

due to logarithmic sampling. Consequently, errors for image sequences with high speeds such as 'Grove', 'Urban', and 'Teddy' are larger. This is especially visible in the high EE for these three sequences (highlighted by using a bold font style). In addition the sequence 'Grove' contains many fine structures from a modeled bush moving at fast speed which are smoothed out in the model's velocity estimates; see also an earlier comment on the model's smoothness constraint. Overall, the model can process scenes with opaque materials; however, we do not claim to compete with computer vision algorithms that are optimized for this task. We emphasize that the newly proposed model architecture is capable to process transparent as well as opaque surface appearances without specific parameter changes of the model mechanisms. It is demonstrated that the architecture successfully explains experimental findings using artificial test stimuli designed to probe the perception of stereo and motion transparency. Furthermore, the model is also able to process captured videos and particularly suggests a new approach to treat crowding as a special case of semi-transparent motion. The final demonstration closes the range of evaluation by demonstrating the successful processing of benchmark sequences from computer vision repositories.

FUTURE RESEARCH DIRECTIONS

Future research on binocular and motion transparency processing could combine the two pathways of stereo and motion signaling. Such an approach has been demonstrated for opaque surface motions (Qian & Andersen, 1997). Furthermore, physiological data shows that area MT has neurons selective for disparity (Born & Bradley, 2005) and their role for motion transparency processing might be important (Bradley et al., 1995). Suppression effects for the anti-preferred motion direction for motion and disparity tuned neurons were strong if the stimulus depth was near the preferred depth. This suggests that opponent motion directions could be represented in parallel; however, in different depths. This parallel representation relates to studies about contextual influences on perceptual judgments about figure motion and the underlying neural responses in area MT (Duncan et al., 2000). In this study a barber-pole pattern in diamond shape has been designed that is composed of vertical stripe patterns moving horizontally. The stripe terminators are stereoscopically defined by texture panels displayed in front or behind the moving diamond. In a nutshell, the terminators, judged as intrinsic or extrinsic to the diamond stripe pattern, influence the perceptual decision of the integrated movement direction so that the extrinsic terminators discard the movement information from being integrated (see the discussion in Albright & Stoner, 2002). The model mechanisms, especially the three step-processing cascade could be combined with the principles to selectively integrate neuronal responses that segregate along a particular feature dimension, such as stereo in the above described stimulus (Beck & Neumann, 2010).

Different data show multiple activations of MT neurons for various angular differences of transparently overlaid motion directions beside the preferred motion direction (Treue et al., 2000). In the current model, MT neurons are purely selective for only motion directions and speeds. By adding a disparity selective modality to the motion sensitive neurons the possible space of interactions is extended by another dimension. Whether the proposed local center-surround interaction generalizes for such a 3D feature space defined by motion direction, motion speed, and disparity remains to be explored. Even further, it is yet an open issue whether such a model mechanism uses a localized or a distributed code. In a localized representation, each neuron would directly operate on a 3D feature representation while in the latter case motion sensitive neurons would operate on a 2D (speed, direction) velocity representation and might additionally receive and send projections from and to remote representations of disparity or stimulus depth in general (e.g., in area V2).

In the current model disparity and motion gradients can be represented without applying explicit mechanisms. Recent investigations demonstrate that neurons show explicit selectivity to these stimulus properties for stereo (Jenssen et al., 2001) and motion stimuli (Sereno et al., 2002). An extension of the current model could use the gradient information contained in model areas V2 and MT representations and project them into a space of cells that are explicitly tuned to gradient information. For disparity gradients, a prototypical cell from this space could sum activity that is continuously changing in disparity and horizontal spatial location, but homogeneously integrating over vertical spatial locations, which would represent the selectivity for the tilted planes in the scenario displayed in Figure 5. Such a population of neurons explicitly representing gradients could be also useful for further read-out and separation of transparently overlaid planes, as it enables to sum activation selectively for a specific gradient plane configuration over the visual field. This summation effectively increases the signal-to-noise ratio and, thus, increases the reliability of detecting tilted planar object structures in image pairs or image streams.

Another strategy of a gradient representation could use local operators to represent gradients locally, instead of projecting activity into a set of predefined gradient patterns. Evidence for such local mechanisms in area MT is provided by physiology (Born & Tootell, 1992) and a model thereof (Buracas & Albright, 1996). The same mechanism is also used to define motion opponent operators for models of ego-motion and depth estimation (Royden, 1997). However, these previous models do not use a biologically plausible mechanism for the detection or representation of optic flow. Thus, the gradient processing by local difference operators with detected and population encoded motions remains an open yet unresolved issue, especially considering the ambiguity provided in transparency stimuli. Experiments with a transparent rotating cylinder that is viewed frontally show that disambiguation of gradients in motion transparency processing are possible (Treue et al., 1995).

CONCLUSION

We propose a new generic model for binocular transparency and motion transparency processing, with a local center-surround interaction as key mechanism. This interaction supports similar disparities or motions and suppresses dissimilar ones. The local center-surround interaction enables to resolve noisy and ambiguous perceptual input on one hand and allows for establishing a stable representation of multiple activations for transparent surfaces on the other hand. This mechanism has been shown to be general enough to be applied in the disparity and motion domain; furthermore, suggesting that both modalities share a common neural mechanism.

Simulation results show that such a mechanism along with an appropriate read-out method can explain effects of attraction and repulsion for disparity and motion signals in stimuli with transparent layers in different depths or moving into different directions. Video sequences that include complex geometry and realistic surface textures are successfully processed with the same model. Besides the processing of scenes with transparent materials, scenes with fully opaque materials leading to opaque disparity or motion can be processed with the same model and parameters as well. This makes the model also interesting for technical applications.

ACKNOWLEDGMENT

The authors wish to express their gratitude to Ennio Mingolla and Isao Hayashi for comments and discussions on the manuscript. The constructive criticism of three reviewers of the manuscript is also gratefully acknowledged. FR is supported in part by CELEST, a National Science Foundation Science of Learning Center (NSF SMA-0835976) and the Office of Naval Research (ONR N00014-11-1-0535). H.N. acknowledges support by the European Community in the 7th framework program ICT-project no. 215866-SEARISE and the Transregional Collaborative Research Center SFB/TRR 62 "Companion-Technology for Cognitive Technical Systems" funded by the German Research Foundation (DFG).

REFERENCES

Adelson, E., & Bergen, J. (1985). Spatiotemporal energy models for the perception of motion. *Journal of the Optical Society of America, Series A, 2*, 284–299. doi:10.1364/JOSAA.2.000284

Albright, T. (1984). Direction and orientation selectivity of neurons in visual area MT of the macaque. *Journal of Neurophysiology, 52*, 1106–1130.

Albright, T., & Desimone, R. (1987). Local precision of visuotopic organization in middle temporal area (MT) of the macaque. *Experimental Brain Research, 65*, 582–592. doi:10.1007/BF00235981

Albright, T. D., & Stoner, G. R. (2002). Contextual influences on visual processing. *Annual Review of Neuroscience, 25*, 339–379. doi:10.1146/annurev.neuro.25.112701.142900

Angelucci, A., Levitt, J., Walton, E., Hupe, J.-M., Bullier, J., & Lund, J. (2002). Circuits for local and global signal integration in primary visual cortex. *The Journal of Neuroscience, 22*, 8633–8646.

Baker, S., Scharstein, D., Lewis, J. P., Roth, S., Black, M. J., & Szeliski, R. (2011). A database and evaluation methodology for optical flow. *International Journal of Computer Vision, 92*, 1–31. doi:10.1007/s11263-010-0390-2

Bayerl, P., & Neumann, H. (2004). Disambiguating visual motion through contextual feedback modulation. *Neural Computation, 16*, 2041–2066. doi:10.1162/0899766041732404

Beck, C., & Neumann, H. (2010). Interactions of motion and form in visual cortex – A neural model. *The Journal of Physiology*, *104*, 61–70.

Black, M., & Anandan, P. (1993). A framework for the robust estimation of optical flow. *In Fourth International Conference on Computer Vision, ICCV-93, Berlin, Germany*, May, 1993, (pp. 231-236).

Black, M., & Anandan, P. (1996). The robust estimation of multiple motions: parametric and piecewise-smooth flow fields. *Computer Vision and Image Understanding*, *63*, 75–104. doi:10.1006/cviu.1996.0006

Born, R. T., & Bradley, D. C. (2005). Structure and function of visual area MT. *Annual Review of Neuroscience*, *28*, 157–189. doi:10.1146/annurev.neuro.26.041002.131052

Born, R. T., & Tootell, R. B. H. (1992). Segregation of global and local motion processing in primate middle temporal visual area. *Nature*, *357*, 497–499. doi:10.1038/357497a0

Braddick, O., Wishart, K., & Curran, W. (2002). Directional performance in motion transparency. *Vision Research*, *42*, 1237–1248. doi:10.1016/S0042-6989(02)00018-4

Bradley, D. C., Qian, N., & Andersen, R. A. (1995). Integration of motion and stereopsis in middle temporal cortical area of macaques. *Nature*, *373*, 609–611. doi:10.1038/373609a0

Brox, T., Weickert, J., Burgeth, B., & Mrazek, P. (2006). Nonlinear structure tensors. *Image and Vision Computing*, *24*, 41–55. doi:10.1016/j.imavis.2005.09.010

Bruhn, A., Weickert, J., Kohlberger, T., & Schnörr, C. (2006). A multigrid platform for real-time motion computation with discontinuity-preserving variational methods. *International Journal of Computer Vision*, *70*(3), 257–277. doi:10.1007/s11263-006-6616-7

Bullier, J., Hupe, J., James, A., & Girard, P. (2001). The role of feedback connections in shaping the responses of visual cortical neurons. *Progress in Brain Research*, *134*, 193–204. doi:10.1016/S0079-6123(01)34014-1

Buracas, G. T., & Albright, T. D. (1996). Contribution of area MT to perception of three-dimensional shape: A computational study. *Vision Research*, *36*(6), 869–887. doi:10.1016/0042-6989(95)00192-1

Chen, Y., & Qian, N. (2004). A coarse-to-fine disparity energy model with both phase-shift and position-shift receptive field mechanisms. *Neural Computation*, *16*, 1545–1577. doi:10.1162/089976604774201596

Cheng, K., Hasegawa, T., Saleem, K. S., & Tanaka, K. (1994). Comparison of neuronal selectivity for stimulus speed, length, and contrast in the prestriate visual cortical areas V4 and MT of the macaque monkey. *Journal of Neurophysiology*, *71*(6), 2269–2280.

Cumming, B. G., & Parker, A. J. (1999). Binocular neurons in V1 of awake monkeys are selective for absolute, not relative, disparity. *The Journal of Neuroscience*, *19*(13), 5602–5618.

Danielsson, P.-E., & Segera, O. (1990). Rotation invariance in gradient and higher order derivative detectors. *Computer Vision Graphics and Image Processing*, *49*(2), 198–221. doi:10.1016/0734-189X(90)90137-K

Darrell, T., & Pentland, A. (1991). *Robust estimation of a multi-layered motion representation*. In IEEE Workshop on Visual Motion, Princeton, New Jersey, October.

Darrell, T., & Simoncelli, E. (1993). *Separation of transparent motion into layers using velocity-tuned mechanisms*. Technical report, M.I.T. Media Laboratory, Vision and Modeling Group, Technical Report No. 244.

Daugman, J. (1985). Uncertainty relation for resolution in space, spatial frequency, and orientation optimized by two-dimensional visual cortical filters. *Journal of Optical Society of America, Series A, 2*, 1160–1169. doi:10.1364/JOSAA.2.001160

Duncan, R. O., Albright, T. D., & Stoner, G. R. (2000). Occlusion and the interpretation of visual motion: perceptual and neuronal effects of context. *The Journal of Neuroscience, 20*, 5885–5897.

Durant, S., Donoso-Barrera, A., Tan, S., & Johnston, A. (2006). Moving from spatially segregated to transparent motion: a modeling approach. *Biology Letters, 2*, 101–105. doi:10.1098/rsbl.2005.0379

Eckhorn, R., Reitboeck, H., Arndt, M., & Dicke, P. (1990). Feature linking via synchronization among distributed assemblies: Simulations of results from cat visual cortex. *Neural Computation, 2*, 293–307. doi:10.1162/neco.1990.2.3.293

Edwards, M., & Nishida, S. (1999). Global-motion detection with transparent-motion signals. *Vision Research, 39*, 2239–2249. doi:10.1016/S0042-6989(98)00325-3

Felisberti, F., & Zanker, J. (2005). Attention modulates perception of transparent motion. *Vision Research, 45*, 2587–2599. doi:10.1016/j.visres.2005.03.004

Franken, E., van Almsick, M., Rongen, P., Florack, L., & ter Haar Romeny, B. (2006). An efficient method for tensor voting using steerable filters. In Leonardis, A., Bischof, H., & Pinz, A. (Eds.), *ECCV 2006, Part IV, LNCS 3954* (pp. 228–240). doi:10.1007/11744085_18

Freeman, W. T., & Adelson, E. H. (1991). The design and use of steerable filters. *IEEE Transactions on Pattern Analysis and Machine Intelligence, 13*(9), 891–906. doi:10.1109/34.93808

Greenwood, J., & Edwards, M. (2009). The detection of multiple global directions: Capacity limits with spatially segregated and transparent-motion signals. *Journal of Vision (Charlottesville, Va.), 9*, 1–15. doi:10.1167/9.1.40

Grossberg, S., & Mingolla, E. (1985). Neural dynamics of perceptual grouping: Textures, boundaries, and emergent segmentations. *Perception & Psychophysics, 38*, 141–171. doi:10.3758/BF03198851

Hassenstein, B., & Reichardt, W. (1956). Systemtheoretische Analyse der Zeitreihenfolgen und Vorzeichenauswertung bei der Bewegungsperzeption des Rüsselkäfers, Chlorophanus. *Naturforschung Teil B, 11*, 513–524.

Heeger, D. (1987). Model the extraction of image flow. *Journal of Optical Society of America, Series A, 4*, 1455–1471. doi:10.1364/JOSAA.4.001455

Horn, B., & Schunk, B. (1981). Determining optical flow. *Artificial Intelligence, 17*, 185–203. doi:10.1016/0004-3702(81)90024-2

Hubel, D. H., & Livingstone, M. S. (1987). Segregation of form, color, stereopsis in primate area 18. *The Journal of Neuroscience, 7*(11), 3378–3415.

Hubel, D. H., & Wiesel, T. N. (1962). Receptive fields, binocular interaction and functional architecture in the cat's visual cortex. *The Journal of Physiology, 160*, 106–154.

Hubel, D. H., & Wiesel, T. N. (1970). Stereoscopic vision in macaque monkey. Cells sensitive to binocular depth in area 18 of the macaque monkey cortex. *Nature, 225*, 41–42. doi:10.1038/225041a0

Janssen, P., Vogels, R., Liu, Y., & Orban, G. A. (2011). Macaque inferior temporal neurons are selective for three-dimensional boundaries and surfaces. *The Journal of Neuroscience, 21*(23), 9419–9429.

Johnston, A., McOwan, P., & Benton, C. (1999). Robust velocity computation from a biologically motivated model of motion perception. *Proceedings of Royal Society, Series B*, *266*, 509–518. doi:10.1098/rspb.1999.0666

Ju, S., Black, M., & Jepson, A. (1996). Skin and bones: Multi-layer, locally affine, optical flow and regularization with transparency. In *IEEE Conference on Computer Vision and Pattern Recognition, CVPR'96, San Francisco, CA*, June 1996, (pp. 307-314).

Kiorpes, L., & Movshon, J. A. (2004). Development of sensitivity to visual motion in macaque monkeys. *Visual Neuroscience*, *21*, 851–859. doi:10.1017/S0952523804216054

Langley, K., Fleet, D., & Atherton, T. (1992). On transparent motion computation. In *Proceedings of British Machine Vision Conference (BMVC)*, Leeds, (pp. 247-257). New York, NY: Springer.

Liu, H., Hong, T.-H., Herman, M., & Chellappa, R. (1995). Spatio-temporal filters for transparent motion segmentation. In Proceedings of the *International Conference on Image Processing*, Vol. 3, (pp. 464-467). doi: 10.1109/ICIP.1995.537672

Marr, D., & Poggio, T. (1976). Cooperative computation of stereo disparity. *Science*, *194*, 283–287. doi:10.1126/science.968482

Maunsell, J., & Essen, D. V. (1983). The connections of the middle temporal visual area (MT) and their relationship to a cortical hierarchy in the macaque monkey. *The Journal of Neuroscience*, *3*, 2563–2586.

Mechler, F., Reich, D., & Victor, J. (2002). Detection and discrimination of relative spatial phase by V1 neurons. *The Journal of Neuroscience*, *22*, 6129–6157.

Meso, A., & Zanker, J. (2009). Perceiving motion transparency in the absence of component direction differences. *Vision Research*, *49*, 2187–2200. doi:10.1016/j.visres.2009.06.011

Mestre, D., Masson, G., & Stone, L. (2001). Spatial scale of motion segmentation from speed cues. *Vision Research*, *41*, 2697–2713. doi:10.1016/S0042-6989(01)00162-6

Mota, C., Dorr, M., Stuke, I., & Barth, E. (2004). Categorization of transparent motion patterns using the projective plane. *Journal of Computer and Information Science*, *5*, 129–140.

Mulligan, J. (1992). Motion transparency is restricted to two planes. *Investigative Ophthalmology & Visual Science*, *33*(Supplement), 1049.

Nover, H., Anderson, C. H., & DeAngelis, G. (2005). A logarithmic, scale-invariant representation of speed in macaque middle temporal area accounts for speed discrimination performance. *The Journal of Neuroscience*, *25*, 10049–10060. doi:10.1523/JNEUROSCI.1661-05.2005

Nyquist, H. (2002). Certain topics in telegraph transmission theory. *Proceedings of the IEEE*, *90*, 280–305. doi:10.1109/5.989875

Ohzawa, I., DeAngelis, G. C., & Freeman, R. D. (1990). Stereoscopic depth discrimination in the visual cortex: Neurons ideally suited as disparity detectors. *Science*, *249*, 1037–1041. doi:10.1126/science.2396096

Orban, G. A., Kennedy, H., & Bullier, J. (1986). Velocity sensitivity and direction selectivity of neurons in areas Vl and V2 of the monkey: Influence of eccentricity. *Journal of Neurophysiology*, *56*(2), 462–480.

Pollard, S. B., & Frisby, J. P. (1990). Transparency and the uniqueness constraint in human and computer stereo vision. *Nature*, *347*, 553–556. doi:10.1038/347553a0

Prazdny, K. (1985). Detection of binocular disparities. *Biological Cybernetics*, *52*, 93–99. doi:10.1007/BF00363999

Priebe, J. N., Lisberger, S. G., & Movshon, J. A. (2006). Tuning for spatiotemporal frequency and speed in directionally selective neurons of macaque striate cortex. *The Journal of Neuroscience*, *26*(11), 2941–2950. doi:10.1523/JNEUROSCI.3936-05.2006

Prince, S. J. D., Cumming, B. G., & Parker, A. J. (2002). Range and mechanism of encoding of horizontal disparity in macaque V1. *Journal of Neurophysiology*, *87*, 209–221.

Qian, N. (1994). Computing stereo disparity and motion with known binocular cell properties. *Neural Computation*, *6*, 390–404. doi:10.1162/neco.1994.6.3.390

Qian, N., & Andersen, R. A. (1997). A physiological model for motion–stereo integration and a unified explanation of Pulfrich-like phenomena. *Vision Research*, *37*(12), 1683–1698. doi:10.1016/S0042-6989(96)00164-2

Qian, N., Andersen, R. A., & Adelson, E. (1994). Transparent motion perception as detection of unbalanced motion signals, III- Modeling. *The Journal of Neuroscience*, *14*, 7381–7392.

Qian, N., & Sejnowski, T. J. (1989). Learning to solve random-dot stereograms of dense and transparent surfaces with recurrent backpropagation. In *Proceedings of the 1988 Connectionist Models Summer School,* Morgan Kaufmann.

Ramirez-Manzanares, A., Rivera, M., Kornprobst, P., & Lauze, F. (2006). *Multi-valued motion fields estimation for transparent sequences with a variational approach.* Rapport De Recherche Inria, number RR-5920.

Rauber, H.-J., & Treue, S. (1999). Revisiting motion repulsion: Evidence for a general phenomenon? *Vision Research*, *39*, 3187–3196. doi:10.1016/S0042-6989(99)00025-5

Raudies, F., & Neumann, H. (2010). A model of neural mechanisms in monocular transparent motion perception. *The Journal of Physiology*, *104*, 71–83.

Reeves, A., Lynch, D., Tran, M., & Grayem, R. (2010). Multiple planes in stereo-transparency. *Vision Research*, *10*(7), 375. doi:10.1167/10.7.375

Ringach, D. (2002). Spatial structure and symmetry of simple-cell receptive fields in macaque primary visual cortex. *Journal of Neurophysiology*, *88*, 455–463.

Rodman, H. R., & Albright, T. D. (1987). Coding of visual stimulus velocity in area MT of the macaque. *Vision Research*, *27*(12), 2035–2048. doi:10.1016/0042-6989(87)90118-0

Royden, C. S. (1997). Mathematical analysis of motion-opponent mechanisms used in the determination of heading and depth. *Journal of the Optical Society of America. A, Optics, Image Science, and Vision*, *14*(9), 2128–2143. doi:10.1364/JOSAA.14.002128

Scharstein, D., & Pal, C. (2007). *Learning conditional random fields for stereo*. In IEEE Computer Society Conference on Computer Vision and Pattern Recognition (CVPR 2007).

Scharstein, D., & Szeliski, R. (2002). A taxonomy and evaluation of dense two-frame stereo correspondence algorithms. *International Journal of Computer Vision, 47*(1/2/3), 7-42.

Scharstein, D., & Szeliski, R. (2003). High-accuracy stereo depth maps using structured light. In *IEEE Computer Society Conference on Computer Vision and Pattern Recognition* (CVPR 2003), Vol. 1, (pp. 195-202).

Sereno, M. E., Trinath, T., Augath, M., & Logothetis, N. K. (2002). Three-dimensional shape representation in monkey cortex. *Neuron*, *33*, 635–652. doi:10.1016/S0896-6273(02)00598-6

Simoncelli, E. P., & Heeger, D. J. (1998). A model of neuronal responses in visual area MT. *Vision Research*, *38*, 743–761. doi:10.1016/S0042-6989(97)00183-1

Snowden, R. J., Treue, S., Erikson, R. G., & Andersen, R. A. (1991). The response of area MT and V1 neurons to transparent motion. *The Journal of Neuroscience*, *11*, 2768–2785.

Stafstrom, C. E., Schwindt, P. C., & Crill, W. E. (1984). Receptive firing in layer V neurons from cat neocortex in vitro. *Journal of Neurophysiology*, *2*, 264–277.

Stevenson, S. B., Comack, L. K., & Shorr, C. M. (1991). Depth attraction and repulsion in random dot stereograms. *Vision Research*, *31*, 805–813. doi:10.1016/0042-6989(91)90148-X

Thomas, O. M., Cumming, B. G., & Parker, A. J. (2002). A specialization for relative disparity in V2. *Nature Neuroscience*, *5*(5), 472–478. doi:10.1038/nn837

Treue, S., & Andersen, R. A. (1996). Neural responses to velocity gradients in macaque cortical area MT. *Visual Neuroscience*, *13*, 797–804. doi:10.1017/S095252380000866X

Treue, S., Andersen, R. A., Ando, H., & Hildreth, E. (1995). Structure-from-motion: Perceptual evidence for surface interpolation. *Vision Research*, *35*(1), 139–148. doi:10.1016/0042-6989(94)E0069-W

Treue, S., Hol, K., & Rauber, H.-J. (2000). Seeing multiple directions of motion - physiology and psychophysics. *Nature Neuroscience*, *3*, 270–276. doi:10.1038/72985

Tsai, J. J., & Victor, J. D. (2003). Reading a population code: A multi-scale neural model for representing binocular disparity. *Vision Research*, *43*, 445–466. doi:10.1016/S0042-6989(02)00510-2

Tsirlin, I., Allison, R. S., & Wilcox, L. M. (2008). Stereoscopic transparency: Constraints on the perception of multiple surfaces. *Journal of Vision (Charlottesville, Va.)*, *8*(5), 1–10. doi:10.1167/8.5.5

Tzvetanov, T., Wirmer, A., & Folta, K. (2007). Orientation repulsion and attraction in alignment perception. *Vision Research*, *47*, 1693–1704. doi:10.1016/j.visres.2007.03.003

Watanabe, O. (2008). A neural model for stereo transparency with the population of the disparity energy models. *Neurocomputing*, *71*, 3158–3167. doi:10.1016/j.neucom.2008.04.025

Watanabe, O., & Kikuchi, M. (2005). Nonlinearity of the population activity to transparent motion. *Neural Networks*, *18*, 15–22. doi:10.1016/j.neunet.2004.06.007

Weinshall, D. (1989). Perception of multiple transparent planes in stereo vision. *Nature*, *341*, 737–739. doi:10.1038/341737a0

Westheimer, G. (1986). Spatial interaction in the domain of disparity signals in human stereoscopic vision. *The Journal of Physiology*, *370*, 619–629.

Zanker, J. (2005). A computational analysis of separating motion signals in transparent random dot kinematograms. *Spatial Vision*, *18*, 431–445. doi:10.1163/1568568054389615

ADDITIONAL READING

Braddick, O., & Qian, N. (2001). The organization of global motion and transparency. In Zanker, M., & Zeil, J. (Eds.), *Motion vision - Computational, neural, and ecological constraints*. Berlin, Germany: Springer Verlag. doi:10.1007/978-3-642-56550-2_5

Cumming, B. G., & DeAngelis, G. C. (2001). The physiology of stereopsis. *Annual Review of Neuroscience*, *24*, 203–238. doi:10.1146/annurev.neuro.24.1.203

Howard, I. P. (2002). *Seeing in depth* (*Vol. 1-2*). Thornhill, Canada: I Porteous.

Pack, C. C., & Born, R. T. (2008). Cortical mechanisms for the integration of visual motion. In *The senses: A comprehensive reference*. Oxford, UK: Elsevier Ltd. doi:10.1016/B978-012370880-9.00309-1

Roe, A. W., Parker, A. J., Born, R. T., & DeAnglis, G. C. (2007). Disparity channels in early vision. *The Journal of Neuroscience*, *27*(44), 11820–11831. doi:10.1523/JNEUROSCI.4164-07.2007

Sperling, G. (1970). Binocular vision: A physical and neural theory. *The American Journal of Physiology*, *83*, 461–534.

KEY TERMS AND DEFINITIONS

Binocular Transparency: If multiple surfaces at different depths occur in the same location of the visual field, then binocular transparency occurs.

Feedback (FB): A feedback signal originates from a later stage in a chain of processing steps and enters at an earlier stage in the chain. In engineering feedback occurs for controller systems, where the controller's output signal influence is directly measured and fed back into the controller. Feedback or descending projections in cortex originate from higher areas in the hierarchy of visual processing and project to lower areas.

Gabor Filter: This filter is defined by the combination of a cosine wave (real part) and sine wave (imaginary part) each multiplied together with a Gaussian function. For instance, a one-dimensional Gabor filter is defined by $f^{Gabor}(x) = \exp(i \cdot 2\pi \cdot f) \cdot 1 / (\sqrt{2\pi} \cdot \sigma) \cdot \exp(-x^2 / (2 \cdot \sigma^2))$. Transformed into the Fourier domain this filter covers a Gaussian shaped frequency window centered at the frequency *f*.

Middle Temporal Area (MT): Multiple studies show that MT is the mainly controlling spatial and temporal integration of visual image motion, integrated inputs mainly from area V1. Besides motion integration, cells in area MT show also selectivity for disparity.

Motion Transparency: If at least two motions different in speed and or motion direction occur in the same location of the visual field, then motion transparency occurs. Naturally, this happens for surfaces of transparent material moving in front of an also moving background, e.g. the dusty windows of a bus.

Primary Visual Area (V1): This area is the first stage of cortical 'image processing' extracting end-stops like corners, orientations of edges, spatial frequency, temporal frequency, visual motion, and disparity of stimuli.

Random Dot Kinematogram (RDK): Like in the RDS, dots are randomly distributed on the display plane. Dots are shifted between frames presented in a temporally succeeding order. Note that an RDS and RDK can be combined resulting in a stimulus containing stereo and motion attributes.

Random Dot Stereogram (RDS): Dots of a certain size, shape, and luminosity are randomly distributed on the display plane with a certain density. To generate positive disparity, dots for the left image are displaced to the right according to the disparity value and with respect to their position in the right image.

Second Visual Area (V2): This area processes form, e.g. border ownership encoding, color, and disparity; relative disparity more than absolute.

Semi-Transparency: In contrast to transparency, semi-transparency is generated by the spatial integration by the visual system of motions from small objects. These motions are integrated in a way that they appear as two layers of distinct motions. For disparity in the stereo domain the same semi-transparency happens.

ENDNOTES

1. Assume the detected phase by 1D Gabor filters for left eye's image is denoted by φ_L and the right eye's image by φ_R. Then the horizontal disparity is computed as $\left[\phi_L - \phi_R\right]_{-\pi}^{+\pi} / \omega$, where ω denotes the angular frequency of the Gabor filter and $\left[\ \cdot\ \right]_{-\pi}^{+\pi}$ a circular wrapping into the range of $\pm\pi$.
2. A simplified version of the detector could test only for shifts orthogonal to the orientation that is extracted by the Gabor filters.
3. In our implementation we solve all ODEs by using their steady-state solution. Iterations between different frames of the input sequence are iterations of these steady state solution assumed for each individual frame.
4. Note there is a difference between the increase in RF size and the magnification factor. Here, the RF size in MT is about ten times larger than that in V1, however, the magnification factor in V1 is about one-fifth of that of MT (Albright and Desimone, 1987). This difference between magnification factor and RF size may reflect the Nyquist sampling theorem, where MT applies a low-pass filter which restricts the highest spatial frequency to at least the half of the sampling frequency (Nyquist, 2002).
5. Assume that the maximum normalized frequency is π, then the power in the spectrum of the Gaussian filtered signal with σ at the sampling rate r is $\sigma / \sqrt{2\pi} \cdot \exp(-(\pi / r \cdot \sigma)^2 / 2\cdot)$. For instance, for the sampling rate r=5 we apply a Gaussian filter with σ=5 pixel the power is ~1.43% of the maximum.
6. The density of black dots on a white background is 25%. Black dots have a size of 1 x 1 pixels.
7. Random dot kinematograms have a size of 256 x 256 pixels. White dots appear on a black background at a 10% density and are constructed by (i) randomly and uniformly distributing seed points over the entire stimulus, (ii) enlarging these points to six pixels in diameter by using the morphological dilation operation, and (iii) convolving the resulting discs in the image with a Gaussian filter of three pixels support and ¾ pixels standard deviation. Dots move at a speed of five pixels per frame and the motion direction varies as reported in the simulated experiments.

Chapter 7
Early Perception-Action Cycles in Binocular Vision:
Visuomotor Paradigms and Cortical-Like Architectures

Silvio P. Sabatini
DIBRIS – University of Genoa, Italy

Andrea Canessa
DIBRIS – University of Genoa, Italy

Fabio Solari
DIBRIS – University of Genoa, Italy

Manuela Chessa
DIBRIS – University of Genoa, Italy

Agostino Gibaldi
DIBRIS – University of Genoa, Italy

ABSTRACT

Pushed by ample neurophysiological evidence of modulatory effects of motor and premotor signals on the visual receptive fields across several cortical areas, there is growing attention for moving the active vision paradigm from systems in which just the effects of action influence the perception, to systems where the acting itself, and even its planning, operate in parallel with perception. Such systems could close the loops and take full advantage of concurrent/anticipatory perception-action processing. In this context, cortical-like architectures for both vergence control and depth perception (in the 3D peripersonal space) that incorporate adaptive tuning mechanisms of the disparity detectors are presented. The proposed approach points out the advantages and the flexibility of distributed and hierarchical cortical-like architectures against solutions based on a conventional systemic coupling of sensing and motor components, which in general poses integration problems since processes must be coupled that are too heterogeneous and complex.

INTRODUCTION

There is increasing interest in moving the active vision field from systems in which just the effects of action influence the perception, to systems where the acting itself, and even its planning, operate in parallel with perception, thus really closing the loops and taking full advantage of a concurrent/anticipatory perception-action processing. From this perspective, the motor system of a humanoid should be an integral part of its perceptual machinery (e.g., see Int. Journal of Humanoid Research Special issue on the "Active

DOI: 10.4018/978-1-4666-2539-6.ch007

Vision of Humanoids", 2010). Traditionally, however, in robot vision systems, perception-action loops close at a "system level" (by decoupling *de facto* the vision modules from those dedicated to motor control and motor planning), and the computational effects of the eye movements on the visual processes are rarely implemented in artificial systems.

The limitation of this approach is that solving specific high-level tasks usually requires sensory-motor shortcuts at the system level, and specific knowledge-based rules or heuristic algorithms have to be included to establish behaviorally consistent relationships among the extracted perceptual features and the desired actions. The risk is to abandon distributed representations of multiple solutions to prematurely construct integrated descriptions of cognitive entities and commit the system to a particular behavior. Conversely, our claim is that early/complex interactions between vision and motor control are crucial in determining the effective performance of an active binocular vision system with a minimal amount of resources and coping with uncertainties and inaccuracies of real systems.

There is ample evidence for the pivotal role of programmed eye movements in the computations that are performed in the process of seeing (as opposite to "looking at"). Yet, how to profitably integrate this accumulating evidence with the computational theories of stereo vision has not been fully exploited, as rectified images are still calculated in current humanoid active-disparity vision modules, relying solely on the encoder's data. The complexity of integrating efficiently and with flexibility the different aspects of binocular active vision indeed prevented until now a full validation of the visuomotor approaches to 3D perception in real world situations. We believe that the advantages of binocular visuomotor strategies could be fully understood only if one jointly analyzes and models the problem of neural computation of stereo information, and if one takes into account the limited accuracy of the motor system. Unfortunately, models in this joint field are few (Theimer & Mallot, 1994; Hansard & Horaud, 2008; Read & Cumming, 2006) and rarely address all the computational issues.

In this work we defend a visuomotor approach to 3D perception by proposing the instantiation of visuomotor optimization principles concurrently with the design of distributed neural models/ architectures that can efficiently embody them. Specifically, we present two case studies that show how large-scale networks of V1-like binocular cells can provide a flexible medium on which to base coding/decoding adaptation mechanisms related to sensorimotor schema. At the coding level, the position of the eyes in the orbits can adapt the disparity tuning to minimize the necessary resources, while preserving reliable estimates (i.e., adjustable tuning mechanisms based on the posture of the eyes to improve depth vision; see Chessa, Sabatini & Solari, 2009). At the decoding level, read-out mechanisms of the disparity population code can specialize to gain vergence control servos over a wider range of disparities than what would be possible through an explicit calculation of the disparity map (Gibaldi, Canessa, Chessa, Solari & Sabatini, 2010).

BACKGROUND

Purposive (active) vision is an important source of information and provides a number of cues about the 3D layout of objects in a scene that could be used for planning and controlling goal-directed behaviors. Although computer and robot vision are today making technological progress, the current active vision solutions are increasingly driven by applications like robotic manipulation or surveillance and are still far from reaching a real purposive behavior. More precisely, research in robot vision is more geared towards active "looking at" scenes and objects rather that "seeing", gathering the visual data and having to act in a limited time and space. According to the sensorimotor theory of perception (O'Regan & Noë, 2001; Noë, 2004), "seeing" is something we do rather than a sequence of hierarchical interpretative processes. From this perspective, the experience of "seeing" in not necessarily generated, but it expresses itself in the behavior. Following these premises, we can study the topic of seeing within an embodied artificial intelligence framework.

Perception-Action Synergies in Purposive Vision

An intelligent perceptual agent must be able to interact with its environment through sensing, processing and transforming information about the surrounding world into different levels of representation, and eventually solve complex problems in a real dynamic world. The idea of constructing such an intelligent system has been the ultimate goal of the Artificial Intelligence (AI) field and has led this community to investigate a number of robot capabilities such as: to generate and execute complex plans; to perform online resource allocation; to deal with problems as they arise in real-time (reaction); and to reason with incomplete information and unpredictable events. In view of the inherent difficulty of the problem, while robots are now commonplace in today's manufacturing industry, these devices are typically characterized by a lack of the ability to adapt to a dynamic environment. In short, they lack intelligent sensing and action. One of the main reasons of this failure must be ascribed to the traditional AI view of an intelligent system as a set of independent cognitive modules: perception, planning, learning, and execution (see Figure 1A). Within this view, complex problems are solved by the execution of individual modules that can exchange information through well-defined interfaces. The assumption of independent processes brought up enormous difficulties because of the unexpected interactions of those parts (Costa, Rillo, Barros & Bianchi, 1998).

The embodiment concept, which describes the ability of the system to acquire knowledge of its world from the consistent coupling of its own action and perception, has been rooted in the scientific community and has characterized many significant advances in recent cognitive vision research. During the last decades, there has been a growing interest in the use of active control of image formation to simplify and accelerate scene understanding. Since the pioneering ideas of Bajcsy (1988) and Aloimonos, Weiss & Bandopadhay (1987), the approach has been extended by several groups (Ballard, 1991; Eklundh & Pahlavan, 1992; Brown, 1990) demonstrating how multiple simple behaviors (e.g., saccadic, vergence, vestibulo-ocular reflex and neck motion) may be used for controlling visual perception. Different computational paradigms have been introduced through the years, by developing the initial concept of "animate vision" in which the visual calculations are embedded in a sensory-motor repertoire that reduces degrees of freedom and yields a number of computational advantages.

In more general terms, an important research direction emerged, with the aim of designing a robotic agent that could autonomously acquire visual skills from its interactions with an uncommitted environment in order to achieve some set of goals. Learning new visual skills in a dynamic, task-driven fashion so as to complete an a priori unknown visual task is known as the purposive vision paradigm. Purposive vision is essentially orthogonal to the reconstructionist approach of computer vision (Marr, 1982).

The goal of reconstructive or recovery vision (Dean, Allen & Aloimonos, 1995) is to derive indeed, from one or more images of a scene, an accurate three-dimensional description of the objects in the world and quantitatively recover its properties from image cues such as shading, contours, motion, stereo, color, etc. Thus recovery emphasizes the study of task-independent visual abilities carried out by a passive observer through

Figure 1. (A) The modular view of an intelligent system: "Complex problems are solved by the execution of individual modules that can exchange information through well defined interfaces" (Costa, Rillo, Barros & Bianchi, 1998). (B) The synergic view of an intelligent system: "Perception should not be considered as a self-contained module, but as an entity containing other intelligent capabilities, i.e., planning, reasoning and learning, all of which cooperate to solve specific tasks" (Costa, Rillo, Barros & Bianchi, 1998).

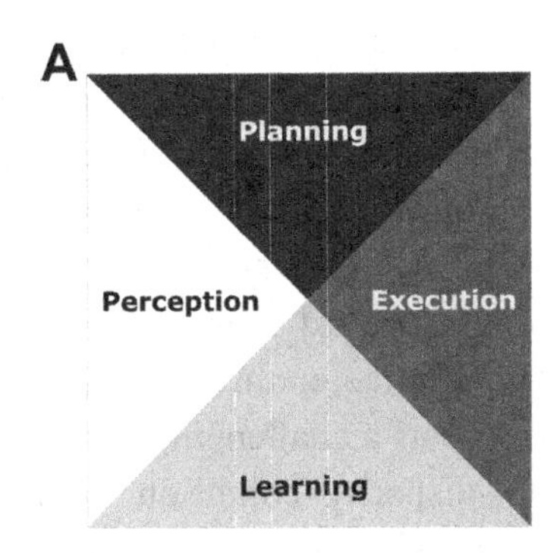

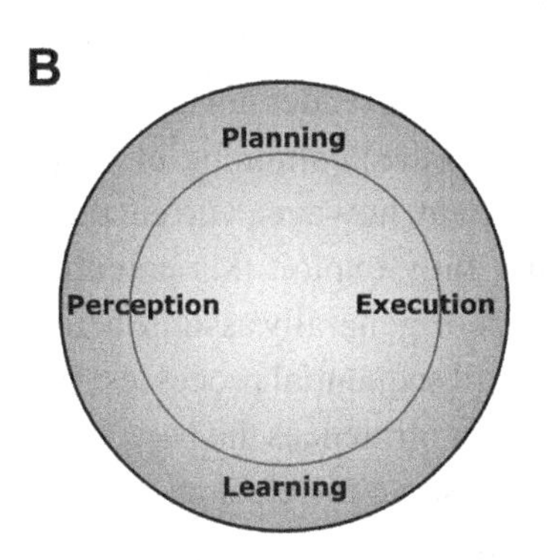

a hierarchy of bottom-up processes (from primal sketch, to 21/2-D, and then to scene interpretation) (Marr, 1982). In contrast, the purposive vision paradigm does not consist in generating a complete, detailed, symbolic 3D model of the surrounding environment; rather it emphasizes the fact that vision is task-oriented and that the performing agent should focus its attention only on the parts of the environment that are relevant to its task. Therefore, purposive vision stresses the dependency between action and perception: selecting actions becomes the inherent goal of the visual sensing process. This paradigm often leads to the breakdown of the visual task into several sub-problems that are managed by a supervision module that ultimately selects the suitable reactions.

According to the purposive approach, vision should not be considered as a self-contained module, but as an entity containing other intelligent capabilities, i.e., planning, reasoning and learning, all of which cooperate to solve specific tasks. Intelligence should not be divided into isolated cognitive modules, but decomposed in terms of behaviors (Polpitiya, Ghosh, Martin & Dayawansa, 2004). Thus a synergic approach replaces the modular one (see Figure 1B). Each ring corresponds to a perception-action-loop that can be associated with specific behaviors decomposed with increasing degrees of complexity.

Purposive vision is very close to active vision, and these concepts are sometimes used interchangeably. Just like purposive vision, active vision criticizes the passive point of view of the reconstructionist approach, and it argues that visual perception is an exploratory activity. However, active vision is essentially interested in experimental setups where the position of the visual sensors can be governed by the effectors. This approach is evidently inspired by human vision, in which muscles can orientate the head, the eyes and the pupils, and the visual sensor is regarded as a component in a larger system, able to make either deliberate actions to simplify the visual sensing process, or to react to visual events. By learning to control such effectors, the agent can acquire better information and resolve ambiguities in the visual data, for example by acquiring images of a scene from different viewpoints. Some ill-posed problems in computer vision become well-posed by employing active vision (Bajcsy, 1988; Krotkov, Henriksen & Kories, 1990; Ballard & Ozcandarli, 1988; Brown, 1990). From this perspective, (1) general perceptual problems that are ill posed and nonlinear for a passive observer become well posed and linear, (2) computational resources are directed to important areas ("attentive" mode; Clark & Ferrier, 1988), therefore improving the efficiency of the visual systems.

In this respect, the concept of "purposive vision" is much more general and powerful than that of "active vision" since it does not essentially confine interactivity to the positioning of visual sensors. To a large extent, however, current models of vision do not fully exploit this potential. Indeed, models of vision generally assume action and perception are still sequential processes: it is the effect of action that influences the perception (e.g., eye movements serve to select a scene for perception) and not the acting itself, even less its planning (but see Hamker, 2005a, and Hamker, 2005b).

A Visuomotor Approach to 3D Perception

In absence of motion parallax, and disposing of a binocular stereo vision system, 3D information can be gathered without introducing active components (except for covering a larger field of view). In such conditions, stereopsis (i.e., position parallax) is usually thought as a static problem, since the disparity map obtained by a fixed-geometry stereo camera pair, with (nearly) parallel axes, is sufficient to reconstruct the 3D spatial layout of the observed scene, and camera movements are often regarded as unnecessary complicating factor. Things are dramatically different if we consider a binocular, foveated system with a vergent stereo geometry. In such conditions, the perceptual process intrinsically gains a motor dimension as the 3D information is collected dynamically with respect to the fixation point. The eye rotations, although insufficient *per se* to provide depth cues (but see Santini & Rucci, 2007), strongly constrain the stereo vision processing, and visual information is gathered through a continuous interaction with the environment. This is especially true for visual exploration of the peripersonal space when large values of vergence occur, and disparity geometry strongly depends on the viewing geometry.

In general, the importance of the visuomotor aspects of 3D visual perception can be understood not just to develop algorithms that enable robots to cope with changes in the environment, but, and more importantly, to acquire task-independent skills as a living being. Even while the problem of controlling on a visual basis the vergence of a stereo camera system has specific and rather straightforward solutions, the joint treatment of the vergence control and of 3D perception still represents a challenging cognitive problem. The zero-disparity condition in the fixation point solves indeed the vergence task, but nullifies the visually-based information for the 3D position of the fixated target point. Only the residual disparities elsewhere in the visual field are cues for stereopsis. The momentarily existing (and continuously changing) fixation point, i.e., the position where the system verges, becomes a reference that can be parameterized by the relative orientations of the eyes. Moreover, how the system verges in terms of the full three-dimensional rotational position of the cameras impacts the accuracy of stereopsis. Changing camera positions influences the local shape of the zero disparity surface near the fixation point (i.e., the surface horopter), and optimal motor control provides several advantages for vision, such as optimal use of the range over which the disparity detectors operate, or a "corrective" warping of the images to adjust the slant of the observed surface when it deviates from the stereotypical frontoparallel case.

Although these facts have been understood in the psychological literature for a long time (Howard & Rogers, 2002), it is only recently that computational and theoretical approaches attempted an engineering formulation of these concepts in order to provide operative guidelines to quantitatively analyze their visual (and motor) advantages, and optimal design criteria for active artificial vision systems (Schreiber, Crawford, Fetter & Tweed, 2001; Schor, Maxwell, McCandless & Graf, 2002; Read & Cumming, 2004; Hansard & Horaud, 2008; Hansard & Horaud, 2010). From a behavioural point of view, the empirical derivation of the horopter has been used to simulate the optimally stereo-viewed surface in foveal vision (Schreiber, Tweed & Schor, 2006; Schreiber, Hillis, Filippini, Schor & Banks, 2008), and complementary non-visual information has been exploited to estimate absolute distances when the system is engaged in reaching tasks towards extrafoveally viewed targets (Greenvald & Knill, 2009; Blohm, Khan, Ren, Schreiber & Crawford, 2008). From a computational point of view, a debate on the role of vertical disparities to calibrate depth perception pointed out that the vertical disparity is not simply tolerated, but it is actively detected and used in perception (Read & Cumming, 2006; Read, Phillipson & Glennerster, 2009; Serrano-Pedraza & Read, 2009; Serrano-Pedraza, Phillipson, & Read, 2010) and to guide vergence behaviour (Yang, FitzGibbon & Miles 2003; Sheliga & Miles, 2003; Gibaldi, Canessa, Chessa, Solari & Sabatini, 2010, but see Rambold and Miles, 2008). As a whole, the 2D vector disparity pattern should be recovered when incorporating eye movements since limiting the search of the binocular correspondences on the epipolar lines predicted by the current position of the eyes would be vulnerable to any inaccuracies in the sensed eye position. Exploiting mutual dependencies between the disparity patterns and the epipolar geometry, e.g., by adapting the computational resources or the processing to the fixation constraint, can be a viable solution to the inaccuracy of eye position sensing (cf. the approach proposed in Chessa, Canessa, Gibaldi, Solari, and Sabatini, 2009). In general, to overcome the difficulties in obtaining an accurate estimation of epipolar geometry, Monaco, Bovik and Cormack (2009) demonstrated a symbiotic relation between foveation and uncalibrated active vision systems to minimize the number of points per epipolar space and thus improve the efficiency of the search for stereo matches.

Phase-Based Stereo Vision Processing

Depth perception derives from the differences in the positions of corresponding points in the stereo image pair projected onto the two retinas of a binocular system. When the camera axes are parallel, on the basis of a local approximation of the Fourier Shift Theorem, the phase-based stereopsis defines the disparity $\delta(\mathbf{x})$ as the one-dimensional (1D) shift necessary to align, along the direction of the horizontal epipolar lines, the phase values of bandpass filtered versions of the stereo image pair $I^R(\mathbf{x})$ and $I^L\left[\mathbf{x}+\delta(\mathbf{x})\right]$ (Sanger, 1988). In general, this type of local measurement of the phase yields stable results, and a quasilinear behavior of the phase *vs.* space is observed over relatively large spatial extents, except around singular points where the amplitude vanishes and the phase becomes unreliable (Fleet, Jepson & Jenkin, 1991). This property of the phase signal yields good predictions of binocular disparity by

$$\delta\left(\mathbf{x}\right)=\frac{\left\lfloor\varphi^L\left(\mathbf{x}\right)-\varphi^R\left(\mathbf{x}\right)\right\rfloor_{2\pi}}{k\left(\mathbf{x}\right)}=\frac{\left\lfloor\Delta\varphi\left(\mathbf{x}\right)\right\rfloor_{2\pi}}{k\left(\mathbf{x}\right)},$$

where φ^L and φ^R are the local phase in the left and right image, respectively, and $k\left(\mathbf{x}\right)$ is the average instantaneous frequency of the bandpass signal, measured by using the phase derivative φ_x from the left and right filter outputs:

$$k\left(\mathbf{x}\right)=\frac{\varphi_x^L\left(\mathbf{x}\right)+\varphi_x^R\left(\mathbf{x}\right)}{2}.$$

As a consequence of the linear phase model, the instantaneous frequency is generally constant and close to the tuning frequency of the filter $\left(\varphi_x\approx k_0\right)$, except near singularities where abrupt frequency changes occur as a function of spatial position. Therefore, a disparity estimate at a point

$\mathbf{x}$ is accepted only if $\left|\varphi_x - k_0\right| < k_0\mu$, where μ is a proper threshold (Fleet, Jepson & Jenkin, 1991).

When the camera axes are moving freely, as it occurs in a binocular active vision system, stereopsis cannot longer be considered a 1D problem and the disparities have both horizontal and vertical components. Therefore, the 1D phase difference approach must be extended to the 2D case. Still relying upon the local approximation of the Fourier Shift Theorem, the 2D local vector disparity $\boldsymbol{\delta}(\mathbf{x})$ between the left and right images can be detected as a phase shift $\mathbf{k}^T\boldsymbol{\delta}(\mathbf{x})$ in the local spectrum, where $\mathbf{k}(\mathbf{x})$ is the local (i.e., instantaneous) frequency vector defined as the phase gradient:

$$\mathbf{k}(\mathbf{x}) = \nabla\varphi(\mathbf{x}) = \left(\frac{\partial\varphi(x,y)}{\partial x}, \frac{\partial\varphi(x,y)}{\partial y}\right)^T \quad (1)$$

with

$$\varphi(\mathbf{x}) = \frac{\varphi^L(\mathbf{x}) + \varphi^R(\mathbf{x})}{2},$$

Given the 1D character of both the local phase and the instantaneous frequency, their measures strictly depend on the choice of one reference orientation axis, thus preventing the determination of the full disparity vector by a punctual single-channel measurement. Only the projected disparity component on the direction orthogonal to the dominant local orientation of the filtered image can be detected.

Let us distinguish two cases. When the image structure is intrinsically 1D, with a dominant orientation θ_s (let us think of an oriented edge or an oriented grating with frequency $\mathbf{k}_s = (k_s \sin\theta_s, k_s \cos\theta_s)^T$, as extreme cases), the aperture problem (Morgan & Castet, 1997) restricts detectable disparity to the direction orthogonal to the edge (i.e., to the direction of the dominant frequency vector $\mathbf{k}_s$):

$$\boldsymbol{\delta}_{\theta_s}(\mathbf{x}) = \frac{\mathbf{k}_s}{k_s}\frac{\left[\Delta\varphi_{\theta_s}(\mathbf{x})\right]_{2\pi}}{k(\mathbf{x})} \approx \frac{\mathbf{k}_s}{k_s}\frac{\left[\Delta\varphi_{\theta_s}(\mathbf{x})\right]_{2\pi}}{k_s}, \quad (2)$$

where $k(\mathbf{x})$ is the magnitude of the instantaneous frequency. That is, only the projection $\boldsymbol{\delta}_{\theta_s}$ of the disparity $\boldsymbol{\delta}$ onto the direction of the stimulus frequency $\mathbf{k}_s$ is observed. A spatial disparity in a direction orthogonal to $\mathbf{k}_s$ cannot be measured. For an intrinsic 1D image structure, indeed, the spectrum energy is confined within a very narrow bandwidth and it is gathered by the bandwidth of a single activated channel. This is a realistic assumption for a relatively large number of orientation channels. Moreover, in this condition, when the dominant frequency of the stimulus $\mathbf{k}_s$ is unknown, it can be approximated by k_0, and thus Equation 2 becomes:

$$\boldsymbol{\delta}_{\theta_s}(\mathbf{x}) \approx \frac{\mathbf{k}_0}{k_0}\frac{\left[\Delta\varphi_{\theta_s}(\mathbf{x})\right]_{2\pi}}{k_0}.$$

When the image structure is intrinsically 2D (let us think of a rich texture or white noise, as an extreme case), the visual signal has local frequency components in more than one direction and the dominant direction is given by the orientation of the Gabor filter. Similarly, the only detectable disparity by a band-pass oriented channel is the one orthogonal to the filter's orientation θ, i.e., the projection in the direction of the filter's frequency:

$$\boldsymbol{\delta}_{\theta}(\mathbf{x}) = \frac{\mathbf{k}_0}{k_0}\frac{\left[\Delta\varphi_{\theta}(\mathbf{x})\right]_{2\pi}}{k(\mathbf{x})}.$$

Again, $\mathbf{k}(\mathbf{x})$ can be derived by Equation 1 or approximated by the peak frequency of the Gabor filter k_0.

By considering the whole set of oriented filters, we can derive the projected disparities in the directions of all the frequency components of the multi-channel band-pass representation, and obtain the full disparity vector by intersection of constraints (Theimer & Mallot, 1994; Sabatini, Gastaldi, Solari, Pauwels, Van Hulle, Diaz, Ros, Pugeault & Krueger, 2010), thus solving the aperture problem. Without measurement errors, the vector disparity determined by each orientation channel consists of projection $\boldsymbol{\delta}_\theta(\mathbf{x})$ on the $\mathbf{k}_0$ direction and unknown orthogonal component. The full disparity vector $\boldsymbol{\delta}(\mathbf{x})$ can be recovered from at least two projections $\boldsymbol{\delta}_\theta(\mathbf{x})$, which are not linearly dependent. Taking into account measurement errors of $\Delta\varphi_\theta$ and the fact that the redundancy of more than two projections can be used to minimize the mean square error for $\boldsymbol{\delta}(\mathbf{x})$, we obtain:

$$\boldsymbol{\delta}(\mathbf{x}) = \arg\min_{\boldsymbol{\delta}(\mathbf{x})} \sum_\theta c_\theta(\mathbf{x}) \left(\delta_\theta(\mathbf{x}) - \frac{\mathbf{k}_0^T}{k_0} \boldsymbol{\delta}(\mathbf{x}) \right)^2,$$

where the coefficient $c_\theta(\mathbf{x}) = 1$ when the component disparity along direction θ for pixel $\mathbf{x}$ is a valid (i.e., reliable) component on the basis of a confidence measure, and is null otherwise. In this way, the influence of erroneous filter responses is reduced.

CORTICAL ARCHITECTURES FOR 3D ACTIVE MEASUREMENTS IN THE PERIPERSONAL SPACE

Distributed Representation of Binocular Disparity

The phase-based disparity estimation approach presented in the previous section implies, for each spatial orientation channel θ (and for any given scale), explicit measurements of the local phase difference $\Delta\varphi$ in the image pairs, from which we obtain the direct measure of the binocular disparity component δ_θ. Similarly, we can consider a distributed approach in which the binocular disparity δ is never measured, but implicitly coded by the population activity of cells that act as "disparity detectors" - over a proper range of disparity values. Such models are inspired by the experimental evidence on how the brain and, specifically, the primary visual cortex (V1) implements early mechanisms for stereopsis. Using such a distributed code, it is possible to achieve a very flexible and robust representation of binocular disparity for each spatial position in the retinal image.

An abundance of neurophysiological evidence indicates that the cortical cells' sensitivity to binocular disparity is related to interocular phase shifts in the Gabor-like receptive fields (RFs) of V1 simple cells (Sanger, 1988; Fleet, 1994; Fleet, Wagner & Heeger, 1996a; Qian, 1994; Ohzawa Freeman & DeAngelis, 1990; Prince, Cumming & Parker, 2002). The phase-shift model posits that the center of the left and right eye RFs coincides, but the arrangements of the RF subregions are different. Formally, the response of a simple cell with RF center in $\mathbf{x}$ and oriented along θ can be written as:

$${}^{\theta}_{\Delta\psi} r_{s,\psi_0}(\mathbf{x}) = {}^{\theta} r_{l,\psi^L}(\mathbf{x}) + {}^{\theta} r_{r,\psi^R}(\mathbf{x})$$

where

$$ {}^{\theta}r_{l,\psi^L}(\mathbf{x}) = I^L * h^L(\mathbf{x};\theta,\psi_0+\psi^L) $$
$$ {}^{\theta}r_{r,\psi^R}(\mathbf{x}) = I^R * h^R(\mathbf{x};\theta,\psi_0+\psi^R) \quad (3) $$

and

$$ h(\mathbf{x}) = h(\mathbf{x};\theta,\psi) = = \eta \exp\left(-\frac{1}{2\sigma^2}\mathbf{x}^T\Theta\mathbf{x}\right)\cos(\mathbf{k}_0\mathbf{x}+\psi) $$

is a real-valued RF, ψ_0 is a "central" value of the phase of the RF, ψ^L and ψ^R are the phases that characterize the binocular RF profile, and Θ is the rotation matrix defined by:

$$ \Theta = \begin{pmatrix} \cos\theta & \sin\theta \\ -\sin\theta & \cos\theta \end{pmatrix} $$

In order to make the disparity tuning independent of the monocular local Fourier phase of the images (but only on the interocular phase difference), binocular energy complex cells play a crucial role. Such "energy units" are defined as the squared sum of a quadrature pair of simple cells (see Figure 2A) and their response is defined as:

$$ {}^{\theta}_{\Delta\psi}r_c(\mathbf{x}) = {}^{\theta}_{\Delta\psi}r^2_{s,0}(\mathbf{x}) + {}^{\theta}_{\Delta\psi}r^2_{s,\pi/2}(\mathbf{x}) $$

For any fixed orientation, if we characterize a "quadrature pair" of simple cells by a complex-valued RF:

$$ h(\mathbf{x}) \equiv h_C(\mathbf{x}) + jh_S(\mathbf{x}) = g(\mathbf{x};\psi) $$

where:

$$ g(\mathbf{x};\psi) = g(\mathbf{x};\theta,\psi) = = \eta \exp\left(-\frac{1}{2\sigma^2}\mathbf{x}^T\Theta\mathbf{x}\right)\left(\cos(\mathbf{k}_0\mathbf{x}+\psi) + i\sin(\mathbf{k}_0\mathbf{x}+\psi)\right) $$

then we can write the expression of the response of the "quadrature pair" as:

$$ Q(\mathbf{x}) = I^L * g^L(\mathbf{x}) + I^R * g^R(\mathbf{x}) = = I^L * g(\mathbf{x})e^{j\psi^L} + I^R * g(\mathbf{x})e^{j\psi^R} = = Q^L(\mathbf{x})e^{j\psi^L} + Q^R(\mathbf{x})e^{j\psi^R} $$

The response of a complex "energy" cell is then

$$ {}^{\theta}_{\Delta\psi}r_c(\mathbf{x}) = \left|{}^{\theta}_{\Delta\psi}r_{s,0}(\mathbf{x}) + {}^{\theta}_{\Delta\psi}r_{s,\pi/2}(\mathbf{x})\right|^2 = \left|Q^L(\mathbf{x})e^{j\psi^L} + Q^R(\mathbf{x})e^{j\psi^R}\right|^2 = = \left|e^{j\psi^L}\left(Q^L(\mathbf{x}) + Q^R(\mathbf{x})e^{j\Delta\psi}\right)\right|^2 = \left|Q^L(\mathbf{x}) + Q^R(\mathbf{x})e^{j\Delta\psi}\right|^2 \quad (4) $$

where $\Delta\psi = \psi^L - \psi^R$. Therefore, complex cells' responses depend on $\Delta\psi$ only, instead of on ψ^L and ψ^R individually.

Equation 4 formally establishes the equivalence between phase-based techniques and energy-based models (Qian & Mikaelian, 2000). Indeed, the maximum of r_c responses is obtained when the two phasors Q^L and Q^R are aligned in the complex plane (see Figure 2B), that is, when $\Delta\psi$ compensates for the different Fourier phases of the left and right image patches within the cell's RF (cf. Sanger, 1988). Notwithstanding the formal equivalence between phase-based techniques and energy-based models, the latter prove themselves more robust to noise and more flexible, since they can intrinsically embed adap-

Figure 2. (A) The complex cell response is constructed as the squared sum of a quadrature pair of simple cells. The light and dark grey pathways relate to the monocular "quadrature pair" of simple cell RFs, g_L and g_R, respectively. (B) LEFT: The responses of the two "quadrature pairs" for the left and the right eye are characterized by a phase shift $\Delta\varphi$ proportional to the disparity. RIGHT: The maximum response of a complex cell is obtained when the two phasors are aligned. This is obtained when the RF phase shift $\Delta\psi$ equals $\Delta\varphi$ (RIGHT). (C) The population of binocular receptive fields for each retinal location.

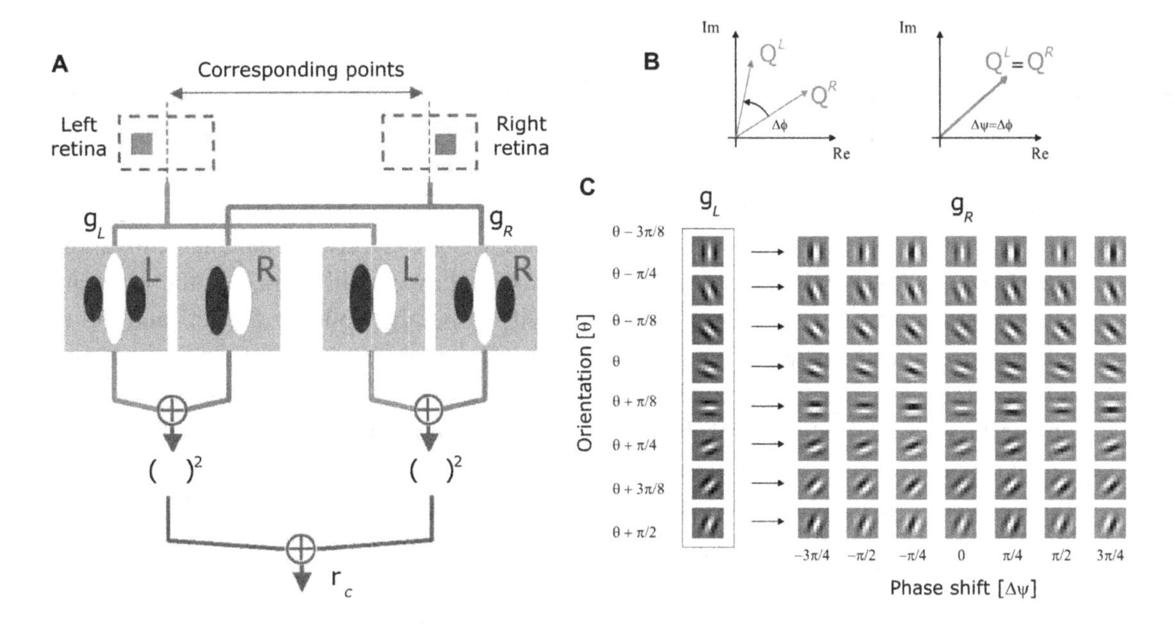

tive mechanisms both at the coding and decoding levels of the population code.

Based on these computational principles, a large-scale cortical network has been designed to encode disparity information from a stereo image pair. For each pixel, the network employs a population of simple and complex cells sensitive to $N_O \times N_P$ vector disparities $\boldsymbol{\delta} = (\delta_H, \delta_V)$ with N_P magnitude values distributed in the range $[-\Delta, \Delta]$ pixels and along N_O orientations, uniformly distributed between 0 and π (see Figure 2C). For each simple cell we can control the orientation θ of the binocular RF $h(\mathbf{x})$ with respect to the horizontal axis, and the interocular phase shift $\Delta\psi$ along the rotated axis, which confers to the cell its specific tuning to a disparity $\delta_{pref} = \Delta\psi_\theta / k_0$, along the direction orthogonal to θ. The spatial frequency k_0 and the spatial envelope are fixed on the basis of optimal design criteria described in Sabatini, Gastaldi, Solari, Pauwels, Van Hulle, Diaz, Ros, Pugeault, and Krueger (2010). The complex cell inherits the spatial properties of the simple cells, and its response $r_c(\mathbf{x})$ is given by Equation 4. For each orientation, the population is, in this way, capable of providing reliable disparity estimates in the range between $\pm\Delta$, where $\Delta = \Delta\psi_{\max} / k_0$ can be defined as the maximum detectable disparity of the population.

Embedding Fixation Constraints in Binocular Energy-Based Models of Depth Perception

When we look around in a cluttered environment, or when we inspect a small object, the eyes coordinate to make the lines of sight intersect in the target dynamically, thus ensuring binocular fusion and accurate scanning of the object. In general (but in particular for relatively large vergence angles), binocular coordinated movements of the eyes affect the two-dimensional (horizontal and vertical) disparity pattern in the peripheral part of the image of the fixated object, as well as in the background,. Consequently, the strategy adopted to move the eyes can directly influence the perception of depth, the visual behavior, and eventually the 3D spatial awareness of the world around us.

The epipolar lines, defined as the loci of all the possible matching points for every retinal location, represent the most convenient/immediate way to characterize the disparity patterns experienced by a binocular vergent system (see Figure 3A). When we look straight ahead at infinity (i.e., with parallel optical axes) all the epipolar lines are horizontal. Conversely, whenever the gaze changes and the vergence increases the epipolar lines move and become more and more tilted. This movement causes an increase of the observed disparities, and, as a consequence, the vision system has to cope with larger search zones within which the stereo correspondences have to be found. From this perspective, having a general design strategy for the oculomotor system behavior that minimizes the motion of the epipolar lines would reduce the search zone and thus the computational cost of finding visual correspondences (see Figure 3C). Vice versa, the predictable components of disparity, depending on the relative position of the eyes, may be used as *priors* to optimally allocate the computational resources to ease the recovery of the (unpredictable) components of disparity, which are dependent only on the structure of the scene. This suggests the possibility of a *mutual calibration* of the vision and the oculomotor system to compensate disparity components due to the epipolar geometry.

The eye with its three degrees of freedom could, in principle, assume an infinite number of torsional postures for any gaze direction. However, Listing's Law states that the eye assumes only those orientations that can be reached from the primary position by a single rotation about an axis in a plane called Listing's plane (Tweed & Vilis, 1990). This corresponds, according to Donders, to a single possible torsional position for each combination of the azimuth and the elevation angles. During binocular convergence, Listing's Law is still valid, but the plane is rotated temporally both for the left and the right eye. These convergent-dependent changes of orientation of Listing's plane have been referred to as the binocular extension of Listing's Law or L2 (Mok, Ro, Cadera, Crawford & Vilis, 1992). From a functional point of view, Listing's Law can be understood as a limiter of the degrees of freedom of the oculomotor system (when the behavioral situation demands or permits it), which constrains torsional components to reduce rotation (Listing's Law, or LL) (Tweed & Vilis, 1990), or to reduce the cyclovergence and restrict the motion of the epipolar lines (Binocular LL, or L2) (Mok, Ro, Cadera, Crawford & Vilis, 1992), thus permitting stereo matching to work with smaller search zones.

Although, from a conceptual point of view, the oculomotor parameterization of active stereopsis is a well-established issue (Jenkin, 1996; Hansard & Horaud, 2008), mapping the oculomotor constraints into the neural population coding and decoding strategies is still an open problem. In this section, we describe how it is possible to exploit such oculomotor information in the specification of the architectural parameters/resources of the distributed representation of disparity information. To this end, we have calculated natural scene disparity statistics for a binocular vergent system engaged in natural viewing in a peripersonal workspace. For

Figure 3. (A) Given an image point on the left retina, all its possible corresponding points on the right one lie on a line: the epipolar line (heavy black line). The epipolar lines change their orientation depending on the relative position of the eyes in the orbits. (B) In the three represented cases the eyes fixate the same point in the world, but in different ways, following a Helmholtz (or Tilt-Pan), a Listing, and a L2 system. (C) The viewed surface is always orthogonal to the gaze line. In case of perfect alignment (as it occurs for Helmholtz and L2), the two projections of the horizontal and vertical meridians for the left and right eye on the surface superimpose each other. For the three systems in (B) the epipolar lines for a grid of 3x3 retinal points of the left eye are depicted for different gaze directions. The reference point on the left eye is represented by an open circle, the epipolar lines are represented in gray. The values of version and elevation angles vary in a range [-40°, 40°]. The epipolar lines tilt and move depending on the version and the elevation of the gaze direction, spanning an area that defines the correspondence search zone. It is possible to see how the size of the search zone depends on the geometry of the system.

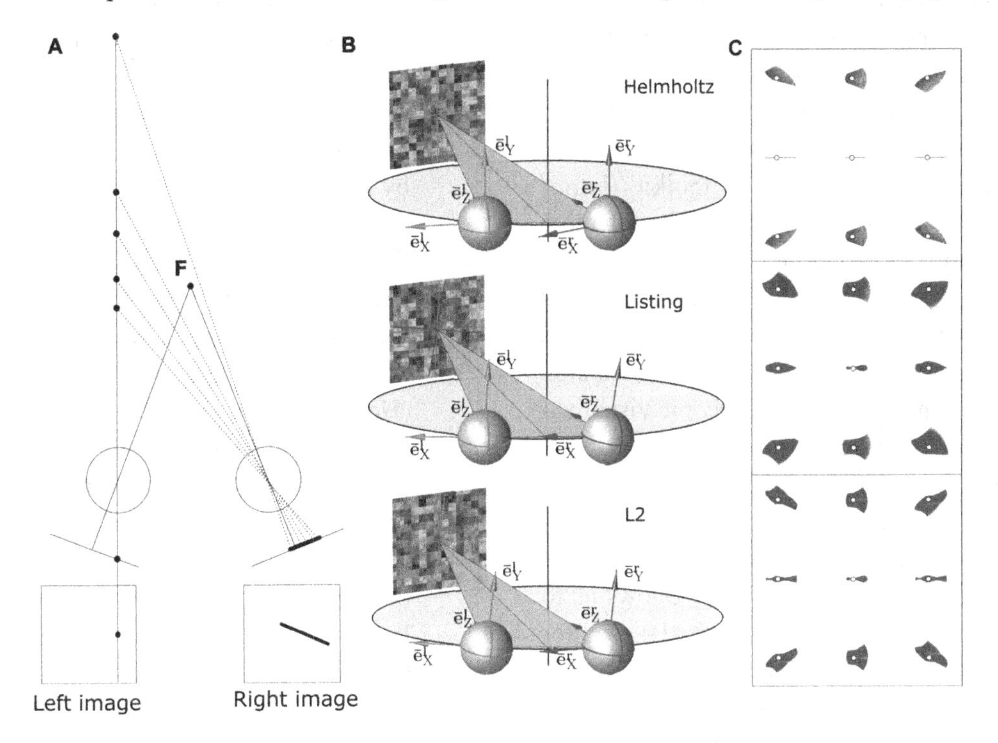

comparison, both the Helmholtz (i.e., tilt-pan, zero torsion) and the more sophisticated oculomotor models based on LL and its binocular extension L2 have been considered (see Figure 3B).

- **Data Acquisition:** For the simulations shown in the following, we first captured 3D data from a real-world scene by using a 3D laser scanner (Konica Minolta Vivid 910), with the optimal 3D measurement operating range from 0.6 m to 1.2 m, which is appropriate for analyzing the disparity information experienced by an active observer in his/her peripersonal space. The system allows also capturing the color textures at a resolution of 640 × 480 pixels. Each scan contained up to 307,200 points within a variable field of view, which was adjusted with respect to the size of the object to be scanned. For this work, we considered cluttered desks with a collection of one hundred real-world objects. The whole scene as well as the single objects were scanned, registered and merged together to obtain full models of more than 13,000,000 points each (see Figure 4A). Off-line registrations of data guaranteed an accuracy of about 0.1 mm. A full 360-degree view of the scene was acquired to minimize the occlusion problems that occur when one simulates changes in the vantage point of the virtual observer.

- **Simulated Fixations in the Acquired Peripersonal Scenes**: The real-world environment, captured by the 3D laser scanner, is then "explored" through an active vision simulator. Such simulator has been implemented in C++, using OpenGL libraries and the Coin3D toolkit (http://www.coin3d.org/) developed for effective 3D graphics rendering. This system is capable of handling the commonly used 3D modeling formats (e.g., VRML), and thus the data acquired by the 3D laser scanner. To obtain the toe-in stereoscopic visualization of the scene, useful to mimic an active stereo vision system rather than to make humans perceive depth, we have modified the SoCamera node of the Coin3D toolkit. Moreover, the developed tool allows us to access the buffers (see Figure 4B) used for the 3D rendering of the scenes. The 3D data and the textures are loaded in the active vision simulator, and then the left and right projections, the horizontal and the vertical ground truth disparity maps are obtained for each possible fixation point. More details on the simulator are reported in (Chessa, Sabatini & Solari, 2011). The developed tool has been used to create a database of real-world range data and stereo image pairs for a variety of fixations (see Figure 4C), in order to guide modeling and for algorithmic and behavioral benchmarks in real-world but fully measured environments.
- **Statistical Analysis:** For a given eye posture, we computed the distribution of the horizontal and vertical disparities for all the objects whose images fell within an angle of ±22.5° in both retinas. The other parameters used were: a resolution of 601 × 601 pixels, a focal length of 10 mm, and an interocular distance of 6 cm. We repeated the calculation for 100 different vantage points, corresponding to different positions and orientations of the cyclopean visual axis, and for a set of fixation points. The fixation points varied in the range of 0° to 360° for the azimuth angle, and in the range of 0° to 32° for the polar angle. More precisely, the fixation points were obtained by backprojecting an 11×11 grid of equally spaced points of the cyclopean retina on the closest visible surface of the scene. Under the same experimental conditions, the disparity patterns were calculated for three different eye movement paradigms (Helmholtz, i.e., Tilt-Pan, Listing and L2). Figures 14 and 15 demonstrate that large vertical disparities can occur in the peripheral field of view, especially for tertiary eye positions. The mean vector disparity patterns, together with their standard ellipses (measuring the joint dispersion of the bivariate distribution) are shown in Figure 4E. It is worth noting that, as expected, the mean disparity patterns calculated for each fixation are characterized by significant differences (not shown), these are attenuated averaging over all the fixations we considered.

From the analysis of the simulation data, it is worth noting that the mean value of the disparities changes with the fixation point, thus it is possible to distinguish two disparity components: the first (δ_s), unpredictable, due to the structure of the 3D scene and the second (δ_e), more predictable, due to the geometry of the binocular system (see Figure 4D):

$$\delta = \delta_s + \delta_e .$$

- **Adjustable Energy Models:** The component of the disparity due to the epipolar geometry can be embedded in the distributed representation of disparity information with the position shift mechanisms (Fleet et al., 1996). The position-shift model assumes that there is a population of simple cells whose left and right RFs are always identical in shape, but can be centered at different spatial locations. Accordingly, we can consider a family of binocular energy neurons whose right monocular receptive field is shifted by a set of offsets $\mathbf{d} = \delta_e$ with respect to the center of the corresponding monocular receptive field in the left retina. Formally, the response of a simple cell with RF center in $\mathbf{x}$ and oriented along θ, can be written as:

$$^{\theta}r_{s,\psi_0}(\mathbf{x};\mathbf{d}) \;=\; ^{\theta}r_{L,\psi_0}(\mathbf{x}) + ^{\theta}r_{R,\psi_0}(\mathbf{x}-\mathbf{d})$$

where $^{\theta}r_{L,\psi_0}(\mathbf{x})$, $^{\theta}r_{R,\psi_0}(\mathbf{x})$ are expressed as in Equation 3. Still, we can define the response of a binocular energy complex cell as the squared sum of a quadrature pair of simple cells:

$$^{\theta}r_c(\mathbf{x};\mathbf{d}) \;=\; ^{\theta}r^2_{s,0}(\mathbf{x};\mathbf{d}) + ^{\theta}r^2_{s,\pi/2}(\mathbf{x};\mathbf{d}) .$$

Accordingly, for the direction θ, the stimulus disparity to which the cell is tuned is:

$$\delta^{\theta}_{pref} = d^{\theta} .$$

By using jointly the position-shift and the phase-shift disparity encoding mechanisms, the spatial relationships between target points on the left eye and the mean of the corresponding points for the right eye are embedded into a hybrid energy-based model where phase-shifts and position-shifts play a different role: position-shifts are used to compensate the global components of the averaged disparity pattern over all the fixations, whereas phase-shifts are used to estimate the residual 2D disparity.

Figure 5A shows the distribution of the estimated disparities between the left and the right retinas without and with a compensation of the predictable components of the disparity pattern. For different points of the left retina (open circles) we estimated the corresponding point for the right retina (colored dots) by a population of disparity detectors. The disparity relates to point image projections of randomly oriented surfaces in the peripersonal space. The red dots represent the mean of the estimated disparities, whereas the black dots represent the true mean disparity. It is worth noting that, by embedding the mean values computed with respect to the reference situation, the mean values of the estimated disparities (red dots) become closer to the true values of disparities (black dots). Figure 5B shows the estimation of the 2D disparity without global components compensation and by embedding these components into the model, for a frontoparallel plane and for an in-door scenario obtained by the active vision simulator. It is worth noting that the reliability of the disparity representation is improved by embedding the component due to the epipolar geometry of the system.

Moreover, the activity of the population of neurons in the distributed representation can be adapted by changing the distribution of the units to minimize the necessary resources while preserving reliable estimates. To this aim, we have also tested if a prior knowledge of a particular feature (e.g., the sign of the disparity values, or their range) can be used to redistribute the sensitivity coverage of the cells' population and its density, by properly choosing the phase-shifts, while keeping fixed the other parameters. To

Figure 4. Example of a real-world scene acquired by the laser scanner. (A) Together with the 3D data, the system is able to attach the real color texture to the scanned objects. Two outputs of the active vision system simulator: the Z buffer (B) and the left and right image pairs (C). (D) The disparity δ can be divided into two components: one, unpredictable, due to the scene, called residual disparity δ_s, and another one, predictable, due the geometry of the adopted vision system, called epipolar disparity δ_e. (E) The mean vector disparity patterns and the standard ellipses, averaged over all the fixation, are depicted for a Helmholtz, a Listing and a L2 system. Here only a grid of 7x7 retinal points are shown for the sake of clarity (E).

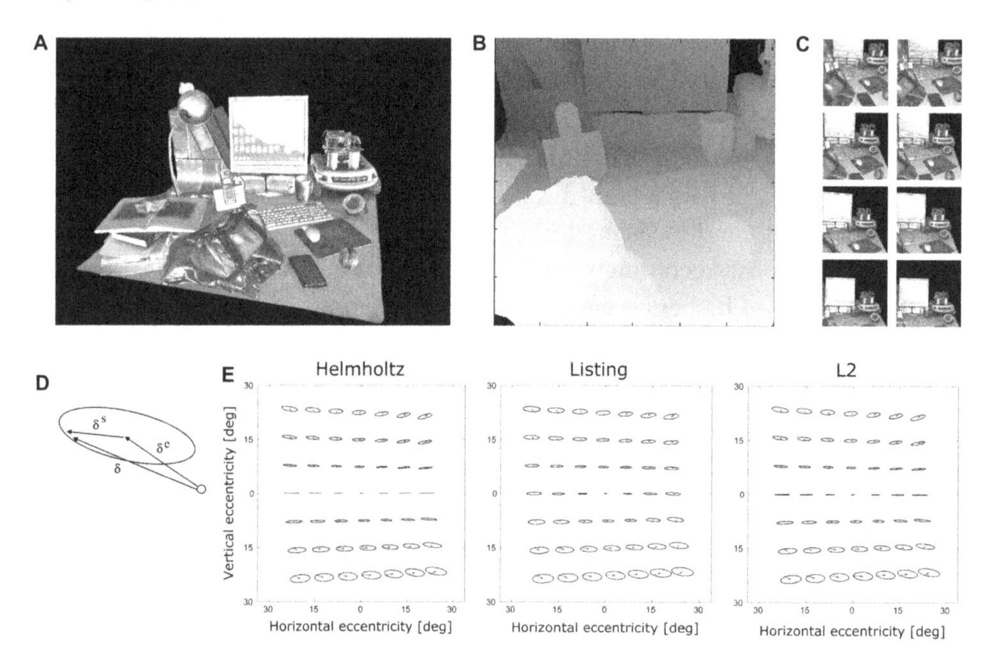

compare the results, we have used two standard benchmark stereo image pairs (Venus and Tsukuba) for which the ground truth is available (Scharstein & Szeliski, 2002). We have redistributed the cells of the population accordingly to the (known) sign of the disparity, and we have compared the results with the ground truth disparity maps. Table 1 shows how the same (and in certain cases better) reliability is obtained by halving the units of the population. In conclusion, the position shift mechanism can be seen as a pre-wired design strategy that takes into account an initial adaptation of the system with respect to a "typical" viewing condition.

Reading-Out the Disparity Population Code to Specialize Vergence Control Servos

Previous vergence models that are based on a population of disparity detectors require first the computation of the disparity map for the extraction of the control signals (Theimer & Mallot, 1994; Patel, Ogmen & Jiang, 1996), thus limiting the functionality of the vergence system within the range of disparities in which the system is able to fuse the left and right images. Making a parallel with the biological system, this means that vergence eye movements would be reliable only inside Panum's area, where they are not necessary. Although each neuron of the Medial Superior Temporal area (MST) is sensitive to

Figure 5. (A) The subplots represent a grid of 7x7 retinal points for a value of the gaze corresponding to zero elevation and zero version angles. For different points of the left retina (open circles) we estimated the corresponding point for the right retina (color dots) by a population of disparity detectors. The disparity relates to point image projections of randomly positioned planes in the peripersonal space, when the fixation point is in the primary position. The red dots represent the mean of the disparities, whereas the black dots represent the true mean disparity. Distribution of the estimated disparities between the left and the right retina are depicted without and with the compensation of the predictable components of the disparity pattern. (B) Disparity estimation by embedding fixation constraints into the binocular energy model for a stereo pair representing a fronto-parallel plane and an in-door scenario obtained by the active vision simulator. (TOP) Ground truth horizontal and vertical disparity maps. (MIDDLE) Estimation of the disparity by using the distributed architecture without embedding any fixation constraint. (BOTTOM) Estimation of the disparity by using the distributed architecture by embedding the fixation constraints: a position shift derived from the mean values of disparities averaged over all the fixation points. The results are obtained by using 43×43 pixels receptive fields, tuned to a ±8 pixel disparity range.

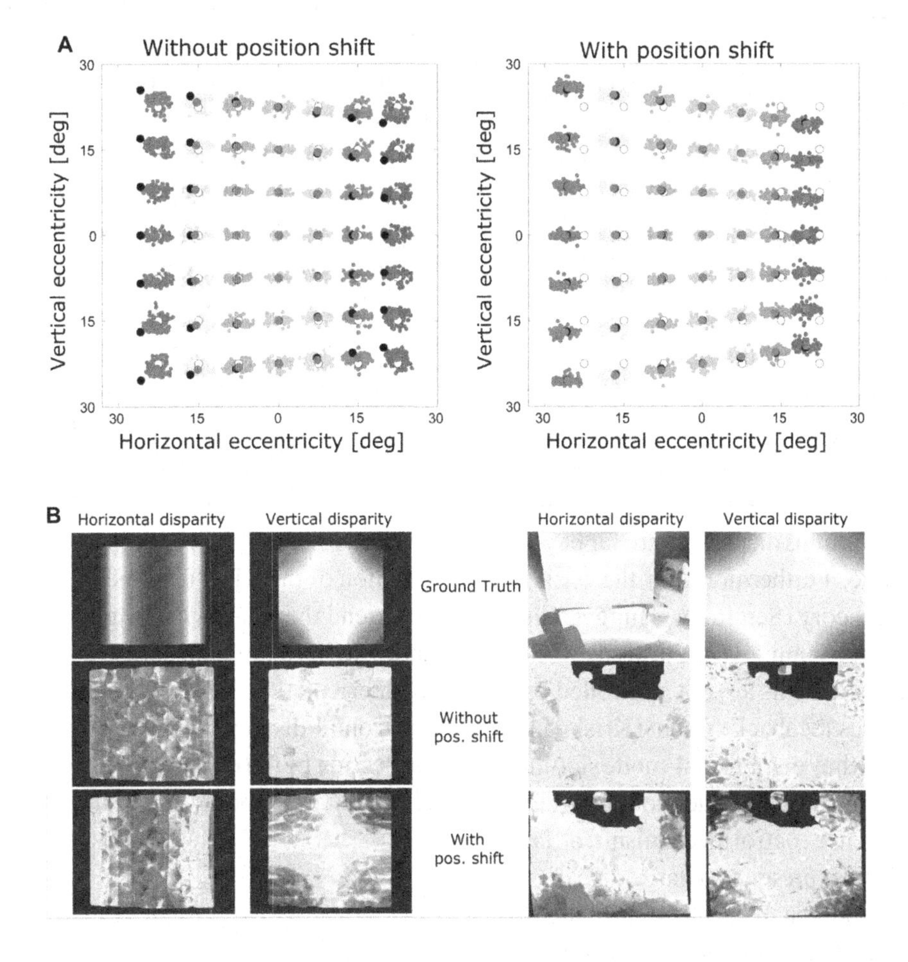

retinal disparity, it has been found to encode only some limited aspects of the motor response for vergence eye movements; the activity of the whole population directly correlates with the magnitude, direction, and time course of the initial vergence motor response (Takemura, Inoue, Quaia & Miles, 2001; Takemura, Kawano, Quaia & Miles, 2006). Mimicking the behavior of the cells of the MST

Table 1. Average error (AVG), standard deviation of the error (STD) and density (expressed as the percentage of estimated values with respect to the total number of pixels in the image) for the Venus and the Tsukuba stereo pairs, without and with the redistribution of the cells. The redistribution has been performed by taking into account the known sign of the true disparity values. The first column shows the number of cells (for each spatial orientation) necessary to obtain the estimation of the disparity.

	# cells	AVG	STD	%
Venus stereo pair				
without phases shifts redistribution	33	0.84	0.63	91
with phases shifts redistribution	17	0.72	0.56	91
Tsukuba stereo pair				
without phases shifts redistribution	33	0.36	0.37	56
with phases shifts redistribution	17	0.28	0.20	91

area, we present a model that, by combining the response of a population of complex cells, does not make a decision on the disparity values (disparity map), but extracts disparity-vergence responses that allows us to nullify the disparity in the fovea, even when the stimulus disparities are far beyond the fusible range. Furthermore, on the basis of the Dual Mode theory (Semmlow, Hung & Ciuffreda, 1986; Hung, Semmlow & Ciuffreda, 1986), vergence eye movements are not controlled by a simple continuous feedback system (Krishnan & Stark, 1977), but they exhibit dual-mode slow and fast responses. Accordingly, the model provides two distinct vergence control mechanisms: a "fast" mode enabled in the presence of large disparities, and a "slow" mode enabled in the presence of small disparities. An additional signal provides the switch between the two modes, according to the stimulus disparities.

The population used is made of complex cells that are, by construction, tuned to oriented disparities, i.e., jointly tuned to horizontal and vertical disparities δ_H and δ_V, respectively. By recovering the full disparity vector, the disparity detectability range would still be limited to $\pm\Delta$, and the horizontal component of the full disparity vector will then be used for the control of horizontal vergence. Unless one uses computationally expensive multiscale techniques for widening the disparity detectability range, this approach would considerably limit the working range of the vergence control.

As for the control of vergence, larger disparities have to be discriminated while keeping sufficient accuracy around the fixation point for allowing finer refinement and achieving stable fixations. Alternative strategies might be employed to gain effective vergence signals directly from the complex cell population responses, without solving the aperture problem and thus without explicit computation of the disparity map. To this end, we can consider that to drive horizontal vergence, the meaningful feature is δ_H only; thus we can map the 2D disparity feature space onto the 1D space of the projected horizontal disparities, where the orientation θ plays the role of a parameter. More precisely, by assuming $\delta_V = 0$, the dimensionality of the problem of disparity estimation reduces to one, and the orientation of the RF is used as a degree of freedom to extend the sensitivity range of the cells' population to horizontal disparity stimuli. In this way, each orientation channel has a sensitivity for the horizontal disparity that can be obtained by the projection of the oriented phase difference on the (horizontal) epipolar line in the following way:

$$\delta_H = \frac{\Delta\psi}{2\pi k_0 \cos\theta}.$$

Figure 6C shows the horizontal disparity tuning curves obtained by the population for different orientations of the receptive fields (blue lines).

To decode the horizontal disparity at a specific image point, the whole activity of the population of cells, with receptive fields centered in that location, is considered. By using a COM decoding strategy, the estimated horizontal disparity δ_H^{est} is obtained by:

$$\delta_H^{est} = \frac{\sum_{j=1}^{N_O} \sum_{i=1}^{N_P} \frac{\Delta\psi}{2\pi k_0 \cos\theta} r_c^{ij}}{\sum_{i=1}^{N_P} r_c^{ij}}$$

where r_c^{ij} denotes the response of the complex cell characterized by the ith phase difference and by the jth orientation. The estimate of the disparity can be considered correct when the stimulus disparity is within $\left[-\Delta, \Delta\right]$. By analyzing the tuning curves of the population we observe that the peak sensitivity of cells that belong to a single orientation channel is uniformly distributed in a range that increases with the orientation angle θ of the receptive field, as the horizontal projection of the frequency of the Gabor function declines to zero. Thus, applying the center of mass decoding strategy, separately for each orientation, we can obtain N_O different estimates of the disparity:

$$\delta_{H,\theta_j}^{est} = \frac{\sum_{i=1}^{N_P} \frac{\Delta\psi}{2\pi k_0 \cos\theta_j} r_c^{ij}}{\sum_{i=1}^{N_P} r_c^{ij}}$$

It is worth noting that the increase of the sensitivity range, as the orientation of the receptive fields deviates from the vertical, comes at the price of a reduced reliability and accuracy of the measure (as an extreme case, horizontal receptive fields are unable to detect horizontal disparities, i.e., $\delta_H^{\theta=0} \to \infty$). Moreover, since the 1D tuning curves of the population were obtained under the assumption of horizontal disparity only, when the vertical disparity in the images differs from zero, the correctness of te estimate of the actual component of the horizontal disparity has to be taken into account.

- **Control Signal Extraction:** A desired feature of the disparity tuning curves for vergence is an odd symmetry with a linear segment passing smoothly through zero disparity (see Figure 6D), which defines a critical servo range over which changes in the stimulus horizontal disparity elicit roughly proportional changes in the amount of horizontal vergence eye movements, $\Delta\alpha = p\delta_H$, where α is the vergence angle. Given a stimulus with a horizontal disparity δ_H, we want to combine the population responses in order to extract a vergence control proportional to the disparity to be reduced, regardless of a possible non-zero vertical disparity δ_V. To this end, starting from the 2D (multichannel) responses of the population of binocular cells, we exploit the responses at different orientations to design linear servos that work outside the reliability range of disparity estimation. Yet, to cope with the attendant sensitivity to vertical disparity, which is an undesirable effect that alters the control action, a limiting factor of the influence of vertical disparity must be introduced. The desired disparity vergence response curves r_v^k are approximated by a weighted combination of the population cell responses, where disparity tuning curves act as basis functions:

$$r_v^k = \frac{\sum_{j=1}^{N_O} \sum_{i=1}^{N_P} w_{ij}^k r_c^{ij}}{\sum_{j=1}^{N_O} \sum_{i=1}^{N_P} r_c^{ij}}$$

Figure 6. (A) Simplified scheme of the neural circuitry involved in the control of vergence eye movements. The left and right images are processed by a population of disparity detectors that model complex cells of area V1. The population produces a distributed representation of the retinal disparity, which is decoded through convolutions with weighting kernels to obtain a family of vergence cells able to provide a direct vergence motor response, which is sent to the ocular plant. Since the task is to drive vergence eye movements so as to improve the fixation and the estimation of disparity, the information is gathered only from the central (parafoveal) portion of the visual field. (B) The v_H^K *target curves to be approximated by the LMS minimization in order to obtain the* r_{NE}, r_{FA}, r_{TN}, r_{TF}, r_{T0} *signals. (C) Disparity-tuning curves of the cells of the whole population stimulated by horizontal disparities varying between* $[-\Delta, \Delta]$. *The frequency of the curves decreases as the orientation of the RFs approaches the vertical one. (D) The effective LONG (solid line) and SHORT (dashed line) signals computed by the model, stimulated with random dot stereograms. The short control is able to work in a linear and precise manner for small disparities, while the long one works in a coarse but effective way for larger disparities. (E) The effective* r_{T0} *signal that is able to act as a switch between the two controls. When the disparities are large, the switch signal is below a defined threshold* TH*, and it enables the long control (grey area), otherwise it enables the short control (white area).*

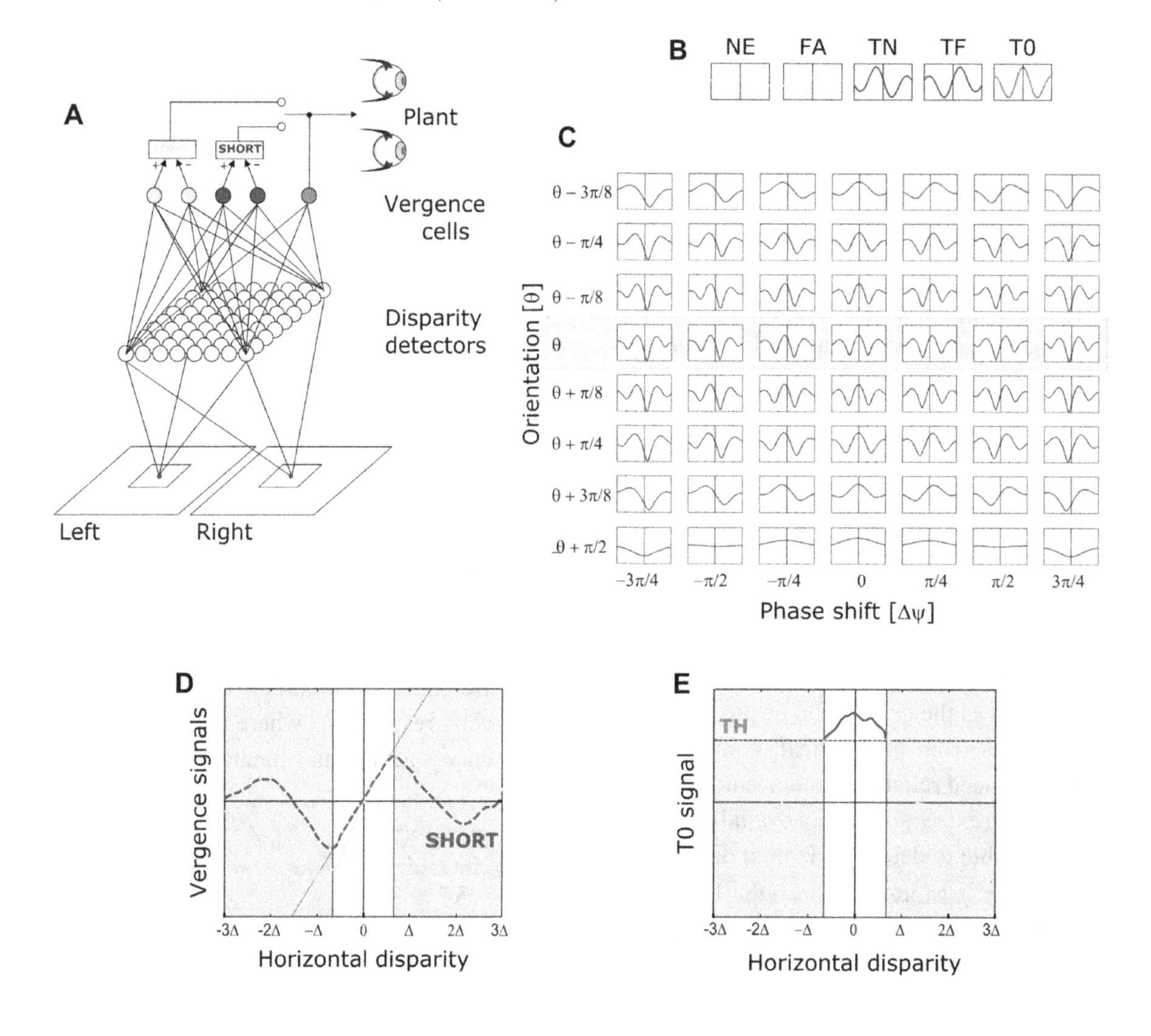

The normalization term is introduced to make the vergence response independent of the image contrast.

The weights w_{ij}^{k} are obtained through a recursive LMS algorithm that minimizes the following function:

$$E\left(\mathbf{w}^{k}\right) = \left\|\sum_{j=1}^{N_O}\sum_{i=1}^{N_P} r_c^{ij}\left(\delta_H\right) w_{ij}^{k} - v_H^{K}\right\|^2 + \lambda\left\|\sum_{j=1}^{N_O}\sum_{i=1}^{N_P} r_c^{ij}\left(\delta_V\right) w_{ij}^{k} - 1\right\|^2$$

where $\lambda > 0$ balances the relevance of the second term over the first. In our simulations we fixed $\lambda = 1$.

More precisely, given the profile of the desired vergence curve $r_v^{k}\left(\delta_H\right)$, such curve is approximated by a weighted sum of the tuning curves for horizontal disparity $r_c^{ij}\left(\delta_H;\theta,\Delta\psi\right)$. To gain the insensitivity to vertical disparity we add a constraint term in the minimization to ensure that the sum of the vertical disparity tuning curves $r_c^{ij}\left(\delta_V;\theta,\Delta\psi\right)$, weighted with the same $\mathbf{w}^{k}$, is approximately constant.

- **Dual-Mode Behavior:** In analogy to the usual classification (Poggio, 1995), we distinguish five categories of r_v cells: near (r_{NE}) and far (r_{FA}) dedicated to coarse vergence, tuned near (r_{TN}), tuned far (r_{TF}) and tuned zero (r_{T0}) for fine vergence. More precisely, r_{NE} and r_{TN} drive convergence movements, whereas r_{FA} and r_{TF} drive divergence movements, in a push-pull system (see Figure 6A-B). In practice the fast-coarse control is given by *LONG* $= r_{NE} - r_{FA}$, while the slow-fine is given by *SHORT*$= r_{TN} - r_{TF}$. The *SHORT* control signal is designed to proportionally generate, in a small range of disparities, the vergence to be achieved, and allows a precise and stable fixation (see Figure 6D). Out of its range of linearity, the short signal decreases and loses efficiency to the point where it changes sign, thus generating a vergence movement opposite to the desired one. Instead, for small disparities the *LONG* control signal yields an overactive vergence signal that makes the system oscillate, whereas for larger disparities it provides a rapid and effective signal. The role of the r_{T0} signal is to act as a switch between the *SHORT* and the *LONG* controls (see Figure 6E). When the binocular disparities are small, r_{T0} is above a proper threshold TH, and it enables the *SHORT* control (see white regions in Figure 6D-E). On the contrary, for large stimulus disparities, r_{T0} is below the threshold and it enables the *LONG* control (see grey regions in Figure 6D-E).
- **Results:** We tested the proposed model in a virtual environment in which the eyes, characterized by random azimuth and elevation angles, look at a plane with a random dot texture. The plane is at a distance Z with respect to the cyclopic position, and perpendicular to the binocular line of sight (see Figure 7A-B). In the first experiment, at the beginning of each trial, the plane and the fixation point are at the same Z, then the plane is moved to a new depth, and the vergence angle starts to change step by step, until the fixation point reaches the depth of the plane. In the second and in the third experiments, on the contrary, the plane is free to move along the gaze line as a ramp or a sinusoid, and the fixation point has to follow it in depth (see Figure 7G-H). Considering that the gaze direction is allowed to span the entire environment, and it is not constrained to null azimuth and elevation, the vertical disparity

components are not negligible and it may strongly affect the population response, as can be seen from the disparity patterns (see Figure 7C-D).

We considered the gaze direction for a primary fixation (Azimuth = 0° and Elevation = 0°), and for a tertiary fixation (Azimuth = 40° and Elevation = 40°). Even if in tertiary position, the vertical disparity pattern has a non-negligible value, and the vergence control is able to work properly for disparities in a range three times larger than the control gathered from the estimation of disparity (see Figure 7E-F).

FUTURE RESEARCH DIRECTIONS

Because humans and primates outperform the best machine vision systems by almost any measure, building a system that emulates cortical visual processing has always been an attractive idea. However, for the most part, the use of visual neuroscience in computer vision has been limited to a justification of Gabor filters for early vision tasks. Perhaps an interesting exception relates to the research on the basic processing mechanisms of binocular vision where relevant breakthroughs in recent years have been reached by a synergic dialogue across disciplines (mixing "engineering" and "experimental" approaches). This dialogue primed experiments and scientific debates, which eventually converged to the understating/formulation of the basic principles of neuronal coding of motion and stereopis, as well as to powerful bio-inspired algorithms for depth and optic flow (Ohzawa, DeAngelis & Freeman, 1997; Qian & Mikaelian, 2000; Fleet & Jepson, 1993; Fleet, Wagner & Heeger, 1996; Fleet & Jepson, 1990; Heeger, 1988; Simoncelli & Heeger, 1998; Gautama & Van Hulle, 2001; Chen & Qian, 2004; Jepson, Fleet & Jenkin, 1991; Sabatini & Solari, 2004; Perrone, 2004).

In this framework, phase-based computational paradigms became very popular for the reliability of the extracted stereo motion features and for the interesting correlations with the properties of simple and complex cells in primary visual cortex. A general fresh view of complex cells as phase-insensitive units, but effective encoders of differential phase properties, has been recently proposed (Sabatini, Gastaldi, Solari, Pauwels, Van Hulle, Diaz, Ros, Pugeault & Krueger, 2010). On this basis, consolidated direct phase-based measure techniques imposed themselves (e.g., Sanger, 1988; Fleet, Jepson, and Jenkin, 1991), corresponding to distributed coding approaches (Fleet, Wagner & Heeger, 1996; Chen & Qian, 2004) based on populations of binocular energy units (Ohzawa, Freeman & DeAngelis, 1990; Ohzawa, DeAngelis & Freeman, 1997; Qian, 1994) in which the output from receptive fields in both eyes is linearly combined by V1 simple cells and this sum is then passed through an output non-linearity. The equivalence between phase-based techniques and energy-based models has been formally demonstrated (Qian & Mikaelian, 2000). Yet, the latter prove themselves more robust to noise and more flexible, since they can intrinsically embed adaptive mechanisms both at the coding and decoding levels of the population code.

Binocular energy units are now consolidated models of complex cells in area V1 as demonstrated by the numerous recent studies that propose architectural variants to enrich their functionality or that adopt them to describe complex perceptual behaviors (Read, 2002; Read, Parker & Cumming, 2002; Tanabe & Cumming, 2008; Bridge & Cumming, 2008; Haefner & Cumming, 2008; Read & Cumming, 2006; Serrano-Pedraza & Read, 2009; Nishimoto, Ishida & Ohzawa, 2006; Sanada & Ohzawa, 2006; Miura, Sugita, Matsuura, Inaba, Kawano & Miles, 2008).

Similarly, in the ICT community there are several examples of neuromorphic (i.e., distributed) approaches profitably used to challenge conventional solutions to computer vision problems, by

Figure 7. Eyes fixating on a plane perpendicular to the binocular gaze line, with a RDS texture attached. The gaze direction, for a primary fixation, is defined by an Azimuth = 0° and an Elevation = 0° (A), and by an Azimuth = 40° and an Elevation = 40° for a tertiary fixation (B). In the first case the horizontal disparity pattern δ_x is quasi-constant and the vertical one δ_y has a value close to zero (C), while in the second case the horizontal is no more constant and the vertical has a not negligible value (D). The disparity-vergence response in case of a constant disparity pattern with zero vertical component, is close to the desired one for both the LONG and the SHORT controls (E). Indeed, in case of a tertiary fixation, thanks to the reduced sensitivity to vertical disparity, the vergence control is able to be effective with more complicate disparity patterns (F). Time course of the fixation point (solid line) with respect to the depth of the stimulus (dashed line), in case of a step, a ramp and a sinusoid for the primary and a tertiary position of the gaze line (G and H, respectively).

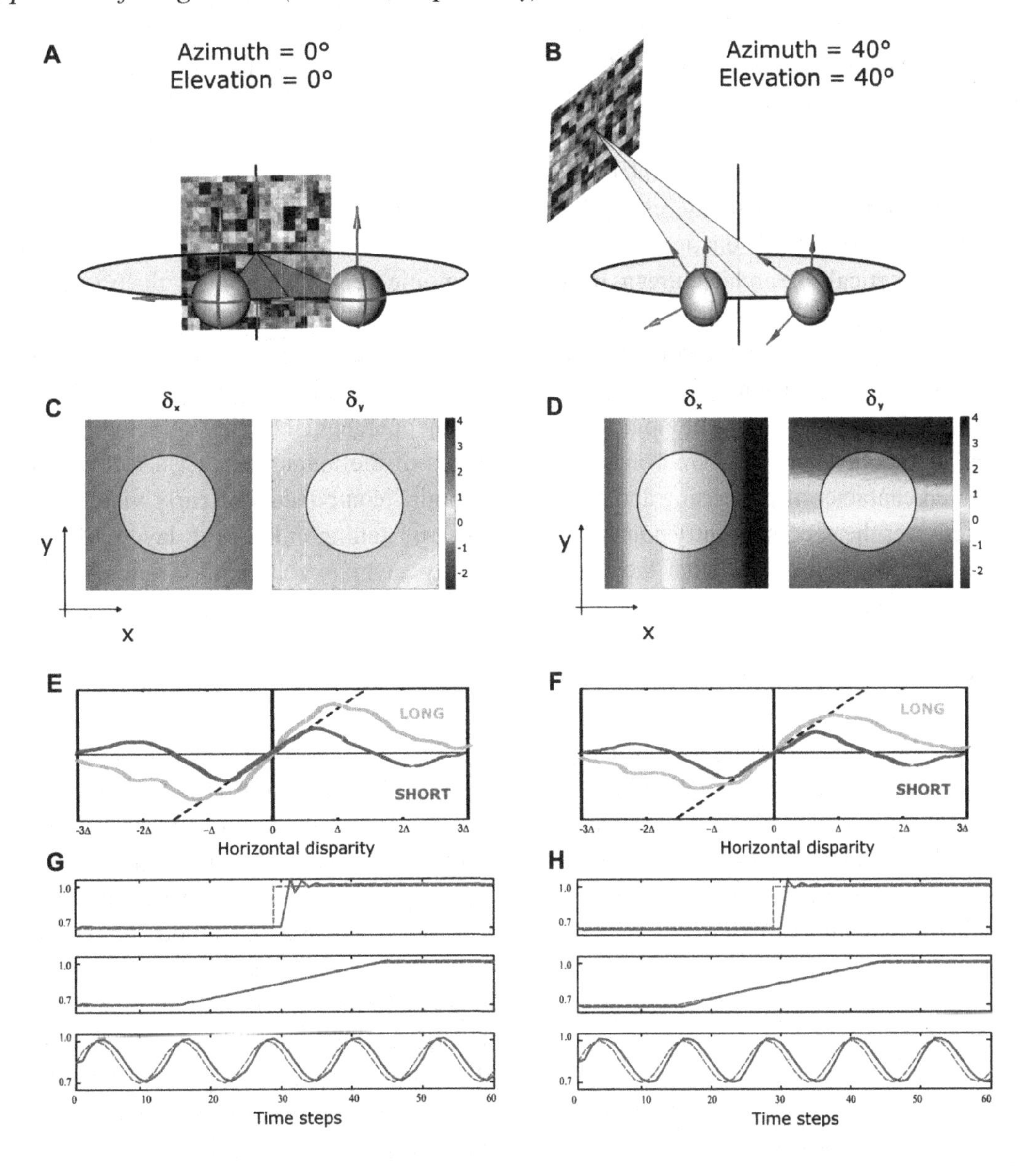

introducing sophisticated interpretation of biologically plausible operations (e.g., Tsang and Shi, 2007; Tsang and Shi, 2009; Bayerl and Neumann, 2007; see also Franz and Triesh, 2007; Wang and Shi, 2009; Solgi and Weng, 2008). Although the performances of these models were promising, the models have never been largely employed in real-world applications. This is mainly due to their high computational cost. The specific design approach followed to implement the distributed architecture presented in this chapter demonstrated that it is possible to implement 'neuromorphic' solutions that are characterized by an affordable computational cost, to be efficiently employed in closed-loop robotic applications. Pilot GPU-based implementations of the distributed architecture for the computation of 2D disparity, using the Nvidia CUDA Library yielded encouraging results. Therefore, cortical-like architectures as bio-inspired structural paradigms to solve computer vision tasks can represent a viable solution for the next-generation robot vision systems, which are capable to calibrate and adapt autonomously through the interaction with the environment. The distributed character of processing and representation ensures the necessary entry points for closing perception-action cycles from the very initial processing stages.

From a broader sensorimotor perspective, the challenge is to extend the problem of a visuomotor awareness of the 3D peripersonal space to other body parts, e.g. head and arms, so possibly using multisensory feedback, to extract information useful to build representations of the 3D space which are coherent and stable with respect to time, towards an egocentric and heterogeneous multimodal representation of space.

CONCLUSION

In this chapter, we presented two case studies that show how large-scale networks of V1-like binocular cells can provide a flexible medium on which to base coding/decoding adaptation mechanisms related to sensorimotor schema. At the coding level, the position of the eyes in the orbits can adapt the disparity tuning to minimize the necessary resources, while preserving reliable estimates (i.e., adjustable tuning mechanisms based on the posture of the eyes to improve depth vision (Chessa, Canessa, Gibaldi, Solari & Sabatini, 2009). At the decoding level, specialized read-out mechanisms can be obtained for directly extracting disparity-vergence responses without explicit calculation of the disparity map, to gain (1) linear servos with fast reaction and precision, and (2) wide working range with a reduced amount of resources (Gibaldi, Canessa, Chessa, Solari & Sabatini, 2010).

The extraction of binocular features relies upon a full (i.e., amplitude, orientation and phase) harmonic representation of the visual signal, operated by a set of "simple cell" units (S-cells). Such representation allows us to reconsider and analyze the flexibility and robustness of the multichannel perceptual coding, adopted by the early stages of the mammalian visual cortex, for the "atomic" components of early vision. Oriented disparity tuning emerges in layers of binocular energy "complex cell" units (C-cells) which gather S-cells outputs according to specific architectural schemes.

From a methodological point of view, the proposed approach points out the advantages and the flexibility of distributed and hierarchical cortical-like architectures against solutions based on a conventional systemic coupling of sensing and motor components, which in general poses integration problems since highly heterogeneous and complex processes must be coupled. Through the distributed coding, indeed, it is possible to avoid a sequentialization of sensorial and motor processes, which is certainly desirable for the development of cognitive abilities at a pre-interpretative (i.e., sub-symbolic) level, e.g., when a system must learn (binocular) eye coordination, handling the inaccuracies of the motor system, calibrating the active measurements of the space around it. The design strategy of these active visual cortical networks jointly involves three concurrent aspects: (i) *signal processing*, by defining the proper descriptive elements of the visual signal (in the Gibsonian sense) and the operators to measure them (cf. the Plenoptic Function; Adelson & Bergen, 1991), (ii) the *geometry of the system* and its kinematics, which directly relates to the embodiment concept, and (iii) the *connectionism paradigms*, which define neuromorphic architectural solutions for information processing and representation. The connectionism paradigm (i.e., hierarchical, distributed computing) is crucial to guarantee accessibility and interaction of the information at different levels of coding and decoding, by postponing decisions as much as possible.

REFERENCES

Adelson, E. H., & Bergen, J. R. (1991). *Computational models of visual processing*. Cambridge, MA: MIT Press.

Aloimonos, J. Y., Weiss, I., & Bandopadhay, A. (1987). Active vision. *International Journal of Computer Vision*, *1*(4), 333–356.

Bajcsy, R. (1988) Active perception. *IEEE Proceedings, 76*(8), 996-1006.

Ballard, D. (1991). Animate vision. *Artificial Intelligence*, *48*(1), 1–27.

Ballard, D. H., & Ozcandarli, A. (1988, December). *Eye fixation and early vision: Kinematic depth*. Paper presented at the meeting of the IEEE 2nd International Conference on Computer Vision, Tarpon Springs, Fla.

Bayerl, P., & Neumann, H. (2007). A fast biologically inspired algorithm for recurrent motion estimation. *IEEE Transactions on Pattern Analysis and Machine Intelligence*, *29*(2), 246–260.

Blohm, G., Khan, A. Z., Ren, L., Schreiber, K. M., & Crawford, J. D. (2008). Depth estimation from retinal disparity requires eye and head orientation signals. *Journal of Vision, 8*(16), 3, 1-23.

Bridge, H., & Cumming, B. C. (2008). Representation of binocular surfaces by cortical neurons. *Current Opinion in Neurobiology*, *18*(4), 425–430.

Brown, C. (1990). Prediction and cooperation in gaze control. *Biological Cybernetics*, *63*(1), 61–70.

Chen, Y., & Qian, M. (2004). A coarse to fine energy model with both phase-shift and position-shift receptive field mechanisms. *Neural Computation*, *16*, 1545–1577.

Chessa, M., Sabatini, S. P., & Solari, F. (2009). A fast joint bioinspired algorithm for optic flow and two-dimensional disparity estimation. In J. Piater (Ed.), *7th International Conference on Computer Vision Systems (ICVS'09), Lecture Notes in Computer Science, Vol. 5815*, (pp. 13-15).

Chessa, M., Solari, F., & Sabatini, S. P. (2011). Virtual reality to simulate visual tasks for robotic systems. In Kim, J.-J. (Ed.), *Virtual reality* (pp. 71–92). InTech.

Clark, J. J., & Ferrier, N. J. (1988). Modal control of attentive vision system. In *Proceedings of the International Conference on Computer Vision* (pp. 514–523).

Costa, A. H. R., Rillo, C., Barros, L. N. D., & Bianchi, R. A. C. (1998). Integrating purposive vision with deliberative and reactive planning: Engineering support for robotic applications. *Journal of the Brazilian Computer Society*, *4*(3).

Dean, T., Allen, J., & Aloimonos, Y. (1995). *Artificial intelligence: Theory and practice*. Redwood City, CA: Benjamin/Cummings Publishing Co.

Eklundh, J. O., & Pahlavan, K. (1992, April). *Eye and head-eye system.* SPIE Applications of AI X: Machine Vision and Robotics, Orlando, Fla.

Fleet, D. (1994). Disparity from local weighted phase-correlation. In *Proceedings of the IEEE International Conference on Systems, Man and Cybernetics,* Vol. 1, (pp. 48–54).

Fleet, D. J., & Jepson, A. D. (1990). Computation of component image velocity from local phase information. *International Journal of Computer Vision, 5*(1), 77–104.

Fleet, D. J., & Jepson, A. D. (1993). Stability of phase information. *IEEE Transactions on Pattern Analysis and Machine Intelligence, 15*(12), 1253–1268.

Fleet, D. J., Jepson, A. D., & Jenkin, M. R. M. (1991). Phase-based disparity measurement. *CVGIP: Image Understanding, 53*(2), 198–210.

Fleet, D. J., Wagner, H., & Heeger, D. J. (1996). Neural encoding of binocular disparity: Energy models, position shifts and phase shifts. *Vision Research, 36*(12), 1839–1857.

Franz, A., & Triesch, J. (2007). *Emergence of disparity tuning during the development of vergence eye movements.* In International Conference on Development and Learning.

Gautama, T., & Van Hulle, M. M. (2001). Function of center-surround antagonism for motion in visual area MT/V5: A modeling study. *Vision Research, 41*(28), 3917–3930.

Gibaldi, A., Chessa, M., Canessa, A., Sabatini, S. P., & Solari, F. (2010). A cortical model for binocular vergence control without explicit calculation of disparity. *Neurocomputing, 73*, 1065–1073.

Greenwald, H. S., & Knill, D. C. (2009). Cue integration outside central fixation: A study of grasping in depth. *Journal of Vision, 9*(2), 11, 1-16.

Haefner, R. M., & Cumming, B. G. (2009). An improved estimator of variance explained in the presence of noise. *Advances in Neural Information Processing Systems, 21*, 585–592.

Hamker, F. H. (2005a). The reentry hypothesis: The putative interaction of the frontal eye field, ventrolateral prefrontal cortex, and areas V4, IT for attention and eye movement. *Cerebral Cortex, 15*, 431–447.

Hamker, F. H. (2005b). A computational model of visual stability and change detection during eye movements in real world scenes. *Visual Cognition, 12*, 1161–1176.

Hansard, M., & Horaud, R. (2008). Cyclopean geometry of binocular vision. *Journal of the Optical Society of America, 25*, 2357–2369.

Hansard, M., & Horaud, R. (2010). Cyclorotation models for eyes and cameras. *IEEE Transactions on Systems, Man, and Cybernetics. Part B, Cybernetics, 40*, 151–161.

Heeger, D. (1988). Optical flow using spatiotemporal filters. *International Journal of Computer Vision, 1*, 270–302.

Howard, I. P., & Rogers, B. J. (2002). Seeing in depth: *Vol. 2. Depth perception.* Ontario, Canada: I Porteous Publishing.

Hung, G. K., Semmlow, J. L., & Ciuffreda, K. J. (1986). A dual-mode dynamic model of the vergence eye movement system. *IEEE Transactions on Bio-Medical Engineering, 36*(11), 1021–1028.

Jenkin, M. R. M. (1996). Stereopsis near the horoptor. *Proceedings of the 4th ICARCV.*

Jepson, A. D., Fleet, D. J., & Jenkin, R. M. (1991). Phase-based disparity measurement. *CVGIP: Image Understanding, 53*, 198–210.

Krishnan, V. V., & Stark, L. A. (1977). A heuristic model for the human vergence eye movement system. *IEEE Transactions on Bio-Medical Engineering, 24*, 44–49.

Krotkow, E., Henriksen, K., & Kories, R. (1990). Stereo ranging from verging cameras. *IEEE Transaction on PAMI, 12*(12), 1200–1205.

Marr, D. (1982). *Vision*. New York, NY: W.H. Freeman and Company.

Miura, K., Sugita, Y., Matsuura, K., Inaba, N., Kawano, K., & Miles, F. A. (2008). The initial disparity vergence elicited with single and dual grating stimuli in monkeys: Evidence for disparity energy sensing and nonlinear interactions. *Journal of Neurophysiology*, *100*(5), 2907–2918.

Mok, D., Ro, A., Cadera, W., Crawford, J. D., & Vilis, T. (1990). Rotation of listing's plane during vergence. *Vision Research*, *32*, 2055–2064.

Monaco, J. P., Bovik, A. C., & Cormack, L. K. (2009). Active, foveated, uncalibrated stereovision. *International Journal of Computer Vision*, *85*(2), 192–207.

Morgan, M. J., & Castet, E. (1997). The aperture problem in stereopsis. *Vision Research*, *37*, 2737–2744.

Nishimoto, S., Ishida, T., & Ohzawa, I. (2006). Receptive field properties of neurons in the early visual cortex revealed by local spectral reverse correlation. *The Journal of Neuroscience*, *26*(12), 3269–3280.

Noë, A. (2004). *Action in perception*. Cambridge, MA: MIT Press.

O'Regan, K., & Noë, A. (2001). A sensorimotor account of vision anvisual consciousness. *The Behavioral and Brain Sciences*, *24*(5), 883–917.

Ohzawa, I., DeAngelis, G. C., & Freeman, R. D. (1997). Encoding of binocular disparity by complex cells in the cat's visual cortex. *Journal of Neurophysiology*, *77*, 2879–2909.

Ohzawa, I., Freeman, R. D., & DeAngelis, G. C. (1990). Stereoscopic depth discrimination in the visual cortex: Neurons ideally suited as disparity detectors. *Science*, *249*, 1037–1041.

Perrone, J. A. (2004). A visual motion sensor based on the properties of V1 and MT neurons. *Vision Research*, *44*, 1733–1755.

Poggio, G. F. (1995). Mechanism of stereopsis in monkey visual cortex. *Cerebral Cortex*, *5*, 193–204.

Polpitiya, A. D., & Ghosh, B. K. (2002, May). *Modelling and control of eye-movement with muscolotendon dynamics*. Paper presented at the meeting of the American Control Conference, Anchorage, AK.

Prince, S. J. D., Cumming, B. G., & Parker, A. J. (2002). Range and mechanism of encoding of horizontal disparity in macaque v1. *Journal of Neurophysiology*, *87*, 209–221.

Qian, N. (1994). Computing stereo disparity and motion with known binocular cell properties. *Neural Computation*, *6*(3), 390–404.

Qian, N., & Mikaelian, S. (2000). Relationship between phase and energy methods for disparity computation. *Neural Computation*, *12*, 303–316.

Rambold, H. A., & Miles, F. (2008). A human vergence eye movements to oblique disparity stimuli: Evidence for an anisotropy favoring horizontal disparities. *Vision Research*, *48*, 2006–2019.

Read, J. C. A. (2002). A Bayesian approach to the stereo correspondence problem. *Neural Computation*, *14*, 1371–1392.

Read, J. C. A., & Cumming, B. G. (2004). Understanding the cortical specialization for horizontal disparity. *Neural Computation*, *16*(10), 1983–2020.

Read, J. C. A., & Cumming, B. G. (2006). Does depth perception require vertical disparity detectors? *Journal of Vision (Charlottesville, Va.)*, *6*(12), 1323–1355.

Read, J. C. A., & Cumming, B. G. (2006). Does depth perception require vertical disparity detectors? *Journal of Vision (Charlottesville, Va.)*, *6*(12), 1323–1355.

Read, J. C. A., Parker, A. J., & Cumming, B. G. (2002). A simple model accounts for the response of disparity-tuned V1 neurons to anti-correlated images. *Visual Neuroscience*, *19*, 735–753.

Read, J. C. A., Phillipson, G. P., & Glennerster, A. (2009). Latitude and longitude vertical disparities. *Journal of Vision (Charlottesville, Va.)*, *9*(13), 1–37.

Sabatini, S. P., Gastaldi, G., Solari, F., Pauwels, K., Van Hulle, M. M., & Diaz, J. (2010). A compact harmonic code for early vision based on anisotropic frequency channels. *Computer Vision and Image Understanding*, *114*, 681–699.

Sabatini, S. P., & Solari, F. (2004). Emergence of motion-in-depth selectivity in the visual cortex through linear combination of binocular energy complex cells with different ocular dominance. *Neurocomputing*, *58–60*, 865–872.

Sanada, T. M., & Ohzawa, I. (2006). Encoding of three-dimensional surface slant in cat visual areas 17 and 18. *Journal of Neurophysiology*, *95*, 2768–2786.

Sanger, T. D. (1988). Stereo disparity computation using Gabor filters. *Biological Cybernetics*, *59*, 405–418.

Santini, F., & Rucci, M. (2007). Active estimation of distance in a robotic system that replicates human eye movement. *Robotics and Autonomous Systems*, *55*(2), 107–121.

Scharstein, D., & Szeliski, R. (2002). A taxonomy and evaluation of dense two-frame stereo correspondence algorithms. *International Journal of Computer Vision, 47*(1/2/3), 7-42.

Schor, C. M., Maxwell, J. S., McCandless, J., & Graf, E. (2002). Adaptive control of vergence in humans. *Annals of the New York Academy of Sciences*, *956*, 297–305.

Schreiber, K., Crawford, J. D., Fetter, M., & Tweed, D. (2001). The motor side of depth vision. *Nature*, *410*, 819–822.

Schreiber, K. M., Hillis, J. M., Filippini, H. R., Schor, C. M., & Banks, M. S. (2008). The surface of the empirical horopter. *Journal of Vision (Charlottesville, Va.)*, *8*(3), 1–20.

Schreiber, K. M., Tweed, D. B., & Schor, C. M. (2006). The extended horopter: Quantifying retinal correspondence across changes of 3d eye position. *Journal of Vision (Charlottesville, Va.)*, *6*, 64–74.

Semmlow, J. L., Hung, G. K., & Ciuffreda, K. J. (1986). Quantitative assessment of disparity vergence components. *Investigative Ophthalmology & Visual Science*, *27*, 558–564.

Serrano-Pedraza, I., Phillipson, G. P., & Read, J. C. A. (2010). A specialization for vertical disparity discontinuities. *Journal of Vision (Charlottesville, Va.)*, *10*(3), 1–25.

Serrano-Pedraza, I., & Read, J. C. A. (2009). Stereo vision requires an explicit encoding of vertical disparity. *Journal of Vision (Charlottesville, Va.)*, *9*(4), 1–13.

Sheliga, B. M., & Miles, F. A. (2003). Perception can influence the vergence responses associated with open-loop gaze shifts in 3-d. *Journal of Vision (Charlottesville, Va.)*, *3*, 654–676.

Simoncelli, E. P., & Heeger, D. J. (1998). A model of neuronal responses in visual area MT. *Vision Research*, *38*(5), 743–761.

Solgi, M., & Weng, J. (2008, Nov). *Developmental stereo: Topographic iconic-abstract map from top-down connection.* In International Neural Network Society, Symposia Series New developments in Neural Networks, Auckland, New Zealand.

Takemura, A., Inoue, Y., Kawano, K., Quaia, C., & Miles, F. A. (2001). Single-unit activity in cortical area MST associated with disparity vergence eye movements: Evidence for population coding. *Journal of Neurophysiology*, *85*, 2245–2266.

Takemura, A., Kawano, K., Quaia, C., & Miles, F. A. (2006). Population coding of vergence eye movements in cortical area MST. In Harris, L., & Jenkin, M. (Eds.), *Levels of perception*.

Tanabe, S., & Cumming, B. G. (2008). Mechanisms underlying the transformation of disparity signals from V1 to V2 in the macaque. *The Journal of Neuroscience*, *28*(44), 11304–11314.

Theimer, W. M., & Mallot, H. A. (1994). Phase-based vergence control and depth reconstruction using active vision. *CVGIP. Image Understanding*, *60*(3), 343–358.

Tsang, E. K. C., & Shi, B. E. (2007). *Estimating disparity with confidence from energy neurons*. NIPS2007.

Tsang, E. K. C., & Shi, B. E. (2009). Disparity estimation by pooling evidence from energy neurons. *IEEE Transactions on Neural Networks*, *20*(11), 1772–1782.

Tweed, D., & Vilis, T. (1990). Geometric relations of eye position and velocity vectors during saccades. *Vision Research*, *30*(1), 111–127.

Wang, Y., & Shi, B. E. (2009). Autonomous development of vergence control driven by disparity energy neuron populations. *Neural Computation*, *22*, 1–22.

Yang, D. S., FitzGibbon, E. J., & Miles, F. A. (2003). Short-latency disparity vergence eye movements in humans: Sensitivity to simulated orthogonal tropias. *Vision Research*, *43*(3).

ADDITIONAL READING

Adelson, E. H., & Bergen, J. R. (1985). Spatiotemporal energy models for the perception of motion. *Journal of the Optical Society of America*, *2*(2), 284–299.

Anzai, A., Ohzawa, I., & Freeman, R. D. (2001). Joint-encoding of motion and depth by visual cortical neurons: neural basis of the Pulfrich effect. *Nature Neuroscience*, *4*, 513–518.

Daugman, J. G. (1985). Uncertainty relation for resolution in space, spatial frequency, and orientation optimized by two-dimensional visual cortical filters. *Journal of the Optical Society of America*, *2*(7), 1160–1169.

De Valois, R., & De Valois, K. (1988). *Spatial vision*. Oxford University Press.

Emerson, R. C., Bergen, J. R., & Adelson, E. H. (1992). Directionally selective complex cells and the computation of motion energy in cat visual cortex. *Vision Research*, *32*, 203–218.

Heeger, D. J. (1987). Model for the extraction of image flow. *Journal of the Optical Society of America*, *4*, 1455–1471.

Li, Z. (1996). A theory of the visual motion coding in the primary visual cortex. *Neural Computation*, *8*(4), 705–730.

Li, Z., & Atick, J. J. (1994). Towards a theory of striate cortex. *Neural Computation*, *6*, 127–146.

Priebe, N. J., Lisberger, S. G., & Movshon, J. A. (2006). Tuning for spatiotemporal frequency and speed in directionally selective neurons of macaque striate cortex. *The Journal of Neuroscience*, *26*, 2941–2950.

Raiguel, S. E., Van Hulle, M. M., Xiao, D. K., Marcar, V. L., & Orban, G. A. (1995). Shape and spatial distribution of receptive fields and antagonistic surrounds in area MT (V5) of the macaque. *The European Journal of Neuroscience*, *7*, 2064–2082.

Rust, N. C., Mante, V., Simoncelli, E. P., & Movshon, J. A. (2006). How MT cells analyze the motion of visual patterns. *Nature Neuroscience*, *9*, 1421–1431.

Simoncelli, E. P. (1993). *Distributed analysis and representation of visual motion.* Unpublished doctoral dissertation, Massachusetts Institute of Technology, Cambridge MA.

Zhu, Y., & Qian, N. (1996). Binocular receptive field models, disparity tuning and characteristic disparity. *Neural Computation*, *8*, 1611–1641.

Section 3
Visual Cortical Structures

Chapter 8
The Roles of Endstopped and Curvature Tuned Computations in a Hierarchical Representation of 2D Shape

Antonio J. Rodríguez-Sánchez
University of Innsbruck, Austria

John K. Tsotsos
York University, Canada

ABSTRACT

Computational models of visual processes are of interest in fields such as cybernetics, robotics, computer vision, and others. This chapter argues for the importance of intermediate representation layers in the visual cortex that have direct impact on the next generation of object recognition strategies in computer vision. Biological inspiration - and even biological realism - is currently of great interest in the computer vision community. The authors propose that endstopping and curvature cells are of great importance for shape selectivity and show how their combination can lead to shape selective neurons, providing an approach that does not require learning between early stages based on Gabor or Difference of Gaussian filters and later stages closer to object representations.

INTRODUCTION

Over the last fifteen years, many models inspired by advances in the anatomy of the visual cortex have been presented (Cadieu, Kouch, Connor, Riesenhuber, & Poggio, 2007; Heinke & Humphreys, 2003; Murphy & Finkel, 2007; Olshausen, Anderson, & Van Essen, 1993; Riesenhuber & Poggio, 1999, 2000, 2002; E. T. Rolls & G. Deco, 2002; Serre, Wolf, Bileschi, & Riesenhuber, 2007; Wallis & Rolls, 1997). But none of the models presented until now fully explore the possible

DOI: 10.4018/978-1-4666-2539-6.ch008

contributions of intermediate representations as are known in the brain.

In the past decade we have seen a resurgence of interest in shape representation and analysis in the object recognition literature. At the same time, an important number of influential studies in neuroscience have shed new light into how the brain performs the analysis of visual objects (Peissig & Tarr, 2007). Due to the latter, several models have appeared which are inspired to some degree on how neurons achieve object recognition (see the compendium of articles edited by (Dickinson, Leonardis, Schiele, & Tarr, 2009). By understanding how specific simple objects are analyzed by the brain, we may construct subsystems that emulate that behavior. 2D shapes (closed contours) are an important feature for recognizing objects (Connor, Brincat, & Pasupathy, 2007). But until recently there was no substantial proof that the biological visual system analyzes curvature in areas that are involved in the object recognition pathway, such as V4 (Pasupathy & Connor, 1999, 2002) and IT (Connor, et al., 2007).

There are several hypotheses on how, starting with neurons that may be modeled in V1 through a set of Gabor filters, we may achieve shape and object representation. We explore here one of those hypotheses, that of endstopping as an intermediate neural computation. The work of (Dobbins, Zucker, & Cynader, 1987, 1989) provides a framework where we can represent curvature from a combination of simple and complex neurons. Simple, complex, endstopped and curvature neurons are well known to exist in the visual cortex (Hubel & Wiesel, 1968; Kato, Bishop, & Orban, 1978; Pasupathy & Connor, 1999) in different areas of the object recognition pathway. Surprisingly, endstopped neurons have been neglected during the past 20 years in the modeling literature, and the models introduced up to this date achieve object representation by combining the responses of Gabor filters in different ways but not through a combination of cell responses which achieve a direct computation of curvature.

We propose here a direct way of achieving curvature and shape-selective neurons - through intermediate endstopping stages - in a biologically plausible manner which has not been explored before through the role of intermediate layers that may shed a new light into future models of human vision as well as object recognition systems.

BACKGROUND

Contour and Curvature Computation in the Visual Cortex and Computer Vision

Since the foundation of modern neuroanatomy by Ramón y Cajal (Jones, 2007; Ramon y Cajal, 1888, 1894, 1904), who gave a detailed description of nerve cell organization in the central and peripheral nervous system, great progress has been achieved in understanding the human brain.

The visual cortex is organized into different areas. V1 and V2 are the largest, each having an area of approximately 11-12% of the macaque neocortex (Felleman & Van Essen, 1991). Physiological studies show two different pathways with connections between them: The occipitotemporal pathway (V1, V2, V4, TEO and TE) is related with object recognition features (color, shape, etc.) (Logothetis & Sheinberg, 1996; Tanaka, 1996a), while the occipitoparietal pathway (V1, V2, V3, MT and MST) is associated with spatiotemporal characteristics of the scene (direction of motion, speed gradients, etc.) (Webster & Ungerleider, 1998).

Along this hierarchical architecture, neurons become increasingly selective to more complex stimuli and less sensitive to stimulus variation. At the bottom of the hierarchy, neurons in V1 are selective for edges (among other features), and at the top, TE neurons respond to complex objects with significant variation in their orientation, size, illumination and foreshortening. How is this early visual information transformed into whole objects?

Concerning orientation selection, V1 neurons can be classified into three types: simple cells, complex cells, and endstopped cells (Hubel & Wiesel, 1959, 1962, 1965, 1968): (1) Simple cells have small receptive fields (0.1°-1°) (Hubel & Wiesel, 1965; Schiller, Finlay, & Volman, 1976), are close to the fovea, and their response is based on small areas relative to the background (Hubel & Wiesel, 1968). They respond to bars and edges with different orientations as well as to spatial frequency (K. DeValois, DeValois, & Yund, 1979). (2) Complex cells are also sensitive to bars and orientations, but with a lower sensitivity (Hubel & Wiesel, 1959, 1965, 1968). Their receptive fields are larger than those of simple cells (0.2°-2°) (R. DeValois, Albrecht, & Thorell, 1982). In contrast to simple cells, a complex neuron responds irrespective of the particular position at which a bar is flashed inside its receptive field (Hubel & Wiesel, 1968). (3) Endstopped cells are sensitive to the termination of an edge or a bar (Hubel & Wiesel, 1965, 1968). Endstopped cells are also known as hypercomplex and have been described in great detail for the cat (Bishop, Kato, & Orban, 1980; Kato, et al., 1978; Orban, Kato, & Bishop, 1979a, 1979b). Later evidence supports the role of endstopped cells in curvature estimation (Dobbins, Zucker & Cynader, 1987; Versavel, Orban & Lagae, 1990).

V2 neurons respond to contours, both real and illusory (von der Heydt, Peterhans, & Baumgartner, 1984). Area V2 contains endstopped cells as well, which are very similar to the ones found in V1 (Heider, Heitger & Peterhans, 1998; Heider, Meskenaite & Peterhans, 2000). More recent studies (Boynton & Hegde, 2004; Ito & Komatsu, 2004) have found that V2 neurons are mainly selective for angles and corners, and that these neurons also showed submaximal responses for bars. V4 neurons have receptive fields that range from 2° to 4°. Some of the qualities of V4 neurons include that they show selectivity to luminance (Heywood, Gadotti, & Cowey, 1992; Motter, 1994; Schein & Desimone, 1990) and color constancy (Zeki, 1983). They also exhibit sensitivity to length, width, orientation, direction of motion and spatial frequency (Desimone, Schein, Moran, & Ungerleider, 1985). Later experiments in monkeys where area V4 was ablated showed that V4 is important for the perception of form and pattern/shape discrimination (Merigan & Pham, 1998). Neurons in V4 respond to those simple shapes and their responses can be fit by a curvature position function (Pasupathy & Connor, 1999, 2001, 2002). In this representation, the object's curvature is attached to a certain angular position relative to the object center of mass. Most V4 neurons represent individual parts or contour fragments (Connor, et al., 2007).

The macaque monkey's inferotemporal cortex (IT) receives inputs mainly from V2 and V4 (Felleman & Van Essen, 1991). IT is the main area involved in object recognition and discrimination (Brincat & Connor, 2004; Dean, 1976; Gross, Rocha-Miranda, & Bender, 1972; Logothetis & Sheinberg, 1996; Tanaka, 1996b). IT neurons are view-independent, translation, space and size invariant and respond mainly to objects and faces (E. Rolls & G. Deco, 2002). IT can be divided in two main parts (Tanaka, Saito, Fukada, & Moriya, 1991): (1) In Posterior IT (PIT or TEO) most of the neurons are primary cells which are activated maximally by a simple combination of features such as bars or disks varying in size, orientation and color (Tanaka, et al., 1991). TEO is responsible for medium complexity features and integrates information about the shapes and relative positions of multiple contour elements. Recent experiments (Connor, et al., 2007) support parts-based shape theories. (2) Anterior IT (AIT or TE) neurons comprise two-thirds to three-quarters of the IT area and they require more complex features for maximal activation. These neurons are called elaborate cells. TE is responsible for high complexity features (Kobatake, Wang, & Tanaka,

1998; Tanaka, 1996a) including faces, hands and other body parts. TE receives inputs from V4 and TEO neurons at different retinal positions (Tanaka, 1996b), which may explain its scale, position and view invariance (Booth & Rolls, 1998). All this evidence shows that areas V4 and TEO are involved in curvature and shape analysis.

But shape and curvature have been popular in vision sciences for object recognition for decades. As early as 1967, (Blum, 1967) already points out the difference between biological and physical representations regarding shape. In this work he presents the Medial Axis transform that can describe any pattern by the envelope of circles of proper radius associated with each point. In this paper, Blum discusses psychological and physiological implications regarding illusions and cortical cell responses reported by (Hubel & Wiesel, 1962, 1965). In a recent book (Siddiqi & Pizer, 2008) summarize many of the later findings that point to a role of the medial loci (also known as skeletons) in shape perception. In what follows we provide a brief historical overview of curvature and shape methods in computer vision.

Early studies approximated curves using line segments or chain encoding (Freeman, 1974; McKee & Aggarwal, 1977). Polygonal approximations (Pavlidis, 1972) were used early as well, where each segment is considered a graph with branches connecting the nodes corresponding to segments with overlapping boundaries, and where various criteria determine the breakpoints that define the best polygon. Other early approximations to shape and curvature are through skeletons (Blum, 1973), shape descriptors such as area and perimeters (Danielsson, 1978) or angles and sides (Davis, 1977). Fourier descriptors have been widely used since (Persoon & Fu, 1974) for boundary representation; a curve is represented by the Fourier expansion of a parametric representation of a curve. A similar approach is the use of principal components which uses the strongest set of eigenvectors (Darroch & Mosimann, 1985). (Ballard, 1981) proposed a method to detect shapes using the Hough transform. The Hough transform is a method for detecting curves by exploiting the duality between points on a curve and parameters of that curve. A mapping between image space and Hough transform space through the boundaries of a shape can be performed, and this mapping can be used to detect instances of a particular shape.

The Curvature Primal Sketch (Asada & Brady, 1984) followed the primal sketch proposed by (Marr & Nishihara, 1978) for curves. A curve is approximated using a library of analytic curves, the curvature function is then computed and convolved with a Gaussian of varying standard deviation. Darboux vectors have been used for contour descriptions (Kehtarnavaz & de Figueiredo, 1988) since they contain information regarding curvature and torsion properties. Hype (Ayache & Faugeras, 1986) used segmented descriptions of the object contours to generate and recursively evaluate a number of selected hypotheses. (Mehrotra & Grosky, 1989) also presented a system of hypothesis generation and testing based on dynamic programming.

Curvature extrema were used by (Richards, Dawson, & Whittingham, 1988) which were based on the codons from human perception (Richards & Hoffman, 1984). Codons are sequences of curvature extrema separated by curvature minima and zeroes, whose combinations provide the type of codon. A list of curvature extrema provides a "vocabulary" for curves. (Leyton, 1987) exploits curvature extrema and symmetry structure as descriptors of shape and presents the Symmetry-Curvature Duality Theorem that proposes a relationship between symmetry and curvature extrema. Landmarks (Ansari & Delp, 1990) are points of interest with important shape attributes such as points of high curvature. (Ansari & Delp, 1990) used sphericity for matching. Sphericity is a measure of similarity between triangles.

A popular strategy for curve-based representations in object recognition are splines. Splines are piecewise polynomials in an interval connected smoothly by knots (joining points). Smoothed splines have been proposed to parametrize the curve (Shahraray & Anderson, 1989). To obtain the optimal degree of regularization (the smoothing term), cross-validation was used. Cross-validation is a method where the goodness of a set of parameters is measured in terms of the ability of the model to predict some of the observations. This work also first presented the idea of analyzing a shape by a curvature-position histogram, a representation later proposed for V4 neurons (Pasupathy & Connor, 1999, 2001, 2002). (Marimont, 1984) presented a framework that extracted curvatures at different scales. The Curvature Scale Space, or CSS (Mokhtarian, 1995; Mokhtarian & Mackworth, 1984) is a multiscale representation of shape curvatures, a curve is described at varying levels of detail through features invariant to transformations. The features used for matching are the maxima of CSS contours. A three-stage, coarse-to-fine matching algorithm prunes the search space in stage one by applying the CSS aspect ratio test.

Dudek and Tsotsos (Dudek & Tsotsos, 1997) introduced an approach in which curvature is represented at multiple spatial scales. Curved objects are described by a group of segments that encode length, position and curvature. Kimia and colleages (Kimia & Siddiqi, 1994; Kimia, Tannenbaum, & Zucker, 1992, 1995) proposed a theory of shape based on deformations, parts, bends and seeds. Contour deformations are characterized by a deformation along the normal and a deformation that varies in proportion to curvature. A space of shapes is constructed in which similar shapes are arranged according to the different axes of deformation. (Belongie, Malik, & Puzicha, 2002) captured the subset of points from object shapes sampled from the internal or external contours. Shape samples are performed through uniform spacing. A descriptor (shape context) is attached to each point that captures the distribution of the remaining points relative to it such that similar shapes have similar descriptors. (Elder, Krupnik, & Johnston, 2003) used prior knowledge of objects for contour grouping. An approximate constructive search technique computes the candidate object boundaries.

For a more complete and detailed overview on shape representation, the reader may refer to (Zhang & Lu, 2004).

Related Work: Biologically Inspired Models

The last three decades have seen the resurgence of neural networks, which originated in 1962 with the Perceptron (Rosenblatt, 1962). Soon afterwards, the first models inspired by biological systems were presented (Grossberg, 1968, 1970, 1971, 1975). Computer modeling of the visual cortex is related to artificial neural networks since the elements to be modeled are neurons, although they are quite different from the classical neural networks such as the Perceptron. An important early model while still being influenced from classical artificial neural networks is Fukushima's Neocognitron (Fukushima, 1980). The Neocognitron is a self-organizing neural network model that achieves object position invariance and was later shown to perform well on digit recognition (Fukushima, Miyake, & Ito, 1983). Later models that included backpropagation (Rumelhart & Mcclelland, 1986) were also successful at this task (Lecun et al., 1989; Lecun, Bottou, Bengio, & Haffner, 1998). Over the last fifteen years, many models inspired by advances in the anatomy of the visual cortex have been presented.

One of the first such models was proposed by Olshausen and colleagues (Olshausen, et al., 1993). They developed a model that is based on (Anderson & Van Essen, 1987), the model is position and scale invariant and performs a transformation from the retinal reference frame to an object-centred frame. To accomplish this, shifter circuits and control neurons are used. The control neurons dynamically conduct information from lower levels of a hierarchical network to higher levels of the network. By means of the shifter circuits and the control neurons, the window of attention changes in size for scale invariance and position. This model was later extended in the SIAM system (Heinke & Humphreys, 2003) which is a combination of networks (one for an attentional window, a second one for storing objects and a third one for selecting contents) that achieve translation invariant object recognition.

Visnet (Wallis & Rolls, 1997) consists of a four layer network that achieves invariant object recognition. The most crucial part of such a method is a trace learning rule that is Hebbian based. Lateral inhibition is performed following (von der Malsburg, 1973), and competition is applied by means of a soft winner take-all. To achieve translation invariance, the network is trained with inputs at different positions. A later review includes a top-down attentional strategy (E. Rolls & G. Deco, 2002).

A very popular model is the one proposed by (Riesenhuber & Poggio, 1999, 2000, 2002). The model is an extension of Fukushima's Neocognitron consisting of five hierarchical levels of neurons that are connected through linear and non-linear MAX operations (the strongest units determine the response of the system). The first level receives input from the retina and is composed of simple neuron receptive fields that analyze orientations. The next levels account for more complex features (e.g. junctions). The last level is composed of view-tuned neurons that achieve position and scale invariance. The original model included a Radial Basis Function (RBF) (Riesenhuber & Poggio, 1999) for classification, and a later update included a Support Vector Machine (SVM) (Serre, Wolf, & Poggio, 2005). The model has been recently extended by the inclusion of an unsupervised learning stage (Serre, Wolf, Bileschi, & Riesenhuber, 2007).

Suzuki and colleagues (Suzuki, Hashimoto, Kashimori, Zheng, & Kambara, 2004) construct a model of the form pathway based on predictive coding (Rao & Ballard, 1997, 1999). Predictive coding hypothesizes that feedback connections from high to lower order cortical areas carry predictions of lower-level neural activities. Feedforward connections carry residual errors between predictions and the actual lower-level activities. (Murphy & Finkel, 2007) implement a set of feature vectors of contours: mean polar angle, mean curvature of region, mean curvature of adjacent clockwise region, mean curvature of counter-clockwise region, mean direction of curvature region, mean distance from center of mass and indication of inner or outer contour. Recognition is then performed through matching using comparison of segments, histogram cross-correlations, minimum sum of squared differences, image cross-correlation, parametric eigenspaces and support vector machines (SVM). Results are reported using Earth Mover's distance which is motivated by human perceptual studies (Kahana & Sekuler, 2002).

Even if this review may look somewhat extensive, there are many other methods and improvements over the exposed ones that have not been considered, the reader may refer to (Tsotsos & Rothenstein, 2011) and (Frintop, Rome, & Christensen, 2010) for more detailed information.

We think that models have achieved the sufficient maturity as to take them to next level and include intermediate representations as are known in the ventral stream of the visual cortex. We present a model that incorporates endstopping as a direct way to compute curvature for shape selectivity.

INCLUDING ENDSTOPPING IN THE OBJECT RECOGNITION PATHWAY

Issues, Controversies, Problems

Recent advances in neuroscience have provided a framework from which to understand how the human visual system performs the analysis of object recognition. These advances have led to models which are inspired to some degree by how neurons achieve object recognition. At the same time, there has been in the last decade a resurgence of interest in shape representation and analysis in the object recognition literature. How do we achieve object recognition in area TE with invariance to translation, rotation, scale, illumination, etc. starting from neurons in V1 that perform edge detection? What if we include an intermediate stage that computes curvatures in V4?

Biologically-inspired models have found their way in the computer vision community. But it may be too early for biologically-plausible models to be directly compared in terms of results against classical computer vision systems. and it may even be counterproductive for the advance of biological plausible modeling. Common to most models is a first step that performs edge-detection in a similar way to some V1 neurons in the brain. But after this first step there is little consensus. It is difficult to interpret results from neurophysiology, and even when the behavior of cells in one layer may be determined, it is difficult for modelers to decide how to connect one layer to the next. In addition to this, there is some pressure from the computer vision community in terms of obtaining results from real-world images, meaning invariance to affine transformations, illumination, clutter, occlusions, etc. and at the same time comparing them with state of the art computer vision systems. As a result some models must resort to complex computational methods such as classifiers, learning and others in order to achieve real-world results. Due to this, even though the starting point is biological plausibility, we find ourselves diverting from it for the sake of results and sometimes reducing the biological plausibility of the model to a pool of Gabor filters.

Consider the recent study conducted by (Pinto, Cox, & Dicarlo, 2008). They constructed a very simple V1-like model (edge detectors). The model was a neuroscience null model in the sense that it was a simple thresholded Gabor function over 16 different orientations and 6 spatial frequencies. The model did not contain a representation of shape and no mechanisms for recognition under position, size or pose variation. As it was expected, such a simple system performed poorly when tested on a easy task of differentiating just two categories (planes from cars) that introduced real-world variability (position, scale, in-plane rotation and depth rotation). But surprisingly this system performed better than five state of the art systems (Grauman & Darrell, 2006; Lazebnik, Schmid, & Ponce, 2006; Mutch & Lowe, 2006; Wang, Zhang, & Fei-Fei, 2006; Zhang, Berg, Marie, & Malik, 2006) when using the popular Caltech 101 database that included those two categories among the 102 categories in that database. The reason behind this is that even though such a database contains pictures taken from real-world scenarios, it does not include the random variability found in the real world, while the basic two-category test did. The authors warn us about the risks of such biased datasets when performing tests on real-world images, and they show this to be especially true in the case of biologically-inspired systems.

Many biologically inspired object recognition systems have been proposed over the years. The performance of biologically plausible models is not yet comparable to other, more computationally "pure", systems of object recognition, such as (Fidler, Berginc, & Leonardis, 2006; Lowe, 1999, 2004; Mekuz & Tsotsos, 2007) and others. There is starting to be a large amount of evidence on how the visual system works, which allows us to establish the basis of future systems that emulate the human visual system. In addition to this, top-down attention operating on a finer grain set of intermediate level representation will lead to more powerful computer vision recognition systems.

An example of a model that has been successfully compared with neuronal data as well as successfully tested to provide similar responses to neurons in area V4 is that of (Cadieu, et al., 2007). The authors claim that units in layer S2 in their model become selective to boundary conformations. But their model does not achieve a shape representation through any explicit form of curvature computation. Rather, they rely on the repeated convergences layer by layer of approximate straight-line fits to boundaries beginning with edge elements. This strategy does not explicitly include either curvature or end-stopped units, both well-known to exist in the visual cortex. Units that may appear similar may be learned; however, this is not necessarily so and depends on the training data selection.

We present here a study that includes end-stopping as an intermediate step for the direct computation of curvature values and shape representation. This may be considered as an evolution with respect to current models of the object recognition pathway, incorporating intermediate representations that fill the gap between the Gabor filter-like V1 representation and the later areas.

Solutions and Recommendations

It is fair to conclude that current models do not fully explore the possible contributions of intermediate representations as are known in the brain.

We propose a model of intermediate representations and computations to bridge the gap between the common very early orientation representations found in most categorization systems, and the higher object level representations. Curvature is considered an important component in order to achieve object recognition in the human brain, along with corners, edges, color, texture and other important features (Connor, et al., 2007; Wolfe, 1998). A group of studies has shown that neurons in visual area V4 in monkeys are involved with analyzing curvature (Pasupathy & Connor, 1999, 2001, 2002). In the hierarchical object recognition pathway, V4 is the area just below the inferotemporal cortex (IT), where object recognition is achieved (Felleman & Van Essen, 1991; Tanaka, 1996a; Tanaka, et al., 1991).

We have recently presented a model (Rodríguez-Sánchez & Tsotsos, 2011) (Figure 1) comprising the following types of cells organized into a hierarchy and following their function in the brain as proposed in neurophysiology studies: 1) Simple cells are linear filters with the functional form of Differences of Gaussians; 2) Complex cells are the result of the combination of spatially displaced simple cells; 3) Endstopped cells respond to variations of straightness; 4) Local curvature neurons receive input from the different types of endstopped cells; 5) Shape-selective neurons respond to curvature configurations with respect to their angular position. These cells are organized in layers in a similar way as they appear in the primate visual cortex and are explained in detail elsewhere (Rodríguez-Sánchez, 2010; Rodríguez-Sánchez & Tsotsos, 2011). Here we provide a summary of the model. In what follows whenever a neuron is referred to as model neuron it is one developed for our theory. A neuron referred to without the model adjective is a biological one.

Simple Cells (V1)

We modeled simple cells using a Difference of Gaussians formulation (Hawken & Parker, 1987):

$$G(x,y) = \frac{1}{2\pi\sigma_{x_1}\sigma_y} e^{-\frac{1}{2}\left(\left(\frac{x'}{\sigma_{x_1}}\right)^2 + \left(\frac{y'}{\sigma_y}\right)^2\right)} - \frac{1}{2\pi\sigma_{x_2}\sigma_y} e^{-\frac{1}{2}\left(\left(\frac{x'}{\sigma_{x_2}}\right)^2 + \left(\frac{y'}{\sigma_y}\right)^2\right)}$$

$$x' = x\cos(\theta) + y\sin(\theta)$$
$$y' = -x\sin(\theta) + y\cos(\theta)$$

where σ_y is the height and σ_{x1} and σ_{x2} are the width of each Gaussian function. θ is their orientation. For our experiments, we used 12 orientations and 4 different sizes, this gives a total of 48 types of V1 model simple neurons.

Complex Cells (V1)

Complex cells may be the result of the addition of simple cells along the axis perpendicular to their orientation (Spitzer & Hochstein, 1985). In our model, a complex cell is the sum of 5 laterally

Figure 1. Architecture of the shape representation model

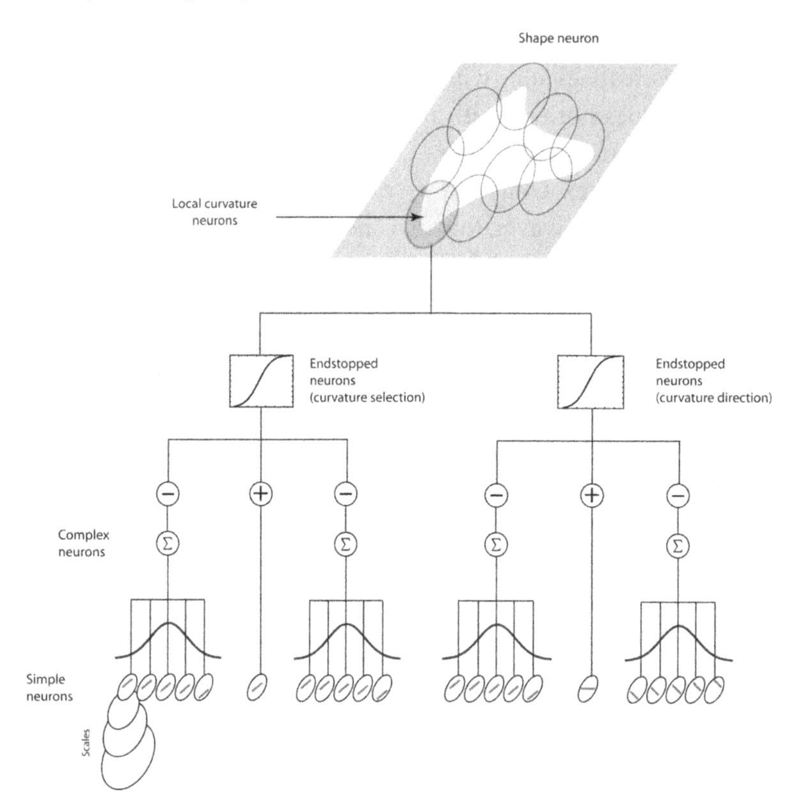

displaced model simple cells. The model complex cell response is given by (Dobbins, 1992):

$$(R_{ES_{dir2}} > R_{ES_{dir1}}) \tag{1}$$

R_i is the response of the i-th cell and c_i is its weight. Model cells are Gaussian weighted with position, with weight inversely proportional to distance to the center. ϕ is a rectification function, where any value less than 0 is set to 0.

Endstopped Cells (V2)

We propose two different types of curvature computations using the endstopped structure:

1. **Curvature Selection:** Model endstopped cells provide us with a coarse curvature estimation so that we can divide contours into curvature classes. For the design of the model endstopped cells we followed the work of (Dobbins, 1992):

$$R_{ES} = \mathbf{\Phi}\left[c_c\phi\left(R_c\right) - (c_{d1}\phi\left(R_{d1}\right) + (c_{d2}\phi\left(R_{d2}\right))\right] \tag{2}$$

c_c, c_{d1} and c_{d2} are the gains for the center and displaced cells. R_c, R_{d1} and R_{d2} are the responses of the center and the two displaced cells. The center cell is a model simple cell and the displaced cells are model complex cells. ϕ is the same rectification function as before (Complex cells), Φ is the common sigmoidal function (Wilson, 1999).
The center simple cell has an excitatory effect while the two complex cells have an inhibitory effect. The response shows a good selectivity to curvature due to the inhibitory

effect of the displaced cells, which we may note are wider than the center cell, following (Orban, et al., 1979a). Model endstopped cells provide us with a coarse curvature estimation.

2. **Direction of Curvature:** We refer to direction as the direction of the normal to the curve. The same model endstopped cells are used adding a rotated component on each displaced complex cell with opposite directions (e.g. 45° and 135° for the 0° model endstopped neurons). These cells provide valuable information in order to compute convexity/concavity at a later stage. Two types of model direction cells are used, and we will use the term *sign* to specify if the curvature is in one direction or the opposite, positive or negative. These different directions are obtained by changing the order of the displaced subtracted neurons (e.g. Figure 2a vs Figure 2d). If the orientations of the displaced cells lie between the tangent to the curve and the normal to the curve (in the positive direction within the coordinate system), then the sign is defined as positive, the neuron's response is R_+, otherwise sign is defined as negative and its response is R_- cells lie between the tangent to the curve and the normal (e.g. 45° and 135° for the 0° model endstopped neurons, Figure 2).

$$R_+ = \Phi\left[c_c\phi\left(R_c\right) - (c_{d1_{45}}\phi\left(R_{d1_{45}}\right) + (c_{d2_{135}}\phi\left(R_{d2_{135}}\right))\right]$$
$$R_- = \Phi\left[c_c\phi\left(R_c\right) - (c_{d1_{135}}\phi\left(R_{d1_{135}}\right) + (c_{d2_{45}}\phi\left(R_{d2_{45}}\right))\right] \quad (3)$$

where c_c, c_{d1} and c_{d2} are the gains for the center and displaced cells as before. R_c, R_{d1} and R_{d2} are the responses of center and displaced cells. The difference here is that the displaced cells are at different orientations of the preferred center simple cell, for the positive sign model endstopped neuron, the displaced model complex neuron *d1* is at 45°, while the model complex component *d2* is at 135°. Figure 2e shows the response of direction selective cells over a circular shape for direction positive vs negative.

Local Curvature Cells

Curvature cells are obtained due to the neural convergence of the model endstopped cells selective for curvature selection and the model endstopped cells selective for curvature orientation:

$$R_{curv_i} = R_{ES_i} \bigcap (R_{ES_{dir1}} > R_{ES_{dir2}})$$
$$R_{curv_{i+n}} = R_{ES_i} \bigcap (R_{ES_{dir2}} > R_{ES_{dir1}}) \quad (4)$$

where n is the number of model endstopped cell types, R_{ESi} is the response of the model endstopped cell i and R_{ESdir1}, R_{ESdir2} are the responses of the model direction selective endstopped neurons.

Shape-Selective Neurons

Our shape cells integrate the responses from model local curvature cells. The proposed response of a model's shape neuron is:

$$R_{shape} = \sum_{i=1}^{n} c_i R_{curv_i}(\lambda) \quad \lambda = max_{j=1}^{m}(\lambda_j)$$
$$c_i = \frac{1}{2\pi} e^{-(x^2+y^2)} \quad (5)$$

where R_{curvi} is the response of the *ith* model curvature neuron from the set of all possible n model curvature neurons at the preferred curvature direction (λ) inside the model shape neuron receptive field, and c_i is a Gaussian weight that

Figure 2. Direction selective neurons. Endstopped configuration of cells whose curve's normal direction selectivity is in the direction of the solid line (a), if the normal is in the direction of the dashed line, it is inhibited; (b), (c) and (d) show other configurations, e) An example of a circle, positive sign corresponds to the curve in blue. Negative sign is shown in red.

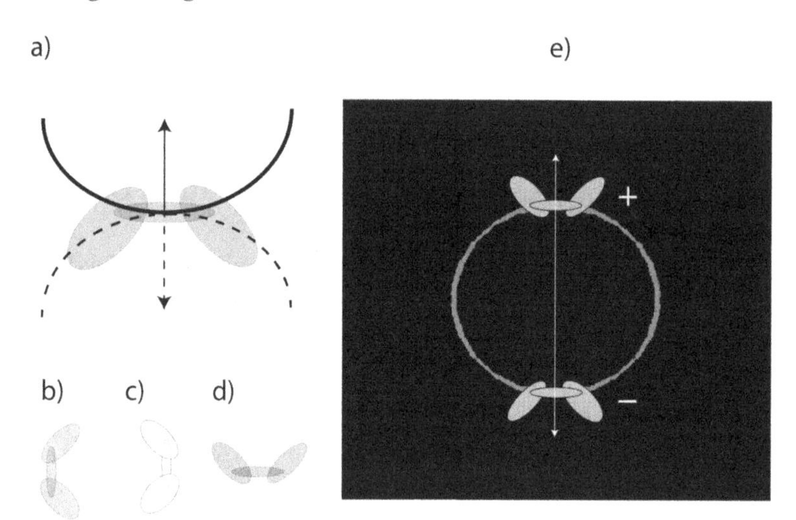

would account for partial excitation depending on the selective curvature in distance-angular position (Figure 3).

To summarize: Model simple neurons perform edge analysis. In the experiments to follow, 4 sizes and 12 orientations are used. Responses from model simple neurons are integrated into model complex neurons receptive fields. By combining model simple and complex neurons we achieve endstopping. Responses of model endstopped cells are used to get different curvature classes (8 in the experiments). The main element in this architecture is that of shape-selective neurons, they represent curvature parts in a curvature × position (radial and angular) domain. The possible number of shapes that may be represented by our model Shape neurons is very large, given the limited type of neurons at each level of the architecture. A models shape neuron has a response depending on the position and curvature of the stimulus component parts. The response to a shape from a model shape-selective neuron depends on how similar a stimulus is to a preferred stimulus.

Response of a Model Shape Neuron in Curvature Space

In addition to being sensitive to location inside the model shape's neuron receptive field, a model shape neuron has a response depending on how close the stimulus is to its curvature selectivity. For example, consider a model neuron selective to a sharp curvature at the top left. This neuron would respond maximally when that feature is present at that specific location, but it would respond also to a broader curvature at that location with a lower value and would have a small response to a very broad curvature or a straight line.

Model shape neurons exhibit band-pass tuning for curvature information. Their responses achieve a peak at a specific curvature, then decay providing a decreasing response for curvature values of increasing distance. No response is provided for

Figure 3. Model shape-selective neurons respond to different curvatures at different positions. The response is maximal when those curvatures are present at their selective positions (dark gray). If they are in nearby positions the neuron provides some response as well (gray and light gray). Numbers attached to curvature segments correspond to the curvature class of those segments.

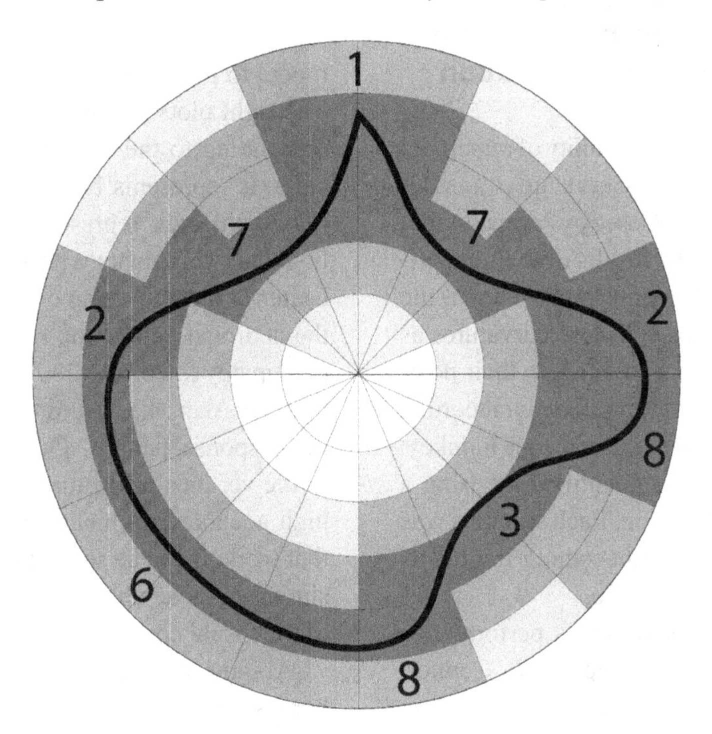

curvatures very far from the optimal. The model shape neuron in our example is then selective for those model endstopped neurons that respond strongly to sharp curvatures at that position. Since a model endstopped neuron with a high response to a sharp curvature has also some response to a slightly broader type of curvature, model shape neurons will not provide a binary response but a range or responses depending on the distance between curvatures in curvature space.

Response of a Model Shape Neuron based on Curvature Locations

Features (curvatures) included in a model shape neuron's receptive field are weighted with respect to a factor c_i (Equation 5) depending on how close the desired curvature is to the desired position. Let's continue with our example of a model shape neuron selective for a sharp curvature at the top left. This model neuron will have a high response to any stimuli that contain such sharp curvature at that position, but some response will still be elicited in a nearby position, e.g. a sharp curvature at the top mid-left, but no response will be obtained for a sharp curvature present at far away positions (e.g. the sharp curvature is at the bottom).

The curvatures that fall into the preferred cell's positions are considered in their full value (dark gray in Figure 3), but if they fall close, they are weighted in a Gaussian manner depending on how far from the preferred position they are (gray and light gray in Figure 3). For this task we used polar coordinates (Pasupathy & Connor, 2002), that is, the radial distance to the center of the Shape neuron and its angular position.

Capability of the Model for Representing Shapes on a Curvature x Angular Position Representation

We wanted to first test the capability of our model to encode curvature in the Curvature × angular position representation proposed by Pasupathy and Connor (2002). From the results of their experiments, Pasupathy and Connor proposed that the representation of shapes in V4 are curvatures as parts of boundary patterns relative to their position in the object. Pasupathy and Connor recorded from neurons in area V4 of the macaque monkey. The response pattern was quantified by using a 2D Gaussian tuning function. Each stimulus was decomposed into four to eight contour fragments of relatively constant curvature.

Here we compare our model's performance against the results from (Pasupathy & Connor, 2002). The stimuli were constructed combining convex and concave boundary elements to form closed shapes. Boundary elements include sharp convex angles, and medium and high convex and concave curvatures. The combination of these boundary elements gave rise to 49 different stimuli. Stimuli were composed of white edges against a black background, the inside was black as well but it is shown from now on in our figures as white-filled for illustration purposes. For details on the methods, please consult (Rodríguez-Sánchez, 2010; Rodríguez-Sánchez & Tsotsos, 2011).

Figure 4 shows a comparison the output of the model to Pasupathy and Connor (2002) stimuli. The right plots are the output of the model corresponding to the stimuli on the left. the vertical axis represents boundary curvature and the horizontal axis represents angular position of boundary fragments with respect to the shape's center of mass. We can compare this figure with the neuronal population response in Figure 3 of (Pasupathy & Connor, 2002), their figure includes the Gaussian shape-tuning function describing the response pattern. Our line plots are close to the veridical curvature function and fits with high accuracy the neural population data from that work. It can be seen that the results are quite similar to those obtained for neurons in area V4 of the visual cortex.

At some angular positions our plots show small bumps this is an effect of sampling (we use only 12 orientations), in fact those bumps occur at those orientations and provides a limitation on shape representation. Nevertheless, we observe here that the model performs closely to neuronal data, fitting very well in almost every case the Gaussian shape response pattern (Figure 3 of (Pasupathy & Connor, 2002)). The peaks of our

Figure 4. For every stimulus (left image), we provided the response our model corresponding to its curvature components with respect to its angular position with respect to the center of the stimulus. Compare this figure with Figure 3 of (Pasupathy & Connor, 2002)

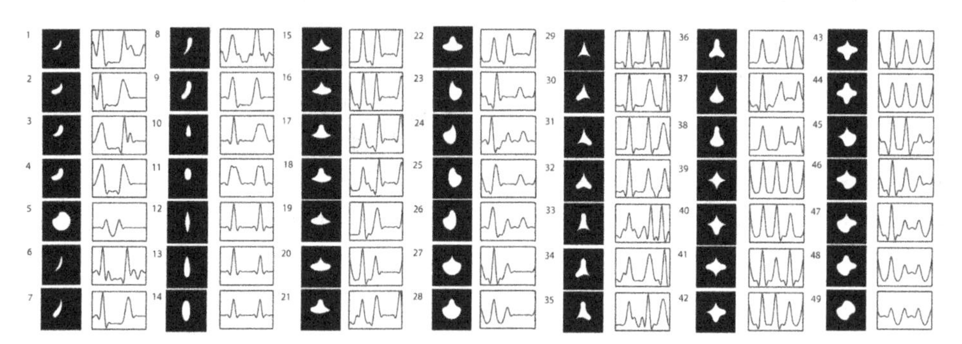

model are highly correlated to the cells response patterns. Another important observation of these results is that the shapes of the model plots are very close to the ones from (Pasupathy & Connor, 2002). This fact is further supported by the quantitative analysis provided next, where we measured the difference between the results from the model and the data from neurons that Pasupathy and colleagues used to draw their plots.

The original data provided included the angular position and curvature for four to eight different angular positions. For such a task we averaged the Euclidean distance between these four to eight angular position values and the results from our model in curvature and angular position. Both terms were normalized to 1. That is, for those position values provided in Dr. Pasupathy's data we measured how far our values were in terms of curvature and position, these distances were averaged over the total number of values. The worst case scenario would be one where the plot provided by the model would be completely the opposite from the plot in (Pasupathy & Connor, 2002) (*distance*=1). The case where our results completely overlap Pasupathy's plot would mean that Shape neurons have the same exact response pattern as real cells (*distance*=0). Normalized distances for each one of the 49 stimuli in Figure 4 (left column) are shown in the blue bars of Figure 5. The maximum error is 1 and a perfect match is 0. Total average error for all stimuli was 0.074 (*stdev* = 0.037). In order to further test the validity of the analysis, we compared the results from our model to each stimulus with those data corresponding to all the other stimuli different to the selected one (e.g., stimulus 1 model values vs data from the other 2-49 stimuli), if the analysis is correct, we should obtain much higher error values than the ones reported. When we performed this analysis between each stimulus and the other 48 different stimuli, values were much higher (*average*=0.218, *stdev*=0.087). When comparing both populations (stimulus paired correctly vs stimuli paired wrongly) they are statistically different (*t-test*=1, $p<0.0001$).

These results show that the proposed hierarchical representation - which is based on endstopping to achieve curvature - provides very similar results to neuronal data, only 5 out of the 49 stimulus distances were over 10% error (or 0.10 distance), and all of them were below 19%. Most errors are on the range 0.02-0.08.

The model has been also successfully tested as a computer vision system and compared with other models in a previously published study (Rodríguez-Sánchez & Tsotsos, 2011).

Capability of the Model for Encoding V4 Neuron Responses

In a more detailed study and related to the previous one, (Pasupathy & Connor, 2001) recorded the

Figure 5. Euclidean distance from the model to Pasupathy and Connor's data

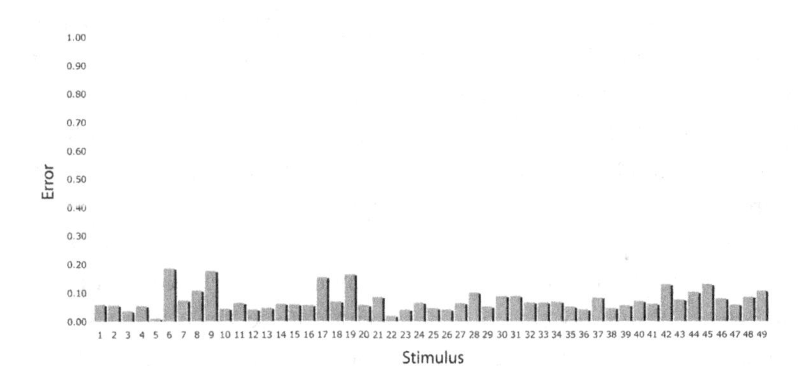

responses of 109 neurons to 366 different shapes. The stimuli were the same 49 shapes used in the previous experiment but rotated 8 orientations (some only 2 or 4 due to redundancies) in 45° increments. Each cell in the sample responded to a variety of very different shapes. No cell displayed a response pattern that could be characterized in terms of a single type of global shape. However, for most cells the effective stimuli showed some degree of shape consistency at one position. In other words, these cells were tuned for boundary configuration in one part of the shape.

In order to prove the plausibility of our model shape neurons, we study the behavior of the model shape neurons by comparing their responses against real neuron responses. If model shape neurons provide similar responses to those of neurons in area V4, we can summarize that they faithfully mimic the behavior of real neurons. For this, Dr. Pasupathy kindly provided the data corresponding to the 109 cells they recorded in area V4. Cells responses were normalized to 1 (although 1 was not always the highest value), the responses to the mentioned 366 stimuli were recorded. We found that the selectivity of 34 of those neurons was unclear for our purposes, for this reason we used 75 out the 109 of neurons.

The absolute difference between the responses of our model shape neurons and that of real cells is first obtained. For each cell, mean and standard deviation were computed and results will be provided next as error percentages, meaning mean difference between our model shape neurons and real cells. The results for all the 75 cells considered in this study are shown in Figure 6. We did two subsets of experiments, the first one, model neuron responses were recorded using the curvature parts with respect to the center of the neuron (blue bars). For the second subset, model neuron responses were with respect the centroid of the shape (green bars). Note that the stimuli from (Pasupathy & Connor, 2001) are not always at the receptive field center. We did not find difference from using curvature parts with respect to the center of the model neurons or the centroid of the object.

For both cases we can see that there are only a few model shape neurons with over 20% error, most of the differences between the model and that of real cells fall in the range 10-20%. Average error for all model shape neurons was 16.95% for the center of the model neuron (*stdev*=12.61) and almost the same when using the centroid of the shape (*error*=16.98%, *stdev*=12.25). This shows that even for such a large number of neurons the model performs successfully and the difference between the response of the model shape-selective neurons and that of real cells is small.

FUTURE RESEARCH DIRECTIONS

We have presented a model that tries to fill the gap between early and later visual representations in the object recognition pathway. Other models have been presented that provide some insight into how object recognition may be achieved through a hierarchical structure of biologically-inspired neurons. But these models have neglected the importance of endstopping to perform curvature computation. Before there was good evidence that V4 and TEO neurons performed curvature analysis, some authors considered that endstopping could be important for such analysis (Dobbins, et al., 1987, 1989). Pasupathy and Connor also consider that - among other hypothesis - endstopping may be a way to achieve curvature selection in the brain (Pasupathy & Connor, 1999). We propose that endstopped neurons provide a valuable hypothesis to achieve curvature and shape selectivity in later areas of the visual cortex. We have shown how this can be achieved and provided several experiments that may support our hypothesis.

Our model local curvature neurons do not provide an exact value of curvature but can discriminate between degrees of curvature. This was done using a starting point where V1 is composed

Figure 6. Difference between the model's shape-selective neurons and 75 real cells responses from area V4. On the left is the difference between the real cells and the model shape cells when the center of the cell is used as the center of the representation. On the right is the difference between the real and model cell shape cells when using the shape centroid as the center of the representation.

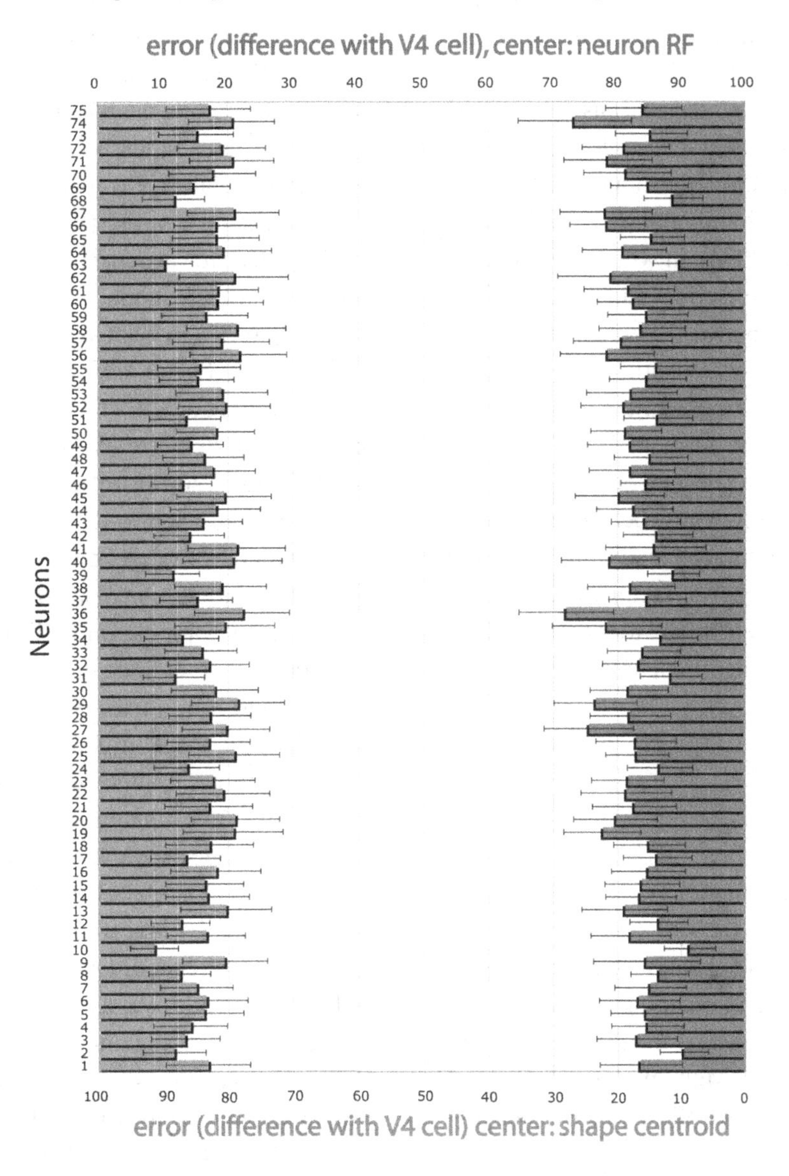

of neurons of different sizes. Through the use of different neuronal sizes and the integration of model simple neurons into model complex neurons we obtained model endstopped neurons able to bandpass between degrees of curvature, from very sharp to very broad.

Our model shape neurons can represent a very large number (14,400!) of possible shapes but this poses the problem of combinatorial explosion as a computer vision system. Even though the primate visual system and our model has the capability to represent a virtual infinity of shapes, the way to handle the large but finite number of shapes in the world is through learning, selecting those configurations of curvatures and corners relevant to recognize the shapes around us. Since the representation has the capability to represent any shape, a new shape can be easily incorporated into the system.

All responses from model neurons are summed for the response of a model shape selective neuron, but cells in area TEO of the brain have shown to integrate information in a more complex way (Brincat & Connor, 2004), in which some curvatures have a subtractive effect and there can be a nonlinear interaction between the elements as well. The way the brain works is still more complex than what we have proposed here and it would be interesting to study also inhibitory features and provide a more heterogeneous model of the shape-selective neurons whose behavior would be even closer to real neurons than the one proposed here. There are a number of factors that could be included into the present model for a more faithful and similar performance to neurons in areas V4 and TEO of the brain.

CONCLUSION

We have presented a model of 2D Shape Representation that follows the structure and behavior of the visual cortex. In our aim was to implement a model with a high degree of biological plausibility. We would like to stress next the differences with other existing models. Most models use a set of Gabor filters or Difference of Gaussians at the lowest level and then, incorporate a learned classifier at the top. In those models, the in-between layers are non-existent or their biological plausibility is questionable. In our case, from a starting point of edge detectors, we provide a set of endstopped neurons to obtain sets of neurons that are sensitive to different curvatures and their direction to finally obtain Shape-selective neurons.

Due to the nature of the representation there is a transformation from a pure retinotopic representation in V1 and V2 to a non-cartesian representation in V4 as proposed in the literature (Gallant, Connor, Rakshit, Lewis, & Van Essen, 1996), which may be the intermediate stage to the less retinotopic representation found in later areas (Tanaka, 1996b). In V4, representation is based on neurons depending on distance from the center of the neuron and angular position following recent studies in that area (Pasupathy & Connor, 2001). The model supports a recognition by parts strategy, in which the parts are curvature values at different positions, whose support comes from Connor's group as well (Brincat & Connor, 2004). The differences between our model and other recent models, e.g. (Cadieu, et al., 2007; Serre, Oliva, & Poggio, 2006; Serre, Wolf, Bileschi, Riesenhuber, & Poggio, 2007) are several. Whereas Serre, Cadieu and colleagues define their cell types as combinations of edge zenith responses successively over 7 hierarchical layers, here our neurons in each layer compute quite different quantities. The goal was to include curvature computations directly, and not indirectly as Serre and Cadieu does through the conjunctions of edges. How the visual cortex might accomplish this has been extensively investigated, and endstopped cells play a major role. However, except for the notable exception of (Dobbins, et al., 1987), they have not been adequately investigated computationally. Our architecture is not a succession of simple and complex cells over a number of layers, we go further, incorporating into our model endstopped and local curvature cells. This is the main difference where our approach and the one from other authors diverge. This is also what enables our true representation of curvature and 2D shape. Another difference between our model and that of Serre, Cadieu and colleagues is their use of a learning approach needed for all layers except the first. Learning at these levels is not required in our model, since in our model learning combinations of Gabor outputs is not required to model curvatures. We think that in the same way cells do not learn Gabor representations since they are well known, the representation of endstopped and curvature cells is not learned either since their behavior is well known as well.

With our proposal we have taken modeling to a next stage by incorporating the roles of end-stopped and curvature neurons into intermediate layers of a visual hierarchy and proved its validity by comparing our model shape neurons responses with that of neurons in area V4.

ACKNOWLEDGMENT

We would like to thank Allan Dobbins and Steven Zucker for all their input and advice regarding parts of the model. We would also like to thank Anitha Pasupathy for providing us with the code for constructing the stimuli as well as data corresponding to V4 neurons.

REFERENCES

Anderson, C., & Van Essen, D. (1987). Shifter circuits: a computational strategy for dynamic aspects of visual processing. *Proceedings of the National Academy of Sciences of the United States of America*, *84*(17), 6297–6301. doi:10.1073/pnas.84.17.6297

Ansari, N., & Delp, E. (1990). Partial shape recognition: A landmark-based approach. *IEEE Transactions on Pattern Analysis and Machine Intelligence*, *12*(5), 470–483. doi:10.1109/34.55107

Asada, H., & Brady, M. (1984). *The curvature primal sketch. AIM 758: Massachusetts Institute of Technology*. MIT.

Ayache, N., & Faugeras, O. (1986). HYPER: A new approach for the recognition and positioning of two-dimensional objects. *IEEE Transactions on Pattern Analysis and Machine Intelligence*, *8*(1), 44–54. doi:10.1109/TPAMI.1986.4767751

Ballard, D. (1981). Generalizing the Hough transform to detect arbitrary shapes. *Pattern Recognition*, *13*(2), 111–122. doi:10.1016/0031-3203(81)90009-1

Belongie, S., Malik, J., & Puzicha, J. (2002). Shape matching and object recognition using shape contexts. *IEEE Transactions on Pattern Analysis and Machine Intelligence*, *24*, 509–522. doi:10.1109/34.993558

Bishop, P., Kato, H., & Orban, G. (1980). Direction-selective cells in complex family in cat striate cortex. *Journal of Neurophysiology*, *43*, 1266–1283.

Blum, H. (1967). A transformation for extracting new descriptors of shape. *Proceedings of the Symposium on Models for the Perception of Speech and Visual Form* (pp. 362-380). MIT Press.

Blum, H. (1973). Biological shape and visual science, I. *Journal of Theoretical Biology*, *38*(2), 205–287. doi:10.1016/0022-5193(73)90175-6

Booth, M., & Rolls, E. (1998). View-invariant representations of familiar objects by neurons in the inferior temporal visual cortex. *Cerebral Cortex*, *8*(6), 510–523. doi:10.1093/cercor/8.6.510

Boynton, G., & Hegde, J. (2004). Visual cortex: The continuing puzzle of area V2. *Current Biology*, *14*(13), 523–524. doi:10.1016/j.cub.2004.06.044

Brincat, S., & Connor, C. (2004). Underlying principles of visual shape selectivity in posterior inferotemporal cortex. *Nature Neuroscience*, *7*(8), 880–886. doi:10.1038/nn1278

Cadieu, C., Kouch, M., Connor, C., Riesenhuber, M., & Poggio, T. (2007). A model of V4 shape selectivity and invariance. *Journal of Neurophysiology*, *3*(98), 1733–1750. doi:10.1152/jn.01265.2006

Connor, C., Brincat, S., & Pasupathy, A. (2007). Transformation of shape information in the ventral pathway. *Current Opinion in Neurobiology*, *17*(2), 140–147. doi:10.1016/j.conb.2007.03.002

Danielsson, P. E. (1978). A new shape factor. *Computer Graphics and Image Processing*, *7*, 292–299. doi:10.1016/0146-664X(78)90119-3

Darroch, J. N., & Mosimann, J. (1985). Canonical and principal components of shape. *Biometrika*, *72*(2), 241–252. doi:10.1093/biomet/72.2.241

Davis, L. S. (1977). Understanding shape: Angles and sides. *IEEE Transactions on Computers*, *C*(26), 236–242. doi:10.1109/TC.1977.1674812

Dean, P. (1976). Effects of inferotemporal lesions on the behavior of monkeys. *Psychological Bulletin*, *83*(1), 41–71. doi:10.1037/0033-2909.83.1.41

Desimone, R., Schein, S., Moran, J., & Ungerleider, L. (1985). Contour, color and shape analysis beyond the striate cortex. *Vision Research*, *25*(3), 441–452. doi:10.1016/0042-6989(85)90069-0

DeValois, K., DeValois, R., & Yund, E. (1979). Responses of striate cortex cells to grating and checkerboard patterns. *The Journal of Physiology*, *291*(1), 483–505.

DeValois, R., Albrecht, D., & Thorell, L. (1982). Spatial frequency selectivity of cells in macaque visual cortex. *Vision Research*, *22*(5), 545–559. doi:10.1016/0042-6989(82)90113-4

Dickinson, S., Leonardis, A., Schiele, B., & Tarr, M. J. (2009). *Object categorization, computer and human vision perspectives*. Cambridge University Press. doi:10.1017/CBO9780511635465

Dobbins, A. (1992). *Difference models of visual cortical neurons.* PhD doctoral dissertation, Department of Electrical Engineering. McGill University.

Dobbins, A., Zucker, S., & Cynader, M. (1987). Endstopped neurons in the visual cortex as a substrate for calculating curvature. *Nature*, *329*(6138), 438–441. doi:10.1038/329438a0

Dobbins, A., Zucker, S., & Cynader, M. (1989). Endstopping and curvature. *Vision Research*, *29*(10), 1371–1387. doi:10.1016/0042-6989(89)90193-4

Dudek, G., & Tsotsos, J. (1997). Shape representation and recognition from multiscale curvature. *Computer Vision and Image Understanding*, *68*(2), 170–189. doi:10.1006/cviu.1997.0533

Elder, J. H., Krupnik, A., & Johnston, L. A. (2003). Contour grouping with prior models. *IEEE Transactions on Pattern Analysis and Machine Intelligence*, *25*(6), 661–674. doi:10.1109/TPAMI.2003.1201818

Felleman, D., & Van Essen, D. (1991). Distributed hierarchical processing in the primate cerebral cortex. *Cerebral Cortex*, *1*(1), 1–47. doi:10.1093/cercor/1.1.1-a

Fidler, S., Berginc, G., & Leonardis, A. (2006). Hierarchical statistical learning of generic parts of object structure. *IEEE Conference on Computer Vision and Pattern Recognition* (pp. 182-189).

Freeman, H. (1974). Computer processing of line-drawing images. *Computer Surveys, 6.*

Frintop, S., Rome, E., & Christensen, H. I. (2010). Computational visual attention systems and their cognitive foundations: A survey. *ACM Transactions on Applied Perception*, *7*(19), 1–39. doi:10.1145/1658349.1658355

Fukushima, K. (1980). Neocognitron: A self organizing neural network model for a mechanism of pattern recognition unaffected by shift in position. *Biological Cybernetics*, *36*(4), 193–202. doi:10.1007/BF00344251

Fukushima, K., Miyake, S., & Ito, T. (1983). Neocognitron: A neural network model for a mechanism of visual patter recognition. *IEEE Transactions on Systems, Man, and Cybernetics*, *13*, 826–834.

Gallant, J., Connor, C., Rakshit, S., Lewis, J., & Van Essen, D. (1996). Neural responses to polar, hyperbolic, and Cartesian gratings in area V4 of the macaque monkey. *Journal of Neurophysiology*, *76*(4), 2718–2739.

Grauman, K., & Darrell, T. (2006). *Pyramid match kernels: Discriminative classification with sets of image features*. MIT Technical Report, CSAIL-TR-2006-20.

Gross, C., Rocha-Miranda, C., & Bender, D. (1972). Visual properties of neurons in inferotemporal cortex of the macaque. *Journal of Neurophysiology*, *35*, 96–111.

Hawken, M., & Parker, A. (1987). Spatial properties of neurons in the monkey striate cortex. *Proceedings of the Royal Society of London. Series B, Biological Sciences*, *231*, 251–288. doi:10.1098/rspb.1987.0044

Heinke, D., & Humphreys, G. (2003). Attention, spatial representation, and visual neglect: simulating emergent attention and spatial memory in the selective attention for identification model (SAIM). *Psychological Review*, *110*(1), 29–87. doi:10.1037/0033-295X.110.1.29

Heywood, C., Gadotti, A., & Cowey, A. (1992). Cortical area V4 and its role in the perception of color. *The Journal of Neuroscience*, *12*(10), 4056–4065.

Hubel, D., & Wiesel, T. (1959). Receptive fields of single neurones in the cat's striate cortex. *The Journal of Physiology*, *148*, 574–591.

Hubel, D., & Wiesel, T. (1962). Receptive fields, binocular interaction and functional architecture in the cat's visual cortex. *The Journal of Physiology*, *160*, 106–154.

Hubel, D., & Wiesel, T. (1965). Receptive fields and functional architecture in two nonstriate visual areas (18 and 19) of the cat. *Journal of Neurophysiology*, *28*, 229–289.

Hubel, D., & Wiesel, T. (1968). Receptive fields and functional architecture of monkey striate cortex. *The Journal of Physiology*, *195*(1), 215–243.

Ito, M., & Komatsu, H. (2004). Representation of angles embedded within contour stimuli in area V2 of macaque monkeys. *The Journal of Neuroscience*, *24*(13), 3313–3324. doi:10.1523/JNEUROSCI.4364-03.2004

Jones, E. (2007). Neuroanatomy: Cajal and after Cajal. *Breain Research Reviews*, *55*(2), 248–255. doi:10.1016/j.brainresrev.2007.06.001

Kahana, M., & Sekuler, R. (2002). Recognizing spatial patterns: a noisy exemplar approach. *Vision Research*, *42*(18), 2177–2192. doi:10.1016/S0042-6989(02)00118-9

Kato, H., Bishop, P., & Orban, G. (1978). Hypercomplex and simple/complex cells classifications in cat striate cortex. *Journal of Neurophysiology*, *41*(5), 1071–1095.

Kehtarnavaz, N., & de Figueiredo, R. (1988). A framework for surface reconstruction from 3D contours. *Computer Vision Graphics and Image Processing*, *42*(1), 32–47. doi:10.1016/0734-189X(88)90141-7

Kimia, B., & Siddiqi, K. (1994). Geometric heat equation and nonlinear diffusion of shapes and images. *IEEE Conference on Computer Vision and Pattern Recognition*, (pp. 113-120).

Kimia, B., Tannenbaum, A., & Zucker, S. W. (1992). On the evolution of curves via a function of curvature, 1: The classical case. *Journal of Mathematical Analysis and Applications*, *163*(2), 438–458. doi:10.1016/0022-247X(92)90260-K

Kimia, B., Tannenbaum, A., & Zucker, S. W. (1995). Shapes, shocks and deformations I: The components of two-dimensional shape and the reaction-diffusion space. *International Journal of Computer Vision*, *15*, 189–224. doi:10.1007/BF01451741

Kobatake, E., Wang, G., & Tanaka, K. (1998). Effects of shape-discrimination training on the Selectivity of inferotemporal cells in adult monkeys. *Journal of Neurophysiology*, *80*, 324–330.

Lazebnik, S., Schmid, C., & Ponce, J. (2006). Beyond bags of features: Spatial pyramid matching for recognizing natural scenes categories. *IEEE Conference on Computer Vision and Pattern Recognition*, 2169-2178.

Lecun, Y., Boser, B., Denker, J., Henderson, D., Howard, R., Hubbard, W., & Jackel, L. (1989). Backpropagation applied to handwritten zip code recognition. *Neural Computation*, *1*(4), 541–551. doi:10.1162/neco.1989.1.4.541

Lecun, Y., Bottou, L., Bengio, Y., & Haffner, P. (1998). Gradient-based learning applied to document recognition. *Proceedings of the IEEE*, *86*(11), 2278–2324. doi:10.1109/5.726791

Leyton, M. (1987). Symmetry-curvature duality. *Computer Vision Graphics and Image Processing*, *38*(3), 327–341. doi:10.1016/0734-189X(87)90117-4

Logothetis, N., & Sheinberg, D. (1996). Visual object recognition. *Annual Review of Neuroscience*, *19*, 577–621. doi:10.1146/annurev.ne.19.030196.003045

Lowe, D. (1999). Object recognition from local scale-invariant features *International Conference on Computer Vision* (pp. 1150-1157).

Lowe, D. (2004). Distinctive image features from scale-invariant keypoints. *International Journal of Computer Vision*, *60*(2), 91–110. doi:10.1023/B:VISI.0000029664.99615.94

Marimont, D. (1984). A representation for image curves. *Association for the Advancement of Artificial Intelligence*, 237-242.

Marr, D., & Nishihara, H. (1978). Representation and recognition of the spatial organization of three-dimensional shapes. *Proceedings of the Royal Society of London. Series B, Biological Sciences*, *200*(1140), 269–294. doi:10.1098/rspb.1978.0020

McKee, J. W., & Aggarwal, J. K. (1977). Computer recognition of partial views of curved objects. *IEEE Transactions on Computers*, *C*(26), 790–800. doi:10.1109/TC.1977.1674917

Mehrotra, R., & Grosky, W. (1989). Shape matching utilizing indexed hypothesis generation and testing. *IEEE Transactions on Robotics and Automation*, *5*(1), 70–77. doi:10.1109/70.88019

Mekuz, N., & Tsotsos, J. (2007). Hierarchical learning of dominant constellations for object class recognition. *Asian Conference on Computer Vision*, (pp. 492-501).

Merigan, W. H., & Pham, H. H. (1998). V4 lesions in macaques affect both single- and multiple-viewpoint shape discriminations. *Visual Neuroscience*, *15*, 359–367. doi:10.1017/S0952523898152112

Mokhtarian, F. (1995). Silhouette-based isolated object recognition through curvature scale space. *IEEE Transactions on Pattern Analysis and Machine Intelligence*, *17*(5), 539–544. doi:10.1109/34.391387

Mokhtarian, F., & Mackworth, A. (1984). Scale-based description and recognition of planar curves and two-dimensional objects. *IEEE Transactions on Pattern Analysis and Machine Intelligence*, *8*(1), 34–43. doi:10.1109/TPAMI.1986.4767750

Motter, B. (1994). Neural correlates of attentive selection for color or luminance in extrastriate area V4. *The Journal of Neuroscience*, *14*(4), 2178–2189.

Murphy, T., & Finkel, L. (2007). Shape representation by a network of V4-like cells. *Neural Networks*, *20*, 851–867. doi:10.1016/j.neunet.2007.06.004

Mutch, J., & Lowe, D. (2006). Multiclass object recognition with sparse, localized features. *IEEE Conference on Computer Vision and Pattern Recognition*, (pp. 11-18).

Olshausen, B., Anderson, C., & Van Essen, D. (1993). A neurobiological model of visual attention and invariant pattern recognition based on dynamic routing of information. *The Journal of Neuroscience*, *13*(11), 4700–4719.

Orban, G., Kato, H., & Bishop, P. (1979a). Dimensions and properties of end-zone inhibitory areas of hypercomplex cells in cat striate cortex. *Journal of Neurophysiology*, *42*, 833–849.

Orban, G., Kato, H., & Bishop, P. (1979b). End-zone region in receptive fields of hypercomplex and other striate neurons in the cat. *Journal of Neurophysiology*, *42*, 818–832.

Pasupathy, A., & Connor, C. (1999). Responses to contour features in macaque area V4. *Journal of Neurophysiology*, *82*(5), 2490–2502.

Pasupathy, A., & Connor, C. (2001). Shape representation in area V4: Position-specific tuning for boundary conformation. *Journal of Neurophysiology*, *86*(5), 2505–2519.

Pasupathy, A., & Connor, C. (2002). Population coding of shape in area V4. *Nature Neuroscience*, *5*(12), 1332–1338. doi:10.1038/nn972

Pavlidis, T. (1972). Segmentation of pictures and maps through functional approximation. *Computer Graphics and Image Processing*, *1*, 360–372. doi:10.1016/0146-664X(72)90021-4

Peissig, J., & Tarr, M. (2007). Visual object recognition: Do we know more now than we did 20 years ago? *Annual Review of Psychology*, *58*, 15–96. doi:10.1146/annurev.psych.58.102904.190114

Persoon, E., & Fu, K. (1974). Shape discrimination using Fourier descriptors. *Second International Joint Conference on Pattern Recognition*, (pp. 126-130).

Pinto, N., Cox, D., & Dicarlo, J. (2008). Why is real-world visual object recognition hard? *PLoS Computational Biology*, *4*(1), 151–156. doi:10.1371/journal.pcbi.0040027

Ramon y Cajal, S. (1888). Sobre las fibras nerviosas de la capa molecular del cerebelo. *Rev Trim Histol Norm Patol*, *1*, 33–49.

Ramon y Cajal, S. (1894). The Croonian lecture: La fine structure des centres nerveux. *Royal Society of London Proceedings Series I*, *55*, 444–468. doi:10.1098/rspl.1894.0063

Ramon y Cajal, S. (1904). Variaciones morfologicas, normales y patologicas del reticulo neurofibrilar. *Trab Lab Investig Biol Madrid*, *3*, 9–15.

Rao, R., & Ballard, D. (1997). Dynamic model of visual recognition predicts neural response properties in the visual cortex. *Neural Computation*, *9*(4), 721–763. doi:10.1162/neco.1997.9.4.721

Rao, R., & Ballard, D. (1999). Predictive coding in the visual cortex: a functional interpretation of some extra-classical receptive-field effects. *Nature Neuroscience*, *2*(1), 79–87. doi:10.1038/4580

Richards, W., Dawson, B., & Whittingham, D. (1988). *Encoding contour shape by curvature extrema.* Paper presented at the Natural Computations.

Richards, W., & Hoffman, D. D. (1984). *Codon constraints on closed 2D shapes*. MIT, AI lab.

Riesenhuber, M., & Poggio, T. (1999). Hierarchical models of object recognition in cortex. *Nature Neuroscience*, *2*(11), 1019–1025. doi:10.1038/14819

Riesenhuber, M., & Poggio, T. (2000). Models of object recognition. *Nature Neuroscience*, *3*(Suppl), 1199–1204. doi:10.1038/81479

Riesenhuber, M., & Poggio, T. (2002). Neural mechanisms of object recognition. *Current Opinion in Neurobiology*, *12*(2), 162–168. doi:10.1016/S0959-4388(02)00304-5

Rodríguez-Sánchez, A. (2010). *Intermediate visual representations for attentive recognition systems.* PhD, York University. Retrieved from http://www.cse.yorku.ca/techreports/2010/?abstract=CSE-2010-06

Rodríguez-Sánchez, A., & Tsotsos, J. (2011). The importance of intermediate representations for the modeling of 2D shape detection: Endstopping and curvature tuned computations. *IEEE Conference on Computer Vision and Pattern Recognition (CVPR 2011)* (pp. 4321-4326).

Rolls, E., & Deco, G. (2002). *Computational neuroscience of vision*. Oxford.

Rolls, E. T., & Deco, G. (2002). *Computational neuroscience of vision*. Oxford, UK: Oxford University Press.

Rosenblatt, F. (1962). *Principles of neurodynamics: Perceptrons and the theory of brain mechanisms*. Spartan Books.

Rumelhart, D., & Mcclelland, J. (1986). *Parallel distributed processing: Explorations in the microstructure of cognition: Foundations*. MIT Press.

Schein, S., & Desimone, R. (1990). Spectral properties of V4 neurons in the macaque. *The Journal of Neuroscience*, *10*(10), 3369–3389.

Schiller, P., Finlay, B., & Volman, S. (1976). Quantitative studies of single-cell properties in monkey striate cortex, I: Spatiotemporal organization of receptive fields. *Journal of Neurophysiology*, *39*(6), 1288–1319.

Serre, T., Oliva, A., & Poggio, T. (2006). A feedforward architecture accounts for rapid categorization. *Proceedings of the National Academy of Sciences of the United States of America*, *104*(15), 6424–6429. doi:10.1073/pnas.0700622104

Serre, T., Wolf, L., Bileschi, S., & Riesenhuber, M. (2007). Robust object recognition with cortex-like mechanisms. *IEEE Transactions on Pattern Analysis and Machine Intelligence*, *29*(3), 411–426. doi:10.1109/TPAMI.2007.56

Serre, T., Wolf, L., Bileschi, S., Riesenhuber, M., & Poggio, T. (2007). Object recognition with cortex-like mechanism. *IEEE Transactions on Pattern Analysis and Machine Intelligence*, *29*(3), 411–426. doi:10.1109/TPAMI.2007.56

Serre, T., Wolf, L., & Poggio, T. (2005). *Object recognition with features inspired by visual cortex*. IEEE Conference on Computer Vision and Pattern Recognition.

Shahraray, B., & Anderson, D. J. (1989). Optimal estimation of contour properties by cross-validated regularization. *IEEE Transactions on Pattern Analysis and Machine Intelligence*, *11*, 600–610. doi:10.1109/34.24794

Siddiqi, K., & Pizer, M. (2008). *Medial representations: Mathematics, algorithms and applications*.

Spitzer, H., & Hochstein, S. (1985). A complex-cell receptive-field model. *Journal of Neurophysiology, 53*(5), 1266–1286.

Suzuki, N., Hashimoto, N., Kashimori, Y., Zheng, M., & Kambara, T. (2004). A neural model of predictive recognition in form patway of visual cortex. *Bio Systems, 76*, 33–42. doi:10.1016/j.biosystems.2004.05.004

Tanaka, K. (1996a). Inferotemporal cortex and object vision. *Annual Review of Neuroscience, 19*, 109–139. doi:10.1146/annurev.ne.19.030196.000545

Tanaka, K. (1996b). Representation of visual features of objects in the inferotemporal cortex. *Neural Networks, 9*(8), 1459–1475. doi:10.1016/S0893-6080(96)00045-7

Tanaka, K., Saito, H., Fukada, Y., & Moriya, M. (1991). Coding visual images of objects in the inferotemporal cortex of the macaque monkey. *Journal of Neurophysiology, 66*(1), 170–189.

Tsotsos, J. K., & Rothenstein, A. (2011). Computational models of visual attention. *Scholarpedia, 6*(1). doi:10.4249/scholarpedia.6201

von der Heydt, R., Peterhans, E., & Baumgartner, G. (1984). Illusory contours and cortical neuron responses. *Science, 224*(4654), 1260–1262. doi:10.1126/science.6539501

von der Malsburg, C. (1973). Self-organization of orientation sensitive cells in the striate cortex. *Kybernetik, 14*(2), 85–100. doi:10.1007/BF00288907

Wallis, G., & Rolls, E. (1997). Invariant face and object recognition in the visual system. *Progress in Neurobiology, 51*(2), 167–194. doi:10.1016/S0301-0082(96)00054-8

Wang, G., Zhang, Y., & Fei-Fei, L. (2006). Using dependent regions for object categorization in a generative framework. *IEEE Conference on Computer Vision and Pattern Recognition*, (pp. 1597-1604).

Webster, M., & Ungerleider, L. (1998). Neuroanatomy of visual attention. In Parasuraman, R. (Ed.), *The attentive brain*. MIT Press.

Wilson, H. R. (1999). *Spikes, decisions, and actions: The dynamical foundations of neuroscience*. Oxford University Press.

Wolfe, J. (1998). Visual search. In De Valois, K. K. (Ed.), *Attention*. Unversity College London Press.

Zeki, S. (1983). Colour coding in the cerebral cortex: the responses of wavelength-selective and colour-coded cells in monkey visual cortex to changes in wavelength composition. *Neuroscience, 9*(4), 767–781. doi:10.1016/0306-4522(83)90266-X

Zhang, H., Berg, A., Marie, M., & Malik, J. (2006). SVM-KNN: Discriminative nearest neighbor classification for visual category recognition. *IEEE Conference on Computer Vision and Pattern Recognition*, (pp. 2126-2136).

Chapter 9
A Measure of Localization of Brain Activity for the Motion Aperture Problem Using Electroencephalograms

Isao Hayashi
Kansai University, Japan

Hisashi Toyoshima
Japan Technical Software, Co., Ltd., Japan

Takahiro Yamanoi
Hokkai Gakuen University, Japan

ABSTRACT

When viewed through a limited-sized aperture, bars appear to move in a direction normal to their orientation. This motion aperture problem is an important rubric for analyzing the early stages of visual processing particularly with respect to the perceptual completion of motion sampled across two or more apertures. In the present study, a circular aperture was displayed in the center of the visual field. While the baseline bar moved within the aperture, two additional circular apertures appeared; within each aperture, a "flanker bar" appeared to move. For upwards movement of the flanker lines, subjects perceived the flanker bar to be connected to the base bar, and all three parts to move upward. The authors investigated the motion perception of the moving bars by changing the line speeds, radii of the apertures, and distances between the circular apertures and then analyzed spatio-temporal brain activities by electroencephalograms (EEGs). Latencies in the brain were estimated by using equivalent current dipole source (ECD) localization for one subject. Soon after the flankers appear, ECDs, assumed to be generated by the recognition of the aperture's form, were localized along the ventral pathway. After the bars moved, the ECDs were localized along the dorsal pathway, presumably in response to motion of the bars. In addition, for the perception of grouped motion and not normal motion, ECDs were localized to the middle frontal gyrus and the inferior frontal gyrus.

DOI: 10.4018/978-1-4666-2539-6.ch009

INTRODUCTION

The brain perceives information from the outside world and translates this information into intelligence and knowledge (Wilson, R.A. 1999, Palmer, S.E. 1999, Eysenck, M. 2006). If we want to construct a computational model of brain function, there are two kinds of approaches: a bottom-up layered model which identifies the higher brain function from the neuronal network level by analysis of synaptic transmission of the neuronal network and a top-down layered model which identifies the lower layer of brain function by perceptional experiments. In addition, both approaches include a center layer model. We call these models Biologically Inspired Models (BIMs). The authors have proposed BIMs that use soft computing approaches (Kudoh, S.N. 2006, Hayashi, I. 2007a, Kudoh, S.N. 2007). The aperture problem (Ben-av, M.B. 1995, Okada, M. 2003, Pack, C.C. 2001, Chey, J. 1997) is a psychological paradigm to analyze the binding mechanism of spatial recognition in an early stage of the visual pathway. The authors are interested in a hierarchical model related to the early vision system of the brain, particularly, the ventral and dorsal pathways. To discuss this model, we need to analyze the data of psychological experiments such as those derived from the aperture problem.

In the aperture problem, a circular aperture is displayed in the center of the visual field, and, in its baseline condition, a bar initially appears to move from the lower-left to the upper-right inside the aperture. We call this the normal motion direction. While the baseline bar is moving, two additional circular apertures appear; within each aperture, a "flanker bar" moves in one of three orientations: horizontally, vertically, or in the same direction as the ends of the baseline bar. The ends of the flanker bars are visible in the two apertures and thus the motion of the base bar depends on the motion of the flanker bars. Subjects may perceive the base bar to be connected to the flanker bars with all three parts moving together as one line, changing the perceived movement of the base bar to match the orientation of the flanker bars. Even though parts of the line are actually obscured by the foreground, humans "fill in" the gaps of the line based on the outline information of the line in all three apertures. This perception phenomenon is called "a modal supplement." We can treat the aperture perception as an example for the construction of a hierarchical model that describes the ability of the modal supplement.

Okada and Nishina et al. (Okada, M. 2003) have already claimed that perception strongly depends on the radii of the circular aperture, the distance between circles, and the display time of the flanker bars. In this paper, we investigate motion perception of the moving bars by changing the line speed, the radii of the circular apertures, and the distances between circles while recording activities by electroencephalograms (EEGs) (Hayashi, I. 2002a, Hayashi, I. 2004a) and then analyze spatio-temporal brain activities (Moritaka, A. 2008, Hayashi, I. 2007b). In particular, we should note that the motion perception drops at display times greater than 550 ms. Therefore, we should discuss the change of the motion perception accuracy as a function of display time, and we will specifically analyze the experimental data for the delay time using trend analysis.

Latencies in the brain are estimated using equivalent current dipole source (ECD) localization for one subject (Moritaka, A. 2008, Hayashi, I. 2007b). Soon after the base bar and flankers appear, the localization of ECDs, e.g., the visual evoked potential (VEP) and event related potential (ERP) which are assumed to be generated by recognition of the aperture's form and the bar motions, respectively, are estimated. In addition, for the perception of grouped motion, the ECDs are localized to the frontal gyrus. Finally, from the results provided by the two kinds of experiments, we discuss all experimental results of the aperture perception.

METHODS

A brief summary of the aperture experiment is shown in Figure 1. The sequence of the steps in Figure 1 follows. (a) A circular aperture is displayed at the center of the visual field, and the subject fixates on the fixation point. (b) In the baseline condition, a bar initially appears to move from the lower-left to the upper-right (normal motion direction). (c) While the baseline bar is moving, two additional circular apertures appear; within each aperture, a "flanker bar" appears. For these flanker bars, one line end of each flanker bar is visible in each of the two apertures, which can disambiguate the motion of the base bar. For an upwards movement of the flanker lines, the subjects perceive the flanker bars to be connected with the base bar, and all three parts of the line move upward. Similarly, when the flanker bars and base bar move in the horizontal direction, all three line segments appear to move horizontally. (d) When the baseline bar reaches the end of the aperture, the two circular apertures disappear. (e) After the central circular aperture disappears, the subject states the perceived motion of the base bar to the observer. As shown in Figure 2, the subjects' heads are placed on a chinrest to fix the distance between the subject and the computer display at 100 cm. The stimuli are shown at a resolution of 1280 x 960 pixels with a 17 inch computer display, FMV-DP9713, made by Fujitsu Ltd. with a vertical frequency of 85.0 Hz and a horizontal frequency of 68.7 KHz. Figure 3 shows the location of the base bar, apertures, and flanker bars.

We investigate the motion perception of the moving bars by changing the line speed, the radii of the circular apertures, and the distance between the apertures while recording and analyzing spatio-temporal brain activities by electroencephalograms (EEGs). Latencies in the brain are estimated using equivalent current dipole source (ECD) localization for one subject.

RESULTS

Behavioral Experiments

At first, we performed a perception experiment for orientation selectivity. Fixing the radius of the circular aperture at 35 mm, we investigated motion perception for five subjects (20 to 22 years old) by conducting three trials with parameters as follows: display time: 50, 100, 200, 400, 600, 800, 1000, and 1200 ms, distance between endpoints of circular apertures: 160, 170, 190, 200, and 220 mm, orientation of base bar: 0 degrees (upper-right), 45, 90, 135, 180, 225, 270, and 315 degrees, and configuration angles of flanker bars: -45 degrees, 0 degrees, and +45 degrees.

In Figure 4, Figure 5, and Figure 6, we show the results of display time at 1000 ms by changing the distance between the circular apertures, orientation of the base bar, and configuration angle of flanker bars, where the radius and distance between apertures are shown in the legend of each figure in the form (radius / distance). The results of flanker bar orientation -45 degrees in Figure 4 and +45

Figure 1. Stimuli used in the aperture problem experiment

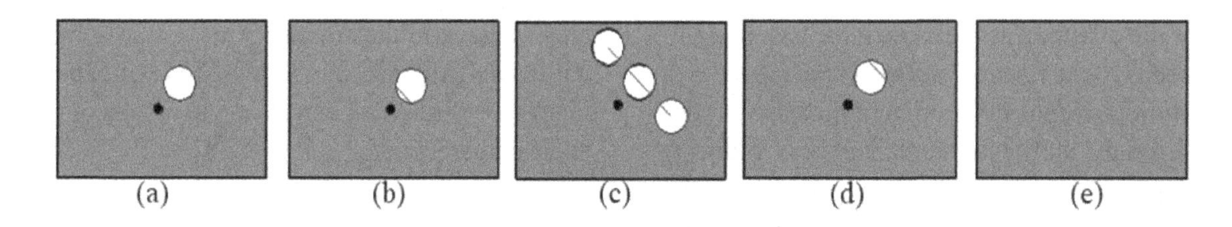

Figure 2. Subject and experimental set-up

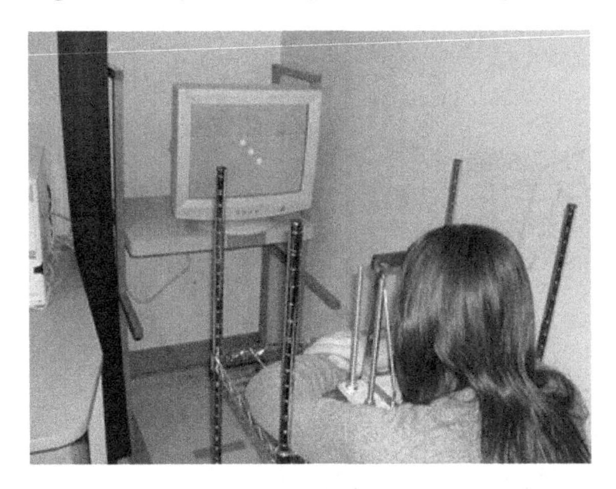

Figure 3. Geometry of the aperture problem

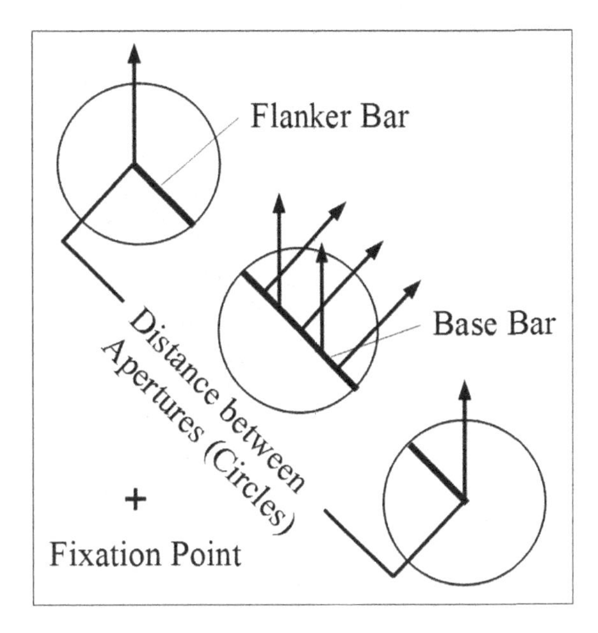

degrees in Figure 6 show that subjects recognize motion perception a high percentage of the time. In particular, with a horizontal orientation (0 degrees and 180 degrees) and with a vertical orientation (90 degrees and 270 degrees), perceptual recognition is high whereas the perception is lower in other orientations. This result agrees with the study by Castet (Castet, E. 1993). Furthermore, these results are not surprising since the subjects do not recognize most of the motion perceptions in the control experiment at zero degrees in Figure 5.

Next, we experimented with perceptual recognition by changing the display time. Ten subjects (18 to 22 years old) specified their perceptual recognition using the measurement program that we developed. We summarize the experiments as follows.

Exp. 1: Fixing the speed of the moving bars at 14.28 mm/sec and the radius of circular apertures at 8.7 mm, we investigated the motion perception by changing the display times: 100, 200, 300, 400, 500, and 600 ms, and the distance between circular apertures: 40.4, 80.8, 121.2, and 161.6 mm.

Exp. 2: Fixing the speed of the moving bars at 14.28 mm/sec and the distance between circular apertures at 121.2 mm, we investigated the motion perception by changing the display times: 100, 200, 300, 400, 500, and 600 ms, and the radius of the circular apertures: 8.7, 11.4, 14.3, and 17.1 mm.

Exp. 3: Fixing the radius of the circular apertures at 8.7 mm and the distance between circular apertures at 80.8 mm, we investigated the motion perception by changing the display length while the bar was moving: 5.7,7.1, and 14.3 mm and display times: 100, 200, 300, 400, 500, 600, 800, 1000, and 1200 ms.

In addition, in Exp. 1 to Exp. 3, the perceptual recognition was calculated from the average of all 150 answers of all subjects in five trials with the base bar at 90 degrees and the flanker bars at 0 degrees, 45 degrees, and 90 degrees. The perceptual accuracies of Exp. 1 are shown in Figure 7. Even when varying distances between the circular apertures, the perceptual recognition increases as display time increases. In addition, the perceptual recognition is higher when the distance between apertures is shortened at the same display times. In other words, the perceptual recognition increases monotonically with display time and

Figure 4. Perceptual recognition at flanker bar orientation -45 degrees

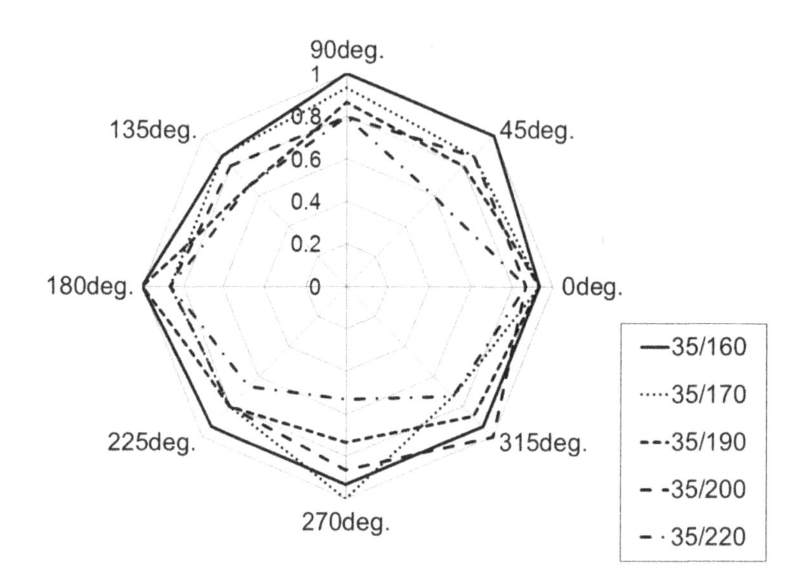

Figure 5. Perceptual recognition at flanker bar orientation 0 degrees

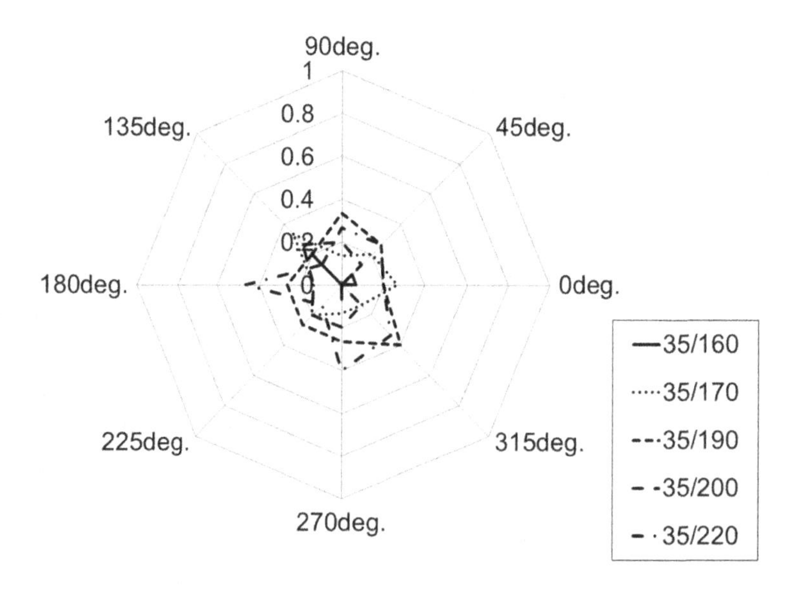

is inversely related to the distance between the circular apertures.

In Exp. 2, we investigated motion perception by changing the display time and aperture radii; perceptual recognition is shown in Figure 8. Across all sizes of radii, the perceptual recognition increases as display time increases. In addition, perceptual recognition is higher when radii are longer at the same display times. In other words, perceptual recognition depends on the length of radii and display time, and increases monotonically with both factors. These results agree with

Figure 6. Perceptual recognition at flanker bar orientation +45 degrees

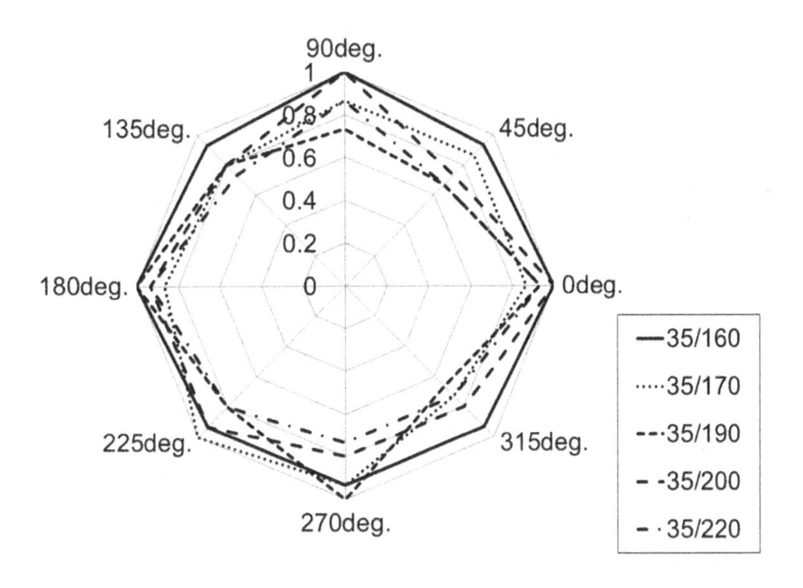

Figure 7. Perceptual recognition as a function of display time and distance between apertures

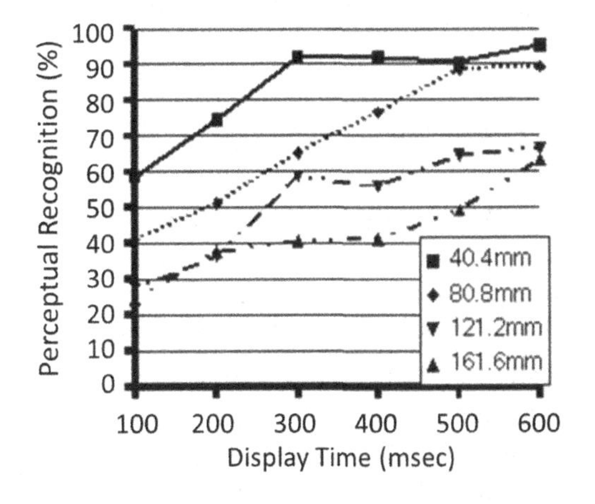

Figure 8. Perceptual recognition as a function of display time and aperture radius

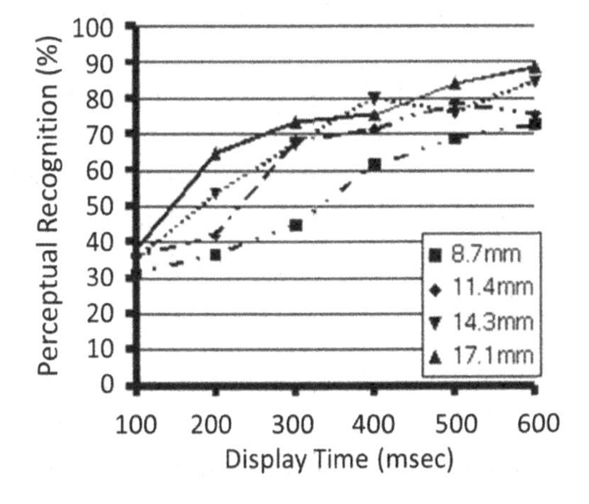

the experiments of Okada and Nishina (Okada, M. 2003). Since perceptual recognition depends on the distance between circular apertures and the radius size, it seems that motion perception depends on the balance of the visible domain and the non-visible domain.

The results of Exp. 3, in which we varied the speed of the bars, are less clear. In general, it is thought that a subject can easily and accurately recognize motion when the speed of the bars is slow. However, while the present results show a decline in perceptual performance with faster bars when the speed is high, the results are different for slow bars. We applied a trend analysis to confirm the nonmonotonicity of motion perception. Table 1 shows the result of the trend analysis by fixing the display length at 5.7 mm with changing bar speeds. The F-test value of percep-

Table 1. Influence of speed of bars on recognition performance

Elements		Sq. Sum	Free Deg.	Ave. Sq. Val.	F Val.	p Val.
Speed of Bar		158.4	8	19.8	5.6	< 0.01
Order	1	1.9	1	19.3	5.5	n.s.
	2	72.1	1	72.1	20.4	< 0.01
	3	37.5	1	37.5	10.3	< 0.01
	4	39.5	1	39.5	11.2	< 0.01
	5	2.0	1	2.0	0.6	n.s.
Error		254.1	72	3.5		
Total			85			

tual recognition for the quadratic function, cubic function, and quartic function of the speed of bars is greater than the critical value 7.00 at p = 0.01 for the degrees of freedom (1.0, 72). In other words, the trend for the quadratic function, cubic function, and quartic function for perceptual recognition is accepted at p= 0.01, and the non-monotonicity of motion perception by changing the speed of bars is statistically confirmed (Figure 9).

Perceptual recognition deteriorates with increased speed of the bars in high-speed domains greater than 30 mm/sec consistent with Okada and Nishina et al. On the other hand, motion perception also fails if the base bar stands still because the base bar does not bind with the flanker. Therefore, perceptual recognition become a convex function at a certain speed of bar movement, and there is a speed of bars that enables easy recognition. When we construct a hierarchical model realizing a modal supplement, a multi-structural complex based on the dynamics of the time attribute is necessary as well as a balance of the visible and non-visible domains. Hawken (Hawken, M.J. 1994) argues that mechanisms treating color and brightness are different with respect to motion stimuli at low speeds and high speeds. In addition, Cropper (Cropper, S.J. 1994) states that there is usually a different vision mechanism for the fixation of short-stimuli signals. According to these reports, the vision system may

Figure 9. Perceptual recognition as a function of bar speed and aperture radius

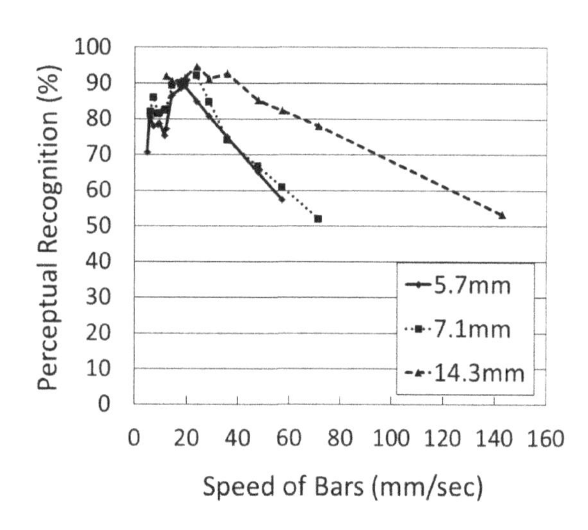

have the ability of changing processing depending on the speed of the stimulus; it is interesting to note that our results are in line with this possibility.

EEG Analysis

In the previous section, we investigated the trends in recognizing a circular aperture perception using a psychological experiment and data analysis. From latencies in the brain estimated using equivalent current dipole source (ECD) which we detected by averaging electroencephalogram (EEG) data, we measured the reaction latency of the visual-evoked potential (VEP) and event-related potential (ERP). We estimated the latency of VEP and ERP in one subject by EEG analysis, and ECD was simultaneously localized in Exp. 4 to Exp. 7. Using the experiment process from (a) to (e) in Figure 1, we measured aperture perception and we obtained the EEG data from a subject at the same time. We summarize the experiments as follows:

Exp. 4: Fixing the speed of bars at 14.28 mm/sec, the radius of the circular apertures at 8.7 mm, and the display time at 500 ms, we measured the latency of VEP and ERP while changing the distance between circular apertures: 28.6, 57.2, and 85.7 mm.

Exp. 5: Fixing the speed of bars at 14.28 mm/sec, the distance between the circular apertures at 85.7 mm, and the display time at 500 ms, we measured the latency of VEP and ERP while changing the radius of the circular apertures: 8.7, 11.5, and 14.3 mm.

Exp. 6: Fixing the distance between the circular apertures at 57.1 mm, the radius of the circular apertures at 11.4 mm, and the display time at 500 ms, we measured the latency of VEP and ERP while changing the speed of bars: 2.9 and 5.7 mm/sec.

Exp. 7: Fixing the distance between circular apertures at 57.1 mm, the radius of the circular apertures at 11.4 mm, the display time at 500 ms, and the speed of bars at 14.28 mm/sec, we estimated the localized equivalent current dipole (ECD) in the visual pathway.

We estimated the latency of VEP and ERP of the subject, and ECD was simultaneously localized in Exp. 4 to Exp. 7. In the measurements, we generated four orientations by random number: three kinds of orientations of the flanking bar and no flanking bar, and the ECD was localized by averaging across 60 experiments. A change of the amplitude of the VEP with the change of visual stimulation was detected in all conditions. In particular, VEP was constantly detected after 340 ms of reaction latency (RL) when the base bar appeared. In addition, we assumed that the subject recognized "the bar's moving orientation is diagonal" in the case of a single circular aperture, and the subject recognized "the bar's orientation was changed" in the case of horizontal orientation (0 degrees) or vertical orientation (90 degrees) when two circular apertures were added.

In Exp. 4 when the flanker bars appeared in the display, the amplitude of the ERP reached its peak at 900 ms. In particular, the ECD was localized along the right inferior frontal gyrus (RL: 1,160 ms to 1,170 ms) and the left middle frontal gyrus (RL: 1,230 ms to 1,250 ms) when the flanker bars shifted to the horizontal orientation (0 degrees) and the vertical orientation (90 degrees). Figure 10 shows the localized ECD at the middle frontal gyrus when the flanker bars shifted to the horizontal orientation (0 degrees) and the vertical orientation (90 degrees). However, the amplitude of VEP was not detected in the case of 45 degrees. By these results, when the flanker bars shifted to either the horizontal orientation or the vertical orientation, a more active VEP was detected at the frontal gyrus primarily related to spatial recognition.

In Exp. 5, the amplitude of ERP reached its peak at RL: 1,300 ms when the flanker bars appeared. ECD was then localized along the right superior frontal gyrus (RL: 1,640 ms to 1,650 ms) and the left middle frontal gyrus (RL: 2,040 ms to 2,050 ms) particularly when the flanker bars moved in the horizontal orientation (0 degrees) or the vertical orientation (90 degrees). Figure 11 shows the localized ECD at the superior frontal gyrus when the flanker bars shifted to the horizontal orientation (0 degrees) and the vertical orientation (90 degrees). However, the amplitude of VEP was not detected in the case of 45 degrees. By these results, when the flanker bars shifted to either the horizontal orientation or the vertical orientation, the more active VEP was detected at the frontal gyrus primarily related to spatial recognition.

In Exp. 6, VEP and ERP were constantly detected after the appearance of the base bar, but no large changes of amplitude were detected at any orientation including 0 and 90 degrees. In Exp. 7, we estimated the propagated localization related to the movement of the flanker bars after an RL of 340 ms in the condition that fixed the orientation of the movement of flanker bars at 90

Figure 10. Localization of ECD in experiment 4

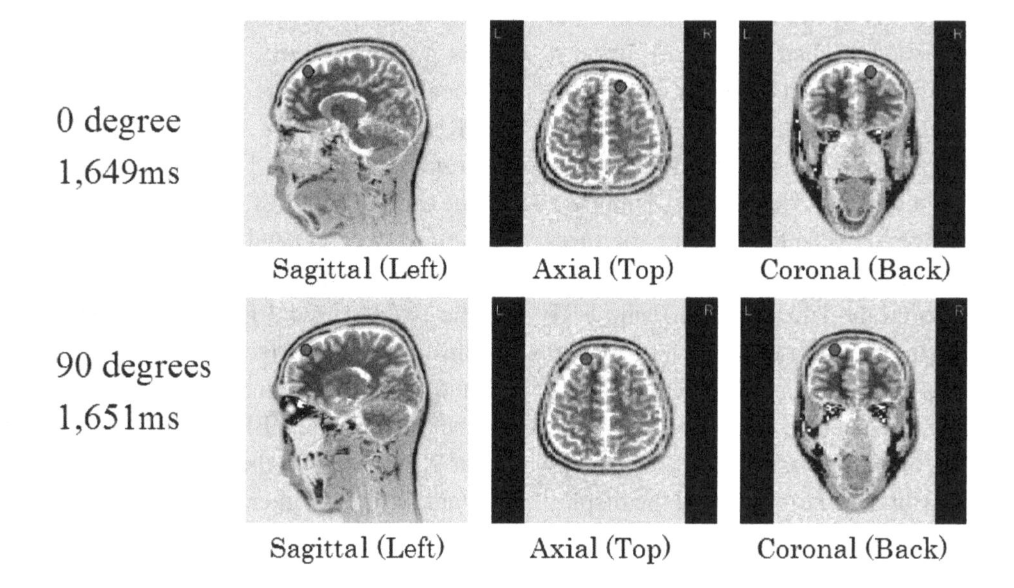

Figure 11. Localization of ECD in experiment 5

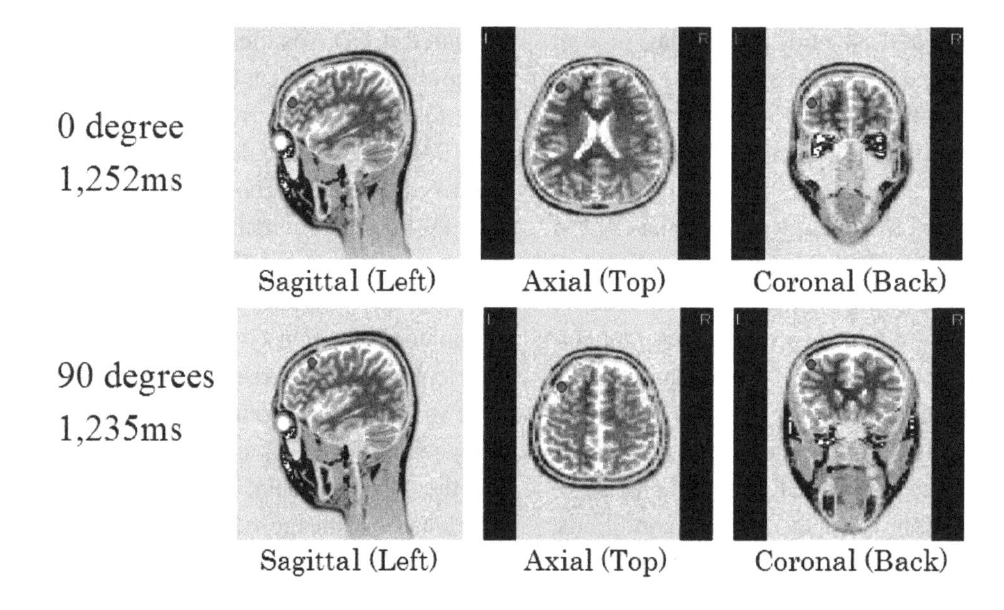

degrees. The amplitude of VEP reached its peak at reaction latencies of 100 ms to 400 ms, and the amplitude of ERP reached its peak at two periods of reaction latency, that is at 500 ms to 700 ms and at 1,000 ms to 1,300 ms. Figure 12 shows VEP and ECD at an RL of 245 ms in V4, while Figure 13 shows ERP and ECD at an RL of 625 ms (at an RL of 285 ms after appearance of the flanker bar) in V5.

In general, visual stimulation input from the retina propagates to the prefrontal cortex through the optic chiasm, LGN, and the primary visual

Figure 12. VEP and ECD in V4

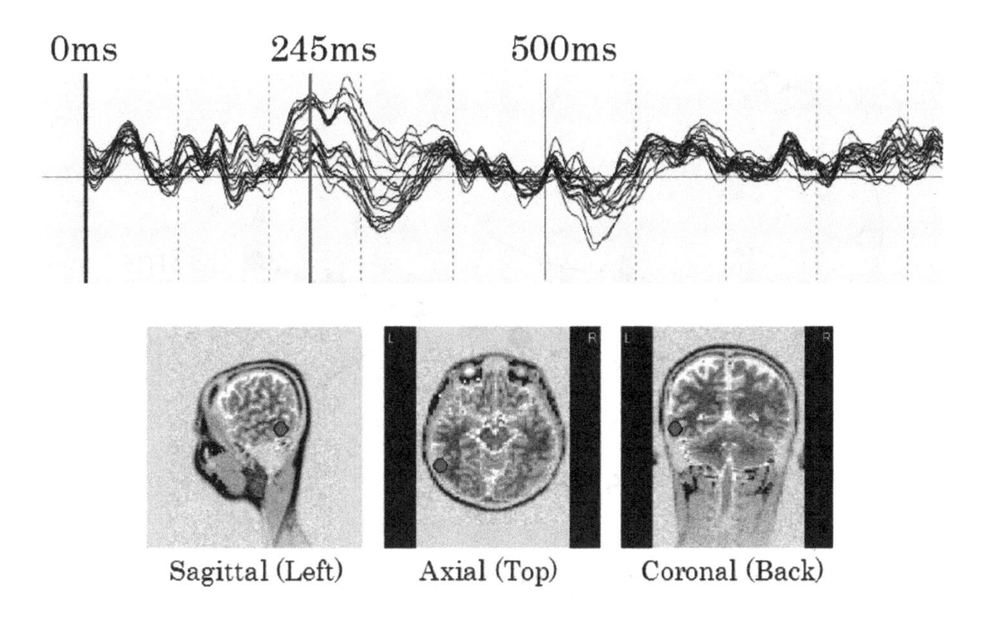

Figure 13. ERP and ECD in V5

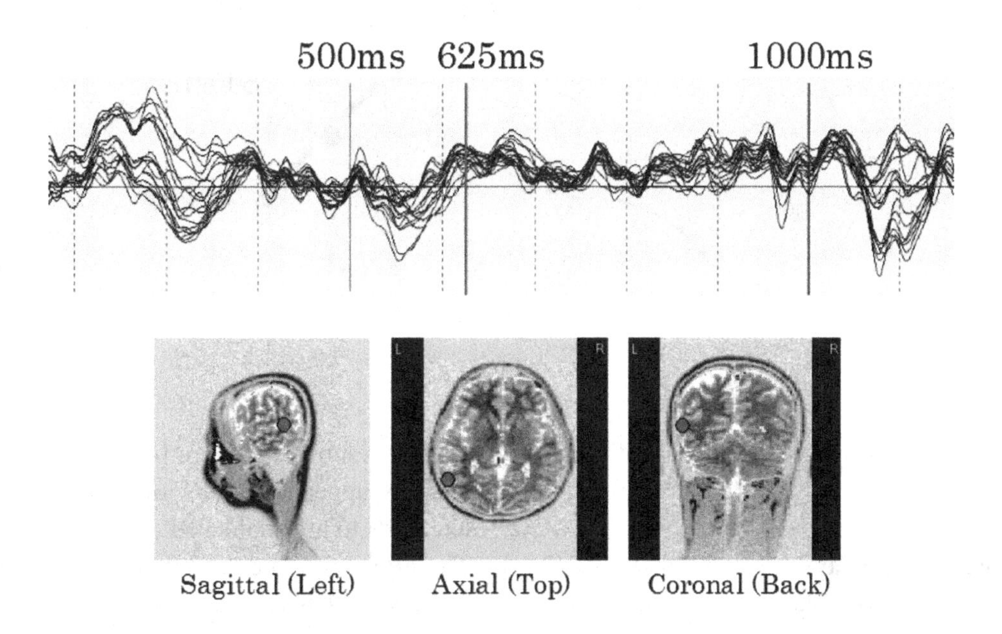

cortex. In particular, the propagated signal at the primary visual cortex is divided in two pathways: the ventral pathway from the primary visual cortex to the prefrontal cortex through the temporal lobe and the dorsal pathway from the primary visual cortex to the prefrontal cortex through the parietal lobe. In general, the ventral pathway relates to symbolic recognition, and the dorsal pathway relates to spatial recognition. From the ECD of Exp. 7, the following ventral pathway

Figure 14. Localization of ECD in the ventral pathway

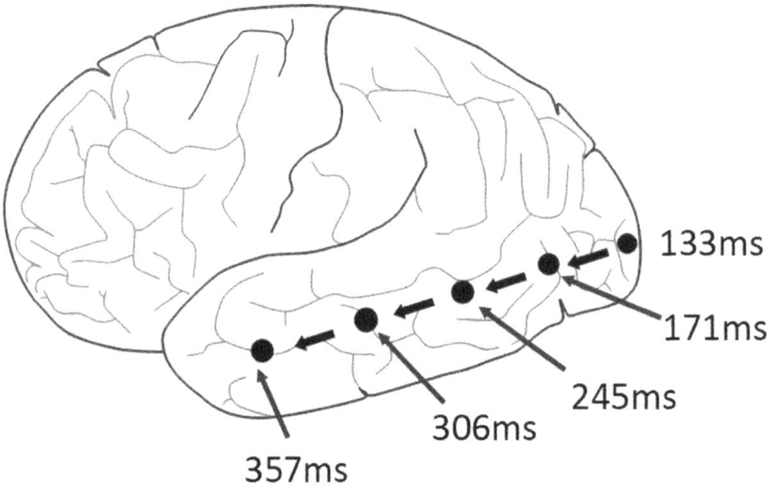

Figure 15. Localization of ECD in the dorsal pathway

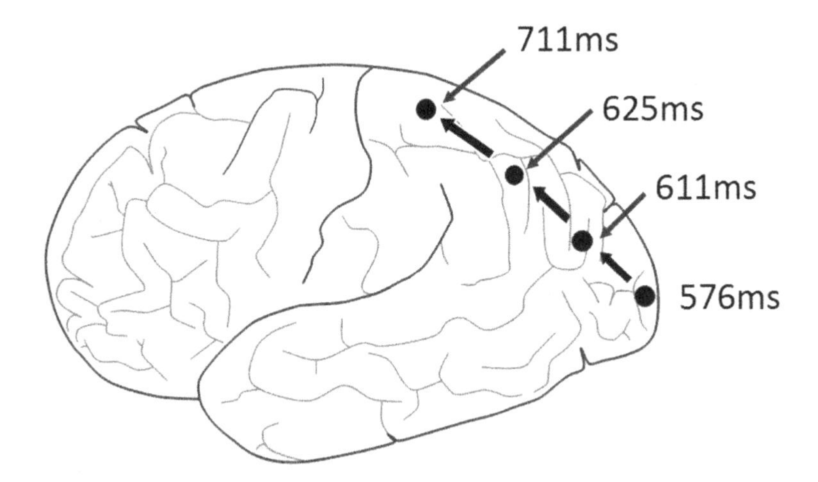

and the dorsal pathway were estimated with reaction latencies.

- **Ventral Pathway:** V1 (133 ms) → V2 (171 ms) → V4 (245 ms) → TEO (306 ms) → TE (357 ms)
- **Dorsal Pathway:** V1 (576 ms) → V2 (611 ms) → V5 (625 ms) → Occipital Lobe (711 ms)

The signal propagation to the temporal lobe from the primary visual cortex with each reaction latency is shown in Figure 14. The center circular aperture appears at an RL of 0 ms, and the base bar starts to move at an RL of 340 ms in Exp. 7. Therefore, we concluded that the localized ECD in Figure 14 is derived from the appearance of the center circular aperture. The propagation in the dorsal pathway is shown in Figure 15. We concluded that the localized ECD in Figure 15 is related to the movement of the base bar because the base bar starts at an RL of 340 ms.

By comparing the latencies of VEP, ERP, and the localized ECD, we note that the active signal

Figure 16. Localization of ECD by movement of the flanker bars

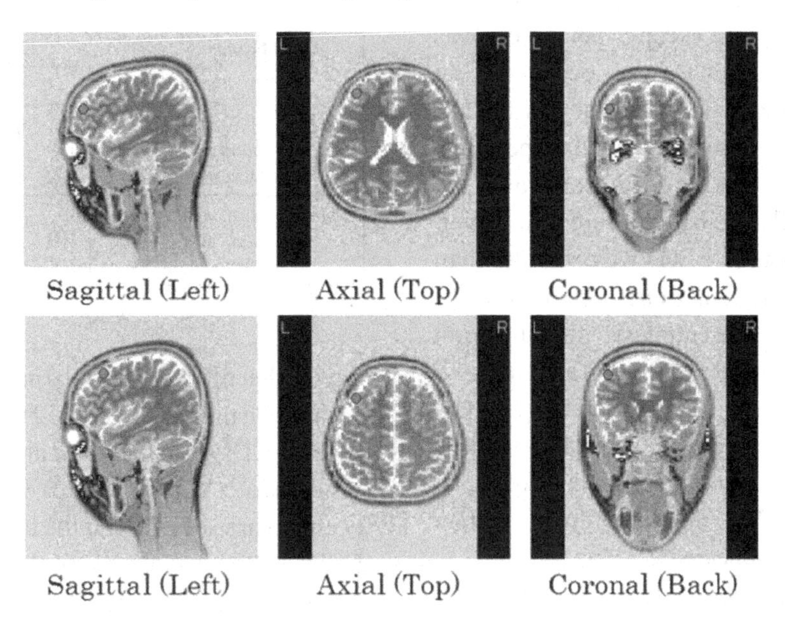

propagated to the temporal lobe through the ventral pathway at latencies of 100 ms to 400 ms from the primary visual cortex, and the active signal is related to the appearance of the center circular aperture. Similarly, we should note that the signal that propagated to the parietal lobe through the dorsal pathway at latencies of 500 ms to 700 ms is related to movement of the base bar. Since the ventral pathway primarily relates to symbolic recognition, and the dorsal pathway primarily relates to spatial recognition, this consideration should be acceptable.

Which part of brain relates to the peak amplitude of ERP at the latency period of 1,000 ms to 1,300 ms? To answer this question, we estimated the localization of ECD after the flanker bars shifted. The localizations of ECD were estimated at the right superior frontal gyrus (RL: 1,165 ms to 1,172 ms) and the left middle frontal gyrus (RL: 1,235 ms to 1,252 ms) when the flanker bars moved in the horizontal orientation (0 degrees) and the vertical orientation (90 degrees). Figure 16 shows the localized ECD induced by movement of the flanker bars. We should note that the active signal propagated to the frontal lobe at the latency interval of 1,000 ms to 1,300 ms and is assumed to be related to movement of the flanker bars.

This tendency is very similar to brain activity during perception of straight moving visual stimuli. In the case of straight moving visual stimuli, ECDs were estimated to be associated with the right frontal lobe regardless of the shifting orientation. However, when comparing VEPs of opposing orientations, the peak latencies for marked amplitude changes were predominantly similar, but the polarities were opposite. In this investigation, comparing VEPs between the horizontal orientation (0 degrees) and the vertical orientation (90 degrees), the peak latencies for marked amplitude changes were predominantly similar, but the polarities were also different. However, in comparing localized ECDs between the horizontal orientation (0 degrees) and the vertical orientation (90 degrees), the areas of brain activity are similar. Therefore, these results suggest that the right frontal lobe activities relate to dynamic stimuli.

In all cases, ECDs were localized to the ventral pathway at the latency of the center circular aperture appearance. In addition, ECDs were localized to the dorsal pathway at the latency of the base bar appearance except when no bar was presented. In all cases, ECDs were localized again to the ventral pathway at the latency in the appearance of the two additional circular apertures. ECDs were localized to the dorsal pathway at the latency when the flanker bars appeared. However, the peaks of measured EEGs were smaller than at the latency of the center circular aperture appearance. These results emphasize that the brain activities in early visual recognition area relay all changes of visual stimuli, and the dorsal pathway relays only changes of dynamic visual stimuli. In addition, in the case of continuous change of visual stimuli, changes of EEG amplitude are lower than when new stimuli appeared.

When the flanker bars shifted to the horizontal orientation (0 degrees) and the vertical orientation (90 degrees), ECDs were estimated at the right superior frontal gyrus, the right middle frontal gyrus, and the right inferior frontal gyrus at the latency of the flanker bar appearance. However, in the case of diagonal orientation (45 degrees), ECDs were not estimated in any of these areas. These results suggest that the subject recognizes “the bar’s moving orientation was not changed” in the case of diagonal orientation (45 degrees), and our assumptions about “the bar’s moving orientation is diagonal” are correct.

For additional experiments, we recorded EEGs of a subject who had recognized changes in the speed and orientation of the bar’s movement. EEGs were summed and averaged according to line speeds and moving patterns in order to obtain ERPs. We also estimated their sources and latencies using the equivalent current dipole source localization (ECDL) method. Two different speeds were used, 10 ms/pixel and 20 ms/pixel, and four bar orientations, 0, 45, 90 degrees, and no bar. Stimuli were presented in random order, and measurements were repeated sixty times in each condition.

ERPs of 20 ms/pixel showed the same tendency as those for 10 ms/pixel. However, their latencies

Table 2. ECDs localized along ventral pathway

Orientations		Latencies				
		V1	V2	V4	TEO	TE
10ms/p	Horizontal	33	86	97	147	215
	Vertical	54	109	165	314	400
	Diagonal	52	130	239	281	369
20ms/p	Horizontal	30	75	175	259	364
	Vertical	44	103	232	261	319
	Diagonal	78	121	152	239	312

were rather different from 10 ms/pixel. Therefore, we applied the ECDL method to their latencies of ERPs. ECDs were localized at visual area 1 (V1), visual area 2 (V2), visual area 4 (V4), the temporal occipital area (TEO) and the temporal area (TE); ECDs were localized along the ventral pathway. The ventral pathway is related to the recognition of static stimuli. In both speed conditions, the center circle and the fixation point appeared at a latency of 0 ms. ECDs localized along the ventral pathway were derived from the appearance of the center circle and the fixation point. Table 2 shows the ECDs’ localization along the ventral pathway with changing bar speeds.

ECDs were localized at V1, V2, the middle temporal gyrus (MT), and the postcentral gyrus (PstCG); ECDs were localized along the dorsal pathway. The dorsal pathway relates to the recognition of dynamic stimuli. The base bar appeared at 120 ms in the 10 ms/pixel condition and at 340 ms in the 20 ms/pixel condition. Table 3 shows the ECDs’ localization along the dorsal pathway with changing bar speeds.

ECDs localized along the dorsal pathway were derived from the movement of the base bar. Some ECDs were localized at the middle frontal gyrus (MFG) and the inferior frontal gyrus (IFG) at latencies from 1,000 ms to 1,100 ms in the 10 ms/pixel condition and at latencies from 1,800 to 1,900 ms in the 20 ms/pixel condition.

The areas MFG and IFG are thought to relate to spatial recognition as it involves working memory. These latencies are estimated just after

Table 3. ECDs localized along dorsal pathway

Orientations		Latencies			
		V1	V2	MT	PstCG
10ms/p	Horizontal	232	319	426	619
	Vertical	216	267	369	577
	Diagonal	225	271	401	511
20ms/p	Horizontal	457	498	592	638
	Vertical	481	538	587	709
	Diagonal	481	518	587	636

two circles were presented, with the subject's task being the recognition of the bar's orientation. ECDs localized at the MFG and the IFG were derived from the perception of orientation of the bar's movement. We analyzed the brain activity of the perception on aperture problem depending on the bar's speed and direction. However, no difference was recognized to estimate the areas regardless of bar speed and orientation.

From these experimental results, we concluded that perception originates at the prefrontal lobe because the left middle frontal gyrus is thought to relate to spatial recognition using temporal memory and the right inferior frontal gyrus is thought to relate to motor recognition using temporal memory.

DISCUSSION

We discuss a hierarchical model that includes a modal supplement (Hayashi, I. 2004b, Hayashi, I. 2005). The results of the current experiments on the aperture problem suggest that the size of a circular aperture radius and the distance between circles affects human perception. As Okada et al. (2003) claim that the binding mechanism in the non-visible domain is influenced by extrapolation of the visible domain to explain the propagation function, and this function is constructed with repetitive extrapolation, we should consider that the continuity of a processing loop extrapolation process is important to the construction of the hierarchical model. A similar discussion is described by Fukushima (Fukushima, K. 2010), Neumann (Neumann, H. 1999) and Hayashi (Hayashi, I. 2001a, Hayashi, I. 2001b, Hayashi, I. 2002b). Fukushima et al. (2010) state that a modal supplement can be achieved by repetitive processing to predict both curvature and position of an occluded domain with the hierarchical model. In addition, we realize that there is a velocity of bar movement that facilitates motion perception by nonmonotonicity of the speed of bars. As for this discussion, besides the occupancy classification of the visible domain and the non-visible domain, the structure of the multi-complex structure based on the time series dynamic is necessary to construct a hierarchical model.

Furthermore, the EEG analysis confirmed that the ventral pathway and the dorsal pathway are involved in aperture perception, and we realized that the hierarchical model needs a layer structure integrating these two pathways. In addition, we concluded that perception originates at the prefrontal lobe because the left middle frontal gyrus relates spatial recognition to temporal memory, and the right inferior frontal gyrus relates motor recognition to temporal memory. Furthermore, we need a layer structure including the prefrontal lobe in the hierarchical model. Therefore, to construct a model incorporating a modal supplement, it is thought that an attention signal (Grossberg, S. 1999) of the feedback type is necessary between an upper layer including the prefrontal lobe and a lower layer incorporating the ventral and dorsal pathways to achieve an extrapolation process.

CONCLUSION

Our behavioral experiments indicate that motion perception in the aperture problem depends on the display time and the speed of bar movement. We conclude that the perceptual recognition particularly depends on the quadratic function, cubic function, and quartic function of the speed of the bars. In addition, the nonmonotonicity of motion perception is shown by varying the speed of the bars.

ECDs are localized in the ventral pathway at the latency of the center circular aperture appearance and in the dorsal pathway at the latency of the base bar appearance. We conclude that perception originates at the prefrontal lobe because the left middle frontal gyrus relates spatial recognition to temporal memory and the right inferior frontal gyrus relates motor recognition to temporal memory. However, it is necessary to improve the precision of the hypothesis by repeating experiments with more subjects in the near future.

ACKNOWLEDGMENT

This work was partially supported by the Ministry of Education, Culture, Sports, Science, and Technology of Japan under Grant-in-Aid for Scientific Research 19200018. In addition, this work was also partially supported by a grant from the Ministry of Education, Sports, Science and Technology of Japan to the national project of advanced improvements of vision, image, speech and language information processing and the application to the technologies for intelligent instrument and control in the High-tech Research Center of Hokkai-Gakuen University, and to the strategic project to support the formation of research bases at private universities, 2008-2012, and the Organization for Research and Development of Innovative Science and Technology (ORDIST) of Kansai University.

REFERENCES

Ben-av, M. B., & Shiffrar, M. (1995). Disambiguating velocity estimates across image space. *Vision Research*, *35*(20), 2889–2895. doi:10.1016/0042-6989(95)00048-5

Castet, E., Lorenceau, J., Shiffrar, M., & Bonnet, C. (1993). Perceived speed of moving lines depends on orientation, length, speed and luminance. *Vision Research*, *33*, 1921–1936. doi:10.1016/0042-6989(93)90019-S

Chey, J., Grossberg, S., & Mingolla, E. (1997). Neural dynamics of motion grouping: From aperture ambiguity to object speed and direction. *Optical Society of America A*, *14*(10), 2570–2594. doi:10.1364/JOSAA.14.002570

Cropper, S. J., & Derrington, A. M. (1994). Motion of chromatic stimuli: First-order or second-order? *Vision Research*, *34*, 49–58. doi:10.1016/0042-6989(94)90256-9

Eysenck, M. (2006). *Fundamentals of cognition*. East Sussex, UK: Psychology Press.

Fukushima, K. (2010). Neural network model for completing occluded contours. *Neural Networks*, *23*, 528–540. doi:10.1016/j.neunet.2009.10.002

Grossberg, S. (1999). How does the cerebral cortex work? Learning, attention, and grouping by the laminar circuits of visual cortex. *Spatial Vision*, *12*(2), 163–185. doi:10.1163/156856899X00102

Hawken, M. J., Gegenfurtner, K. C., & Tang, C. (1994). Contrast dependence of colour and luminance motion mechanisms in human vision. *Nature*, *367*, 268–270. doi:10.1038/367268a0

Hayashi, I., Maeda, T., & Williamson, J. R. (2004b). A formulation of receptive field type input layer for TAM Network using gabor function. *Proceedings of 2004 IEEE International Conference on Fuzzy Systems* (FUZZ-IEEE2004), No.FUZZ1335.

Hayashi, I., & Shinpaku, G. (2004a). Structuralization of early vision for perceptual grouping in apertures. *Proceedings of the International Workshop on Fuzzy Systems and Innovational Computing 2004* (FIC2004), (pp. 254-258).

Hayashi, I., Taguchi, T., & Kudoh, S. N. (2007a). Learning and memory in living neuronal networks connected to moving robot. *Proceedings of 8th International Symposium on Advanced Intelligent Systems* (ISIS2007), (pp. 79-81).

Hayashi, I., Toyoshima, H., & Yamanoi, T. (2007b). Recognition of perception and the localization for aperture problem in visual pathway of brain. *Proceedings of 2007 IEEE International Conference on Systems, Man and Cybernetics* (SMC2007) (pp. 1872-1877).

Hayashi, I., & Williamson, J. R. (2001a). A study on pruning methods for TAM network. *Proceedings of the Fifth International Conference on Cognitive and Neural Systems* (CNS2001).

Hayashi, I., & Williamson, J. R. (2001b). Acquisition of fuzzy knowledge from topographic mixture networks with attentional feedback. *Proceedings of the International Joint Conference on Neural Networks* (IJCNN2001), (pp. 1386-1391).

Hayashi, I., & Williamson, J. R. (2002a). An analysis of aperture problem using fuzzy rules acquired from TAM network. *Proceedings of 2002 IEEE International Conference on Fuzzy Systems* (FUZZ-IEEE2002) *in 2002 World Congress on Computational Intelligence* (WCCI2002), (pp. 914-919).

Hayashi, I., & Williamson, J. R. (2002b). Knowledge restructuring in fuzzy TAM network, *Proc. of the 9th International Conference on Neural Information Processing* (ICONIP2002), (No. ICONIP1918).

Hayashi, I., & Williamson, J. R. (2005). Orientation selectivity of TAM network with extensive receptive field. *Proceedings of the International Conference on Computational Intelligence for Modelling Control and Automation* (CIMCA2005), (pp. 1184-1189).

Kudoh, S. N., Hosokawa, C., Kiyohara, A., Taguchi, T., & Hayashi, I. (2007). Biomodeling system: Interaction between living neuronal network and outer world. *Journal of Robotics and Mechatronics, 19*(5), 592–600.

Kudoh, S. N., Taguchi, T., & Hayashi, I. (2006). Interaction and intelligence in living neuronal networks connected to moving robot. *Proceedings of 2006 IEEE International Conference on Fuzzy Systems* (FUZZ-IEEE2006) *in 2006 IEEE World Congress on Computational Intelligence* (WCCI2006), (pp. 6271-6275).

Moritaka, A., Yamanoi, T., Toyoshima H., & Nonaka, H. (2008). Spatio-Temporal Analysis of Brain Activities on Aperture Problem. Proceedings of Joint 4th International Symposium on Soft Computing and Intelligent Systems and 9th International Symposium on Advanced Intelligent Systems (SCIS & ISIS2008), (pp. 144-147).

Neumann, H., & Sepp, W. (1999). Recurrent V1-V2 interaction in early visual boundary processing. *Biological Cybernetics, 81*, 425–444. doi:10.1007/s004220050573

Okada, M., Nishina, S., & Kawato, M. (2003). The neural computation of the aperture problem: An iterative process. *Neurology Report, 14*(4), 1767–1771.

Pack, C. C., & Born, R. T. (2001). Temporal dynamics of a neural solution to the aperture problem in visual area MT of macaque brain. *Nature, 409*, 1040–1042. doi:10.1038/35059085

Palmer, S. E. (1999). *Vision science*. London, UK: MIT Press.

Wilson, R. A., & Keil, F. C. (Eds.). (1999). *The MIT encyclopedia of the cognitive sciences (MITECS)*. London, UK: MIT Press.

Chapter 10
Mathematical Foundations Modeled after Neo-Cortex for Discovery and Understanding of Structures in Data

Shubha Kadambe
Rockwell Collins, USA

ABSTRACT

Even though there are distinct areas for different functionalities in the mammalian neo-cortex, it seems to use the same algorithm to understand a large variety of input modalities. In addition, it appears that the neo-cortex effortlessly identifies the correlation among many sensor modalities and fuses information obtained from them. The question then is, can we discover the brain's learning algorithm and approximate it for problems such as computer vision and automatic speech recognition that the mammalian brain is so good at? The answer is: it is an orders of magnitude problem, i.e., not a simple task. However, we can attempt to develop mathematical foundations based on the understanding of how a human brain learns. This chapter is focused along that direction. In particular, it is focused on the ventral stream – the "what pathway" - and describes common algorithms that can be used for representation and classification of signals from different sensor modalities such as auditory and visual. These common algorithms are based on dictionary learning with a beta process, hierarchical graphical models, and embedded hidden Markov models.

1. INTRODUCTION

In this chapter, we provide the results of applicability of dictionary learning in processing images by filling in the missing pixels and enhancing noisy images. Some example applications of hierarchical graphical models are also provided. Moreover, we demonstrate that the same learning algorithm can be used in representing both visual and audio signals. This indicates that it is possible to approximate how the neo-cortex processes multi-sensory data. The results provided in this

DOI: 10.4018/978-1-4666-2539-6.ch010

chapter are promising and the described algorithms may constitute a step in the right direction for approximating the brain's learning, understanding and inferring algorithms.

Even though the neo-cortex of the mammalian brain has distinct areas for different functionalities it seems to use the same algorithm to understand a large variety of input modalities (Mountcastle, 1978; Hawkins & Blakeslee, 2004). For example, in the ferret experiments conducted by Roe *et al* (1992) it was shown that the auditory cortex learned to "see" by plugging in outputs of vision sensors into the auditory part of the brain. Similarly, it has been shown that by sensory remapping in the human brain the functionality of that part of the brain can be altered. For example, by remapping touch sensors with visual cortex it was shown that blind persons can get visual perception by touch (Sadato et al., 1996). In addition, it appears that the neo-cortex effortlessly identifies the correlation among many sensor modalities and fuses information obtained from them. The question then is, can we discover the brain's learning algorithm and approximate it for solving problems such as computer vision and automatic speech recognition that the mammalian brain is so good at? The answer is: it is an orders of magnitude problem, i.e., not a simple task. (a) The human brain has 10^{14} synapses; (b) Humans live approximately 10^{9} seconds; (c) If each synapse has just one bit to parameterize, humans would need to learn 10^{14} bits in 10^{9} seconds. That is, humans have to learn at the speed of 10^{5} bits per second (Hinton, n.d.). This tremendous amount of information is learned by humans mostly in unsupervised fashion. To achieve the same feat by a computer is an orders of magnitude problem indeed! However, we can attempt to develop mathematical foundations based on the understanding of how a human brain learns. This chapter is focused along that direction.

The visual cortex of the mammalian brain is part of the cerebral cortex responsible for processing visual information. It is located in the occipital lobe in the back of the brain. There is a visual cortex on each hemisphere of the brain. The left hemisphere visual cortex receives signals from the right visual field and vice versa. The primary visual cortex V1, which is a small portion of the brain as can be seen in Figure 1, is located in and around the calcarine fissure in the occipital lobe. Each hemisphere's V1 transmits information to two primary pathways – the dorsal and ventral streams. The dorsal stream begins with V1, goes through visual area V2, then to the dorsomedial area next to the visual area V5 and then to the posterior parietal cortex. This dorsal pathway is sometimes referred to as "where pathway" or "how pathway". It is associated with motion, representation of object locations and control of the eyes and arms, especially when visual information is used to guide saccades or reaching (Milner, 1992). The ventral stream begins with V1, goes through V2, V4 and Inferior Temporal (IT) cortex. This ventral stream is sometimes referred to as "what pathway". It is associated with form recognition and object representation. It is also involved with storage of long-term memory. In this chapter we are focusing on this ventral stream as we are interested in the common algorithm that the brain applies for recognition and representation. The regions in the ventral stream V1, V2, V4 and IT are believed to be connected hierarchically with both feed forward and backward pathways as depicted in a simplified form in Figure 2.

As can be seen from Figure 2, V1 is the first stage in the visual processing pipeline. It finds a "sparse code" of the input image and represents it succinctly (Olushen & Field, 1996). This can be interpreted mathematically as sparse representation of an image in the form of a weighted linear combination of bases ϕ_is. By definition, the sparse representation of an image means that most of the weights a_is have to be zero or very close to zero. Based on the above argument, for example, an image X can be mathematically represented as:

Figure 1. Primary visual cortex V1

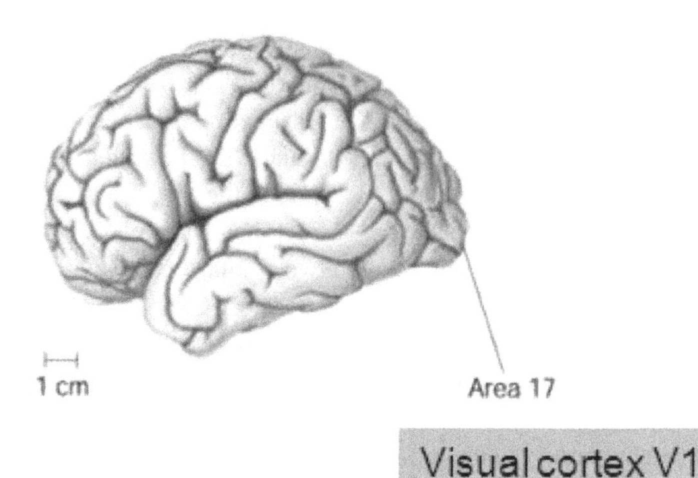

$$\hat{X} = \sum_i a_i \varphi_i \text{ where } a_i\text{s are the weights. (1)}$$

Thus, in order to mimic the processing and representation of an image in the V1 region, we need to learn bases ϕ_is that sparsely represent a given image.

Several algorithms have been developed for basis learning. Most of these algorithms optimally select a set of bases from a predefined dictionary of basis functions such as wavelets or discrete cosine. These predefined basis functions may not match physically how a V1 region would have processed and represented images optimally and sparsely. Some of the recent de-noising and in-painting research in the area of image processing has demonstrated the significant advantages of learning an often over-complete dictionary matched to signals of interest (*e.g.*, images) (Duarte-Carvajalino & Sapiro, 2008; Elad & Aharon, 2005; Mairal et al., 2009; Ranzato et al., 2006). Hence, we are proposing a technique to learn bases from a set of training images. These learned bases would correspond to building blocks of images such as edges and basic shapes. Hence, they are general and can represent any image sparsely at the lowest level similar to the V1 region. A technique similar to our proposed approach has been developed in (Raina et al., 2007). The authors there use convex optimization principles to learn bases from a given

Figure 2. Hierarchical connections of the regions in the visual processing along the ventral stream ("what pathway")

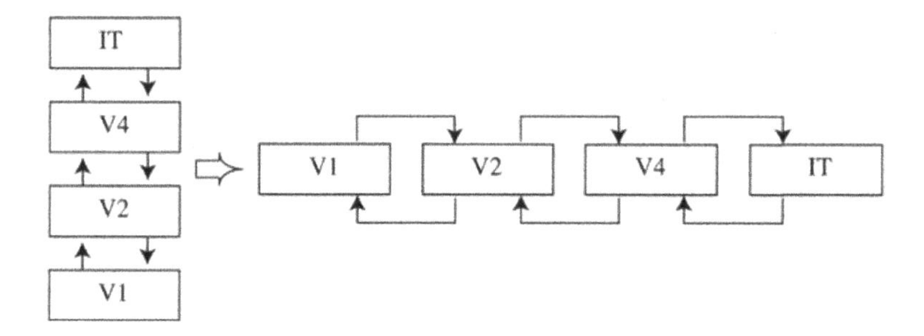

set of images. This optimization corresponds to minimizing convex functions over convex sets. A real-valued function $f(x)$ defined on an interval x_1 and x_2 is called convex (or convex downward or concave upward) if the graph of the function $f(x)$ lies below the line segment joining any two points (i.e., x_1 and x_2) of the graph as shown in Figure 3. The following statements are true about the convex minimization problem:

- If a local minimum exists then it is also a global minimum
- The set of all global minima is convex
- For each strictly convex function, if the function has a minimum then the minimum is unique

The convex minimization or optimization problem corresponds to minimizing a convex function over its variable under inequality or equality constraints. That is:

$$\underset{x}{minimize} \quad f(x)$$

$$subject\,to \quad \begin{array}{l} g_i(x) \leq 0, i = 1, \cdots, m \ or \\ h_i(x) = 0, \quad i = 1, \cdots, p \end{array}$$

Figure 3. Example of a convex function

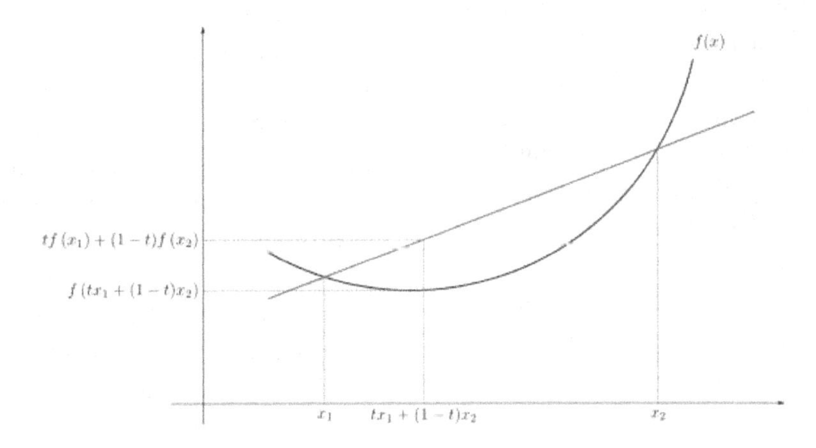

The standard form of the convex optimization problem mentioned above can be cast into a Lagrangian function using Lagrange multipliers λ_is as follows: Consider a convex optimization problem given in a standard form by a cost function $f(x)$ and inequality constraints $g_i(x) \leq 0, where\, i = 1, \cdots, m$. Then the Lagrangian function for the optimization problem is:

$$L(x, \lambda_0, \lambda_1, \cdots, \lambda_m) = \lambda_0 f(x) + \lambda_1 g_1(x) + \cdots + \lambda_m g_m(x).$$

For each point x in X that minimizes f over X, there exist real numbers $\lambda_0, \lambda_1, \ldots, \lambda_m$, called Lagrange multipliers. The authors in (Raina et al., 2007) use the above described Lagrangian function for the optimization to learn the basis functions and weights. In particular, they minimize the following equation:

$$\min_{\phi a} \sum_{i=1}^{m} \left\| x_i - \sum_{j=1}^{n} a_j^{(i)} \phi_j \right\|^2 - \lambda \sum_{i=1}^{m} \left\| a^i \right\|_1 \quad (2)$$

In the above equation the first term corresponds to $\lambda_0 f(x) with\, \lambda_0 = 1$ and the second term corresponds to $\lambda_1 g_1(x) + \cdots + \lambda_m g_m(x) with\, \lambda_i = 1, i = 1, \ldots, m\, and\, g_i(x) = a^{(i)}$.

From this equation it can be seen that this optimization problem is convex in each of the two parameters ϕ and a. To optimize ϕ_is the authors use the Lagrangian dual whereas to optimize a_is they use quadratic programs. These approaches are computationally expensive.

We have developed a technique based on statistical processing – Beta processing and non-parametric Bayesian technology (Paisley & Carin, 2009; Thibaux & Jordan, 2007) to learn bases. Our approach is computationally less expensive as compared to (Raina et al., 2007). In addition our approach offers the following advantages over the other bases learning approaches briefly discussed above:

1. The number of dictionary elements - in other words, the number of bases and their relative importance - can be inferred non-parametrically.
2. No need to assume a priori the knowledge of noise variance, and noise can be non-stationary.
3. The spatial inter relationships between different components in images are exploited by the Drichlet (Paisley & Carin, 2009) and probit stick breaking statistical processes.

In the next section our dictionary learning approach is described in detail. In Section 3 an overview of the mathematical foundation for the hierarchical representation of other regions of the visual processing is provided. In both Sections 2 and 3 some of the applications and results are provided. In section 4 we conclude and indicate that even though learning and mimicking the complete functionality of the human brain is an orders of magnitude problem, the mathematical foundations described in this chapter are a step in the right direction.

To implement the learning algorithms, hierarchical architecture and inferring using a network of a large number of nodes (which relates to millions of neurons involved in the visual processing in the brain), require cloud computing. Since cloud computing is possible now, there is some hope to achieve the same feat of the human brain by computers in the future!

2. DICTIONARY LEARNING WITH A BETA PROCESS

In traditional sparse coding (sparse representation) tasks a signal $\boldsymbol{x} \in R^n$ (real space of dimension n) and a fixed dictionary (basis functions) matrix $\mathbf{D} = (\boldsymbol{d}_1, \boldsymbol{d}_2, \ldots, \boldsymbol{d}_M)$ where each $\boldsymbol{d}_m$ is a real vector of size n i.e., $\in R^n$, are considered and it is assumed that any $\boldsymbol{x} \in R^n$ can be represented approximately as $\hat{x} = \boldsymbol{D}$ - weighted linear combination of basis functions similar to Equation (1). Here $\boldsymbol{\alpha}$ is a vector of real values of size M ***i.e.,*** $\in R^M$, and is sparse (most elements of $\alpha = 0$). Our objective is to learn bases by minimizing the L_2 error $\left\|\hat{x} - x\right\|_2$ – the first term in Equation (2) (sum of magnitude square of difference between a signal x and its estimate as a weighted linear combination of basis functions). With a proper dictionary a sparse $\boldsymbol{\alpha}$ often manifests robustness to noise. The above model also yields effective inference of $\boldsymbol{\alpha}$ even when $\boldsymbol{x}$ is partially or indirectly observed via a small number of measurements.

To the author's knowledge, all previous work in this direction has been performed in the following manner: (*i*) If $\mathbf{D}$ is given, the sparse vector $\boldsymbol{\alpha}$ is estimated via a point estimate (without a posterior distribution). For this purpose, typically techniques based on Orthogonal Matching Pursuits (OMP), basis pursuits or related methods are applied. These techniques need a stopping criterion. This is defined by assuming knowledge (or off-line estimation) of the noise variance or the sparsity level of $\boldsymbol{\alpha}$. (*ii*) When the dictionary $\mathbf{D}$ is to be learned, the dictionary size M must be set *a priori*, and a point estimate is achieved for $\mathbf{D}$. In practice one can infer M via cross-validation.

Our technique described below avoids this extra step in inferring the dictionary size *M*.

The main disadvantages of previous work that follow the two steps mentioned above are as follows: 1. In many applications we may not know the noise variance or an appropriate sparsity level of $\boldsymbol{\alpha}$. 2. In many applications we would be interested in the confidence of the estimate (*e.g.*, "error bars" on the estimate of $\boldsymbol{\alpha}$) to validate the performance. To overcome these disadvantages, we apply a non-parametric Bayesian formulation to this problem, in terms of the Beta process – a statistical approach. This lets us infer the appropriate values of M and $\|a\|_0$ (sparsity level) jointly. It also provides a full posterior density function on the learned dictionary of bases **D** and the inferred $\boldsymbol{\alpha}$ (for a particular $\boldsymbol{x}$). This yields a measure of confidence in the inversion in other words in the estimates of α and x. As discussed further below, the non-parametric Bayesian formulation also allows us to relax other assumptions that have been made in the field of learning **D** and $\boldsymbol{\alpha}$ in the case of inpainting (filling in the missing information), de-noising (enhancing signal/image by removing noise) and compressive sensing (projecting a signal in to a sparse domain or sparse sampling). Furthermore, the addition of other goals (i.e., applications such as image compression and object classification) can be readily addressed within the non-parametric Bayesian paradigm, such as designing **D** for joint compression *and* classification.

2.1 Beta Process (BP) Formulation

As mentioned above any $\boldsymbol{x} \in R^n$ can be represented approximately as $\hat{x} = D\alpha$. Using this we can model $\boldsymbol{x} = \mathbf{D}\boldsymbol{\alpha}+\varepsilon$, where ε is the error between x and $\hat{x}$ and $\mathbf{D} \in R^{nXM}$ is a matrix of size n x M. Using this model we wish to learn **D** and in so doing infer *M*, the number of basis functions needed to represent $\boldsymbol{x}$ optimally. Toward this end, we consider an over-complete dictionary **D** (of size n x K)$\in R^{nXK}$, with $K \rightarrow \infty$. By estimating the number of columns of **D** that are required for accurate representation of $\boldsymbol{x}$, the appropriate value of *M* is implicitly inferred. We also impose a condition that $\boldsymbol{\alpha} \in R^K$ is sparse, and therefore only a small fraction of the columns of **D** are used for representation of a given $\boldsymbol{x}$. We assume that we have a training set $D = \{\boldsymbol{x}_i, y_i\}_{i=1,N}$, where $\boldsymbol{x}_i \in R^n$ and $y_i \in \{1, 2, \ldots, N_c\}$, where $N_c \geq 2$ represents the number of classes from which data $\boldsymbol{x}$ arise. While learning the dictionary we ignore the class labels y_i, and later discuss how they may be considered in the learning process that helps in object classification applications.

The two-parameter beta process (BP) was developed in (Paisley & Carin, 2009), to which the reader is referred for further details. Here, we only provide details of those that are relevant for the current application of dictionary learning. The BP with parameters $a > 0$ and $b > 0$, and base measure H_0, is represented as BP(a, b, H_0), and a draw $H \sim$ BP(a, b, H_0) may be represented as:

$$H\left(\Psi\right) = \sum_{k=1}^{K} \delta_{\Psi_k}\left(\Psi\right)$$
$$\pi_k \sim Beta\left(a / K, b(K-1)/k\right) \; \Psi_k \sim H_0 \quad (3)$$

with a valid measure as $K \rightarrow \infty$. $\delta_{\Psi_k}\left(\Psi\right) = 1$ if $\psi = \psi_k$ and is zero otherwise. Therefore $H(\psi)$ represents a vector of K probabilities, each associated with a respective atom - basis function ψ_k. In the limit $K \rightarrow \infty$, $H(\psi)$ corresponds to an infinite-dimensional vector of probabilities and each probability has an associated atom ψ_k drawn independently and identically distributed (i.i.d.) from H_0.

Using $H(\psi)$, we may now draw N *binary* vectors, the ith of which is denoted by $z_i \in \{0, 1\}^K$ and the kth component of z_i is drawn $z_{ik} \sim$ Bernoulli(π_k). These N binary column vectors are used to constitute a matrix $\mathbf{Z} \in \{0, 1\}^{KXN}$ with the ith column corresponding to z_i; and the kth row of **Z** being associated with an atom ψ_k, drawn as discussed above. For our problem the atoms ψ_k

$\in R^n$ will correspond to candidate members of our dictionary **D**, and the binary vector z_i defines which members of the dictionary are used to represent sample $x_i \in D$.

Consider the above model: $x = \mathbf{D}\alpha + \varepsilon$. Let $\Psi = (\psi_1, \psi_2, \ldots, \psi_K)$, and we may consider the limit $K \rightarrow \infty$. By substituting for $\mathbf{D}\alpha$ using ψ and z in our model for representation of sample $x_i \in D$, we get $x_i = \Psi z_i + \epsilon_i$. However, this is highly restrictive, as it imposes that the coefficients of the dictionary expansion must be binary since z is binary. To address this limitation, we draw weights using a normal distribution $w_i \sim N\left(0, \gamma_w^{-1} I_K\right)$ where γ_w is the precision or inverse variance. Using this, the dictionary weights are now $\alpha_i = z_i \circ w_i$, and $x_i = \Psi \alpha_i + \epsilon_i$ where $\circ$ represents the Hadamard (element-wise) multiplication of two vectors. Note that, by construction, α is sparse (z_i has a binary value 0 or 1, and many can be 0s). This imposition of sparseness is distinct from the widely used Laplace shrinkage prior (Tibshirani, 1996). The Laplace shrinkage prior imposes that many coefficients are small but not necessarily exactly zero.

For simplicity we assume that the dictionary elements, defined by the atoms ψ_k, are drawn from a multivariate Gaussian base (distribution) H_0, and the components of the error vectors ϵ_i are drawn i.i.d. from a zero-mean Gaussian. The hierarchical form of our model now can be expressed as:

$$x_i = \psi \alpha_i + \epsilon_i \; ; \; \alpha_i = z_i o w_i \; ; \; \Psi = (\psi_1, \psi_2, \ldots, \psi_K) \; ; \; \psi_k \sim \aleph\left(0, n^{-1} I_n\right) \; ;$$

$$w_i \sim \aleph\left(0, \gamma_w^{-1} I_K\right) \; ; \; \epsilon_i \sim \aleph\left(0, \gamma_{\in}^{-1} {}_n\right) \; ;$$
$$z_i \sim \prod_{k=1}^{K} Bernoulli\left(\pi_k\right) \; ;$$

$$\pi_k \sim Beta\left(a / K, b(K-1) / k\right) \qquad (4)$$

Non-informative gamma hyper-priors are typically placed on γ_w and γ_{ε}. Consecutive elements in the above hierarchical model are in the conjugate exponential family, and therefore inference may be implemented via a Variational Bayesian (Beal, 2003) or Gibbs-sampling analysis, with analytic update equations. After performing such inference, we retain those columns of Ψ that are used in the representation of the data in D, thereby inferring **D** and hence M. To impose our desire that the vector of dictionary weights α is sparse, one may adjust the parameters a and b. Particularly, as discussed in (Pailsey & Carin, 2009), in the limit $K \rightarrow \infty$, the number of elements of z_i that are non-zero is a random variable drawn from the Poisson distribution Poisson(a/b).

The steps of the dictionary or basis learning using the hierarchical form of our model given in Equation (4) are:

1. Randomly select N patches from the training images to construct x (we use1280 patches sampled from 25 128*128 images in the examples below)
2. Select a, b, K, and N that correspond to:
   - The number of basis N
   - The sparsity level K of the representation under the learned dictionary
   - a and b parameters of the Beta distribution provided in Equation (4)
3. From the chosen a, b, get the value of π_k from the Beta distribution ($\pi_k \sim Beta\left(a / K, b(K-1) / k\right)$)
4. From the π_k compute the value of z_i - $z_i \sim \prod_{k=1}^{K} Bernoulli\left(\pi_k\right)$
5. Draw ψ_K using the multivariate Gaussian distribution - ${}_k \sim \left(0, \boldsymbol{n}^{-1}{}_{\boldsymbol{n}}\right)$ and from the N patches of training images and w_i using the normal distribution - $w_i \sim \left(0, {}_w^{-1} {}_K\right)$
6. Compute $\alpha_i = \boldsymbol{z_i} \boldsymbol{o} \boldsymbol{w_i}$ by substituting for w_i and z_i obtained from steps 4 and 5

7. Estimate x_i as $\psi\alpha_i$ by substituting for and α_i that are obtained from steps 5 and 6
8. Compute the error ϵ_i – the difference between x_i and its estimate obtained from step 7 and repeat the process (steps 3-7) till the error is minimized
9. The resulting Ψ that minimizes the error is the learned basis.
10. By modifying a, b, and K, we can get different kinds of dictionaries.
    - One extreme is large reconstruction error but very sparse representation under the dictionary.
    - The other extreme is small reconstruction error but the representation under the dictionary is not very sparse.

The examples of these two extremes are shown below in Figures 4 and 5. In these two figures, the subplot with title "Z" corresponds to the binary values drawn from the Bernoulli process, the subplot with title "A" is the weight w drawn from a normal distribution, the subplot with title "S" is α= (z o w), the subplot bar graph corresponds to error ε and the subplot with the title "Learned basis functions" corresponds to D that results after the learning iteration is stopped.

Notice that S is sparse in Figure 4 but dense in Figure 5; however, the error is large (0.13462) versus 0.029288 after 300 iterations for the values of a_0 and b_0 equal to 0.5 & 0.5 in Figure 4 and 0.75 and 0.5 in Figure 5, respectively. Also notice that the learned basis functions represent the building blocks of images (horizontal, vertical, edges and some basic shapes, etc.). Also notice from Figure 5, most of the learned bases look random (grainy) without any specific structure hence, it is not necessary to choose the BP processing parameters that represent the extreme case of non-sparse representation.

It was mentioned before that there is evidence to indicate that the neo-cortex uses the same algorithm to process other sensory data. To show that this is indeed possible under our assumptions, we applied the above described learning algorithm for audio (speech) signals. In Figure 6 an example of learned dictionary for such a signal is shown.

In the following section two applications of dictionary learning – inpainting and de-noising are provided. The first application, inpainting, corresponds to recovering the mixing pixels and the second application, de-noising, corresponds to enhancing noisy images. These two applications are similar to the visual processing that human brain performs in filling in the missing information and enhancing the noisy images while sparsely representing images in the V1 region.

2.2 Inpainting

In the discussions in Section 2.1, we implicitly assumed all data $D = \{x_i, y_i\}_{i=1,..N}$ are used together to learn the dictionary **D**. However, in some applications such as inpainting and denoising N may be large, and therefore such a "batch" approach is undesirable due to computational complexity. To address this issue we partition the data into $D = D_1 \cup D_2 \cup \ldots D_{J-1} \cup D_J$, with each partition of the data processed sequentially. Here ∪ corresponds to the union operation. Note that the sequential inference is handled naturally via our proposed Bayesian analysis similar to the V1 region. Specifically, let $p(\mathbf{D}|D,\mathbf{\Theta})$ represent the posterior probability on the desired dictionary, with all other model parameters marginalized out (*e.g.*, the sample-dependent coefficients $\boldsymbol{\alpha}$). The vector $\mathbf{\Theta}$ represents the model hyper parameters. In a Bayesian analysis, rather than evaluating $p(\mathbf{D}|D,\mathbf{\Theta})$ directly, we employ the same model (prior) to infer $p(\mathbf{D}|D1,\mathbf{\Theta})$. This posterior then serves as a prior for **D** when considering next $D2$, inferring $p(\mathbf{D}|D1 \cup D2,\mathbf{\Theta})$. When performing Variational Bayesian (VB) inference we have an analytic approximate representation for posteriors such as $p(\mathbf{D}|D1,\mathbf{\Theta})$ whereas for Gibbs sampling

Figure 4. Example of dictionary learning in the case of large reconstruction error and very sparse representation

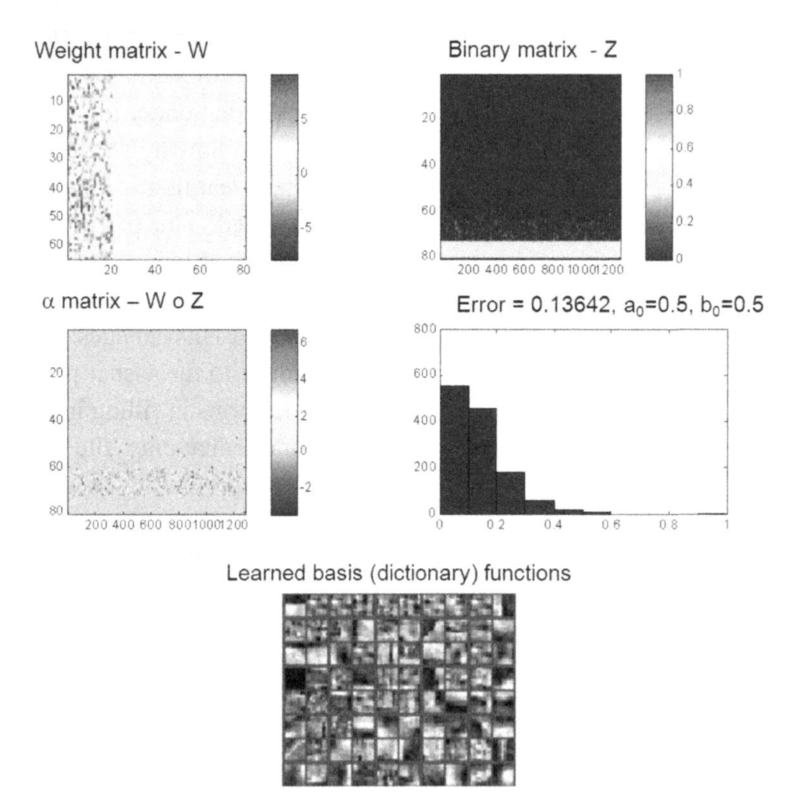

we use the inferred samples. This sequential approach is used in inpainting and de-noising applications and is described below.

Assume we are given an image $\mathbf{I} \in R^{Ny \times Nx}$ with additive noise and missing pixels; we here assume a monochrome image for mathematical simplicity, but color images are also readily handled, as demonstrated when presenting results. As is done typically (Duarte-Carvajalino & Sapiro, 2008; Thibaux & Jordan, 2007), we partition the image into $N_B = \left(N_y - B + 1\right) X \left(N_x - B + 1\right)$ overlapping blocks $\left\{x_i\right\}_{i=1\ldots N_B}$, for each of which $\boldsymbol{x}_i \in R^{B2}$ ($B = 8$ is typically used). If there is only additive noise but no missing pixels, then the model in Equation (4) can be readily applied for simultaneous dictionary learning and image denoising. If there are both noise and missing pixels, instead of directly observing $\boldsymbol{x}_i$, we observe a subset of the pixels in each $\boldsymbol{x}_i$. Note that here $\boldsymbol{\Psi}$ and $\left\{\alpha_i\right\}_{i=1\ldots N_B}$ which are used to recover the original noise-free and complete image, are directly inferred from the data under test. One may also employ an appropriate training set with which to learn a dictionary $\mathbf{D}$ offline, or for initialization of *in situ* learning.

In de-noising and inpainting studies of this type (see for example [Elad & Aharon, 2006; Mairal, Elad, & Sapiro, 2008] and references therein), it is often assumed that either the variance is known and used as a "stopping" criterion, or the (often fixed for all $i \in \{1,N_B\}$) sparsity level is pre-determined. While these may be practical in some applications, we feel it is more desirable to not make these assumptions as they are not practical in all applications. In Equation (4) the noise precision (inverse variance), γ_ε, is assumed to be

Figure 5. Example of dictionary learning in the case of very small reconstruction error and a non-sparse representation

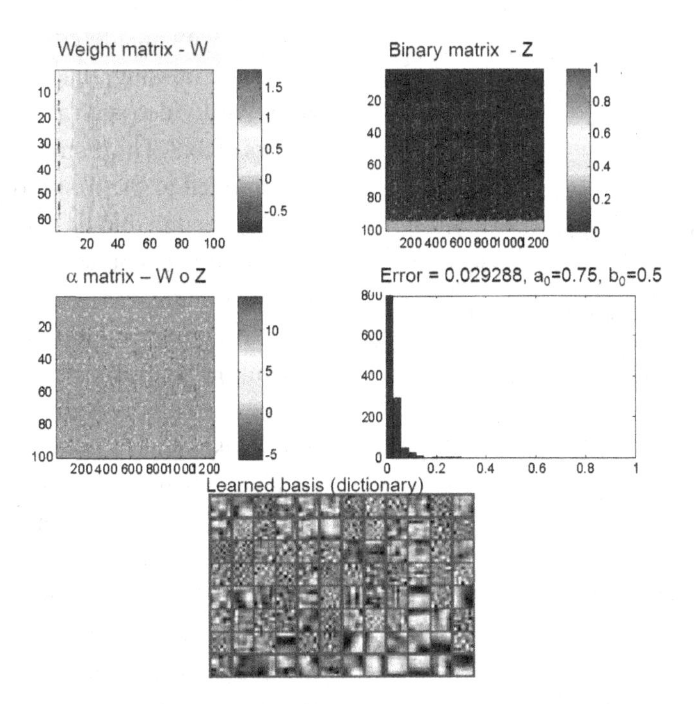

drawn from a non-informative gamma distribution, and a full posterior density function is inferred for γ_ε (and all other model parameters). In addition, the problems of addressing spatially non-uniform noise as well as non-uniform noise across color channels are of interest (Mairal, Elad, & Sapiro, 2008); they are readily handled in the proposed model by drawing a separate precision γ_ε for each color channel in each $B \times B$ block, each of which is drawn from a shared gamma prior.

The sparsity level of the representation in our model, *i.e.*, $\left\{\alpha_{i0}\right\}_{i=1,..N_B}$ is influenced by the parameters a and b in the beta prior in Equation (4). Examining the posterior (presented in Box 1) conditioned on all other parameters, we find that most settings of a and b tend to be non-informative. Therefore, the average sparsity level of the representation is inferred by the data itself and each sample $\boldsymbol{x}_i$ has its own unique sparse representation based on the posterior, which renders more flexibility than enforcing the same sparsity level for each sample.

In brief the steps of the algorithm for inpainting are:

Figure 6. Example of learned dictionary for an audio signal

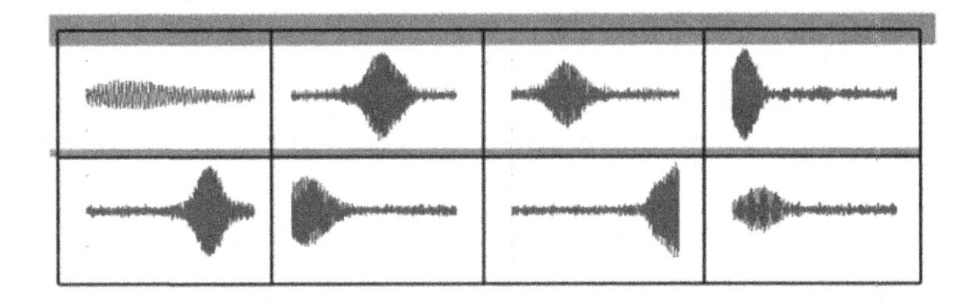

Table 1. Peak signal-to-noise reconstructed image measure (PSNR) for the data in Figure 8, for K-SVD and the proposed BP method. The true standard deviation was 15, 25 and 50, respectively, from the top to the bottom row. For the mismatched K-SVD results, the noise standard deviation was fixed at 30.

Original noisy image dB	K-SVD Denoising mismatched variance (dB)	K-SVD Denoising matched variance (dB)	Our approach - Beta Process denoising (dB)
24.58	30.67	34.22	34.19
20.19	31.52	32.08	31.89
14.56	19.60	27.07	27.85

1. Given image with missing pixels (e.g., bad sensor) or noisy image (e.g, image corrupted by the packet losses in communication channel) is divided into blocks of 8x8
2. First iteration of learning
   a. Use the first block
   b. Initialize ψ and w using Singular Value Decomposition (SVD)
   c. Learn ψ iteratively using the model in Equation (4)
3. Consider the union of blocks 1 and 2 (augment data)
   a. Use the learned ψ and w of the previous block as the initialization for the next round of learning (retain the last sample)
   b. Learn ψ and w on this expanded version
4. Retain the last sample and augment the data and repeat the process

In the following Figure 7, the results of the above described inpainting algorithm are provided. For this we considered an image in which 80% pixels are missing, that is, those pixels are set to zero. We divided such a missing pixels image into blocks of 8x8. The dictionary learning algorithms was applied to the first block. It was augmented by the second block. The dictionary learning algorithm was applied to this augmented block. This procedure was repeated for all the blocks. By comparing the resulted image after applying the inpainting algorithm with the original image, it can be seen it is very close to the original image. The Peak Signal to Noise Ratio (PSNR) that is obtained by our algorithm after 64 rounds of learning is 28.66 dB. This example is also considered in (Mairal, Elad, & Sapiro, 2008). The best result reported in (Mairal, Elad, & Sapiro, 2008) is a PSNR of 29.65 dB which is approximately one dB higher than ours. To achieve those results a training data set was employed for initialization in (Mairal, Elad, & Sapiro, 2008). However, our results are achieved with no *a priori* training data.

2.3 Image De-Noising

We consider a 256 × 256 image for the de-noising application. We compare the results of our approach with Kernel-SVD (K-SVD) (Elad & Aharon, 2006), a state-of the-art technique. This K-SVD approach assumes that the noise variance is known and fixed. The *true* noise standard deviation is set at 15, 25 and 50 in the examples provided below. In Figure 8, we show the results of three algorithms: (*i*) mismatched K-SVD (with noise standard deviation of 30), (*ii*) K-SVD when the standard deviation of the noise

Box 1.

$$\left(\pi_k \middle| -\right) \sim Beta\left(a/k + \sum_{i=1}^{N_B} z_{ik}, b\left(K-1\right)/K + N_B - \sum_{i=1}^{N_B} z_{ik}\right)$$

Figure 7. Example of inpainting results

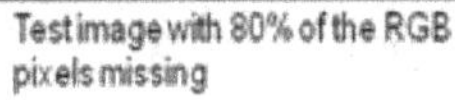

Test image with 80% of the RGB pixels missing

Results of inpainting after 64 rounds of learning (PSNR = 28.66 dB)

Original uncontaminated image

is properly matched, and (*iii*) our BP approach. For (*iii*) a non-informative prior is placed on the noise precision, and the same BP model is run for all three noise levels (with the underlying noise levels inferred). The BP and K-SVD employed no *a priori* training data. A preset large dictionary size $K = 256$ is used in both K-SVD and our algorithms. For the BP results, we inferred that approximately M = 219, 143, and 28 dictionary elements were important for noise standard deviations 15, 25, and 50, respectively; the remaining elements of the dictionary were used less than 0.1% of the time. As seen within the bottom portion of the right part of Figure 8, the unused dictionary elements appear as random draws from the prior. Note that K-SVD works well when the set noise variance is at or near truth. However, our proposed BP approach is robust to changing noise levels. Quantitative performance is summarized in Table 1. The BP de-noiser estimates a full posterior density function on the noise standard deviation. For the examples considered here, the modes of the inferred standard-deviation posteriors were 15.52, 25.33, and 48.13, for true standard deviations 15, 25, and 50, respectively.

In summary, the above described dictionary or bases learning approach can be used to represent different sensory data – visual, audio, etc. – succinctly, similar to the V1 region. From this we can build up a hierarchy and model areas V2, V4 and IT of the visual processing pathway of the neo-cortex. For this, a graphical approach based on a hierarchical Bayesian network has been developed in (Lee & Mumford, 2003; Dean, Caroll, & Washington, 2007). In the next section we provide the overview of that work.

3. HIERARCHICAL GRAPHICAL MODELS OF VISUAL PROCESSING OF THE VENTRAL STREAM

The basic concepts that are used in developing the Bayesian network based graphical models described below are: 1. The regions of the visual pathway V1, V2, V4 and IT are connected both bottom up and top down (i.e., there is feedback

Figure 8. Results of de-noising using the K-SVD algorithm and our BP algorithm. Left: Representative de-noising results, with the top through bottom rows corresponding to noise standard deviations of 15, 25 and 50, respectively. The second and third columns represent K-SVD results with assumed standard deviation equal to 30 and the ground truth, respectively. The fourth column represents the proposed BP reconstructions. The original noisy images are in the first column. Right: Inferred BP dictionary elements (mean from the posterior) for noise standard deviation 25, in order of importance from the top-left.

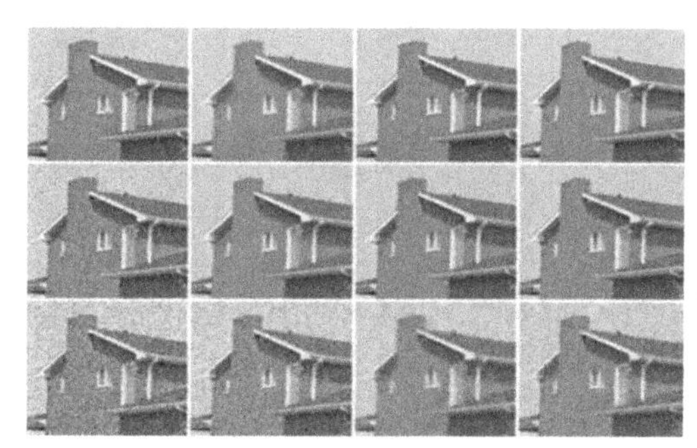

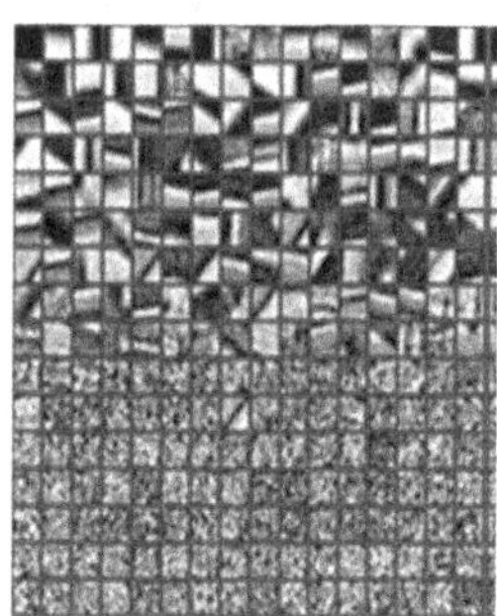

from the one region to the other); 2. The neurons associated with each region can be represented as graphical nodes; 3. The information processed by neurons can be represented in a probabilistic way (i.e., non-deterministic); 4. There are time durations associated with each neuron which relate to different levels of details of processing information.

If v_1, v_2, v_3, v_4 represent four cortical areas in the visual pathway – V1, V2, V4 and IT and if x_0 is the observed data then the joint probability distribution equation relating to these four regions is:

$$P\left(x_0, v_1, v_2, v_3, v_4\right) = P\left(\left(x_0|v_1\right)\right)P\left(\left(v_1|v_2\right)\right)P\left(\left(v_3|v_2\right)\right)P\left(\left(v_3|v_4\right)\right)P\left(v_4\right).$$

In the above equation it is assumed that in the sequence (x_0, v_1, v_2, v_3, v_4) each variable is independent of the other variables given its immediate neighbor in the sequence (i.e., a first order Markov process). The above equation results in a graphical model or a Bayesian network. The activity in the ith region is influenced by the bottom-up feed-forward data v_{i-1} and top-down probabilistic priors representing feedback from region v_{i+1}. This is shown pictorially in Figure 9.

Each region in the above figure can be modeled graphically as a subnet with k nodes, and each subnet can be connected hierarchically as shown in Figures 10a & 10b below. In these two Figures z_i corresponds to nodes (representing neurons) in region v_1, y_i nodes in region v_2 and x_i nodes in region v_3.

The time duration - t, t-LΔ(L = 1,2 ...) in each of these subnets is modeled using embedded hidden Markov models as shown in Figure 11 below. By inserting these models within subnets one can account for the possibility that the inter slice duration can vary among subnets. This results in a spatially extended version of a hierarchical hidden Markov model (Fine, Singer, & Tishby, 1998).

The model parameters are learned and inferencing is carried out on the subnet graph in two passes using a variant of generalized belief propagation. For the details readers are referred to (Yedidia, Freeman, & Weiss, 2003). This hierarchical representation and inferencing can be used in describing and understanding or interpreting images similar to the human visual processing pathway as shown in Figure 12.

In (Jin & Geman, 2006) the authors have used this type of hierarchical graphical model approach for the application of recognizing license plates

Figure 9. Mathematical representation of the relationship between four regions of the visual processing of ventral stream ("what pathway")

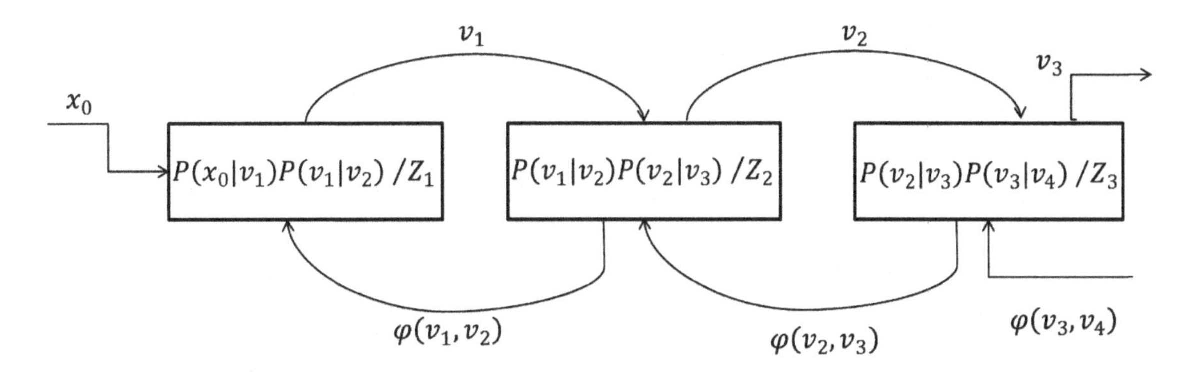

Figure 10. Hierarchical Bayesian graphical model and decomposition into tractable sub-structures: (a) One stage; (b) multiple stages

(a)

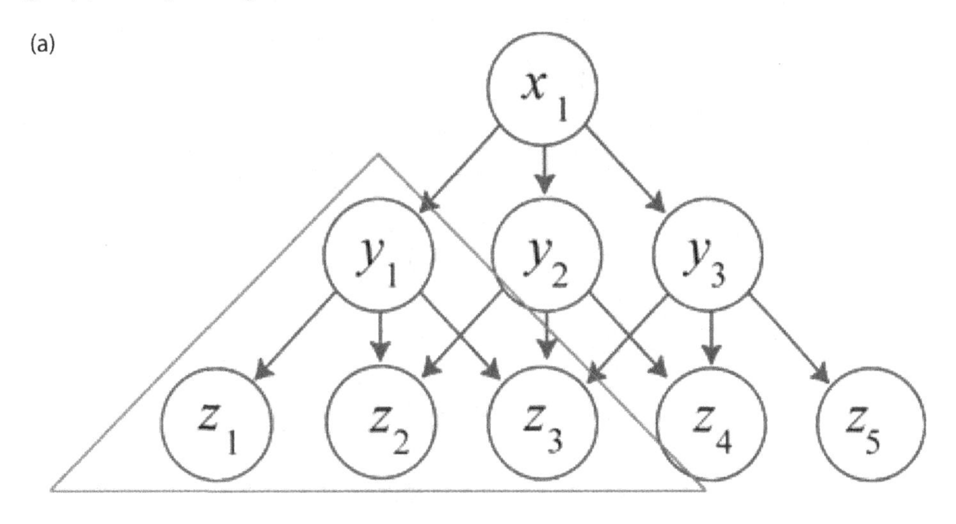

(b)

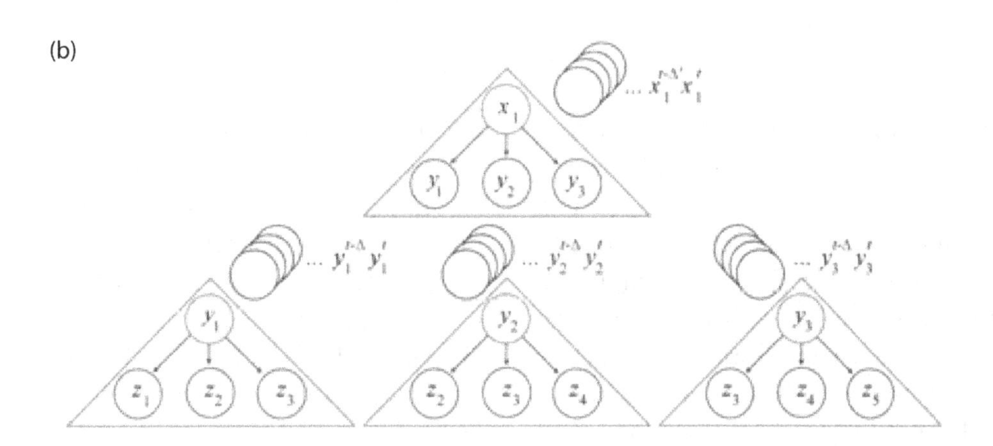

Figure 11. Embedded hidden Markov models

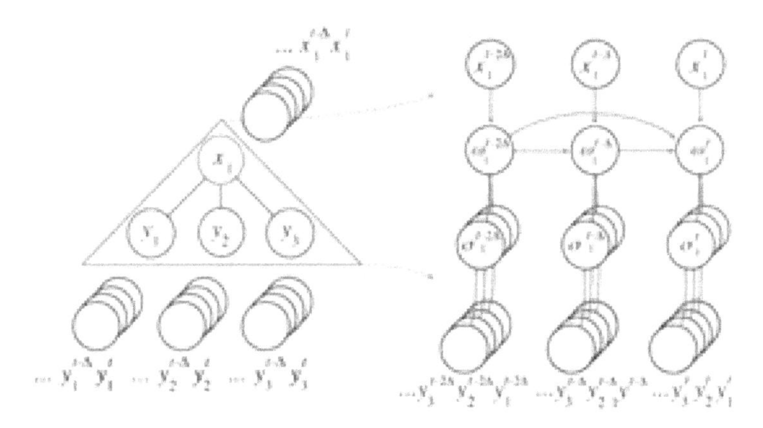

Figure 12. Example of an application of hierarchical models for image understanding/interpretation

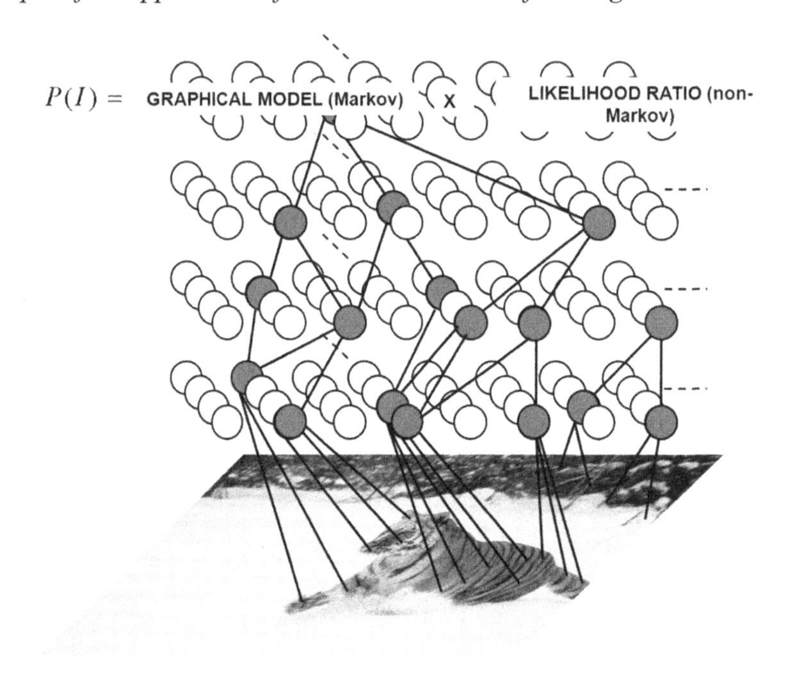

with 95% accuracy. An example hierarchical model of a license plate is as shown in Figure 13.

Instead of the above described subnet and embedded hidden Markov models, the hierarchical abstractions can also be modeled similar to the V1 region as described in Section 2 and can be learned using either our learning approach or the one described in (Elad & Aharon, 2006) at each level. An example of learned features or dictionary at V2 using the approach in (Elad & Aharon, 2006) is as shown in Figure 14 below.

In this example, V1 detects edges which are the most basic elements of images. In V2 edges are aggregated to learn more complex concepts.

To implement the above described hierarchical models with a large number of nodes to approximate the processing of the visual cortex to some extent there is a need for at least 60 dual core

Figure 13. Example of an application of hierarchical models for license plate recognition

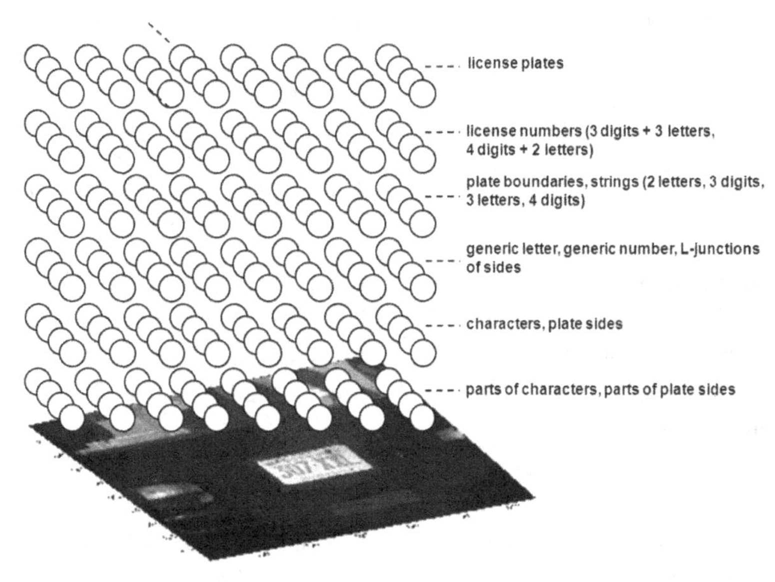

Figure 14. Example of an application of same learning algorithm of V1 at V2

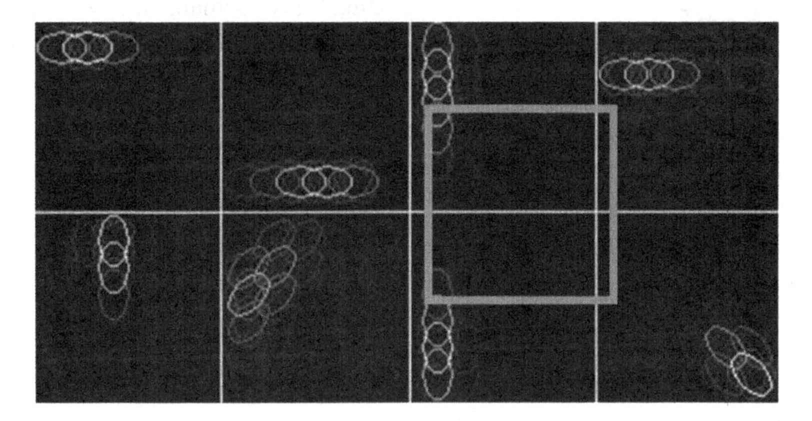

computing nodes each with 8 Gigabytes of shared memory. This should not be a problem now with the availability of cloud computing.

4. CONCLUSION

In this chapter, we have provided a brief description of the mammalian visual cortex and visual processing pathway. We have also shown how mathematical foundations can be developed based on some understanding of how the neo-cortex processes sensory data. These mathematical foundations are based on dictionary or basis learning and on hierarchical Bayesian graphical modeling and embedded hidden Markov modeling. We have demonstrated the applicability of dictionary learning in processing images by filling in the missing pixels and enhancing noisy images. Some of the applications of hierarchical Bayesian graphical models – image interpretation/understanding and license plate recognition are also provided in this chapter. Furthermore, we have shown how the same learning algorithm can be used in succinctly representing audio signals. These results suggest that it is possible to approximate the way in which the neo-cortex processes multi-sensory data. The techniques described in this chapter are promising and seem to be a step in the right direction even though it is a very hard problem (orders of magnitude) to approximate the brain's learning, understanding and inferring algorithms for the applications such as computer vision or automatic speech recognition that the mammalian brain excels at. With the availability of cloud computing it should be possible to implement large networks of the type described in the previous section, if not the same size as 10^{14} synapses of the human brain. Hence, it seems possible that in the near future we will be able to mimic at least some learning and inferring aspects of the human brain.

ACKNOWLEDGMENT

The work on BP based basis learning and its application to inpaiting and denosing that are described in this chapter is a collaboration with Prof. Lawrence Carin, Duke University, Durham, NC. I would like to acknowledge his help and contribution to this technology.

REFERENCES

Beal, M. J. (2003). *Variational algorithms for approximate Bayesian inference.* PhD thesis, Gatsby Computational Neuroscience Unit, University College London, 2003.

Dean, T., Caroll, G., & Washington, R. (2007). *On the prospects for building a working model of the visual cortex.* American Association for Artificial Intelligence.

Duarte-Carvajalino, J. M., & Sapiro, G. (2008). Learning to sense sparse signals: Simultaneous sensing matrix and sparsifying dictionary optimization. *IMA Preprint Series*, 2211.

Elad, M., & Aharon, M. (2006). Image denoising via sparse and redundant representations over learned dictionaries. *IEEE Transactions on Image Processing*, 15.

Ferguson, T. (1973). A Bayesian analysis of some nonparametric problems. *Annals of Statistics.* doi:10.1214/aos/1176342360

Fine, S., Singer, Y., & Tishby, N. (1998). The hierarchical hidden Markov model: Analysis and applications. *Machine Learning, 32*(1), 41–62. doi:10.1023/A:1007469218079

Hawkins, J., & Blakeslee, S. (2004). *On intelligence.* Times Books.

Hinton, G. (n.d.). The next generation of neural networks. Retrieved from www.cs.toronto.edu/~hinton/talks/msr10.ppt

Jin, Y., & Geman, S. (2006). Context and hierarchy in a probabilistic image model, In *IEEE international Conference on Computer Vision and Pattern Recognition,* Vol. 2.

Lee, T. S., & Mumford, D. (2003). Hierarchical Bayesian inference in the visual cortex. *Journal of the Optical Society of America, 2*(7), 1434–1448.

Mairal, J., Bach, F., Ponce, J., & Sapiro, G. (2009). Online dictionary learning for sparse coding. In *Proceedings of the International Conference on Machine Learning.*

Mairal, J., Elad, M., & Sapiro, G. (2008). Sparse representation for color image restoration. *IEEE Transactions on Image Processing*, 17.

Milner, A. D. (1992). Separate pathways for perception and action. *Trends in Neurosciences, 15*(1), 20–25. doi:10.1016/0166-2236(92)90344-8

Mountcastle, V. (1978). The unit model and the distributed system. In Edelman, G. M., & Mountcastle, V. B. (Eds.), *The mindful brain.* MIT Press.

Olushen, B. A., & Field, D. J. (1996). Emergence of simple –cell receptive field properties by learning a sparse code for natural images. *Nature, 381*, 607–609. doi:10.1038/381607a0

Paisley, J., & Carin, L. (2009). Nonparametric factor analysis with beta process priors. In *Proceedings of the International Conference on Machine Learning*.

Raina, R., Battle, A., Lee, H., Packer, B., & Ng, A. Y. (2007). Self-taught learning: Transfer learning from unlabeled data. In *Proceedings of the International Conference on Machine Learning*.

Ranzato, M., Poultney, C., Chopra, S., & Lecun, Y. (2006). Efficient learning of sparse representations with an energy-based model. In *Proceedings of the Neural Information Processing Systems*.

Roe, A. W., Pallaqb, S. L., Kwon, Y. H., & Sur, M. (1992). Visual projections routed to the auditory pathway in ferrets: Receptive fields of visual neurons in primary auditory cortex. *The Journal of Neuroscience, 12*(g), 3651-3664

Sadato, N., Pascual-Leone, A., & Grafman, J. (1996). Activation of the primary visual cortex by Braille reading in blind subjects. *Nature, 380*, 526–528. doi:10.1038/380526a0

Thibaux, R., & Jordan. (2007). *Hierarchical beta processes and the Indian buffet process*. In International Conference on Artificial Intelligence and Statistics.

Tibshirani, R. (1996). Regression shrinkage and selection via the lasso. *Journal of the Royal Statistical Society. Series B. Methodological, 58*, 267–288.

Yedidia, J. S., Freeman, W. T., & Weiss, Y. (2003). Understanding belief propagation and its generalizations. In Lakemeyer, G., & Nebel, B. (Eds.), *Exploring artificial intelligence in the new millennium* (pp. 239–269). San Francisco, CA: Morgan Kaufmann Publishers.

Section 4
Artificial Vision Systems

Chapter 11
Visual Behavior Based Bio-Inspired Polarization Techniques in Computer Vision and Robotics

Abd El Rahman Shabayek
Université de Bourgogne, France

Olivier Morel
Université de Bourgogne, France

David Fofi
Université de Bourgogne, France

ABSTRACT

For long time, it was thought that the sensing of polarization by animals is invariably related to their behavior, such as navigation and orientation. Recently, it was found that polarization can be part of a high-level visual perception, permitting a wide area of vision applications. Polarization vision can be used for most tasks of color vision including object recognition, contrast enhancement, camouflage breaking, and signal detection and discrimination. The polarization based visual behavior found in the animal kingdom is briefly covered. Then, the authors go in depth with the bio-inspired applications based on polarization in computer vision and robotics. The aim is to have a comprehensive survey highlighting the key principles of polarization based techniques and how they are biologically inspired.

INTRODUCTION

Bio-inspiration is an established concept which is developing to meet the needs of many applications, particularly in machine vision. Polarization vision is one of the most important biological features in the animal kingdom. A broad range of applications has been inspired by it. What is polarization? Polarization is the phenomenon that describes the oscillations of orientation in light (or other radiation) waves which are restricted in direction (Goldstein, 2003). Light's vector orienta-

DOI: 10.4018/978-1-4666-2539-6.ch011

tion can be surprisingly weakly detected by some humans with their naked eyes (Haidinger, 1844), but humans need the help of polarizing optics to visualize most invisible polarization effects (Green, Ohmann, Leininger, & Kavanaugh, 2010).

Many fish, cephalopods, crustaceans, insects, and other animals are capable of perceiving polarized light (Horváth & Varjú, 2004). Most animal photoreceptors are able to differentially react to partially linearly polarized light (Goldsmith, 1975; Nilsson & Warrant, 1999; Waterman, 1981; Wehner, 2001). The photoreceptors of ish (Hawryshyn, 1992) and birds (Phillips & Waldvogel, 1988) respond to polarized light patterns and hence are able to analyze linear polarization (Cronin et al., 2003).

Firstly, we will briefly cover the polarization based visual behavior in the animal kingdom, especially behaviors that can be mapped directly to the machine vision world such as orientation and navigation, water and transparent object detection, camouflage breaking, and communication. Secondly, a comprehensive review of polarization-inspired machine vision applications will be given. Finally, future research directions in bio-inspired machine vision applications based on polarization will be discussed.

The main part of the chapter will go into details regarding bio-inspired polarization techniques in robotics applications. We start with a short survey of how to visualize polarization information. Then a detailed complete survey of robot orientation and navigation techniques based on polarization will be given due to their importance to computer vision and robotics communities and ongoing research. A comprehensive survey of underwater polarization vision is also given due to the challenging problem of enhancing vision underwater and how it is greatly improved using polarization. A moderate survey of communication (few methods are clearly bio-inspired) and camouflage breaking techniques based on polarization are then covered. Finally, examples of general computer vision techniques based on polarization are mentioned.

Our objective is to give a overview of polarization applications in computer vision and robotics, especially the bio-inspired polarization dependent techniques in order to have comprehensive coverage of such an important and active area of research.

POLARIZATION BASED VISUAL BEHAVIOR IN THE ANIMAL KINGDOM

Orientation and Navigation

Sky polarization patterns are used by many insects for navigation. Honeybees use celestial polarization to move between the hive and foraging locations (Cronin et al., 2003; Rossel,1989; Wehner, 2001). Cataglyphis ants (Cronin et al., 2003) and nocturnal ball-rolling dung beetle (Dacke, Byrne, Baird, Scholtz, & Warrant, 2011) use the sun and moon, respectively, celestial polarization for similar tasks. See Figure 1.

Salmon fishes (Figure 1) may have a similar ability (Hawryshyn, 1992), which allows them to orient in underwater light fields (Novales & Hawryshyn, 1997). Light reflection from water surfaces results in horizontally polarized light which is utilized by water beetles and other insects for orientation. (Schwind, 1983; Schwind, 1984; Schwind, 1991).

Water and Transparent Object Detection

Water surfaces can be discriminated from virtual surfaces (like mirages) by flying insects using their polarization vision ability (Horváth & Wehner, 1997; Cronin et al., 2003). Reflected polarized light is used by aquatic insects such as dragonflies, mayflies, and backswimmers to detect calm water surfaces (Horváth & Varjú 2004). (Lythgoe & Hemmings, 1967) were the first to propose enhancing the visibility of transparent targets in

Figure 1. Polarization in the animal kingdom

water using polarization. It was found that there are some objects which strongly reflect polarized light underwater (Cronin & Shashar, 2001; Cronin et al., 2003). It is has been proven that squids and their relatives see obscure objects using polarized light (Shashar, Adessi, & Cronin, 1995, Shashar, Milbury, & Hanlon, 2002).

Camouflage Breaking

Camouflage is a tool to defeat visual detection by predators. (Lythgoe & Hemmings, 1967) proposed that polarization could be used to detect well-camouflaged targets in water. Polarization vision helps to detect transparent preys (Shashar, Hanlon, & Petz, 1998). Cephalopods (squid, cuttlefish, and octopus) can produce a variety of body patterns for camouflage using their optically malleable skin that contains neutrally controlled pigmented chromatophores as well as structural light reflectors. Some of these cephalopods are able to see camouflaged objects (Hanlon & Messenger, 1996; Shashar & Hanlon, 1997; Shashar et al. 1998; Shashar, Hagan, Boal, & Hanlon, 2000). (Mäthger, & Hanlon, 2006) have shown that the polarized aspect of iridescent color in squid skin produces highly dynamically changeable camouflaged patterns.

Communication

Polarization patterns are used for signaling by some animals. Some of these signals are controlled by the reflection of linearly polarized light. Forest butterflies use their wings as identifying markers by utilizing their polarization-dependent reflectivity (Sweeney, Jiggins, & Johnsen, 2003; Douglas, Cronin, Chiou, & Dominy, 2007). Males appear to recognize females based on these markers (Sweeney et al., 2003; Cronin et al., 2003; Douglas et al., 2007).

Although spectral irradiance varies strongly underwater with depth, signal constancy is stable and predictable thanks to polarization (Ivanoff & Waterman, 1958). Linked to specific communications, polarized light is strongly reflected from many stomatopod species' body parts that are specialized for that kind of reflection (Cronin et al., 2003). Polarized-light signals and color signals are used in much the same way by mantis shrimps (Cronin et al., 2003). Cephalopods can produce body patterns for signaling using their skin which contains controlled pigmented chromatophores and structural light reflectors (Hanlon & Messenger, 1996).

POLARIZATION-INSPIRED MACHINE VISION APPLICATIONS

It is clear that the polarized patterns seen by some animals have an important impact on image formation as they are significant image features within the animals' visual fields. These significant polarized features can be transferred to the computer world leading tonumerous biologically inspired applications in camera technology, image formation, computer vision and robotics. Many researchers have already made use of polarization features in nature inspired artificial vision techniques e.g (Lambrinos et al. 1997; Goldstein, 2000; Taylor & wolff 2001; Furukawa & Sakamoto 2010). Some of the current applications which imitate the natural animal behavior are found in robot orientation and navigation, camouflage breaking, communication, and underwater vision. Scene segmentation and object detection, recognition, and tracking are also active research areas e.g (Ben-Ezra2000; Ahmad, & Takakura, 2007; Terrier, Devlaminck, & Charbois, 2008; Subramaniam, & Hancock, 2010; Shabayek, Demonceaux, Morel, & Fofi, 2012).

There are many applications that utilize polarization but are not biologically inspired (e.g. camera calibration, fiber optics communication, etc). Therefore these methods are beyond the scope of this chapter, however, a section will be dedicated to list different examples of polarization based applications in computer vision. This chapter mainly covers methods that imitate animal's behavior.

Visualizing Polarization Information

Polarization-Difference Imaging (PDI) inspired by polarization vision of certain animal species was introduced by (Rowe, Pugh, Tyo, & Engheta, 1995). They demonstrated that PDI techniques may facilitate target detection in scattering media even if targets show very weak polarization or are located far from the optical setup (Wehner, 1987; Lin, Yemelyanov, Pugh, & Engheta, 2004; Rowe et al., 1995).

In order to represent polarization without affecting other visual information such as color and brightness, special sensory substitution forms are required. (Yemelyanov, Lo, Pugh, & Engheta, 2003; Yemelyanov, Lin, Luis, Pugh, & Engheta, 2003) investigated several bio-inspired representational methodologies for mapping polarization information into visual cues readily perceived by the human visual system. The visual cues and strategies they explored were a) using coherently moving dots superimposed on image to represent various range of polarization signals, b) overlaying textures with spatial and/or temporal signatures to isolate image regions with differing polarization, c) modulating luminance and/or scene color contrast in terms of certain aspects of polarization values, and d) fusing polarization images into intensity-only images. (Yemelyanov et al., 2003) tried to determine which mappings are most suitable for specific applications such as object detection, navigation, sensing, scene classification, and surface deformation. (Lin et al., 2004) proposed to use these visual cues to enhance visual surveillance techniques using polarization.

Robot Orientation and Navigation

Many researchers have made theoretical and experimental investigations on skylight polarization for autonomous orientation and navigation. The sky is polarized due to the scattering of sunlight by particles and air molecules in the atmosphere. Sky polarization patterns present us with polarization information which can be used as an external compass. The location of the sun mainly determines the celestial skylight polarization pattern. It is visible and stable even in open sky patches when the sun is occluded by clouds, and it also appears beneath dark objects in air that is illuminated by the sun (Pomozi, Horváth, & Wehner, 2001; Suhai & Horváth, 2004). The benefit of using the skylight polarization pattern, rather than directly using the sun is that only patches of sky are sufficient for orientation task (Cronin, Warrant, & Greiner, 2006; Wu, Gao, Fan, & Xie, 2010).

Firstly, orientation techniques using photodiodes as a primary sensor to read polarization data will be covered. Secondly, as camera technology has become less expensive and more advanced, new techniques using CCD, CMOS, and/or Fish-eye lens to obtain polarization information will be covered. Thirdly, water and mud detection for off-road navigation will be covered. Methods that require a rotating polarizer as a primary optic combined with the mentioned sensors will be explained.

Sensors USING Photodiodes

Inspired by the basic biological neuronal circuit, (Lambrinos et al. 1997; Lambrinos et al. 1998; Möller, Lambrinos, Pfiefer, Labhart, & Wehner, 1998; Lambrinos, Möller, Labhart, Pfeifer, & Wehner, 2000) have developed polarization-opponent units (POL- OP units) as input devices that are functionally similar to the POL-neurons found in insects. Each POL-OP unit consists of a pair of polarized light sensors (POL-sensors) followed by a log-ratio amplifier. POL-sensors are explained in Table 1.

There are two models to obtain compass direction from the POL-OP responses: a) scanning models and b) simultaneous models. Scanning models (Lambrinos et al. 1997) are explained in Table 2.

In contrast, the heading direction can be determined continuously and no scanning movements are necessary in a simultaneous model. (Lambrinos et al. 2000) implemented a simultaneous model which does not require a lookup table, but uses an analytical procedure to derive compass information from the values of the POL-OP units. The change in the polarization pattern during the day has to be taken into account. This can be done by either regularly updating the lookup table or by normalizing the outputs of the POL-OP units as explained in Table 3.

(Chu, Zhao, Zhang, & Wang, 2007a; Chu, Zhao, Wang & Zhang, 2007b; Chu, Zhao, Zhang, & Wang, 2008; Chu, Wang, Chen, & Li, 2009; Zhao, Chu, Wang, & Zhang, 2009) have a bionic navigation sensor which is similar to (Lambrinos et al. 1997; Lambrinos et al. 1998; Möller et al. 1998; Lambrinos et al. 2000) with the same POL-OP unit (see Figure 2) and used the same mathematical formulation. Their design is explained in Table 4.

Chu et al. simulated their design in Simulink® and analyzed the output error. Then outdoor experiments were carried out.

All outdoor experiments performed by (Lambrinos et al. 1997; Lambrinos et al. 1998; Möller et al. 1998; Lambrinos et al. 2000) and (Chu et al. 2007a; Chu et al. 2007b; Chu et al. 2008; Chu et al. 2009; Zhao et al. 2009) proved to have high accuracy in obtaining directional information from polarization and the error is independent of the traveling distance.

Table 1. Polarized light sensors (POL-sensors)

	POL-sensors
1	The POL-sensors consisted of photodiodes with a linear polarizer and a blue transmitting filter on the top.
	o In each POL-OP unit, the polarizing axis of one POL-sensor was adjusted 90° to the polarizing axis of the other sensor, thus mimicking the crossed-analyzer configuration in the POL-area of insect eyes.
2	The signals of each pair of POL-sensors were fed into a log ratio amplifier.
3	The three pairs of POL-sensors were mounted on a mobile robot and adjusted such that the polarizing axis of the positive channel was 0°, 60° and 120° (similar to the insect layout) with respect to the robot's body axis. The visual fields of the POL-OP units are about 60° and are centered on the zenith.

Table 2. Scanning models (Lambrinos et al. 1997)

	Scanning Models **The agent has to:**
1	find the solar meridian to use it as a reference direction 0° for its proprioceptive system.
	o To that it has to actively scan the sky by rotating around its vertical body axis.
	o When the output signal of one POL-OP unit (or a combination of multiple POL-OP units) reaches its maximum, the robot is known to be aligned with the solar meridian.
2	use proprioceptive information to find its heading direction based on the solar meridian.
3	obtain the compass direction by comparing the current output values of the POL-OP units with a lookup table that associates the output values of the POL-OP units with the corresponding orientation of the robot.
4	record the lookup table before each experiment by a single 360° rotation of the robot.

Table 3. Simultaneous models (Lambrinos et al. 2000)

	Simultaneous model **normalizing the outputs of the POL-OP units**
1	The POL-OP signals are delogarithmized by applying a sigmoid function.
2	Find the two candidate orientations (an ambiguity of π exists) from the equation derived in (Lambrinos et al. 2000) $\phi = \frac{1}{2}\arctan\frac{\bar{p}_1(\phi) + 2\bar{p}_2(\phi) - \frac{3}{2}}{\sqrt{3}(\bar{p}_1(\phi) - \frac{1}{2})}$ where $\bar{p}_i$ is the delogarithmized sensors' output and *i=1,2, or 3.*
3	Solve the ambiguity by employing a set of ambient-light sensors on the robot.
	o The values from eight ambient-light sensors, arranged in two half-circles covering a visual field of 180°, are used to obtain a rough estimate of the robot's heading with respect to the sun (ambient-light sensors with the visual field enclosing the solar meridian will have a stronger response).
4	Transform the current POL-OP readings to signals that are independent of the degree of polarization as shown in (Lambrinos et al. 2000).

Figure 2. Diagrammatic description of POL OP unit (Adapted from Lambrinos et al., 2000; Chu et al., 2007)

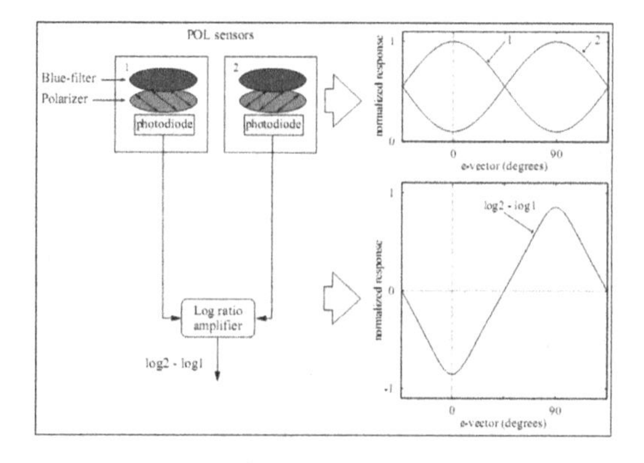

Table 4. Bionic navigation sensor design (Chu et al.)

	Bionic navigation sensor design
1	Three polarization direction analyzers whose polarizing axis of the positive channel is adjusted to 60° difference from one to one.
	Each one consists of two POL-sensors which have the shape of regular triangular prisms (total of six sensors).
	For each direction analyzer, the polarizing axis of one POL-sensor was adjusted 90° to the polarizing axis of the other sensor.
2	A POL-OP unit consists of a pair of POL-sensors and a log-ratio amplifier.
	The log-ratio amplifier receives input from the two POL-sensors and delivers the difference of their logarithmized signals (exactly the same idea technique of Lambrinos et al).
3	The three direction analyzers are mounted on a base plate.
4	Six ambient-light sensors are arranged in a ring and mounted in the metal cylinder of the six POL-sensors.
	Each ambient-light sensor consists of standard photoresistors with blue filter in front.

Table 5. Mimicking polarization vision in the head of a dragonfly called Hemianax Papuensis (Chahl & Mizutani, 2010)

	Polarization sensor in the mimicked head of a dragonfly called Hemianax Papuensis
1	It used three photodiodes each with their own optics and polarization filters.
	o The output of the photodiode amplifiers was digitized and processed on a microcontroller.
	o Each photodiode had a voltage bias and gain that required calibration.
2	(Chahl & Mizutani, 2010) considered the direction computation from three samples from an assembly of diode, filter, and amplifier at known angles (0°, 60°, and 120°) relative to the orientation of the polarization axis of the polarization filter.

In (Schmolke & Mallot, 2002), the performance of the path integration without external reference is compared with the performance using a polarization compass. As a proprioceptive estimate, wheel revolutions were used in both cases. The experiments were carried out using a Khepera miniature robot. They found that the e-vector (the observed regular pattern across the entire celestial hemisphere formed by the directions of polarization) compass was more accurate.

(Chahl & Mizutani, 2010) developed two biomimetic sensors and made flight tests for stabilization and navigation of an aircraft using the spatial, polarization, and spectral distribution of light in the environment. They tried to mimic the head of a dragonfly called Hemianax Papuensis. Here we only consider the polarization sensor which is explained in Table 5.

Each photodetector response to incident light in terms of voltage v is $v=b+ P.F +q$, which includes the response to unpolarized light q and a bias term b which is due to the electronics. The sensor response to the polarized component of the light is given by the dot product $P\cdot F$ where F is a column vector representing the orientation of the polarization axis of the filter and P is a row vector representing the direction and magnitude of the incident polarized light. To eliminate electronic and optical biases (b and q) the difference between the responses of the three samples v_1 to v_3 was taken. Solving for P gives:

$$P^T = \begin{bmatrix} v_1 - v_2 \\ v_1 - v_3 \end{bmatrix} \begin{bmatrix} F_1 - F_2 & F_1 - F_3 \end{bmatrix}^{-1}$$

where F_1-F_2 is a column vector.

This solution assumes a calibrated system. To test their sensor, a remotely piloted aircraft was instrumented with a calibrated polarimeter and attitude reference that included a magnetic compass. The flight was run early in the morning when the sun was low. The polarization compass produced a discontinuity several times during the flight as the solution passed through 180°. There were minor differences between the two measures. They concluded that the absence of any correction for attitude probably contributed to most deviation between the magnetic and north-aligned polarization heading.

CCD, Fisheye and CMOS Sensors

(Usher, Ridley, & Corke, 2001) proposed to perceive sky polarization pattern using a color CCD video camera and a linear polarizing film as a filter. The blue component was used for analysis as the sunlight polarization is most apparent at UV and blue wavelengths (350-450 nm). They smoothed all images by using a 2D Gaussian function to overcome the poor response at these short wavelengths. Two images were taken at a time, with the second image having its polarizing filter axis orthogonal to the first. Taking a set of images, they modeled the response as $f(\Phi) = K[1 + d\cos(2\Phi)]$ where K is a scaling factor dependent on camera shutter settings and ambient conditions, d is the degree of polarization, Φ is the orientation of the polarizing filter with respect to the solar meridian (line connection the zenith and the sun), and $f(\Phi)$ is the mean intensity of an image. Their model had the same form for the photosensitive diodes of (Lambrinos et al. 2000). Their initial experiments proved that it is possible to locate the solar meridian using a digital camera applying the scanning method of (Lambrinos et al. 1997) and hence extracting a reference bearing from an arbitrary orientation.

The mentioned methods simulate insect strategy by taking advantage of the skylight polarization through single numerical values rather than patterns. (Wu et al., 2010) presented a method to obtain navigation orientations by gradient vectors of skylight polarization maps even if the sun is invisible or occluded by clouds. The maps were provided by a zenith centered imaging polarimeter with a narrow field of view. The imaging polarimeter was constructed by a sensitive industrial CCD camera (Daheng-SV1400FC) with a short focus lens (LM6NCL) and a linearly polarizing filter (DHC-GCL-05). Assisted by a compass and gradienter, the imaging polarimeter was kept horizontal with the local sea level so its field of view center was adjusted to the zenith of the sky area during the experiments. Then the linear polarizer mounted in front of the objective lens was rotated. For a given sky area, four images were taken by rotating the linear polarizer to four different relative positions (0°, 45°, 90°, and 135°) following the method in (Lee, 1998). They estimated the solar azimuth by searching the maximum attenuation gradient vector among different azimuths relative to the zenith in the degree of polarization (DOP) map or the symmetrical axis in the angle of polarization (AOP) map, making use of the attenuation from zenith to horizon along the local meridian in the DOP maps and the symmetrical distribution of AOP along the local meridian. They concluded that the skylight polarization maps are able to supply stable solar azimuth information and if aided by calendar (insect circadian clock), the real body orientation could be located.

In (Sarkar, Bello, Hoof, & Theuwissen, 2010a; Sarkar, Bello, Hoof, & Theuwissen, 2010b; Sarkar, Bello, Hoof, & Theuwissen, 2010c; Sarkar, Bello, Hoof, & Theuwissen, 2010d) a polarization analyzing CMOS image sensor was proposed. It is able to sense polarization information in real time using a metallic wire grid micro-polarizer oriented in various directions on top of the pixel. The DOP and AOP can be computed using three intensity images (0°, 45°, and 90°) using the Stokes parameters as in (Malacara, 1989; Gerhart & Matchko, 2002; Damask, 2005), the variations of which can be used as compass clues. The image sensor consists of an array of 128x128 pixels, occupies an area of 5x4 mm^2, and it has been designed and fabricated in a 180 nm CMOS process. They concluded that the computed polarization information can be used as a clue for autonomous robot navigation.

Unlike previous investigations, (Miyazaki, Ammar, Kawakami, & Ikeuchi, 2009) analyzed sky polarization patterns with the fisheye lens. They have tilted the measurement system based on a fisheye lens, a CCD camera, and a linear polarizer, in order to analyze the transition of the 180° sky polarization patterns while tilting. The used is similar to one described in (Pomozi et al. 2001; Hegedüs, Åkesson, & Horváth, 2007). Three photographs were taken for three different alignments (0°, 45°, and 90°) of the transmission axis of the polarizer clockwise from the top view of the camera. Their main contribution was to analyze the sky polarization patterns when the camera was tilted from the horizon. They presented a method to determine the solar meridian orientation from photos taken outdoors, while only a small part of the sky was available and the camera sensor was not horizontal. Therefore, the orientation of the camera could be determined from the solar meridian.

Water and Mud Detection for Off-Road Navigation

Water and mud detection based on polarization depends on the physical principle that the light reflected from the water surface is partially linearly polarized and the polarization phases of them are more similar than those from the surrounding scenes. These hazards can be detected by comparing polarization degree and similarity of the polarization phases. There is a comparison between different approaches of water and mud hazards detection in (Matthies, Bellutta, & Mchenry, 2003; Rankin & Matthies, 2008) and a survey in (Iqbal, Morel, & Meriaudeau, 2010).

Icy or wet roads present dangerous situations as there is an increased danger of losing control of the vehicle and the glare from wet roadway may hide path markings and other road features. A polarizing filter can considerably reduce reflections due to the fact that water tends to horizontally polarize reflected light. (Huber et al., 1997) have developed a spectro-polarimetric imager. It is a portable machine vision system that operates at video frame rates. It contains only electronically controllable components, including an imaging acousto-optic tunable filter, a phase retarder, and a standard CCD-based camera. The system operates much like an ordinary CCD camera, except that the spectral and polarimetric content of light to be viewed is electronically controlled using computers. During operation, the host computer sends commands to the controller to select the desired spectral and polarization parameters. They proposed glare reduction and glare detection in which their imaging system could be applied to wet or icy road conditions. Glare reduction works similarly to a polarizing filter inserted in the optical path. However, the phase retarder accomplishes this electronically and can be programmatically enabled and disabled, which is beneficial since an additional filter reduces the overall intensity of the image. For glare detection, they identify horizontally polarized reflections, thereby detecting possible dangerous road conditions. In a computer-assisted driving scenario, this additional information could be used to alert the driver of the danger, or in an autonomous vehicle, the controller could modify its driving habits accordingly.

In (Yamada, Ueda, Horiba, & Sugie, 2001) to discriminate wet road, the ratio between horizontal and vertical polarization image intensity for each pixel was used. This algorithm obtained good discrimination accuracy when applied to highway environment where most of the water reflects the sky. A drawback of this polarization ratio based method is that it becomes imprecise when water reflects other aspects of the environment, which is common in off-road navigation.

(Sarwal, Nett, & Simon, 2004) have made use of two approaches for the detection of small water bodies. The first one requires use of an existing custom camera with three polarization filters (0°, 45°, and 90°) that is intrinsically mounted such that these filters and connected optics view exactly the same scene. The other approach requires the use of three physically distinct cameras mounted with similar optics, running with certain geometric approximations due to the flat-earth assumption. There are pros and cons for each approach. Both approaches used the formulas from (Wolff, 1995).

In order to detect water hazards for autonomous off-road navigation, especially bodies of water that are roofed with tree canopy, (Xie, Xiang, Pan, & Liu, 2007) presented another polarization method based on the similarity between polarization patterns reflected from the water's surface than those from other scenes. Their detection algorithm is based on the comparison of DOP and similarity of the AOP using the formulas from (Wolff, 1995).

In (Pandian, 2008) the author used polarization imaging and stereo vision to detect water hazards for robot navigation. He investigated the conventional single camera polarization imaging setup employing a mechanically rotated polarizer, polarization contrast imaging using two cameras, a three camera setup enabling the complete characterization of partially linearly polarized light, and a four camera setup employing two polarizers with identical orientations. The main challenge in their proposed system was to improve the pixel correspondence across the polarization images. They obtained good results for water detection, however, further in-depth experiments are still required.

Robust mud detection is also a critical perception requirement for autonomous navigation. Mud is highly polarized and hence polarization based techniques can be used. (Rankin, & Matthies, 2008) proposed to use multiple sensors for mud detection including a polarization camera. At a pixel level, partial linear polarization is measured by the radiance transmitted through a polarization filter. To determine the polarization state (orientation, intensity, and DOP), three images of a scene are acquired, each with the polarization filter at a different orientation. To calculate "polarization contrast" as a simplified measurement, only two images are required where the polarization filter orientations differ by 90°. The "polarization contrast" at each pixel can be calculated by dividing the absolute value of the difference between the 0° and 90° intensity values by the sum of them. Regions that have a significantly higher DOP can be a potential cue for water or mud. In the experiments of (Rankin, & Matthies, 2008), two polarization sensors were used: SAMBA and SALSA polarization cameras produced by Bossa Nova Technologies. The SAMBA camera provides a "polarization contrast" image and the SALSA camera provides DOP, intensity, and AOP images.

Underwater Polarization Vision

Underwater imaging is widely used in scientific research and technology. Computer vision methods are used for a variety of applications, such as automated swimming pool life guards, mine detection, inspection of underwater power and telecommunication cables, pipelines, nuclear reactors, research in marine biology, archaeology and mapping.

The underwater polarized light distribution is mainly affected by a) the position of the sun or the moon in the sky, b) the water optical properties, c) the viewing depth, and d) surface reflections (Waterman, 1988; Novales & Hawryshyn, 1997; Cronin & Shashar, 2001; Shashar, Sabbah, & Cronin, 2004). There are two distinct polarization patterns underwater, one inside Snell's window (underwater natural lighting comes from a limited cone above the scene which is caused by the illuminating rays' refraction through the water surface, and is called the optical manhole or Snell's window) and one outside it. Generally, the polarization pattern inside Snell's window in a few meters depths is assumed to be determined by the same factors as those influencing the sky polarization (Waterman, 1988). (Cronin & Shashar, 2001) found small differences between the polarization patterns within Snell's window and outside it. With increasing depth, the polarization pattern simplifies rapidly, tending to become horizontal everywhere (Timofeeva, 1969; Shashar et al., 2004).

(Lerner, Sabbah, Erlick, & Shashar, 2010) found that, only in clear waters, the polarization is correlated with the sun's elevation and the maximum value of the e-vector orientation angle equals the angle of refraction in the horizontal viewing direction. They concluded that navigation by means of underwater polarization is possible under restricted conditions like being in clear waters, mainly near the horizontal viewing direction, and in locations where the sea floor has limited effects on the light's polarization. In underwater vision, the scattering of light largely degrades contrast between the observer and any object observed (Lythgoe & Hemmings, 1967; Wehner, 2001). As a result of the existing horizontal polarization, a vertical analyzer would reduce the amount of scattered light perceived and, hence, would increase contrast.

In order to improve airborne underwater target detection, a proper polarization filter should be selected. This reduces line of sight problems and false alarms. Detection processing by a polarization filter that gives mostly surface related detections can be used to filter the final detection list as proposed in (Crosby & Stetson, 2002). They found that reducing the effect of the surface reflections is possible using a linear horizontal and a linear vertical polarizer. One of them contains surface reflection and one does not. If the system is active, the choice is the image from the polarizer that aligns with the light source. Otherwise (if passive), the linear horizontal polarizer image contains the most surface effects. They chose an algorithm called FX target detection (Crosby, & Riley, 2001) along with the linear polarizers to improve the detection of underwater targets.

The SHallow water Real-time IMagIng Polarimeter (SHRIMP), developed at the Office of Naval Research in 2000, can measure underwater partial polarization imagery (Taylor & Wolff, 2001). This sensor is a passive, three-channel device that concurrently measures the three Stokes vector components needed to find out the partial linear polarization of the scene. The testing of this sensor was completed in 2002 and the data were analyzed in (Taylor, Davis, & Wolff, 2002; Taylor, Davis, & Wolff, 2003). They presented performance results which showed a high probability for detecting the target with a low probability of a false alarm. The tests were done in very shallow water and surf zone regions. Their results support that a) the passive polarization signature is a range dependent quantity that decreases with increased range which does not impact performance greatly, and it is reflective (it is a function of target shape, surface characteristics, and light source level) and b) the polarization magnitude signature is higher for the more turbid water.

(Shashar et al., 2004) studied how polarization signals vary when seen from different distances in water. To check how polarization changes as a function of distance in water, a polarization target was created. The target was set at different locations and types of water (clear and turbid). The target was videotaped over a range of distances with a custom-built underwater imaging polarimeter where the polarizer was rotated automatically at (0°, 45°, and 90°). Images were analyzed based on (Wolff & Andreou, 1995). Based on these measurements, (Shashar et al., 2004) expect that polarization sensitivity will be most useful in a few meters distance for visual tasks in water. It will be much less useful for detecting objects, signals, or structures from far away. Celestial polarization patterns for navigation and orientation are expected to be limited to shallow waters, while solar navigation is possible through a deeper range.

In order to improve underwater visibility, some methods applied image enhancement either by showing the DOP (Rowe et al., 1995; Taylor & wolff 2001) or showing the polarization contrast by subtracting two orthogonal polarization images (Denes, Gottlieb, Kaminsky, & Metes, 1998; Harsdorf, Reuter, & Tönebön, 1999). The previous solutions assumed that polarization is associated with object radiation, rather than the causes which degrade this signal. This assumption is not valid with increasing distance (Morgan, Khong, & Somekh, 1997). In natural illumination, underwater polarization is associated with the visibility disturbance (Können, 1985). The approach in (Schechner & Karpel, 2004; Schechner & Karpel, 2005; Treibitz & Schechner, 2009) uses the captured polarization components using an underwater polarimetric camera (Karpel & Schechner, 2004; Treibitz & Schechner, 2009) to delete that disturbance and inverts the physical model to recover an image similar to the clear visibility appearance. In their methods, they use two images maintaining the same viewing position while varying the polarization filter orientation. (Sarafraz, Negahdaripour & Schechner, 2009) integrate polarization analysis with stereovision by extending the single-camera method in (Treibitz & Schechner, 2006) to a pair of cameras displaced by a finite base line where each camera makes use of a different polarization setting. The stereo disparity and polarization analyses are used to construct enhanced de-scattered views.

(Li & Wang, 2009) propose a method for backscatter rejection where the difference between object and background depolarization characteristics is used to improve image contrast. If the object and the background differ considerably in their depolarization properties, the signal-to-noise ratio (SNR) of the image may increase. (Li & Wang, 2010) propose a polarization image fusion for the intensity (first Stokes component), DOP, and AOP in a false RGB image to enhance the underwater image contrast.

Communication

From a communications perspective, polarization modulation of an optical signal is an old concept that was proposed in (Niblack, & Wolf, 1964). A basic theoretical treatment of a polarization modulation system can be found in (Pratt, 1969; Benedetto & Poggiolini, 1992). The use of light polarization for sending data is common in fiber optic systems (Chow, Kwok, Liu, Tsang, & Chinlon, 2006) and has previously been proposed for free space communications (Uehara, Seto, Ohtsuki, Sasase, & Mori, 1992), but is rarely implemented due to concerns about depolarization in free space communications (Pun, Chan, & Chen, 2005). Intensity modulation schemes are usually implemented and the polarization of the signal is usually ignored. A comparison of intensity and polarization modulation can be found in (Grosinger, 2008) which proved that polarization modulation outperforms intensity modulation.

Due to the high conductivity of seawater, which limits the electromagnetic waves propagation, radio frequency communications in seawater are impractical. Current methods, such as acoustic communication, are limited in bandwidth, data rate, and have a high latency (Heidemann, Ye, Wills, Syed, & Li, 2006). The use of cables is impractical for autonomous vehicles. Optical wireless communications that utilize the blue/green transparency window of seawater offer high bandwidth, short range communications (Hanson, & Radic, 2008).

One useful feature of optical communications is the ability to exploit light beam polarization to differentiate the received signal from backscatter, other transmitters, or surface light. (Cox, Hughes, & Muth, 2009) demonstrate a simple and low-cost system to explore light polarization for underwater communication. The system uses diode lasers and is portable. It consists of a transmitter (which uses two diode lasers mounted to the faces of a polarizing beam splitter (PBS) to combine the orthogonal polarizations) and a receiver (which is constructed using another PBS with two detectors mounted to the faces that detect the imposed modulated data on the orthogonal polarizations). Their work is based on (Cox, Simpson, Domizioli, Muth, & Hughes, 2008).

In (Furukawa & Sakamoto 2010) the authors proposed a communication method using an invisible polarization code which is drawn on the eyes of the robot. A special graphics display for showing expression of robot's eyes was developed. The mobile robots are able to send and receive data, using the invisible polarization code, in order to establish an environment for cooperative robots. The code is a variation of QR (Quick Response) Code which is a kind of 2D symbology developed by Denso Wave in 1994. QR Code contains information in both the vertical and horizontal directions. This QR Code was used to establish the communication between the mobile robots. To embed the invisible polarization code within the displayed data, they used a polarized symbol image to overlap additional data on the display. Their display consists of a conventional LCD panel, an additional liquid crystal (LC) layer and some optics. The LC layers can rotate the direction of the polarization axis according to the applied voltage. The LC layer in the LCD panel is responsible for showing visual data. The additional LC layer changes the direction of polarization from LCD outputs to generate invisible symbol patterns which are horizontal or vertical linear polarized light waves. This difference of orientation creates a binary symbol image. The invisible code can be perceived using a polarizer.

Camouflage Breaking

Polarization has a strong role to play in camouflage breaking specially in remote sensing. Camouflage technology has exposed the conventional remote sensing drawback because the natural background makes the target detection very complicated. Scattering light polarimetric characteristics of camouflaged targets are very different from that of natural backgrounds. Polarimetric imaging can remove the background's influence and improve the inspection efficiency. Compared with reflectance images, polarization images have advantages in camouflage targets detection. Polarimetric imaging has proven to be the most effective approach as it strongly reveals camouflaged targets embedded in complex backgrounds (Egan, 1992; Brun, Jeune, Cariou, & Lotrian, 1992; Weidemann, Fournier, Forand, & Mathieu, 2005; Zhang, Cheng, Chen, & Zheng, 2009a).

In different remote sensing applications, polarimetric techniques were studied to find the optimum polarization for rain cancellation (Tang & Rubin, 1972), to enhance the image visibility of ocean waves (Schuler, Lee, & Hoppel, 1993), and to find optimum polarizations in the bistatic scattering from layered random media (Lee & Mudaliar, 1994). (Dehmollaian & Sarabandi, 2009) tried to find an optimum polarization set that is able to enhance the signal-to-clutter ratio of a foliage-camouflaged stationary target. They employed a genetic algorithm to find optimum polarization configurations which minimize the effect of forests on the backscattered radar cross section response of a camouflaged hard target.

A field study of polarimetric characteristics was done by many researchers. It indicated that polarimetric imaging in hot infrared can eliminate the influence of background and enhance the efficiency of detection. (Goldstein, 2000) tested military coatings on aluminous plates. (Egan & Duggin, 2000; Egan & Duggin, 2002) studied the polarimetric characteristics of aircraft and camouflaged vehicles. (Forssell & Karlsson, 2003) carried out polarimetric experiments on vehicles and (Aron & Gronau, 2005) tents.

In order to set up a portable polarimetric camera, (Cronin, Shashar, & Wolff, 1994) placed two twisted nematic liquid crystals and a fixed polarizing filter in front of a CCD camera. They presented two configurations: an autonomous sensor that uses a small camcorder for recording images; and an on-line sensor that uses a digital camera connected to a personal computer. For the same purpose (Zhang et al., 2009a) used a multispectral CCD polarization camera, a trisection prism to divide the scattering light from targets into three parts, and a polarizer. The simplest polarimetric

Table 6. Examples of the usage of polarization in several computer vision and robotics applications

Application	References
analyze speculiarities	speculiarities (Wolff, 1989; Nayar, Fang, & Boult, 1997; Saito, Sato, Ikeuchi, & Kashiwagi, (1999a; 1999b))
separate transparent and semi-reflected scenes	(Farid, & Adelson, 1999; Schechner, Shamir, & Kiryati, (1999; 2000))
classify materials	(Wolff, 1997; Sarkar2010b)
catadioptric camera calibration and 3D reconstruction	(Morel, Stolz, & Gorria, 2004a ; Morel, Meriaudeau, Stolz, & Gorria, 2005; Atkinson, & Hancock, 2005; Morel, Ferraton, Stolz, & Gorria, 2006; Morel, Stolz, Meriaudeau, & Gorria, 2006; Morel, & Fofi, 2007; Morel, Seulin, & Fofi, (2007a; 2007b; 2008); Shabayek, Morel, & Fofi, (2009; 2010); Shabayek, 2010)
industrial inspection	(Morel, Stolz, & Gorria, 2004b; Morel, Stolz, Meriaudeau, & Gorria, 2005; Morel, Stolz, & Gorria, 2006; Meriaudeau, Ferraton, Stolz, Bigué, & Morel, 2008)
segmenting scenes	(Ben-Ezra, 2000; Ahmad, & Takakura, 2007; Terrier et al., 2008; Subramaniam, & Hancock, 2010; Shabayek et al., 2012)
dehazing	Schechner, Narasimhan, & Nayar, (2001; 2003; 2008))
polarimetric cameras which enable acquisition of polarization information in real time to be applied in any of the polarized based machine vision applications	(Shutov, 1993; Cronin et al., 1994; Wolff, Mancini, Pouliquen, & Andreou, 1997; Ben-Ezra, 2000; Zhang et al., 2009a)

camera may consist of a rotating linear polarizer and a CCD camera.

(Cronin et al., 1994) used their polarimetric camera to break color camouflage. An orange caterpillar camouflaged on an orange leaf show a case where polarization can be used where the orientation of polarization difference is significantly larger than the differences that appear in the brightness of the natural, full colored image. Moreover, the AOP variation in the light reflected from the caterpillar is much larger than that reflected from the leaf.

(Zhang et al., 2009a) studied the properties of polarization scattering in camouflaged targets according to the change of incidence angle and observational angle. They concluded that the spectra of camouflage targets can simulate that of backgrounds. Polarization remote sensing proved that camouflage targets with the same spectra most likely have very different polarimetric characteristics with background. Camouflage targets can be identified clearly in DOP imaging and AOP imaging. The camouflage effect is lost when it comes from traditional remote sensing to polarization remote sensing.

The spectral scattering light polarization signature is affected by the incidence angle, azimuth and the characteristics of materials. In (Zhang, Cheng, Chen, & Zheng, 2009b) the coating DOP was studied, and the results indicated that the coating DOP represented a reverse trend with surface reflectance and azimuth angle. A model based on Fresnel reflection equation was set up to describe the coating's polarization scattering behavior, which can be predicted by the model up to visible light and infrared wavelengths.

Miscellaneous

Polarization filtered images analysis proved to be useful for computer vision. Hence, in this section we will cover different applications in computer vision based on polarization, which are not necessarily bio-inspired, to give the flavor of polarization in this important research area. See Table 6 for some examples.

Summary

This section will summarize the different areas of bio-inspired, polarization based computer vision and robotics applications, highlighting the important points in each area.

Visualizing Polarization Information

A short survey was given on available methods to visualize polarization information in order to map it into visual cues such as polarization-difference imaging, coherently moving dots superimposed on an image, overlaying textures with spatial and/or temporal signatures, modulating luminance and/or scene color contrast in terms of certain aspects of polarization measured values, and fusing polarization images into intensity-only images.

Robot Orientation and Navigation

We surveyed the different bio-inspired polarization techniques for robot orientation and navigation. Photodiodes, CCD/CMOS, and special sensors were used. The methods using photodiodes are cheap; however, they simulate the strategy of insects by taking advantage of skylight polarization through single numerical values rather than patterns. The techniques based on CCD/CMOS sensors are more expensive, but they can analyze the sky polarization patterns giving polarization maps (DOP, AOP, polarization contrast) in order to obtain various orientation and navigation clues. Using a fisheye lens with a CCD sensor is a good solution to obtain an omni-directional polarization image up to 180°. CMOS based techniques are promising for miniature robots as size is important for practical situations; however, the viewing angle is limited. Stereo vision based techniques provide different points of view but require more equipment, and they are not practical especially if the cameras do not share the same baseline. Polarimetric cameras are a good solution as they acquire the polarization information in one shot, which is better than conventional sensors that need at least three acquisitions. The spectro-polarimetric imager is good in the sense that it is possible to obtain both polarimetric and spectral information to be fused to obtain various clues for orientation and navigation.

Underwater Polarization Vision

The effect of water surface reflections can be reduced using a linear horizontal and a linear vertical polarizer. The passive polarization signature decreases with increased range, and it is a function of target shape, surface characteristics, and light source level. Polarization sensitivity will be most useful at a distance of a few meters for visual tasks in water. In short distances, it is valid to assume that polarization is associated with object radiation, and hence it is possible to use DOP, AOP, and DPI to enhance the image. However it is not valid at long distances; therefore, the visibility disturbance should be deleted and the physical model of the disturbance cause should be inverted to obtain a clear image.

Communication

Polarization modulation outperforms intensity modulation. Optical communications are able to exploit light beam polarization in order to differentiate the received signal from any other signal in air and underwater. It is possible to show invisible polarization code on a display (e.g robot's eyes) to be embedded within visual information. Polarization information can be used effectively for cooperative robots.

Camouflage Breaking

Polarization has a strong role to play in camouflage breaking specially in remote sensing. Polarimetric imaging has proven to be the most effective approach as it strongly reveals camouflaged targets embedded in complex backgrounds. The camouflaged targets with the same spectra most likely have very different polarimetric characteristics with background. The camouflage effect can be lost when it comes from traditional sensing to polarization sensing.

Miscellaneous

Polarization filtered image analysis proved to be useful for computer vision and robotics applications. It has been used in a broad range of applications such as specularities analysis, separation of transparent and semi-reflected scenes, material classification, camera calibration, 3D reconstruction, industrial inspection, scene segmentation, dehazing, and development of new camera technologies (e.g polarimetric cameras).

FUTURE RESEARCH DIRECTIONS

We think that there are three important fields of polarization research which will evolve in the next few years: spectral-polarization vision, omni-polarization vision, and a combination of both (omni-spectro-polarization vision).

Independently, polarimetric and spectral features do not completely represent an object of interest (Zhao, Gong, & Pan, 2008). The object's elemental composition defines the reflected spectral signature. The polarization characteristics depend on surface features, such as smoothness and conductance. These features can be combined to reduce false alarms, improve target identification, and enhance scene description. Some work has already been done on this combination in (Giakos, 2006; Zhao, Pan, & Zhang, 2006; Zhao et al., 2008; Zhao, Zhang, L., Zhang, D. & Pan, 2009; Cummings et al., 2009).

Omni-directional polarization vision is required to perceive the surrounding 360° polarization features. Omni-vision can be obtained by wide angle lenses, a fisheye lens, multi-cameras, and catadioptric sensors (a combination of mirror and lens). Catadioptric sensors provide the best omni-vision view as it is able to completely capture the surrounding which is up to 360° with minimal occlusions. Omni-directional polarization vision has been established by combining a fisheye lens and polarization filter in (Miyazaki et al., 2009). It has been also proposed as a combination of sspecially designed mirror placed into a cylindrical polarization filter in (Horita et al., 2008; Horita, Shibata, Maeda, & Hayashi, 2009). Another design based on cone mirror and CCD camera for surveillance in (Lin et al., 2004) is equipped with a linear/circular polarizer. They capture three images at (0°, 45°, and 90°). However, in (p.220) it was wrongly stated that "For reflective mirror with metallic reflection surface, however, the effects on polarization are simpler. For many highly reflective metallic surfaces the polarization of reflected light is the mirror image of the original polarization pattern." The light polarization state is changed after being reflected from metallic surfaces (e.g. a linearly polarized light reflects as an elliptically polarized light) (Born & Wolf, 1999, p.741). This problem has been solved by calibrating the original incident light polarization state from the reflected state in (Shabayek, Morel, & Fofi, 2012a).

The future of polarization vision is going to be omni-directional due to its wide range of applications and the amount of information captured at one location and in one shot. It takes conventional vision applications into the omni-directional dimension. To overcome the special design, and multiple captures (at least three) requirements, a novel omni-polarization catadioptric sensor is proposed in the next section.

Finally, we propose to have an omni-spectro-polarimetric camera (e.g combining a mirror with FD-1665 3CCD Multispectral Cameras with a linear polarizer at 0°, 60°, 120° in front of each camera configured by the manufacturer). It is inspired by the birds' field of view which can reach 360°, spectral vision of the Daphnia magna, and polarization vision of Cataglyphis ants. The proposed sensor will be able to show the spectral and polarimetric features from an omni-directional window. This means that we will be able to sense 360° of the surrounding environment at one shot. Imagine the power of such sensor! It can be used in almost all machine vision applications enhancing the quality of perceived images and fusing comprehensive information into a single image. It may greatly enhance the autonomous robotics world especially in open environments. To the best of our knowledge, this is the first time such sensor is proposed.

Non-Central Omni-Polarization Catadioptric Sensor

We propose to use a non-central omni-polarization catadioptric sensor composed of a mirror and a polarimetric camera at (0°, 60°, and 120°) as an optimal combination (Tyo, 1998). It can be used for most machine vision applications. We have recently proposed to use it for sky/ground segmentation for unmanned air vehicle (UAV) attitude estimation (Shabayek, Demonceaux, Morel, & Fofi, 2012).

Polarization information is directly computed from three intensity images taken at three different angles (0°, 45°, and 90°) or (0°, 60°, and 120°) in one shot using a polarimetric camera. The polarization patterns consist of the AOP ϕ and the DOP ρ are defined as:

$$\phi = \arctan(\frac{S_2}{S_1}), \rho = \frac{\sqrt{S_1^2 + S_2^2}}{S_0}$$

where S_i are called the Stokes components (Goldstein, 2003) that can be computed from:

$$I_0 = 0.5(S_0 + S_1 \cos(2\alpha) + S_2 \sin(2\alpha))$$

where α is the polarizer angle. Hence:

$$S_0 = I_0 + I_{90}, \; S_1 = I_0 - I_{90}, \; S_2 = 2I_{45} - I_0 - I_{90},$$

or

$$S_0 = \frac{I_{60}}{2} + \frac{I_{120}}{2} + I_0, \; S_1 = \frac{I_{60}}{2} - \frac{I_{120}}{2} + I_0, \; S_2 = \frac{2}{\sqrt{3}}(\frac{I_{60}}{2} - \frac{3 * I_{120}}{2} + 3 * I_0)$$

where I_0, I_{45}, and I_{90} are intensity images taken at (0°, 45°, and 90°) or I_0, I_{60}, and I_{120} are intensity images taken at (0°, 60°, and 120°) in one shot using a polarimetric camera (e.g FluxData FD-1665 series like FD-1665P-M which has three monochrome CCDs with 0°, 45°, 90° or 0°, 60°, 120° linear polarizers) .

Figure 3. Sky/Ground segmentation and horizon extraction based on polarization from non-central catadioptric images. a) The used Catadioptric sensor. b) Segmentation based on DOP which is between 0 and 1 as shown in the colorbar. c) Segmentation based on AOP which is between -90° (-1.5 rad) and 90° (1.5 rad) as shown in the colorbar d) The extracted horizon

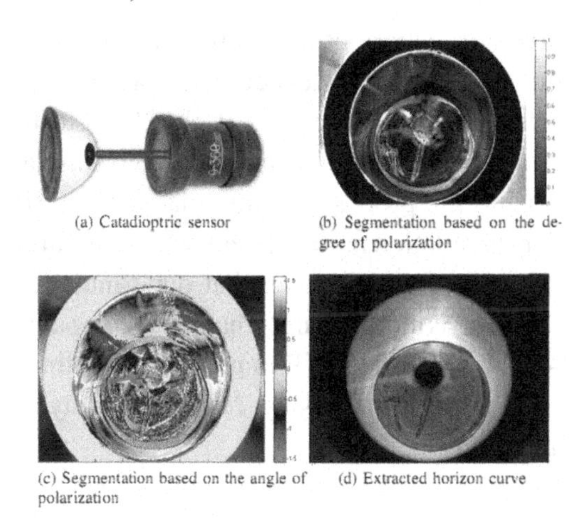

(a) Catadioptric sensor (b) Segmentation based on the degree of polarization (c) Segmentation based on the angle of polarization (d) Extracted horizon curve

Figure 4. Simulation of the sky AOP pattern in the University of Tokyo, institute of industrial science at sunset using a pola-catadioptric sensor. a) Theoretical Sky AOP pattern by Miyazaki et al. (2009) b) Actual captured Sky AOP pattern by Miyazaki et al. (2009) using a fisheye lens; c) Simulated theoretical Sky AOP

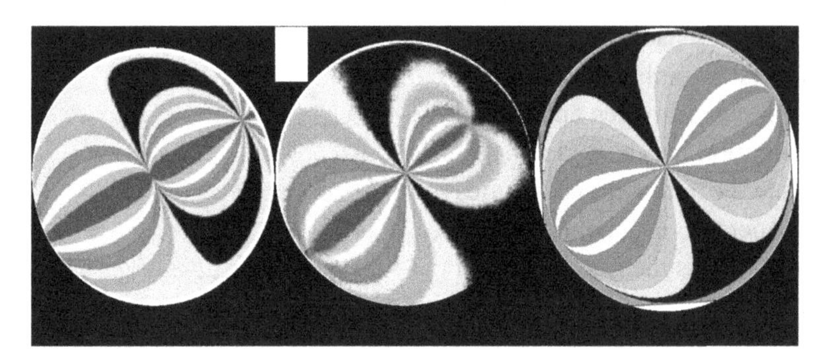

Figure 3 shows the segmentation results for non-central catadioptric images with the horizon detected by detecting the polarization transition areas. Unlike conventional segmentation methods, thanks to polarization, the illumination problem caused by the sun is solved in the image domain.

Sky polarization patterns can be obtained using the proposed sensor; however, in order to use it, the original incident polarization state should be calibrated as the reflected light from the metallic mirror has a different polarization state from the incident light (Born & Wolf, 1999, p.741). Once the pattern is obtained the sun azimuth and zenith angle can be computed. Given a built-in calendar in the autonomous robot with the extracted sun information, the orientation information can be obtained. Figure 4 shows the sky polarization pattern at the University of Tokyo Institute of Industrial Science at sunset as captured and simulated by (Miyazaki et al., 2009) to be taken as a ground truth. It also shows our simulation using the proposed omni-pola-catadioptric sensor. Simulation attributes are shown in Table 7. It is clear from Figure 4 that our simulation pattern (4-c) is more accurate than (4-a) compared to (4-b). This work is still in progress, and there are unpublished promising results (Shabayek, Morel, & Fofi, 2012b).

We believe that polarization information has strong cues for orientation and navigation. In the near future, it will be possible to use the sky polarization patterns at night for robot autonomous navigation like day light using the moon polarization patterns (Dacke et al., 2011).

CONCLUSION

Animal behavior is extremely flexible and robust for facing environmental contingencies. By adopting some of these behaviors for machines, it is possible to obtain similar flexibility and robustness. Many aspects of animals lead to biological inspiration like a) behavioral strategies, b) physical design, and c) the nervous system organization. In this chapter, we focused on the animals' polarization based visual behavior strategies.

Human visual awareness can be greatly expanded by augmenting different sensor models by the different capabilities of computer vision systems. Polarization vision represented in polarimetric cameras becomes available to a broad audience, specifically for outdoor and underwater applications. Thanks to polarimetric cameras, it will be easier to have real time bio-inspired robotics. Unmanned robots for surveillance or for

Table 7. Simulation attributes of the sky AOP pattern in the University of Tokyo, institute of industrial science at sunset using a pola-catadioptric sensor

Simulation attributes	Values
Date	6\July\2008
Time	1:0:0 GMT
Time Zone	-9
Sunset Time	1h 0m 24.5745s
Location	Latitude +N: 35.667 Longitude +E: 139.667

exploring tasks may greatly benefit from such sensors.

Polarization information has strong cues for orientation and navigation. It can be used efficiently in communication, remove backscattering for underwater vision, break camouflage in complex backgrounds, and adapted to various machine vision applications where polarization filtered images proved to be useful.

A complete, dedicated survey of one of the most important bio-inspired visual features in current applications was presented and future views of possible sensors were proposed.

REFERENCES

Ahmad, J. E., & Takakura, Y. (2007). Improving segmentation maps using polarization imaging. In *IEEE International Conference on Image Processing,* Vol. 1 (pp. I -281 -I -284).

Aron, Y., & Gronau, Y. (2005). Polarization in the LWIR. *Proceedings of the Society for Photo-Instrumentation Engineers, 5783,* 653–661. doi:10.1117/12.605316

Atkinson, G. A., & Hancock, E. R. (2005). Multiview surface reconstruction using polarization. In *Proceedings of the IEEE International Conference on Computer Vision.*

Ben-Ezra, M. (2000). Segmentation with invisible keying signal. In *Proceedings of IEEE Conference on Computer Vision and Pattern Recognition* (pp. 32-37).

Benedetto, S., & Poggiolini, P. (1992). Theory of polarization shift keying modulation. *IEEE Transactions on Communications, 40,* 708–721. doi:10.1109/26.141426

Born, M., & Wolf, E. (1999). *Principles of optics: Electromagnetic theory of propagation, interference and diffraction of light* (7th ed.). Cambridge University Press. doi:10.1063/1.1325200

Brun, G. L., & Jeune, L. B., Cariou, J., & Lotrian, J. (1992). Analysis of polarization signature of immersed targets. In *Proceedings of SPIE Polarization and Remote Sensing, Vol. 1747* (pp. 128-139).

Chahl, J., & Mizutani, A. (2010). Biomimetic attitude and orientation sensors. *Sensors Journal, 99,* 1.

Chow, C. W., Kwok, C. H., Liu, Y., Tsang, H. K., & Chinlon, L. (2006). *3-bit/symbol optical modulation-demodulation simultaneously using DRZ, DPSK and PolSK.* In Conference on Lasers and Electro-Optics (CLEO).

Chu, J., Wang, H., Chen, W., & Li, R. (2009). Application of a novel polarization sensor to mobile robot navigation. In *International Conference on Mechatronics and Automation, ICMA 2009* (pp. 3763 -3768).

Chu, J., Zhao, K., Wang, T., & Zhang, Q. (2007b). *Research on a novel polarization sensor for navigation.* In IEEE International Conference on Information Acquisition.

Chu, J., Zhao, K., Zhang, Q., & Wang, T. (2007a). *Design of a novel polarization sensor for navigation.* In IEEE International Conference on Mechatronics and Automation.

Chu, J., Zhao, K., Zhang, Q., & Wang, T. (2008). Construction and performance test of a novel polarization sensor for navigation. *Sensors and Actuators. A, Physical*, *148*, 75–82. doi:10.1016/j.sna.2008.07.016

Cox, W. C., Hughes, B. L., & Muth, J. F. (2009). *A polarization shift-keying system for underwater optical communications*. In OCEANS 2009, MTS/IEEE Biloxi - Marine Technology for Our Future: Global and Local Challenges.

Cox, W. C., Simpson, J., Domizioli, C. P., Muth, J., & Hughes, B. (2008). An underwater optical communication system implementing Reed-Solomon channel coding. In *Proceedings of OCEANS Conference*.

Cronin, T. W., & Shashar, N. (2001). The linearly polarized light field in clear, tropical marine waters: Spatial and temporal variation of light intensity, degree of polarization, and e-vector angle. *Journal of Experimental Biology*, *204*, 2461 2467.

Cronin, T. W., Shashar, N., Caldwell, R. L., Marshall, J., Cheroske, A. G., & Chiou, T.-H. (2003). Polarization vision and its role in biological signaling. *Integrative and Comparative Biology*, *43*(4), 549–558. doi:10.1093/icb/43.4.549

Cronin, T. W., Shashar, N., & Wolff, L. B. (1994). Portable imaging polarimeters. In *Pattern Recognition, 1994. Vol. 1 - Conference A: Computer Vision Image Processing, Proceedings of the 12th IAPR International Conference,* Vol. 1 (pp. 606 -609).

Cronin, T. W., Warrant, E. J., & Greiner, B. (2006). Celestial polarization patterns during twilight. *Optical Society of America. Applied Optics*, 45.

Crosby, F., & Riley, S. (2001). Signature Adaptive mine detection at a constant false alarm rate. In *Proceeding of SPIE Conference on Detection and Remediation Technologies for Mines and Minelike Targets*.

Crosby, F., & Stetson, S. (2002). Surface effect subtraction for airborne underwater target detection. In *OCEANS MTS*. IEEE. doi:10.1109/OCEANS.2002.1191865

Cummings, M. E., Ahmed, S. A., Dierssen, H. M., Gilerson, A., Gilly, W. F., Kattawar, G. W., & Sullivan, J. M. (2009). *Biological response to the dynamic spectral-polarized underwater light field*. Texas University at Austin.

Dacke, M., Byrne, M. J., Baird, E., Scholtz, C. H., & Warrant, E. (2011). How dim is dim? Precision of the celestial compass in moonlight and sunlight. *Philosophical Transactions of The Royal Society. Biological Sciences B*, *366*, 697–702. doi:10.1098/rstb.2010.0191

Damask, J. N. (Ed.). (2005). *Polarization optics in telecommunications* (*Vol. 101*). Springer.

Dehmollaian, M., & Sarabandi, K. (2009). Optimum polarizations for discrimination of a foliage-camouflaged target, using genetic algorithms. *IEEE Geoscience and Remote Sensing Letters*, *6*(1), 82–86. doi:10.1109/LGRS.2008.2008402

Denes, L. J., Gottlieb, M., Kaminsky, B., & Metes, P. (1998). AOTF polarization difference imaging. *SPIE*, *3584*, 106–115. doi:10.1117/12.339812

Douglas, J. M., Cronin, T. W., Chiou, T.-H., & Dominy, N. J. (2007). Light habitats and the role of polarized iridescence in the sensory ecology of neotropical nymphalid butterflies (Lepidoptera: Nymphalidae). *The Journal of Experimental Biology*, *210*, 788–799. doi:10.1242/jeb.02713

Egan, W. G. (1992). Polarization in remote sensing. In *Proceedings of SPIE, 1747*. Elsevier. doi:10.1117/12.142571

Egan, W. G., & Duggin, M. J. (2000). Optical enhancement of aircraft detection using polarization. *Proceedings of the Society for Photo-Instrumentation Engineers*, *4133*, 172–178. doi:10.1117/12.406624

Egan, W. G., & Duggin, M. J. (2002). Synthesis of optical polarization signatures of military aircraft. *Proceedings of the Society for Photo-Instrumentation Engineers, 4481*, 188–194. doi:10.1117/12.452888

Farid, H., & Adelson, E. H. (1999). Separating reflections and lighting using independent components analysis. In *Proceedings of IEEE Conference on Computer Vision and Pattern Recognition* (pp. 262-267).

Forssell, G., & Karlsson, E. H. (2003). Measurements of polarization properties of camouflaged objects and of the denial of surfaces covered with cenospheres. *Proceedings of the Society for Photo-Instrumentation Engineers, 5075*, 246–258. doi:10.1117/12.487312

Furukawa, T., & Sakamoto, K. (2010). Eye contact communication system between mobile robots using invisible code display. In Yang, H., Malaka, R., Hoshino, J., & Han, J. (Eds.), *Entertainment Computing - ICEC 2010* (*Vol. 6243*, pp. 468–471). Berlin, Germany: Springer. doi:10.1007/978-3-642-15399-0_62

Gerhart, G., & Matchko, R. (2002). Visualization techniques for four Stokes parameter polarization. In *Proceedings of the Ground Target Modeling and Validation Conference* (pp. 216-225).

Giakos, G. C. (2006). Multifusion, multispectral, optical polarimetric imaging sensing principles. *IEEE Transactions on Instrumentation and Measurement, 55*, 1628–1633. doi:10.1109/TIM.2006.881030

Goldsmith, T. (1975). The polarization sensitivity-dichroic absorption paradox in arthropod photoreceptors. In Snyder, A. W., & Menzel, R. (Eds.), *Photoreceptor optics* (pp. 98–125). Berlin, Germany: Springer Verlag. doi:10.1007/978-3-642-80934-7_23

Goldstein, D. (2003). *Polarized light, revised and expanded (optical science and engineering)*. CRC. doi:10.1201/9780203911587

Goldstein, D. H. (2000). Polarimetric characterization of federal standard paints. *Proceedings of the Society for Photo-Instrumentation Engineers, 4133*, 112–123. doi:10.1117/12.406618

Green, A. S., Ohmann, P. R., Leininger, N. E., & Kavanaugh, J. A. (2010). Polarization imaging and insect vision. *The Physics Teacher, 48*(1), 17–20. doi:10.1119/1.3274352

Grosinger, J. (2008). *Investigation of polarization modulation in optical free space communications through the atmosphere.* Unpublished Master's thesis, Institut fur Nachrichtentechnik und Hochfrequenztechnik, eingereicht an der Technischen Universitat Wien, Fakultat fur Elektrotechnik und Informationstechnik.

Haidinger, W. (1844). Über das directe Erkennen des polarisirten Lichts und der Lage der Polarisationsebene. *Poggendorfs Annalen, 63*, 29–39. doi:10.1002/andp.18441390903

Hanlon, R. T., & Messenger, J. B. (1996). *Cephalopod behaviour*. Cambridge, UK: Cambridge University Press.

Hanson, F., & Radic, S. (2008). High bandwidth underwater optical communication. *Applied Optics, 47*, 277–283. doi:10.1364/AO.47.000277

Harsdorf, S., Reuter, R., & Tönebön, S. (1999). Contrast-enhanced optical imaging of submersible targets. *SPIE, 3821*, 378–383. doi:10.1117/12.364201

Hawryshyn, C. (1992). Polarization vision in fish. *American Scientist, 80*, 164–175.

Hegedüs, R., Åkesson, S., & Horváth, G. (2007). Polarization patterns of thick clouds: Overcast skies have distribution of the angle of polarization similar to that of clear skies. *Journal of the Optical Society of America*, *24*, 2347–2356. doi:10.1364/JOSAA.24.002347

Heidemann, J., Ye, W., Wills, J., Syed, A., & Li, Y. (2006). Research challenges and applications for underwater sensor networking. In *Proceedings of the IEEE Wireless Communications and Networking Conference* (pp. 228--235).

Horita, Y., Hayashi, Y., Shibata, K., Hayashi, K., Morohashi, K., & Doi, T. (2008). Omni-directional polarization image capture using omni-directional camera and polarization filter. In *ITST 2008, 8th International Conference on ITS Telecommunications,* (pp. 99 -102).

Horita, Y., Shibata, K., Maeda, K., & Hayashi, Y. (2009). Omni-directional polarization image sensor based on an omni-directional camera and a polarization filter. In *IEEE International Conference on Advanced Video and Signal Based Surveillance* (pp. 280 -285).

Horváth, G., Gál, J., & Wehner, R. (1997). Why are water-seeking insects not attracted by mirages? The polarization properties of mirages. *Naturwissenschaften*, *84*, 300–303. doi:10.1007/s001140050398

Horváth, G., & Varjú, D. (2004). *Polarized light in animal vision: Polarization patterns in nature*. Springer.

Huber, D. F., Denes, L., Hebert, M., Gottlieb, M., Kaminsky, B., & Metes, P. (1997). A spectro-polarimetric imager for intelligent transportation systems. In *SPIE International Symposium on Intelligent Systems and Advanced Manufacturing, Intelligent Transportation Systems, Vol. 3207*.

Iqbal, M., Morel, O., & Meriaudeau, F. (2010). *A survey on outdoor water hazard detection*. In The 5th International Conference on Information & Communication Technology and Systems.

Ivanoff, A., & Waterman, T. H. (1958). Factors, mainly depth and wavelength, affecting the degree of underwater light polarization. *Journal of Marine Research*, *16*, 283–307.

Karpel, N., & Schechner, Y. Y. (2004). Portable polarimetric underwater imaging system with a linear response. In *Proceedings of SPIE Polarization: Measurement, Analysis and Remote Sensing VI*.

Können, G. P. (1985). *Polarized light in nature*. Cambridge University Press.

Lambrinos, D., Maris, M., Kobayashi, H., Labhart, T., Pfeifer, R., & Wehner, R. (1997). An autonomous agent navigation with a polarized light compass. *Adaptive Behavior*, *6*, 131–161. doi:10.1177/105971239700600104

Lambrinos, D., Maris, M., Kobayashil, H., Labhart, T., Pfeifer, R., & Wehner, R. (1998). Navigating with a polarized light compass. In *Self-Learning Robots II: Bio-robotics (Digest No. 1998/248), IEE* (pp. 7/1 -7/4).

Lambrinos, D., Möller, R., Labhart, T., Pfeifer, R., & Wehner, R. (2000). A mobile robot employing insect strategies for navigation. *Robotics and Autonomous Systems*, *30*, 39–64. doi:10.1016/S0921-8890(99)00064-0

Lee, J. K., & Mudaliar, S. (1994). Optimum polarizations in the bistatic scattering from layered random media. *IEEE Transactions on Geoscience and Remote Sensing*, *32*, 169–176. doi:10.1109/36.285199

Lee, R. L. (1998). Digital imaging of clear-sky polarization. *Applied Optics*, *37*, 1465–1476. doi:10.1364/AO.37.001465

Lerner, A., Sabbah, S., Erlick, C., & Shashar, N. (2010). Navigation by light polarization in clear and turbid waters. *Philosophical Transactions of The Royal Society Biological Sciences*, *366*, 671–679. doi:10.1098/rstb.2010.0189

Li, Y., & Wang, S. (2009). Underwater polarization imaging technology. In *Conference on Lasers Electro Optics The Pacific Rim.*

Li, Y., & Wang, S. (2010). Underwater object detection technology based on polarization image fusion. In *5th International Symposium on Advanced Optical Manufacturing and Testing Technologies: Optoelectronic Materials and Devices for Detector, Imager, Display, and Energy Conversion Technology, Proceedings of SPIE.*

Lin, S.-S., Yemelyanov, K. M., Pugh, J. E. N., & Engheta, N. (2004). Polarization enhanced visual surveillance techniques. In *Proceedings of the IEEE International Conference on Networking, Sensing & Control.*

Lythgoe, J. N., & Hemmings, C. C. (1967). Polarized light and underwater vision. *Nature, 213,* 893–894. doi:10.1038/213893a0

Malacara, D. (1989). *Physical optics and light measurements* (p. 157). Academic Press.

Mäthger, L. M., & Hanlon, R. T. (2006). Anatomical basis for camouflaged polarized light communication in squid. *Biology Letters, 2*(4), 494–496. doi:10.1098/rsbl.2006.0542

Matthies, L., Bellutta, P., & Mchenry, M. (2003). Detecting water hazards for autonomous off-road navigation. In *Proceedings of SPIE Conference 5083: Unmanned Ground Vehicle Technology V* (pp. 263-352).

Meriaudeau, F., Ferraton, M., Stolz, C., Bigué, L., & Morel, O. (2008). Polarization imaging for industrial inspection. In *SPIE Electronic Imaging - Machine Vision Applications in Industrial Inspection XIII, Vol. 6813.*

Miyazaki, D., Ammar, M., Kawakami, R., & Ikeuchi, K. (2009). Estimating sunlight polarization using a fish-eye lens. *IPSJ Transactions on Computer Vision and Applications, 1,* 288–300. doi:10.2197/ipsjtcva.1.288

Möller, R., Lambrinos, D., Pfiefer, R., Labhart, T., & Wehner, R. (1998). Modeling ant navigation with an autonomous agent. In *Proceedings of the Fifth International Conference on Simulation of Adaptive Behavior: From Animals to Animats.*

Morel, O., Ferraton, M., Stolz, C., & Gorria, P. (2006). Active lighting applied to shape from polarization. In *IEEE International Conference on Image Processing* (pp. 2181-2184).

Morel, O., & Fofi, D. (2007). Calibration of catadioptric sensors by polarization imaging. In *IEEE International Conference on Robotics and Automation.*

Morel, O., Meriaudeau, F., Stolz, C., & Gorria, P. (2005). Polarization imaging applied to 3D reconstruction of specular metallic surfaces. In *SPIE Electronic Imaging* (*Vol. 5679,* pp. 178–186). Machine Vision Applications in Industrial Inspection XIII, Electronic Imaging. doi:10.1117/12.586815

Morel, O., Seulin, R., & Fofi, D. (2007a). *Measurement of the three-dimensional mirror parameters by polarization imaging applied to catadioptric camera calibration.* In IEEE/SPIE 8th International Conference on Quality Control by Artificial Vision (QCAV'2007).

Morel, O., Seulin, R., & Fofi, D. (2007b). *Catadioptric camera calibration by polarization imaging.* In Iberian Conference on Pattern Recognition and Image Analysis.

Morel, O., Seulin, R., & Fofi, D. (2008). Measurement of three-dimensional mirror parameters by polarization imaging applied to catadioptric camera calibration. *Journal of Electronic Imaging, 17*(3). doi:10.1117/1.2958290

Morel, O., Stolz, C., & Gorria, P. (2004a). *Polarization applied to 3D reconstruction of highly reflective metallic objects.* In OSAV.

Morel, O., Stolz, C., & Gorria, P. (2004b). Application of polarimetric imaging to 3D inspection of highly reflective metallic surface. In *SPIE Optics East - Two- and Three-Dimensionale Vision Systems for Inspection, Control, and Metrology II, Vol. 5606* (pp. 82-89).

Morel, O., Stolz, C., & Gorria, P. (2006). Polarization imaging for 3D inspection of highly reflective metallic objects. *Optics and Spectroscopy, 101*(1), 15–21. doi:10.1134/S0030400X06070034

Morel, O., Stolz, C., Meriaudeau, F., & Gorria, P. (2005). Three-dimensional inspection of highly-reflective metallic objects by polarization imaging. *Electronic Imaging Newsletter, 15*(2), 4.

Morel, O., Stolz, C., Meriaudeau, F., & Gorria, P. (2006). Active lighting applied to 3D reconstruction of specular metallic surfaces by polarization imaging. *Applied Optics, 45*(17), 4062–4068. doi:10.1364/AO.45.004062

Morgan, S. P., Khong, M. P., & Somekh, M. G. (1997). Effects of polarization state and scatterer concentration on optical imaging through scattering media. *Applied Optics, 36*, 1560–1565. doi:10.1364/AO.36.001560

Nayar, S. K., Fang, X. S., & Boult, T. (1997). Separation of reflection components using color and polarization. *International Journal of Computer Vision, 21*, 163–186. doi:10.1023/A:1007937815113

Niblack, W., & Wolf, E. (1964). Polarization modulation and demodulation of light. *Applied Optics, 3*, 277–277. doi:10.1364/AO.3.000277

Nilsson, D.-E., & Warrant, E. J. (1999). Visual discrimination: Seeing the third quality of light. *Current Opinions in Biology, 9R535-R537*, 9, 535-537.

Novales, F. I., & Hawryshyn, C. W. (1997). Is the use of underwater polarized light by fishes restricted to crepuscular time periods? *Vision Research, 37*, 975–989. doi:10.1016/S0042-6989(96)00236-2

Phillips, J. B., & Waldvogel, J. A. (1988). Celestial polarized light patterns as a calibration reference for sun compass of homing pigeons. *Journal of Theoretical Biology, 131*, 55–67. doi:10.1016/S0022-5193(88)80120-6

Pomozi, I., Horváth, G., & Wehner, R. (2001). How the clear-sky angle of polarization pattern continues underneath clouds: Full-sky measurements and implications for animal orientation. *The Journal of Experimental Biology, 204*, 2933–2942.

Pratt, W. K. (1969). *Laser communication systems*. New York, NY: Wiley.

Pun, S., Chan, C., & Chen, L. (2005). A novel optical frequency shift keying transmitter based on polarization modulation. In *Optical Fiber Communication Conference. Technical Digest. OFC/NFOEC*, Vol. 3.

Rankin, A., & Matthies, L. (2008). Daytime mud detection for unmanned ground vehicle autonomous navigation. In *Proceedings of the 26th Army Science Conference*.

Rossel, S. (1989). Polarization sensitivity in compound eyes. In Stavenga, D. G., & Hardie, R. C. (Eds.), *Facets of vision* (pp. 298–316). Berlin, Germany: Springer Verlag. doi:10.1007/978-3-642-74082-4_15

Rowe, M. P., Pugh, E. N., Tyo, J. S., & Engheta, N. (1995). Polarization-difference imaging: A biologically inspired technique for observation through scattering media. *Optics Letters, 20*, 608–610. doi:10.1364/OL.20.000608

Saito, M., Sato, Y., Ikeuchi, K., & Kashiwagi, H. (1999a). Measurement of surface orientations of transparent objects using polarization in highlight. *Journal of the Optical Society of America, 16*(9), 2286–2293. doi:10.1364/JOSAA.16.002286

Saito, M., Sato, Y., Ikeuchi, K., & Kashiwagi, H. (1999b). Measurement of surface orientations of transparent objects using polarization in highlight. In *Proceedings of IEEE Conference on Computer Vision and Pattern Recognition.*

Sarafraz, A., Negahdaripour, S., & Schechner, Y. Y. (2009). Enhancing images in scattering media utilizing stereovision and polarization. In *Proceedings of IEEE Workshop on Applications of Computer Vision.*

Sarkar, M., Bello, D. S. S., Hoof, C. V., & Theuwissen, A. (2010a). Biologically inspired autonomous agent navigation using an integrated polarization analyzing CMOS image sensor. *Procedia Engineering, 5*, 673–676. doi:10.1016/j.proeng.2010.09.199

Sarkar, M., Bello, D. S. S., Hoof, C. V., & Theuwissen, A. (2010b). Integrated polarization-analyzing CMOS image sensor for detecting incoming light ray direction. In *Sensors Applications Symposium, 2010 IEEE* (pp. 194-199).

Sarkar, M., Bello, D. S. S., Hoof, C. V., & Theuwissen, A. (2010c). Integrated polarization-analyzing CMOS image sensor. In *Proceedings of 2010 IEEE International Symposium on Circuits and Systems* (pp. 621-624).

Sarkar, M., Bello, D. S. S., Hoof, C. V., & Theuwissen, A. (2010d). Integrated polarization analyzing CMOS Image sensor for autonomus navigation using polarized light. In *IEEE Conference of Intelligent Systems* (pp. 224-229).

Sarwal, A., Nett, J., & Simon, D. (2004). *Detection of small water-bodies*. Littleton, CO: PercepTek Robotics.

Schechner, Y. Y., & Karpel, N. (2004). Clear underwater vision. In *IEEE Conference on Computer Vision and Pattern Recognition* (pp. 536 543).

Schechner, Y. Y., & Karpel, N. (2005). Recovery of underwater visibility and structure by polarization analysis. *IEEE Journal of Oceanic Engineering, 30*, 631–636. doi:10.1109/JOE.2005.850871

Schechner, Y. Y., Narasimhan, S. G., & Nayar, S. K. (2001). Instant dehazing of images using polarization. In *Proceedings of IEEE Conference on Computer Vision and Pattern Recognition* (pp. 325-332).

Schechner, Y. Y., Narasimhan, S. G., & Nayar, S. K. (2003). Polarization-based vision through haze. *Applied Optics, 42*, 511–525. doi:10.1364/AO.42.000511

Schechner, Y. Y., Narasimhan, S. G., & Nayar, S. K. (2008). Polarization-based vision through haze. In *Proceeding of ACM SIGGRAPH Asia,* Vol. 42.

Schechner, Y. Y., Shamir, J., & Kiryati, N. (1999). Polarization-based decorrelation of transparent layers: The inclination angle of an invisible surface. In *Proceedings of IEEE International Conference on Computer Vision* (pp. 814-819).

Schechner, Y. Y., Shamir, J., & Kiryati, N. (2000). Polarization and statistical analysis of scenes containing a semi-reflector. *Journal of the Optical Society of America. A, Optics, Image Science, and Vision, 17*, 276–284. doi:10.1364/JOSAA.17.000276

Schmolke, A., & Mallot, H. A. (2002). Polarisation compass for robot navigation. In D. Polani, J. Kim, & T. Martinez (Eds.), *Fifth German Workshop on Artificial Life*.

Schuler, D. L., Lee, J. S., & Hoppel, K. W. (1993). Polarimetric SAR image signatures of the ocean and Gulf Stream features. *IEEE Transactions on Geoscience and Remote Sensing, 31*, 1210–1221. doi:10.1109/36.317442

Schwind, R. (1983). Zonation of the optical environment and zonation in the rhabdom structure within the eye of the backswimmer, Notonecta glauca. *Cell and Tissue Research*, *232*, 53–63. doi:10.1007/BF00222373

Schwind, R. (1984). The plunge reaction of the backswimmer Notonecta glauca. *Journal of Comparative Physiology. A, Neuroethology, Sensory, Neural, and Behavioral Physiology*, *155*, 319–321. doi:10.1007/BF00610585

Schwind, R. (1991). Polarization vision in water insects and insects living on a moist substrate. *Journal of Comparative Physiology. A, Neuroethology, Sensory, Neural, and Behavioral Physiology*, *169*, 531–540. doi:10.1007/BF00193544

Shabayek, A. E. R. (2010). *Non-central catadioptric sensors auto-calibration*. LAP Lambert Academic Publishing.

Shabayek, A. E. R., Demonceaux, C., Morel, O., & Fofi, D. (2012). Vision based UAV attitude estimation: Progress and insights. *Journal of Intelligent & Robotic Systems*, *65*, 295–308. doi:10.1007/s10846-011-9588-y

Shabayek, A. E. R., Fofi, D., & Morel, O. (2009). *A novel non-central catadioptric auto-calibration approach*. In 9th Workshop on Omnidirectional Vision (OMNIVIS) in conjunction with International Conference on Computer Vision (ICCV).

Shabayek, A. E. R., Morel, O., & Fofi, D. (2010). *Auto-calibration and 3D reconstruction with non-central catadioptric sensors using polarization imaging*. In 10th Workshop on Omnidirectional Vision (OMNIVIS) in conjunction with Robotics Systems and Science RSS.

Shabayek, A. E. R., Morel, O., & Fofi, D. (2012a). *Polarization in the eye of a catadioptric sensor*. Unpublished work.

Shabayek, A. E. R., Morel, O., & Fofi, D. (2012b). *Polarization as seen by a catadioptric sensor: A simulation and calibration toolbox*. Unpublished work.

Shashar, N., Adessi, L., & Cronin, T. W. (1995). Polarization vision as a mechanism for detection of transparent objects. In Gulko, D., & Jokiel, P. L. (Eds.), *Ultraviolet radiation and coral reefs* (pp. 207–211).

Shashar, N., Hagan, R., Boal, J. G., & Hanlon, R. T. (2000). Cuttlefish use polarization sensitivity in predation on silvery fish. *Vision Research*, *40*, 71–75. doi:10.1016/S0042-6989(99)00158-3

Shashar, N., & Hanlon, R. (1997). Squids (Loligo pealii and Euprymna scolopes) can exhibit polarized light patterns produced by their skin. *The Biological Bulletin*, *193*, 207–208.

Shashar, N., & Hanlon, R., & Petz, de M. A. (1998). Polarization vision helps detect transparent prey. *Nature*, *393*, 222–223. doi:10.1038/30380

Shashar, N., Milbury, C., & Hanlon, R. (2002). Polarization vision in cephalopods: Neuroanatomical and behavioral features that illustrate aspects of form and function. *Marine and Freshwater Behaviour and Physiology*, *35*, 57–68. doi:10.1080/10236240290025617

Shashar, N., Sabbah, S., & Cronin, T. W. (2004). Transmission of linearly polarized light in seawater: Implications for polarization signaling. *The Journal of Experimental Biology*, *207*, 3619–3628. doi:10.1242/jeb.01187

Shutov, A. M. (1993). Videopolarimeters. *Soviet Journal of Optical Technology*, *60*, 295–301.

Subramaniam, N., & Hancock, E. (2010). Surface material segmentation using polarisation. *Lecture Notes in Computer Science*, *6256*, 115–124. doi:10.1007/978-3-642-15992-3_13

Suhai, B., & Horváth, G. (2004). How well does the Rayleigh model describe the E-vector distribution of skylight in clear and cloudy conditions? A full-sky polarimetric study. *Optical Society of America A*, *21*, 1669–1676. doi:10.1364/JOSAA.21.001669

Sweeney, A., Jiggins, C., & Johnsen, S. (2003). Insect communication: Polarized light as a butterfly mating signal. *Nature*, *423*, 31–32. doi:10.1038/423031a

Tang, C. H., & Rubin, M. D. (1972). Optimum polarization for rain cancellation. In *Proceedings of IEEE Antennas and Propagation Society International Symposium*, Vol. 10.

Taylor, J. S. J., Davis, P., & Wolff, L. (2002). Underwater partial polarization signatures from the SHallow water Real-time IMaging Polarimeter (SHRIMP). In *OCEANS MTS*. IEEE. doi:10.1109/OCEANS.2002.1191863

Taylor, J. S. J., Davis, P., & Wolff, L. (2003). Underwater partial polarization signatures from the shallow water real-time imaging polarimeter (SHRIMP). In *SPIE Proceedings, Detection and Remediation Technologies for Mines and Minelike Targets VIII*.

Taylor, J. S. J., & Wolff, L. (2001). *Partial polarization signature results from the field testing of the SHallow water Real-time IMaging polarimeter (SHRIMP)*. In OCEANS MTS/IEEE Conference and Exhibition.

Terrier, P., Devlaminck, V., & Charbois, J. M. (2008). Segmentation of rough surfaces using a polarization imaging system. *Optical Society of America*, *25*(2), 423–430. doi:10.1364/JOSAA.25.000423

Timofeeva, V. A. (1969). Plane of vibrations of polarized light in turbid media. *Izvestiya. Atmospheric and Oceanic Physics*, *5*, 603–607.

Treibitz, T., & Schechner, Y. Y. (2006). Instant 3descatter. In *Proc. IEEE Computer Vision and Pattern Recognition*.

Treibitz, T., & Schechner, Y. Y. (2009). Active polarization descattering. *IEEE Transactions on Pattern Analysis and Machine Intelligence*, *31*, 385–399. doi:10.1109/TPAMI.2008.85

Tyo, J. S. (1998). Optimum linear combination strategy for an N-channel polarization-sensitive imaging or vision system. *Journal of Optical Society*, *15*, 359–366. doi:10.1364/JOSAA.15.000359

Tyo, J. S., Rowe, M. P., Pugh, E. N. Jr, & Engheta, N. (1996). Target detection in optically scattered media by polarization-difference imaging. *Applied Optics*, *35*, 1855–1870. doi:10.1364/AO.35.001855

Uehara, H., Seto, I., Ohtsuki, T., Sasase, I., & Mori, S. (1992). *Phase noise insensitive multilevel POLSK based on QAM mapping in coherent optical systems*. In Singapore ICCS/ISITA: Communications on the Move.

Usher, K., Ridley, P., & Corke, P. (2001). *A camera as a polarized light compass: Preliminary experiments*. In Australian Conference on Robotics and Automation.

Waterman, T. H. (1981). Polarization sensitivity. In Autrum, H. (Ed.), *Handbook of sensory physiology* (pp. 281–463). Berlin, Germany: Springer Verlag.

Wehner, R. (1987). Matched filters' -Neural models of the external world. *Journal of Comparative Physiology. A, Neuroethology, Sensory, Neural, and Behavioral Physiology*, *161*, 511–531. doi:10.1007/BF00603659

Wehner, R. (2001). Polarization vision a uniform sensory capacity? *The Journal of Experimental Biology*, *204*, 2589–2596.

Weidemann, A., Fournier, G. R., Forand, L., & Mathieu, P. (2005). In harbor underwater threat detection/ identification using active imaging. In *Proceedings of SPIE, Photonics for Port and Harbor Security, Vol. 5780* (pp. 59-70).

Wolff, L., Mancini, T., Pouliquen, P., & Andreou, A. (1997). Liquid crystal polarization camera. *IEEE Transactions on Robotics and Automation*, *13*(2), 195–203. doi:10.1109/70.563642

Wolff, L. B. (1989). Using polarization to separate reflection components. In *Proceedings of IEEE Conference on Computer Vision and Pattern Recognition* (pp. 363-369).

Wolff, L. B. (1995). Applications of polarization camera technology. *IEEE Expert*, *10*(5), 30–38. doi:10.1109/64.464928

Wolff, L. B. (1997). Polarization vision: A new sensory approach to image understanding. *Image and Vision Computing*, *15*, 81–93. doi:10.1016/S0262-8856(96)01123-7

Wolff, L. B., & Andreou, A. G. (1995). Polarization camera sensors. *Image and Vision Computing*, *13*, 497–510. doi:10.1016/0262-8856(95)94383-B

Wu, L., Gao, J., Fan, Z., & Xie, Z. (2010). How to get navigation information within patches of sky as insects do? A primitive orientation by skylight polarization maps. In *2nd International Conference on Signal Processing Systems*.

Xie, B., Xiang, Z., Pan, H., & Liu, J. (2007). Polarization-based water hazards detection for autonomous off-road navigation. In *IEEE/RSJ International Conference on Intelligent Robots and Systems*.

Yamada, M., Ueda, K., Horiba, I., & Sugie, N. (2001). Discrimination of the road condition toward understanding of vehicle driving environments. *IEEE Transactions on Intelligent Transportation Systems*, *2*(1), 26–31. doi:10.1109/6979.911083

Yemelyanov, K. M., Lin, S.-S., Luis, W. Q., Pugh, J. E. N., & Engheta, N. (2003). Bio-inspired display of polarization information using selected visual cues. In *Proceedings of SPIE - The International Society for Optical Engineering, 5158*.

Yemelyanov, K. M., Lo, M. A., Pugh, J. E. N., & Engheta, N. (2003). Display of polarization information by coherently moving dots. *Optics Express*, *11*, 1577–1584. doi:10.1364/OE.11.001577

Zhang, Z. Y., Cheng, H. F., Chen, Z. H., & Zheng, W. W. (2009a). Analysis of polarimetric characteristics of camouflage targets. In *Proceedings of SPIE 4th International Symposium on Advanced Optical Manufacturing and Testing Technologies: Optical Test and Measurement Technology and Equipment, Vol. 7283*.

Zhang, Z. Y., Cheng, H. F., Chen, Z. H., & Zheng, W. W. (2009b). Analysis of polarimetric scattering for backgrounds and camouflage materials. In *Proceedings of SPIE International Symposium on Photoelectronic Detection and Imaging: Advances in Infrared Imaging and Applications, Vol. 7383*.

Zhao, K., Chu, J., Wang, T., & Zhang, Q. (2009). A novel angle algorithm of polarization sensor for navigation. *IEEE Transactions on Instrumentation and Measurement*, *58*, 2791–2796. doi:10.1109/TIM.2009.2016299

Zhao, Y., Pan, Q., & Zhang, H. (2006). Object detection by fusion spectral and polarimetric imagery. In *Proceedings of SPIE, Vol. 6031*.

Zhao, Y., Zhang, L., Zhang, D., & Pan, Q. (2009). Object separation by polarimetric and spectral imagery fusion. *Computer Vision and Image Understanding*, *113*, 855–866. doi:10.1016/j.cviu.2009.03.002

Zhao, Y.-Q., Gong, P., & Pan, Q. (2008). Object detection by Spectropolarimeteric imagery fusion. *IEEE Transactions on Geoscience and Remote Sensing*, *46*, 3337–3345. doi:10.1109/TGRS.2008.920467

ADDITIONAL READING

Born, M., & Wolf, E. (1999). *Principles of optics: Electromagnetic theory of propagation, interference and diffraction of light* (7th ed.). Cambridge University Press. doi:10.1063/1.1325200

Cox, W. C., Hughes, B. L., & Muth, J. F. (2009). *A polarization shift-keying system for underwater optical communications*. In OCEANS 2009, MTS/IEEE Biloxi - Marine Technology for Our Future: Global and Local Challenges.

Cronin, T. W., Shashar, N., Caldwell, R. L., Marshall, J., Cheroske, A. G., & Chiou, T.-H. (2003). Polarization vision and its role in biological signaling. *Integrative and Comparative Biology, 43*(4), 549–558. doi:10.1093/icb/43.4.549

Furukawa, T., & Sakamoto, K. (2010). Eye contact communication system between mobile robots using invisible code display. In Yang, H., Malaka, R., Hoshino, J., & Han, J. (Eds.), *Entertainment Computing - ICEC 2010* (*Vol. 6243*, pp. 468–471). Berlin, Germany: Springer. doi:10.1007/978-3-642-15399-0_62

Giakos, G. C. (2006). Multifusion, multispectral, optical polarimetric imaging sensing principles. *IEEE Transactions on Instrumentation and Measurement, 55*, 1628–1633. doi:10.1109/TIM.2006.881030

Goldstein, D. (2003). *Polarized light, revised and expanded (optical science and engineering)*. CRC. doi:10.1201/9780203911587

Horváth, G., & Varjú, D. (2004). *Polarized light in animal vision: Polarization patterns in nature*. Springer.

Können, G. P. (1985). *Polarized light in nature*. Cambridge University Press.

Lambrinos, D., Möller, R., Labhart, T., Pfeifer, R., & Wehner, R. (2000). A mobile robot employing insect strategies for navigation. *Robotics and Autonomous Systems, 30*, 39–64. doi:10.1016/S0921-8890(99)00064-0

Lerner, A., Sabbah, S., Erlick, C., & Shashar, N. (2010). Navigation by light polarization in clear and turbid waters. *Philosophical Transactions of The Royal Society Biological Sciences, 366*, 671–679. doi:10.1098/rstb.2010.0189

Li, Y., & Wang, S. (2010). Underwater object detection technology based on polarization image fusion. In *5th International Symposium on Advanced Optical Manufacturing and Testing Technologies: Optoelectronic Materials and Devices for Detector, Imager, Display, and Energy Conversion Technology, Proceedings of SPIE.*

Miyazaki, D., Ammar, M., Kawakami, R., & Ikeuchi, K. (2009). Estimating sunlight polarization using a fish-eye lens. *IPSJ Transactions on Computer Vision and Applications, 1*, 288–300. doi:10.2197/ipsjtcva.1.288

Schechner, Y. Y., Narasimhan, S. G., & Nayar, S. K. (2008). Polarization-based vision through haze. In *Proceeding of ACM SIGGRAPH ASIA, Vol. 42.*

Shabayek, A. E. R. (2010). *Non-central catadioptric sensors auto-calibration*. LAP Lambert Academic Publishing.

Tyo, J. S. (1998). Optimum linear combination strategy for an N-channel polarization-sensitive imaging or vision system. *Journal of Optical Society, 15*, 359–366. doi:10.1364/JOSAA.15.000359

Yemelyanov, K. M., Lin, S.-S., Luis, W. Q., Pugh, J. E. N., & Engheta, N. (2003). Bio-inspired display of polarization information using selected visual cues. In *Proceedings of SPIE - The International Society for Optical Engineering 5158.*

Zhang, Z. Y., Cheng, H. F., Chen, Z. H., & Zheng, W. W. (2009a). Analysis of polarimetric characteristics of camouflage targets. In *Proceedings of SPIE 4th International Symposium on Advanced Optical Manufacturing and Testing Technologies: Optical Test and Measurement Technology and Equipment, Vol. 7283*.

Zhao, Y.-Q., Gong, P., & Pan, Q. (2008). Object detection by spectropolarimeteric imagery fusion. *IEEE Transactions on Geoscience and Remote Sensing*, *46*, 3337–3345. doi:10.1109/TGRS.2008.920467

KEY TERMS AND DEFINITIONS

Camouflage: The ability to hide.

Catadioptric Camera: A combination of mirror and lens to obtain omni-directional images up to 360°.

Communication: The ability to exchange a simple message.

Navigation: The ability to decide on correct route.

Omni-Directional Image: An image which has a wide extent of the surrounding environment.

Omni-Directional Polarization Vision: The ability to perceive the surrounding environment, up to 360°, in terms of its polarimetric values.

Omni-Spectro-Polarization Vision: The ability to perceive the surrounding environment, up to 360°, in terms of its spectral and polarimetric values.

Orientation: The ability to decide on correct direction.

Polarimetic Camera: A camera that is able to capture polarization characteristics represented in intensity images.

Polarization: It is the phenomenon that describes the oscillations orientation of waves which are restricted in direction.

Chapter 12
Implementation and Evaluation of a Computational Model of Attention for Computer Vision

Matthieu Perreira Da Silva
IRCCyN – University of Nantes, France

Vincent Courboulay
L3i – University of La Rochelle, France

ABSTRACT

In the field of scene analysis for computer vision, a trade-off must be found between the quality of the results expected and the amount of computer resources allocated for each task. Using an adaptive vision system provides a more flexible solution as its analysis strategy can be changed according to the information available concerning the execution context. The authors describe how to create and evaluate a visual attention system tailored for interacting with a computer vision system so that it adapts its processing according to the interest (or salience) of each element of the scene. The authors propose a new set of constraints called 'PAIRED' to evaluate the adequacy of a model with respect to its different applications. The authors then justify why dynamical systems are a good choice for visual attention simulation, and we show that predator-prey models provide good properties for simulating the dynamic competition between different kinds of information. They present different results (cross-correlation, Kullback-Leibler divergence, normalized scanpath salience) that demonstrate that, in spite of being fast and highly configurable, their results are as plausible as existing models designed for high biological fidelity.

INTRODUCTION

While machine vision systems are becoming increasingly powerful, in most regards they are still far inferior to their biological counterparts. In human, the mechanisms of evolution have generated the visual attention system which selects the most important information in order to reduce both cognitive load and scene understanding ambiguity. Thus, studying the biological systems and applying the findings to the construction of computational vision models and artificial vision

DOI: 10.4018/978-1-4666-2539-6.ch012

systems are a promising way of advancing the field of machine vision.

In the field of scene analysis for computer vision, a trade-off must be found between the quality of the results expected, and the amount of computer resources allocated for each task. It is usually a design time decision, implemented through the choice of pre-defined algorithms and parameters. However, this way of doing it limits the generality of the system. Using an adaptive vision system provides a more flexible solution as its analysis strategy can be changed according to the information available concerning the execution context. As a consequence, such a system requires some kind of guiding mechanism to explore the scene faster and more efficiently.

In this chapter, we propose a first step to building a bridge between computer vision algorithms and visual attention. In particular, we will describe how to create and evaluate a visual attention system tailored for interacting with a computer vision system so that it adapts its processing according to the interest (or salience) of each element of the scene.

Somewhere in between hierarchical salience based and competitive distributed models, we propose a hierarchical yet competitive model. Our original approach allows us to generate the evolution of attentional focus points without the need of either saliency map or explicit inhibition of return mechanism. This new real-time computational model is based on a dynamical system. The use of such a complex system is justified by an adjustable trade-off between nondeterministic attentional behavior and properties of stability, reproducibility and reactiveness.

In the first two sections, we start by giving a brief overview of the main theories and concepts of human visual attention and we provide the forces and weaknesses of state of the art attention models. This analysis is based on their potential of integration into adaptable computer vision system. We propose a new set of constraints called 'PAIRED' to evaluate the adequacy of a model with respect to its different applications. In a third section, we provide an in-depth description of our model and its implementation. We justify why dynamical systems are a good choice for visual attention simulation, and we show that predator-prey models provide good properties for simulating the dynamic competition between different kinds of information. This dynamical system is also used to generate a focus point at each time step of the simulation. In order to show that our model can be integrated in an adaptable computer vision system, we show that this architecture is fast and allows a flexible real time visual attention simulation. In particular, we present a feedback mechanism used to change the scene exploration behavior of the model. This mechanism can be used to maximize the scene coverage (explore each and every part) or maximize focalization on a particular salient area (tracking).

In a last section we present the evaluation results of our model. Since the model is highly configurable, its evaluation will cover not only its plausibility (compared to human eye fixations), but also the influence of each parameter on a set of properties (stability, reproducibility, scene exploration, dynamic behavior). But let's start by presenting attention.

THEORIES AND MECHANISMS OF BIOLOGICAL VISUAL ATTENTION

Why Visual Attention?

Does what we see really represent the world? Our perception of scenes seems accurate, continuous and consistent; however, the study of the various components of our visual system reveals a very different situation.

Eye and retina do not capture a perfect representation of the world. Actually, the distribution of different photoreceptor cells on the retina is not homogeneous: the center of it (the *fovea*) contains many more cone cells than the periphery.

One major consequence is that representation of scene in human vision is more accurate in the center than in periphery. Thus, it is necessary to move our eyes to capture every detail of the scene to construct a coherent representation (Rensink, 2000). Another interesting characteristic is that our visual cortex splits the electrically received signal, which *codes* the scene into features which have an increasing complexity (intensity, color, orientation, and corners, line intersections, etc.). All these features are generated in separate but interconnected areas of the brain (VanRullen, 2003). These different treatments have led scientists to speak about specialization. This concept is also used when dealing with the process of object recognition and location (central and dorsal pathway). Our brain must reconstruct a coherent representation from a relatively heterogeneous set of information.

As a consequence, in order to interpret what we see, our visual system has developed mechanisms to select and optimize information partially captured from the world. One of the most important is *attention*. Attention is the cognitive process of selectively concentrating on one aspect of the environment while ignoring other things. Attention has also been referred to as the allocation of processing resources. Attention theories are mainly based on two dual approaches.

Attention through Selection as a Consequence of Limited Abilities to Process Information (Broadbent, 1958; Treisman, 1969; Tsotsos, 1990)

This most widespread theory is referred to as an early selection model because irrelevant messages are filtered out before the stimulus information is processed for meaning. In other words, if our brain were bigger and/or more powerful, we would not need attentional mechanisms. In this context, attention selects some information in order not to overload our cognitive system. This is also the basic premise of a large number of computational models of visual attention (Frintrop, Klodt, & Rome, 2007;Itti, Koch, Niebur, & Others, 1998; Ouerhani, 2003).

We would like to mention here the theory of simplexity (Berthoz, 2009) which also places attention among the key mechanisms to *simplify complexity*. Yet, this theory does not describe attention as the result of our limited brain capacities, but as a *tool* to wisely use our skills to suit our needs.

Attention as a Functional Objective

This second family of attention theories (Allport, 1987; van der Heijden & Bem, 1997; Neumann, 1987) considers that our processing capabilities are unlimited. For proponents of this theory, having a bigger brain does not prevent us from having attentional mechanisms. Attention would not be a filter for our limited brain capacities, but would be a filter for our limited capacities of action. In reality, we construct a representation of the world in order to interact with it through actions. However, our motor skills are limited by our morphology (for example: our hands can only handle one (or two) objects simultaneously). Thus, our action capacities are limited and require the collecting of a selection of information in order to treat it accurately.

Whatever paradigms chosen, attentional processes are essential. They help remove ambiguities (Van Rullen & Koch, 2005), they are also essentials to build a coherent representation of our environment (Rensink, 2000) and to detect changes in it (Rensink, Regan, & Clark, 1997).

As previously mentioned, attentional processes are involved in many areas of our brain. Attention adapts both visual perception and hearing; it is also engaged in many cognitive tasks – perception, storage and retrieval, motion control, *etc.* Its study is a complex area in which are found many disciplines (neuropsychology, neurobiology, cognitive neuroscience etc.). We have decided not to mention here either anatomy or underlying theoretical models. Readers requiring additional information may consult (Driver, 2001; Tsotsos, Itti, & Rees, 2005; Tsotsos, 2007) or (Styles, 2006).

Attention Characteristics

Although far from exhaustive, the subset chosen illustrate the main characteristics of attention. Mole (2009) provides a more complete list for interested readers:

- Our brain does not have a single area dedicated to attention. This is the result of the interaction between different cortical areas involved in perception, motor control, or action planning (Laberge, 1995; Mesulam, 1981; Posner & Petersen, 1990);
- Attention is a selective mechanism. It adjusts the binding problem by performing a spatial relationship between different and unlocalized attributes computed in separate areas of our visual cortex;
- Attention is a multifaceted phenomenon. Most of its characteristics can be presented in a dual way. It can be: endogenous and automatic or exogenous and controlled, spatially guided or localized on objects, centralized or distributed, deployed in an overt or covered way.
- Features that guide attention are numerous: intensity/contrast, color, orientation, but can also be: form, fine lines, curvature or face and semantic category (Wolfe & Horowitz, 2004).

As we see, the complexity of attentional phenomenon opens the door to a multiplicity of theoretical interpretation.

In the late nineties, computers became powerful enough to consider a computational implementation of these multiple models. New theories still emerged and they were almost coupled with an implementation for computer simulation and thus allowed validation. In the next section, we explore a wide selection of models to determine the advantages and disadvantages of each ones.

COMPUTATIONAL MODELS OF ATTENTION

An Ideal Attention Model for Vision...

At the beginning of this chapter, we mentioned the apparent ease with which we perceive the world. But the world is complex: we must analyze a large amount of constantly-changing and often ambiguous information. To manage this complexity and react quickly and effectively to the different situations it faces, our brain need simplifying principles. Alain Berthoz proposes grouping together, in a single theory, the various mechanisms for managing this complexity (Berthoz, 2009). According to the 'simplexity' theory, a simplex system should: be modular/separate its different functions; be fast; be reliable; be flexible; have memory; have generalization properties.

Attention perfectly meets this characterization. Berthoz even defines this selective mechanism as a core function of our existence and proposes replacing the famous 'I think therefore I am' by 'I choose therefore I am'.

From a computational point of view, it is necessary to use some criteria in order to classify or evaluate attention models. Usually, processing time, robustness or plausibility is used. Nevertheless, we can use the properties of a simplex system in order to derive a set of constraints which will help evaluate the adequacy of a model with respect to its different applications. We have named this set 'PAIRED', it is composed of the following elements:

- Plausible when compared to human behavior an neurobiology;
- Adaptable in real-time to varying contexts;
- Invariant through different transforms (rotation, translation and scale);

Table 1. PAIRED constraints balance for some application of attention models

	Plausible	Adaptable	Invariant	Rapid	Extensible	Dynamic
Attention modeling	●●●	●	●	●	●	●●●
Ergonomics / advertisement	●●●	●	●	●	●●	●●
Vision	●●	●●●	●●	●●●	●●●	●●●
Content based image retrieval	●	●	●●●	●●	●●●	●
Image processing	●●	●●	●●	●●	●●●	●●

- Rapid to compute the focus of attention;
- Extensible concerning its ability to take into account new characteristics;
- Dynamic and capable of producing results at any time.

Once these criteria are presented, we can define their importance in several applications (Table 1). One dot means a weak constraint opposed to a strong one represented by three dots. Later in this chapter, we use this set of constraints to evaluate the fitness between different families of attention model and our target application: computer vision. The 'ideal' attention model will have to meet all of the PAIRED constraints.

A Taxonomy of Existing Models

We have separated the presentation of the various computational models of attention in two families. Supporters of the distributed models view attention as an emergent property of the biased competition (by evolution, winner takes all, learning or context) between different visual stimuli. Attention is not specifically encoded in a single topographic map. Proponents of central representation models support an opposite hypothesis. Attention is encoded in a 2D topographic map that serves as a reference for allocating attention through various mechanisms (winner takes all, inhibition of return, etc.). In this subsection, we conduct an (non-comprehensive) overview of existing models belonging to these two families.

Distributed Attention: Models Based on Biased Competition

Distributed models of attention were rooted in neuroscientific and connectionist schools. They are generally developed using a neuromimetic approach. Their level of granularity can be up to that of neurons, these being sometimes very accurately simulated (Rolls & Stringer, 2006). As a consequence, the experimental study of such models can be compared with that of the human brain, allowing the measurement of individual signals of each cell. The majority of these models are inspired by the biased competition theory proposed by Desimone and Duncan (1995). It can be summarized as follows:

- Attention is not a mental beam (as described by Treisman and Gelade, 1980) traversing the visual scene at high speed. It is rather an emergent property of a slow competition between parallel visual processing on the entire visual field.
- Objects in the visual field compete for the allocation of limited cognitive resources and the motor control of attention.
- This competition is biased by bottom-up mechanisms allowing objects to be separated from their background, and top-down mechanisms allowing the most suitable object for the current task/context to be selected. This bias can be controlled by the position and / or various other features of the objects in the scene.

These principles are applied in two sub-categories of models: those studying the response of isolated neurons, without worrying too much about the macroscopic behavior of the system (Bundesen, 1987, 1998; Spratling & Johnson, 2004; VanRullen, 2003); and computational models, more concerned with real-life performances on natural images (Deco, 2004; Ji & Weng, 2008; Navalpakkam, Arbib, & Itti, 2005; Stringer & Rolls, 2000; Tsotsos et al., 1995). Attention can also be modeled in a less competitive and more centralized way. We discuss the models using this paradigm in the remainder of this section.

Central Representation: Saliency Map Based Models

Saliency map based models lie in the continuity of the seminal work of Treisman and Gelade (1980). According to the Feature-Integration Theory, attention is encoded in a central map which represents the entire visual field (its name is dependent on the theory used: master map of locations, saliency map, etc.). Although more recent studies still fail to prove the uniqueness of the representation of saliency in our brain, this model is very popular because if offers a simple explanation which is computationally efficient and has a proven explanatory power.

As the central representation hypothesis is more popular than its distributed counterpart, the number of models based on this paradigm is important. We propose a taxonomy split into five sub-families:

- Hierarchical models build a hierarchy of various feature maps which are progressively combined in order to obtain a unique central representation of attention: the saliency map. Many influent attention models are based on this approach (Achanta, Estrada, Wils, & Süsstrunk, 2008; Belardinelli, Pirri, & Carbone, 2009; Choi, Jung, & Ban, 2006; Dong, Ban, & Lee, 2006; Frintrop, 2005; Frintrop et al., 2007; Geerinck, Sahli, Henderickx, Vanhamel, & Enescu, 2009; Itti, 2000; Itti et al., 1998; Koch & Ullman, 1985; Kootstra, Nederveen, & Boer, 2008; F. Liu & Gleicher, 2006; Marat et al., 2008; Le Meur, Castellan, Le Callet, & Barba, 2006; Milanese, Wechsler, Gill, Bost, & Pun, 1994; Ouerhani & Hugli, 2003; Rapantzikos & Tsapatsoulis, 2003; Sun & Fisher, 2003; Treisman & Gelade, 1980; Walther & Christof Koch, 2006);
- Statistical and probability based models consider that saliency is related to the least frequent or probable features events or objects in a scene (Avraham & Lindenbaum, 2010; Baldi & Itti, 2005; Hamker, 2005; Itti & Baldi, 2005; Park, An, & Lee, 2002; Torralba, Oliva, Castelhano, & Henderson, 2006);
- Information theory-based models are linked to probabilistic models by express attention as a means to maximize the quantity of information acquired (Bruce & Jernigan, 2003; Bruce & Tsotsos, 2008, 2009; Gilles, 1996; Kadir & Brady, 2001; Mancas, 2007; Park et al., 2002);
- Connectionist models are generally based on neural networks which are used for generating the dynamics of the focus of attention (Ahmad, 1992; Fix, 2008; Mozer & Sitton, 1998; Vitay, Rougier, & Alexandre, 2005);
- Algorithmic models propose various methods which are usually deeply linked to a specific application (Aziz & Mertsching, 2009; Aziz & Mertsching, 2008; Kootstra et al., 2008; Lopez, Fernandezcaballero, Fernandez, Mira, & Delgado, 2006; Orabona, Metta, & Sandini, 2008; Sela & Levine, 1997).

Other classifications exist (Bruce & Tsotsos, 2009; Chamaret & Meur, 2009), and some algo-

Table 2. Advantages and weaknesses of 'central representation' based models

Model sub-family	Advantages(s)	Weakness(es)
Hierarchical	Simplicity Computational efficiency Extensibility	Methods used for map normalization and fusion are subject to discussion
Statistical	Models difference from neighborhood Easy integration of top-down influence	Explanatory capacity Biological plausibility
Information theory based	Strong theoretical framework Formalism for information scarceness Easy integration of top-down influence	Explanatory capacity Biological plausibility
Connectionist	Good handling of the competition between different kinds of information Possibility to couple attention modeling and pattern recognition Dynamical evolution	Usually works on pre-computed saliency maps
Algorithmic	Well suited to computer vision applications	Often far from biological model

rithms are difficult to place into a single category. But the taxonomy proposed in this chapter is focused on distinguishing the various basic theory used for attention modeling. Table 2 summarizes the advantages and disadvantages of each type of saliency based model of attention. Despite the diversity of approaches used in each of the families, it is possible to identify some common characteristics.

Comparative Study

Table 3 summarizes the advantages and disadvantages of the two major approaches for modeling visual attention. The distributed approach is close to biological reality, effectively handles the problem of competition, but is more cumbersome to implement and extend. The centralized approach is usually computationally more efficient, but it does not take into account dynamics (evolution of the focus of attention in time) and requires the addition of expensive connectionist methods (WTA + inhibition of return).

Table 4 summarizes how each attentional model family and sub-family meets the requirements of the PAIRED constraints for computer vision applications. We notice that no single approach is perfectly adequate to this application.

Table 3. Advantages and weaknesses of the two main attention model families

Model family	Advantages(s)	Weakness(es)
Distributed	Good handling of the competition between different kinds of information Dynamical evolution	Complexity Easy addition of new features
Central representation	Computational efficiency Extensibility	No / poor dynamical evolution

Given the properties of fidelity, invariance, and dynamic adaptation of distributed models, and properties of speed and scalability of hierarchical models we can conclude that a hybrid approach between these two alternatives would allow the desired model to be obtained.

Such an approach has already been partially explored by some connectionist models: they usually combine a hierarchical model to generate a saliency map and a distributed approach to handle the dynamics of the focus of attention. However in these models, it's the hierarchical system which is responsible for the competition between the different features (intensity, color, orientation etc). Therefore, we do not benefit from

Table 4. Set of constraints with regards to computer vision applications. First row corresponds to our objective. Criteria reached or exceeded by each family of model are represented in gray.*

	Plausible	Adaptable	Invariant	Rapid	Extensible	Dynamic
Target	**	***	***	***	***	***
Distributed	●●●	●●●	●●●	○	○	●●●
Hierarchical	○○	○○	○○	○○	●●●	○
Statistical	●●	○	●●	○○	○○	○
Information theory based	●●	○	●●	○○	○○	○
Connexionist	●●	●●●	●●	○○	○○	●●●
Algorithmic	○	○○	●●	●●●	○	○

* represented in this table by lighter dots.

the principle of biased competition between these different sources of salience.

To overcome this problem, we think we should avoid using a central representation of salience. Instead, we propose linking conspicuity or feature maps in a competitive model which can fully play its role of managing the dynamics of the focus of attention as well as the competition between different features. In the remainder of this chapter, we present this solution and study its properties and plausibility with respect to the PAIRED criteria.

A COMPETITIVE YET HIERARCHICAL ATTENTION MODEL

Dynamical Systems, Predator-Prey Models, and Visual Attention

As was introduced at the end of the previous section, we propose a new hybrid model which allows the study of the temporal evolution of the visual focus of attention. We have modified the classical algorithm proposed by Itti (1998), in which the first part of his architecture relies on the extraction of three conspicuity maps based on low-level computation. These three conspicuity maps are representative of the three main human perceptual channels: color, intensity and orientation.

The second part of Itti's architecture proposes a medium level system which allows merging conspicuity maps and then simulates a visual attention path on the observed scene. The focus is determined by a 'winner takes all' and an 'inhibition of return' algorithms. We propose to substitute this second part with a competitive approach: a predator-prey system (Figure 1).

Predator-prey equations are particularly well-adapted for such a task. The main reasons are:

- Predator-prey systems are dynamic, they intrinsically include time evolution of their activities. Thus, the visual focus of attention, seen as a predator, can evolve dynamically;
- Without any objective (top-down information or pregnancy), choosing a method for conspicuity maps fusion is hard. A solution consists in developing a competition between conspicuity maps and waiting for a natural balance in the predator-prey system, reflecting the competition between emergence and inhibition of elements that either do, or do not, engage our attention;
- Discrete dynamic systems can have a chaotic behavior. Despite the fact that this property is not often interesting, it is an important one for us. In fact, it allows the emergence of original paths and explora-

Figure 1. Architecture of the computational model of attention

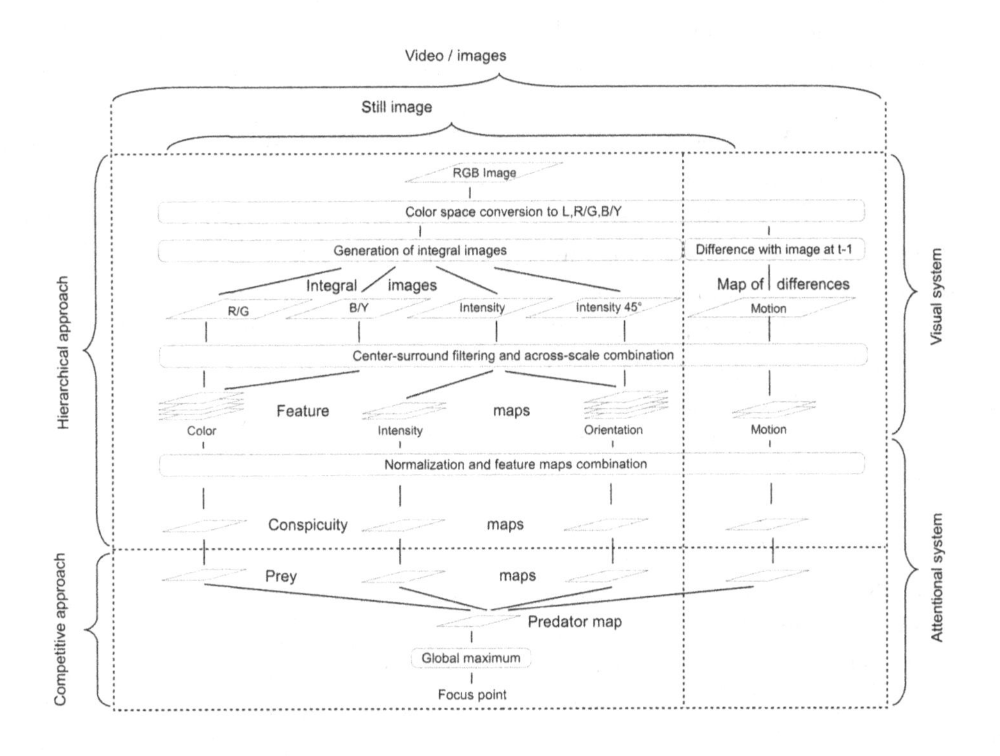

tion of visual scene, even in non-salient areas, reflecting something like curiosity.

Model Description and Implementation

Conspicuity Maps Processing

The 'visual system' part of our model provides two ways of generating its conspicuity maps:

- The classical one, treating the whole visual field with the same accuracy;
- The retina-inspired one, simulating the varying resolution of the human retina using a log-polar transform (as used in (Sela & Levine, 1997; Sun, Fisher, Wang, & Gomes, 2008). The proposed solution allows both retinal blur simulation and computational load reduction.

This section describes both methods, starting with common pre-processing and following on with the classical and the retina based approaches.

Pre-Processing

Human color processing is based on opponent color coding. Thus, our first pre-processing step is a color space conversion one. Some computational models (Frintrop, 2005) use perceptual color spaces like *Lab* in order to be as close as possible to the human visual system. However, our goal is to create a fast (but still plausible) attention model. For this reason we have chosen the L,R/G,B/Y space. This color space is similar to the one used in (Laurent Itti et al., 1998) except that it uses a faster subtraction-based normalization instead of a division-based one.

After color space conversion, we obtain one achromatic channel I_L and two chromatic channels $I_{R/G}$ and $I_{B/Y}$. These will serve as a basis for the generation of intensity, color, orientation and motion feature maps. These maps are usually obtained using Gaussian pyramids (Choi et al., 2006; Itti et al., 1998), but in order to speed up processing we have used an integral image-based approach democratized by Viola and Jones (2002) and proposed by Frintrop (2007) in an attention modeling context. However, this latter model was initially built with multi-resolution pyramids and later optimized with integral images; hence the full potential of this technique is not exploited. Consequently, our model was designed to massively use integral images for all of its feature maps.

Four integral images are necessary to compute all the feature maps:

- An intensity image II_L, derived from I_L helps generate intensity maps as well as 0° and 90° orientation maps;
- Two color images $II_{R/G}$ and $II_{B/Y}$, derived from $I_{R/G}$ and $I_{B/Y}$, used for color feature maps;
- One 45° rotated intensity image IIR_L, derived from I_L, allow the processing of 45° and 135° orientation maps. These images use an oriented extension of "basic" integral images, proposed by Lienhart and Maydt (2002).

Next, processing depends on whether the varying resolution of the retina is taken into account. In the next sub-section, we start by describing the 'classical' case, without retinal blur.

Map Generation without Retinal Blur

Intensity and Color Pyramids

Integral images are used to compute, quickly and in constant time, the sum of any rectangular area of an image. Consequently, our implementation of the centre-surround filters found in the human visual system is not based on the classical difference of Gaussians filter (DoG) but on a difference of boxes filter (DoB). Each level (r_0 to r_{N-1}) of the multi-resolution pyramid is thus computed from the integral image II_L, $II_{R/G}$ and $II_{B/Y}$. r_0 is the finest resolution, r_{N-1} the coarsest. For an image I of size WxH, we have N=1+log$_2$(min(W,H)). Due to the use of integral images, pyramids are not generated by iteratively reducing the size of images, but conversely by varying the size of the DoB filter. In our implementation, this filter is the difference of two filter $B_{1,r}$ and $B_{2,r}$:

$$S_{B_{1,r}} = \begin{cases} 1 & if\ r = 0 \\ 2^{r-1} \times 3 & otherwise \end{cases} \quad (1)$$

with $r \in \{1, N-3\}$.

Positive response of the DoB filter corresponds to on/off center-surround filters, negative response corresponds to off/on filters. In order to avoid information loss, these responses are stored in two different pyramids $P_{L_{on}}$, $P_{L_{off}}$:

$$P_{L_{on}}(x,y,r) = \begin{cases} CS_{L,r}(x,y) & if\ CS_{L,r}(x,y) > 0 \\ 0 & otherwise \end{cases}$$
$$P_{L_{off}}(x,y,r) = \begin{cases} -CS_{L,r}(x,y) & if\ CS_{L,r}(x,y) \leq 0 \\ 0 & otherwise \end{cases} \quad (2)$$

with

$CS_{L,r} = I_L * (B_{1,r} - B_{2,r}) = (I_L * B_{1,r}) - (I_L * B_{2,r})$.

Color pyramids P_R, P_G and P_B, P_Y are processed similarly.

Orientation Pyramids

(Itti et al., 1998) and (Frintrop, 2005) generate orientation pyramids from Gabor filters applied to a Laplacian pyramid. Itti also uses an additional center-surround filtering step, but, as pointed out by Frintrop, center-surround filtering is already performed by Gabor filter. Consequently, the latter is not necessary.

Figure 2. Harr-like filters used for oriented pyramids processing

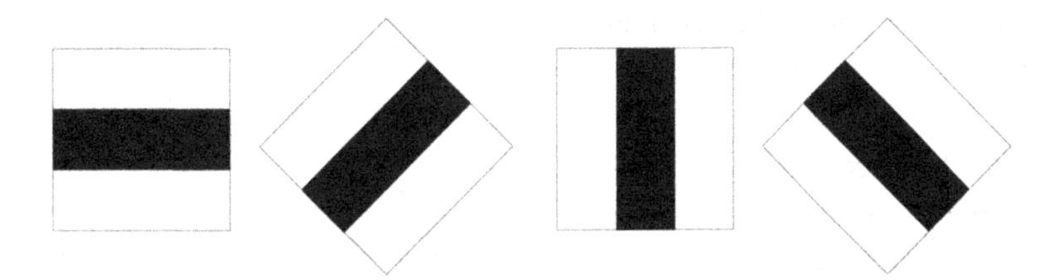

As Gabor filters computation is relatively slow, we favored the reuse of integral images generated during the pre-processing stage. The latter allows using orientation selective Harr-like filters in order to generate oriented pyramids efficiently (Figure 2).

For each resolution level $r \in \{1, N-3\}$, we can then generate four oriented pyramids P_{Ori0}, P_{Ori45}, P_{Ori90} and P_{Ori135}, corresponding to 0°, 45°, 90° et 135° orientations. The resulting pyramids are less accurate than Gabor based pyramids, but require much less computational power.

Motion Pyramids

Due to the center-surround nature of our visual system, motion saliency is primarily linked to speed or motion changes. Consequently an attentional system does not necessarily need an accurate description of the optical flow. Our model uses a simple and fast image differences-based motion detector which, although not biologically justified, is an effective way to obtain an acceptable estimate of motion in a video stream.

The image-differences image I_{Diff_L} is obtained by subtracting the intensity channel images of two successive video frames: $I_{Diff_L} = \left| I_{L_t} - I_{L_{t-1}} \right|$

The motion pyramids $P_{M_{on}}$ and $P_{M_{off}}$ are then processed in a classical way (i.e. with standard box filter and not integral images). In fact, the computational cost of building an integral image dedicated to motion pyramids processing would be too high.

Feature Maps, Singularity Maps, and Normalization

Intensity feature maps $FM_{L_{on}}$, $FM_{L_{off}}$, color feature maps FM_R, FM_G, FM_B, FM_Y, orientation feature maps FM_{Ori0}, FM_{Ori45}, FM_{Ori90}, FM_{Ori135} and motion feature maps $FM_{M_{on}}$, $FM_{M_{off}}$ are processed by a simple across-scale attention. Unlike (Laurent Itti et al., 1998), and similarly to (Frintrop, 2005), the addition is not performed relative to the coarsest resolution, but at an intermediate scale (usually r_2). This prevents losing too much information during the map addition process. For example, $FM_{L_{on}}$ is processed in the following way:

$$FM_{L_{on}}(x,y) = \bigoplus_r P_{L_{on}}(x,y,r) \tag{3}$$

where $r \in \{1, N-2\}$ and $\oplus$ is the across-scale addition operator.

In order to match the target resolution (usually r_2), each resolution level is respectively over-sampled or sub-sampled using bilinear interpolation or box filters. The resulting feature maps represent the most salient elements of the source image / video whatever the observation scale.

These maps could be used to directly feed the predator/prey attention system. However, using only four basic features (intensity, color, orientation and motion) leads to 12 feature maps. Running the competition on these 12 maps is possible but would unnecessarily complexify the model.

Consequently, and as proposed by Itti (1998) and Frintrop (2005), we merge the various feature maps into four singularity maps: intensity SM_L, color SM_C, orientation SM_O and motion SM_M.

As was demonstrated (Bruce & Jernigan, 2003; Frintrop, 2005; Laurent Itti et al., 1998), singularity maps cannot be reduced to a simple sum (or linear combination) of feature maps. A normalization step must be applied in order to emphasize the most salient elements of the scene. Different solutions have been proposed in (Itti & Koch, 2001; Itti et al., 1998) or (Frintrop, 2005), but they are either are too simplistic or have a high computational cost. To overcome these problems, we proposed an information theory based normalization operator inspired by (Mancas, 2007). The idea behind this operator is that salient elements / features are rare. In terms of information theory, rarity corresponds to self-information. For each pixel of a feature map FM_i, self-information $SI(x,y)$ is processed as follows:

$$SI_i(x,y)=-\log(p(FM_i'(x,y))) \quad (4)$$

where $p(x)$ is the probability that a pixel has gray-level x, FM_i' a 16 gray-level version of the feature map FM_i, and

$$i \in \{L_{on}, L_{off}, R, G, B, Y, Ori_0, Ori_{45}, Ori_{90} Ori_{135}, M_{on}, M_{off}\}.$$

The normalized feature map FM_i'' is then:

$$FM_i''(x,y) = \frac{FM_i(x,y) \times SI_i(x,y)}{\log(Card(FM_i))} \quad (5)$$

As SI_i reaches its maximum value when:

$$SI_i(x,y) = -\log(p(FM_i'(x,y))) = -\log(\frac{1}{Card(FM_i')}) = \log(Card(FM_i')) \quad (6)$$

The divider $\log(Card(FM_i))$ allows the keeping of

$$\frac{SI_i(x,y)}{\log(Card(FM_i))}$$

in the [0,1] interval.

After this normalization step, each singularity maps is computed as the average of its corresponding feature maps

(for example, $SM_L = \frac{FM''_{L_{on}} + FM''_{L_{off}}}{2}$).

Figure 3 illustrates the effect of this normalization step.

Computational Retinal Blur

Most computational models of attention perform the same processing on all the pixels of their source image/video. However, some use the log polar transform in order to simulate the internal structure of the retina whose spatial resolution is variable. From an attention modeling point of view, this kind of representation is worth studying because the gradual loss of information due to the non-uniform representation of image may have an impact on the allocation of the focus of attention.

Nevertheless, the log polar transform is not very well adapted to the structure of our model of visual attention: the use of integral images complexifies the processing of center-surround filter in the log polar domain. We propose a much more efficient technique, based on the replacement of the classical multi-resolution pyramids by multi-resolution columns (Figure 4). The following paragraph describes how this approach can be applied to the intensity channel, but it is also valid (and used) for color and orientation channels.

In the case of standard multi-resolution pyramids the integral image II_L is used to process the response of the center-surround filtering for each pixel of each resolution level. In the case of the multi-resolutions column, this processing is only

Figure 3. Effect of scarcity-based normalization on intensity feature maps (on/off and off/on, top row) and singularity map (bottom row).

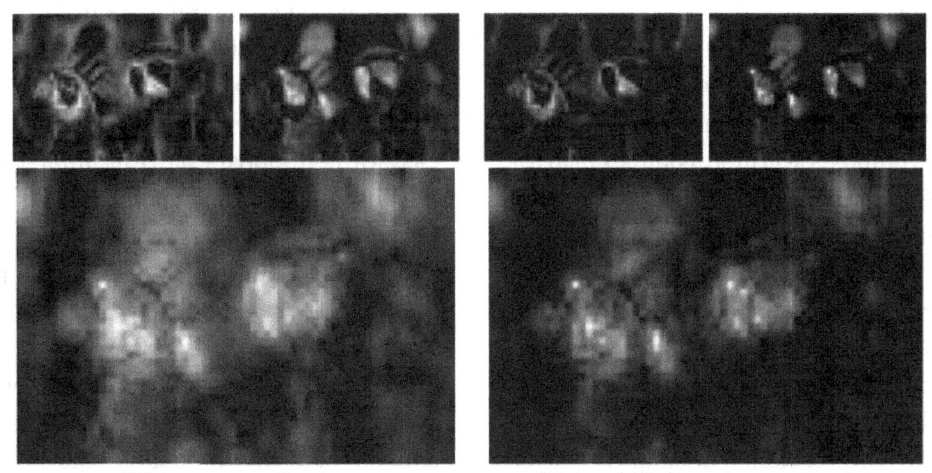

applied to a fixed size area (for example 16×16 pixels) whatever the resolution. This area is centered on the coordinates of the last focus of attention. When performing the final across-scale addition of the resolution levels of the multi-resolution analysis, this columnar representation generates a blur effect due to the fact that the amount of information available at each resolution is variable. For pixels close to the focus of attention, information from all scales is available. But for pixels further from this reference point, information from the finest resolution is missing: the across-scale addition is performed only from the coarsest resolutions.

This representation considerably reduces the computational resources needed. For example, for 256x256 pixels image and 5 resolution levels we process:

- 256×256+128×128+64×64+32×32+16×16=87296 pixels in the case of the multi-resolutions pyramid;

Figure 4. Multi-resolution pyramid versus multi-resolution column. In the column case, only a fixed size patch is calculated for each resolution.

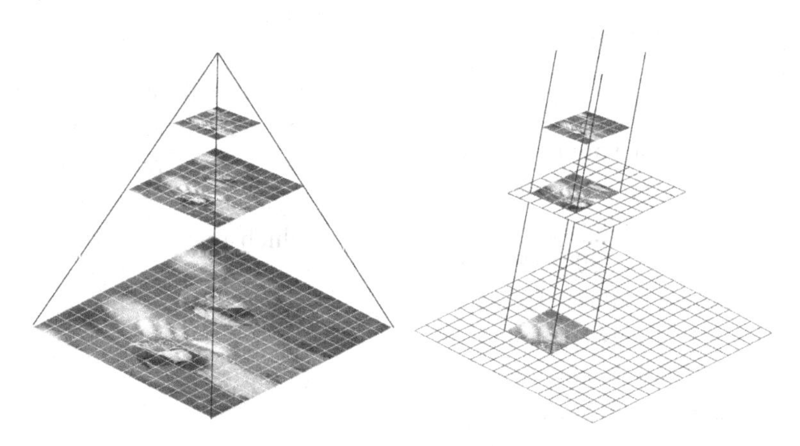

- $16\times16\times5=256\times5=$pixels in the case of the multi-resolutions column, that is 98.5% less processing!

Real computational gain is however more limited because across-scale addition of multi-resolution pyramids is a bit more complex than for pyramids. Additionally, integral images processing represents a significant and uncompressible time when compared to center-surround filtering. When taking into account the full processing pipeline, column-based processing is still 33% faster than classical pyramid-based processing.

It should be noted that motion maps are not processed using multi-resolution columns because:

- Even if the retina has a variable resolution, human motion sensitivity is still important in the periphery of the field of view;
- The column-based approach is computationally efficient when combined with integral-images based filtering which is not the case of motion maps.

Singularity maps, generated by the visual system part, are only the first part of our computational model of attention. A competition between these maps is then run in order to determine the evolution of the focus of attention. This is the role of the attentional system part of our model.

The Attentional System

Visual attention can be regarded as a competition between different sources of information. This point of view is, for example, shared by models based on the biased competition paradigm. They usually solve this competition problem by using a neural network approach (Deco, 2004; Spratling & Johnson, 2004; Tsotsos, Itti, et al., 2005; Tsotsos, Liu, et al., 2005; VanRullen, 2003). However this approach implies a complex modeling of the biological model which we do not need (our model should have a plausible behavior, but is not intended to be a neurobiological replica of the human visual system). Additionally such a complex system may impact the computational performances of the attention model.

An alternative approach is to consider the brain as a dynamic system whose behavior can be modeled at a more global scale (Eliasmith, 1995; Lesser & Dinah, 1998). The microscopic representation provided by neural networks is then replaced by a differential equation system, which provides a mesoscopic view of the attentional phenomenon (Fix, 2008; Vitay et al., 2005). In this context, we propose to model attentional competition with a competitive dynamical system inspired from animal food web modeling: the predator-prey system. Its architecture is represented in Figure 5.

The remainder of this section justifies the analogy between attention and the predator-prey model and describes the equations governing the evolution of the system.

How to Build a 2D Predator-Prey System

Predator-prey systems are defined by a set of equations whose objective is to simulate the evolution and the interactions of some colonies of prey and predators (Murray, 2003a, 2003b). For our system, we have based our work on (Lesser & Dinah, 1998) so as to represent the time evolution of the focus of attention.

Traditionally, the evolution of predator-prey systems is governed by a small set of simple rules, inspired from Volterra-Lotka equations (Volterra, 1928):

- The growth rate of prey is proportional to their population C and to a growth factor b;
- The growth rate of predators I is proportional to their predation rate CI (rate at which prey and predators encounter) and to a predation factor s;
- The mortality rate of predators is proportional to their population I and to a mortality factor m_I;

Figure 5. Competitive predator-prey attention model. Singularity maps are the resources that feed a set of prey which are themselves eaten by predators. The maximum of the predators' map represents the location of the current focus of attention.

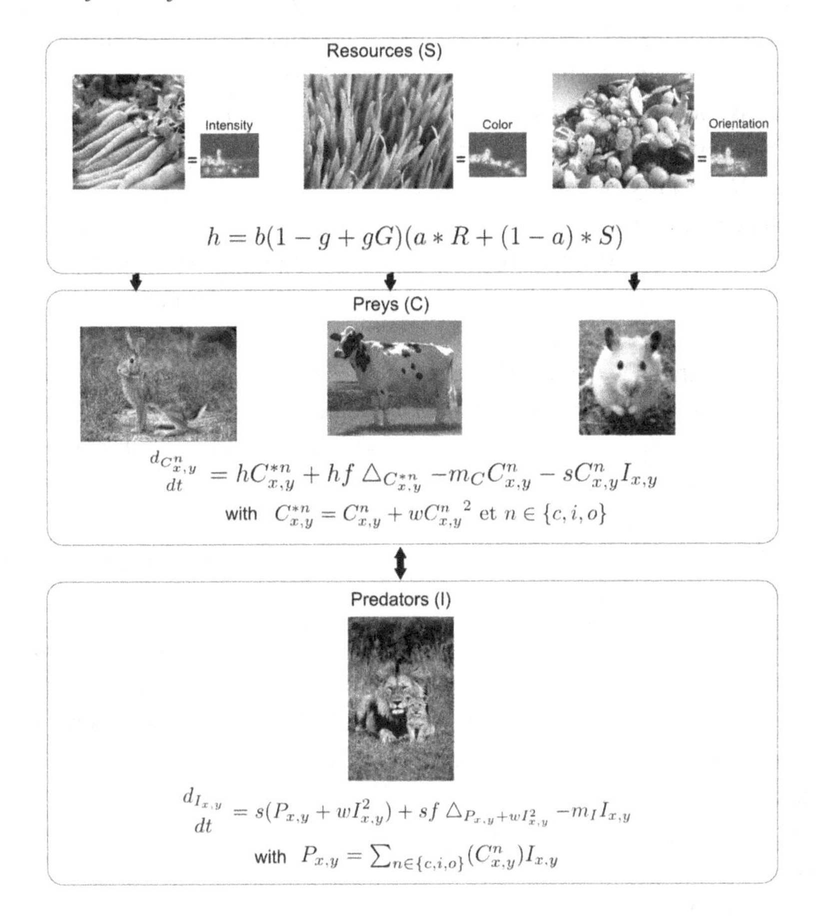

- The mortality rate of prey is proportional to the predation rate CI and a mortality factor s';

Formalizing these rules leads to Volterra-Lotka equations:

$$\frac{dC}{dt} = bC - s'CI$$
$$\frac{dI}{dt} = sCI - m_I I \tag{7}$$

This 'basic' version of predator-prey equations can be enriched in several ways:

- The number of parameters can be reduced by replacing s' by s. Indeed, mortality rate differences between prey and predators can be modeled by an adjustment of factors b and m_I
- The original model represents the evolution of a single quantity of prey and predators over time. It can be spatially extended in order to be applied to 2D maps where each point represents the amount of prey or predators at a given place and time. Prey and predators can then 'move' on this map using a classical diffusion rule, proportional to their Laplacian Δ_C and a diffusion factor f.

- Natural mortality of prey in the absence of predation is not taken into account. If the model only changes temporally, mortality is negligible when compared to predation. However, when the model is applied to a 2D map (which is the case in our system), some areas of the map may not contain any predator. Natural mortality of prey can no longer be considered negligible. A new mortality term $-m_c$ needs to be added to the model.

This yields the following set of equations, modeling the evolution of predator-prey populations on a two dimensional map:

$$\begin{cases} \frac{dC_{x,y}}{dt} = bC_{x,y} + f\Delta_{C_{x,y}} - m_C C_{x,y} - sC_{x,y} I_{x,y} \\ \frac{dI_{x,y}}{dt} = sC_{x,y} I_{x,y} + sf\Delta_{P_{x,y}} - m_I I_{x,y} \end{cases} \quad (8)$$

A last phenomenon can be added to this model: a positive feedback, proportional to C^2 or I^2 and controlled by a factor w. This feedback models the fact that (provided that there are unlimited resources) the more numerous a population is, the better it is able to grow (more efficient hunting, higher encounter rates favoring reproduction etc.). The new predator-prey system is now:

$$\begin{cases} \frac{dC_{x,y}}{dt} = b(C_{x,y} + w(C_{x,y})^2) + f\Delta_{C_{x,y}} - m_C C_{x,y} - sC_{x,y} I_{x,y} \\ \frac{dI_{x,y}}{dt} = s(C_{x,y} I_{x,y} + w(I_{x,y})^2) + sf\Delta_{P_{x,y}} - m_I I_{x,y} \end{cases} \quad (9)$$

In order to simulate the evolution of the focus of attention, we propose a predator-prey system (as described above) with the following features:

- The system is comprised of four types of prey and one type of predator;
- These four types of prey represent the spatial distribution of the curiosity generated by our four types of conspicuity maps (intensity, color, orientation and motion);
- The predators represent the interest generated by the consumption of curiosity (prey) associated to the different conspicuity maps;
- The global maximum of the predators maps (interest) represents the focus of attention at time t.

The equations described in the next sub-section are obtained by building a predator-prey system which integrates the above-cited features.

Simulating the Evolution of the Attentional Focus with a Predator-Prey System

For each of the three conspicuity maps (color, intensity, orientation and motion), the prey population C evolution is governed by the following equation:

$$\frac{dC^n_{x,y}}{dt} = hC^{*n}_{x,y} + hf\Delta_{C^{*n}_{x,y}} - m_C C^n_{x,y} - sC^n_{x,y} I_{x,y} \quad (10)$$

with $C^{*n}_{x,y} = C^n_{x,y} + w(C^n_{x,y})^2$ and $n \in \{c, i, o, m\}$, which means that this equation is valid for C^c, C^i, C^o and C^m which represent respectively color, intensity, orientation and motion populations.

C represents the curiosity generated by the image's intrinsic conspicuity. It is produced by a sum h of four factors:

$$h = b(1 - g + gG)(aR + (1 - a)SM_n)(1 - e) \quad (11)$$

- The image's conspicuity SM_n (with $n \in \{c, i, o, m\}$) is generated using our real time visual system, previously described in this chapter. Its contribution is inversely proportional to *a*;

- A source of random noise *R* simulates the high level of noise that can be measured when monitoring our brain activity (Fox, Snyder, Vincent, & Raichle, 2007). Its importance is proportional to *a*. Equations that model the evolution of our system become stochastic differential equations. A high value for *a* gives some 'freedom' to the attentional system, so it can explore less salient areas. On the contrary, a lower value for *a* will constrain the system to only visit high conspicuity areas;
- A Gaussian map *G* which simulates the central bias generally observed during psycho-visual experiments (Le Meur, Castellan, et al., 2006; Tatler, 2007). The importance of this map is modulated by *g*.
- The entropy *e* of the conspicuity map (color, intensity, orientation or motion). This map is normalized between 0 and 1. *C* is modulated by 1-*e* in order to favor maps with a small number of local minimums. Explained in terms of predator-prey system, we favor the growth of the most organized populations (grouped in a small number of sites). This mechanism is the predator-prey equivalent to the feature maps normalization presented above.

The population of predators *I*, which consume the 4 kinds of prey, is governed by the following equation:

$$\frac{dI_{x,y}}{dt} = s(P_{x,y} + wI_{x,y}^2) + sf\Delta_{P_{x,y}+wI_{x,y}^2} - m_I I_{x,y} \quad (12)$$

with $P_{x,y} = \sum_{n\in\{c,i,o\}} C_{x,y}^n I_{x,y}$.

As already mentioned the positive feedback factor *w* enforces the system dynamics and facilitates the emergence of chaotic behaviors by speeding up saturation in some areas of the maps. Lastly, please note that curiosity *C* is consumed by interest *I*, and that the maximum of the interest map *I* at time *t* is the location of the focus of attention.

To allow less frequent changes of the position of the focus of attention, we added an optional hysteresis mechanism. The latter changes the focus of attention only if the new maximum of the predators map exceeds its previous value by more than a certain threshold as presented in Box 1.with (x_{max}, y_{max}) the coordinates of the maximum of $P_{x,t}(t)$. $T_{Hysteresis}$ is the hysteresis threshold and *Focus(t)* are the coordinates of the current focus of attention.

Default Parameters of the Predator-Prey System

During the experiments presented at the end of this chapter, the following (empirically determined) parameters were used (Table 5):

These parameters represent reasonable values that can be used to obtain a system at equilibrium. This equilibrium is obtained when the system is run without any input image. Other parameter combinations are possible. In particular, experi-

Box 1. Equation 13

$$Focus(t) = \begin{cases} (x_{\max}, y_{\max}) & if\ \max_{x,y}(P_{x,y}(t)) > (1 + T_{Hysteresis}) \times \max_{x,y}(P_{x,y}(t-1)) \\ Focus(t-1) & otherwise \end{cases} \quad (13)$$

Table 5. Default parameters of the predator-prey model

a	b	g	w	m_C	m_I	s	f	$T_{Hysteresis}$
0.5	0.007	0.1	0.001	0.3	0.5	0.025	0.25	0.0

ments have shown that these values can be varied within a wide range without compromising the system's stability (see below for details). The system is thus quite robust against parameter variations.

Please note that our implementation of the model evolves according to the Euler method using a step size of 0.33 and that 3 sub-iterations are run before computing each simulated focus of attention.

Top-Down Feedback

The attention model presented in this chapter is computationally efficient and plausible. It provides many tuning possibilities (adjustment of curiosity, central preferences, etc.) that can be exploited in order to adapt the behavior of the system to a particular context. This adaptation is however somewhat limited. In this sub-section, we propose extending our bottom-up model so that it can take into account more information concerning its objectives.

This top-down influence can be expressed as a simple modification of the model parameters, but it can also reuse information generated by the system itself in order to modify its behavior. In the latter case, a feedback loop is created (auto-adaptation).

In the following, we define the adaptation mechanisms used in our model. We will also explore how previously-visited locations can be used as inputs to an attentional feedback mechanism aimed at controlling the scene exploration capabilities of the model.

Adaptation Mechanisms

In this sub-section, we describe the different mechanisms that can be used in order to adapt the model behavior to external constraints (e.g. top-down information).

Top-Down Map

Usually, top-down information is included in hierarchical computational attention models in either of these two ways:

- Global weighting of feature maps which allows a bias of the attentional system in favor of the distinctive features of a target object. This mechanism is used, for example, in (Frintrop, Backer, & Rome, 2005) in order to learn which features are salient, depending on the context.
- Local weighting of feature maps. This approach is an extension of the global weighting scheme which allows specifying prior knowledge about the target localization. This mechanism is exploited by (Navalpakkam & Itti, 2005) where it is called task-relevance maps.

Other extensions are also possible, for example using prior knowledge about the intensity of some expected features (Navalpakkam & Itti, 2006).

Even if the conspicuity maps fusion part of our model of attention is competitive (and thus non-hierarchical), it can be biased using top-down maps. This can be done using a map (different for each kind of prey) which will favor the growth of one kind of prey against anther (eventually at preferred locations):

Figure 6. Effects of global weighting. a) heatmap generated with default parameters ($W^c=W^i=W^o=1.0$), b) heatmap generated with lower color weights ($W^c=0.5$), c) heatmap generated with high color weight ($W^i=W^o=0.5$)

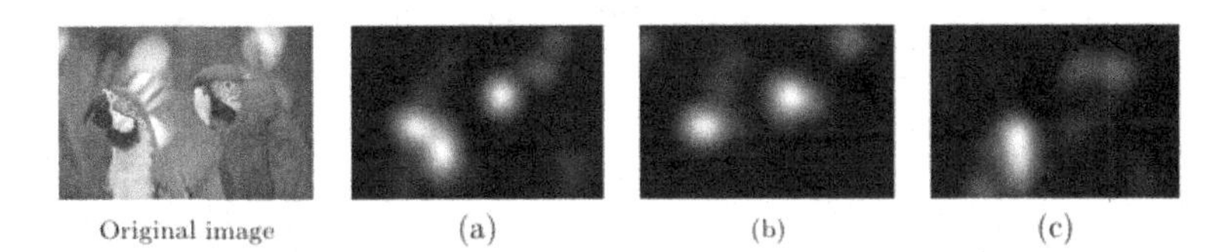

$$\frac{dC^n_{x,y}}{dt} = T^n_{x,y}\left(1-\frac{C^n_{x,y}}{Max_{population}}\right)\left(hC^{*n}_{x,y}+hf\Delta_{C^{*n}_{x,y}}\right)- m_C C^n_{x,y} - sC^n_{x,y}I^n_{x,y} \quad (14)$$

where $T^n_{x,y}$ is the top-down map associated with a prey type,

$n \in \{c,i,o,m\}$, and $\max_{x,y}(T^n_{x,y}) = 1.0$.

If $T^n_{x,y} = W^n \ \forall\ (x,y)$ then the evolution of prey n is constrained by a global weight (Figure 6).

Otherwise, saliency boosting is local (Torralba et al., 2006). It can be used, for example, to favor colored targets located in the right part of the scene.

Feedback Maps

Top-down maps as described in the previous paragraphs help modify the attentional system behavior using contextual prior-knowledge (external to the model of attention). But the system can also be biased using information generated by the model itself or the computer vision system it is connected to.

This mechanism can be implemented using a global feedback map *R* which will be used as a facilitation or inhibition mechanism. The prey growth equation now becomes:

$$\frac{dC^n_{x,y}}{dt} = R_{x,y}T^n_{x,y}\left(1-\frac{C^n_{x,y}}{Max_{population}}\right)\left(hC^{*n}_{x,y}+hf\Delta_{C^{*n}_{x,y}}\right)- m_C C^n_{x,y} - sC^n_{x,y}I^n_{x,y} \quad (15)$$

where $R_{x,y}$ is built according to one or more feedback criteria. An example criterion, based on scene exploration is given in the next sub-section.

A Feedback Criterion: Scene Exploration

In this sub-section, we describe how we can use a scene exploration feedback criterion based on the history of attentional focus points generated by our system. If we build a map of previously visited locations and modulate (negatively or positively) its influence in the prey growing equation, we can define two complementary attentional strategies (and all intermediate states):

- Scene exploration maximization: the attentional system will favor unvisited areas;
- Focalization stability: the attentional system will favor areas already visited.

We now describe how this visited areas map is constructed, and how it can be used as a feedback map.

Box 2. Equation 16

$$M_{visit}(x,y,t) = \max\left(M_{visit}(x,y,t-1), \frac{N_{Levels} - \min\left(\frac{dist(x,y,x_f,y_f)}{BlurSize}, N_{Levels}\right)}{N_{Levels}}\right) \quad (16)$$

$$M_b(x,y,t-1), N_{Levels} - \min\left(\frac{dist(x,y,x_f,y_f)}{BlurSize}, N_{Levels}\right)$$

Box 3. Equation 17

$$M_{visit}(x,y,t) = \max\left(F_{forget} \times M_{visit}(x,y,t-1), \frac{N_{Levels} - \min\left(\frac{dist(x,y,x_f,y_f)}{BlurSize}, N_{Levels}\right)}{N_{Levels}}\right) \quad (17)$$

Visited Areas Map

The visited areas map construction is based on the following hypothesis: During an attentional focus, most of the information is acquired at the center of a circular area (equivalent to the fovea in the retina). In the rest of this circular area, information linearly loses importance as we move away from the center.

The visited areas map is constructed incrementally in order to keep a memory of all the information acquired in the scene as presented in Box 2.where (x_f,y_f) are the coordinates of the focus of attention at time *t*; $dist(x_1,y_1,x_2,y_2)$ is the Euclidian distance between (x_1,y_1) and (x_2,y_2); *BlurSize* the size of the retinal area (fixed to 10% of the largest image dimension; this value may be associated with human fovea size (about 2 degrees of visual field)); *NbLevels*=*ceiling*($\log_2$(min(*W*,*H*)) and (*W*,*H*) the size of the input image.

It guarantees that $M_{Visit}(x,y) \in [0,1]\ \forall x,y$.

However, human memory is limited, and thus the attentional focus is most probably influenced by only the most recent focus points. To improve the plausibility of M_{visit}, we should take into account this fact and update the M_{visit} equation by introducing a "forgetting" factor $F_{forget} \in [0,1]$ which will iteratively attenuate the role of the oldest focus points as presented in Box 3.

Figure 7 shows the influence of F_{forget} on the visited areas map $M_{visites}$.

Feedback Map Processing

The feedback map *R* is built upon $M_{visites}$. Its parameter $F_{feedback}$ allows modulating the influence of the visited areas map in intensity and feedback type (positive or negative):

Figure 7. Influence of F_{forget} on the visited areas map, after 100 attention simulation iterations

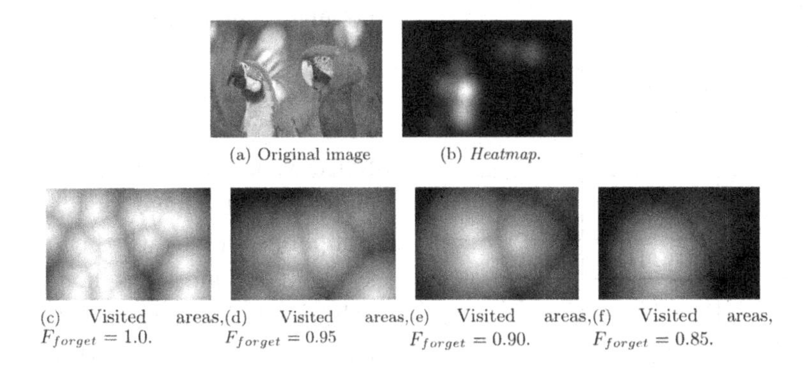

(a) Original image (b) *Heatmap*.

(c) Visited areas, $F_{forget} = 1.0$. (d) Visited areas, $F_{forget} = 0.95$ (e) Visited areas, $F_{forget} = 0.90$. (f) Visited areas, $F_{forget} = 0.85$.

$$R(x,y) = \begin{cases} \dfrac{1+\left|F_{feedback}\right| \times M_{visit}(x,y)}{1+\left|F_{feedback}\right|} & if\ F_{feedback} \geq 0 \\ \dfrac{1+\left|F_{feedback}\right| \times (1-M_{visit}(x,y))}{1+\left|F_{feedback}\right|} & otherwise \end{cases} \quad (18)$$

with $R(x,y) \in \left[0,1\right] \forall x,y$.

A positive feedback value will lead to a focalization or tracking behavior because previously visited objects / locations are preferred. A negative feedback value will lead to an exploration behavior because unknown (unvisited) objects or locations will be favored.

The computational model of attention described in this chapter provides many tuning parameters and adaptation mechanisms. In order to validate this model we need to evaluate its plausibility by comparing its prediction with human fixations; but we also need to study the way it reacts when its parameters are adjusted. In fact, the model is dedicated to computer vision and as such we should provide some clues concerning its general behavior (plausibility, reproducibility, etc.). This is the purpose of the next section.

EVALUATION OF THE MODEL

Model Properties

In order to evaluate our model, it is necessary to define one or more observation levels (microscopic or macroscopic) as well as a set of properties. In this chapter we study macroscopic properties, since we are interested in the overall behavior of the model (competition between different sources of attention). The properties studied are derived from the PAIRED constraint set defined at the beginning of this chapter:

- **Stability:** Do the values of the dynamical system stay within their nominal range when the different parameters of the model are changed ?
- **Reproducibility:** As discrete dynamical system can have a chaotic behavior, what is the influence of the various parameters of the model (in particular, noise) on the variability of the focus paths generated during different simulations on the same data ?
- **Scene Exploration:** Which parameters influence the scene exploration strategy of our model?
- **System Dynamics:** How can we influence the reactivity of the system? In particular how do we deal with mean fixation time?

Table 6. Stability range of the main parameters of the predator-prey system

Parameter	Default value	Min stable value	Max stable value
Prey natality (b)	0.007	0.006	0.013
Prey mortality (m_C)	0.3	0.3	0.36
Predation (s)	0.025	0.017	0.05
Predator natality (m_I)	0.5	0.1	1.5
Positive feedback (w)	0.001	0	0.003

For all of these properties we have also studied the influence of top-down feedback.

All the measures presented in this section were done on two image databases. The first one is proposed by Bruce and Tsotsos (2009). It is made up of 120 color images whose contexts are streets, gardens, vehicles or buildings, more or less salient. The second one, proposed by Le Meur et al. (2006), contains 26 color images. They represent sport scenes, animals, buildings, indoor scenes or landscapes. Unless otherwise stated, the system is run using the parameters defined in Table 5.

Stability

Volterra-Lotka equations are only stable in a predefined range of parameter values (Idema, 2005). This statement is also true for our attention model. For example, if prey's birth rate is too small compared to predation rate and natural mortality of predators is high, neither prey nor predators will see their populations grow.

We have studied the stability of our system by monitoring the mean value of the prey maps Cn and the predator map I. If these values stay within a finite range, the system is stable. Table 6 gives an overview of the system behavior for different values of natality, mortality and predator parameters b, m_C, m_I, s. Outside of the stability ranges defined in this table prey and/or predator population gradually saturate.

Reproducibility

Since we are using a discrete dynamical system and because we have added a random map when computing the growth factor of the attentional system, our model is non-deterministic. This behavior is interesting because it simulates the natural variability observed when performing multiple eye-tracking experiments on the same person and the same data set. It is also a way to adjust the curiosity of our attentional system by encouraging the exploration of relatively low saliency areas of an image.

However, giving more 'curiosity' to our system also leads to less reproducibility. In order to study this phenomenon, we have used the same measures as when studying attentional models plausibility. We have compared heatmaps generated from eye-tracking measures, with heatmaps generated from various simulations with our model. We have used classical similarity / dissimilarity measures: cross-correlation (Le Meur, Le Callet, et al., 2006), Kullback-Leibler divergence (Tatler, Baddeley, & Gilchrist, 2005) and normalized scanpath salience (Peters, Iyer, Itti, & Koch, 2005).

During our experiments, we used ground truth heatmaps included in Bruce and LeMeur datasets. Simulated heatmaps were generated using the same method as for ground truth maps: integrating all focalizations on a single map, and then filtering this map with a Gaussian filter $G_{\sigma x, \sigma y}$ where:

$$\sigma_x = \sigma_y = 0.3 \times \mathit{foveaSize} \times \max(W,H)$$

With W and H the width and height of the source image, and $\mathit{foveaSize} = 0.15$ (which correspond to a Gaussian width of approximately 15% of the source image).

As the number of parameters studied is important (retinal filter, central bias, diffusion, hysteresis, noise, positive feedback and top-down

Table 9. Summary of the influence of each parameter on the model

Parameters	Default value	Plausibility	Reproducibility	Exploration	Dynamics
Retinal blur	Not used	⇗	⇘	⇗	⇨
Central bias (g)	0.1	⇧	⇨	⇧	⇩
Diffusion (f)	0.25	⇨	⇘	⇗	⇘
$T_{Hysteresis}$	0	⇨	⇨/⇘	⇘	⇘
Noise (a)	0.5	⇧/⇩	⇩	⇧	⇗
Positive feedback (w)	0.0001	⇗/⇩	⇘/⇩	⇗/⇘	⇗/⇩
Simulation step	1/3	×	×	×	⇧
# of sub-iterations	3	×	×	×	⇧
Top-down feedback	0	⇨	⇨	⇩	⇩

Box 4. Equation 19

$$M_b(x,y,t) = \max\left(M_b(x,y,t-1), N_{Levels} - \min\left(\frac{dist(x,y,x_f,y_f)}{BlurSize}, N_{Levels}\right)\right) \tag{19}$$

feedback) we have decided not to include detailed results of our measures in this chapter. A summary of the analysis of these results is however available in Table 9.

Scene Exploration

Scene exploration validation is based on a measure of the quantity of information lost between the original image and a 'reconstruction' of this image through the evolution of the attentional focus. To 'reconstruct' the image during the dynamic simulation, we start from a completely blurred image and 'add' details from the image in areas which get the focus. The 'reconstruction' becomes sharper and sharper through time evolution.

In fact, we update a blurring mask M_b whose maximum values represent non blurred areas and minimum values represent highly-blurred area. Its iterative construction is similar to the one used for M_{visit} equation, as demonstrated in Box 4.

Reconstructed image I_R is then generated through a convolution between the source image I_S and a mean filter B_s:

$$I_R(x,y) = I_s(x,y) * B_s(x,y) \tag{20}$$

With s the size of the filter, $s(x,y) = 2^{N_{Levels} - M_b(x,y)}$. Examples of image 'reconstruction' are presented in Figure 8.

After generating these "reconstructed images", we have used the minimum description length (MDL) principle inspired by (Rissanen, 1978). Following this principle, the simpler a data is, the easier it is to compress. We have decided to adapt this principle to images using two compression technics: JPEG (lossy compression) and PNG (lossless compression). An estimator between 0 and 1 is obtained at any t:

Figure 8. Example of image 'reconstruction'. Left, source image and current focus point; middle, blur mask; right, 'reconstructed' image.

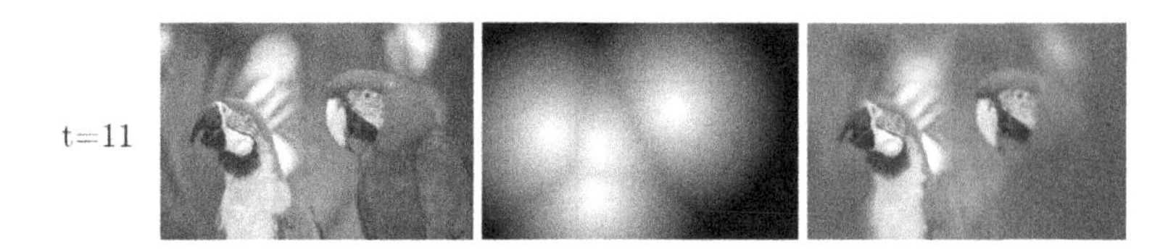

Table 7. Influence of feedback on scene exploration

Feedback	PNG			JPG		
	t=50	t=150	t=300	t=50	t=150	t=300
-1.0	0,940	0,983	0,992	0,779	0,915	0,955
-0.8	0,941	0,983	0,992	0,778	0,914	0,955
-0.6	0,930	0,978	0,987	0,772	0,913	0,955
-0.4	0,922	0,980	0,991	0,752	0,906	0,950
-0.2	0,914	0,977	0,988	0,736	0,894	0,939
0.0	0,899	0,963	0,978	0,714	0,860	0,911
0.2	0,810	0,900	0,935	0,609	0,751	0,817
0.4	0,763	0,856	0,902	0,550	0,684	0,767
0.6	0,739	0,830	0,871	0,522	0,648	0,721
0.8	0,722	0,807	0,840	0,500	0,611	0,668
1.0	0,703	0,792	0,826	0,481	0,594	0,645

$$InformationRatio_{JPEG} = \frac{size(compress_{JPEG}(I_S))}{size(compress_{JPEG}(I_R))}$$
$$InformationRatio_{PNG} = \frac{size(compress_{PNG}(I_S))}{size(compress_{PNG}(I_R))} \quad (21)$$

where I_S the source image and I_R the reconstructed image.

The feedback mechanism aims to control the way in which visual scene is explored. Results obtained from measures described above (JPEG and PNG ratio) confirm this expected behavior (Table 7):

- Positive feedback leads to a faster but not necessarily a more exhaustive exploration. Without any feedback, the scene is already almost covered after 300 simulation steps;
- Negative feedback can greatly reduce the explored area. For a feedback value $F_{feedback}$=-1, even after 300 simulation steps, the scene exploration ratio is still inferior to the one obtained without any feedback.

Other parameters also play a role in scene exploration, in particular noise and central bias. Their influence is summarized in Table 9.

Dynamics

Even if our system does not generate saccades and fixations which are directly comparable to human eye fixations (we do not take into account eye movements constraints), we can estimate the average time *FixationTime* between two changes

Table 8. Influence of a few parameters on simulated fixation time

Parameters	Default	CentralBias =0.5	Feedback= -1.0	Feedback =1.0	Step=0.1 Iterations=1	Hysteresis =0.5
Fixation time (ms)	70.1	142.88	52.98	416.57	806.76	102.02

of position of the simulated focus of attention. New fixations detection can be done:

- When the position of the focus of attention changes, regardless of the distance to the next position;
- If the distance between the current focus and the next exceeds a threshold S_{Fixing}.

We have chosen the second method because it allows canceling the effect of small movements that would otherwise bias the estimation of the average time between two fixations. The value of S_{Fixing} (15% of the longest side of the source image) was determined so as to be consistent with the *foveaSize* parameter used to generate heatmaps from the focus of attention output by our attention model.

We measured the effect of the different parameters of our model on the mean fixation time for the Bruce and Le Meur image databases. The results of this study are summarized in Table 9. Table 8 gives a few examples for some representative parameters. These results should be compared to mean human fixation time (300 ms; Dorr, Gegenfurtner, & Barth, 2010).

Dynamics can be fine-tuned using many parameters, but the most efficient ones are differential equation evolution parameters (simulation step and number of sub-iterations), feedback, and central bias. However, these parameters do not have the same side-effects on other properties such as plausibility and scene exploration.

Summary

Table 9 summarizes the influence of each parameter on the system behavior. We have not mentioned the influence of birth and death factors b, s, M_C and M_I since they only affect stability.

The arrows used have the following meanings:

⇧ strong positive influence
⇩ strong negative influence
⬀ weak positive influence
⬂ weak negative influence
⇨ no significant influence
✖ non-tested / theoretically non-influent

In the case of the retinal filter, arrows correspond to the influence of activating the filter. Arrows separated by a slash (for example: ⇨/⬂) represent a first type of influence for small increases of the parameters, followed by a second type of influence for higher increases.

Model Plausibility

Comparison to Existing Models

In (Perreira Da Silva, Courboulay, Prigent, & Estraillier, 2010) we have presented a subjective validation of the plausibility of our model. In this chapter we confirm the latter by a more classical objective evaluation. This validation consists of checking the plausibility of the system, i.e. checking if it is apparently reasonably-valid, and truthful.

Cross-correlation, Kullback-Leibler divergence and normalized scanpath saliency were used to compare six algorithms to an eye-tracking

Figure 9. Plausibility of computational models. Comparison of the saliency maps and heatmaps generated by the six algorithms tested.

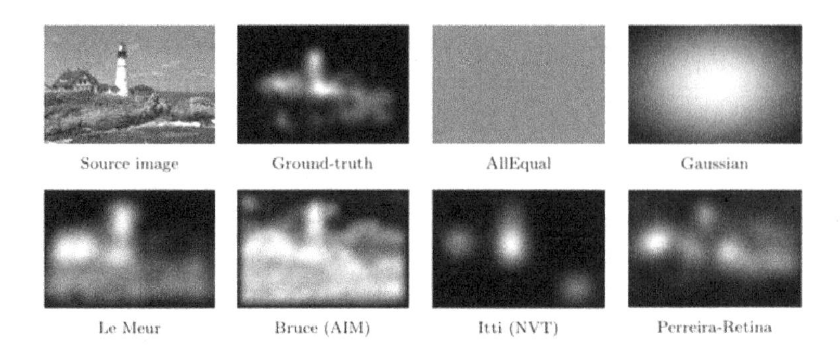

Table 10. Comparison of different algorithms to ground-truth (Please note that for KLD, lower values mean more plausibility)

	CC		KLD		NSS	
	Bruce	**LeMeur**	**Bruce**	**LeMeur**	**Bruce**	**LeMeur**
Bruce	0,40	0,45	1,59	1,08	0,98	0,89
LeMeur	0,37	0,43	1,61	1,08	0,90	0,84
Itti	0,31	0,27	2,74	2,52	0,79	0,54
AllEqual	0,00	0,00	2,15	1,55	0,00	0,00
Gaussian	0,46	0,60	1,55	0,94	1,02	1,10
Perreira-Retina	0,43	0,38	1,61	1,40	1,17	0,73

ground-truth (Figure 9). The models evaluated were:

- Two naïve models. 'AllEqual' correspond to a constant saliency map, consider all points as equally salient. 'Gaussian' model considers the central part of the image as the most salient area. Saliency is distributed using a centered Gaussian distribution, scaled in order to cover all the image ($\sigma_x = \frac{imageWidth}{3}$ and $\sigma_y = \frac{imageHeight}{3}$);
- Le Meur model (Le Meur, Le Callet, et al., 2006), in its 'coherent normalization' version;
- The AIM model of Bruce and Tsotsos (2009);
- The NVT model of Itti et al. (1998).
- Our model (with fast retinal blur).

All models were tested using their default parameters.

Table 10 is a summary of the performance of each algorithm over all the images of the two test databases. The analysis of the latter table leads to the following observations:

- Kullback-Leibler divergence is sensitive to maps normalization: the 'AllEqual' model seems to perform better than Itti's model whereas it obtains a null score with the two other measures;

Table 11. Influence of model parameters on plausibility. Gains are relative to default parameters defined in Table 5.

Parameters	CC		KLD		NSS		Mean gain
	Bruce	LeMeur	Bruce	LeMeur	Bruce	LeMeur	
Default	0,35	0,30	1,80	1,76	0,95	0,56	0%
RetinalFilter	0,43	0,38	1,61	1,40	1,17	0,73	22%
CentralBias=0.00	0,20	0,14	2,33	2,29	0,57	0,27	-41%
CentralBias=0.25	0,48	0,44	1,57	1,49	1,29	0,82	32%
CentralBias=0.50	0,55	0,53	1,92	1,66	1,49	1,01	45%
Diffusion=0.00	0,33	0,23	2,06	2,26	0,96	0,47	-14%
Diffusion=0.125	0,35	0,29	1,77	1,70	0,95	0,55	0%
Diffusion=0.50	0,35	0,31	1,83	1,72	0,94	0,59	1%
Noise=0.00	0,17	0,06	4,32	4,77	0,49	0,13	-95%
Noise=0.25	0,16	0,07	4,21	4,49	0,48	0,15	-90%
Noise=0.75	0,46	0,44	1,61	1,17	1,25	0,83	33%
Noise=1.00	0,27	0,35	1,89	1,30	0,68	0,64	0%

- The ‘AllEqual’ model is (quite unsurprisingly) the worst performer;
- Despite its simplicity, the ‘Gaussian’ model is quite a plausible model. This central preference is a well-known bias when evaluating computational attention models over eye-tracking data. It may be due to the type of images included in the databases, the experimental protocol, the photographer bias (which tends to center its subject in the picture), or a real attentional bias toard the central position. This effect can however be attenuated by using an alternative metric: the area under ordinal dominant score (Berg, Boehnke, Marino, Munoz, & Itti, 2009);
- Our model’s performance is comparable to other state of the art models and even outperforms them on the ‘Bruce’ database (NSS measure).

Influence of Parameters

We have shown that our model is as plausible as other state of the art models. However, this model (and in particular its dynamical system) depends on numerous parameters. Table 11 summarizes the influences of some of these parameters on the plausibility of the model. The following conclusions can be drawn:

- Using a retinal filter during the generation of feature and conspicuity maps significantly improves plausibility. This tends to prove that each new attentional focus depends on the location of the previous attentional focus;
- Using central biasing in an attention model can significantly improve its plausibility, but this bias is partly due to the experimental protocol;
- The dynamical system used in our attention model needs some diffusion in order to work correctly, but adding more diffusion does not improve plausibility;
- Similarly, noise is an important factor for the plausibility of the model. However, the influence of noise on the repeatability of the system (variation in behavior between different runs) is still an open question.

Table 12. Influence of top-down feedback on plausibility. Gains are relative to the bottom-up only version of the model.

Gain / Feedback	-1.0	-0.8	-0.6	-0.4	-0.2	0	0.2	0.4	0.6	0.8	1.0
CC+NSS	-19%	-18%	-16%	-13%	-7%	0%	9%	10%	12%	14%	20%
KLD	-1%	0%	1%	1%	3%	0%	-10%	-26%	-40%	-55%	-64%

Influence of Feedback

The influence of feedback on the plausibility of our model is quite complicated to explain. In fact, as can be seen in Table 12, the mean changes observed seem contradictory:

- For cross-correlation and normalized scanpath salience, the use of top-down feedback appears to improve the plausibility of our model;
- For the Kullback Leibler divergence, it seems rather to reduce it.

Our explanation is the following: NSS and correlation are similarity measures while Kullback-Leibler divergence is a dissimilarity measure, as a consequence they react differently to a change in the exploration strategy of our model.

It is therefore difficult to judge the influence of feedback, as it is twofold. However, we can conclude that feedback slightly improves correlation of our model with ground truth in the most salient areas, the price of increasing the difference with ground truth in the less salient areas.

CONCLUSION

In this chapter, we have presented a complete implementation and evaluation of a computational model of attention for computer vision. Concerning implementation, we have shown that predator-prey models provide good properties for simulating the dynamic competition between different kinds of information. We have described the architecture of our model which can be divided into two parts. The first one is hierarchical, it improves the model of Itti by providing much faster processing times while allowing the computation of more scales during its multi-resolution analysis of the scene. The second part is our major contribution: it makes use of a dynamical system (inspired from a predator-prey competition analogy) to handle the fusion of conspicuity maps generated by the first part of the model. This dynamical system is also used to generate a focus point at each time step of the simulation. Concerning evaluation, we have presented different results (cross-correlation, Kullback-Leibler divergence, normalized scanpath salience) which demonstrate that, in spite of being fast and highly configurable, our results are as plausible as existing models designed for high biological fidelity.

REFERENCES

Achanta, R., Estrada, F., Wils, P., & Süsstrunk, S. (2008). Salient region detection and segmentation. *6th International Conference on Computer Vision Systems, ICVS* (pp. 66-75). Berlin, Germany: Springer.

Ahmad, S. (1992). *VISIT: An efficient computational model of human visual attention*. University of Illinois at Urbana-Champaign, Champaign, IL, (510). Citeseer.

Allport, D. A. (1987). Selection for action: Some behavioral and neurophysiological considerations of attention and action. In H. Heuer & S. A.F. (Eds.), *Perspectives on perception and action* (pp. 395-419). Hillsdale, NJ: Lawrence Erlbaum Associates.

Avraham, T., & Lindenbaum, M. (2010). Esaliency (extended saliency): Meaningful attention using stochastic image modeling. *IEEE Transactions on Pattern Analysis and Machine Intelligence*, *32*(4), 693–708. doi:10.1109/TPAMI.2009.53

Aziz, M. Z., & Mertsching, B. (2008). Fast and robust generation of feature maps for region-based visual attention. *IEEE Transactions on Image Processing: A Publication of the IEEE Signal Processing Society, 17*(5), 633-644. doi:10.1109/TIP.2008.919365

Aziz, M. Z., & Mertsching, B. (2009). *Towards standardization of evaluation metrics and methods for visual attention models. Attention in Cognitive Systems* (pp. 227–241). Springer.

Baldi, P., & Itti, Laurent. (2005). Attention: Bits versus wows. *2005 International Conference on Neural Networks and Brain* (pp. 56-61). IEEE.

Belardinelli, A., Pirri, F., & Carbone, A. (2009). *Motion saliency maps from spatiotemporal filtering. Lecture Notes in Artificial Intelligence* (pp. 112–123). Springer.

Berg, D. J., Boehnke, S. E., Marino, R. A., & Munoz, D. P., & Itti, Laurent. (2009). Free viewing of dynamic stimuli by humans and monkeys. *Journal of Vision (Charlottesville, Va.)*, *9*, 1–15. doi:10.1167/9.5.19

Berthoz, A. (2009). *La simplexité* (pp. 1–256). Paris: Odile Jaco.

Broadbent, D. E. (1958). *Perception and communication* (p. 340). Elmsford, NY: Pergamon Press. doi:10.1037/10037-000

Bruce, B., & Jernigan, E. (2003). Evolutionary design of context-free attentional operators. *Proceedings of ICIP '03* (pp. 0-3). Citeseer.

Bruce, N. D. B., & Tsotsos, J. K. (2008). Spatiotemporal saliency: Towards a hierarchical representation of visual saliency. *Proceedings of the 5th International Workshop on Attention in Cognitive Systems* (pp. 98-111). Springer.

Bruce, N. D. B., & Tsotsos, J. K. (2009). Saliency, attention, and visual search: An information theoretic approach. *Journal of Vision (Charlottesville, Va.)*, *9*(3), 5. doi:10.1167/9.3.5

Bundesen, C. (1987). Visual attention: Race models for selection from multi-element displays. *Psychological Research*, *49*, 113–121. doi:10.1007/BF00308676

Bundesen, C. (1998). A computational theory of visual attention. *Philosophical Transactions of the Royal Society of London. Series B, Biological Sciences*, *353*(1373), 1271–1281. doi:10.1098/rstb.1998.0282

Chamaret, C., & Meur, O. L. (2009). *Attention-based video reframing: validation using eye-tracking. Pattern Recognition, ICPR* (pp. 1–4). IEEE.

Choi, S.-B., Jung, B.-S., & Ban, S.-W. (2006). Biologically motivated vergence control system using human-like selective attention model. *Neurocomputing*, *69*(4-6), 537–558. doi:10.1016/j.neucom.2004.12.012

Deco, G. (2004). A neurodynamical cortical model of visual attention and invariant object recognition. *Vision Research*, *44*(6), 621–642. doi:10.1016/j.visres.2003.09.037

Desimone, R., & Duncan, J. (1995). Neural mechanisms of selective visual attention. *Annual Review of Neuroscience*, *18*, 193–222. doi:10.1146/annurev.ne.18.030195.001205

Dong, L., Ban, S. W., & Lee, M. (2006). Biologically inspired selective attention model using human interest. *International Journal of Information Technology*, *12*(2), 140–148.

Dorr, M., Gegenfurtner, K. R., & Barth, E. (2010). Variability of eye movements when viewing dynamic natural scenes. *Journal of Vision (Charlottesville, Va.)*, *10*, 1–17. doi:10.1167/10.10.28

Driver, J. (2001). A selective review of selective attention research from the past century. *The British Journal of Psychology*, *92*(1), 53–78. doi:10.1348/000712601162103

Eliasmith, C. (1995). *Mind as a dynamical system*. University of Waterloo.

Fix, J. (2008). *Mécanismes numériques et distribués de lanticipation motrice*. Université Henri Poincaré - Nancy 1.

Fox, M. D., Snyder, A. Z., Vincent, J. L., & Raichle, M. E. (2007). Intrinsic fluctuations within cortical systems account for intertrial variability in human behavior. *Neuron*, *56*(1), 171–184. doi:10.1016/j.neuron.2007.08.023

Frintrop, S. (2005). *VOCUS: A Visual attention system for object detection and goal-directed search*. University of Bonn. doi:10.1007/11682110

Frintrop, S., Backer, G., & Rome, E. (2005). Selecting what is important: Training visual attention. *28th Annual German Conference on AI (KI)* (pp. 351-366). Koblenz, Germany: Springer Verlag.

Frintrop, S., Klodt, M., & Rome, E. (2007). A real-time visual attention system using integral images. *5th International Conference on Computer Vision Systems (ICVS)*. Bielefeld, Germany: Applied Computer Science Group.

Geerinck, T., Sahli, H., Henderickx, D., Vanhamel, I., & Enescu, V. (2009). *Modeling attention and perceptual grouping to salient objects. Attention in Cognitive Systems* (p. 166). London, UK: Springer, Limited.

Gilles, S. (1996). *Description and experimentation of image matching using mutual information*. Oxford: Entropy.

Hamker, F. (2005). The emergence of attention by population-based inference and its role in distributed processing and cognitive control of vision. *Computer Vision and Image Understanding*, *100*(1-2), 64–106. doi:10.1016/j.cviu.2004.09.005

Idema, T. (2005). *The behaviour and attractiveness of the Lotka-Volterra equations. ilorentz.org*. Universiteit Leiden.

Itti, L. (2000). *Models of bottom-up and top-down visual attention*. California Institute of Technology.

Itti, Laurent, & Baldi, P. (2005). A principled approach to detecting surprising events in video. *2005 IEEE Computer Society Conference on Computer Vision and Pattern Recognition (CVPR'05)* (pp. 631-637). IEEE. doi:10.1109/CVPR.2005.40

Itti, L., & Koch, C. (2001). Computational modelling of visual attention. *Nature Reviews. Neuroscience*, *2*(3), 194–204. doi:10.1038/35058500

Itti, L., Koch, C., & Niebur, E. (1998). A model of saliency-based visual attention for rapid scene analysis. *IEEE Transactions on Pattern Analysis and Machine Intelligence*, *20*(11), 1254–1259. doi:10.1109/34.730558

Ji, Z., & Weng, J. (2008). Where-what network 1 : Where and what assist each other through top-down connections. *7th IEEE International Conference on Development and Learning*, (pp. 61-66).

Kadir, T., & Brady, M. (2001). Saliency, scale and image description. *International Journal of Computer Vision*, *45*(2), 83–105. doi:10.1023/A:1012460413855

Koch, C., & Ullman, S. (1985). Shifts in selective visual attention: towards the underlying neural circuitry. *Human Neurobiology*, *4*(4), 219–227.

Kootstra, G., Nederveen, A., & Boer, B. D. (2008). Paying attention to symmetry. In M. Everingham, C. Needham, & R. Fraile (Eds.), *19th British Machine Vision Conference* (Vol. 284). Leeds, UK: University of Leeds. doi:10.1126/science.284.5419.1429k

Laberge, D. (1995). *Attentional processing: The brain's art of mindfulness* (1st ed., p. 256). Harvard University Press.

Le Meur, O., Castellan, X., Le Callet, P., & Barba, D. (2006). Efficient saliency-based repurposing method. *IEEE International Conference on Image Processing* (pp. 421-424). Atlanta, USA.

Le Meur, O., Le Callet, P., Barba, D., & Thoreau, D. (2006). A coherent computational approach to model bottom-up visual attention. [Piscataway, NJ: IEEE.]. *IEEE Transactions on Pattern Analysis and Machine Intelligence*, *28*(5), 802–817. doi:10.1109/TPAMI.2006.86

Lesser, M., & Dinah, M. (1998). Mind as a dynamical system: Implications for autism. In Shattock, P., & Linfoot, G. (Eds.), *Psychobiology of autism: Current research & practice*.

Lienhart, R., & Maydt, J. (2002). An extended set of Haar-like features for rapid object detection. *Proceedings of the International Conference on Image Processing* (pp. 900-903). IEEE.

Liu, F., & Gleicher, M. (2006). Region enhanced scale-invariant saliency detection. *Proceedings of IEEE ICME* (pp. 1-4).

Lopez, M., Fernandezcaballero, A., Fernandez, M., Mira, J., & Delgado, A. (2006). Motion features to enhance scene segmentation in active visual attention. *Pattern Recognition Letters*, *27*(5), 469–478. doi:10.1016/j.patrec.2005.09.010

Mancas, M. (2007). *Computational attention : Towards attentive computers*. Faculté Polytechnique de Mons.

Marat, S., Phuoc, T. H., Granjon, L., Guyader, N., Pellerin, D., & Gu, A. (2008). Spatio-temporal saliency model to predict eye movements in video free viewing. *Proceedings of the International Conference on Signal Processing*.

Mesulam, M. M. (1981). A cortical network for directed attention and unilateral neglect. *Annals of Neurology*, *10*, 309–325. doi:10.1002/ana.410100402

Milanese, R., Wechsler, H., Gill, S., Bost, J.-M., & Pun, T. (1994). Integration of bottom-up and top-down cues for visual attention using non-linear relaxation. *Proceedings of IEEE Conference on Computer Vision and Pattern Recognition* (pp. 781-785). IEEE Computer Society Press.

Mole, C. (2009). Attention. *The Stanford encyclopedia of philosophy* (2009 ed., Vol. 37). doi:10.3928/00904481-20080101-02

Mozer, M. C., & Sitton, M. (1998). Computational modeling of spatial attention. In Pashler, H. (Ed.), *Attention* (pp. 341–393). London, UK: UCL Press.

Murray, J. D. (2003a). *Mathematical biology: Spatial models and biomedical applications. Interdisciplinary applied mathematics*. Springer Verlag.

Murray, J. D. (2003b). *Mathematical biology: An introduction* (pp. 1–551). Berlin, Germany: Springer Verlag.

Navalpakkam, V, & Itti, Laurent. (2006). Top-down attention selection is fine grained. *Journal of Vision (Charlottesville, Va.)*, *6*(11), 4. doi:10.1167/6.11.4

Navalpakkam, V., Arbib, M., & Itti, L. (2005). Attention and scene understanding. In Itti, L., Rees, G., & Tsotsos, J. K. (Eds.), *Neurobiology of attention* (pp. 197–203). Academic Press. doi:10.1016/B978-012375731-9/50037-9

Navalpakkam, V., & Itti, L. (2005). Modeling the influence of task on attention. *Vision Research*, *45*(2), 205–231. doi:10.1016/j.visres.2004.07.042

Neumann, O. (1987). Beyond capacity: A functional view of attention. Perspectives on perception and action. In Heuer, H., & Sanders, A. F. (Eds.), *Perspectives on perception and action* (pp. 361–394). Hillsdale, NJ: Lawrence Erlbaum Associates.

Orabona, F., Metta, G., & Sandini, G. (2008). A proto-object based visual attention model. In Paletta, L. (Ed.), *Attention in cognitive systems. Theories and systems from an interdisciplinary viewpoint (WAPCV)* (pp. 198–215). Berlin, Germany: Springer. doi:10.1007/978-3-540-77343-6_13

Ouerhani, N. (2003). *Visual attention: From bio-inspired modeling to real-time implementation*. Université de Neuchâtel.

Ouerhani, N., & Hugli, H. (2003). *A model of dynamic visual attention for object tracking in natural image sequences* (pp. 702–709). Lecture Notes in Computer Science Springer. doi:10.1007/3-540-44868-3_89

Park, S. J., An, K. H., & Lee, M. (2002). Saliency map model with adaptive masking based on independent component analysis. [Elsevier.]. *Neurocomputing*, *49*(1), 417–422. doi:10.1016/S0925-2312(02)00637-9

Perreira Da Silva, M., Courboulay, V., Prigent, A., & Estraillier, P. (2010). Evaluation of preys / predators systems for visual attention simulation. In P. Richard & J. Braz (Eds.), *VISAPP 2010 - International Conference on Computer Vision Theory and Applications* (Vol. 2, pp. 275-282). Angers, France: INSTICC.

Peters, R. J., Iyer, A., Itti, L., & Koch, C. (2005). Components of bottom-up gaze allocation in natural images. *Vision Research*, *45*(18), 2397–2416. doi:10.1016/j.visres.2005.03.019

Posner, M. I., & Petersen, S. E. (1990). The attention system of the human brain. *Annual Review of Neuroscience*, *13*, 25–42. doi:10.1146/annurev.ne.13.030190.000325

Rapantzikos, K., & Tsapatsoulis, N. (2003). *On the implementation of visual attention architectures*. Tales of the Disappearing Computer Conference, Santorini.

Rensink, R. A. (2000). The dynamic representation of scenes. *Visual Cognition*, *7*, 17–42. doi:10.1080/135062800394667

Rensink, R. A., Regan, J. K. O., & Clark, J. J. (1997). To see or not to see: The need for attention to perceive changes in scenes. *Psychological Science*, *8*(5), 1–6. doi:10.1111/j.1467-9280.1997.tb00427.x

Rissanen, J. (1978). Modeling by shortest data description. *Automatica*, *14*, 465–471. doi:10.1016/0005-1098(78)90005-5

Rolls, E. T., & Stringer, S. M. (2006). Invariant visual object recognition: a model, with lighting invariance. *The Journal of Physiology*, *100*(1-3), 43–62. doi:doi:10.1016/j.jphysparis.2006.09.004

Sela, G., & Levine, M. D. (1997). Real-time attention for robotic vision. *Real-Time Imaging*, *3*, 173–194. doi:10.1006/rtim.1996.0057

Spratling, M. W., & Johnson, M. H. (2004). A feedback model of visual attention. *Journal of Cognitive Neuroscience*, *16*(2), 219–237. doi:10.1162/089892904322984526

Stringer, S. M., & Rolls, E. T. (2000). Position invariant recognition in the visual system with cluttered environments. *Neural Networks: The Official Journal of the International Neural Network Society*, *13*(3), 305–315. doi:10.1016/S0893-6080(00)00017-4

Styles, E. A. (2006). *The psychology of attention* (2nd ed., p. 351). New York, NY: Psychology Press.

Sun, Y., & Fisher, R. (2003). Object-based visual attention for computer vision. [Elsevier.]. *Artificial Intelligence*, *146*(1), 77–123. doi:10.1016/S0004-3702(02)00399-5

Sun, Y., Fisher, R., Wang, F., & Gomes, H. (2008). A computer vision model for visual-object-based attention and eye movements. *Computer Vision and Image Understanding, 112*(2), 126-142. Elsevier Inc. doi:10.1016/j.cviu.2008.01.005

Tatler, B. W. (2007). The central fixation bias in scene viewing : Selecting an optimal viewing position independently of motor biases and image feature distributions. *Journal of Vision (Charlottesville, Va.)*, *7*, 1–17. doi:10.1167/7.14.4

Tatler, B. W., Baddeley, R. J., & Gilchrist, I. D. (2005). Visual correlates of fixation selection: Effects of scale and time. *Vision Research*, *45*(5), 643–659. doi:10.1016/j.visres.2004.09.017

Torralba, A., Oliva, A., Castelhano, M. S., & Henderson, J. M. (2006). Contextual guidance of eye movements and attention in real-world scenes: The role of global features in object search. *Psychological Review*, *113*(4), 766–786. doi:10.1037/0033-295X.113.4.766

Treisman, A. (1969). Strategies and models of selective attention. *Psychological Review*, *76*, 282–299. doi:10.1037/h0027242

Treisman, A., & Gelade, G. (1980). A feature-integration theory of attention. *Cognitive Psychology*, *136*(12), 97–136. doi:10.1016/0010-0285(80)90005-5

Tsotsos, J. K. (1990). Analysing vision at the complexity level. *The Behavioral and Brain Sciences*, *13*, 423–469. doi:10.1017/S0140525X00079577

Tsotsos, J. K. (2007). *A selective history of visual attention*. France: Les Houches.

Tsotsos, J. K., Culhane, S. M., Kei Wai, W. Y., Lai, Y., Davis, N., & Nuflo, F. (1995). Modeling visual attention via selective tuning. [Elsevier.]. *Artificial Intelligence*, *78*(1-2), 507–545. doi:10.1016/0004-3702(95)00025-9

Tsotsos, J. K., Itti, L., & Rees, G. (2005). A brief and selective history of attention. In Itti, L., Rees, G., & Tsotsos, J. K. (Eds.), *Neurobiology of attention*. Elsevier Press. doi:10.1016/B978-012375731-9/50003-3

Tsotsos, J. K., Liu, Y., Martinez-Trujillo, J., Pomplun, M., Simine, E., & Zhou, K. (2005). Attending to visual motion. *Computer Vision and Image Understanding*, *100*(1-2), 3–40. doi:10.1016/j.cviu.2004.10.011

van der Heijden, a H., & Bem, S. (1997). Successive approximations to an adequate model of attention. *Consciousness and Cognition*, *6*(2-3), 413–428. doi:10.1006/ccog.1996.0284

Van Rullen, R., & Koch, C. (2005). Visual attention and visual awareness. In Celesia, G. (Ed.), *Disorders of visual processing* (*Vol. 5*, pp. 65–83). Elsevier.

VanRullen, R. (2003). Visual saliency and spike timing in the ventral visual pathway. *The Journal of Physiology*, *97*(2-3), 365–377. doi:doi:10.1016/j.jphysparis.2003.09.010

Viola, P., & Jones, M. (2002). Robust real-time object detection. *International Journal of Computer Vision*, *57*(2), 137–154. doi:10.1023/B:VISI.0000013087.49260.fb

Vitay, J., Rougier, N. P., & Alexandre, F. (2005). A distributed model of spatial visual attention. *Biomimetic Neural Learning for Intelligent Robots Conference* (pp. 54-72). Springer.

Volterra, V. (1928). Variations and fluctuations of the number of individuals in animal species living together. *ICES Journal of Marine Science*, *3*(1), 3–51. doi:10.1093/icesjms/3.1.3

Walther, D., & Koch, C. (2006). Modeling attention to salient proto-objects. *Neural Networks: The Official Journal of the International Neural Network Society*, *19*(9), 1395–1407. doi:10.1016/j.neunet.2006.10.001

Wolfe, J. M., & Horowitz, T. S. (2004). What attributes guide the deployment of visual attention and how do they do it? *Nature Reviews. Neuroscience*, *5*(6), 495–501. doi:10.1038/nrn1411

KEY TERMS AND DEFINITIONS

Adaptation: A system is said adaptive when it is able to change its behavior when faced to a change in its environment.

Dynamical System: System whose evolution can be modeled using a set of fixed, time dependent, rules.

Feedback: Mechanism in which the past output of a system is used to influence its current evolution.

Heatmap: In visual attention studies, a heatmap is a 2D map in which the value of each pixel represents its attentional attractiveness. It can be generated from eye-tracking experiments or attention model simulations.

Saliency: Quality of an object (or scene location) to 'pop-out' from its neighborhood. This phenomenon is linked to bottom-up visual attention.

Simplexity: The theory of 'simplexity' from Alan Berthoz describes the set of mechanisms created by nature in order to simplify the complexity of the world we are living in.

Visual Attention: Selective process in which our brain discards (fully or partially) some visual information in order to focus more effectively on others.

Chapter 13
Implementation of Biologically Inspired Components in Embedded Vision Systems

Christopher Wing Hong Ngau
The University of Nottingham, Malaysia

Li-Minn Ang
Edith Cowan University, Australia

Kah Phooi Seng
Sunway University, Malaysia

ABSTRACT

Studies in the area of computational vision have shown the capability of visual attention (VA) processing in aiding various visual tasks by providing a means for simplifying complex data handling and supporting action decisions using readily available low-level features. Due to the inclusion of computational biological vision components to mimic the mechanism of the human visual system, VA processing is computationally complex with heavy memory requirements and is often found implemented in workstations with unapplied resource constraints. In embedded systems, the computational capacity and memory resources are of a primary concern. To allow VA processing in such systems, the chapter presents a low complexity, low memory VA model based on an established mainstream VA model that addresses critical factors in terms of algorithm complexity, memory requirements, computational speed, and salience prediction performance to ensure the reliability of the VA processing in an environment with limited resources. Lastly, a custom softcore microprocessor-based hardware implementation on a Field-Programmable Gate Array (FPGA) is used to verify the implementation feasibility of the presented low complexity, low memory VA model.

INTRODUCTION

Imaging and semiconductor technologies have matured substantially throughout the previous decade, paving the way for revolutionary vision applications. Whenever static images or videos are of concern, most vision systems perform some form of processing on the immense amount of visual information received in order to remove data redundancies or to select useful information to be used in subsequent actions of the system. While vision systems are given artificial vision by

DOI: 10.4018/978-1-4666-2539-6.ch013

means of image processing algorithms, research efforts are constantly undertaken to create intelligent vision systems which are able to interpret visual information similar to humans. Even for current vision systems, the selection of useful information from a large information pool can be rather complicated. Taking a system performing the task of object detection and recognition, for example, multiple sliding windows and trained classifiers have to be used to determine regions of the visual input that consist parts of an object before the object can be recognized (Frintrop, 2011). Although the approach is fairly straightforward for visual inputs containing simple objects, specifically trained classifiers are required for complex visual scenes. Furthermore, the multiple sliding window approach may not be efficient for large visual inputs. Therefore, there is a need for an approach that can efficiently select relevant information to be used in higher processing such as classification, intelligent compression, and recognition without relying on pre-determined data or parameters.

Research in visual attention (VA) provides insight into the challenges faced by many vision systems by identifying priority regions in the visual input without any prior training through the use of artificial visual attention processing. The artificial visual attention processing is achieved by a VA model comprised of biologically inspired components of the retina and the V1 cortex. The use of VA in vision systems also helps to aid action decisions (Frintrop, 2011). Often, vision systems operate in complex and probably unknown environments. Therefore, it is necessary for the system to locate and interpret relevant parts of the visual scene to decide on the actions to be taken. VA allows relevant parts to be detected with ease using models of attention based on the human visual system. Various studies on VA related vision processing have shown the importance of implementing an attentional mechanism in a general vision system working with complex visual data (Frintrop, 2011; Begum & Karray, 2011; Frintrop & Jensfelt, 2008).

While VAs offered an artificial visual attention mechanism that can be applied to a wide range of vision systems, it has a disadvantage in terms of computational complexity. Complex and parallel algorithm structures of the VA models have to be taken into consideration when implementing in an environment with limited computational capabilities. Computational time of the VA processing increases by three to four folds when processed in a serial manner and therefore, has to be evaluated for feasibility in real-time applications. Furthermore, blob-like detected conspicuous regions seen in early VA models (Itti, Koch, & Neibur, 1998; Ma & Zhang, 2003) are being out-phased by high resolution outputs in newer models to serve a wider range of vision applications. This indirectly resulted in the increase of computational cost and memory requirements (Huang, He, Cai, Zou, Liu, Liang, & Chen, 2011); hence, making the implementation of VA in embedded systems challenging. In order to utilize the advantages of the attentional mechanism for vision processing in a resource constrained system, a low complexity, low memory VA model has be first developed without compromising on prediction performance.

VISUAL ATTENTION AND SALIENCE

Among the five senses – vision, hearing, touch, smell, and taste; vision is undeniably the sense upon which humans rely most. With vision, a person is able to perceive information leading to responses to daily activities; from locating objects to danger avoidance. The human visual system (HVS) consisting of the eye and the brain, is a highly complex physiological system that is responsible for gathering visual information and translating them into useful responses. Furthermore, the human eye is capable of capturing a massive amount of visual information with each glance, probably exceeding ten megabits per second in continuous viewing (Davies, 2005). Although the eye has the capability of capturing and delivering a tremendous amount of visual information for processing, the brain itself has a limited processing capacity to handle all the information that is passed to it.

Therefore, to avoid bottlenecking and to promote efficient utilization of processing resources the brain only selects relevant information to be processed at a time. In the early cognitive study by Broadbent (Broadbent, 1985), information selection by the brain is illustrated with a computational HVS where information in the form of stimuli is selected via selective filters for processing. With the brain having no prior knowledge of the content of the captured visual information, in order for a part of the information to have a chance of being processed, it must have a quality that makes it stand out. This quality, which is rather subjective in nature, is called salience. Since the introduction of the computational HVS model by Broadbent, researchers in the field of psychophysics and vision have conducted a considerable amount of research towards understanding the mechanism of the HVS. This works eventually led to the first neurally plausible visual attention system (Koch & Ullman, 1985).

Research on the underlying mechanism of visual attention has been ongoing since 1890s, when early psychological studies on the nature of attentive process were carried out (James, 1890). From these initial studies, visual attention was shown to guide the actions of perceiving, conceiving, distinguishing, and remembering parts of a visual scene. For a visual scene seen by an observer, attention will cause the allocation of processing resources to salient areas rather than the entire scene as a strategy to work around the limited processing capacity of the human brain (Pashler, 1998). As a result, parts of the visual scene can be broken down to a series of localized and computationally less demanding information for rapid processing (Itti, Koch, & Neibur, 1998). Ultimately, the purpose of attention is to shorten the reaction time for the HVS to process a visual scene (James, 1890), by first attending to salient areas which would bring about a visual awareness and understanding of the entire scene (Itti, 2005; Rapantzikos, Avrithis, & Kollias, 2007).

COMPUTATIONAL VISUAL ATTENTION

Computational visual attention (CVA) can be defined as algorithmic models that provide a means of selecting parts of the visual input information for further higher vision processing or investigation based on the principles of the human selective attention (Frintrop, 2011). In contrast to separate theoretical biological and mathematical computer vision attention models, CVA models span both branches allowing the validation of the modeled attention by comparing the output of the model to the results of experiments using visual stimuli such as images and video frames as inputs (Rothenstein & Tsotsos, 2011). Due to the ability to produce attention outputs rapidly and without the need for additional stimuli other than the input image, CVA models are widely studied and expanded upon in the fields of cognitive science, computer vision, and psychology. Since this chapter focuses only on CVA models, the term visual attention (VA) is understood in the place of CVA.

High-Level and Low-Level Features

Features present in a visual stimulus can be divided into two categories: high-level and low-level. High level features allow a semantic bridge between the extracted visual information and the interpretation of same information by the user (Zheng, Li, Si, Lin, & Zhang, 2006); resulting in comprehension of the entire visual scene (Nystrom & Holmqvist, 2008). These features exist in various subjective forms and are often defined by data or image representations (Li, Su, Xing, & Fei-Fei, 2010). While high-level features provide a more accurate and semantic understanding of the visual scene, extraction of these features is time consuming and involves large training databases (Zheng, Li, Si, Lin, & Zhang, 2006; Li, Su, Xing, & Fei-Fei, 2010).

In contrast, low-level features are distinctive attributes that can be readily and easily extracted from objects or particular regions of a visual scene. Low-level features, unlike the high-level ones, contribute minimally to the understanding of the visual scene. Although unable to provide full semantic understanding of the entire visual scene, low-level features play an important role in providing the quality of "uniqueness" for the information, locations, and objects comprising the visual stimuli (Wolfe, 1998). Color, edge, luminance, orientation, scale, shape, and texture are among the low-level features humans can efficiently detect with ease.

Bottom-Up Visual Attention

Visual attention can be computed with two different approaches: a bottom-up approach and a top-down approach. For the bottom-up approach, attention is driven by the low-level features present in the visual stimuli (Koch & Ullman, 1985; Itti, Koch, & Neibur, 1998). The method is often reflexive and can be said to be task-independent since the observer would have no prior knowledge of the visual stimuli or the actions to be performed. In contrast, the task-driven, top-down approach is related to recognition processing (Fang, Lin, Lee, Lau, Chen, & Lin, 2012) and is more complex to model since it integrates high level processes such as task, cognitive state, and visual context (Navalpakkam & Itti, 2005; Torralba, Castelhano, Oliva, & Henderson, 2006; Kanan, Tong, Zhang, & Cottrell, 2009).

Bottom-up visual attention is closely related to areas early in the visual processing stream (the retina and some parts of the cortical area V1) where visual features are extracted and analyzed. Top-down visual attention can be associated with the higher-order visual areas (cortical areas V2, V3, and V4) in which task specific operations are performed (Ho-Phuoc, Guyader, & Guerin-Dugue, 2010). Figure 1 illustrates a basic biologically inspired architecture of a vision system containing both early and higher vision processing.

Center-Surround Process

The center-surround (CS) process is an operation that resembles the preference in stimuli of cells found in the lateral geniculate nucleus (LGN) of the thalamus, a major player in the visual processing stream (Treisman & Gelade, 1980). In computational visual attention, the CS process generally provides an enhancement of fine feature details found at higher resolutions and coarse feature details at lower resolutions prior to the combination of multiple features that leads to a global contribution of salience. The CS process can be conducted in different ways but all have the same goal of enhancing locations consisting of both fine and coarse details relative to their

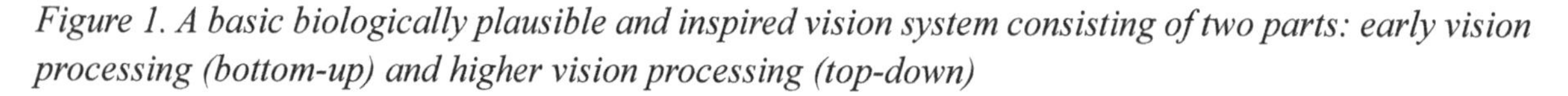

Figure 1. A basic biologically plausible and inspired vision system consisting of two parts: early vision processing (bottom-up) and higher vision processing (top-down)

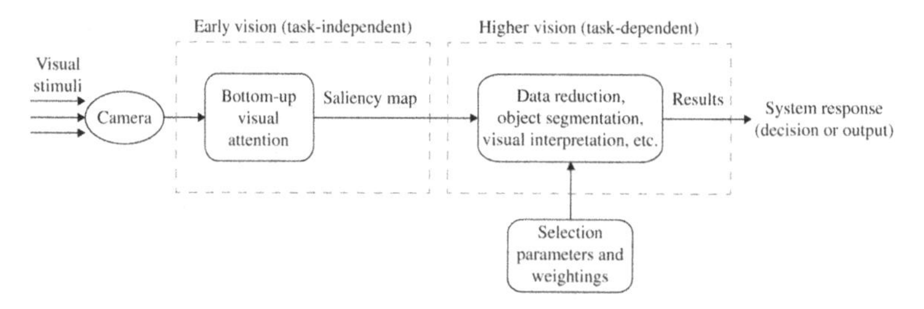

surroundings indicated by the CS differences (also known as contrast differences). Among the methods used for computing CS differences are the point-to-point subtraction of locations between fine and coarse scales (Itti, Koch, & Neibur, 1998; Itti & Koch, 2000; Tsapatsoulis, Rapantzikos, & Pattichis, 2007), the use of a sliding window (Urban, Follet, Chamaret, Meur, & Baccino, 2011; Achanta, Estrada, Wils, & Susstrunk, 2008), and the use of morphological operators (Tsapatsoulis & Rapantzikos, 2006). Figure 2 illustrates the CS process of (Urban, Follet, Chamaret, Meur, & Baccino, 2011) which uses the sliding window method.

Saliency Map

The saliency map is the end result of the VA processing performed in a bottom-up manner. The concept of a saliency map was introduced in 1985 to provide a measure of visual salience from selected contributing features present in a visual stimulus. In the framework of Treisman, the saliency map is defined as a master map consisting of conspicuous locations based on the contributions of local salience of each separable feature maps (Treisman, 1985). Similarly, in the works of Koch and Ullman (Koch & Ullman, 1985), the saliency map is a topographical map containing information on the available features in the visual stimuli with the aim of providing a global measure of salience. The saliency map can be used as a control mechanism for selective attention (Koch & Ullman, 1985; Itti, 2005) or for vision tasks such as the prediction of eye movements (Foulsham & Underwood, 2008; Urban, Follet, Chamaret, Meur, & Baccino, 2011; Judd, Ehinger, Durand, & Torralba, 2009) and computer vision applications involving content based information retrieval and object segmentations (Tsapatsoulis, Rapantzikos, & Pattichis, 2007; Achanta, Hemami, Estrada, & Susstrunk, 2009; Liu, Yuan, Sun, Wang, Zheng, Tang, & Shum, 2011). Figure 3 provides an illustration of a saliency map that is VA processed with contributing features from color, luminance, and orientation using the bottom-up VA model of (Tsapatsoulis, Rapantzikos, & Pattichis, 2007).

Figure 2. An illustration of the center-surround process. Fine and coarse details arising from the luminance feature are emphasized.

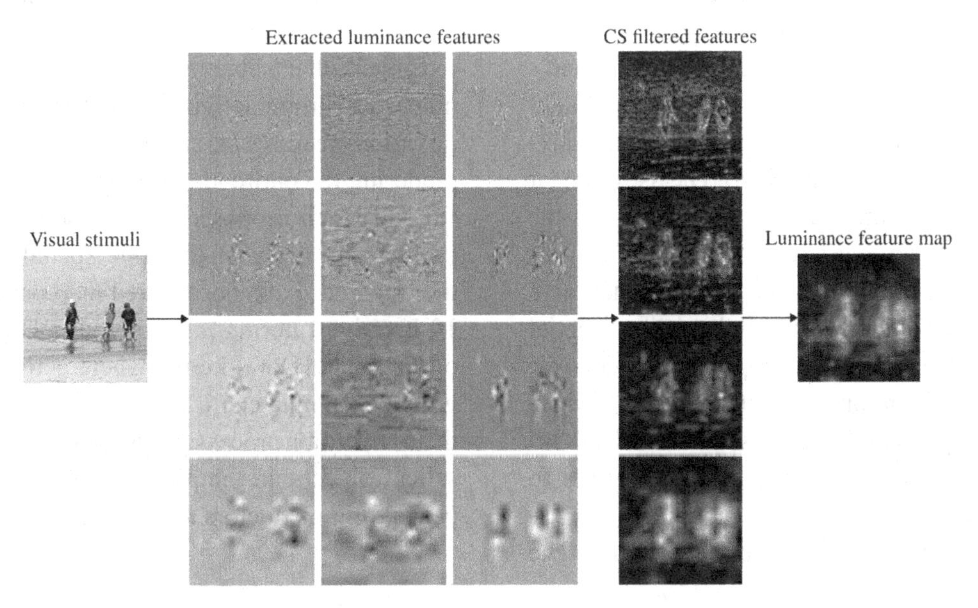

Figure 3. (a) Input image for VA processing (visual stimuli) and (b) its saliency map where global salience is computed from the color, luminance, and orientation features. Bright peaks in the surface plot of the saliency map indicate location of high salience (conspicuous locations in the visual stimuli).

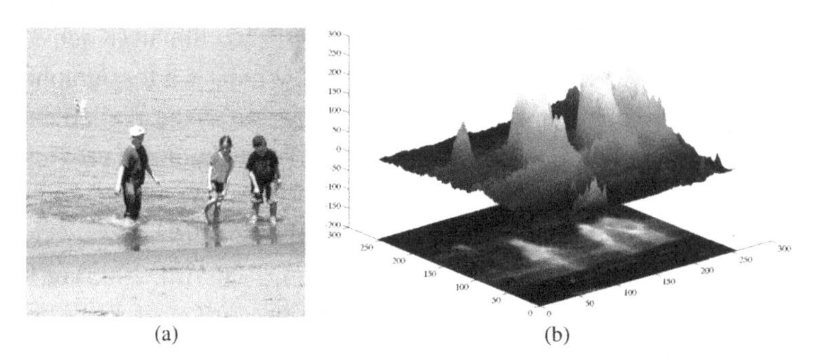

Development of Visual Attention Models

Most bottom-up VA models are based on the Feature Integration Theory (FIT) of Treisman and Gelade (Treisman & Gelade, 1980). The FIT describes the pre-attentive stage of the visual system where separable features present in the visual stimuli can be detected and identified in parallel. Treisman and Gelade also described attention with a spotlight metaphor whereby the attention of the observer moves around the field of vision like the beam from spotlight. The awareness of the objects that falls within the spotlight beam can then be manifested through either a stimulus-driven focal attention or a top-down processing.

Using the framework of the Koch and Ullman's VA model, Itti et al. introduced a newer implementation of the initial VA model for rapid scene analysis (Itti, Koch, & Neibur, 1998). The use of linear filtering and center-surround structures in the feature computations allowed low-level features consisting of color, luminance, and orientation to be computed quickly in parallel across 42 spatial maps. With the absence of top-down processing, feature combinations over different modalities tend to be biased. To address the problem, Itti et al. proposed a map normalization operator to eliminate modality-dependent amplitudes by setting a fixed dynamic range for all the maps. The normalization operator also globally promotes strong activity peaks which are small in number while suppressing comparable peak responses. A vision system called the Neuromorphic Vision C++ Toolkit (NVT) implementing the improved VA model is available publicly for benchmarking and development purposes.

Later on, Itti and Koch improved on the Itti et al. VA model by further investigating the feature combination structure across several modalities (Itti & Koch, 2000). They discovered that the attention system suffered from a severe signal-to-noise ratio problem when a large number of maps is used in the combination process. The locations of salient objects consisting of strong activity peaks arising from a few distinctive features of the objects themselves are found competing with numerous strong activity peaks from distractors of various features at non-salient locations; thus, rendering the entire attention system unreliable. Itti and Koch proposed a novel solution to the problem by using an iterative spatial competition method. Each normalized map undergoes a 10 iterative filtering process with a Difference-of-Gaussian (DoG) kernel where activity peaks within each map compete with each other. After the competition process, strong peaks arising from salient objects are amplified while the activity peaks from distractors are suppressed.

The difficulty of attending to an object before it can be recognized is described in the work of Walther and Koch (Walther & Koch, 2006). According to the authors, attending to an object can be difficult without considering the shape or the properties binding the object that is to be attended. However, the shape and the area covered by the attended object can be established with the use of proto-objects. Based on the proto-objects described by Rensink (Rensink, 2000), Walther and Koch developed a new model using the Itti et al. VA model (Itti, Koch, & Neibur, 1998) as a platform and applying iterative spatial competition (Itti & Koch, 2000). In their model, the equations for the opponent color computations were redefined to operate based on the maximum values from the R, G, and B channels instead of using the average of the channels. The new VA model generates salient proto-objects based on the winning locations provided by the WTA network, which then can be used for object recognition tasks. Walther and Koch also developed the Saliency Toolbox (STB) for modeling attention to salient proto-objects in the MATLAB environment.

Tsapatsoulis et al. proposed a wavelet based approach for efficient extraction of early visual features and computation of the feature maps (Tsapatsoulis, Rapantzikos, & Pattichis, 2007). The authors suggested that the use of multi-resolution wavelet decomposition instead of the Gaussian pyramid scheme found in the Itti and Koch VA models will provide a more natural process of mimicking the center-surround process in the HVS. The normalization operator was replaced with a saturation function to preserve the contribution independency of each feature towards the final saliency map. While a deviation is observed in the feature computation and normalization processes, the framework of Itti et al. (Itti, Koch, & Neibur, 1998) was retained. Tsapatsoulis et al. also had extended the model to emulate visual search for human faces in video encoding applications by implementing an additional skin feature computed with a top-down process.

Recently, Urban et al. proposed an attention model based on the framework of Koch and Ullman that operates on medium to high frequency features to predict the best fixation locations in free-viewing tasks (Urban, Follet, Chamaret, Meur, & Baccino, 2011). Similar to the VA model in (Tsapatsoulis, Rapantzikos, & Pattichis, 2007), their proposed model utilizes wavelet decomposition for early feature extraction. A window CS filtering method is used in the place of the commonly seen point-to-point subtractions of fine and coarse scales approach. To validate the biological plausibility of their proposed model, Urban et al. conducted an eye fixation experiment to allow a comparison of fixation points to the saliency maps generated. From the eye fixation evaluations, their model was able to provide high predictability of the fixated eye locations while outperforming several mainstream VA models. From their research, it was concluded that the fixation locations are best predicted with medium to high frequencies for man-made scene and low to medium frequencies for natural scenes.

Deviating from the FIT and the framework of Koch and Ullman, Bruce and Tsotsos proposed a computational model called the Attention Based on Information Maximization (AIM) which is based on information theory (Bruce & Tsotsos, 2009). As opposed to the use of low-level visual features in FIT based VA models, salience in this model is fundamentally driven by information. The AIM predicts salience using a self-information map consisting of a measure of localized information obtained through a density estimation and a joint likelihood computation. Locations within the map that contain the most information indicate spatial locations of high salience in the visual stimuli. Besides the AIM model, there are other computational VA models that are not based on the FIT. Reputable works on non-FIT models can be found in the research of Meur et al. (Meur, Callet, Barba, Member, & Thoreau, 2006) and Aziz and Mertsching (Aziz & Mertsching, 2008) where VA processing is performed with frequency and region based methods respectively.

BOTTOM-UP VISUAL ATTENTION MODELS

Bottom-up VA models allow the quantification of visual conspicuity of each location in a visual stimulus in the form of feature contrast between a location and its surroundings (Foulsham & Underwood, 2008) resulting in a saliency map that can be used to aid and complete vision tasks. Since the saliency map is the common outcome of the processing in most bottom-up VA models, the elements that differentiate the nature of these models are the strategies employed to selectively filter the features present in the visual stimuli and the method of salience extraction (Itti, 2005). This section reviews four mainstream computational bottom-up VA models that are commonly encountered in VA literature.

Walther-Koch Visual Attention Model

The Walther-Koch VA model (Walther & Koch, 2006) is an extension of the successful Itti et al. (Itti, Koch, & Neibur, 1998) and the Itti-Koch (Itti & Koch, 2000) VA models which are commonly used as a standard in visual attention comparisons. The algorithm of the Walther-Koch model, which is very much similar to the Itti-Koch, is briefly reviewed as follows: using intensity, color, and orientation as the operating features.

The input image I is first repeatedly sub-sampled by means of convolution and decimation by factor of two into a nine-scale dyadic Gaussian pyramid. Normally, a linearly separable 6×6 Gaussian kernel of $\left[1\ 5\ 10\ 10\ 5\ 1\right] / 32$ will be used in creating the image pyramid. In the Gaussian pyramid hierarchy, the image at level zero corresponds to the input image and the image at peak of the pyramid corresponds to the sub-sampled image at level eight.

Given the channels of the RGB as *r* (red), *g* (green), and *b* (blue) of the input image, then the intensity map is computed as

$$M_I = \frac{r + g + b}{3} \tag{1}$$

This operation is repeated for all level σ in the image pyramid, forming an intensity pyramid $M_I\left(\sigma\right)$.

For the color features, two opponent color pyramids for red-green (RG) and blue-yellow (BY) are created using (2a) and (2b):

$$M_{RG} = \frac{r - g}{\max\left(r, g, b\right)} \tag{2a}$$

$$M_{BY} = \frac{b - \min\left(r, g\right)}{\max\left(r, g, b\right)} \tag{2b}$$

In order to avoid fluctuations of color opponency values at low luminance, M_{RG} and M_{BY} are set to zero at pixel locations with $\max\left(r, g, b\right)$ < 1/10 for a dynamic range of $\left[0,\ 1\right]$.

The orientation maps are computed by convolving the levels of the intensity pyramid with Gabor filters shown in (3) and (4). Four maps of orientation 0°, 45°, 90°, and 135° are the result of the convolution.

$$O\left(\sigma\right) = \left\|I\left(\sigma\right) * G_0\left(\theta\right)\right\| + \left\|I\left(\sigma\right) * G_{\pi/2}\left(\theta\right)\right\| \tag{3}$$

where

$$G_\psi\left(x, y, \theta\right) = \exp\left(-\frac{x'^2 + \gamma^2 y'^2}{2\delta^2}\right)\cos\left(2\pi\frac{x'}{\lambda} + \psi\right) \tag{4}$$

is a Gabor filter with an aspect ratio γ, wavelength λ, standard deviation δ, phase ψ, and the transformed coordinates $\left(x', y'\right)$ with respect to orientation θ:

$$x' = x\cos(\theta) + y\sin(\theta) \quad (5a)$$

$$y' = -x\sin(\theta) + y\cos(\theta) \quad (5b)$$

In Walther-Koch algorithm, $\gamma = 1$, $\lambda = 7$ pixels, $\delta = 7 / 3$ pixels, and $\psi \in \{0, \pi / 2\}$. The filters are truncated to 19×19 pixels.

Once the visual features are extracted and grouped into their own respective feature pyramids, a CS structure is applied to the pyramids to compute a set of feature maps. In the Walther-Koch model, the CS operations are implemented using across level-subtraction (Θ) between two maps at the center (c) and the surround (s) scales of each feature pyramid. The center corresponds to a pixel at level $c \in \{2, 3, 4\}$ of the pyramid and the surround corresponds to a pixel at level $s = c + \alpha$ where $\alpha \in \{3, 4\}$. For example, the CS operation for the intensity feature is given as:

$$I(c,s) = |I(c) \Theta I(s)| \quad (6)$$

It is important not to confuse the across level subtraction in (6) with the arithmetic subtraction.

Color feature maps are computed in the same manner as the intensity feature in (6). For the orientation feature maps, the CS process is computed for all four orientations:

$$O(c,s,\theta) = |O(c,\theta) \ \Theta \ O(s,\theta)| \quad (7)$$

where $\theta \in \{0°, 45°, 90°, 135°\}$.

In total, there will be 42 feature maps computed; six for intensity, 12 for color, and 24 for orientation. All the feature maps are normalized using the normalization operator $N(\cdot)$ to globally promote maps that have strong peaks of activities and to suppress maps with numerous comparable peak responses (Itti & Koch, 2001). The normalization operator is given as follows:

$$N(\cdot) = \frac{I - I_{min}}{I_{max} - I_{min}} \times 255 \quad (8)$$

where I_{min} is the lowest valued pixel in the image and I_{max} is the highest valued pixel in the image.

The feature maps are summed according to individual feature using the across scale addition ($\oplus$) and the sums are normalized once more to form the conspicuity maps:

$$\bar{I} = \bigoplus_{c=2}^{4} \bigoplus_{s=c+3}^{c+4} N(I(c,s)) \quad (9)$$

$$\bar{C} = \bigoplus_{c=2}^{4} \bigoplus_{s=c+3}^{c+4} \left[N(RG(c,s)) + N(BY(c,s))\right] \quad (10)$$

$$\bar{O} = \sum_{\theta=\{0°, 45°, 90°, 135°\}} N\left(\bigoplus_{c=2}^{4} \bigoplus_{s=c+3}^{c+4} N(O(c,s,\theta))\right) \quad (11)$$

Finally, the three conspicuity maps are normalized and summed. The sum of these maps is averaged, giving a single saliency map.

$$S = \frac{1}{3}\left(N(\bar{I}) + N(\bar{C}) + N(\bar{O})\right) \quad (12)$$

Tsapatsoulis et al. Wavelet Based Saliency Map Estimator Model

While the Itti-Koch model (Itti & Koch, 2000) and its derived VA models performs well in detecting locations of conspicuous objects in a given image, its overall process is rather lengthy, especially the need to extract and group visual features into their respective pyramids before feature maps can be computed. Noticing the inefficiency of computing feature maps in the Itti-Koch model, Tsapatsoulis et al. proposed an alternative approach to computing visual salience while maintaining the biological framework of the model.

In their proposed model (Tsapatsoulis, Rapantzikos, & Pattichis, 2007), the Gaussian pyramid is replaced with a multi-resolution pyramid created through a series of wavelet filtering and sub-sampling. With the discrete wavelet transform (DWT), image pyramids can be computed more efficiently for static images as well as for video sequences. The DWT is a viable alternative to the Gaussian pyramid as the HVS appears to process visual input in a multi-resolution manner similar to the wavelet transform (Cassereau, 1993). The following paragraphs describe the algorithm used in the wavelet based saliency map estimator model (WBSME).

Instead of the RGB input found in many visual attention models, the WBSME takes in a YCbCr input. This particular color space is chosen to conform to the face detection scheme of the model's application in video coding. In addition to the coding requirements, the color space is preferred because the decorrelated luminance channel Y and the chrominance channels Cb and Cr provide a more accurate representation of the intensity and opponent colors features. At the starting stage of the model, a pair of low-pass $h_{\varphi}(\cdot)$ and high-pass $h_{\psi}(\cdot)$ filters is applied to the input image channels Y, Cb, and Cr in both horizontal and vertical directions. The filter outputs are then sub-sampled by a factor of two.

For one level of wavelet decomposition, there will be four resultant sub-bands: LL, HL, LH, and HH. The LL sub-band (approximate coefficients, A) is a coarser representation of the input image. The LL sub-band of the Y channel is used to compute the intensity feature whereas the LL sub-bands of the Cb and Cr channels are used to compute the color features. The other three sub-bands: HL (vertical detail coefficients, V); LH (horizontal detail coefficients, H); and HH (diagonal detail coefficients, D) will be used in the computation of the orientation feature. Similar to the Walther-Koch model, the orientation features are computed from the intensity feature; in this case, the orientation sub-bands of the Y channel. Equations (13) to (16) describe the visual feature extraction using the wavelet transform:

$$Y_A^{-(j+1)}(m,n) = \left(h_{\phi}(-m) * \left(Y_A^{-j}(m,n) * h_{\varphi}(-n)\right)\downarrow^{2n}\right)\downarrow^{2m} \quad (13)$$

$$Y_H^{-(j+1)}(m,n) = \left(h_{\psi}(-m) * \left(Y_A^{-j}(m,n) * h_{\varphi}(-n)\right)\downarrow^{2n}\right)\downarrow^{2m} \quad (14)$$

$$Y_V^{-(j+1)}(m,n) = \left(h_{\phi}(-m) * \left(Y_A^{-j}(m,n) * h_{\psi}(-n)\right)\downarrow^{2n}\right)\downarrow^{2m} \quad (15)$$

$$Y_D^{-(j+1)}(m,n) = \left(h_{\psi}(-m) * \left(Y_A^{-j}(m,n) * h_{\psi}(-n)\right)\downarrow^{2n}\right)\downarrow^{2m} \quad (16)$$

where $*$ denotes convolution, $Y_A^{-j}(m,n)$ is the approximate of Y channel at the j-th level (with $Y_A^{0}(m,n) = Y$), $\downarrow^{2m}$ and $\downarrow^{2n}$ each denoting a downsample by factor of two along rows and column respectively. The number of decomposition level required is dependent on the dimension of the input image. The equation describing the number of decomposition level is presented in a more appropriate paragraph later on.

The next step of the algorithm consists of the CS operation where the CS differences are computed at level j using a point-to-point subtraction between the approximation at the next coarser level ($j + 1$) with the approximation of the current j-th level.

The CS operation for the three intensity, color, and orientation features are shown in (17) to (24).

$$I^{-j} = \left|Y_A^{-j}(m,n) - \left(\left(Y_A^{-(j+1)}(m,n) \uparrow^{2m}\right) * h_\varphi(m)\right) \uparrow^{2n} * h_\varphi(n)\right| \quad (17)$$

$$C^{-j} = w_{C_r} C_r + w_{C_b} C_b \quad (18)$$

$$C_r^{-j} = \left|C_{rA}^{-j}(m,n) - \left(\left(C_{rA}^{-(j+1)}(m,n) \uparrow^{2m}\right) * h_\varphi(m)\right) \uparrow^{2n} * h_\varphi(n)\right| \quad (19)$$

$$C_b^{-j} = \left|C_{bA}^{-j}(m,n) - \left(\left(C_{bA}^{-(j+1)}(m,n) \uparrow^{2m}\right) * h_\varphi(m)\right) \uparrow^{2n} * h_\varphi(n)\right| \quad (20)$$

$$O^{-j} = w_{Y_D}\left|Y_D^{-j} - \hat{Y}_D^{-j}\right| + w_{Y_V}\left|Y_V^{-j} - \hat{Y}_V^{-j}\right| + w_{Y_H}\left|Y_H^{-j} - \hat{Y}_H^{-j}\right| \quad (21)$$

$$\hat{Y}_D^{-j} = \left|\left(\left(Y_D^{-(j+1)}(m,n) \uparrow^{2m}\right) * h_\varphi(m)\right) \uparrow^{2n} * h_\varphi(n)\right| \quad (22)$$

$$\hat{Y}_V^{-j} = \left|\left(\left(Y_V^{-(j+1)}(m,n) \uparrow^{2m}\right) * h_\varphi(m)\right) \uparrow^{2n} * h_\varphi(n)\right| \quad (23)$$

$$\hat{Y}_H^{-j} = \left|\left(\left(Y_H^{-(j+1)}(m,n) \uparrow^{2m}\right) * h_\varphi(m)\right) \uparrow^{2n} * h_\varphi(n)\right| \quad (24)$$

In (17) to (24), I^{-j}, C^{-j}, and O^{-j} denote the intensity, color, and orientation features at level j respectively; C_r^{-j} and C_b^{-j} are the approximation for the chromatic channels Cb and Cr at level j; $\uparrow^{2m}$ and $\uparrow^{2n}$ denote up-sampling of both row and column respectively; while $\hat{Y}_D^{-j}$, $\hat{Y}_V^{-j}$, and $\hat{Y}_H^{-j}$ are the up-sampled approximations of $Y_D^{-(j+1)}$, $Y_V^{-(j+1)}$, and $Y_H^{-(j+1)}$ respectively. The weightings w_{C_r}, w_{Cb}, w_{Y_D}, w_{Y_V}, and w_{Y_H} are the feature modulating gains of the top-down skin/face detection subsystem. These weightings are set to a value of one in a bottom-up saliency map estimation.

Feature maps at various levels j are combined to compute the conspicuity maps for the intensity, color, and orientation features. In this model, the conspicuity maps are achieved by interpolating the feature maps to the finer level, summed using a point-to-point addition, and then undergo a saturation function. The saturation function, as the authors of this model stressed, is a more accurate way of combining features from different modalities. Tsapatsoulis et al. believe the normalization, summation, and averaging method used in the Itti and Koch model though simple, creates inaccurate results as it weakens the importance of salient peaks from individual modalities.

To preserve the independence of the salient peaks from each feature, the saturation function is used in generating the conspicuity maps and the final saliency map for this model. Equations (25) to (27) describe the steps in achieving the intensity conspicuity map C_I. The same steps are also applied to the color and orientation features to achieve the color conspicuity map C_C and the orientation conspicuity map C_O.

$$C_I = \frac{2}{1 + e^{\sum_{j=Jmaz}^{-1} C_I^j}} \quad (25)$$

$$C_I^{-j} = I^{-j}(m,n) - \left(\left(Y_D^{-(j+1)}(m,n) \uparrow^{2m}\right) * h_\varphi(m)\right) \uparrow^{2n} * h_\varphi(n) \quad (26)$$

$$C_I^{J\max} = I^{J\max} \quad (27)$$

In (26), J_{max} is the maximum analysis depth where R and C the number of rows and columns of the input image respectively. J_{max} is computed as

$$J_{\max} = \left\lfloor \frac{\log_2 N}{2} \right\rfloor \text{ with } N = \min\left(R, C\right) \quad (28)$$

Once more, the saturation function is used, applying to the conspicuity maps to obtain the final saliency map S, as described in (29):

$$S = \frac{2}{1 + e^{-\left(C_I + C_C + C_O\right)}} - 1 \quad (29)$$

Urban et al. Medium Spatial Frequencies: A Predictor of Salience Model

In the prediction of fixation location in free-viewing tasks, it is often believed that high frequency components such as edges and luminance contrasts contribute greatly in locating salient locations of a given visual field. However, in the research study of Einhauser and Konig (Einhauser & Konig, 2003), it was found that luminance contrasts of high frequency components provide little significance to the saliency map for prediction of fixation. Saliency works involving the frequency domain in (Bruce, Loach, & Tsotsos, 2007) showed that that fixated locations contain large differences in horizontal and vertical frequency contents than for random locations at medium frequencies. In contrast, saliency works of Hou and Zhang (Hou & Zhang, 2007) favor low frequency components whereby in their model, salient locations are detected through spectral residuals in the low frequency range. In another study, Achanta et al. (Achanta, Hemami, Estrada, & Susstrunk, 2009) stressed that low frequency components in the input image are vital to efficiently detect and wholly highlight salient objects.

With many controversial claims on which spatial frequency contributes most to the prediction of attention, Urban et al. conducted an eye-tracking study on 40 participants using different scene categories defined by their Fourier spectrum in order to provide a more definite and reliable answer (Urban, Follet, Chamaret, Meur, & Baccino, 2011). From the study, it was concluded that medium spatial frequencies globally allowed the best prediction of salience. Furthermore, medium to high frequencies were found to contribute more to salience predictions in scenes containing man-made objects whereas low to medium frequencies work best for natural scenes. Urban et al. also proposed a VA model based on the Koch and Ullman VA framework to verify their claims. The proposed model is able to predict salient locations well in complex natural scenes and performing as well as other state-of-the-art models in general visual scenes. The framework of the model (termed as MSF) is fairly simple and straightforward yet biologically-plausible. The following paragraphs describe the model's structure.

Similar to the Tsapatsoulis et al.'s model (Tsapatsoulis, Rapantzikos, & Pattichis, 2007), the MSF extracts early visual features by means of wavelet transform. Assuming that the YCbCr color space is used, the 9/7 Cohen-Daubechies-Feauveau (CDF) is applied to each individual Y, Cb, and Cr channels. For each channel, a five-level decomposition is applied. As medium spatial frequencies are of interest, only the orientation sub-bands: HL, LH, and HH are retained for processing. Once the five-level feature pyramid for each channel is computed, a CS process is applied to each orientation sub-band of the three channels, resulting in orientation maps. For each location, the CS is computed as the difference between the current pixel coefficient value and the mean coefficient value of the neighbouring pixels as shown in (30).

$$CS(x) = \left| \left| I(x) \right| - \frac{1}{s} \sum_{k \in S} \left| I(k) \right| \right| \tag{30}$$

where $I(x)$ is the pixel coefficient value at location x, S is the center-surround support, and s is the surround area. The surround area for this model is fixed to the size of 5×5 pixels for each pyramid level.

The next step of the algorithm consists of summing up the orientation maps according to pyramid level and channel to form level (feature) maps. For each level, a filtering process is applied to give the same spatial impact regardless of the pyramid level. Equation (31) defines the filtering process.

$$L(x) = \frac{1}{d} \sum_{k \in D(x)} \left(\sum_{o \in (1,\ 2,\ 3)} CS_o(k) \right) \tag{31}$$

In (31), $CS_o(k)$ is the center-surround response at location k for the orientation sub-bands, $D(x)$ is a disk of radius 1° centered on k, and d is the surface area of the disk.

The final step of the algorithm is the fusion of the level maps. The fusion step consists of two stages: level fusion and channel fusion. The level fusion step is applied first by averaging the sum of level maps performed through successive bilinear up-sampling and point-to-point addition. This gives rise to a channel map described by (32).

$$C(x) = \frac{1}{Nb\_L} \oplus L_l(x) \tag{32}$$

where Nb_L is the number of decomposition level and $L_l(x)$ is the map at level l.

The saliency map is then computed by summing all three channel maps and averaging them (channel fusion). Finally, the saliency map is normalized to the range of [0, 255] where the normalization operator $N(\cdot)$ used is found in (8).

Equation (33) shows the computation of the saliency map $S(x)$.

$$S(x) = N\left(\frac{1}{3}\left(C_Y(x) + C_{Cr}(x) + C_{Cb}(x) \right) \right) \tag{33}$$

where $C_Y(x)$, $C_{Cb}(x)$, and $C_{Cr}(x)$ are the channel maps for channels Y, Cb, and Cr respectively.

Bruce-Tsotsos Attention Based on Information Maximization Model

Computational visual attention work found in various research literatures are often based on the computational framework of the Itti-Koch VA model. However in (Bruce & Tsotsos, 2009), Bruce and Tsotsos proposed an entirely different computational framework that is, nonetheless, biologically-plausible and takes the properties of the V1 cortical cells into consideration. Their proposed Attention Based On Information Maximization (AIM) model is based on Shannon's theory of self-information (Shannon, 2001), where the model predicts salience based on spatial locations that carry the most information. The AIM model consists of three main stages: independent feature extraction, density estimation, and joint likelihood and self-information.

In the independent feature extraction stage, each pixel location $I(m,n)$ of the input image I is computed for the response to a set of various basis functions B_k. The response at each pixel location to the B_k is akin to measuring the response of information coding of each spatial location performed by various V1 cortical cells. This measure of response is similar to the activities of oriented Gabor filters and color opponent cells occurring at a specific frequency band.

To compute the basis functions B_k, 31×31 and 21×21 RGB patches are sampled from a set of 3,600 natural scene images picked randomly from the Corel Stock Photo Database. A Joint Approximate Diagonalization of Eigenmatrices (JADE)-based Independent Component Analysis (ICA) (Cardoso, 1999) is then applied to these patches, retaining a variance of 95%, with (Principle Component Analysis) PCA as a pre-processing step. The ICA results in a set of basis components where mutual dependence of features is minimized. The retention of 95% variance yields 54 basis filters for patches of 31 × 31 and 25 basis filters in the case of 21 × 21.

The basis functions, also called the mixing matrix, are then pseudoinversed. Pseudoinversing the mixing matrix provides an unmixing matrix, which can be used to separate the information within any local region of the input I into independent components. The function of the unmixing matrix corresponds to the oriented Gabor filters and color opponent cells found in the V1 cortical cells.

The matrix product between the local neighbourhood of the pixel and the unmixing matrix gives the independent feature of an image pixel as a set of basis coefficients. This output of the independent feature extraction stage is computed as shown in (34).

$$a_{m,n,k} = P * C_k \tag{34}$$

where $a_{m,n,k}$ is the set of basis coefficients for the pixel at location $I(m,n)$, P is the unmixing matrix computed by the pseudoinverse of the basis functions $B_{m,n,k}$ for location (m,n), is the linear product between two matrices, and C_k is a 21 × 21 local neighborhood centered at (m,n).

The next stage of the AIM involves determining the amount of information carried by a pixel. The information may correspond to features such as edges and contrast, and is measured in terms of coefficient densities of the pixel. For a local neighborhood $C_{m,n,k}$ at pixel location (m,n), the content of this neighbourhood corresponding to the image I is characterized by a number of basis coefficients a_k resulting from the matrix multiplication with the unmixing matrix. Each basis coefficient a_k can be related to a basis filter.

Surrounding this local neighborhood, another larger neighborhood $S_{m,n,k}$ exists with $C_{m,n,k}$ at its centre. From (Bruce, 2010), the size of S_k is determined to span over the entire image I. The surrounding neighborhood $S_{m,n,k}$ also possesses a number of basis coefficients a_k that are also possessed by $C_{m,n,k}$. In order to estimate the coefficient density (likelihood) of a pixel at (m,n), basis coefficients corresponding to the same filter type in spatial locations of both $C_{m,n,k}$ and $S_{m,n,k}$ are observed and distributions of these coefficients are computed by means of histogram density estimates.

A joint likelihood of all the coefficients within a neighborhood C_k that corresponds to a pixel location is found from the product of all individual likelihoods (coefficient density). The computation of the joint likelihood for a particular pixel is assumed to have non-dependency between individual likelihoods due to the sparse representation of the ICA. Hence, each coefficient density contributes independently to the joint likelihood of a location situated in the image I. Equation (35) shows the computation of joint likelihood for a particular pixel $I(m,n)$.

$$P(I(m,n)) = \prod_{k=1}^{N_B} P(C_{m,n,k}) \tag{35}$$

where $P(I(m,n))$ is the joint likelihood of pixel $I(m,n)$, $P(C_{m,n,k})$ is the coefficient density (likelihood) corresponding to the basis function k, and NB is the total number of basis functions.

The joint likelihood is then translated into Shannon's measure of Self Information using (36) giving the self-information map.

$$-\log\left(P\left(I\left(m,n\right)\right)\right)=\sum_{k=1}^{N_B}-\log\left(P\left(C_{m,n,k}\right)\right) \tag{36}$$

The resulting self-information map is convolved with a Gaussian envelope that corresponds to an observed drop-off in visual acuity. This encodes the amount of information gained for a target location, which is similar to saccade viewing. The self-information map represents the salience of spatial locations in the input image. Locations that have higher self-information is regarded to contain more information, hence, more salient.

Saliency Maps of the Reviewed Models

Figure 4 and Figure 5 each show the saliency maps of the AIM, MSF, Walther-Koch, and the WBSME VA models for simple and complex scenes. The simple scene images were taken from the Berkeley Segmentation Dataset and Benchmarks (Martin, Fowlkes, Tal, & Malik, 2001) whereas the complex scene images were from the MIT Indoor Scene Recognition Database (Quattoni & Torralba, 2009). Five images for the simple and complex scenes respectively were picked at random from the datasets. Prior to VA processing in MATLAB, all test images involved were resized to the dimension of 256×256. As the saliency maps generated by the Walther-Koch model were smaller in dimension compared to their inputs, the maps of this model were upsampled by means of bilinear interpolation for the visual evaluation.

Simulations for Figures 4 and 5 only consider saliency maps that were computed in a bottom-up manner; therefore, all weightings were set to a value of one and task-dependent computations, if any, were ignored. The type of wavelet transform and the normalization range for the WBSME were not documented in its published literature. In order for a fair comparison, the 9/7 CDF wavelet transform used in the MSF was applied to the WBSME. The normalization range was set to $\left[0,255\right]$ for all four VA models. The conditions for the VA models described are also used for the evaluations in the next section.

From Figure 4 and Figure 5, it can be observed that the saliency maps of the four VA models were able to provide predictions on the locations of the salient objects by indicating the conspicuous regions using high amplitude salient pixels. The AIM VA was able to predict the conspicuous objects easily; however, the boundaries enclosing the objects can be seen spilling over to the regions of non-importance. The precision of the predictions worsen with multiple, cluttered objects as seen in Figure 5. The Walther-Koch VA encodes conspicuous locations and objects in a blob-like manner. Instead of predicting the objects as a whole, the model only predicts locations based on importance. The blob size also determines the area coverage of salient peaks. For the MSF and WBSME VA, their saliency maps are very much similar. Instead of encoding conspicuous locations in down-scaled maps seen in the Walther-Koch model, these two models resize the maps to the dimension of the input at each combination stage. Because of this, the final saliency map is much higher in resolution than the ones in the AIM and Walther-Koch VA. One advantage of this is that the boundary of salient objects can be made out from the salient pixels, allowing these two models to be used in region or point-based applications. Nonetheless, the WBSME saliency map was seen to contain significant amount of noise arising from the background texture.

Figure 4. Visual comparison of saliency maps for the AIM, MSF, Walther-Koch, and the WBSME VA models using simple scene images as inputs

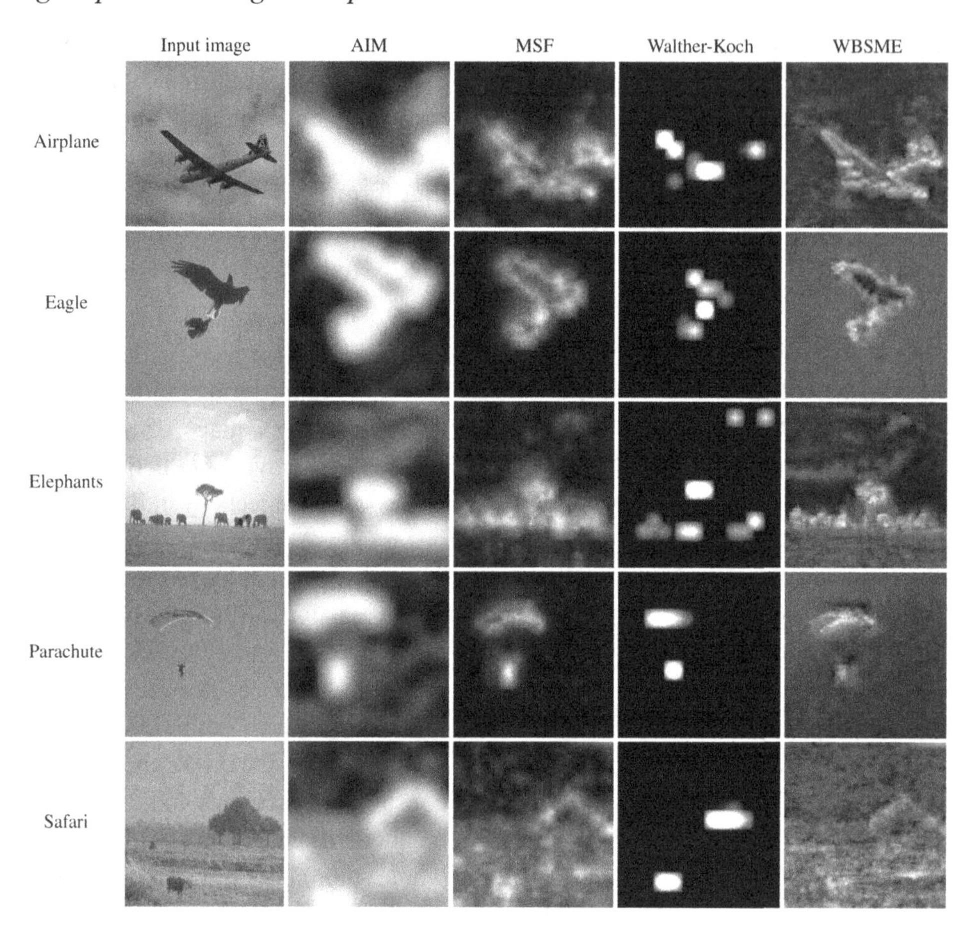

EVALUATIONS ON THE SALIENCE PREDICTION OF VISUAL ATTENTION MODELS

Salience predictions are very subjective in nature and the performance of individual VA models is usually measured based on its specific application. Therefore, a standardized evaluation on the VA performance is difficult to be established. For example, the Walther-Koch and the MSF VA models are suited for fixation applications whereby interesting locations fixated upon by humans are predicted using the computed saliency map. These particular VA models are normally verified using the pattern of eye fixations obtained from multiple observers (Urban, Follet, Chamaret, Meur, & Baccino, 2011; Ho-Phuoc, Guyader, & Guerin-Dugue, 2010). On the other hand, VA models that are targeted at content based segmentation and retrieval, such as the AIM and WBSME, use application performance oriented evaluations. In the case of WBSME where visual telephony coding is targeted, its saliency performance is measured by the compression efficiency achieved (Tsapatsoulis, Rapantzikos, & Pattichis, 2007).

Nonetheless, the aim of most VA models is the same; that is to predict locations containing possible important or interesting information for a given visual stimulus. The reviewed VA models of interest are subjected to two quantitative evaluations covering object-oriented and eye fixation aspects to determine the best candidate

Figure 5. Visual comparison of saliency maps for the AIM, MSF, Walther-Koch, and the WBSME VA models using complex scene images as inputs

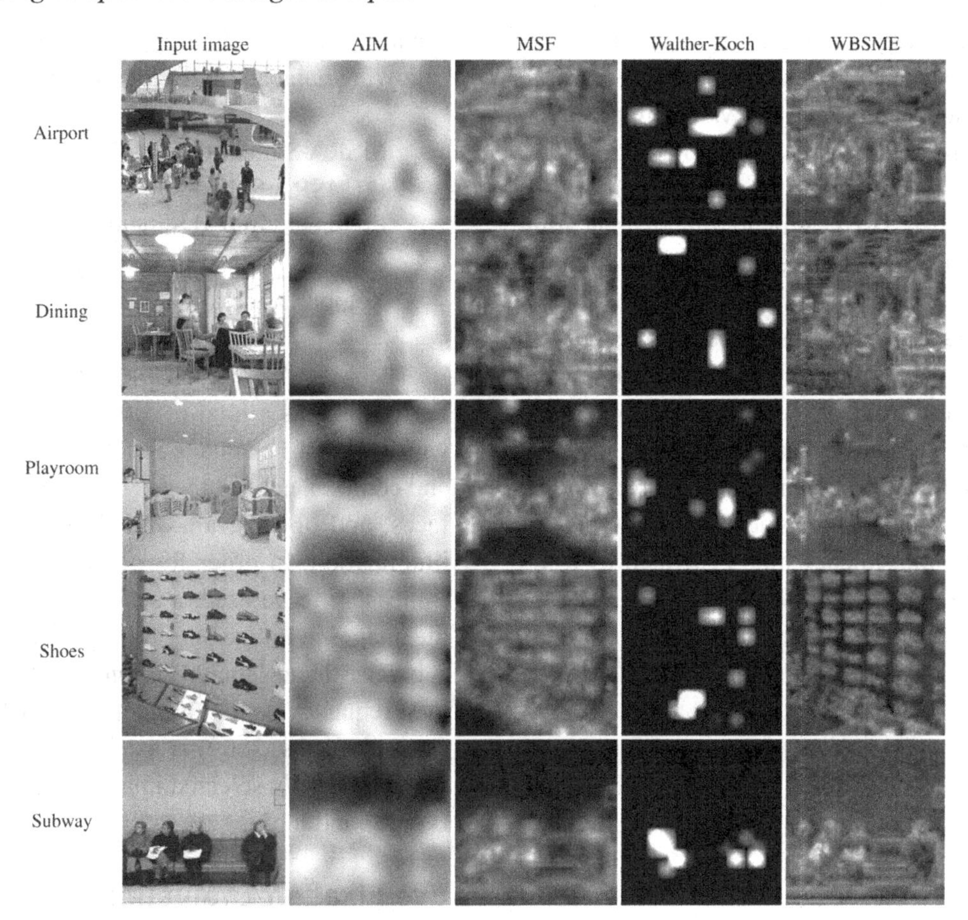

for algorithm modification to achieve a low complexity-low memory implementation in a resource constrained embedded system. The VA model with the best salience prediction performance should be used for modification since simplifications to the algorithms are likely to reduce the performance of the model.

Object-Oriented Evaluation

In computer vision applications, the saliency map can be used to aid object-oriented tasks involving content-based image retrieval (CBIR) and image segmentation (Liu, Yuan, Sun, Wang, Zheng, Tang, & Shum, 2011; Achanta, Hemami, Estrada, & Susstrunk, 2009). Such tasks usually require the saliency map to highlight the objects of interest; covering the body of the objects while establishing clear object boundaries. To evaluate the prediction performance of VA models in object-oriented tasks, a statistical evaluation in terms of precision, recall, and F-measure is used. While the evaluation method is normally used for benchmarking VA models involving image segmentations and object retrieval, it can also be used to provide a measure of salient point precision and coverage regardless of VA application type.

For the evaluation, consider an image I which is the input to a specific VA model. Then, the saliency map S will be the topological map resulted from the VA processing; indicating the possible locations of important objects in I.

Similarly, the ground truth G for I is found by hand-labeling and object annotation by human observers. With S and G, the VA model can be evaluated through the calculations of precision, recall, and F-measure. The value of precision directly shows how the salience predictions fare (how many salient points are correctly predicted) when compared to the ground truth by indicating the consistency of the predictions in locating the important objects of I. Similarly, the recall indicates the ratio of correctly predicted salient points to the number of points in the observer's annotated ground truth of I. The F-measure is the overall performance measurement and is computed as the ratio of precision to recall. The precision, recall, and F-measure equations for evaluating the saliency map generated by a VA model are given as follows:

$$\text{Precision} = \frac{n_s}{N_S} \tag{37}$$

$$\text{Recall} = \frac{n_s}{N_G} \tag{38}$$

$$\text{F-measure} = \left(1+\beta^2\right)\cdot\frac{\text{Precision} \times \text{Recall}}{\left(\beta^2 \cdot \text{Precision}\right) + \text{Recall}} \tag{39}$$

where n_s is the number of salient points in S that corresponds to the annotated object(s) in G, N_S is the number of salient points in S, N_G is the number of points in the annotated object(s) of G that indicate locations of importance, and β is the weighting that emphasizes precision over recall. Figure 6 illustrates and describes on the evaluation steps.

Object-Oriented Evaluation Dataset

For a statistical evaluation of the VA models, the following database and ground truths are used:

1. MSRA Salient Object Database Image Set B (MSRA Salient Object Database, 2007)
2. Frequency-tuned Salient Region Detection Ground Truths (Frequency-Tuned Salient Region Detection Ground Truths, 2009)

The MSRA Salient Object Database Image Set B contains a total of 5,000 color images of various sizes. The Image Set B consists of simple and complex natural scenes of animals, humans, faces, and objects; all with different levels of illumination. In order for precision, recall, and F-measure to be used, a set of ground truths of the images in Image Set B is required. Therefore, a precise hand-labeled ground truth set found in (Frequency-Tuned Salient Region Detection Ground Truths, 2009) is used. Ground truths of 1,000 randomly selected images from Image Set B are found in this set.

Eye Fixation Evaluation

To evaluate the performance of salience predictions with fixation data collected from eye movement experiments, the normalized scanpath saliency (NSS) evaluation metric is used (Peters, Iyer, Itti, & Koch, 2005; Zhao & Koch, 2011). The NSS estimates the relevance of the predicted salient points to the fixated locations. To use the NSS evaluation, the saliency map of the VA model is first normalized to have zero mean and unit standard deviation. The NSS value at each location of the normalized saliency map is given in (40) as:

$$NSS\left(x\right) = \frac{M_S\left(x\right) - \mu_S}{\sigma_S} \tag{40}$$

Figure 6. An illustration on steps involved in the object-oriented evaluation. For a given input image I, its saliency map S is first computed. Similarly, a ground truth G and a watershed segmented image of I are found. The saliency map is thresholded to obtain a binary saliency map which is then used to extract possible salient regions from the watershed segmented image. The saliency map threshold value in this case is set to 2 × avg sal. Having the extracted salient region image, each salient point of this image is compared to the points within the annotated regions of the ground truth. Finally, the precision, recall, and F-measure scores are calculated from the comparison data collected.

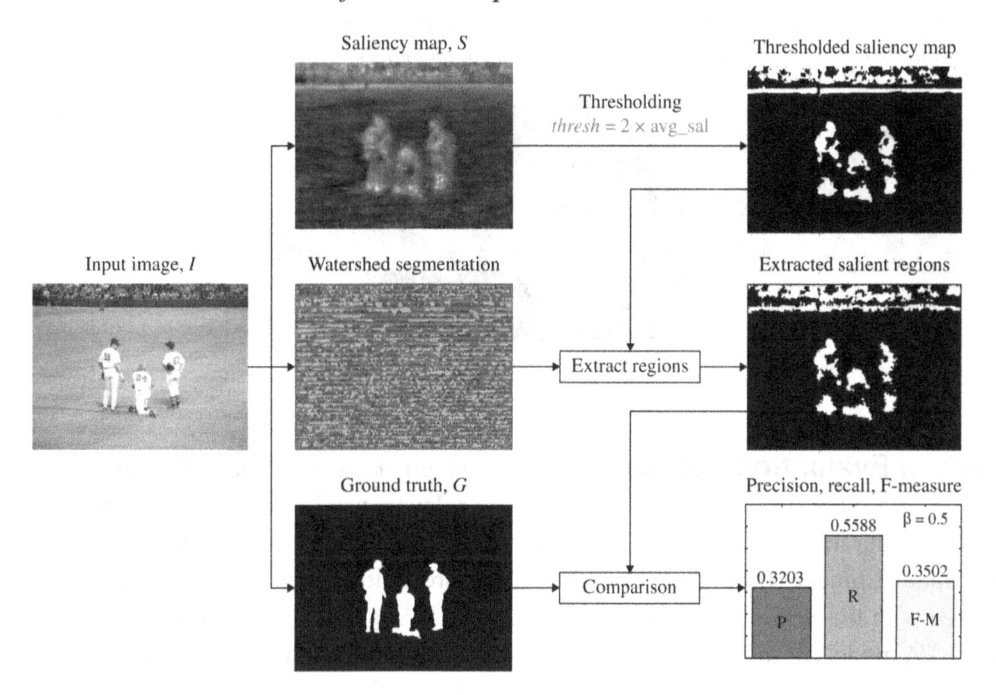

where $NSS(x)$ is the NSS value at location x, $M_S(x)$ is the empirical mean of the saliency map S, and σ_S is the empirical standard deviation of S.

The NSS value at each point corresponding to fixated locations along the observer's scanpath for a certain visual stimuli is summed and then averaged by the number fixation locations to obtain a NSS score. This is described in (41):

$$\text{NSS score} = \sum_{g=1}^{G} NSS(x_g) / G \tag{41}$$

where G is the number of fixation for a particular visual stimuli and $NSS(x_g)$ is the NSS value at the fixated location g.

The NSS score is the average distance between the fixation saliency and zero and is a direct comparison to the saliency distribution of the entire image (Zhao & Koch, 2011). In the case where fixation data from multiple observers are used for the same visual stimuli, the NSS score is found by averaging the summed individual NSS scores. If the NSS score is close to zero, the salience predictions have poor relevance to the eye fixations whereas a score larger than zero implies greater relevance. A score of zero indicates that the salience predictions have no relevance to the eye fixations. Figure 7 illustrates on using the NSS evaluation metric.

Figure 7. Using the normalized scanpath saliency (NSS): (a) The visual stimuli shown to the observer. The dots are the observer's eye scanpaths with the fixated locations marked by the rectangle markers. (b) The saliency map of (a) normalized to zero mean and unit standard deviation. The fixation locations of the observer are extracted and mapped to the normalized saliency map (shown by the circles). Then the NSS values for the fixated locations are computed (shown by the numerical values). (c) The NSS score is found by averaging the summed NSS values for all fixated locations. The score is then compared against the distribution of salience values across the normalized saliency map. For the scanpath shown in (a), the NSS metric indicated that the VA model is able to predict the salience at the fixated locations with 0.7493 standard deviations above chance level on average.

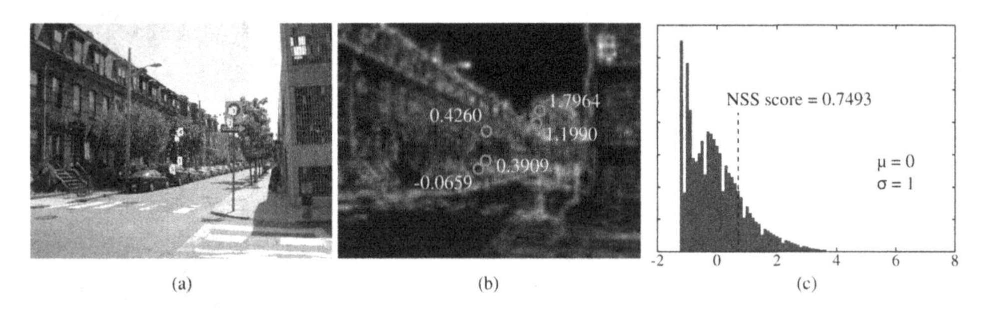

Eye Fixation Evaluation Dataset

Eye movement data from the MIT Eye Tracking Database (Judd, Ehinger, Durand, & Torralba, 2009) is used with the NSS evaluation metric to evaluate the VA models of interest. The database contains 1,003 high resolution color images consisting of a variety of complex visual scenes involving animals, faces, people, objects, as well as indoor and outdoor scenes. Compiled eye movement data of 15 observers for the 1,003 images is available with the dataset.

VA Model Evaluations Results

For the object-oriented evaluation, all four VA models were run for 1,000 iterations to obtain the average precision, recall, and F-measure scores. To segment the image into regions for the extraction of salient regions, the watershed using rainfall simulation (Yeong, Ngau, Ang, & Seng, 2009) was used. This version of the watershed segmentation produces seamless regions compared to the immersion watershed found in MATLAB; therefore, resulting in a more accurate segmentation result. Two thresholds of 1 × avg sal and 2 × avg sal were used in the saliency map thresholding as an observation for segmentation with different threshold values. To emphasize precision over recall, which is more practical in real life situations where conspicuous locations are predicted by eye fixations; the precision is weighted more than the recall by setting $\beta = 0.5$ (Liu, Yuan, Sun, Wang, Zheng, Tang, & Shum, 2011). Table 1 shows the precision, recall, and F-measure for the AIM, MSF, Walther-Koch, and WBSME VA models averaged over 1,000 images using a saliency map threshold of 1 and 2.

Similarly, a total of 1,003 iterations were conducted for each VA model of interest using the eye movement data from 15 observers per image. For the Walther-Koch model, 600 × 800 pixels was the recommended maximum input dimension. Since the visual stimuli from the Eye Tracking Database were all high resolution images (> 700 × 1000 pixels), two simulations were conducted for the Walther-Koch model; with the non-resized images and the recommended resized images as inputs respectively. The saliency maps for the resized inputs were up-sampled back to

Table 1. Precision, recall, and F-measure scores for the AIM, MSF 9/7, Walther-Koch, and WBSME VA models. Both MSF 9/7 and the WBSME use the 9/7 CDF as means of early visual feature extraction. Evaluations are performed using $\beta = 0.5$ and with a saliency map threshold of 1 and 2.

VA model	Saliency map threshold = 1			Saliency map threshold = 2		
	Precision	Recall	F-measure	Precision	Recall	F-measure
AIM	0.3175	0.7651	0.3596	0.3155	0.2061	0.2852
MSF 9/7	0.3975	0.7510	0.4388	0.5245	0.3888	0.4903
Walther-Koch	0.5200	0.2743	0.4410	0.5408	0.2412	0.4332
WBSME	0.3812	0.6546	0.4159	0.4931	0.2696	0.4230

their original dimensions before normalization for the NSS evaluation. For the WBSME and MSF models, no modifications were done for their evaluations. Table 2 shows the average NSS scores for the VA models evaluated. The notation "9/7 CDF" for WBSME and MSF models indicate that the 9/7 CDF wavelet transform is used for the early visual feature extraction.

For a saliency map threshold of 1, the Walther-Koch obtained the highest precision among the four evaluated VA models with a score of 0.5200 in comparison to the AIM with 0.3175, the WBSME with 0.3812 and the MSF with 0.3975. However, Walther-Koch obtained the lowest recall score of 0.2743, followed by WBSME with 0.6546, MSF with 0.7510, and AIM with 0.7651. The overall salience prediction performance given by the F-measure score indicated that the Walther-Koch has the best performance, which was biased towards eye fixations. Similarly, the MSF ranked second with a difference of −0.0022 and WBSME third, with a difference of −0.0251. The AIM recorded the lowest performance score of 0.3596, which differs by −0.0814, −0.0792, and −0.0563

Table 2. NSS scores for the AIM, MSF 9/7, Walther-Koch, and WBSME VA models

AIM	MSF (9/7 CDF)	Walther Koch (non-resized)	Walther-Koch (resized)	WBSME (9/7 CDF)
0.7782	0.7810	0.3609	0.3555	0.6059

when compared to the Walther-Koch, MSF, and WBSME respectively.

With the saliency map threshold of 2, an increase in precision score was observed for all the VA models with the exception for the AIM. Likewise, the recall scores for the models had decreased. The Walther-Koch observed an increase in precision by 4% and a drop of 12.07% in recall scores. For the WBSME, the precision had increased by 29.36% and a steep drop of 58.82% was observed in the recall score. A similar pattern was also observed in the MSF scores, with a 31.95% increase in precision and a 48.36% reduction in recall. In the case for AIM, both precision and recall scores observed a drop of 0.63% and 73.06% respectively. In the overall performance measure, the MSF ranked the highest with a F-measure score of 0.4903; indicating an increase of 7.44% compared to its performance score at a saliency map threshold of 1. The WBSME observed an increase of 1.71% in performance score while the Walther-Koch and the AIM suffered a drop of 1.77% and 20.69% in performance respectively.

The precision score reflects the consistency of the saliency map in predicting the locations within the ground truth. A high precision score shows that most of the predicted locations are true positives. High precision scores are normally seen in fixation based VA models where the locations of interesting objects are predicted accurately despite low number of predictions generated. High compactness in the predicted locations will result in the consequence of a low recall. A low recall score indicates minimal coverage of the regions enclosed by the objects' boundary.

From Table 2, the MSF has the highest NSS score of 0.7810, followed by AIM with 0.7782, WBSME with 0.6059, and finally the Walther-Koch with 0.3609 for the non-resized inputs. While the Walther-Koch algorithm predicts salient locations with higher precision using images of smaller dimensions, it obtained a lower NSS score of 0.3555 with the resized inputs; displaying a 0.0054 drop from the score with non-resized inputs. The drop in NSS score is likely to be a direct effect of the saliency map up-sampling. Even though the saliency map at 600 × 800 pixels may have a high NSS score, up-sampling it back to the original input dimension will cause a neighbourhood averaging among the salience values; hence, flattening the saliency distribution curve and resulting in a lower NSS score.

The NSS score is dependent on two factors: the eye fixations and the statistical distribution of the salience values. For a saliency map with sparse predictions but with most of the predictions falling on the location of the eye fixations, the NSS score will be high; indicating high relevance between the predicted locations and the fixations. If the salience predictions fall on all the fixated locations but also cover wide unrelated areas, the saliency distribution curve will likely be flat. This results in a low NSS score even though all the fixated locations are correctly predicted. The NSS can be used to show the precision of VA models by gauging their prediction coverage for a given visual stimulus.

The MSF VA achieved the highest performance scores for object-oriented tasks at a high saliency map threshold and eye fixation evaluations in comparison to the other evaluated VA models. The tabulated results from Tables 1 and 2 showed that the MSF is capable of providing good salient region coverage for given visual scenes while having a high relevance to the human eye fixation. The MSF model will then be used as the base model for modification to be implemented in hardware. The next section will describe the modifications performed in order to achieve a low complexity low memory version of the MSF.

HARDWARE IMPLEMENTATION OF VISUAL ATTENTION PROCESSING

Despite the excellent performances of the four reviewed VA models in the previous sections, several factors have to be considered when implementing a VA algorithm in resource constrained hardware to ensure performance and reliability. In order to successfully implement VA processing into embedded systems, critical factors such as algorithm complexity, memory requirements, and computational speed have to be taken into consideration while retaining the performance of salience predictions.

With the limited computational capacity of low-cost embedded systems, the complexity of the VA algorithm should be as low as possible in order to be accommodated by the on-board processor. Using more computationally powerful processors will result in higher power consumptions; hence, is undesirable for battery-powered platforms and should be avoided. Limited memory capacity is another implementation challenge faced in such systems. The amount of external memory for data storage in embedded systems can be increased by using high capacity miniaturized flash memory. However, the internal on-chip memory used in data processing remains limited. While data can be transferred to and from the internal and external memory to provide greater memory capacity for processing, the large amount of read and write operations involved will significantly affect the throughput of the overall system. A low memory algorithm or an alternative processing approach is therefore required to reduce the amount of memory used by the VA processing stages.

The computational speed involved in the VA processing is vital for real-time applications.

Careful selection of features to be used in the VA processing allows the computation time to be reduced. For models based on the FIT, three features are normally used in the VA processing. Each feature accounts for approximately 1/3 of the overall salience computation time and can be removed from processing when necessary. In contrast, the AIM VA utilizes integrated information over multiple features in its computation, which can be difficult to isolate. High prediction performance is also important in sustaining the reliability of the vision application. While most VA models are versatile, their algorithms have to be evaluated for the best performance in both computer vision and eye fixations tasks to ensure that the predicted regions are useful to vision processing while having high human perception relevance.

Using the MSF VA as the base model due to its high evaluation scores obtained for the object-oriented and eye fixation tasks, making modifications to reduce computation time, lowering algorithm complexity, and reducing the total memory required are performed to obtain a low complexity-low memory that is able to operate reasonably in real-time for resource constrained embedded systems.

Computation Time Reduction through Selected Feature Processing

Color serves as one of the main contributing features in the prediction of conspicuous locations in a given visual stimulus. While other features such as edges, symmetry, and texture can be used, most VA models use blue-yellow and red-green opponent colors or chrominance channels alongside the basic luminance in salience computations. In most VA works, transformation from the RGB color space is usually performed to obtain a more perceptually uniform color space. This allows accurate contrast computations involving Euclidean distances (Ma & Zhang, 2003).

While perceptually uniform color spaces indeed provide a better approximation to Euclidean space as seen in technical references, the question on whether the transformation of color spaces has a definite impact on the prediction performance is raised. Similarly, the contribution of a single non-color feature in the form of luminance should be investigated to observe the necessary color feature inclusion in VA processing. Minimizing the use of multiple features would reduce the amount of memory required for hardware implementation and overall computation time. Furthermore, the increase in overall complexity has to be reviewed and justified should the transformation of color spaces be found to have a significant contribution to the salient predictions.

In order to observe the contribution of the color feature to the prediction of salience, the object-oriented and eye fixation evaluations were performed on the MSF VA with seven different color spaces. This is primarily done to observe the contribution of different color spaces against RGB and whether the color features are necessary in addition to basic luminance. Evaluations were conducted with the same parameters and number of iterations as in the previous section's MSF VA model for seven different color spaces: RGB; HSV; LUV; YUV; YCbCr; YCoCg; and CIELAB. For the RGB color space, the intensity and opponent-color equations of the Walther-Koch model were used. Table 3 and Table 4 show the precision, recall, F-measure scores, and the NSS scores for the evaluations, respectively.

Also, an investigation into the relative contributions of the luminance and the color features to the human eye fixations was performed. Table 5 and Table 6 show the precision, recall, F-measure scores, and the NSS scores for the grayscale inputs using the luminance feature from the RGB, YUV, and the CIELAB color spaces, respectively. Two different grayscale inputs were used for the RGB color space, consisting of the luminance feature from the intensity equation of (Walther & Koch, 2006) and the green channel

Table 3. Precision, recall, and F-measure scores for seven different color spaces using the MSF 9/7 VA. Evaluations are performed using $\beta = 0.5$ and with a saliency map threshold of 1 and 2.

VA model	Saliency map threshold = 1			Saliency map threshold = 2		
	Precision	Recall	F-measure	Precision	Recall	F-measure
CIELAB	0.3869	0.7356	0.4274	0.5080	0.3758	0.4746
HSV	0.3429	0.6888	0.3812	0.4536	0.3301	0.4220
LUV	0.3872	0.7140	0.4262	0.4864	0.3673	0.4568
RGB	0.3743	0.6917	0.4121	0.4717	0.3498	0.4410
YCbCr	0.3964	0.7489	0.4376	0.5218	0.3861	0.4875
YCoCg	0.4035	0.7618	0.4454	0.5440	0.4018	0.5080
YUV	0.3975	0.7510	0.4388	0.5245	0.3888	0.4903

Table 4. NSS scores for seven different color spaces using the MSF 9/7 VA

CIELAB	HSV	LUV	RGB	YCbCr	YCoCg	YUV
0.7646	0.6464	0.6862	0.7095	0.7774	0.7932	0.7810

component. The luminance channel of the YUV was used as the representative luminance from the YCbCr, YCoCg, and YUV color spaces, since its equation provided the most accurate values. The CIELAB and the LUV share the same brightness component; hence, the L component of the CIELAB was used as the representative of the two color spaces. The grayscale inputs from the RGB, YUV, and the CIELAB color spaces were denoted as RGB-L (luminance), RGB-G (green component), YUV-Y, and CIELAB-L respectively.

From the scores tabulated for a saliency map threshold of 1 in Table 4, the YCoCg had the highest precision, recall, and F-measure scores, followed by YUV and then the YCbCr. The LUV ranked fourth and followed by the CIELAB. The RGB and HSV each ranked sixth and seventh respectively. A similar ranking pattern was observed in the tabulated scores for a saliency map threshold of 2 with the exception of the LUV and CIELAB color spaces when a saliency map threshold of 2 was used. Here, the CIELAB ranked fourth, followed by the LUV. For the eye fixation evaluation conducted, the YCoCg was found to have the highest relevance to human eye fixations, followed by the YUV and then the YCbCr. The CIELAB ranked fourth, followed by RGB, LUV, and finally the HSV color space.

The YCbCr, YCoCg, and the YUV color spaces were found to have high salience prediction performances while having significant relevance to the human eye fixations. These three color spaces have the similar valued luma/luminance channel *Y*, with the luma channel of YCoCg computed in integer arithmetic. By observing the evaluation scores of these three color spaces, the minor differences in the scores suggested that the chroma channels (opponent-colors) have a role in the overall prediction performance. While the luma and chroma channels were designed to match human visual perception (Austerberry, 2002), the influence of the green component in the YCoCg is stronger (Malvar, Sullivan, & Srinivasan, 2008) compared to the YCbCr and the YUV. This is likely to explain the high evaluation scores of the YCoCg since human spectral sensitivity peaks at the yellow-green wavelength of the color

Table 5. Precision, recall, and F-measure scores for grayscale inputs consisting of the luminance feature from the CIELAB, RGB, and YUV color spaces using the MSF 9/7 VA. Evaluations are performed using $\beta = 0.5$ and with a saliency map threshold of 1 and 2.

VA model	Saliency map threshold = 1			Saliency map threshold = 2		
	Precision	Recall	F-measure	Precision	Recall	F-measure
CIELAB-L	0.3725	0.6891	0.4102	0.4680	0.3476	0.4377
RGB-Green	0.3835	0.7039	0.4219	0.4908	0.3642	0.4589
RGB-Mean	0.3745	0.6913	0.4123	0.4716	0.3517	0.4415
YUV-Y	0.3779	0.6962	0.4159	0.4761	0.3522	0.4448

Table 6. NSS scores for grayscale inputs consisting of the luminance feature from the CIELAB, RGB, and YUV color spaces using the MSF 9/7 VA

CIELAB-L	RGB-Green	RGB-Mean	YUV-Y
0.7170	0.7247	0.7090	0.7195

spectrum (Giorgianni, Madden, & Kriss, 2009). However, the minor differences in the observed scores also suggested that a large number of the salience predictions may have been contributed by the luminance channel.

The evaluation scores for the perceptually uniform CIELAB and LUV color spaces were observed to have a similar outcome as the YCbCr, YCoCg, and the YUV color spaces. The variation in the CIELAB and LUV scores showed that the color channels had contributed to the prediction of salience as the brightness component L of the two color spaces was computed with the same mathematical equation. While the CIELAB and LUV were developed as a perception based color space, the reason for the noticeable difference in their evaluation scores when compared to the YCbCr, YCoCg, and the YUV color spaces remains uncertain. One possible reason for the score difference could be the effects of the color channel computations. Nonetheless, the brightness component L of the CIELAB and LUV color spaces was to match the human visual perception, similar to the luminance Y. Therefore, their individual contributions to the prediction of salience are likely to differ by a small margin.

The RGB color space was unable to exhibit a similar performance score for the object-oriented evaluation when compared to the perceptual based color spaces. The accuracy of saliency map values was likely affected by the computations of intensity and the opponent color features using multiple non-linear RGB components. Despite the non-linearity in the RGB components, salient predictions can be improved by using a more accurate measure of intensity and opponent colors in computing the input features from the RGB components. By using the RGB opponent color equations initially described by Itti (Itti, Koch, & Neibur, 1998), the relevance score for the RGB color space was raised from 0.7095 to 0.7943 for the eye fixation evaluations. Similarly, the precision and recall scores were increased to 0.3964 and 0.7489 respectively for a saliency map threshold of 1, and to 0.5218 and 0.3861 respectively for a saliency map threshold of 2. With the new relevance score, RGB outperformed the other six color spaces in the eye fixation evaluation. For the object-oriented evaluation, RGB ranked third for both threshold values in comparison to a rank of sixth, after applying opponent-color equations of (Itti, Koch, & Neibur, 1998). As for the HSV, the color space is a linear transformation of the RGB; hence, similarly low evaluation scores were observed.

From the evaluations scores in Table 3 to Table 6 it was determined that the transformation from the RGB color space to more visual perceptual ones do not have significant effects on the increase in salience prediction performance. Although the evaluations initially indicated that most non-RGB color spaces obtained higher performance scores in terms of object-oriented tasks and eye fixations, the differences in the scores were considerably minimal. Furthermore, approximated calculations on the luminance and opponent colors of the RGB were observed to affect the prediction outcomes, leading to low evaluation scores. In fact, corrected computations of these components have resulted in the RGB outperforming the other evaluated color spaces. Therefore, non-approximated equations for the luminance and color computations should be used with RGB to achieve better prediction results instead of performing the transformation of color space. This would not only simplify algorithm complexity but also minimize the use of hardware resources as many optical imager captures in the native RGB format.

In the investigation on the contribution of colors to the prediction of salience, evaluation scores showed that the MSF VA that used three features (two color channels and a luminance channel) performed slightly better than with a single feature of luminance. The inclusion of colors in VA processing resulted in a maximum of only a 16.0612% increment in evaluation scores, indicating that it has minimal contribution to the prediction of salience. In hardware, the green component of the RGB is used to approximate a grayscale image when direct grayscale capture or a luminance computation is not available due to the limitations of the imager. The RGB green component was observed to be capable of outperforming the grayscale inputs from the luminance feature of RGB, YUV, and CIELAB in salience predictions for both object-oriented and eye fixation evaluations. The green component provides a better perception of equal brightness (Lee & Kalva, 2011) when represented as graytones compared to the red and blue components. Since the human eye is more sensitive to variation in intensity than variation in color, the RGB green component may be a more effective representation of a grayscale image than the computed luminance of most colour spaces. To minimize the number of computations and the memory requirements of a VA implementation, a single feature input with the RGB green component can be used. Although slightly lower performance is expected with the use of a single feature, the amount of VA processing is reduced by two-thirds; directly increasing the VA frame rate while decreasing the number of maps to be stored to memory.

Low Complexity Algorithm Based on Integer Arithmetic Computations

An integer-based algorithm for the MSF is proposed in this section, replacing its floating-point computations to reduce the computational complexity for implementation in hardware with limited computational capacity. Modifications of the algorithm are performed in such a way that all required multiplication and division operations are of the order of 2^i where $i = 0, 1, 2, \ldots$ so that these operations can be implemented as bit shift instructions. Figure 8 shows the overview of the proposed integer-based algorithm with each stage illustrated.

The first step of the algorithm is to extract visual features from the input grayscale image. In order to create an image pyramid containing several sets of orientations relating to the medium-high frequency range, the lifting based LeGall 5/3 DWT is applied to the image as opposed to the 9/7 CDF DWT in the original MSF. In our case, we apply a four level DWT decomposition. Similar to the original MSF, the low frequency components are not required; hence, the LL bands are discarded. In the second step of the model, a CS process is applied to each of the orientation sub-bands at all levels. The CS process is an important operation to emphasize fine details at

Figure 8. An overview of the integer-based MSF

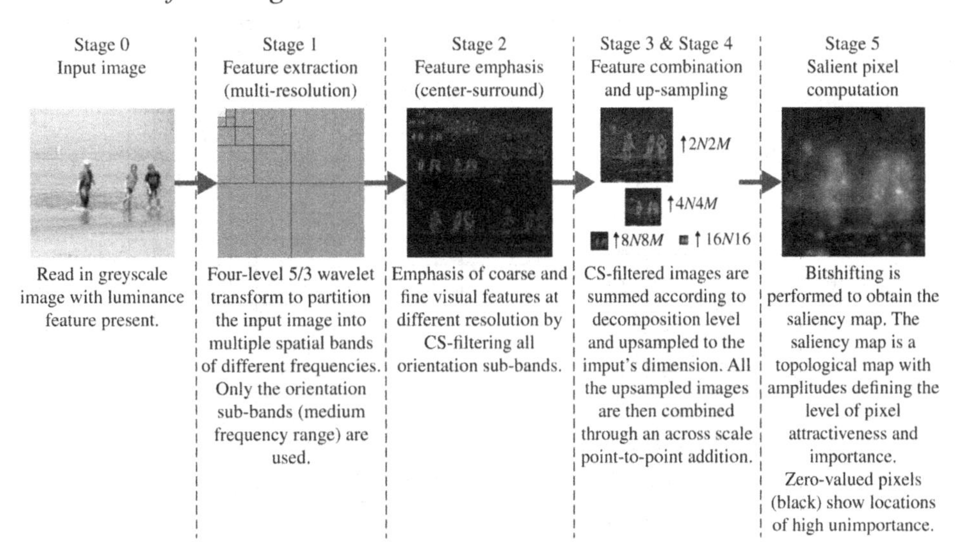

lower levels of the decomposition and coarse details at higher decomposition levels. For each pixel location in the oriented sub-band, a CS filter is applied using (42):

$$CS\left(x\right)=\left|\left|I\left(x\right)\right|-\frac{1}{s}\left(4\cdot\left|I\left(x\right)\right|+\sum_{k\in NE}\left|I\left(k\right)\right|\right)\right| \quad (42)$$

where $I\left(x\right)$ is the pixel value at location x, $I\left(k\right)$ is the pixel value at location k, NE is a set containing neighborhood pixel locations excluding the center pixel found in the structured filter, and s is the total number of elements used in the pixel neighbourhood. Instead of the conventional 5×5 window filter found in many visual saliency algorithms, a proposed diamond-structured filter with two pixels from the origin in our modified algorithm would be used. This is to allow the bit shift operation to be used as a substitute to the floating-point division. Figure 9 illustrates the proposed diamond-structured filter.

Once the CS operation is applied to all the orientation sub-bands, the CS-filtered sub-bands are summed according to their respective levels creating level maps, L_p. Then, each level map is recursively up-sampled to the actual image dimension, doubling the image dimension for each recursion as described in (43):

$$L=\left(L_p\right)\uparrow_l^{2N2M} \quad (43)$$

In (43), L is the up-sampled level map, $\uparrow^{2N2M}$ denotes up-sampling by factor of two, and l is the number of recursions relating to the number of decomposition level of the operated level map L_p. Unlike the original MSF, the smoothing process shown in (31) is skipped.

The final step of the algorithm consists of fusing the up-sampled level maps. The fusion operation is performed by across scale addition of the level maps. The channel map C is then obtained from (44):

$$C\left(x\right)=\frac{1}{ND}\bigoplus_l L_l\left(x\right) \quad (44)$$

where ND is the total number of wavelet decompositions used and L_l is the up-sampled level map at level l.

Figure 9. The diamond-structured filter used in the CS process of the MSF 5/3 VA model. (a) The filter structure and its weighting are shown in the shaded rectangles. (b) CS filtering is conducted in a snake horizontal manner.

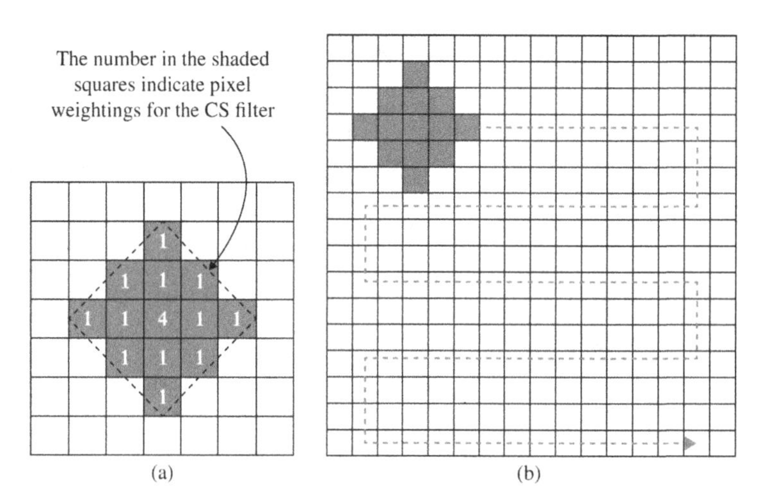

Since only a single luminance feature is used, the final saliency map S is the computed channel map C. Figure 10 shows a visual comparison of saliency maps for the original MSF (MSF 9/7) and the proposed low complexity MSF (MSF 5/3) using the original 5×5 window filter and the proposed CS filter.

Memory Reduction Using Strip-Based Processing Approach

Strip-based processing is an interesting approach which allows high resolution images as well as imaging methods that require extensive memory to be performed in an environment with limited memory resources. The main idea of the approach is to partition the input image into multiple even-sized strips and having each strip processed individually through an iterative loop. The even-sized strips are referred to as image strips and each strip is treated as a valid input for processing. With this approach, the amount of memory required for processing can be proportionally lowered according to the number of image strips partitioned from the input image. Although a minor increase in instruction overhead is expected due to the iteration, the advantage of the strip-based processing is far more attractive, especially for implementing VA in a resource constrained environment.

Figure 11 illustrates the strip-based processing approach applied to the MSF 5/3 algorithm. For a vision-based system employing a VA model, the image captured by the camera is first stored in external memory. In many embedded hardware systems, the external memory is usually detachable for upgradability. This makes them larger in physical size and capacity but relatively lower in cost compared to a system using built-in local memory. Once the image capture has been obtained, a segment of the full image in strip form is loaded from the external memory to the smaller sized local memory for VA processing. When the VA processing has been completed, the processed strip (saliency strip in the case of Figure 11) is released and written back to the external memory for recombination. At the end of the iterative strip-based approach, a fully recombined saliency map will be located in the external memory.

The described case for Figure 11 only illustrates how the strip-based approach is applied to VA processing. Normally for a more realistic implementation, the saliency strip is kept in local

Figure 10. Visual comparison of saliency maps for the MSF 9/7, MSF 5/3 using the original 5 × 5 window CS filter, and the MSF 5/3 using the proposed CS filter with grayscale inputs of the RGB green component

Figure 11. The strip-based processing approach used in visual attention processing as applied to a vision system

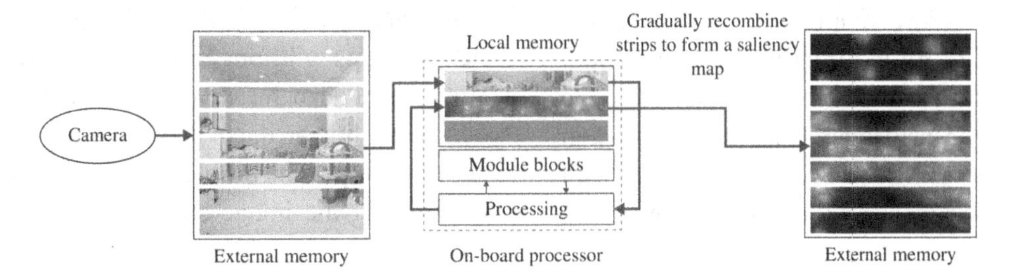

memory for each iteration to be used with task dependent processing of the system. Once task dependent processing has been completed, the final resultant strip will either be written back to external memory for recombination or directly transmitted to the base station before the next iteration begins.

For the MSF 5/3 VA algorithm, a four level wavelet decomposition is used in the feature extraction stage. This in turn, causes the remaining stages to work with maps of four levels. With a carefully designed architecture, the MSF 5/3 VA can be implemented using only two memory arrays, which will be referred to as IMAGE_RAM and STRIP_RAM. The IMAGE_RAM is the external memory of the system and is used to store the image captured by the camera. The STRIP_RAM, on the other hand, is the smaller local memory. The STRIP_RAM is used to hold the data involved in the VA processing as well as other data from tasks that are performed by the on-board processor.

For a single feature used (the RGB green component in this case), the IMAGE_RAM holds a grayscale image. The size of the IMAGE_RAM required is then equal to the dimension of the grayscale image capture as shown in (45):

$$\text{IMAGE\_RAM\_size} = (N \times M) \tag{45}$$

where N and M are the number of rows and columns in the captured grayscale image, respectively.

Considering the scenario where the computed saliency strip is used for additional task dependent processing and the image strip has to be retained in the STRIP_RAM for further use, the size of the STRIP_RAM must be four times larger than the IMAGE_RAM. While the IMAGE_RAM may be used to fill in for an inadequate amount of local memory, situations may arise where the IMAGE_RAM itself is barely sufficient to sustain effective processing in the system. However, with the strip-based processing approach, the size of the STRIP_RAM can be varied according to the number of strips, n, assigned in the hardware architecture as described by (46).

Table 7. Memory requirements against the number of strips for the MSF 5/3 implementation.

Number of strip(s), n	Number of locations	Memory required (kB)	Memory Reduction (%)
1	65,536	131,072	0.000
2	32,768	65,536	50.000
4	16,384	32,768	75.000
8	8,192	16,384	87.500

$$\text{STRIP\_RAM\_size} = 4 \times (\text{IMAGE\_RAM\_size} / n) \tag{46}$$

Table 7 shows the required memory for the MSF 5/3 for $n = 1, 2, 4$, and 8. Calculations are performed using an input image of dimension 128×128 with 16 bits (2 bytes) allocated to each location in the STRIP_RAM. From the tabulated values in Table 7, it can be observed that the memory requirement for the integer-based MSF implementation in hardware decreases significantly with the increase in the number of strips used.

Figure 12 shows the saliency maps computed with the proposed MSF 5/3 using strip-based processing with $n = 1, 2, 4$, and 8. As an input of 128×128 is used in the hardware implementation, the illustration only shows the number of strips used up to eight since the dimension of 16×128 is the smallest image strip that can be used with a four level wavelet decomposition.

For the saliency maps obtained through strip-based processing, most of the predicted salient points are visually similar to the ones in the saliency maps without strip-based processing. However, it can be clearly seen that there are horizontal line artifacts present in the computed saliency maps. The problem occurs due information loss at the image strip borders during the

Figure 12. Visual comparison of saliency maps for the proposed MSF 5/3 using the strip-based processing with n = 1, 2, 4, and 8

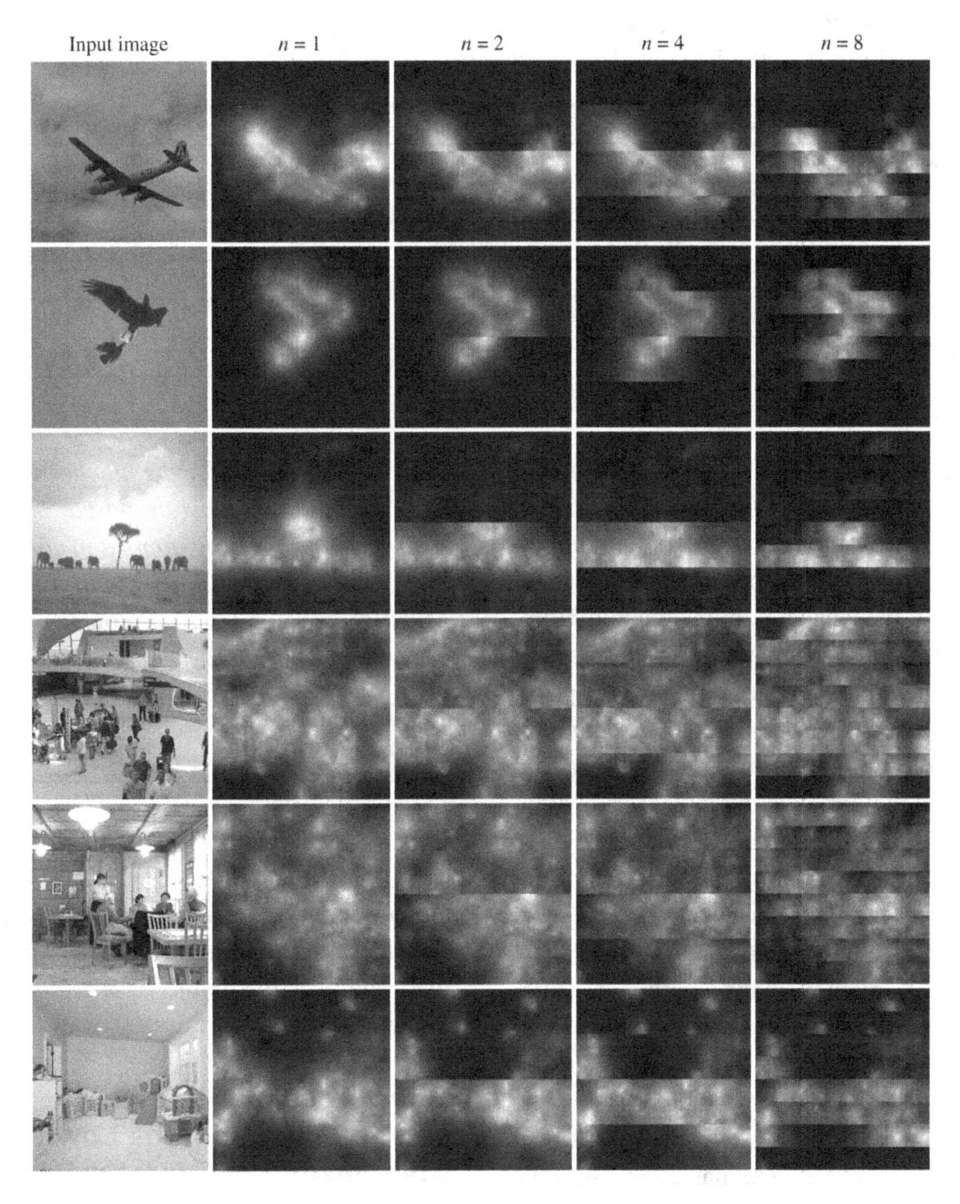

feature extraction stage. When strip-based processing is used, clippings at the image strip borders are also observed. The clipped regions resulted in the distortion of salient point coverage, which in turn, minimized the amount of salient point coverage within the boundaries of the conspicuous objects. Furthermore, normalizing with a local maximum and minimum causes contrast changes at the borders to be computed as salient. With these tradeoffs, the computed saliency map will experience a drop in precision and recall scores.

By doubling the image strip row dimension $2n$ and using only the center portion of the image strip corresponding to the number of rows in n strip after the wavelet decomposition in the feature extraction stage, the problem of the line artifacts can be eliminated entirely. Nonetheless, this method comes with a tradeoff in terms of

Table 8. Precision, recall, and F-measure scores for the number of strips n = 1, 2, 4, and 8 using the proposed MSF 5/3 with strip-based processing applied as compared to the MSF 9/7. The MSF 5/3 with n = 1 and the MSF 9/7 scores are given for the non strip-based processing approach. Evaluations are performed using β = 0.5 and with a saliency map threshold of 1 and 2.

MSF 5/3	Saliency map threshold = 1			Saliency map threshold = 2		
Image strips	Precision	Recall	F-measure	Precision	Recall	F-measure
$n = 1$	0.3992	0.7390	0.4396	0.5273	0.3801	0.4894
$n = 2$	0.3990	0.7345	0.4319	0.5295	0.3795	0.4907
$n = 4$	0.3995	0.7302	0.4393	0.5278	0.3819	0.4903
$n = 8$	0.3995	0.7306	0.4386	0.5230	0.3810	0.4867
MSF 9/7	0.3835	0.7039	0.4219	0.4908	0.3642	0.4589

memory requirement by taking up twice as much memory required by strip-based processing. For the false positives at the image borders, the number of falsely predicted salient points can be reduced by comparing the local maximum and minimum of the image strip which is under VA processing to the local maximum and minimum of the prior processed image strip. The largest maximum and the smallest minimum from the comparison are then used to normalize the image strip being processed. While normalization accuracy progressively increases, leading to the reduction in false positives, additional hardware resources are required for the comparison.

While the saliency maps computed using strip-based processing may seem distorted when observed visually, the distortions do not hinder the salience predictions from providing reliable predictions although a drop in the overall performance score and the relevance to human eye fixation is an expected tradeoff due to the high reduction in memory. Despite the saliency maps' appearance, both object-oriented and eye fixation evaluations in Table 8 and Table 9 showed that the MSF 5/3 with strip-based processing applied was able to outperform the original MSF 9/7 VA model. VA related tasks normally operate on a point basis rather than on regions; hence, inaccuracy in the task is limited to the points located at the strip borders. While drops in both evaluation scores

Table 9. NSS scores for the number of strips n = 1, 2, 4, and 8 using the proposed MSF 5/3 with strip-based processing applied in comparison to the MSF 9/7. The MSF 5/3 with n = 1 and the MSF 9/7 scores are given for the non strip-based processing approach.

MSF 9/	MSF 5/3			
	$n = 1$	$n = 2$	$n = 4$	$n = 8$
0.7247	0.7816	0.7724	0.7712	0.7656

are observed when compared to the MSF 5/3 outputs with no strip-based processing applied, the tradeoff is justifiable for a 87.5% reduction in memory used.

Microprocessor-Based Implementation of the Low Complexity-Low Memory VA Model

The low complexity-low memory MSF 5/3 VA model is implemented in a custom-based microprocessor on a Xilinx Spartan-III FPGA to verify the implementation feasibility in a resource constrained hardware system. The Microprocessor Without Interlocked Stages (MIPS), a form of Reduced Instruction Set Computing (RISC) is used in the implementation. The 32-bit MIPS architecture presented in (Patterson & Hen-

Figure 13. Architecture of the four-stage pipeline custom MIPS

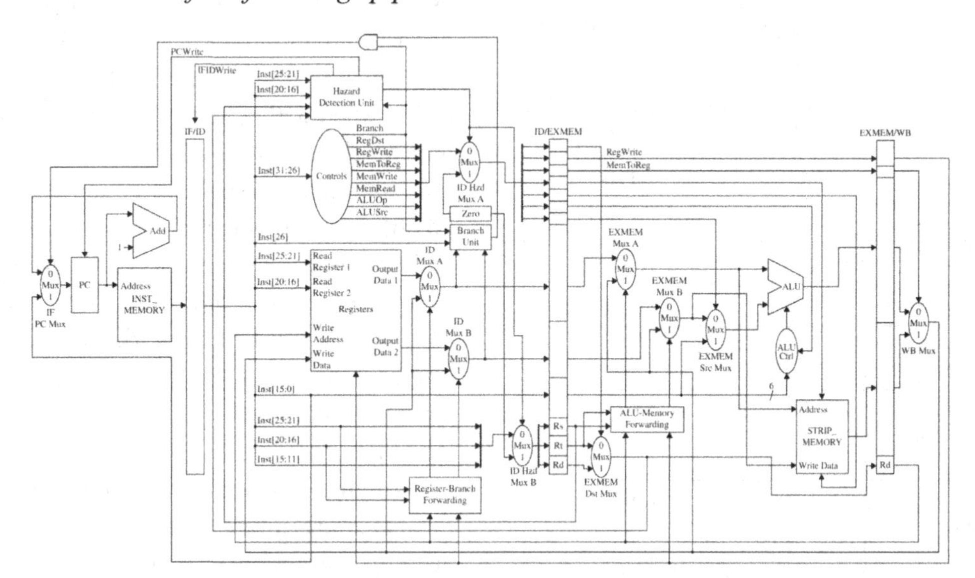

nessy, 2005) is simplified to simulate a resource constrained embedded vision system. Figure 13 gives an overview of the proposed simplified MIPS architecture. Table 10 shows the FPGA utilisation and power summaries for the MIPS implementation on the Xilinx Spartan-III FPGA.

The proposed MIPS was simplified to a four-stage pipeline architecture, merging the data execution and memory access stages. Instead of having to pass through the Data Execution (EX) stage to perform a memory access or the Memory Access (MEM) stage to write back data, the merged stages (EXMEM) now perform either an ALU operation or a memory access operation depending on the instruction given. The custom MIPS is comprised of a basic and a custom instruction set. The basic instruction set includes necessary MIPS instructions such as addition, subtraction, load and store word, add immediate, logical operations, and branch. On the other hand, custom instructions are added to facilitate VA processing. These instructions include absolute, absolute on subtraction result, shift right on addition result, shift right twice on addition result, and dwt address rearranging.

Table 10. Utilization and power summaries for the proposed MIPS implementation on the Xilinx Spartan-III XC3S1500L FPGA

FPGA Utilization Summary	
Target Device	Xilinx Spartan-III XC-3S1500L
Number of Slice Flip Flops	1,433 out of 26,624 (5%)
Number of 4 Input LUTs	2,401 out of 26,624 (9%)
Number of Occupied Slices	2,015 out of 13,312 (15%)
Number of Block RAMs	18 out of 32 (56%)
FPGA Power Summary	
Quiescent (W)	0.159
Dynamic (W)	0.065
Total (W)	0.224

The low complexity-low memory MSF 5/3 VA algorithm described in the previous sections were written in MIPS instructions and stored as binary values in the Instruction Memory of the proposed MIPS. Simulation using the proposed MIPS with pre-loaded images from Figure 12 gave the exact same results for $n = 8$ in Figure 12. The number of MIPS instruction and clock cycles required

Table 11. The number of MIPS instruction and clock cycles required to perform the VA processing on a 128 × 128 image on the FPGA implementation

Stage	Description	Instructions	Clock Cycles	Clock Cycle Proportion (%)
0	Data Copy	14	180,296	3
1	Feature Extraction	191	753,016	14
2	Feature Emphasis	174	1,578,384	28
3	Feature Combination	95	300,568	5
4	Up-sampling & Combination	354	2,524,480	46
5	Salient Pixel Computation	14	196,664	4
Total		842	5,533,408	100

to perform the VA processing on a 128 × 128 is shown in Table 11.

Stage 0 involves the copying of the image strip pixels from the IMAGE_RAM to the STRIP_RAM. Stage 1 is essentially the early visual feature extraction step using the LeGall 5/3 DWT. Equation (42) is performed in Stage 2 using the proposed CS filter. Stages 3 and 4 each involve Equations (43) and (44). Finally, Stage 5 is performed to obtain the final saliency map. In the implementation, a large number of clock cycles are consumed by Stage 2 and Stage 4. The high consumption of clock cycles in these stages is mainly due to the need for loading multiple neighboring pixel values for processing a single pixel location. The overall processing of visual input including Stage 1 can be sped up by approximately two to four times using a multibank memory approach (Yeong, Ngau, Ang, & Seng, 2009).

A similar implementation was performed in (Bae, Cho, Park, Irick, Jin, & Narayanan, 2011) using the AIM VA. In comparison to the works described in this chapter, the AIM VA was implemented on a high-end Xilinx ML605 Development Board fitted with a Xilinx Virtex-6 FPGA. While their work had successfully implemented the VA on a simulated embedded system, more than 4 GB of memory was required for processing. In addition, two system clocks of 100 MHz and 300 MHz were used in order to achieve a pixel rate of 40 Mpps. While their work focused on the VA implementation in hardware, the resource constraints inherent in lower-end embedded systems were not considered.

With the architecture shown in Figure 13 and the hardware implementation of the basic and custom instruction sets, a global clock rate of 37.5 MHz was achieved. If the multiplication and division operations were to be implemented to allow the original DWT and CS computations of the MSF instead of the proposed bit shift variants, a maximum clock rate of only 15.4 MHz can be achieved. This is due to the increase in propagation delay from 26.67 ns (without multiplication and division) to 64.94 ns. In turn, the VA processing frame rate is reduced from 6.5fps to 2.7fps.

Figure 14 illustrates the samples of the low complexity-low memory VA processing with a higher processing of data reduction applied. The real-time simulation was performed using a Celoxica RC10 development board fitted with an onboard Xilinx Spartan-III FPGA implementing the proposed MIPS. A frame rate of 5.8 fps was achieved with the data reduction applied.

CONCLUSION

A biologically-plausible, computationally low complexity-low memory MSF VA model was presented with the aim of introducing artificial visual attention processing into resource limited embedded systems, addressing critical hardware implementation factors such as algorithm complexity, memory requirements, and computational

Figure 14. Samples of the captured images, the low complexity-low memory MSF 5/3 saliency maps, and the corresponding data reduced images. The percentage of data reduction is also shown.

Captured image	Strip-based saliency map	Data-reduced image	Data reduction (%)
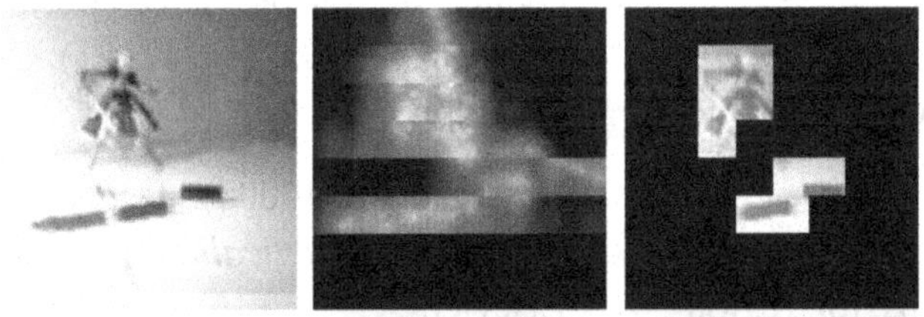			85.9375
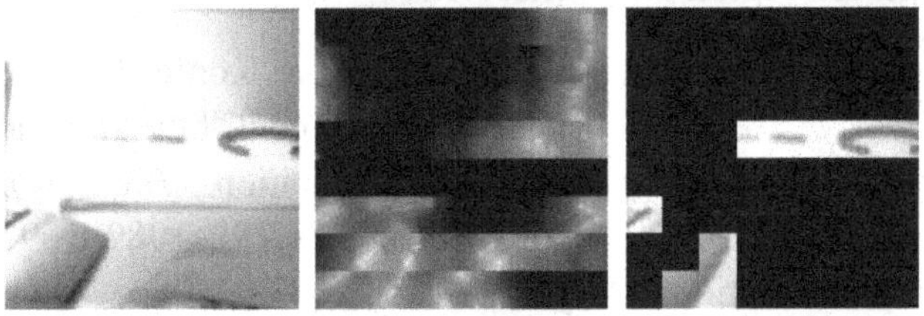			84.3750
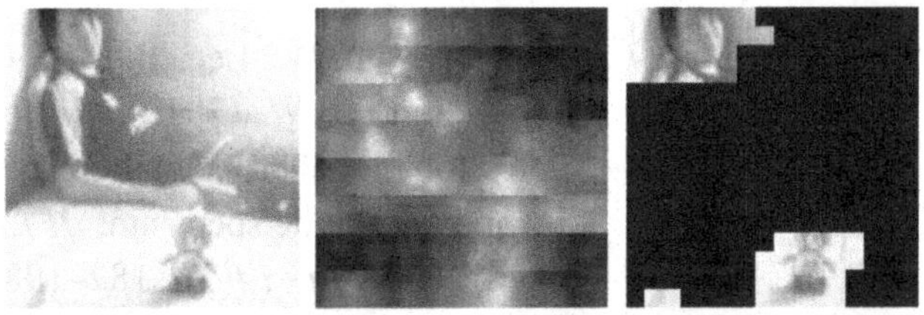			80.4688
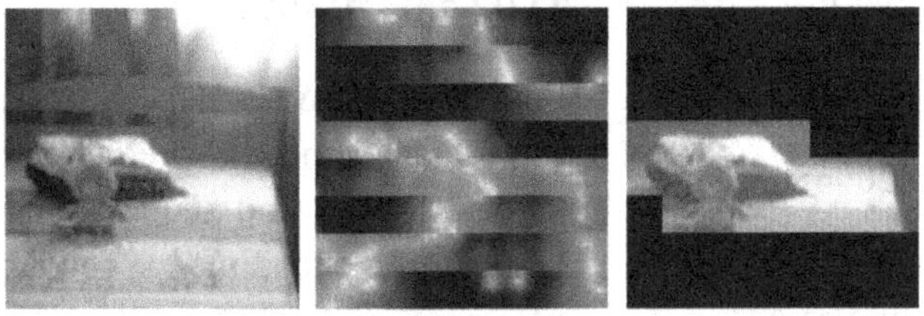			68.7500
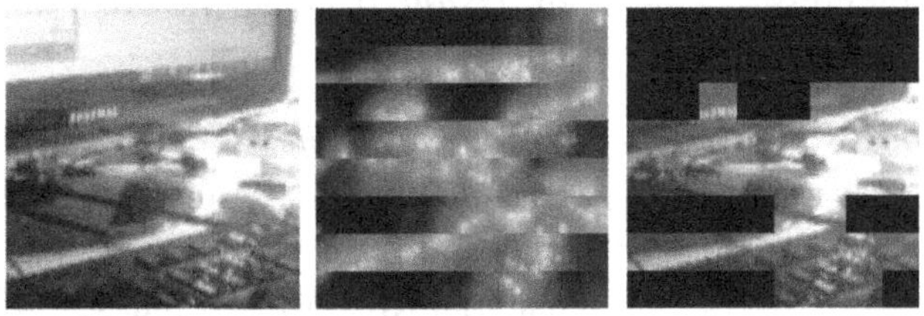			48.4375

speed while retaining high salience prediction performance. The presented model operates entirely on integer computations with a total reduction of 87.5% in overall memory requirements. Hardware implementation of the proposed MSF showed that input images of 128 × 128 can be VA processed at a rate of 6.5 fps at a processor clock of 37.5 MHz.

REFERENCES

Achanta, R., Estrada, F., Wils, P., & Susstrunk, S. (2008). Salient region detection and segmentation. In Gasteratos, A., Vincze, M., & Tsotsos, J. K. (Eds.), *Computer vision systems* (pp. 66–75). Heidelberg, Germany: Springer. doi:10.1007/978-3-540-79547-6_7

Achanta, R., Hemami, S., Estrada, F., & Susstrunk, S. (2009). Frequency-tuned salient region detection. In *The 2009 IEEE International Conference on Computer Vision and Pattern Recognition* (pp. 1597-1604). Miami, FL: IEEE.

Austerberry, D. (2002). *Technology of video and audio streaming* (2nd ed.). Burlington, MA: Focal Press.

Aziz, M., & Mertsching, B. (2008). Fast and robust generation of feature maps for region-based visual attention. *IEEE Transactions on Image Processing*, *17*(5), 633–644. doi:10.1109/TIP.2008.919365

Bae, S., Cho, Y., Park, S., Irick, K., Jin, Y., & Narayanan, V. (2011). An FPGA implementation of information theoretic visual-saliency system and its optimization. In *The Proceedings of the 2011 IEEE 19th Annual International Symposium on Field-Programmable Custom Computing Machines* (pp. 41-48). Salt Lake City, UT: IEEE.

Begum, M., & Karray, F. (2011). Visual attention for robotic cognition: A survey. *IEEE Transactions on Autonomous Mental Development*, *3*(1), 92–105. doi:10.1109/TAMD.2010.2096505

Broadbent, D. E. (1985). *Perception and communication*. London, UK: Pergamon Press.

Bruce, N. D. B. (2010). *Attention based on information maximization source code*. Retrieved January 10, 2012, from http://www-sop.inria.fr/members/Neil.Bruce/

Bruce, N. D. B., Loach, D., & Tsotsos, J. K. (2007). Visual correlates of fixation selection: A look at the spatial frequency domain. In *The Proceedings of the 2007 IEEE International Conference on Image Processing* (pp. 289-292). San Antonio, TX: IEEE.

Bruce, N. D. B., & Tsotsos, J. K. (2009). Saliency, attention, and visual search: An information theoretic approach. *Journal of Vision (Charlottesville, Va.)*, *9*(3), 1–24. doi:10.1167/9.3.5

Cardoso, J.-F. (1999). High-order contrast for independent component analysis. *Neural Computation*, *11*, 157–192. doi:10.1162/089976699300016863

Cassereau, P. M. (1993). Wavelet-based image coding. In Watson, A. B. (Ed.), *Digital images and human vision* (pp. 12–21). Cambridge, MA: MIT Press.

Davies, E. R. (2005). *Machine vision: Theory, algorithms, practicalities* (3rd ed.). Boston, MA: Elsevier.

Einhauser, W., & Konig, P. (2003). Does luminance-contrast contribute to a saliency map for overt visual attention? *The European Journal of Neuroscience*, *17*(5), 1089–1097. doi:10.1046/j.1460-9568.2003.02508.x

Fang, Y., Lin, W., Lee, B.-S., Lau, C. T., Chen, Z., & Lin, C.-W. (2012). Bottom-up saliency detection model based on human visual sensitivity and amplitude spectrum. *IEEE Transactions on Multimedia*, *14*(1), 187–198. doi:10.1109/TMM.2011.2169775

Foulsham, T., & Underwood, G. (2008). What can saliency models predict about eye movements? Spatial and sequential aspects of fixations during encoding and recognition. *Journal of Vision (Charlottesville, Va.)*, *8*(2), 1–17. doi:10.1167/8.2.6

Frequency-Tuned Salient Region Detection Ground Truths. (2009). Retrieved September 21, 2011, from http://ivrg.epfl.ch/supplementary material/RK CVPR09/index.html

Frintrop, S. (2011). Computational visual attention. In Salah, A. A., & Gevers, T. (Eds.), *Computer analysis of human behavior* (pp. 69–101). London, UK: Springer. doi:10.1007/978-0-85729-994-9_4

Frintrop, S., & Jensfelt, P. (2008). Attentional landmarks and active gaze control for visual SLAM. *IEEE Transactions on Robotics*, *24*(5), 1054–1065. doi:10.1109/TRO.2008.2004977

Giorgianni, E. J., Madden, T. E., & Kriss, M. A. (2009). *Digital color management: Encoding solutions* (2nd ed.). New Delhi, India: Wiley.

Ho-Phuoc, T., Guyader, N., & Guerin-Dugue, A. (2010). A functional and statistical bottom-up saliency model to reveal the relative contributions of low-level visual guiding factors. *Cognitive Computation*, *2*(4), 344–359. doi:10.1007/s12559-010-9078-8

Hou, X., & Zhang, L. (2007). Saliency detection: A spectral residual approach. In *The Proceedings of the 2007 IEEE International Conference on Computer Vision and Pattern Recognition* (pp. 1-8). Minneapolis, MN: IEEE.

Huang, Z., He, F., Cai, X., Zou, Z., Liu, J., Liang, M., & Chen, X. (2011). Efficient random saliency map detection. *Science China Information*, *54*(6), 1207–1217. doi:10.1007/s11432-011-4263-2

Itti, L. (2005). Models of bottom-up attention and saliency. In Itti, L., Rees, G., & Tsotsos, J. K. (Eds.), *Neurobiology of attention* (pp. 576–582). San Diego, CA: Elsevier. doi:10.1016/B978-012375731-9/50098-7

Itti, L., & Koch, C. (2000). A saliency-based search mechanism for overt and covert shifts of visual attention. *Vision Research*, *40*, 1489–1506. doi:10.1016/S0042-6989(99)00163-7

Itti, L., & Koch, C. (2001). Feature combination strategies for saliency-based visual attention systems. *Journal of Electronic Imaging*, *10*(1), 161–169. doi:10.1117/1.1333677

Itti, L., Koch, C., & Neibur, E. (1998). A model of saliency-based visual attention for rapid scene analysis. *IEEE Transactions on Pattern Analysis and Machine Intelligence*, *20*(11), 1254–1259. doi:10.1109/34.730558

James, W. (1890). *The principles of psychology*. Cambridge, MA: Harvard University Press. doi:10.1037/11059-000

Judd, T., Ehinger, K., Durand, F., & Torralba, A. (2009). Learning to predict where humans look. In *The Proceedings of the 12th IEEE International Conference on Computer Vision* (pp 2106-2113). Kyoto, Japan: IEEE.

Kanan, C., Tong, M. H., Zhang, L., & Cottrell, G. W. (2009). Sun: Top-down saliency using natural statistics. *Visual Cognition*, *17*(6), 979–1003. doi:10.1080/13506280902771138

Koch, C., & Ullman, S. (1985). Shifts in selective visual attention - Towards the underlying neural circuitry. *Human Neurobiology*, *4*(4), 219–227.

Lee, J.-B., & Kalva, H. (2011). *Video coding techniques and standards - Introduction- The need for compression, perceptual redundancies, the human visual system, sensitivity to temporal frequencies*. Retrieved March 5, 2011, from http://encyclopedia.jrank.org/articles/pages/6922/VideoCoding-Tech niques-and-Standards.html

Li, L.-J., Su, H., Xing, E. P., & Fei-Fei, L. (2010). Object bank: A high-level image representation for scene classification and semantic feature sparsification. In Lafferty, J., Williams, C. K. I., Shawe-Taylor, J., Zemel, R. S., & Culotta, A. (Eds.), *NIPS) 2010* (pp. 1–9). Advances in Neural Information Processing Systems British Columbia, Canada: Curran Associates Inc.

Liu, T., Yuan, Z., Sun, J., Wang, J., Zheng, N., Tang, X., & Shum, H.-Y. (2011). Learning to detect a salient object. *IEEE Transactions on Pattern Analysis and Machine Intelligence*, *33*(2), 353–367. doi:10.1109/TPAMI.2010.70

Ma, Y.-F., & Zhang, H.-J. (2003). Contrast-based image attention analysis by using fuzzy growing. In L. A. Rowe, H. M. Vin, T. Plagemann, P. J. Shenoy, & J. R. Smith (Eds.), *Proceedings of the Eleventh ACM International Conference on Multimedia 2003* (pp. 374-381). ACM.

Malvar, H. S., Sullivan, G. J., & Srinivasan, S. (2008). Lifting-Based reversible color transformations for image compression. In Tescher, A. G. (Ed.), *Proceedings of SPIE 7073* (p. 707307). San Diego, CA: SPIE. doi:10.1117/12.797091

Martin, D., Fowlkes, C., Tal, D., & Malik, J. (2001). A database of human segmented natural images and its application to evaluating segmentation algorithms and measuring ecological statistics. In *Proceedings of the Eighth International Conference On Computer Vision* (pp. 416-423), Vancouver, Canada: IEEE.

Meur, O. L., Callet, P. L., Barba, D., Member, S., & Thoreau, D. (2006). A coherent computational approach to model the bottom-up visual attention. *IEEE Transactions on Pattern Analysis and Machine Intelligence*, *28*(5), 802–817. doi:10.1109/TPAMI.2006.86

MSRA Salient Object Database. (2007). Retrieved September 21, 2011, from http://research.microsoft.com /en-us/um/people/jiansun/SalientObject/salient object.htm

Navalpakkam, V., & Itti, L. (2005). Modeling the influence of task on attention. *Vision Research*, *45*(2), 205–231. doi:10.1016/j.visres.2004.07.042

Nystrom, M., & Holmqvist, K. (2008). Semantic override of low-level features in image viewing both initially and overall. *Journal of Eye Movement*, *2*(2), 1–11.

Pashler, H. E. (1998). *The psychology of attention*. Cambridge, MA: MIT Press.

Patterson, D. A., & Hennessy, J. L. (2005). *Computer organization and design: The hardware/software interface* (3rd ed.). Amsterdam, The Netherlands: Morgan Kaufmann.

Peters, R. J., Iyer, A., Itti, L., & Koch, C. (2005). Components of bottom-up gaze allocation in natural images. *Vision Research*, *45*(8), 2397–2416. doi:10.1016/j.visres.2005.03.019

Posner, M. I., Rafal, R. D., Choate, L. S., & Vaughan, J. (1985). Inhibition of return: Neural basis and function. *Cognitive Neuropsychology*, *2*(3), 211–228. doi:10.1080/02643298508252866

Quattoni, A., & Torralba, A. B. (2009). Recognising indoor scenes. In *Proceedings of the 2009 IEEE Computer Society Conference on Computer Vision and Pattern Recognition* (pp. 413-420). Miami, FL: IEEE.

Rapantzikos, K., Avrithis, Y., & Kollias, S. (2007). Spatiotemporal saliency for event detection and representation in the 3D wavelet domain: Potential in human action recognition. In N. Sebe & M. Worring (Eds.), *Proceedings of the 6th ACM International Conference on Image and Video Retrieval, CIVR 2007* (pp. 294-301). New York, USA: ACM.

Rensink, R. (2000). The dynamic representation of scenes. *Visual Cognition*, *7*(1-3), 17–42. doi:10.1080/135062800394667

Rothenstein, A., & Tsotsos, J. K. (2011). Computational models of visual attention. *Scholarpedia*, *6*(1), 6201. Retrieved March 15, 2012, from http://www.scholarpedia.org/article/Computational_models_ of_ visual_attention

Shannon, C. E. (2001). A mathematical theory of communication. *SIGMOBILE Mobile Computer Communication Review*, *5*, 3–55. doi:10.1145/584091.584093

Torralba, A., Castelhano, M. S., Oliva, A., & Henderson, J. M. (2006). Contextual guidance of eye movements and attention in real-world scenes: The role of global features in object search. *Psychological Review*, 113.

Treisman, A. (1985). Preattentive processing in vision. *Computer Vision Graphics and Image Processing*, *31*(2), 156–177. doi:10.1016/S0734-189X(85)80004-9

Treisman, A. M., & Gelade, G. (1980). A feature-integration theory of attention. *Cognitive Psychology, 12*(1), 97–136. doi:10.1016/0010-0285(80)90005-5

Tsapatsoulis, N., & Rapantzikos, K. (2006). Wavelet based estimation of saliency maps in visual attention algorithms. In Kollias, S. (Ed.), *Artificial neural networks* (pp. 538–547). Heidelberg, Germany: Springer. doi:10.1007/11840930_56

Tsapatsoulis, N., Rapantzikos, K., & Pattichis, C. S. (2007). An embedded saliency map estimator scheme: Application to video encoding. *International Journal of Neural Systems, 17*(4), 289–304. doi:10.1142/S0129065707001147

Urban, F., Follet, B., Chamaret, C., Meur, O. L., & Baccino, T. (2011). Medium spatial frequencies: A strong predictor of salience. *Cognitive Computation, 3*(1), 34–47. doi:10.1007/s12559-010-9086-8

Walther, D., & Koch, C. (2006). Modeling attention to salient proto-objects. *Neural Networks, 19*, 1396–1407. doi:10.1016/j.neunet.2006.10.001

Wolfe, J. (1998). Visual search in attention. In Pashler, H. (Ed.), *Attention* (pp. 13–74). London, UK: University College London Press.

Yeong, L. S., Ngau, C. W. H., Ang, L.-M., & Seng, K. P. (2009). Efficient processing of a rainfall simulation watershed on a FPGA-based architecture with fast access to neighbourhood pixels. *EURASIP Journal on Embedded Systems, 7*(4).

Zhao, Q., & Koch, C. (2011). Learning a saliency map using fixated locations in natural scenes. *Journal of Vision (Charlottesville, Va.), 11*(3), 1–15. doi:10.1167/11.3.9

Zheng, W., Li, J., Si, Z., Lin, F., & Zhang, B. (2006). Using high-level semantic features in video retrieval. In Sundaram, H., Naphade, M. R., Smith, J. R., & Rui, Y. (Eds.), *Image and video retrieval* (pp. 370–379). Tempe, AZ: Springer. doi:10.1007/11788034_38

Chapter 14
Replicating the Role of the Human Retina for a Cortical Visual Neuroprosthesis

Samuel Romero
University of Granada, Spain

Christian Morillas
University of Granada, Spain

Antonio Martínez
University of Alicante, Spain

Begoña del Pino
University of Granada, Spain

Francisco Pelayo
University of Granada, Spain

Eduardo Fernández
University Miguel Hernández, Spain

ABSTRACT

Neuroengineering is an emerging research field combining the latest findings from neuroscience with developments in a variety of engineering disciplines to create artificial devices, mainly for therapeutical purposes. In this chapter, an application of this field to the development of a visual neuroprosthesis for the blind is described. Electrical stimulation of the visual cortex in blind subjects elicits the perception of visual sensations called phosphenes, a finding that encourages the development of future electronic visual prostheses. However, direct stimulation of the visual cortex would miss a significant degree of image processing that is carried out by the retina. The authors describe a biologically-inspired retina-like processor designed to drive the implanted stimulator using visual inputs from one or two cameras. This includes dynamic response modeling with minimal latency. The outputs of the retina-like processor are comparable to those recorded in biological retinas that are exposed to the same stimuli and allow estimation of the original scene.

INTRODUCTION

Nature is a source of inspiration for a variety of engineering fields, such as aerospace engineering, robotics, civil engineering, architecture, optics, etc. From nature, we can obtain a series of efficient, functional, and tested designs. In some cases, these bio-inspired designs are far superior to conventional engineering models, offering better solutions that improve current designs or even become the first approach to problems remaining unsolved.

DOI: 10.4018/978-1-4666-2539-6.ch014

Biomedical engineering is one of the research fields that has looked to biology for solutions. In particular, this discipline has built models for addressing a number of questions that have long been posed by the scientific community. A novel research field named neuroengineering (Sanguineti, Giugliano, Grattarola, & Morasso, 2001) has emerged from the intersection of nature and engineering and is aimed at creating artificial systems able to interact with the central or peripheral nervous systems. A connection between an electronic device and some point of the nervous system could be established by means of invasive (intra- or extracellular electrodes) or non-invasive (surface electrodes) interfaces. This method communication can be used to create therapeutic solutions in which a lost or damaged function in a patient is at least partially restored. Examples of these neuroengineering systems include cochlear implants for the deaf, deep brain stimulation for individuals with Parkinson's disease, brain-computer interfaces for communication and control in paralyzed patients.

Computer vision research has used bio-inspired models to explore issues such as optical flow, object segmentation, etc. The study of natural vision can also take advantage of engineering models to explain how visual processing is carried out at different levels along the visual processing stream. These bio-inspired models can serve not only as a simulator for understanding functional vision, but also as means for understanding and developing solutions for visual impairments. Visual neuroprostheses are aimed at restoring vision in the blind by means of sending the proper neural-like signals to the remaining functional elements of the visual pathway. Building an electronic stimulator able to translate images into neural spike trains requires an interdisciplinary approach involving neuroscientists, neurophysiologists, as well as computer and electrical engineers.

For decades, different research groups throughout the world have pursued the creation of visual neuroprostheses. Although there are some differences in their approaches, they all follow a common principle. The systems proposed take as basis the electrical stimulation of neurons carrying visual information to the cortical areas of the brain in the occipital lobe. It has long been known that electrically stimulating the visual cortex (or neurons arriving at this area) elicits the perception of visual in the form of bright spots, similar to stars in the darkness, known as phosphenes (Löwenstein & Borchart, 1918). Based on that principle, some attempts have been made to provide controlled stimulation of different parts of the visual cortex, in the hope of helping blind individuals perceive shape as a form of rudimentary artificial vision (Brindley & Lewin, 1968), (Dobelle, Mladejovsky, & Girvin, 1974).

VISUAL NEUROPROSTHETICS

Currently, there are three major approaches for restoring sight to the blind by electrical neurostimulation. The major difference between these approaches lies in the location at which the neural interface for electrical stimulation is implanted, as represented in Figure 1.

Thus, we can distinguish retinal implants, optic nerve implants and cortical implants. The first type of neuroprosthesis uses the retina as an entry point for electrical neurostimulation. Depending on the side of the retina receiving the implant, these are named as epi-retinal prostheses (Eckmiller, 1997; Rizzo, Wyatt, Loewenstein, Kelly, & Shire, 2003), (Delbeke, Oozeer, & Veraart, 2003) or sub-retinal prostheses (Chow et al., 2001; Zrenner et al., 2001). Optic nerve implants (Delbeke et al., 2003; Veraart, Wanet-Defalque, Gerard, Vanlierde, & Delbeke, 2003), (Delbeke et al., 2003) use cuff electrodes embracing the nerve bundle travelling from the eye to the visual cortex. The combined activation of several of these electrodes elicits the stimulation

Figure 1. Representation showing the complexity of the primary visual system in humans, including a number of structures conforming the visual pathways. The big arrows mark the location of the electrode arrays for stimulation according to the three kinds of implants (retinal, optic nerve and cortical prostheses). Image modified from a plate from Gray's Anatomy (Gray, 1918).

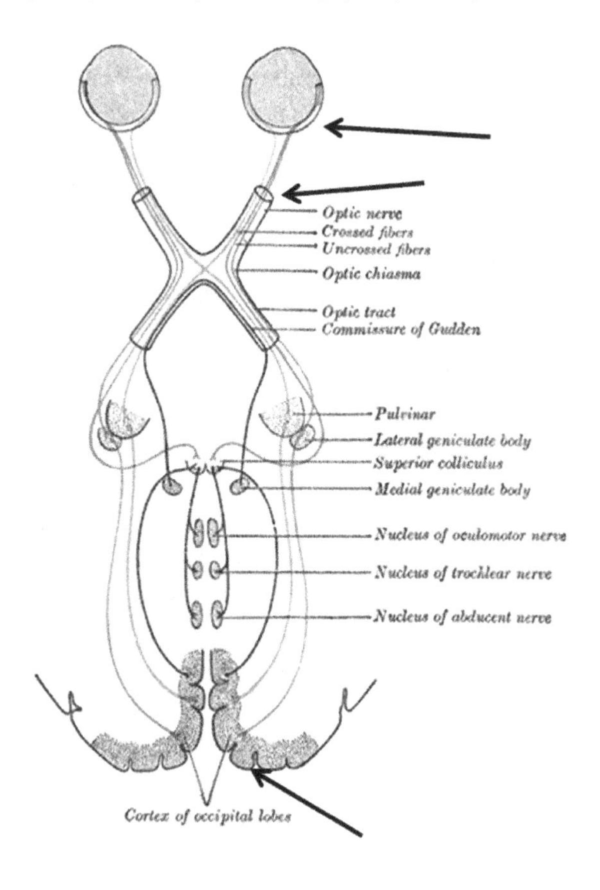

of some of the fibers in the optic nerve, creating visual sensations in the patient. In the case of cortical implants, electrodes might be placed on the surface of the visual cortex (Dobelle, 2000) or penetrate the cortical surface to reach the proper layer of neurons (Bradley et al., 2005), (Fernandez et al., 2005). An excellent review of the approaches used by different groups can be found in (Dagnelie, 2006).

BIO-INSPIRED RETINAL PROCESSING

The Role of the Retina in Vision

The retina (Dowling, 1987) is a delicate tissue covering part of the inner surface of the eye, where light from the visual field is translated into bioelectrical activity and neural responses. The eye is usually compared to photographic cameras in order to explain its function as a system that provides image focusing and light regulation. However, the processing of visual information in the eye is not limited to the direct transduction of light into neural spikes. The set of photoreceptors and the subsequent retinal circuits provide a pre-processing of vision regarding spatial and temporal aspects of the image (Meister, 1999; Famiglietti, 1976). These aspects include intensity detection, color contrast enhancement, and temporal change sensation. This pre-processing is achieved thanks to the distribution and connection of different layers of retinal cells and their organization into receptive fields, which provides a single response channel for a neighborhood of retinal tissue. The output of the retina is a bundle of more than one million ganglion cells per eye, which transmits information to the primary visual cortex (V1) after passing through the Lateral Geniculate Nucleus (LGN) of the thalamus, which acts as a relay station. In V1, further and more complex image analysis is carried out, and its output is sent to a number of subsequent visual areas of the brain.

The organization of the natural visual system has implications for the design of visual neuroprostheses, especially in the case of cortical implants, in which the neuroelectrical interface is directly connected to the visual cortex, so all the pre-processing usually performed by the retina is missing. For this reason, direct stimulation of the visual cortex for a given visual input, should include similar pre-processing by a bio-inspired retina-like processor.

In the rest of the chapter, we give details on the design and results of such a retina-like pre-processor.

An Architecture for a Visual Neuroprosthesis

The inspiration for the work described in this chapter is the European research project CORTIVIS (Fernandez et al., 2005) as well as in previous proposals (Maynard, 2001; Normann, Maynard, Guillory, & Warren, 1996), aiming to develop a complete cortical visual neuroprosthesis for the blind. The implant proposed by the CORTIVIS consortium is composed of several building blocks, as shown in Figure 2.

The first stage of the prosthetic system consists of one or two cameras recording the visual scene (visual stimulus) in front of the subject. Standard cameras are useful for prototyping purposes, although logarithmic imagers or similar high-dynamic range cameras are preferable, in order to avoid saturation and information loss in high contrast scenes. The next stage is devised to perform retina-like filtering and encoding (image capture & processing block). This block applies a set of spatio-temporal filters to the frames grabbed by the first stage. The output of this retinal encoder is a "perceptual map" marking the most relevant features of the image. This map of features is then translated into a spiking code (stimulus encoder), corresponding to the activity of ganglion cells at the output of the retina. Additionally, the full resolution image is divided into small areas that will produce the corresponding spiking output for every implanted electrode, resembling the concept of receptive field. Then, a radio-frequency link (serial link sender) transmits this information, along with power, to the implanted segment of the prosthesis. Finally, the stage after the implanted RF receiver (serial link receiver) performs signal decoding and stimulation waveform shaping for the corresponding channel of the microelectrode array implanted on the visual cortex. In the case of the CORTIVIS implant, this neuroelectrical interface is the Utah Electrode Array (UEA), (Normann & Branner, 1999).

Figure 2. Schematic organization of the CORTIVIS visual neuroprosthesis. The system has an external segment and an internal (implanted) segment. The external section of the prosthetic system provides image analysis and bio-inspired pre-processing, including neuromorphic encoding and serial radio-frequency (RF) transmission to the implanted section. The internal segment receives the serial RF link signal, and selects the activation of stimulation waveforms for the corresponding channels in the microelectrode array implanted on the visual cortex.

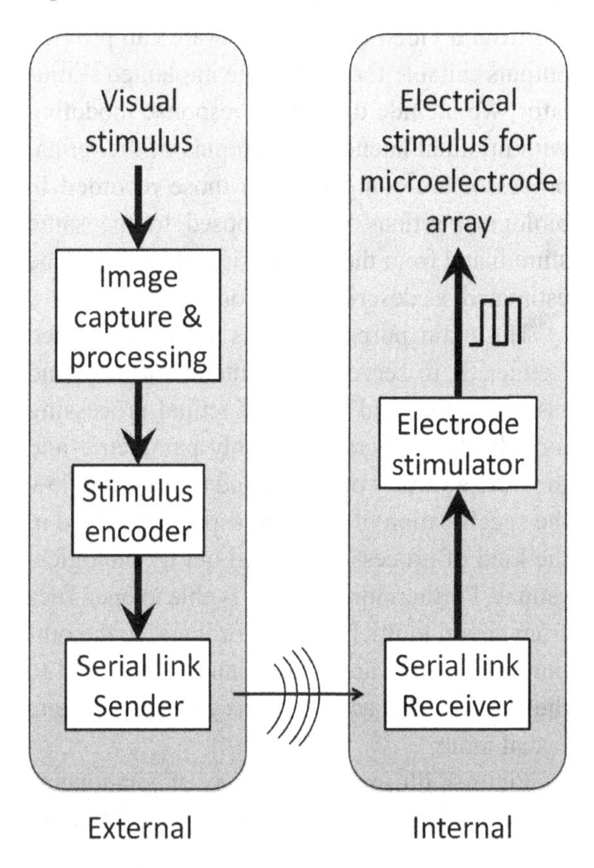

A Simulation Environment to Design and Test Bio-Inspired Artificial Retinas

In order to assist in the design and testing of a bio-inspired retina model for the CORTIVIS neuroprosthesis, a Matlab program was designed (C. Morillas, Romero, Martínez, Pelayo, & Fernandez, 2005; C. A. Morillas et al., 2007), allowing the definition of an algebraic expression for the combination of different spatio-temporal filters over the image sequence acquired by cameras or fed from a video file. The software can provide outputs suitable for driving the implanted stimulator. We include dynamical response modeling with minimal latency. The outputs of the retinal processor are comparable to those recorded in biological retinas when exposed to the same stimuli and from these, the original scene can be estimated, as described later on.

The main purpose of this software, named Retiner, is to serve as a frontend for easy and fast designing and testing of retinal processing models. The program is highly parametric and includes a variety of menus and utilities to allow the specification of different aspects involved in the kind of processing carried out by biological retinae. Furthermore, Retiner is able to open files from neural multichannel recordings, so the output produced by any model can be compared to the response that actual retinas give for the same visual input.

Figure 3 illustrates the variety of components of the configurable architecture of the Retiner environment. Every block in the figure contains a number of parameters that can be selected to influence the results of the retinal processing over the input.

The input for the retinal processor (Video input) is obtained, corresponding to the prosthesis architecture mentioned above, from one or two cameras recording images from the visual field of the subject. For simulation and design purposes, any digital camera is a valid device.

Figure 3. The upper half represents the architecture of the Retiner platform for the design and test of retina-like processing models. The lower half corresponds to an example of application of the main blocks to a given scene for a 20x20 array of electrodes and a basic color-contrast filtering. Every step in this example is labeled with a number, also shown in the corresponding step of the architecture (further explained in text).

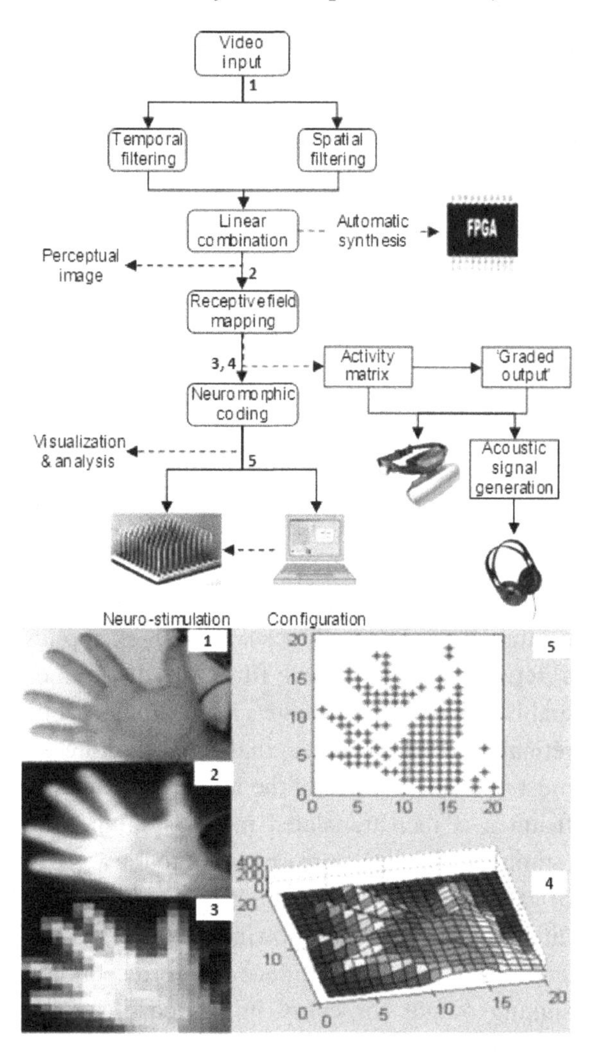

This input can also be fed from static images or video files.

The input video signal is then processed by a set of modules in order to detect or enhance image features, according to different processing models. The first module is in charge of applying temporal filtering, given that natural retinas are sensitive to temporal changes in the visual field. This temporal enhancement is implemented by computing the differences between two or more consecutive frames, with varying strength in the periphery of the visual field. Thus this tool includes emulation of foveated distribution of photoreceptors, following its biological counterpart.

The spatial filtering block performs intensity and colour-contrast filtering over different combinations of the three colour planes of the image frame. This spatial processing acts by implementing the function of bipolar cells in the retina, where a difference of Gaussians (Spillman, 1987) is calculated, although any other filters in the form of any Matlab-valid expression on colour or intensity channels are admitted.

Equations 1, 2, and 3 describe the three built-in bio-inspired filters included in Retiner, corresponding to Gaussian (1), Difference of Gaussians or DoG (2), and Laplacian of Gaussian or LoG (3).

$$G_{\sigma 1}\left(x,y\right)=\frac{1}{\sqrt{2\pi\sigma_1^2}}\exp\left[-\frac{x^2+y^2}{2\sigma_1^2}\right] \tag{1}$$

$$DoG=G_{\sigma 1}-G_{\sigma 2}=\frac{1}{\sqrt{2\pi}}\left[\frac{1}{\sigma_1}e^{-\left(x^2+y^2\right)/2\sigma_1^2}-\frac{1}{\sigma_2}e^{-\left(x^2+y^2\right)/2\sigma_2^2}\right] \tag{2}$$

$$LoG=\Delta G_{\sigma}\left(x,y\right)=\frac{x^2+y^2-2\sigma^2}{\sigma^4}e^{-\left(x^2+y^2\right)/2\sigma^2} \tag{3}$$

where σ is the standard deviation of the distribution, and (x,y) are the spatial coordinates of the current position in the image. In the DoG expression (2), Gaussians $G_{\sigma 1}$ and $G_{\sigma 2}$ might be applied to the same input or to different color channels (Red, Green or Blue), according to the choice made by the experimenter.

In the case of using two cameras, the stereo processing module acts by marking closer objects. This is achieved by computing disparity maps (Trucco, 199) at different resolutions, starting from image pairs captured by a couple of head mounted cameras (optionally assisted by a sonar rangefinder) (C. Morillas, Pelayo, Cobos, Prieto, & Romero, 2009).

After all the spatio-temporal enhancements have been applied to the original input, a synthesis of their corresponding results is obtained through a linear combination, so the most relevant features of the input scene are put together into a single compact representation. We call this representation "perceptual image", as it gives an idea of the relevant information in the visual field to be transmitted to the implant, which would be located in V1. This perceptual image resembles saliency maps, in a similar way to those described in (Itti & Koch, 2001). We use this approach due to the bandwidth limitation when using a relatively low number of channels. So our approach up to this point is not oriented to bio-mimesis, but to a practical engineering solution to encode as much relevant information as possible in a compact form. The contribution of each of these components can be modulated to note the most convenient features.

When dealing with a neuroprosthesis, usually a very limited number of electrodes is available in the neuroelectrical interface. This fact imposes the need for a reduction in the resolution of the original image size down to the number of electrodes in the implant. This process of resolution reduction matches the concept of a receptive field, contributing to the calculation of the output value resulting in the low resolution representation, named "activity matrix". By default, Retiner creates a partition of the image into rectangular non-overlapping areas of fixed size. Nevertheless, it allows defining receptive fields with a variety of shapes and sizes, which also can be variable, depending on its localization, from the center of the visual field to its periphery. An example of this feature is shown in Figure 4.

Figure 4. Foveated processing in Retiner. Upper left image is the visual input. Upper right figure is the distribution of different receptive field sizes from center to periphery of the visual field. Bottom figures show the output after bio-inspired filtering with foveated distribution, for 20x20 channels (left) and its corresponding "graded" (right) version (smoothed version, more realistic for the simulation of phosphene based vision).

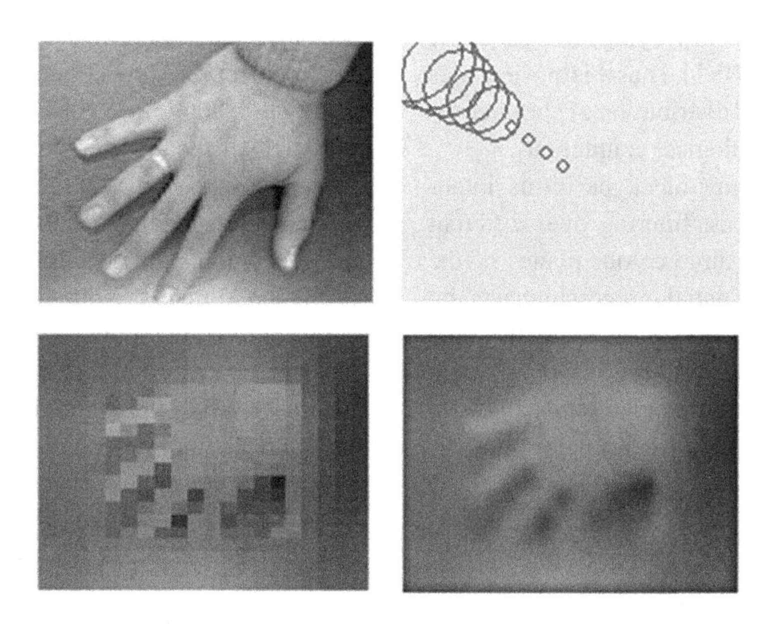

Retiner also creates a smoothed version of the activity matrix for simulation purposes. This version applies Gaussian blurring to the activity matrix to provide a realistic view, suitable for psychophysical experments with volunteers wearing head-mounted displays. Additionally, these outputs can be combined with audio information in stereo sound regarding the location of the most relevant object in the visual field.

The last stage in the retina-like processing platform is the re-encoding of this information into a neuromorphic representation, as a sequence of stimulation events (spike trains), which will be used later to drive a clinical stimulator. For this purpose, we apply a leaky integrate-and-fire spiking neuron model to the activity matrix, which transforms intensity in the matrix (white level) into trains of events (Pelayo et al., 2004).

In this model, every ganglion cell at the output of the retina corresponds to one of the electrodes implanted at the V1 area of the visual cortex. In our case, we are using the Utah Electrode Array (Normann, 1999), which has an area of 4 by 4 mm, bearing 10x10 1.5 mm long electrodes, intended to reach layer IV of the visual cortex. The ganglion cell is modeled as an integrator of the incoming activity matrix levels for its receptive field (gray level, with values ranging from 0 to 255). Whenever the integrated value (resembling the membrane potential in a real ganglion cell) reaches a predefined threshold, the ganglionar output "fires" an event to the corresponding channel and updates its accumulated value down to a resting potential. The model includes a leakage term, so in the absence of close stimulations, there is a constant decay in the integrated potential. This implementation corresponds to the typical behavior of a neuron, which receives a series of afferents from its incoming synapses, increases its membrane potential when those inputs are providing stimulation, and it sends its action potential (spike) through its axon to its outputs, if a certain level of activity is reached. That corresponds to the integrating part of the model, while the leakage term returns the accumulated potential back to a resting baseline when no inputs are received. Models similar to this one can be found in (Victor, 1999), and in (Gerstner, 2002).

Although this is the pre-defined neuromorphic coding model for the Retiner platform, small modifications in its code would allow the implementation of more complex models, closer to the dynamics of biological neurons. For instance, we can make the leakage term depend on the current value of the membrane potential, as shown in Equations 4 and 5:

$$\frac{\partial V_x}{\delta t} = -\frac{1}{\tau} V_x + A_{lin} \qquad (4)$$

$$\frac{\partial V_x}{\delta t} = -\frac{1}{\tau} V_x + \left(V_{\max} - V_x\right) A_{mult} \qquad (5)$$

Where V_x represents the membrane potential, τ is the discharge time constant, V_{max} in Equation 5 corresponds to the saturation or maximum value the membrane potential can reach, and $A_{lin/mult}$ is the instantaneous activity value of the input.

Equation 4 models an additive or linear neuron with a leakage term depending on the membrane potential, so in absence of activity at the input, there is an exponential decay of the membrane potential. Whereas the model defined in Equation 5 has a multiplicative contribution of the input, so the increase rate for the membrane potential is lower as we approach its maximum level, with an exponential evolution of the response for an excitatory constant input. For more details on the models represented by Equations 4 and 5, refer to (Pelayo, Ros, Arreguit, & Prieto, 1997).

Finally, this set of firing events for every electrode is sent to the prosthetic implant, or to an experimentation platform for the adjustment of different bioelectrical and neurostimulation parameters. The scheme used for this communication with the implanted segment of the prosthesis follows an Address-Event Representation (AER), according to (Boahen, 2000; Mortara, Vittoz, & Venier, 1995). This representation is often used in bio-inspired neuromorphic vision systems (Figure 5).

The main advantage of this representation is its efficiency. Instead of performing a scan of the activity matrix for sending every value for every electrode, the serial link only sends “events”, encoded as the addresses of electrodes that must be stimulated at each moment. This results in a considerable acceleration in the data rate, so a high number of channels can be handled with a limited-bandwidth RF link. AER is an adequate technique, given that the number of electrodes implanted is rising, and current arrays can provide over 100 channels. Furthermore, the use of several electrode arrays will considerably increase the resolution of the elicited patterns, requiring an agile and efficient communication protocol.

An additional advantage of this communication technique is the ability to re-order the list of electrode addresses at the decoder. This feature is relevant for the case of cortical visual neuroprostheses, as strong deformations of the elicited patterns with respect to the distribution of activated electrodes is expected when using high density electrode arrays (Warren, Fernandez, & Normann, 2001). We know that the patterns perceived when stimulating with high resolution arrays in the visual cortex suffer non-linear and non-conformal transformations with respect to the stimulation space. So, a given set of electrodes in a certain distribution will elicit a phosphene pattern that might have a quite different spatial distribution, so patterns are not retinotopic. This

Figure 5.Address-Event Representation (AER) scheme. This communication technique is employed in the wireless RF serial link of the prosthetic system. The neuromorphic coding transforms the information contained in the activity matrix into a serialized transmission of activation events for the corresponding channels (electrode addresses). The address decoder selects the activation of the proper electrode of one or more electrode arrays. The table of electrode addresses in the receiver can be re-ordered to provide a re-mapping stage to correct image distortions. This scheme is especially efficient for sending information about a high number of electrodes through a limited bandwidth link in real time.

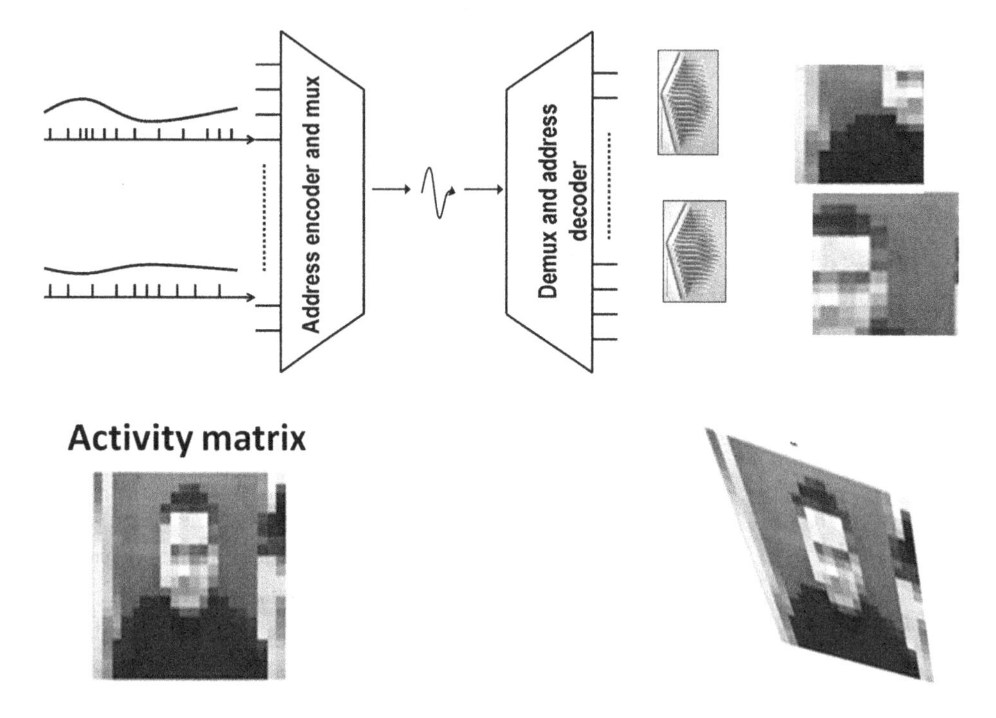

is inconvenient in intra-cortical visual implants, so a method to re-order the electrode-phosphene correspondence is required, to provide patterns in the visual field as similar to the desired shape as possible. In such a case, re-mapping will be required, which can be easily implemented with AER just by re-sorting the electrode addresses table (Romero et al., 2009).

The lower half of Figure 3 shows an example of processing carried out with the Retiner bio-inspired architecture. In this case, the image of a hand (1) is processed with a linear combination of filters that yield an image (2), which enhances the most remarkable information in the visual field (according to color contrast, etc.). This perceptual image is then divided into receptive fields for a 20x20 electrode array (3). The gray level in this activity matrix is an indication of the integrated activity received by a receptive field. An alternative view of these values is shown in Image (4). Each receptive field is connected to a ganglionar output, which fires whenever the accumulated potential (gray level) is over a certain threshold. Image (5) in this figure is a snapshot of firings or events for the array channels in a given moment.

A complete example including temporal filtering is illustrated in Figure 6.

In the example shown in this figure, a video sequence taken at our lab shows the lab (1) without moving objects, a hand approaching the camera (2, 3), the camera lens is completely covered by the hand (4), finally uncovering the lens (5).

Figure 6. A video sequence processed by the retina-like simulation platform. The first row of images corresponds to five snapshots of the original video, with a hand approaching, then occluding the camera, and finally moving away. The second row corresponds to the activity matrix enhancing the most notable spatiotemporal features in the visual field. The third row is a chart where the vertical axis indicates electrode number in a 25x25 array, and the horizontal axis is time (in seconds). The last row is a reconstruction of the activity matrix from the file containing the firing recordings. The input resolution is 320x240 pixels, and the processing combines common color-contrast filtering and temporal filtering (following Spillman, 1987).

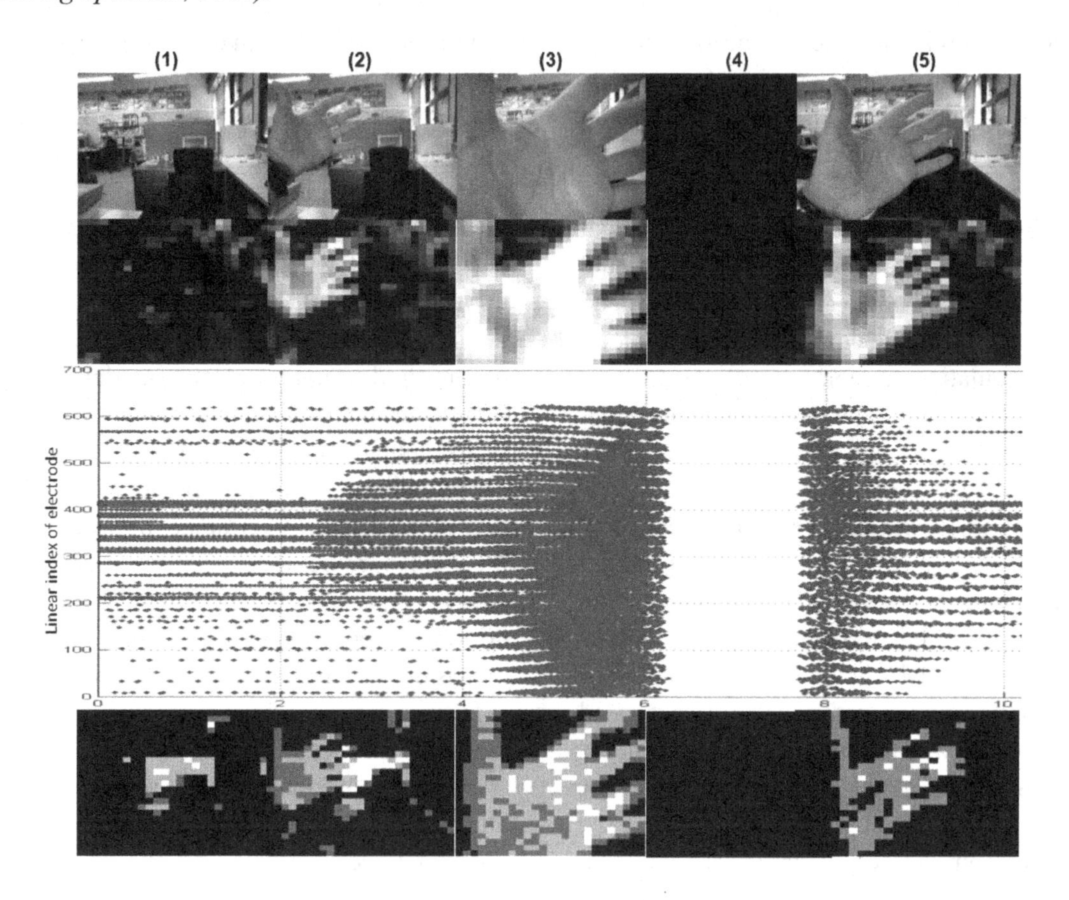

The activity matrix evolves showing the most relevant information in the scene, corresponding to the objects with higher color contrasts and higher motion rates, which are shown as more brilliant objects in the matrices. The activity matrix represents, in every step of this figure, integrative values accumulated by the afferents of the ganglionar outputs, so those over the threshold will fire an event in the middle chart of this figure.

The last row in the image is a reconstruction of the relevant information in the original scene, obtained by applying the same integrate-and-fire model to the events recordings. This image represents the activity integrated by the neurons targeted by a stimulation event. The activity level along time in a neuron is increased by a constant value with every event, and decreases by a leakage term when no stimulation is delivered. This demonstrates that essential information is preserved despite having a very limited number of channels.

ADDITIONAL TOOLS FOR BIO-INSPIRED VISUAL IMPLANTS

Automatic Synthesis of Real-Time Chips for Bio-Inspired Retinal Processing

After applying the steps mentioned above, we commonly obtain a system requiring heavy computational processing. This is in fact the first drawback of having a well tuned bio-inspired model to be used within a wearable visual neuroprosthesis: the need to drive an implanted neurostimulator at a certain speed to produce an appropriate neurostimulation current in visual cortex. The second obvious drawback is the need to develop a wearable device to produce a long lasting stimulation current.

In this way, solutions based on a desktop, laptop or notebook computer architectures are not of interest because of their inherent heaviness (unwearable devices) or their lack of computational power. Note that the original model is being processed using Retiner which runs on top of Matlab. While Retiner gives us enormous flexibility to model, simulate, and validate bio-inspired vision models, unfortunately it lacks speed and portability when simulating, so it is adequate for design and simulation, but not appropriate for actual neurostimulation purposes.

To overcome these two drawbacks we must accelerate the Retiner processing model taking into account both the wearability and the speed-up offered by the solution. The selected solution uses the FPGA (Field Programmable Gate Array) technology as a target for the final implementation of the visual model. This technology not only meets portability and real-time processing requirements, but also offers a number of interesting characteristics such as low power consumption (compared with a general purpose processor architecture) and the possibility of having a highly parameterized hardware model that can be quickly modified.

To translate the selected retina model into a reconfigurable hardware model we have implemented a plug-in for Retiner that automatically performs this task. The plug-in takes a Retiner model, carries out a series of optimizations over it, and generates a synthesizable model in a standard hardware description language (ANSI/IEEE 1076-1993 VHDL). VHDL stands for "VHSIC Hardware Description Language", where VHSIC are "Very High Speed Integrated Circuits". This new model consists of a VHDL hardware description of the model having the same functionality. The model described using VHDL can be processed by a third party tool in order to produce a FPGA or ASIC (Application-specific Integrated Circuit) implementation of the model. At the present, the plug-in is focused on the automatic synthesis of bio-inspired visual processing models using the FPGA technology.

The plug-in interacts with an external application called Hardware–Software Maker (HSM) that performs the interfacing between a high-level software description of the model and its dual low-level hardware version. The top–down synthesis process is performed automatically by means of various software tools, as described in (Martínez, Reynery, Pelayo, Morillas, & Romero, 2006; Morillas et al., 2007)

So the main contribution of the tool described above is that we can obtain a highly accelerated parameterized system using custom hardware, from a high-level description of the visual model that is tuned and tested within a high-level tool, with little or no interaction with the user.

A Testbench for Experimentation with Visual Neuroprostheses

The development of a retina-like image pre-processor is a key step in building a visual neuroprosthesis. However, there are other essential issues that also need to be considered when facing such a complex neuroengineering task.

One of these issues is the need for a research platform allowing manipulation of bioelectrical waveform parameters for neurostimulation and performing a series of tests required to customize the parametric implant for a given patient. To address these needs, another tool has been designed that allows interaction and control of an electronic neurostimulator, which implements a series of procedures and tests to be run with every patient after implantation.

The stimulation waveforms used to evoke visual perceptions can vary in a number of parameters: pulse width, pulse duration, amplitude, number of pulses in a train, etc. The values for these parameters are expected to vary for every channel, so they might take different values for each implanted patient and for each electrode. Even for a given subject, these values might evolve or change in the long term due to electrode encapsulation or breakage.

Given this, a platform for controlling the value of every parameter for each channel is required. In our case, a 100 electrode matrix is employed for research purposes, but future implants might employ several arrays of electrodes, to be able to evoke higher resolution patterns. As the process of finding these parameters is exhaustive, a fast procedure is needed. Previous systems like the one described by (Dobelle, 2000) uses an exhaustive sequential "try and ask" approach, having an operator changing every value and requiring verbal feedback from the patient.

To speed this process up, our system is directly driven by the patient, who uses a feedback device (mouse, keyboard or touch screen). The subject has been previously trained in simulations to respond through this mechanism to sounds (instead of phosphenes) for randomly pre-established thresholds. In this way, the system automatically changes values until the patient stops the process, meaning he/she has perceived a phosphene. The configuration is stored in the computer for later analysis and to be able to "reload" this data whenever the patient gets back to experimentation.

In order to reduce the number of trials, the threshold found for one electrode is selected as the starting point for the next electrodes. This value (if perceived) is considered to be the maximum, so a binary search is performed to find the lowest value that evokes a phosphene.

Once the threshold values are determined for every channel, the patient can start a series of experiences to determine the psychophysical properties of the perceptions evoked by neurostimulation of the visual cortex.

The feedback mechanism in every experiment is similar to the one described above for the threshold finding procedure.

These experiments include:

- Brightness sensitivity
- Spatial resolution
- Phosphene cluster count
- Motion mapping and orientation selectivity
- Simple pattern discrimination
- Basic phosphene mapping

The projection of the perceived image mapping the retina on the primary visual cortex has been traditionally considered to be "retinotopic". This means that two close excited photoreceptors on the retina activate two close neurons at the visual cortex.

However, modern multichannel recording techniques with small inter-electrode separation reveal that this correspondence or mapping results are non-linear and non-conformal (Warren et al., 2001). This fact implies that a regular pattern excited at retinal level (for example, a square) will not preserve its form at cortical level. Thus the patient will perceive a set of phosphenes forming a figure that is quite different from the original pattern. This situation is progressively overcome by the subject, because of plasticity. The patient "learns" the new representation. Such plasticity is quite efficient in children. However, adults show worse and longer adaptation. This would make it more difficult for a prosthesis to recognize patterns.

In order to overcome this drawback and accelerate patient training, a re-mapping between the stimulation and the perceptual spaces must be performed, to get a perceived phosphene combination as close as possible to the original pattern. Once an electrode-to-phosphene map is available, a pattern of phosphenes can be elicited by stimulating the corresponding electrodes. So whenever a specific distribution of phosphenes is required in the visual field of the patient, a list of electrodes has to be determined. This process is called re-mapping (as mentioned earlier, at the AER scheme). The map of phosphenes elicited with intra-cortical microstimulation appears to be stable for a given patient (Schmidt et al., 1996). However, there are a limited number of phosphenes available in specific locations of the visual field, which have to be used to evoke any desired pattern.

Our first approach is to project the desired pattern on the center of the visual field and to then select for every desired point the closest phosphene to it. With a reverse look up at the mapping table its corresponding electrode is found. Instead of selecting the closest phosphene on the map to the desired point, we choose the closest phosphene which hasn't already been selected. Therefore, we can obtain patterns including a maximum number of phosphenes, rather than having more precise locations with fewer percepts. Although the patterns can present some more deformation, its completeness, along with the training of the patient, is expected to lead to better recognition, as illustrated in Figure 7.

Additionally, this selection procedure enhances the response whenever the distribution of the map is highly uneven. So for the case in which there is a region of the visual field covered by a small group of phosphenes and another region with a high density of percepts, a moving object in the visual field should be composed of the same number of phosphenes. Direct selection of the closest phosphene would lead to a different number of points in a pattern, depending on the location of the object in the visual field (which makes it difficult, for example, to recognize a moving object as a unit). With our algorithm, an object of a given size is always composed of the same number of phosphenes, regardless of its location (at a given distance) in the visual field. The shape of the pattern can vary, in an effect similar to looking at a moving objective through a frosted glass.

Figure 7 illustrates the effect of remapping or re-ordering the list of electrodes to be activated for eliciting a desired pattern. As shown for non-conformal and non-linear mappings between the stimulation and perception spaces, direct activation of a pattern of microelectrodes might evoke hardly recognizable shapes that would require lengthy training in order to let neural plasticity make a new interpretation for the meaning of those perceptions. However, after applying a simple re-mapping, the evoked shape is more similar to the desired pattern, so the use and training in recognition of shapes can be made shorter and easier for the user.

FUTURE RESEARCH DIRECTIONS

Developing visual neuroprostheses for the blind is a challenging endeavor requiring an interdisciplinary approach. Ongoing research in this field is starting to give some modest but encouraging results. We can say that neuroengineering is a young research topic, but in order to reach maturity for clinical applications, further efforts need to be made in different aspects. Some neuroengineering developments are now being used in clinical practice (such as deep brain Stimulation or cochlear implants), but the case for vision involves a higher degree of complexity. The design of a visual neuroprosthesis includes a number of issues to be faced before obtaining a clinical solution (Normann, 1996): biocompatibility, chronic stability of the implant, bio-inspired encoding of visual information, portability, reso-

Figure 7. On the left, simulation of a pattern obtained by direct stimulation through the central column and top row of electrodes, corresponding to a T-shaped distribution, for a randomly given mapping (25x25 electrodes). This map of phosphenes has been generated by randomly assigning spatial coordinates in the visual field. As can be seen, this pattern hardly resembles the desired shape. On the right, for the same given mapping, a new set of phosphenes are evoked after a re-mapping procedure, evoking a better recognizable T shape.

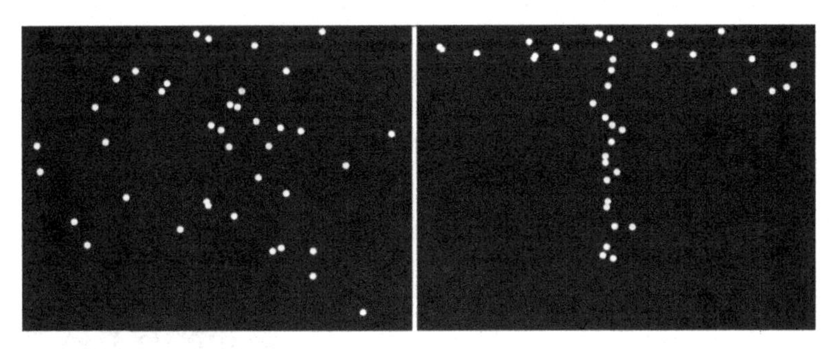

lution (number of simultaneous percepts to be elicited), safety, customization to each patient, training and neuroplasticity, etc. In the case of cortical implants, we might add re-mapping, as well. There are other aspects beyond the scope of bio-engineering, including ethical issues, human experimentation, and insurance for acute experiments for these implants. Currently, this model of neuroprosthesis has some of the components ready for testing or have been already tested in field trials regarding biocompatibility, safety, histological studies, thresholds for stimulation, mappings, etc (Normann, 2009).

Future research in visual neuroprosthetics will include reviewing the latest findings from neuroscience regarding how visual cortex and visual pathways represent different image features, providing valuable information for the design of better bio-inspired image pre-processors. At same the time, we would be able to get a better control of some psychophysical features of the evoked percepts (as color, for example), enriching the kind of patterns that might be perceived by subjects with implants.

Furthermore, the neural interfaces, used as a sort of data port to link between our artificial devices and biological neural networks, can be enhanced by exploring new concepts and materials. One of the issues still requiring better developments is ensuring biocompatibility and making arrays of microelectrodes able to provide useful stimulation and/or recording for longer time, providing durable and stable implantations working for decades, and avoiding health risks. Researchers are working on new generations of microelectrode arrays that include a higher number of channels, wireless communication with the external segment of the prostheses, three-dimensional positioning of electrodes, and new materials apart from microfabricated matrices (such as carbon nanotubes).

Experimentation will probably be the stage in this research providing the biggest and most valuable information, allowing better refinement of every part of the prosthetic implant. Obviously, conducting research with human subjects is desirable given the amount of feedback that can be obtained. However, strong regulations on research involving human beings lead us to think about developing animal models for the initial approaches. Ultimately, human research will be the final step in this process. Until then, animal research and noninvasive and realistic simulations are the tools to advance the design of the prosthesis as well as the calibration, testing, and training procedures for future implants.

Figure 8. The role of bio-inspired image preprocessing in the selection of relevant information. The left column shows the original scene and the output for color image with resolution reduction (20x20). The middle column is the same as before, but in grayscale, given that color is hardly controllable so far in visual neurostimulation implants. The right column applies retina-like bio-inspired filtering to note the most relevant information in the scene, making an efficient use of the implant by stimulation of selected channels.

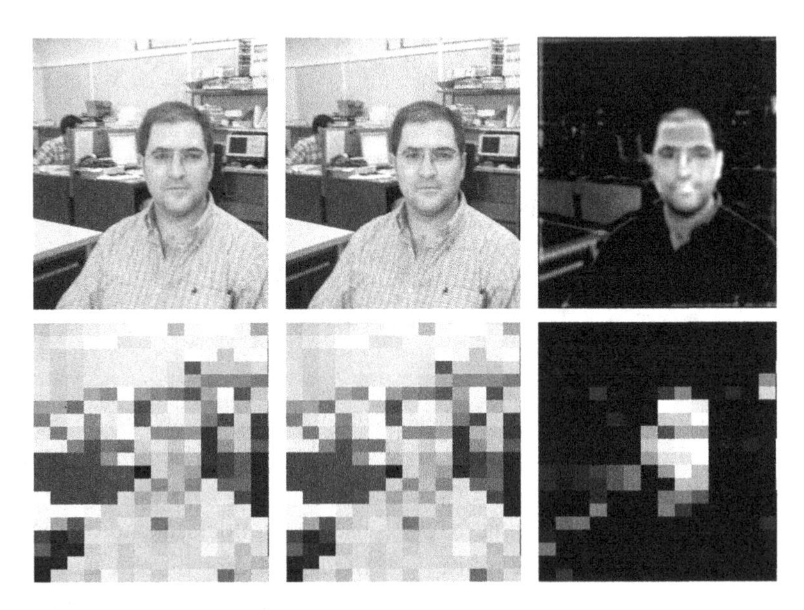

Finally, computing-related parts for the prosthetic system will benefit from the development of smaller, faster and more powerful computing platforms. This will allow handling of more information, so future implants with potentially thousands of channels will be managed with portable, low consumption miniaturized computing devices.

CONCLUSION

This chapter shows an interdisciplinary development of a bio-inspired visual processing model to create an artificial retina, conceived to send electrical stimuli to the visual cortex of blind subjects. In this case, the inspiration by natural for visual processing is mandatory, since ultimate goal is to communicate with the brain. Therefore the response of the visual processor should follow the rules of biology for the same purpose. Our retinal processor models the dynamic response of biological retinae with minimum latency. The results show that the artificial system matches the response of natural retinas for a given stimulus.

The Retiner software has been conceived as a unique tool for modeling retina-like image processing for the purpose of helping to develop a visual neuroprosthesis. It offers the advantage of a flexible environment with a variety of input methods, parameters, and bio-inspired computations. Its output can be easily compared to biological recordings. So our software is not a program that emulates the retina for engineering applications, but a test bench for the design of image pre-processors for visual neuroprostheses.

The development of visual neuroprostheses, especially for cortical implantation, requires engineering efficient multichannel microelectrode implants, refining tools and procedures for surgical implantation, as well as designing safe and efficient stimulation protocols and circuits. However, visual information pre-processing should not be a secondary issue in the whole system. Every step from the acquisition of the image to the delivery of electrical charges to the neural tissue is fundamental and will have an impact on the performance of the visual neuroprosthesis.

This is the reason why we have put great emphasis on the development of the first stage of a visual neuroprosthesis. In this case, biology is performing an image pre-processing that should not be disregarded or over simplified. Simple pre-processing schemes as image thresholding, resolution reduction with sequential scanning for stimulation and border extraction will miss a significant amount of relevant information that might be confused with noisy background details, and the communication with a limited bandwidth implant will be overcharged and inefficient.

This fact is illustrated in Figure 8, in which the same original scene is processed by just performing a resolution reduction (left column in color, central column in grayscale) versus using bio-inspired retina-like processing (right column). In this last case, background noise is removed, so the most relevant object (according to the bio-inspired filtering) is detected and transmitted to the implant.

As the design of a retina model is guided by experiments biological recordings, our environment has been designed to allow easy and flexible definition of retinal with models, with results comparable to those of biological retinas for the same input. This retina-like processor design platform is also useful in other applications such as the development of low vision aids (C. Morillas et al., 2008).

ACKNOWLEDGMENT

The research described in this chapter has been carried out thanks to the financing of the following research projects: EC project CORTIVIS (ref. QLK6-CT-2001-00279), Junta de Andalucia project "HW/SW platform for 3D Vision Sytems in Real Time" (ref. P06-TIC-02007), Spanish National Coordinated Project "RECVIS: Reconfigurable Hw/Sw Platform for Low Vision Aid" (ref. TIN2008-06893-C03-02)", Spanish Ministry of Science and Innovation Project "Aid Systems for th Blind and Low Vision". (ref. GENIL-PYR-2010-19, CEI BioTIC GENIL CEB09-0010), University of Jaén project "VISTA, Visual Implants Simulation for Therapy Advancement" (ref. UJA_08_16_10), and Spanish National Project "DINAM-VISION: Real-time Dynamic Vision Systems and their application to robotics, vehicles and biomedicine" (ref. DPI2007-61683).

REFERENCES

Boahen, K. A. (2000). Point-to-point connectivity between neuromorphic chips using address events. *IEEE Transactions on Circuits and Systems II: Analog and Digital Signal Processing*, *47*(5), 416–434. doi:10.1109/82.842110

Bradley, D. C., Troyk, P. R., Berg, J. A., Bak, M., Cogan, S., Erickson, R., & Xu, H. (2005). Visuotopic mapping through a multichannel stimulating implant in primate V1. *Journal of Neurophysiology*, *93*(3), 1659–1670. doi:10.1152/jn.01213.2003

Brindley, G. S., & Lewin, W. S. (1968). The sensations produced by electrical stimulation of the visual cortex. *The Journal of Physiology*, *196*, 479–493.

Chow, A. Y., Pardue, M. T., Chow, V. Y., Peyman, G. A., Liang, C., Perlman, J. I., & Peachey, N. S. (2001). Implantation of silicon chip microphotodiode arrays into the cat subretinal space. *IEEE Transactions on Neural Systems and Rehabilitation Engineering*, *9*(1), 86–95. doi:10.1109/7333.918281

Dagnelie, G. (2006). Visual prosthetics 2006: Assessment and expectations. *Expert Review of Medical Devices*, *3*(3), 315–325. doi:10.1586/17434440.3.3.315

Delbeke, J., Oozeer, M., & Veraart, C. (2003). Position, size and luminosity of phosphenes generated by direct optic nerve stimulation. *Vision Research, 43*(9), 1091–1102. doi:10.1016/S0042-6989(03)00013-0

Dobelle, W. H. (2000). Artificial vision for the blind by connecting a television camera to the visual cortex. *ASAIO Journal (American Society for Artificial Internal Organs), 46*(1), 3–9. doi:10.1097/00002480-200001000-00002

Dobelle, W. H., Mladejovsky, M. G., & Girvin, J. P. (1974). Artificial vision for the blind: Electrical stimulation of visual cortex offers hope for a functional prosthesis. *Science, 183*, 440–444. doi:10.1126/science.183.4123.440

Dowling, J. E. (1987). *The retina: An approachable part of the brain*. Cambridge, MA: The Belknap Press, Harvard University Press.

Eckmiller, R. (1997). Learning retina implants with epiretinal contacts. *Ophthalmic Research, 29*(5), 281–289. doi:10.1159/000268026

Famiglietti, E. V. Jr, & Kolb, H. (1976). Structural basis for ON-and OFF-center responses in retinal ganglion cells. *Science, 194*, 183–195. doi:10.1126/science.959847

Fernandez, E., Pelayo, F., Ahnelt, P., Ammermuller, J., & Normann, R. A. (2004). Cortical visual neuroprosthesis for the blind. *Restorative Neurology and Neuroscience*.

Fernandez, E., Pelayo, F., Romero, S., Bongard, M., Marin, C., Alfaro, A., & Merabet, L. (2005). Development of a cortical visual neuroprosthesis for the blind: The relevance of neuroplasticity. *Journal of Neural Engineering, 2*(4), R1–R12. doi:10.1088/1741-2560/2/4/R01

Gerstner, W., & Kistler, W. (2002). *Spiking neuron models: single neurons, populations, plasticity*. Cambridge, MA: Cambridge University Press. doi:10.1017/CBO9780511815706

Itti, L., & Koch, C. (2001)... *Nature Reviews. Neuroscience, 2*(3), 194–203. doi:10.1038/35058500

Löwenstein, K., & Borchart, M. (1918). Symptomatologie und elektrische reizung bei einer schubverletzung des histerhauptlappens. *Deutsche Zeitschrift fur Nervenheilkunde, 58*, 264.

Martínez, A., Reynery, L., Pelayo, F., Morillas, C., & Romero, S. (2006). A codesign tool for high level systhesis of vision models on FPL. *Proceedings - 2006 International Conference on Field Programmable Logic and Applications, FPL,* (pp. 829-832).

Maynard, E. M. (2001). Visual prostheses. *Annual Review of Biomedical Engineering, 3*, 145–168. doi:10.1146/annurev.bioeng.3.1.145

Meister, M., & Berry, M. J. (1999). The neural code of the retina. *Neuron, 22*, 435–450. doi:10.1016/S0896-6273(00)80700-X

Morillas, C., Pelayo, F., Cobos, J. P., Prieto, A., & Romero, S. (2008). Bio-inspired image processing for vision aids. *BIOSIGNALS 2008 - Proceedings of the 1st International Conference on Bio-Inspired Systems and Signal Processing, 2,* 63-69.

Morillas, C., Romero, S., Martínez, A., Pelayo, F., & Fernandez, E. (2005). A computational tool to test neuromorphic encoding schemes for visual neuroprosthesis. *8th International Work-Conference on Artificial Neural Networks (IWANN 2005),* Barcelona, (pp. 510-517).

Morillas, C., Romero, S., Martinez, A., Pelayo, F., Reyneri, L., Bongard, M., & Fernandez, E. (2007). A neuroengineering suite of computational tools for visual prostheses. *Neurocomputing, 70*(16-18), 2817–2827. doi:10.1016/j.neucom.2006.04.017

Morillas, C. A., Romero, S. F., Martinez, A., Pelayo, F. J., Ros, E., & Fernandez, E. (2007). A design framework to model retinas. *Bio Systems, 87*(2-3), 156–163. doi:10.1016/j.biosystems.2006.09.009

Mortara, A., Vittoz, E. A., & Venier, P. (1995). A communication scheme for analog VLSI perceptive systems. *IEEE Journal of Solid-state Circuits*, *30*(6), 660–669. doi:10.1109/4.387069

Normann, R. A., & Branner, A. (1999). A multichannel, neural interface for the peripheral nervous system. *Proceedings of the 1999 IEEE International Conference on Systems, Man and Cybernetics, 4*, (pp. 370-375).

Normann, R. A., Greger, B. A., House, P., Romero, S. F., Pelayo, F., & Fernandez, E. (2009). Toward the development of a cortically based visual neuroprosthesis. *Journal of Neural Engineering*, *6*(3), 035001. doi:10.1088/1741-2560/6/3/035001

Normann, R. A., Maynard, E., Guillory, K. S., & Warren, D. J. (1996, May). Cortical implants for the blind. *IEEE Spectrum*, 54–59. doi:10.1109/6.490057

Pelayo, F. J., Romero, S., Morillas, C. A., Martinez, A., Ros, E., & Fernandez, E. (2004). Translating image sequences into spike patterns for cortical neuro-stimulation. *Neurocomputing*, *58-60*, 885–892. doi:10.1016/j.neucom.2004.01.142

Pelayo, F. J., Ros, E., Arreguit, X., & Prieto, A. (1997). VLSI implementation of a neural model using spikes. *Analog Integrated Circuits and Signal Processing*, *13*(1-2), 111–121. doi:10.1023/A:1008240229616

Rizzo, J. F. III, Wyatt, J., Loewenstein, J., Kelly, S., & Shire, D. (2003). Methods and perceptual thresholds for short-term electrical stimulation of human retina with microelectrode arrays. *Investigative Ophthalmology & Visual Science*, *44*(12), 5355–5361. doi:10.1167/iovs.02-0819

Romero, S., Morillas, C., Cobos, J. P., Pelayo, F., Prieto, A., & Fernández, E. (2009). Computer aids for visual neuroprosthetic devices. *Communications in Computer and Information Science*, *25*(2), 96–108. doi:10.1007/978-3-540-92219-3_7

Sanguineti, V., Giugliano, M., Grattarola, M., & Morasso, P. (2001). Neuro-engineering: From neural interfaces to biological computers. In Riva, R., & Davide, F. (Eds.), *Communications through virtual technology: Identity community and technology in the internet age* (pp. 233–246). Amsterdam, The Netherlands: IOS Press.

Schmidt, E. M., Bak, M. J., Hambrecht, F. T., Kufta, C. V., O'Rourke, D. K., & Vallabhanath, P. (1996). Feasibility of a visual prosthesis for the blind based on intracortical microstimulation of the visual cortex. *Brain*, *119*(Pt 2), 507–522. doi:10.1093/brain/119.2.507

Spillman, L., & Werner, J. S. (Eds.). (1987). *Visual perception: The neurophysiological foundations*. New York, NY: Academic Press.

Trucco, E., & Verri, A. (1998). *Introductory techniques for 3-D computer vision*. Prentice Hall.

Veraart, C., Wanet-Defalque, M. C., Gerard, B., Vanlierde, A., & Delbeke, J. (2003). Pattern recognition with the optic nerve visual prosthesis. *Artificial Organs*, *27*(11), 996–1004. doi:10.1046/j.1525-1594.2003.07305.x

Victor, J. D. (1999). Temporal aspects of neural coding in the retina and lateral geniculate. *Network (Bristol, England)*, *10*(4), R1–R66. doi:10.1088/0954-898X/10/4/201

Warren, D. J., Fernandez, E., & Normann, R. A. (2001). High-resolution two-dimensional spatial mapping of cat striate cortex using a 100-microelectrode array. *Neuroscience*, *105*(1), 19–31. doi:10.1016/S0306-4522(01)00174-9

Zrenner, E., Gekeler, F., Gabel, V. P., Graf, H. G., Graf, M., Guenther, E., & Weiss, S. (2001). Subretinal microphotodiode array as replacement for degenerated photoreceptors? *Der Ophthalmologe*, *98*(4), 357–363. doi:10.1007/s003470170141

ADDITIONAL READING

Akay, M. (2007). *Handbook of neural engineering*. Hoboken, NJ: John Wiley & Sons, Inc.

Brindley, G. S., & Lewin, W. S. (1968). The sensations produced by electrical stimulation of the visual cortex. *The Journal of Physiology*, *196*, 479–493.

Canavero, S. (2009). *Textbook of therapeutic cortical stimulation*. New York, NY: Nova Biomedical Books.

Churchland, P. S., & Sejnowski, T. J. (1993). *The computational brain* (2nd ed.). Cambridge, MA: MIT Press.

Dagnelie, G. (2006). Visual prosthetics 2006: Assessment and expectations. *Expert Review of Medical Devices*, *3*(3), 315–325. doi:10.1586/17434440.3.3.315

Dagnelie, G., Keane, P., Narla, V., Yang, L., Weiland, J., & Humayun, M. (2007). Real and virtual mobility performance in simulated prosthetic vision. *Journal of Neural Engineering*, *4*(1), S92–S101. doi:10.1088/1741-2560/4/1/S11

Dario, P., Laschi, C., Menciassi, A., Guglielmelli, E., Carrozza, M. C., & Micera, S. (2003). Interfacing neural and artificial systems: From neuroengineering to neurorobotics. *1st International IEEE EMBS Conference on Neural Engineering 2003, Conference Proceedings,* (pp. 418-421).

Dobelle, W. H. (2000). Artificial vision for the blind by connecting a television camera to the visual cortex. *ASAIO Journal (American Society for Artificial Internal Organs)*, *46*(1), 3–9. doi:10.1097/00002480-200001000-00002

Dobelle, W. H., & Mladejovsky, M. G. (1974). Phosphenes produced by electrical stimulation of human occipital cortex, and their application to the development of a prosthesis for the blind. *The Journal of Physiology*, *243*, 553–576.

Dowling, J. (2005). Artificial human vision. *Expert Review of Medical Devices*, *2*(1), 73–85. doi:10.1586/17434440.2.1.73

Dowling, J. E. (1987). *The retina: An approachable part of the brain*. Cambridge, MA: Belknap Press of Harvard University Press.

Eckmiller, R., Neumann, D., & Baruth, O. (2005). Tunable retina encoders for retina implants: Why and how. *Journal of Neural Engineering*, *2*(1), S91–S104. doi:10.1088/1741-2560/2/1/011

Fernandez, E. (n.d.). *Webvision. The organization of the retina and visual system*. Retrieved April 4, 2011, from http://retina.umh.es

Finkel, L. (2000). Neuroengineering models of brain disease. *Annual Review of Biomedical Engineering*, *2*, 577–606. doi:10.1146/annurev.bioeng.2.1.577

Hamblen, J. O., Hall, T. S., & Furman, M. D. (2008). *Rapid prototyping of digital systems* (2nd ed.). New York, NY: Springer Science+Business Media, LLC.

Horch, K. W., & Dhillon, G. S. (2004). *Neuroprosthetics theory and practice*. River Edge, NJ: World Scientific.

Hubel, D. H. (1988). *Eye, brain, and vision*. New York, NY: Scientific American Library.

Humayun, M. S. (2008). *Artificial sight basic research, biomedical engineering, and clinical advances*. New York, NY: Springer.

Kandel, E., Schwartz, J., Jessell, T., & Mack, S. (2000). *Principles of neural science* (4th ed.). New York, NY: McGraw-Hill.

Kipke, D. R., Vetter, R. J., Williams, J. C., & Hetke, J. F. (2003). Silicon-substrate intracortical microelectrode arrays for long-term recording of neuronal activity in cerebral cortex. *IEEE Transactions on Neural Systems and Rehabilitation Engineering*, *11*(2), 151–155. doi:10.1109/TNSRE.2003.814443

Koch, C., & Mathur, B. (1996). Neuromorphic vision chips. *IEEE Spectrum*, *33*(5), 38–46. doi:10.1109/6.490055

Mahowald, M. (1992). *VLSI analogs of neuronal visual processing: A synthesis of form and function*. Pasadena, CA: California Institute of Technology, Computer Science Dept.

Mead, C. (1989). *Analog VLSI and neural systems*. Reading, MA: Addison-Wesley. doi:10.1007/978-1-4613-1639-8

Normann, R. A., Maynard, E. M., Rousche, P. J., & Warren, D. J. (1999). A neural interface for cortical vision prosthesis. *Vision Research*, *39*(15), 2577–2587. doi:10.1016/S0042-6989(99)00040-1

Oldfield, J. V., & Dorf, R. C. (1995). *Field-programmable gate arrays: Reconfigurable logic for rapid prototyping and implementation of digital systems*. New York, NY: Wiley.

Schmidt, E. M., Bak, M. J., Hambrecht, F. T., Kufta, C. V., O'Rourke, D. K., & Vallabhanath, P. (1996). Feasibility of a visual prosthesis for the blind based on intracortical microstimulation of the visual cortex. *Brain*, *119*(2), 507–522. doi:10.1093/brain/119.2.507

Thakor, N. V. (2008). Neuroengineering: Building interfaces from neurons to brain. *2008 30th Annual International Conference of the IEEE Engineering in Medicine and Biology Society*, Vols. 1-8, (pp. 1602-1603).

KEY TERMS AND DEFINITIONS

AER: Address-Event Representation, an efficient encoding and communication technique often used in bio-inspired neuromorphic vision systems, which serially transmit addresses of electrodes or channels whenever an even is issued.

Cortical Implant: An artificial device placed or inserted at the brain cortex in order to provide neural stimulation and/or recording capabilities.

FPGA: Field-Programmable Gate Array, integrated circuit intended for fast, easy and in-situ reprogramming of its functionality, providing low-power, portable and real-time computing for specific purposes (as, in our case, implementing bioinpired retina-like visual processing).

Microelectrode Array: A set of miniaturized electrodes mounted on a physical support, usually distributed in a matrix form, which can be implanted in a point of the central or peripheral nervous system for stimulation and/or recording.

Neuroengineering: Interdisciplinary field of knowledge that mainly focuses in the connection between biological neural systems and artificial devices for scientific and medical purposes.

Phosphene: Visual sensation elicited by electrical or mechanical stimulation of neural cells related to visual functions. Simple phosphenes usually look like small stars in the darkness.

Remapping: Re-assignment of electrode addresses. This reorganization of the list of available electrodes in cortical visual neuroprostheses is made to elicit better recognizable patterns for a given map of phosphenes, given that the spatial distribution of stimuli in the visual cortex does not necessarily correspond to a pattern of elicited phosphenes with a similar shape in the visual field.

Retina-Like Processing: Bio-inspired computational operations performed over a given visual input with the purpose of producing a response coherent with the activity of ganglion cells for the same stimuli.

Visual Neuroprosthesis: Neuroengineering implant designed to provide a functional form of vision as organized pattern of phosphenes elicited by electrical neurostimulation of neurons at some point of the visual pathways.

Compilation of References

Abraham, F. D. (1990). *A visual introduction to dynamical systems theory for psychology*. Santa Cruz, CA: Aerial Press.

Achanta, R., Estrada, F., Wils, P., & Süsstrunk, S. (2008). Salient region detection and segmentation. *6th International Conference on Computer Vision Systems, ICVS* (pp. 66-75). Berlin, Germany: Springer.

Achanta, R., Hemami, S., Estrada, F., & Susstrunk, S. (2009). Frequency-tuned salient region detection. In *The 2009 IEEE International Conference on Computer Vision and Pattern Recognition* (pp. 1597-1604). Miami, FL: IEEE.

Achanta, R., Estrada, F., Wils, P., & Susstrunk, S. (2008). Salient region detection and segmentation. In Gasteratos, A., Vincze, M., & Tsotsos, J. K. (Eds.), *Computer vision systems* (pp. 66–75). Heidelberg, Germany: Springer. doi:10.1007/978-3-540-79547-6_7

Adami, C. (2004). Information theory in molecular biology. *Physics of Life Reviews*, *1*(1), 3–22. doi:10.1016/j.plrev.2004.01.002

Adelson, E. H., & Bergen, J. R. (1991). *Computational models of visual processing*. Cambridge, MA: MIT Press.

Adelson, E. H., & Movshon, J. A. (1982). Phenomenal coherence of moving visual patterns. *Nature*, *300*, 523–525. doi:10.1038/300523a0

Adelson, E., & Bergen, J. (1985). Spatiotemporal energy models for the perception of motion. *Journal of the Optical Society of America, Series A*, *2*, 284–299.

Ahmad, J. E., & Takakura, Y. (2007). Improving segmentation maps using polarization imaging. In *IEEE International Conference on Image Processing,* Vol. 1 (pp. I -281 -I -284).

Ahmad, S. (1992). *VISIT: An efficient computational model of human visual attention*. University of Illinois at Urbana-Champaign, Champaign, IL, (510). Citeseer.

Albright, T. (1984). Direction and orientation selectivity of neurons in visual area MT of the macaque. *Journal of Neurophysiology*, *52*, 1106–1130.

Albright, T. D., & Stoner, G. R. (2002). Contextual influences on visual processing. *Annual Review of Neuroscience*, *25*, 339–379.

Albright, T., & Desimone, R. (1987). Local precision of visuotopic organization in middle temporal area (MT) of the macaque. *Experimental Brain Research*, *65*, 582–592.

Allport, D. A. (1987). Selection for action: Some behavioral and neurophysiological considerations of attention and action. In H. Heuer & S. A.F. (Eds.), *Perspectives on perception and action* (pp. 395-419). Hillsdale, NJ: Lawrence Erlbaum Associates.

Aloimonos, J. Y., Weiss, I., & Bandopadhay, A. (1987). Active vision. *International Journal of Computer Vision*, *1*(4), 333–356.

Andersen, G. J., & Kramer, A. F. (1993). Limits of focused attention in three-dimensional space. *Perception & Psychophysics*, *53*(6), 658–667. doi:10.3758/BF03211742

Anderson, C., & Essen, D. V. (1987). Shifter circuits: A computational strategy for dynamic aspects of visual processing. *Proceedings of the National Academy of Sciences of the United States of America*, *84*, 6297–6301. doi:10.1073/pnas.84.17.6297

Anderson, C., & Van Essen, D. (1987). Shifter circuits: a computational strategy for dynamic aspects of visual processing. *Proceedings of the National Academy of Sciences of the United States of America*, *84*(17), 6297–6301. doi:10.1073/pnas.84.17.6297

Angelucci, A., Levitt, J., Walton, E., Hupe, J.-M., Bullier, J., & Lund, J. (2002). Circuits for local and global signal integration in primary visual cortex. *The Journal of Neuroscience*, *22*, 8633–8646.

Ansari, N., & Delp, E. (1990). Partial shape recognition: A landmark-based approach. *IEEE Transactions on Pattern Analysis and Machine Intelligence*, *12*(5), 470–483. doi:10.1109/34.55107

Anzai, A., Ohzawa, I., & Freeman, R. D. (2001). Joint encoding of motion and depth by visual cortical neurons: Neural basis of the Pulfrich effect. *Nature Reviews. Neuroscience*, *4*, 513–518.

Arnott, S. R., & Shedden, J. M. (2000). Attention switching in depth using random-dot autostereograms: Attention gradient asymmetries. *Perception & Psychophysics*, *62*(7), 1459–1473. doi:10.3758/BF03212146

Aron, Y., & Gronau, Y. (2005). Polarization in the LWIR. *Proceedings of the Society for Photo-Instrumentation Engineers*, *5783*, 653–661. doi:10.1117/12.605316

Asada, H., & Brady, M. (1984). *The curvature primal sketch. AIM 758: Massachusetts Institute of Technology*. MIT.

Ascher, D., & Grzywacz, N. N. (2000). A Bayesian model for the measurement of visual velocity. *Vision Research*, *40*(24), 3427–3434. doi:10.1016/S0042-6989(00)00176-0

Atchley, P., Kramer, A. F., Andersen, G. J., & Theeuwes, J. (1997). Spatial cuing in a stereoscopic display: Evidence for a depth-aware attentional focus. *Psychonomic Bulletin & Review*, *4*(4), 524 529. doi:10.3758/BF03214343

Atkinson, G. A., & Hancock, E. R. (2005). Multi-view surface reconstruction using polarization. In *Proceedings of the IEEE International Conference on Computer Vision.*

Austerberry, D. (2002). *Technology of video and audio streaming* (2nd ed.). Burlington, MA: Focal Press.

Avraham, T., & Lindenbaum, M. (2010). Esaliency (extended saliency): Meaningful attention using stochastic image modeling. *IEEE Transactions on Pattern Analysis and Machine Intelligence*, *32*(4), 693–708. doi:10.1109/TPAMI.2009.53

Ayache, N., & Faugeras, O. (1986). HYPER: A new approach for the recognition and positioning of two-dimensional objects. *IEEE Transactions on Pattern Analysis and Machine Intelligence*, *8*(1), 44–54. doi:10.1109/TPAMI.1986.4767751

Aziz, M. Z., & Mertsching, B. (2008). Fast and robust generation of feature maps for region-based visual attention. *IEEE Transactions on Image Processing: A Publication of the IEEE Signal Processing Society*, *17*(5), 633-644. doi:10.1109/TIP.2008.919365

Aziz, M. Z., & Mertsching, B. (2009). *Towards standardization of evaluation metrics and methods for visual attention models. Attention in Cognitive Systems* (pp. 227–241). Springer.

Aziz, M., & Mertsching, B. (2008). Fast and robust generation of feature maps for region-based visual attention. *IEEE Transactions on Image Processing*, *17*(5), 633–644. doi:10.1109/TIP.2008.919365

Bae, S., Cho, Y., Park, S., Irick, K., Jin, Y., & Narayanan, V. (2011). An FPGA implementation of information theoretic visual-saliency system and its optimization. In *The Proceedings of the 2011 IEEE 19th Annual International Symposium on Field-Programmable Custom Computing Machines* (pp. 41-48). Salt Lake City, UT: IEEE.

Bajcsy, R. (1988) Active perception. *IEEE Proceedings*, *76*(8), 996-1006.

Baker, S., Scharstein, D., Lewis, J. P., Roth, S., Black, M. J., & Szeliski, R. (2011). A database and evaluation methodology for optical flow. *International Journal of Computer Vision*, *92*, 1–31.

Baldi, P., & Itti, Laurent. (2005). Attention: Bits versus wows. *2005 International Conference on Neural Networks and Brain* (pp. 56-61). IEEE.

Ballard, D. H., & Ozcandarli, A. (1988, December). *Eye fixation and early vision: Kinematic depth.* Paper presented at the meeting of the IEEE 2nd International Conference on Computer Vision, Tarpon Springs, Fla.

Ballard, D. (1981). Generalizing the Hough transform to detect arbitrary shapes. *Pattern Recognition, 13*(2), 111–122. doi:10.1016/0031-3203(81)90009-1

Ballard, D. (1991). Animate vision. *Artificial Intelligence, 48*(1), 1–27.

Bamidele, A., Stentiford, F. W. M., & Morphett, J. (2004). An attention based approach to content based image retrieval. *BT Technology Journal, 22*, 151–160. doi:10.1023/B:BTTJ.0000047129.83260.79

Banks, M. S., & Backus, B. T. (1998). Extra-retinal and perspective cues cause the small range of the induced effect. *Vision Research, 38*, 187–194. doi:10.1016/S0042-6989(97)00179-X

Barker, A. T., Jalinous, R., & Freeston, I. L. (1985). Non-invasive magnetic stimulation of human motor cortex. *Lancet, 1*(8437), 1106–1107. doi:10.1016/S0140-6736(85)92413-4

Barlow, H. B. (1972). Single units and sensation: A neuron doctrine for perceptual psychology? *Perception, 1*(4), 371–394. doi:10.1068/p010371

Bayerl, P., & Neumann, H. (2004). Disambiguating visual motion through contextual feedback modulation. *Neural Computation, 16*, 2041–2066.

Bayerl, P., & Neumann, H. (2007). A fast biologically inspired algorithm for recurrent motion estimation. *IEEE Transactions on Pattern Analysis and Machine Intelligence, 29*(2), 246–260.

Beal, M. J. (2003). *Variational algorithms for approximate Bayesian inference.* PhD thesis, Gatsby Computational Neuroscience Unit, University College London, 2003.

Beck, C., & Neumann, H. (2010). Interactions of motion and form in visual cortex – A neural model. *The Journal of Physiology, 104*, 61–70.

Begum, M., & Karray, F. (2011). Visual attention for robotic cognition: A survey. *IEEE Transactions on Autonomous Mental Development, 3*(1), 92–105. doi:10.1109/TAMD.2010.2096505

Behrmann, M., Zemel, R. S., & Mozer, M. C. (1998). Object-based attention and occlusion: Evidence from normal participants and a computational model. *Journal of Experimental Psychology. Human Perception and Performance, 24*(4), 1011–1036. doi:10.1037/0096-1523.24.4.1011

Belardinelli, A., Pirri, F., & Carbone, A. (2009). *Motion saliency maps from spatiotemporal filtering. Lecture Notes in Artificial Intelligence* (pp. 112–123). Springer.

Belongie, S., Malik, J., & Puzicha, J. (2002). Shape matching and object recognition using shape contexts. *IEEE Transactions on Pattern Analysis and Machine Intelligence, 24*, 509–522. doi:10.1109/34.993558

Ben-av, M. B., & Shiffrar, M. (1995). Disambiguating velocity estimates across image space. *Vision Research, 35*(20), 2889–2895. doi:10.1016/0042-6989(95)00048-5

Benedetto, S., & Poggiolini, P. (1992). Theory of polarization shift keying modulation. *IEEE Transactions on Communications, 40*, 708–721. doi:10.1109/26.141426

Ben-Ezra, M. (2000). Segmentation with invisible keying signal. In *Proceedings of IEEE Conference on Computer Vision and Pattern Recognition* (pp. 32-37).

Ben-Hur, A., Siegelmann, H. T., & Fishman, S. (2002). A theory of complexity for continuous time systems. *Journal of Complexity, 18*, 51–86. doi:10.1006/jcom.2001.0581

Berg, D. J., Boehnke, S. E., Marino, R. A., & Munoz, D. P., & Itti, Laurent. (2009). Free viewing of dynamic stimuli by humans and monkeys. *Journal of Vision (Charlottesville, Va.), 9*, 1–15. doi:10.1167/9.5.19

Berkeley, G. (1975). *Philosophical works; Including the works on vision* (Ayers, M., Ed.). London, UK: Dent. (Original work published 1709)

Berthoz, A. (2009). *La simplexité* (pp. 1–256). Paris: Odile Jaco.

Beverley, K. I., & Regan, D. (1973). Evidence for the existence of neural mechanisms selectively sensitive to the direction of movement in space. *The Journal of Physiology*, *235*, 17–29.

Beverley, K. I., & Regan, D. (1974). Temporal integration of disparity information in stereoscopic perception. *Experimental Brain Research*, *19*, 228–232. doi:10.1007/BF00238537

Beverley, K. I., & Regan, D. (1975). The relation between discrimination and sensitivity in the perception of motion in depth. *The Journal of Physiology*, *249*, 387–398.

Bishop, P., Kato, H., & Orban, G. (1980). Direction-selective cells in complex family in cat striate cortex. *Journal of Neurophysiology*, *43*, 1266–1283.

Black, M., & Anandan, P. (1993). A framework for the robust estimation of optical flow. *In Fourth International Conference on Computer Vision, ICCV-93, Berlin, Germany*, May, 1993, (pp. 231-236).

Black, M., & Anandan, P. (1996). The robust estimation of multiple motions: parametric and piecewise-smooth flow fields. *Computer Vision and Image Understanding*, *63*, 75–104.

Blake, R. (1989). A neural theory of binocular rivalry. *Psychological Review*, *96*, 145–167. doi:10.1037/0033-295X.96.1.145

Bläsing, B., Tenenbaum, G., & Schack, T. (2009). The cognitive structure of movements in classical dance. *Psychology of Sport and Exercise*, *10*, 350–360. doi:10.1016/j.psychsport.2008.10.001

Blohm, G., Khan, A. Z., Ren, L., Schreiber, K. M., & Crawford, J. D. (2008). Depth estimation from retinal disparity requires eye and head orientation signals. *Journal of Vision*, *8*(16), 3, 1-23.

Blum, H. (1967). A transformation for extracting new descriptors of shape. *Proceedings of the Symposium on Models for the Perception of Speech and Visual Form* (pp. 362-380). MIT Press.

Blum, H. (1973). Biological shape and visual science, I. *Journal of Theoretical Biology*, *38*(2), 205–287. doi:10.1016/0022-5193(73)90175-6

Boahen, K. A. (2000). Point-to-point connectivity between neuromorphic chips using address events. *IEEE Transactions on Circuits and Systems II: Analog and Digital Signal Processing*, *47*(5), 416–434. doi:10.1109/82.842110

Booth, M., & Rolls, E. (1998). View-invariant representations of familiar objects by neurons in the inferior temporal visual cortex. *Cerebral Cortex*, *8*(6), 510–523. doi:10.1093/cercor/8.6.510

Born, M., & Wolf, E. (1999). *Principles of optics: Electromagnetic theory of propagation, interference and diffraction of light* (7th ed.). Cambridge University Press. doi:10.1063/1.1325200

Born, R. T., & Bradley, D. C. (2005). Structure and function of visual area MT. *Annual Review of Neuroscience*, *28*, 157–189.

Born, R. T., & Tootell, R. B. H. (1992). Segregation of global and local motion processing in primate middle temporal visual area. *Nature*, *357*, 497–499.

Boynton, G., & Hegde, J. (2004). Visual cortex: The continuing puzzle of area V2. *Current Biology*, *14*(13), 523–524. doi:10.1016/j.cub.2004.06.044

Braddick, O. J. (1974). A short-range process in apparent motion. *Vision Research*, *14*, 519–527. doi:10.1016/0042-6989(74)90041-8

Braddick, O. J. (1980). Low-level and high-level processes in apparent motion. *Philosophical Transactions of the Royal Society of London*, *290B*, 137–151. doi:10.1098/rstb.1980.0087

Braddick, O., Wishart, K., & Curran, W. (2002). Directional performance in motion transparency. *Vision Research*, *42*, 1237–1248.

Bradley, D. C., Qian, N., & Andersen, R. A. (1995). Integration of motion and stereopsis in middle temporal cortical area of macaques. *Nature*, *373*, 609–611.

Bradley, D. C., Troyk, P. R., Berg, J. A., Bak, M., Cogan, S., Erickson, R., & Xu, H. (2005). Visuotopic mapping through a multichannel stimulating implant in primate V1. *Journal of Neurophysiology*, *93*(3), 1659–1670. doi:10.1152/jn.01213.2003

Bradshaw, M. F., & Cumming, B. G. (1997). The direction of retinal motion facilitates binocular stereopsis. *Proceedings. Biological Sciences*, *264*, 1421–1427. doi:10.1098/rspb.1997.0198

Braun, S. M., Beurskens, A. J., Schack, T., Marcellis, R. G., Oti, K. C., Schols, J. M., & Wade, D. T. (2007). It is possible to use the structural dimension analysis of motor memory (SDA-M) to investigate representations of motor actions in stroke patients? *Clinical Rehabilitation*, *21*, 822–832. doi:10.1177/0269215507078303

Bridge, H., & Cumming, B. C. (2008). Representation of binocular surfaces by cortical neurons. *Current Opinion in Neurobiology*, *18*(4), 425–430.

Brincat, S., & Connor, C. (2004). Underlying principles of visual shape selectivity in posterior inferotemporal cortex. *Nature Neuroscience*, *7*(8), 880–886. doi:10.1038/nn1278

Brindley, G. S., & Lewin, W. S. (1968). The sensations produced by electrical stimulation of the visual cortex. *The Journal of Physiology*, *196*, 479–493.

Broadbent, D. E. (1985). *Perception and communication*. London, UK: Pergamon Press.

Brooks, K. R. (2002). Interocular velocity difference contributes to stereomotion speed perception. *Journal of Vision (Charlottesville, Va.)*, *2*, 218–231. doi:10.1167/2.3.2

Brooks, K. R., & Stone, L. S. (2004). Stereomotion speed perception: Contributions from both changing disparity and interocular velocity difference over a range of relative disparities. *Journal of Vision (Charlottesville, Va.)*, *4*, 1061–1079. doi:10.1167/4.12.6

Brown, C. (1990). Prediction and cooperation in gaze control. *Biological Cybernetics*, *63*(1), 61–70.

Brox, T., Weickert, J., Burgeth, B., & Mrazek, P. (2006). Nonlinear structure tensors. *Image and Vision Computing*, *24*, 41–55.

Bruce, B., & Jernigan, E. (2003). Evolutionary design of context-free attentional operators. *Proceedings of ICIP '03* (pp. 0-3). Citeseer.

Bruce, N. D. B. (2010). *Attention based on information maximization source code*. Retrieved January 10, 2012, from http://www-sop.inria.fr/members/Neil.Bruce/

Bruce, N. D. B., & Tsotsos, J. K. (2008). Spatiotemporal saliency: Towards a hierarchical representation of visual saliency. *Proceedings of the 5th International Workshop on Attention in Cognitive Systems* (pp. 98-111). Springer.

Bruce, N. D. B., Loach, D., & Tsotsos, J. K. (2007). Visual correlates of fixation selection: A look at the spatial frequency domain. In *The Proceedings of the 2007 IEEE International Conference on Image Processing* (pp. 289-292). San Antonio, TX: IEEE.

Bruce, N. D. B., & Tsotsos, J. K. (2006). Saliency based on information maximization. *Advances in Neural Information Processing Systems*, *18*, 155–162.

Bruce, N. D. B., & Tsotsos, J. K. (2009). Saliency, attention, and visual search: An information theoretic approach. *Journal of Vision (Charlottesville, Va.)*, *9*(3), 5. doi:10.1167/9.3.5

Bruhn, A., Weickert, J., Kohlberger, T., & Schnörr, C. (2006). A multigrid platform for real-time motion computation with discontinuity-preserving variational methods. *International Journal of Computer Vision*, *70*(3), 257–277.

Bruhn, A., Weickert, J., & Schnörr, C. (2005). Lucas/Kanade meets Horn/Schunck: Combining local and global optic flow methods. *International Journal of Computer Vision*, *61*(3), 211–231. doi:10.1023/B:VISI.0000045324.43199.43

Brun, G. L., & Jeune, L. B., Cariou, J., & Lotrian, J. (1992). Analysis of polarization signature of immersed targets. In *Proceedings of SPIE Polarization and Remote Sensing, Vol. 1747* (pp. 128-139).

Bullier, J. (2001). Integrated model of visual processing. *Brain Research. Brain Research Reviews*, *36*(2-3), 96–107. doi:10.1016/S0165-0173(01)00085-6

Bullier, J., Hupe, J., James, A., & Girard, P. (2001). The role of feedback connections in shaping the responses of visual cortical neurons. *Progress in Brain Research*, *134*, 193–204.

Bundesen, C. (1987). Visual attention: Race models for selection from multi-element displays. *Psychological Research*, *49*, 113–121. doi:10.1007/BF00308676

Bundesen, C. (1998). A computational theory of visual attention. *Philosophical Transactions of the Royal Society of London. Series B, Biological Sciences*, *353*(1373), 1271–1281. doi:10.1098/rstb.1998.0282

Bundesen, C., Habekost, T., & Kyllingsbaek, S. (2005). A neural theory of visual attention: Bridging cognition and neurophysiology. *Psychological Review*, *112*, 291–328. doi:10.1037/0033-295X.112.2.291

Buracas, G. T., & Albright, T. D. (1996). Contribution of area MT to perception of three-dimensional shape: A computational study. *Vision Research*, *36*(6), 869–887.

Burt, P. (1988). Attention mechanisms for vision in a dynamic world. *Proceedings Ninth International Conference on Pattern Recognition*, (pp. 977–987).

Butler, P., & Javitt, D. (2005). Early-stage visual processing deficits in schizophrenia. *Current Opinion in Psychiatry*, *18*, 151–157. doi:10.1097/00001504-200503000-00008

Cadieu, C., Kouch, M., Connor, C., Riesenhuber, M., & Poggio, T. (2007). A model of V4 shape selectivity and invariance. *Journal of Neurophysiology*, *3*(98), 1733–1750. doi:10.1152/jn.01265.2006

Caputo, G., & Guerra, S. (1998). Attentional selection by distractor suppression. *Vision Research*, *38*(5), 669–689. doi:10.1016/S0042-6989(97)00189-2

Carceroni, R. L., & Kutulakos, K. N. (2002). Multi-view scene capture by surfel sampling: From video streams to non-rigid 3D motion, shape and reflectance. *International Journal of Computer Vision*, *49*(2), 175–214. doi:10.1023/A:1020145606604

Cardoso, J.-F. (1999). High-order contrast for independent component analysis. *Neural Computation*, *11*, 157–192. doi:10.1162/089976699300016863

Carney, T., Paradiso, M. A., & Freeman, R. D. (1989). A physiological correlate of the Pulfrich effect in cortical neurons of the cat. *Vision Research*, *29*, 155–165. doi:10.1016/0042-6989(89)90121-1

Case, D. A., Cheatham, T., Darden, T., Gohlke, H., Luo, R., & Merz, K. M. Jr (2005). The Amber biomolecular simulation programs. *Journal of Computational Chemistry*, *26*, 1668–1688. doi:10.1002/jcc.20290

Cassereau, P. M. (1993). Wavelet-based image coding. In Watson, A. B. (Ed.), *Digital images and human vision* (pp. 12–21). Cambridge, MA: MIT Press.

Castet, E., Lorenceau, J., Shiffrar, M., & Bonnet, C. (1993). Perceived speed of moving lines depends on orientation, length, speed and luminance. *Vision Research*, *33*, 1921–1936. doi:10.1016/0042-6989(93)90019-S

Chahl, J., & Mizutani, A. (2010). Biomimetic attitude and orientation sensors. *Sensors Journal*, *99*, 1.

Chamaret, C., & Meur, O. L. (2009). *Attention-based video reframing: validation using eye-tracking. Pattern Recognition, ICPR* (pp. 1–4). IEEE.

Chelazzi, L., Miller, E. K., Duncan, J., & Desimone, R. (2001). Responses of neurons in macaque area V4 during memory-guided visual search. *Cerebral Cortex*, *11*(8), 761–772. doi:10.1093/cercor/11.8.761

Cheng, K., Hasegawa, T., Saleem, K. S., & Tanaka, K. (1994). Comparison of neuronal selectivity for stimulus speed, length, and contrast in the prestriate visual cortical areas V4 and MT of the macaque monkey. *Journal of Neurophysiology*, *71*(6), 2269–2280.

Chen, Y., & Qian, N. (2004). A coarse-to-fine disparity energy model with both phase-shift and position-shift receptive field mechanisms. *Neural Computation*, *16*, 1545–1577.

Chessa, M., Sabatini, S. P., & Solari, F. (2009). A fast joint bioinspired algorithm for optic flow and two-dimensional disparity estimation. In J. Piater (Ed.), *7th International Conference on Computer Vision Systems (ICVS'09), Lecture Notes in Computer Science, Vol. 5815*, (pp. 13-15).

Chessa, M., Solari, F., & Sabatini, S. P. (2011). Virtual reality to simulate visual tasks for robotic systems. In Kim, J.-J. (Ed.), *Virtual reality* (pp. 71–92). InTech.

Chey, J., Grossberg, S., & Mingolla, E. (1997). Neural dynamics of motion grouping: From aperture ambiguity to object speed and direction. *Optical Society of America A, 14*(10), 2570–2594. doi:10.1364/JOSAA.14.002570

Choi, S.-B., Jung, B.-S., & Ban, S.-W. (2006). Biologically motivated vergence control system using human-like selective attention model. *Neurocomputing, 69*(4-6), 537–558. doi:10.1016/j.neucom.2004.12.012

Chow, C. W., Kwok, C. H., Liu, Y., Tsang, H. K., & Chinlon, L. (2006). *3-bit/symbol optical modulation-demodulation simultaneously using DRZ, DPSK and PolSK.* In Conference on Lasers and Electro-Optics (CLEO).

Chow, A. Y., Pardue, M. T., Chow, V. Y., Peyman, G. A., Liang, C., Perlman, J. I., & Peachey, N. S. (2001). Implantation of silicon chip microphotodiode arrays into the cat subretinal space. *IEEE Transactions on Neural Systems and Rehabilitation Engineering, 9*(1), 86–95. doi:10.1109/7333.918281

Chu, J., Wang, H., Chen, W., & Li, R. (2009). Application of a novel polarization sensor to mobile robot navigation. In *International Conference on Mechatronics and Automation, ICMA 2009* (pp. 3763 -3768).

Chu, J., Zhao, K., Wang, T., & Zhang, Q. (2007b). *Research on a novel polarization sensor for navigation.* In IEEE International Conference on Information Acquisition.

Chu, J., Zhao, K., Zhang, Q., & Wang, T. (2007a). *Design of a novel polarization sensor for navigation.* In IEEE International Conference on Mechatronics and Automation.

Chu, J., Zhao, K., Zhang, Q., & Wang, T. (2008). Construction and performance test of a novel polarization sensor for navigation. *Sensors and Actuators. A, Physical, 148*, 75–82. doi:10.1016/j.sna.2008.07.016

Clark, J. J., & Ferrier, N. J. (1988). Modal control of attentive vision system. In *Proceedings of the International Conference on Computer Vision* (pp. 514–523).

Cohen, N. R., Pomplun, M., Gold, B. J., & Sekuler, R. (2009). Sex differences in acquisition of complex skilled movements. *Experimental Brain Research, 205*, 183–193. doi:10.1007/s00221-010-2351-y

Connor, C., Brincat, S., & Pasupathy, A. (2007). Transformation of shape information in the ventral pathway. *Current Opinion in Neurobiology, 17*(2), 140–147. doi:10.1016/j.conb.2007.03.002

Corbeil, J.-C. (1986). *The Stoddart visual dictionary.* Toronto, Canada: Stoddart Publishing.

Costa, A. H. R., Rillo, C., Barros, L. N. D., & Bianchi, R. A. C. (1998). Integrating purposive vision with deliberative and reactive planning: Engineering support for robotic applications. *Journal of the Brazilian Computer Society, 4*(3).

Cox, W. C., Hughes, B. L., & Muth, J. F. (2009). *A polarization shift-keying system for underwater optical communications.* In OCEANS 2009, MTS/IEEE Biloxi - Marine Technology for Our Future: Global and Local Challenges.

Cox, W. C., Simpson, J., Domizioli, C. P., Muth, J., & Hughes, B. (2008). An underwater optical communication system implementing Reed-Solomon channel coding. In *Proceedings of OCEANS Conference.*

Cronin, T. W., & Shashar, N. (2001). The linearly polarized light field in clear, tropical marine waters: Spatial and temporal variation of light intensity, degree of polarization, and e-vector angle. *Journal of Experimental Biology, 204*, 2461 2467.

Cronin, T. W., Shashar, N., & Wolff, L. B. (1994). Portable imaging polarimeters. In *Pattern Recognition, 1994. Vol. 1 - Conference A: Computer Vision Image Processing, Proceedings of the 12th IAPR International Conference,* Vol. 1 (pp. 606 -609).

Cronin, T. W., Shashar, N., Caldwell, R. L., Marshall, J., Cheroske, A. G., & Chiou, T.-H. (2003). Polarization vision and its role in biological signaling. *Integrative and Comparative Biology, 43*(4), 549–558. doi:10.1093/icb/43.4.549

Cronin, T. W., Warrant, E. J., & Greiner, B. (2006). Celestial polarization patterns during twilight. *Optical Society of America. Applied Optics*, 45.

Cropper, S. J., & Derrington, A. M. (1994). Motion of chromatic stimuli: First-order or second-order? *Vision Research*, *34*, 49–58. doi:10.1016/0042-6989(94)90256-9

Crosby, F., & Riley, S. (2001). Signature Adaptive mine detection at a constant false alarm rate. In *Proceeding of SPIE Conference on Detection and Remediation Technologies for Mines and Minelike Targets*.

Crosby, F., & Stetson, S. (2002). Surface effect subtraction for airborne underwater target detection. In *OCEANS MTS*. IEEE. doi:10.1109/OCEANS.2002.1191865

Culhane, S. (1992). *Implementation of an attentional prototype for early vision*. University of Toronto, M.Sc. Thesis.

Cumming, B. G., & Parker, A. J. (1994). Binocular mechanisms for detecting motion in depth. *Vision Research*, *34*, 483–495. doi:10.1016/0042-6989(94)90162-7

Cumming, B. G., & Parker, A. J. (1999). Binocular neurons in V1 of awake monkeys are selective for absolute, not relative, disparity. *The Journal of Neuroscience*, *19*(13), 5602–5618.

Cummings, M. E., Ahmed, S. A., Dierssen, H. M., Gilerson, A., Gilly, W. F., & Kattawar, G. W. … Sullivan, J. M. (2009). *Biological response to the dynamic spectral-polarized underwater light field*. Texas University at Austin.

Cutzu, F., & Tsotsos, J. K. (2003). The selective tuning model of attention: Psychophysical evidence for a suppressive annulus around an attended item. *Vision Research*, *43*(2), 205–219. doi:10.1016/S0042-6989(02)00491-1

Dacke, M., Byrne, M. J., Baird, E., Scholtz, C. H., & Warrant, E. (2011). How dim is dim? Precision of the celestial compass in moonlight and sunlight. *Philosophical Transactions of The Royal Society. Biological Sciences B*, *366*, 697–702. doi:10.1098/rstb.2010.0191

Dagnelie, G. (2006). Visual prosthetics 2006: Assessment and expectations. *Expert Review of Medical Devices*, *3*(3), 315–325. doi:10.1586/17434440.3.3.315

Damask, J. N. (Ed.). (2005). *Polarization optics in telecommunications* (*Vol. 101*). Springer.

Danielsson, P. E. (1978). A new shape factor. *Computer Graphics and Image Processing*, *7*, 292–299. doi:10.1016/0146-664X(78)90119-3

Danielsson, P.-E., & Segera, O. (1990). Rotation invariance in gradient and higher order derivative detectors. *Computer Vision Graphics and Image Processing*, *49*(2), 198–221.

Darrell, T., & Pentland, A. (1991). *Robust estimation of a multi-layered motion representation*. In IEEE Workshop on Visual Motion, Princeton, New Jersey, October.

Darrell, T., & Simoncelli, E. (1993). *Separation of transparent motion into layers using velocity-tuned mechanisms*. Technical report, M.I.T. Media Laboratory, Vision and Modeling Group, Technical Report No. 244.

Darroch, J. N., & Mosimann, J. (1985). Canonical and principal components of shape. *Biometrika*, *72*(2), 241–252. doi:10.1093/biomet/72.2.241

Daugman, J. (1985). Uncertainty relation for resolution in space, spatial frequency, and orientation optimized by two-dimensional visual cortical filters. *Journal of Optical Society of America, Series A*, *2*, 1160–1169.

Davies, E. R. (2005). *Machine vision: Theory, algorithms, practicalities* (3rd ed.). Boston, MA: Elsevier.

Davis, L. S. (1977). Understanding shape: Angles and sides. *IEEE Transactions on Computers*, *C*(26), 236–242. doi:10.1109/TC.1977.1674812

DeAngelis, G. C., & Newsome, W. T. (1999). Organization of disparity-selective neurons in macaque area MT. *The Journal of Neuroscience*, *19*, 1398–1415.

DeAngelis, G. C., & Newsome, W. T. (2004). Perceptual “read-out” of conjoined direction and disparity maps in extrastriate area MT. *PLoS Biology*, *2*, e0394. doi:10.1371/journal.pbio.0020077

DeAngelis, G. C., Ohzawa, I., & Freeman, R. D. (1993). Spatiotemporal organization of simple-cell receptive fields in the cat’s striate cortex. 1. General characteristics and postnatal development. *Journal of Neurophysiology*, *69*, 1091–1117.

Dean, P. (1976). Effects of inferotemporal lesions on the behavior of monkeys. *Psychological Bulletin*, *83*(1), 41–71. doi:10.1037/0033-2909.83.1.41

Dean, T., Allen, J., & Aloimonos, Y. (1995). *Artificial intelligence: Theory and practice*. Redwood City, CA: Benjamin/Cummings Publishing Co.

Dean, T., Caroll, G., & Washington, R. (2007). *On the prospects for building a working model of the visual cortex*. American Association for Artificial Intelligence.

Decartes, R. (1633/1664). *Traité de l'Homme (De Homine, 1662)*.

Deco, G. (2004). A neurodynamical cortical model of visual attention and invariant object recognition. *Vision Research*, *44*(6), 621–642. doi:10.1016/j.visres.2003.09.037

Dehmollaian, M., & Sarabandi, K. (2009). Optimum polarizations for discrimination of a foliage-camouflaged target, using genetic algorithms. *IEEE Geoscience and Remote Sensing Letters*, *6*(1), 82–86. doi:10.1109/LGRS.2008.2008402

Delbeke, J., Oozeer, M., & Veraart, C. (2003). Position, size and luminosity of phosphenes generated by direct optic nerve stimulation. *Vision Research*, *43*(9), 1091–1102. doi:10.1016/S0042-6989(03)00013-0

Denes, L. J., Gottlieb, M., Kaminsky, B., & Metes, P. (1998). AOTF polarization difference imaging. *SPIE*, *3584*, 106–115. doi:10.1117/12.339812

Desimone, R., & Duncan, J. (1995). Neural mechanisms of selective visual attention. *Annual Review of Neuroscience*, *18*, 193–222. doi:10.1146/annurev.ne.18.030195.001205

Desimone, R., Schein, S., Moran, J., & Ungerleider, L. (1985). Contour, color and shape analysis beyond the striate cortex. *Vision Research*, *25*(3), 441–452. doi:10.1016/0042-6989(85)90069-0

Deubel, H., & Schneider, W. X. (1996). Saccade target selection and object recognition: Evidence for a common attentional mechanism. *Vision Research*, *36*, 1812–1837. doi:10.1016/0042-6989(95)00294-4

Deutsch, C. K. (1998). Emergent properties of brain function and development. In S. Soraci & W. J. McIlvane Jr. (Eds.), Perspectives on fundamental processes in intellectual functioning, Vol. 1, (pp. 169-188; 1-86).

Deutsch, C. K., Ludwig, W. W., & McIlvane, W. J. (2008). Heterogeneity and hypothesis testing in neuropsychiatric illness. *The Behavioral and Brain Sciences*, *31*, 266–267. doi:10.1017/S0140525X08004275

Deutsch, C. K., & McIlvane, W. J. (2012. (in press). Non-Mendelian etiologic factors in neuropsychiatric illness: Pleiotropy, epigenetics, and convergence. [in press]. *The Behavioral and Brain Sciences*.

DeValois, K., DeValois, R., & Yund, E. (1979). Responses of striate cortex cells to grating and checkerboard patterns. *The Journal of Physiology*, *291*(1), 483–505.

DeValois, R., Albrecht, D., & Thorell, L. (1982). Spatial frequency selectivity of cells in macaque visual cortex. *Vision Research*, *22*(5), 545–559. doi:10.1016/0042-6989(82)90113-4

Dickinson, S., Leonardis, A., Schiele, B., & Tarr, M. J. (2009). *Object categorization, computer and human vision perspectives*. Cambridge University Press. doi:10.1017/CBO9780511635465

Dickson, C. A., Deutsch, C. K., Wang, S. S., & Dube, W. V. (2006b). Matching-to-sample assessment of stimulus overselectivity in students with intellectual disabilities. *American Journal of Mental Retardation*, *111*, 447–453. doi:10.1352/0895-8017(2006)111[447:MAOSOI]2.0.CO;2

Dickson, C. A., Wang, S. S., Lombard, K. M., & Dube, W. V. (2006a). Overselective stimulus control in residential school students with intellectual disabilities. *Research in Developmental Disabilities*, *27*, 618–631. doi:10.1016/j.ridd.2005.07.004

Dobbins, A. (1992). *Difference models of visual cortical neurons*. PhD doctoral dissertation, Department of Electrical Engineering. McGill University.

Dobbins, A., Zucker, S., & Cynader, M. (1987). End-stopped neurons in the visual cortex as a substrate for calculating curvature. *Nature*, *329*(6138), 438–441. doi:10.1038/329438a0

Dobbins, A., Zucker, S., & Cynader, M. (1989). Endstopping and curvature. *Vision Research*, *29*(10), 1371–1387. doi:10.1016/0042-6989(89)90193-4

Dobelle, W. H. (2000). Artificial vision for the blind by connecting a television camera to the visual cortex. *ASAIO Journal (American Society for Artificial Internal Organs)*, *46*(1), 3–9. doi:10.1097/00002480-200001000-00002

Dobelle, W. H., Mladejovsky, M. G., & Girvin, J. P. (1974). Artificial vision for the blind: Electrical stimulation of visual cortex offers hope for a functional prosthesis. *Science*, *183*, 440–444. doi:10.1126/science.183.4123.440

Dong, L., Ban, S. W., & Lee, M. (2006). Biologically inspired selective attention model using human interest. *International Journal of Information Technology*, *12*(2), 140–148.

Dorr, M., Gegenfurtner, K. R., & Barth, E. (2010). Variability of eye movements when viewing dynamic natural scenes. *Journal of Vision (Charlottesville, Va.)*, *10*, 1–17. doi:10.1167/10.10.28

Douglas, J. M., Cronin, T. W., Chiou, T.-H., & Dominy, N. J. (2007). Light habitats and the role of polarized iridescence in the sensory ecology of neotropical nymphalid butterflies (Lepidoptera: Nymphalidae). *The Journal of Experimental Biology*, *210*, 788–799. doi:10.1242/jeb.02713

Dowling, J. E. (1987). *The retina: An approachable part of the brain*. Cambridge, MA: The Belknap Press, Harvard University Press.

Driver, J. (2001). A selective review of selective attention research from the past century. *The British Journal of Psychology*, *92*(1), 53–78. doi:10.1348/000712601162103

Duarte-Carvajalino, J. M., & Sapiro, G. (2008). Learning to sense sparse signals: Simultaneous sensing matrix and sparsifying dictionary optimization. *IMA Preprint Series*, 2211.

Dube, W. (2009). Stimulus overselectivity in autism: A review of research. In Reed, P. (Ed.), *Behavioural theories and interventions for autism* (pp. 23–46). New York, NY: Nova Science Publishers.

Dube, W. V., Dickson, C. A., Balsamo, L. M., Lombard O'Donnell, K., Tomanari, G. Y., & Farken, K. M. (2010). Observing behavioral and atypically restricted stimulus control. *Journal of the Experimental Analysis of Behavior*, *94*, 297–313. doi:10.1901/jeab.2010.94-297

Dube, W. V., Lombard, K. M., Farren, K. M., Flusser, D., Balsamo, L. M., & Fowler, T. R. (1999). Eye tracking assessment of stimulus overselectivity in individuals with mental retardation. *Experimental Analysis of Human Behaviour Bulletin*, *13*, 267–271.

Dube, W. V., & McIlvane, W. J. (1997). Reinforcer frequency and restricted stimulus control. *Journal of the Experimental Analysis of Behavior*, *68*, 303–316. doi:10.1901/jeab.1997.68-303

Duchowski, A. T., et al. (2010). Scanpath comparison revisited. *Eye Tracking Research & Applications (ETRA 2010)* Austin, USA.

Duchowski, A. (2003). *Eye tracking methodology: Theory AND Practice*. Springer.

Duchowski, A. T. (2007). *Eye tracking methodology: Theory and practice*. New York, NY: Springer Verlag.

Dudek, G., & Tsotsos, J. (1997). Shape representation and recognition from multiscale curvature. *Computer Vision and Image Understanding*, *68*(2), 170–189. doi:10.1006/cviu.1997.0533

Duncan, J. (1984). Selective attention and the organization of visual information. *Journal of Experimental Psychology. General*, *113*(4), 501–517. doi:10.1037/0096-3445.113.4.501

Duncan, R. O., Albright, T. D., & Stoner, G. R. (2000). Occlusion and the interpretation of visual motion: perceptual and neuronal effects of context. *The Journal of Neuroscience*, *20*, 5885–5897.

Durant, S., Donoso-Barrera, A., Tan, S., & Johnston, A. (2006). Moving from spatially segregated to transparent motion: a modeling approach. *Biology Letters*, *2*, 101–105.

Eckhorn, R., Reitboeck, H., Arndt, M., & Dicke, P. (1990). Feature linking via synchronization among distributed assemblies: Simulations of results from cat visual cortex. *Neural Computation*, *2*, 293–307.

Eckmiller, R. (1997). Learning retina implants with epiretinal contacts. *Ophthalmic Research*, *29*(5), 281–289. doi:10.1159/000268026

Edwards, M., & Nishida, S. (1999). Global-motion detection with transparent-motion signals. *Vision Research*, *39*, 2239–2249.

Edwards, M., & Schor, C. M. (1999). Depth aliasing by the transient stereo-system. *Vision Research*, *39*, 4333–4340. doi:10.1016/S0042-6989(99)00149-2

Egan, W. G. (1992). Polarization in remote sensing. In *Proceedings of SPIE, 1747*. Elsevier. doi:10.1117/12.142571

Egan, W. G., & Duggin, M. J. (2000). Optical enhancement of aircraft detection using polarization. *Proceedings of the Society for Photo-Instrumentation Engineers*, *4133*, 172–178. doi:10.1117/12.406624

Egan, W. G., & Duggin, M. J. (2002). Synthesis of optical polarization signatures of military aircraft. *Proceedings of the Society for Photo-Instrumentation Engineers*, *4481*, 188–194. doi:10.1117/12.452888

Einhauser, W., & Konig, P. (2003). Does luminance-contrast contribute to a saliency map for overt visual attention? *The European Journal of Neuroscience*, *17*(5), 1089–1097. doi:10.1046/j.1460-9568.2003.02508.x

Einhäuser, W., Spain, M., & Perona, P. (2008). Objects predict fixations better than early saliency. *Journal of Vision (Charlottesville, Va.)*, *8*, 1–26. doi:10.1167/8.14.18

Eklundh, J. O., & Pahlavan, K. (1992, April). *Eye and head-eye system.* SPIE Applications of AI X: Machine Vision and Robotics, Orlando, Fla.

Elad, M., & Aharon, M. (2006). Image denoising via sparse and redundant representations over learned dictionaries. *IEEE Transactions on Image Processing*, 15.

Elahipanah, A., Christensen, B. K., & Reingold, E. M. (2007). Do patients with schizophrenia have a smaller visual span? *Schizophrenia Bulletin*, *33*(2), 517.

Elder, J. H., Krupnik, A., & Johnston, L. A. (2003). Contour grouping with prior models. *IEEE Transactions on Pattern Analysis and Machine Intelligence*, *25*(6), 661–674. doi:10.1109/TPAMI.2003.1201818

Eliasmith, C. (1995). *Mind as a dynamical system*. University of Waterloo.

Enns, J. T., & Di Lollo, V. (2000). What's new in visual masking? *Trends in Cognitive Sciences*, *4*(9), 345–352. doi:10.1016/S1364-6613(00)01520-5

Essig, K., Pohl, S., & Ritter, H. (2005). EyeDataAnalyser – A general and flexible visualization and analysation tool for eye tracking data-files. *Proceedings 13th European Conference on Eye Movements (ECEM 13)*, Bern, Switzerland.

Essig, K., Berger, A., Hoffmeister, M., Koesling, H., Weigelt, M., & Schack, T. (2010). Der Einflusses der Torwartposition beim 7-Meter im Handball auf das Blick- und Entscheidungsverhalten von Handball-Experten und -Laien. In Mattes, K., & Wollesen, B. (Eds.), *Bewegung und Leistung - Sport, Gesundheit & Alter* (p. 23). Hamburg, Germany: Czwalina.

Evans, K. K., & Treisman, A. M. (2005). Perception of objects in natural scenes: Is it really attention free? *Journal of Experimental Psychology. Human Perception and Performance*, *31*(6), 1476–1492. doi:10.1037/0096-1523.31.6.1476

Eysenck, M. (2006). *Fundamentals of cognition*. East Sussex, UK: Psychology Press.

Famiglietti, E. V. Jr, & Kolb, H. (1976). Structural basis for ON-and OFF-center responses in retinal ganglion cells. *Science*, *194*, 183–195. doi:10.1126/science.959847

Fang, Y., Lin, W., Lee, B.-S., Lau, C. T., Chen, Z., & Lin, C.-W. (2012). Bottom-up saliency detection model based on human visual sensitivity and amplitude spectrum. *IEEE Transactions on Multimedia*, *14*(1), 187–198. doi:10.1109/TMM.2011.2169775

Farid, H., & Adelson, E. H. (1999). Separating reflections and lighting using independent components analysis. In *Proceedings of IEEE Conference on Computer Vision and Pattern Recognition* (pp. 262-267).

Faugeras, O. D. (1992). What can be seen in three dimensions with an uncalibrated stereo rig? In *Proceedings of ECCV 1992*, (pp. 563-578).

Felisberti, F., & Zanker, J. (2005). Attention modulates perception of transparent motion. *Vision Research, 45*, 2587–2599.

Felleman, D., & Van Essen, D. (1991). Distributed hierarchical processing in the primate cerebral cortex. *Cerebral Cortex, 1*(1), 1–47. doi:10.1093/cercor/1.1.1-a

Ferguson, T. (1973). A Bayesian analysis of some nonparametric problems. *Annals of Statistics*. doi:10.1214/aos/1176342360

Fernandez, E., Pelayo, F., Ahnelt, P., Ammermuller, J., & Normann, R. A. (2004). Cortical visual neuroprosthesis for the blind. *Restorative Neurology and Neuroscience*.

Fernandez, E., Pelayo, F., Romero, S., Bongard, M., Marin, C., Alfaro, A., & Merabet, L. (2005). Development of a cortical visual neuroprosthesis for the blind: The relevance of neuroplasticity. *Journal of Neural Engineering, 2*(4), R1–R12. doi:10.1088/1741-2560/2/4/R01

Fernandez, J. M., & Farell, B. (2005). Seeing motion-in-depth using inter-ocular velocity differences. *Vision Research, 45*, 2786–2798. doi:10.1016/j.visres.2005.05.021

Fidler, S., Berginc, G., & Leonardis, A. (2006). Hierarchical statistical learning of generic parts of object structure. *IEEE Conference on Computer Vision and Pattern Recognition* (pp. 182-189).

Fine, S., Singer, Y., & Tishby, N. (1998). The hierarchical hidden Markov model: Analysis and applications. *Machine Learning, 32*(1), 41–62. doi:10.1023/A:1007469218079

Fix, J. (2008). *Mécanismes numériques et distribués de lanticipation motrice*. Université Henri Poincaré - Nancy 1.

Fleet, D. (1994). Disparity from local weighted phase-correlation. In *Proceedings of the IEEE International Conference on Systems, Man and Cybernetics*, Vol. 1, (pp. 48–54).

Fleet, D. J., & Jepson, A. D. (1990). Computation of component image velocity from local phase information. *International Journal of Computer Vision, 5*(1), 77–104.

Fleet, D. J., & Jepson, A. D. (1993). Stability of phase information. *IEEE Transactions on Pattern Analysis and Machine Intelligence, 15*(12), 1253–1268.

Fleet, D. J., Jepson, A. D., & Jenkin, M. R. M. (1991). Phase-based disparity measurement. *CVGIP: Image Understanding, 53*(2), 198–210.

Fleet, D. J., Wagner, H., & Heeger, D. J. (1996). Neural encoding of binocular disparity: Energy models, position shifts and phase shifts. *Vision Research, 36*(12), 1839–1857.

Fleet, D., Wagner, H., & Heeger, D. (1996). Neural encoding of binocular disparity: Energy models. *Vision Research, 36*(12), 1839–1857. doi:10.1016/0042-6989(95)00313-4

Foldiak, P., & Young, M. (1995). Sparse coding in the primate cortex. In Arbib, M. A. (Ed.), *The handbook of brain theory and neural networks* (pp. 895–898). MIT Press.

Forssell, G., & Karlsson, E. H. (2003). Measurements of polarization properties of camouflaged objects and of the denial of surfaces covered with cenospheres. *Proceedings of the Society for Photo-Instrumentation Engineers, 5075*, 246–258. doi:10.1117/12.487312

Foulsham, T., & Underwood, G. (2008). What can saliency models predict about eye movements? Spatial and sequential aspects of fixations during encoding and recognition. *Journal of Vision (Charlottesville, Va.), 8*(2), 1–17. doi:10.1167/8.2.6

Fox, M. D., Snyder, A. Z., Vincent, J. L., & Raichle, M. E. (2007). Intrinsic fluctuations within cortical systems account for intertrial variability in human behavior. *Neuron, 56*(1), 171–184. doi:10.1016/j.neuron.2007.08.023

Franken, E., van Almsick, M., Rongen, P., Florack, L., & ter Haar Romeny, B. (2006). An efficient method for tensor voting using steerable filters. In Leonardis, A., Bischof, H., & Pinz, A. (Eds.), *ECCV 2006, Part IV, LNCS 3954* (pp. 228–240).

Franz, A., & Triesch, J. (2007). *Emergence of disparity tuning during the development of vergence eye movements.* In International Conference on Development and Learning.

Freeman, H. (1974). Computer processing of line-drawing images. *Computer Surveys, 6*.

Freeman, W. T., & Adelson, E. H. (1991). The design and use of steerable filters. *IEEE Transactions on Pattern Analysis and Machine Intelligence, 13*(9), 891–906.

Freiwald, W. A., & Kanwisher, N. (2004). Visual selective attention: Insights from brain imaging and neurophysiology. In Gazzaniga, M. S. (Ed.), *The cognitive neurosciences* (3rd ed.). Cambridge, MA: MIT Press.

Frequency-Tuned Salient Region Detection Ground Truths. (2009). Retrieved September 21, 2011, from http://ivrg.epfl.ch/supplementary material/RK CVPR09/index.html

Frintop, S., Rome, E., & Christensen, H. I. (2010). Computational visual attention systems and their cognitive foundation: A survey. [TAP]. *ACM Transactions on Applied Perception*, *7*, 1–39. doi:10.1145/1658349.1658355

Frintrop, S., Backer, G., & Rome, E. (2005). Selecting what is important: Training visual attention. *28th Annual German Conference on AI (KI)* (pp. 351-366). Koblenz, Germany: Springer Verlag.

Frintrop, S., Klodt, M., & Rome, E. (2007). A real-time visual attention system using integral images. *5th International Conference on Computer Vision Systems (ICVS)*. Bielefeld, Germany: Applied Computer Science Group.

Frintrop, S. (2005). *VOCUS: A Visual attention system for object detection and goal-directed search*. University of Bonn. doi:10.1007/11682110

Frintrop, S. (2011). Computational visual attention. In Salah, A. A., & Gevers, T. (Eds.), *Computer analysis of human behavior* (pp. 69–101). London, UK: Springer. doi:10.1007/978-0-85729-994-9_4

Frintrop, S., & Jensfelt, P. (2008). Attentional landmarks and active gaze control for visual SLAM. *IEEE Transactions on Robotics*, *24*(5), 1054–1065. doi:10.1109/TRO.2008.2004977

Fukushima, K. (1980). Neocognitron: A self organizing neural network model for a mechanism of pattern recognition unaffected by shift in position. *Biological Cybernetics*, *36*(4), 193–202. doi:10.1007/BF00344251

Fukushima, K. (2010). Neural network model for completing occluded contours. *Neural Networks*, *23*, 528–540. doi:10.1016/j.neunet.2009.10.002

Fukushima, K., Miyake, S., & Ito, T. (1983). Neocognitron: A neural network model for a mechanism of visual patter recognition. *IEEE Transactions on Systems, Man, and Cybernetics*, *13*, 826–834.

Furukawa, T., & Sakamoto, K. (2010). Eye contact communication system between mobile robots using invisible code display. In Yang, H., Malaka, R., Hoshino, J., & Han, J. (Eds.), *Entertainment Computing - ICEC 2010* (*Vol. 6243*, pp. 468–471). Berlin, Germany: Springer. doi:10.1007/978-3-642-15399-0_62

Gallant, J., Connor, C., Rakshit, S., Lewis, J., & Van Essen, D. (1996). Neural responses to polar, hyperbolic, and Cartesian gratings in area V4 of the macaque monkey. *Journal of Neurophysiology*, *76*(4), 2718–2739.

Gautama, T., & Van Hulle, M. M. (2001). Function of center-surround antagonism for motion in visual area MT/V5: A modeling study. *Vision Research*, *41*(28), 3917–3930.

Geerinck, T., Sahli, H., Henderickx, D., Vanhamel, I., & Enescu, V. (2009). *Modeling attention and perceptual grouping to salient objects. Attention in Cognitive Systems* (p. 166). London, UK: Springer, Limited.

Gerhart, G., & Matchko, R. (2002). Visualization techniques for four Stokes parameter polarization. In *Proceedings of the Ground Target Modeling and Validation Conference* (pp. 216-225).

Gerstner, W., & Kistler, W. (2002). *Spiking neuron models: single neurons, populations, plasticity*. Cambridge, MA: Cambridge University Press. doi:10.1017/CBO9780511815706

Ghirardelli, T. G., & Folk, C. L. (1996). Spatial cueing in a stereoscopic display: Evidence for a depth-blind attentional spotlight. *Psychonomic Bulletin & Review*, *3*, 81–86. doi:10.3758/BF03210744

Giakos, G. C. (2006). Multifusion, multispectral, optical polarimetric imaging sensing principles. *IEEE Transactions on Instrumentation and Measurement*, *55*, 1628–1633. doi:10.1109/TIM.2006.881030

Gibaldi, A., Chessa, M., Canessa, A., Sabatini, S. P., & Solari, F. (2010). A cortical model for binocular vergence control without explicit calculation of disparity. *Neurocomputing*, *73*, 1065–1073.

Gilles, S. (1996). *Description and experimentation of image matching using mutual information*. Oxford: Entropy.

Giorgianni, E. J., Madden, T. E., & Kriss, M. A. (2009). *Digital color management: Encoding solutions* (2nd ed.). New Delhi, India: Wiley.

Goldsmith, T. (1975). The polarization sensitivity-dichroic absorption paradox in arthropod photoreceptors. In Snyder, A. W., & Menzel, R. (Eds.), *Photoreceptor optics* (pp. 98–125). Berlin, Germany: Springer Verlag. doi:10.1007/978-3-642-80934-7_23

Goldstein, D. (2003). *Polarized light, revised and expanded (optical science and engineering)*. CRC. doi:10.1201/9780203911587

Goldstein, D. H. (2000). Polarimetric characterization of federal standard paints. *Proceedings of the Society for Photo-Instrumentation Engineers*, *4133*, 112–123. doi:10.1117/12.406618

Graf, E. W., Adams, W. J., & Lages, M. (2004). Prior monocular information can bias motion perception. *Journal of Vision (Charlottesville, Va.)*, *4*, 427–433. doi:10.1167/4.6.2

Grauman, K., & Darrell, T. (2006). *Pyramid match kernels: Discriminative classification with sets of image features*. MIT Technical Report, CSAIL-TR-2006-20.

Green, A. S., Ohmann, P. R., Leininger, N. E., & Kavanaugh, J. A. (2010). Polarization imaging and insect vision. *The Physics Teacher*, *48*(1), 17–20. doi:10.1119/1.3274352

Greenwald, H. S., & Knill, D. C. (2009). Cue integration outside central fixation: A study of grasping in depth. *Journal of Vision*, *9*(2), 11, 1-16.

Greenwald, H. S., & Knill, D. C. (2009). Orientation disparity: A cue for 3D orientation. *Neural Computation*, *21*, 2581–2604. doi:10.1162/neco.2009.08-08-848

Greenwood, J., & Edwards, M. (2009). The detection of multiple global directions: Capacity limits with spatially segregated and transparent-motion signals. *Journal of Vision (Charlottesville, Va.)*, *9*, 1–15.

Grill-Spector, K., & Kanwisher, N. (2005). As soon as you know it is there, you know what it is. *Psychological Science*, *16*(2), 152–160. doi:10.1111/j.0956-7976.2005.00796.x

Grill-Spector, K., & Kanwisher, N. (2005). Visual recognition: As soon as you see it, you know what it is. *Psychological Science*, *16*(2), 152–160. doi:10.1111/j.0956-7976.2005.00796.x

Grimson, W. E. L. (1990). *Object recognition by computer-The role of geometric constraints*. Cambridge, MA: MIT Press.

Grosinger, J. (2008). *Investigation of polarization modulation in optical free space communications through the atmosphere*. Unpublished Master's thesis, Institut fur Nachrichtentechnik und Hochfrequenztechnik, eingereicht an der Technischen Universitat Wien, Fakultat fur Elektrotechnik und Informationstechnik.

Grossberg, S. (1999). How does the cerebral cortex work? Learning, attention, and grouping by the laminar circuits of visual cortex. *Spatial Vision*, *12*(2), 163–185. doi:10.1163/156856899X00102

Grossberg, S., & Mingolla, E. (1985). Neural dynamics of perceptual grouping: Textures, boundaries, and emergent segmentations. *Perception & Psychophysics*, *38*, 141–171.

Gross, C., Rocha-Miranda, C., & Bender, D. (1972). Visual properties of neurons in inferotemporal cortex of the macaque. *Journal of Neurophysiology*, *35*, 96–111.

Haefner, R. M., & Cumming, B. G. (2009). An improved estimator of variance explained in the presence of noise. *Advances in Neural Information Processing Systems*, *21*, 585–592.

Haidinger, W. (1844). Über das directe Erkennen des polarisirten Lichts und der Lage der Polarisationsebene. *Poggendorfs Annalen*, *63*, 29–39. doi:10.1002/andp.18441390903

Hamker, F. (2005). The emergence of attention by population-based inference and its role in distributed processing and cognitive control of vision. *Computer Vision and Image Understanding*, *100*(1-2), 64–106. doi:10.1016/j.cviu.2004.09.005

Hamker, F. H. (2005a). The reentry hypothesis: The putative interaction of the frontal eye field, ventrolateral prefrontal cortex, and areas V4, IT for attention and eye movement. *Cerebral Cortex*, *15*, 431–447.

Hamker, F. H. (2005b). A computational model of visual stability and change detection during eye movements in real world scenes. *Visual Cognition*, *12*, 1161–1176.

Hanlon, R. T., & Messenger, J. B. (1996). *Cephalopod behaviour*. Cambridge, UK: Cambridge University Press.

Hansard, M., & Haroud, R. (2008). Cyclopean geometry of binocular vision. *Journal of the Optical Society of America. A, Optics, Image Science, and Vision*, *25*(9), 2357–2369. doi:10.1364/JOSAA.25.002357

Hansard, M., & Horaud, R. (2010). Cyclorotation models for eyes and cameras. *IEEE Transactions on Systems, Man, and Cybernetics. Part B, Cybernetics*, *40*, 151–161.

Hanson, F., & Radic, S. (2008). High bandwidth underwater optical communication. *Applied Optics*, *47*, 277–283. doi:10.1364/AO.47.000277

Harris, J. M. (2006). The interaction of eye movements and retinal signals during the perception of 3-D motion direction. *Journal of Vision (Charlottesville, Va.)*, *6*, 777–790. doi:10.1167/6.8.2

Harris, J. M., & Dean, P. J. A. (2003). Accuracy and precision of binocular 3-D motion perception. *Journal of Experimental Psychology: HPP*, *29*(5), 869–881. doi:10.1037/0096-1523.29.5.869

Harris, J. M., & Drga, V. F. (2005). Using visual direction in three-dimensional motion perception. *Nature Reviews. Neuroscience*, *8*, 229–233. doi:10.1038/nn1389

Harris, J. M., Nefs, H. T., & Grafton, C. E. (2008). Binocular vision and motion-in-depth. *Spatial Vision*, *21*, 531–547. doi:10.1163/156856808786451462

Harris, J. M., & Rushton, S. K. (2003). Poor visibility of motion-in-depth is due to early motion averaging. *Vision Research*, *43*, 385–392. doi:10.1016/S0042-6989(02)00570-9

Harsdorf, S., Reuter, R., & Tönebön, S. (1999). Contrast-enhanced optical imaging of submersible targets. *SPIE*, *3821*, 378–383. doi:10.1117/12.364201

Hartley, R., & Zisserman, A. (2004). *Multiple view geometry in computer vision* (2nd ed.). Cambridge University Press. doi:10.1017/CBO9780511811685

Haspel, N., Ricklin, D., Geisbrecht, B., Lambris, J., & Kavraki, L. (2008). Electrostatic contributions drive the interaction between staphylococcus aureus protein efb-c and its complement target c3d. *Protein Science*, *17*(11), 1894–1906. doi:10.1110/ps.036624.108

Haspel, N., Zanuy, D., Aleman, C., Wolfson, H., & Nussinov, R. (2006). De-novo tubular nanostructure design based on self-assembly of beta-helical protein motifs. *Structure (London, England)*, *14*, 1137–1148. doi:10.1016/j.str.2006.05.016

Hassenstein, B., & Reichardt, W. (1956). Systemtheoretische Analyse der Zeitreihenfolgen und Vorzeichenauswertung bei der Bewegungsperzeption des Rüsselkäfers, Chlorophanus. *Naturforschung Teil B*, *11*, 513–524.

Hawken, M. J., Gegenfurtner, K. C., & Tang, C. (1994). Contrast dependence of colour and luminance motion mechanisms in human vision. *Nature*, *367*, 268–270. doi:10.1038/367268a0

Hawken, M., & Parker, A. (1987). Spatial properties of neurons in the monkey striate cortex. *Proceedings of the Royal Society of London. Series B, Biological Sciences*, *231*, 251–288. doi:10.1098/rspb.1987.0044

Hawkins, J., & Blakeslee, S. (2004). *On intelligence*. Times Books.

Hawryshyn, C. (1992). Polarization vision in fish. *American Scientist*, *80*, 164–175.

Hayashi, I., & Shinpaku, G. (2004a). Structuralization of early vision for perceptual grouping in apertures. *Proceedings of the International Workshop on Fuzzy Systems and Innovational Computing 2004* (FIC2004), (pp. 254-258).

Hayashi, I., & Williamson, J. R. (2001a). A study on pruning methods for TAM network. *Proceedings of the Fifth International Conference on Cognitive and Neural Systems* (CNS2001).

Hayashi, I., & Williamson, J. R. (2001b). Acquisition of fuzzy knowledge from topographic mixture networks with attentional feedback. *Proceedings of the International Joint Conference on Neural Networks* (IJCNN2001), (pp. 1386-1391).

Hayashi, I., & Williamson, J. R. (2002a). An analysis of aperture problem using fuzzy rules acquired from TAM network. *Proceedings of 2002 IEEE International Conference on Fuzzy Systems* (FUZZ-IEEE2002) *in 2002 World Congress on Computational Intelligence* (WCCI2002), (pp. 914-919).

Hayashi, I., & Williamson, J. R. (2002b). Knowledge restructuring in fuzzy TAM network, *Proc. of the 9th International Conference on Neural Information Processing* (ICONIP2002), (No. ICONIP1918).

Hayashi, I., & Williamson, J. R. (2005). Orientation selectivity of TAM network with extensive receptive field. *Proceedings of the International Conference on Computational Intelligence for Modelling Control and Automation* (CIMCA2005), (pp. 1184-1189).

Hayashi, I., Maeda, T., & Williamson, J. R. (2004b). A formulation of receptive field type input layer for TAM Network using gabor function. *Proceedings of 2004 IEEE International Conference on Fuzzy Systems* (FUZZ-IEEE2004), No.FUZZ1335.

Hayashi, I., Taguchi, T., & Kudoh, S. N. (2007a). Learning and memory in living neuronal networks connected to moving robot. *Proceedings of 8th International Symposium on Advanced Intelligent Systems* (ISIS2007), (pp. 79-81).

Hayashi, I., Toyoshima, H., & Yamanoi, T. (2007b). Recognition of perception and the localization for aperture problem in visual pathway of brain. *Proceedings of 2007 IEEE International Conference on Systems, Man and Cybernetics* (SMC2007) (pp. 1872-1877).

Heeger, D. (1987). Model the extraction of image flow. *Journal of Optical Society of America, Series A, 4*, 1455–1471.

Heeger, D. (1988). Optical flow using spatiotemporal filters. *International Journal of Computer Vision, 1*, 270–302.

Hegedüs, R., Åkesson, S., & Horváth, G. (2007). Polarization patterns of thick clouds: Overcast skies have distribution of the angle of polarization similar to that of clear skies. *Journal of the Optical Society of America, 24*, 2347–2356. doi:10.1364/JOSAA.24.002347

Heidemann, J., Ye, W., Wills, J., Syed, A., & Li, Y. (2006). Research challenges and applications for underwater sensor networking. In *Proceedings of the IEEE Wireless Communications and Networking Conference* (pp. 228--235).

Heinke, D., & Humphreys, G. (2003). Attention, spatial representation, and visual neglect: simulating emergent attention and spatial memory in the selective attention for identification model (SAIM). *Psychological Review, 110*(1), 29–87. doi:10.1037/0033-295X.110.1.29

Heinke, D., & Humphreys, G. W. (2004). *Computational models of visual selective attention. A review. Connectionist models in psychology* (pp. 273–312). London, UK: Psychology Press.

Henderson, J. M. (2003). Human gaze control during real-world scene perception. *Trends in Cognitive Sciences, 7*(11), 498–504. doi:10.1016/j.tics.2003.09.006

Henderson, J. M., Weeks, P. A., & Hollingworth, A. (1999). Effects of a semantic consistency on eye movements during scene viewing. *Journal of Experimental Psychology. Human Perception and Performance, 25*, 210–228. doi:10.1037/0096-1523.25.1.210

Heron, S., & Lages, M. (2009). Measuring azimuth and elevation of binocular 3D motion direction. *Journal of Vision (Charlottesville, Va.), 9*(8), 637a. doi:10.1167/9.8.637

Heywood, C., Gadotti, A., & Cowey, A. (1992). Cortical area V4 and its role in the perception of color. *The Journal of Neuroscience, 12*(10), 4056–4065.

Hildreth, E. C. (1984). The computation of the velocity field. *Proceedings of the Royal Society of London. Series B, Biological Sciences*, *221*, 189–220. doi:10.1098/rspb.1984.0030

Hinkle, D. A., & Connor, C. E. (2002). Three-dimensional orientation tuning in macaque area V4. *Nature Reviews. Neuroscience*, *5*, 665–670. doi:10.1038/nn875

Hinton, G. (n.d.). The next generation of neural networks. Retrieved from www.cs.toronto.edu/~hinton/talks/msr10.ppt

Hoffman, J., & Mueller, S. (1994). *An in depth look at attention*. Annual Meeting of the Psychonomic Society, St. Louis, MO.

Hogervorst, M. A., & Eagle, R. A. (1998). Biases in three-dimensional structure-from-motion arise from noise in the early visual system. *Proceedings. Biological Sciences*, *265*, 1587–1593. doi:10.1098/rspb.1998.0476

Holmqvist, K., Nyström, M., Andersson, R., Dewhurst, R., Jarodzka, H., & van de Weijer, J. (2011). *Eye tracking – A comprehensive guide to methods and measures*. New York, NY: Oxford University Press.

Hopf, J. M., Boelmans, K., Schoenfeld, M. A., Luck, S. J., & Heinze, H. J. (2004). Attention to features precedes attention to locations in visual search: Evidence from electromagnetic brain responses in humans. *The Journal of Neuroscience*, *24*(8), 1822–1832. doi:10.1523/JNEUROSCI.3564-03.2004

Ho-Phuoc, T., Guyader, N., & Guerin-Dugue, A. (2010). A functional and statistical bottom-up saliency model to reveal the relative contributions of low-level visual guiding factors. *Cognitive Computation*, *2*(4), 344–359. doi:10.1007/s12559-010-9078-8

Horita, Y., Hayashi, Y., Shibata, K., Hayashi, K., Morohashi, K., & Doi, T. (2008). Omni-directional polarization image capture using omni-directional camera and polarization filter. In *ITST 2008, 8th International Conference on ITS Telecommunications,* (pp. 99 -102).

Horita, Y., Shibata, K., Maeda, K., & Hayashi, Y. (2009). Omni-directional polarization image sensor based on an omni-directional camera and a polarization filter. In *IEEE International Conference on Advanced Video and Signal Based Surveillance* (pp. 280 -285).

Horn, B., & Schunk, B. (1981). Determining optical flow. *Artificial Intelligence*, *17*, 185–203.

Horváth, G., Gál, J., & Wehner, R. (1997). Why are water-seeking insects not attracted by mirages? The polarization properties of mirages. *Naturwissenschaften*, *84*, 300–303. doi:10.1007/s001140050398

Horváth, G., & Varjú, D. (2004). *Polarized light in animal vision: Polarization patterns in nature*. Springer.

Hou, X., & Zhang, L. (2007). Saliency detection: A spectral residual approach. In *The Proceedings of the 2007 IEEE International Conference on Computer Vision and Pattern Recognition* (pp. 1-8). Minneapolis, MN: IEEE.

Howard, I. P., & Rogers, B. J. (2002). Seeing in depth: *Vol. 2. Depth perception*. Ontario, Canada: I Porteous Publishing.

Huang, Z., He, F., Cai, X., Zou, Z., Liu, J., Liang, M., & Chen, X. (2011). Efficient random saliency map detection. *Science China Information*, *54*(6), 1207–1217. doi:10.1007/s11432-011-4263-2

Hubel, D. H., & Livingstone, M. S. (1987). Segregation of form, color, stereopsis in primate area 18. *The Journal of Neuroscience*, *7*(11), 3378–3415.

Hubel, D. H., & Wiesel, T. N. (1962). Receptive fields, binocular interaction and functional architecture in the cat's visual cortex. *The Journal of Physiology*, *160*, 106–154.

Hubel, D. H., & Wiesel, T. N. (1968). Receptive fields and functional architecture of monkey striate cortex. *The Journal of Physiology*, *195*, 215–243.

Hubel, D. H., & Wiesel, T. N. (1970). Stereoscopic vision in macaque monkey. Cells sensitive to binocular depth in area 18 of the macaque monkey cortex. *Nature*, *225*, 41–42.

Hubel, D., & Wiesel, T. (1959). Receptive fields of single neurones in the cat's striate cortex. *The Journal of Physiology*, *148*, 574–591.

Hubel, D., & Wiesel, T. (1962). Receptive fields, binocular interaction and functional architecture in the cat's visual cortex. *The Journal of Physiology*, *160*, 106–154.

Hubel, D., & Wiesel, T. (1965). Receptive fields and functional architecture in two nonstriate visual areas (18 and 19) of the cat. *Journal of Neurophysiology*, *28*, 229–289.

Hubel, D., & Wiesel, T. (1968). Receptive fields and functional architecture of monkey striate cortex. *The Journal of Physiology*, *195*(1), 215–243.

Huber, D. F., Denes, L., Hebert, M., Gottlieb, M., Kaminsky, B., & Metes, P. (1997). A spectro-polarimetric imager for intelligent transportation systems. In *SPIE International Symposium on Intelligent Systems and Advanced Manufacturing, Intelligent Transportation Systems, Vol. 3207*.

Hummel, J. E. (2001). Complementary solutions to the binding problem in vision: Implications for shape perception and object recognition. *Visual Cognition*, *8*, 489–517. doi:10.1080/13506280143000214

Hummel, J. E., & Stankiewicz, B. J. (1996). An architecture for rapid, hierarchical structural description. In Inui, T., & McClelland, J. (Eds.), *Attention and Performance XVI: Information Integration in Perception and Communication* (pp. 93–121). MIT Press.

Hung, G. K., Semmlow, J. L., & Ciuffreda, K. J. (1986). A dual-mode dynamic model of the vergence eye movement system. *IEEE Transactions on Bio-Medical Engineering*, *36*(11), 1021–1028.

Hung, K. P., Kreiman, G., Poggio, T., & DiCarlo, J. J. (2005). Fast readout of object identity from macaque inferior temporal cortex. *Science*, *301*, 863–866. doi:10.1126/science.1117593

Hürlimann, F., Kiper, D. C., & Carandini, M. (2002). Testing the Bayesian model of perceived speed. *Vision Research*, *42*, 2253–2257. doi:10.1016/S0042-6989(02)00119-0

Hwang, A. D., Higgins, E. C., & Pomplun, M. (2009). A model of top-down attentional control during visual search in complex scenes. *Journal of Vision (Charlottesville, Va.)*, *9*(5), 1–18. doi:10.1167/9.5.25

Iavecchia, H. P., & Folk, C. L. (1995). Shifting visual attention stereographic displays: A time course analysis. *Human Factors*, *36*, 606–618.

Idema, T. (2005). *The behaviour and attractiveness of the Lotka Volterra equations. ilorentz.org*. Universiteit Leiden.

Iqbal, M., Morel, O., & Meriaudeau, F. (2010). *A survey on outdoor water hazard detection*. In The 5th International Conference on Information & Communication Technology and Systems.

Ito, M., & Komatsu, H. (2004). Representation of angles embedded within contour stimuli in area V2 of macaque monkeys. *The Journal of Neuroscience*, *24*(13), 3313–3324. doi:10.1523/JNEUROSCI.4364-03.2004

Itti, Laurent, & Baldi, P. (2005). A principled approach to detecting surprising events in video. *2005 IEEE Computer Society Conference on Computer Vision and Pattern Recognition (CVPR'05)* (pp. 631-637). IEEE. doi:10.1109/CVPR.2005.40

Itti, L. (2000). *Models of bottom-up and top-down visual attention*. California Institute of Technology.

Itti, L. (2005). Models of bottom-up attention and saliency. In Itti, L., Rees, G., & Tsotsos, J. K. (Eds.), *Neurobiology of attention* (pp. 576–582). San Diego, CA: Elsevier. doi:10.1016/B978-012375731-9/50098-7

Itti, L., & Koch, C. (2000). A saliency-based search mechanism for overt and covert shifts of visual attention. *Vision Research*, *40*, 1489–1506. doi:10.1016/S0042-6989(99)00163-7

Itti, L., & Koch, C. (2001). Computational modelling of visual attention. *Nature Reviews. Neuroscience*, *2*, 194–203. doi:10.1038/35058500

Itti, L., & Koch, C. (2001). Feature combination strategies for saliency-based visual attention systems. *Journal of Electronic Imaging*, *10*(1), 161–169. doi:10.1117/1.1333677

Itti, L., & Koch, C. (2001)... *Nature Reviews. Neuroscience*, *2*(3), 194–203. doi:10.1038/35058500

Itti, L., Koch, C., & Niebur, E. (1998). A model of saliency-based visual attention for rapid scene analysis. *IEEE Transactions on Pattern Analysis and Machine Intelligence*, *20*, 1254–1259. doi:10.1109/34.730558

Ivanoff, A., & Waterman, T. H. (1958). Factors, mainly depth and wavelength, affecting the degree of underwater light polarization. *Journal of Marine Research*, *16*, 283–307.

Jadhav, S., & Bhalchandra, A. (2008). Blind source separation: Trends of new age - A review. In *IET International Conference on Wireless, Mobile and Multimedia Networks, 2008,* (pp. 251 –254).

James, W. (1890). *The principles of psychology*. Cambridge, MA: Harvard University Press. doi:10.1037/11059-000

Janssen, P., Vogels, R., Liu, Y., & Orban, G. A. (2011). Macaque inferior temporal neurons are selective for three-dimensional boundaries and surfaces. *The Journal of Neuroscience*, *21*(23), 9419–9429.

Jarodzka, H., Holmqvist, K., & Nyström, M. (2010). A vector-based, multidimensional scanpath similarity measure. In C. Morimoto, & H. Instance (Eds.), *Proceedings of the 2010 Symposium on Eye Tracking Research & Applications ETRA '10* (pp. 211-218). New York, NY: ACM.

Jemel, B., Mottron, L., & Dawson, M. (2006). Impaired face processing in autism: Fact or artifact? [Springer Netherlands.]. *Journal of Autism and Developmental Disorders*, *36*(1), 91–106. doi:10.1007/s10803-005-0050-5

Jenkin, M. R. M. (1996). Stereopsis near the horoptor. *Proceedings of the 4th ICARCV*.

Jepson, A. D., Fleet, D. J., & Jenkin, R. M. (1991). Phase-based disparity measurement. *CVGIP: Image Understanding*, *53*, 198–210.

Ji, Z., & Weng, J. (2008). Where-what network 1 : Where and what assist each other through top-down connections. *7th IEEE International Conference on Development and Learning*, (pp. 61-66).

Ji, H., & Fermüller, C. (2006). Noise causes slant underestimation in stereo and motion. *Vision Research*, *46*, 3105–3120. doi:10.1016/j.visres.2006.04.010

Jin, Y., & Geman, S. (2006). Context and hierarchy in a probabilistic image model, In *IEEE international Conference on Computer Vision and Pattern Recognition,* Vol. 2.

Johnston, A., McOwan, P., & Benton, C. (1999). Robust velocity computation from a biologically motivated model of motion perception. *Proceedings of Royal Society, Series B*, *266*, 509–518.

Jones, E. (2007). Neuroanatomy: Cajal and after Cajal. *Breain Research Reviews*, *55*(2), 248–255. doi:10.1016/j.brainresrev.2007.06.001

Ju, S., Black, M., & Jepson, A. (1996). Skin and bones: Multi-layer, locally affine, optical flow and regularization with transparency. In *IEEE Conference on Computer Vision and Pattern Recognition, CVPR '96, San Francisco, CA*, June 1996, (pp. 307-314).

Judd, T., Ehinger, K., Durand, F., & Torralba, A. (2009). Learning to predict where humans look. In *The Proceedings of the 12th IEEE International Conference on Computer Vision* (pp 2106-2113). Kyoto, Japan: IEEE.

Julesz, B. (1971). *Foundations of Cyclopean perception*. Chicago, IL: University of Chicago Press.

Kadir, T., & Brady, M. (2001). Saliency, scale and image description. *International Journal of Computer Vision*, *45*(2), 83–105. doi:10.1023/A:1012460413855

Kahana, M., & Sekuler, R. (2002). Recognizing spatial patterns: a noisy exemplar approach. *Vision Research*, *42*(18), 2177–2192. doi:10.1016/S0042-6989(02)00118-9

Kanai, R., Moradi, F., Shimojo, S., & Verstraten, F. A. J. (2005). Perceptual alternation induced by visual transients. *Perception*, *34*, 803–822. doi:10.1068/p5245

Kanan, C., Tong, M. H., Zhang, L., & Cottrell, G. W. (2009). Sun: Top-down saliency using natural statistics. *Visual Cognition*, *17*(6), 979–1003. doi:10.1080/13506280902771138

Kandel, E. R., Schwartz, J. H., & Jessell, T. M. (2000). *Principles of neural science* (4th ed.). New York, NY: McGraw-Hill.

Kaplan, D., & Glass, L. (1995). *Understanding nonlinear dynamics*. Springer Verlag. doi:10.1007/978-1-4612-0823-5

Karpel, N., & Schechner, Y. Y. (2004). Portable polarimetric underwater imaging system with a linear response. In *Proceedings of SPIE Polarization: Measurement, Analysis and Remote Sensing VI*.

Kasai, T., Morotomi, T., Katayama, J., & Kumada, T. (2003). Attending to a location in three-dimensional space modulates early ERPs. *Brain Research. Cognitive Brain Research, 17*, 273–285. doi:10.1016/S0926-6410(03)00115-0

Kastner, S., De Weerd, P., Desimone, R., & Ungerleider, L. G. (1998). Mechanisms of directed attention in the human extrastriate cortex as revealed by functional MRI. *Science, 282*(5386), 108–111. doi:10.1126/science.282.5386.108

Kato, H., Bishop, P., & Orban, G. (1978). Hypercomplex and simple/complex cells classifications in cat striate cortex. *Journal of Neurophysiology, 41*(5), 1071–1095.

Kehtarnavaz, N., & de Figueiredo, R. (1988). A framework for surface reconstruction from 3D contours. *Computer Vision Graphics and Image Processing, 42*(1), 32–47. doi:10.1016/0734-189X(88)90141-7

Kiani, R., Esteky, H., Mirpour, K., & Tanaka, K. (2007). Object category structure in response patterns of neuronal population in monkey inferior temporal cortex. *Journal of Neurophysiology, 97*, 4296–4309. doi:10.1152/jn.00024.2007

Kimia, B., & Siddiqi, K. (1994). Geometric heat equation and nonlinear diffusion of shapes and images. *IEEE Conference on Computer Vision and Pattern Recognition*, (pp. 113-120).

Kimia, B., Tannenbaum, A., & Zucker, S. W. (1992). On the evolution of curves via a function of curvature, 1: The classical case. *Journal of Mathematical Analysis and Applications, 163*(2), 438–458. doi:10.1016/0022-247X(92)90260-K

Kimia, B., Tannenbaum, A., & Zucker, S. W. (1995). Shapes, shocks and deformations I: The components of two-dimensional shape and the reaction-diffusion space. *International Journal of Computer Vision, 15*, 189–224. doi:10.1007/BF01451741

Kiorpes, L., & Movshon, J. A. (2004). Development of sensitivity to visual motion in macaque monkeys. *Visual Neuroscience, 21*, 851–859.

Klin, A., Jones, W., Schultz, R., Volkmar, F., & Cohen, D. (2002). Visual fixation patterns during viewing of naturalistic social situations as predictors of social competence in individuals with autism. *Archives of General Psychiatry, 59*(9), 809–816. doi:10.1001/archpsyc.59.9.809

Knill, D. C., Kersten, D., & Yuille, A. L. (1996). Introduction: A Bayesian formulation of visual perception. In Knill, D. C., & Richards, W. (Eds.), *Perception as Bayesian inference*. Cambridge, UK: Cambridge University Press. doi:10.1017/CBO9780511984037.009

Knill, D. C., & Richards, W. (1996). *Perception as Bayesian inference*. Cambridge, UK: Cambridge University Press. doi:10.1017/CBO9780511984037

Kobatake, E., Wang, G., & Tanaka, K. (1998). Effects of shape-discrimination training on the Selectivity of inferotemporal cells in adult monkeys. *Journal of Neurophysiology, 80*, 324–330.

Koch, C., & Tsuchiya, N. (2007). Attention and consciousness: Two distinct brain processes. *Trends in Cognitive Sciences, 11*(1), 16–22. doi:10.1016/j.tics.2006.10.012

Koch, C., & Ullman, S. (1985). Shifts in selective visual attention - Towards the underlying neural circuitry. *Human Neurobiology, 4*(4), 219–227.

Koenderink, J. J., & van Doorn, A. J. (1991). Affine structure from motion. *Journal of the Optical Society of America, 8*, 377–385. doi:10.1364/JOSAA.8.000377

Koesling, H., & Ritter, H. (2001). VDesigner – A visual programming environment for eye-tracking experiments. *Proceedings 11th European Conference on Eye Movements ECEM 11*, Turku, Finland.

Können, G. P. (1985). *Polarized light in nature*. Cambridge University Press.

Kootstra, G., Nederveen, A., & Boer, B. D. (2008). Paying attention to symmetry. In M. Everingham, C. Needham, & R. Fraile (Eds.), *19th British Machine Vision Conference* (Vol. 284). Leeds, UK: University of Leeds. doi:10.1126/science.284.5419.1429k

Kreiman, G. (2004). Neural coding: Computational and biophysical perspectives. *Physics of Life Reviews, 2*, 71–102. doi:10.1016/j.plrev.2004.06.001

Kreiman, G., Serre, T., & Poggio, T. (2007). On the limits of feed-forward processing in visual object recognition. *Journal of Vision (Charlottesville, Va.), 9*(7).

Krishnan, V. V., & Stark, L. A. (1977). A heuristic model for the human vergence eye movement system. *IEEE Transactions on Bio-Medical Engineering, 24*, 44–49.

Krotkow, E., Henriksen, K., & Kories, R. (1990). Stereo ranging from verging cameras. *IEEE Transaction on PAMI, 12*(12), 1200–1205.

Kudoh, S. N., Taguchi, T., & Hayashi, I. (2006). Interaction and intelligence in living neuronal networks connected to moving robot. *Proceedings of 2006 IEEE International Conference on Fuzzy Systems* (FUZZ-IEEE2006) *in 2006 IEEE World Congress on Computational Intelligence* (WCCI2006), (pp. 6271-6275).

Kudoh, S. N., Hosokawa, C., Kiyohara, A., Taguchi, T., & Hayashi, I. (2007). Biomodeling system: Interaction between living neuronal network and outer world. *Journal of Robotics and Mechatronics, 19*(5), 592–600.

Laberge, D. (1995). *Attentional processing: The brain's art of mindfulness* (1st ed., p. 256). Harvard University Press.

Lages, M. (2006). Bayesian models of binocular 3-D motion perception. *Journal of Vision (Charlottesville, Va.), 6*(4), 508–522. doi:10.1167/6.4.14

Lages, M., Dolia, A., & Graf, E. W. (2007). Dichoptic motion perception limited to depth of fixation? *Vision Research, 47*, 244–252. doi:10.1016/j.visres.2006.10.001

Lages, M., & Heron, S. (2008). Motion and disparity processing informs Bayesian 3D motion estimation. *Proceedings of the National Academy of Sciences of the United States of America, 105*, E117. doi:10.1073/pnas.0809829105

Lages, M., & Heron, S. (2009). Testing generalized models of binocular 3D motion perception. *Journal of Vision (Charlottesville, Va.), 9*, 636a. doi:10.1167/9.8.636

Lages, M., & Heron, S. (2010). On the inverse problem of local binocular 3D motion perception. *PLoS Computational Biology, 6*(11), e1000999. doi:10.1371/journal.pcbi.1000999

Lages, M., Jenkins, R., & Hillis, J. M. (2008). Anticipation of gravity alters perception of average speed. *Perception, 37*(Supplement), 28.

Lages, M., Mamassian, P., & Graf, E. W. (2003). Spatial and temporal tuning of motion in depth. *Vision Research, 43*(27), 2861–2873. doi:10.1016/j.visres.2003.08.006

Lambrinos, D., Maris, M., Kobayashil, H., Labhart, T., Pfeifer, R., & Wehner, R. (1998). Navigating with a polarized light compass. In *Self-Learning Robots II: Bio-robotics (Digest No. 1998/248), IEE* (pp. 7/1 -7/4).

Lambrinos, D., Maris, M., Kobayashi, H., Labhart, T., Pfeifer, R., & Wehner, R. (1997). An autonomous agent navigation with a polarized light compass. *Adaptive Behavior, 6*, 131–161. doi:10.1177/105971239700600104

Lambrinos, D., Möller, R., Labhart, T., Pfeifer, R., & Wehner, R. (2000). A mobile robot employing insect strategies for navigation. *Robotics and Autonomous Systems, 30*, 39–64. doi:10.1016/S0921-8890(99)00064-0

Land, M. F., & Tatler, B. W. (2009). *Looking and acting. Vision and eye movements in natural behavior*. New York, NY: Oxford University Press. doi:10.1093/acprof:oso/9780198570943.001.0001

Langley, K., Fleet, D., & Atherton, T. (1992). On transparent motion computation. In *Proceedings of British Machine Vision Conference (BMVC),* Leeds, (pp. 247-257). New York, NY: Springer.

Laprevote, V., Oliva, A., Delerue, C., Thomas, P., & Boucart, M. (2010). Patients with schizophrenia are biased towards low spatial frequency to decode facial expression at a glance. *Neuropsychologia, 48*, 4164–4168. doi:10.1016/j.neuropsychologia.2010.10.017

Lazebnik, S., Schmid, C., & Ponce, J. (2006). Beyond bags of features: Spatial pyramid matching for recognizing natural scenes categories. *IEEE Conference on Computer Vision and Pattern Recognition*, 2169-2178.

Le Meur, O., Castellan, X., Le Callet, P., & Barba, D. (2006). Efficient saliency-based repurposing method. *IEEE International Conference on Image Processing* (pp. 421-424). Atlanta, USA.

Le Meur, O., Le Callet, P., Barba, D., & Thoreau, D. (2006). A coherent computational approach to model bottom-up visual attention. *Pattern Analysis and Machine Intelligence*, *28*(5), 802–817. doi:10.1109/TPAMI.2006.86

Lecun, Y., Boser, B., Denker, J., Henderson, D., Howard, R., Hubbard, W., & Jackel, L. (1989). Backpropagation applied to handwritten zip code recognition. *Neural Computation*, *1*(4), 541–551. doi:10.1162/neco.1989.1.4.541

Lecun, Y., Bottou, L., Bengio, Y., & Haffner, P. (1998). Gradient-based learning applied to document recognition. *Proceedings of the IEEE*, *86*(11), 2278–2324. doi:10.1109/5.726791

Ledgeway, T., & Smith, A. T. (1994). Evidence for separate motion-detecting mechanisms for first-order and 2nd-order motion in human vision. *Vision Research*, *34*, 2727–2740. doi:10.1016/0042-6989(94)90229-1

Lee, J.-B., & Kalva, H. (2011). *Video coding techniques and standards - Introduction- The need for compression, perceptual redundancies, the human visual system, sensitivity to temporal frequencies.* Retrieved March 5, 2011, from http://encyclopedia.jrank.org/articles/pages/6922/VideoCoding-Tech niques-and-Standards.html

Lee, J. K., & Mudaliar, S. (1994). Optimum polarizations in the bistatic scattering from layered random media. *IEEE Transactions on Geoscience and Remote Sensing*, *32*, 169–176. doi:10.1109/36.285199

Lee, R. L. (1998). Digital imaging of clear-sky polarization. *Applied Optics*, *37*, 1465–1476. doi:10.1364/AO.37.001465

Lee, T. S., & Mumford, D. (2003). Hierarchical Bayesian inference in the visual cortex. *Journal of the Optical Society of America*, *2*(7), 1434–1448.

Lehky, S. R., & Maunsell, J. H. (1996). No binocular rivalry in the LGN of alert macaque monkeys. *Vision Research*, *36*, 1225–1234. doi:10.1016/0042-6989(95)00232-4

Lerner, A., Sabbah, S., Erlick, C., & Shashar, N. (2010). Navigation by light polarization in clear and turbid waters. *Philosophical Transactions of The Royal Society Biological Sciences*, *366*, 671–679. doi:10.1098/rstb.2010.0189

Le, S., Raufaste, E., & Demonet, J. (2003). Processing of normal, inverted and scrambled faces in a patient with prosopagnosia: Behavioural and eye tracking data. *Brain Research. Cognitive Brain Research*, *17*, 26–35. doi:10.1016/S0926-6410(03)00077-6

Lesser, M., & Dinah, M. (1998). Mind as a dynamical system: Implications for autism. In Shattock, P., & Linfoot, G. (Eds.), *Psychobiology of autism: Current research & practice*.

Leyton, M. (1987). Symmetry-curvature duality. *Computer Vision Graphics and Image Processing*, *38*(3), 327–341. doi:10.1016/0734-189X(87)90117-4

Li, Y., & Wang, S. (2009). Underwater polarization imaging technology. In *Conference on Lasers Electro Optics The Pacific Rim*.

Li, Y., & Wang, S. (2010). Underwater object detection technology based on polarization image fusion. In *5th International Symposium on Advanced Optical Manufacturing and Testing Technologies: Optoelectronic Materials and Devices for Detector, Imager, Display, and Energy Conversion Technology, Proceedings of SPIE*.

Lienhart, R., & Maydt, J. (2002). An extended set of Haar-like features for rapid object detection. *Proceedings of the International Conference on Image Processing* (pp. 900-903). IEEE.

Likova, L. T., & Tyler, C. W. (2007). Stereomotion processing in the human occipital cortex. *NeuroImage*, *38*, 293–305. doi:10.1016/j.neuroimage.2007.06.039

Li, L.-J., Su, H., Xing, E. P., & Fei-Fei, L. (2010). Object bank: A high-level image representation for scene classification and semantic feature sparsification. In Lafferty, J., Williams, C. K. I., Shawe-Taylor, J., Zemel, R. S., & Culotta, A. (Eds.), *NIPS) 2010* (pp. 1–9). Advances in Neural Information Processing SystemsBritish Columbia, Canada: Curran Associates Inc.

Lin, S.-S., Yemelyanov, K. M., Pugh, J. E. N., & Engheta, N. (2004). Polarization enhanced visual surveillance techniques. In *Proceedings of the IEEE International Conference on Networking, Sensing & Control*.

Liu, F., & Gleicher, M. (2006). Region enhanced scale-invariant saliency detection. *Proceedings of IEEE ICME* (pp. 1-4).

Liu, H., Hong, T.-H., Herman, M., & Chellappa, R. (1995). Spatio-temporal filters for transparent motion segmentation. In Proceedings of the *International Conference on Image Processing*, Vol. 3, (pp. 464-467). doi: 10.1109/ICIP.1995.537672

Liu, T., Yuan, Z., Sun, J., Wang, J., Zheng, N., Tang, X., & Shum, H.-Y. (2011). Learning to detect a salient object. *IEEE Transactions on Pattern Analysis and Machine Intelligence*, *33*(2), 353–367. doi:10.1109/TPAMI.2010.70

Logothetis, N. K., Leopold, D. A., & Sheinberg, D. L. (1996). What is rivaling during binocular rivalry? *Nature*, *380*, 621–624. doi:10.1038/380621a0

Logothetis, N., & Sheinberg, D. (1996). Visual object recognition. *Annual Review of Neuroscience*, *19*, 577–621. doi:10.1146/annurev.ne.19.030196.003045

Lopez, M., Fernandezcaballero, A., Fernandez, M., Mira, J., & Delgado, A. (2006). Motion features to enhance scene segmentation in active visual attention. *Pattern Recognition Letters*, *27*(5), 469–478. doi:10.1016/j.patrec.2005.09.010

Lovaas, O., Koegel, R., & Schreibman, L. (1979). Stimulus overselectivity in autism: A review of research. *Psychological Bulletin*, *86*(6), 1236–1254. doi:10.1037/0033-2909.86.6.1236

Lowe, D. (1999). Object recognition from local scale-invariant features *International Conference on Computer Vision* (pp. 1150-1157).

Lowe, D. (2004). Distinctive image features from scale-invariant keypoints. *International Journal of Computer Vision*, *60*(2), 91–110. doi:10.1023/B:VISI.0000029664.99615.94

Löwenstein, K., & Borchart, M. (1918). Symptomatologie und elektrische reizung bei einer schubverletzung des histerhauptlappens. *Deutsche Zeitschrift fur Nervenheilkunde*, *58*, 264.

Lucas, B. D., & Kanade, T. (1981). An iterative image registration technique with an application to stereo vision. *DARPA Image Understanding Workshop*, (pp. 121–130).

Lu, Z.-L., & Sperling, G. (1995). The functional architecture of human visual motion perception. *Vision Research*, *35*, 2697–2722. doi:10.1016/0042-6989(95)00025-U

Lu, Z.-L., & Sperling, G. (2001). Three systems theory of human visual motion perception: Review and update. *Journal of the Optical Society of America. A, Optics, Image Science, and Vision*, *18*, 2331–2370. doi:10.1364/JOSAA.18.002331

Lythgoe, J. N., & Hemmings, C. C. (1967). Polarized light and underwater vision. *Nature*, *213*, 893–894. doi:10.1038/213893a0

Ma, Y.-F., & Zhang, H.-J. (2003). Contrast-based image attention analysis by using fuzzy growing. In L. A. Rowe, H. M. Vin, T. Plagemann, P. J. Shenoy, & J. R. Smith (Eds.), *Proceedings of the Eleventh ACM International Conference on Multimedia 2003* (pp. 374-381). ACM.

Macmillan, N. A., & Creelman, C. D. (2004). *Detection theory: A user's guide*. Routledge.

Maier, A., Logothetis, N. K., & Leopold, D. A. (2005). Global competition dictates local suppression in pattern rivalry. *Journal of Vision (Charlottesville, Va.)*, *5*, 668–677. doi:10.1167/5.9.2

Mairal, J., Bach, F., Ponce, J., & Sapiro, G. (2009). Online dictionary learning for sparse coding. In *Proceedings of the International Conference on Machine Learning*.

Mairal, J., Elad, M., & Sapiro, G. (2008). Sparse representation for color image restoration. *IEEE Transactions on Image Processing*, 17.

Majaj, N., Carandini, M., & Movshon, J. A. (2007). Motion integration by neurons in macaque MT is local not global. *The Journal of Neuroscience*, *27*, 366–370. doi:10.1523/JNEUROSCI.3183-06.2007

Malacara, D. (1989). *Physical optics and light measurements* (p. 157). Academic Press.

Malvar, H. S., Sullivan, G. J., & Srinivasan, S. (2008). Lifting-Based reversible color transformations for image compression. In Tescher, A. G. (Ed.), *Proceedings of SPIE 7073* (p. 707307). San Diego, CA: SPIE. doi:10.1117/12.797091

Mancas, M. (2007). *Computational attention : Towards attentive computers*. Faculté Polytechnique de Mons.

Marat, S., Phuoc, T. H., Granjon, L., Guyader, N., Pellerin, D., & Gu, A. (2008). Spatio-temporal saliency model to predict eye movements in video free viewing. *Proceedings of the International Conference on Signal Processing.*

Marimont, D. (1984). A representation for image curves. *Association for the Advancement of Artificial Intelligence*, 237-242.

Marrara, M. T., & Moore, C. M. (2000). Role of perceptual organization while attending in depth. *Perception & Psychophysics, 62*(4), 786–799. doi:10.3758/BF03206923

Marr, D. (1982). *Vision*. New York, NY: W.H. Freeman and Company.

Marr, D., & Nishihara, H. (1978). Representation and recognition of the spatial organization of three-dimensional shapes. *Proceedings of the Royal Society of London. Series B, Biological Sciences, 200*(1140), 269–294. doi:10.1098/rspb.1978.0020

Marr, D., & Poggio, T. (1976). Cooperative computation of stereo disparity. *Science, 194*, 283–287.

Martin, D., Fowlkes, C., Tal, D., & Malik, J. (2001). A database of human segmented natural images and its application to evaluating segmentation algorithms and measuring ecological statistics. In *Proceedings of the Eighth International Conference On Computer Vision* (pp. 416-423), Vancouver, Canada: IEEE.

Martínez, A., Reynery, L., Pelayo, F., Morillas, C., & Romero, S. (2006). A codesign tool for high level systhesis of vision models on FPL. *Proceedings - 2006 International Conference on Field Programmable Logic and Applications, FPL,* (pp. 829-832).

Martinez-Conde, S., Macknik, S. L., & Hubel, D. H. (2004). The role of fixational eye movements in visual perception. *Nature Reviews. Neuroscience, 5*, 229–240. doi:10.1038/nrn1348

Masson, G. S., & Castet, E. (2002). Parallel motion processing for the intitiation of short-latency ocular following in humans. *The Journal of Neuroscience, 22*, 5149–5163.

Mäthger, L. M., & Hanlon, R. T. (2006). Anatomical basis for camouflaged polarized light communication in squid. *Biology Letters, 2*(4), 494–496. doi:10.1098/rsbl.2006.0542

Matsuoka, K. (1984). The dynamic model of binocular rivalry. *Biological Cybernetics, 49*, 201–208. doi:10.1007/BF00334466

Matthies, L., Bellutta, P., & Mchenry, M. (2003). Detecting water hazards for autonomous off-road navigation. In *Proceedings of SPIE Conference 5083: Unmanned Ground Vehicle Technology V* (pp. 263-352).

Maunsell, J. H., & van Essen, D. C. (1983). Functional properties of neurons in middle temporal visual area of the macaque monkey, part I- Selectivity for stimulus direction, speed, and orientation. *Journal of Neurophysiology, 49*, 1127–1147.

Maunsell, J., & Essen, D. V. (1983). The connections of the middle temporal visual area (MT) and their relationship to a cortical hierarchy in the macaque monkey. *The Journal of Neuroscience, 3*, 2563–2586.

Maycock, J., Bläsing, B., Bockemühl, T., Ritter, H., & Schack, T. (2010). Motor synergies and object representation in virtual and real grasping. *Conference Record of the 1st International Conference on Applied Bionics and Biomechanics (ICABB)*, Venice, Italy.

Mayhew, J. E. W., & Longuet-Higgins, H. C. (1982). A computational model of binocular depth perception. *Nature, 297*, 376–378. doi:10.1038/297376a0

Maynard, E. M. (2001). Visual prostheses. *Annual Review of Biomedical Engineering, 3*, 145–168. doi:10.1146/annurev.bioeng.3.1.145

Mc Mains, S. A., & Somers, D. C. (2004). Multiple spotlights of attentional selection in human visual cortex. *Neuron, 42*, 677–686. doi:10.1016/S0896-6273(04)00263-6

McAdams, C. J., & Maunsell, J. H. (1999). Effects of attention on orientation-tuning functions of single neurons in macaque cortical area V4. *The Journal of Neuroscience, 19*(1), 431–441.

McElree, B., & Carrasco, M. (1999). The temporal dynamics of visual search: Evidence for parallel processing in feature and conjunction searches. *Journal of Experimental Psychology. Human Perception and Performance, 25*(6), 1517–1539. doi:10.1037/0096-1523.25.6.1517

McKee, J. W., & Aggarwal, J. K. (1977). Computer recognition of partial views of curved objects. *IEEE Transactions on Computers, C*(26), 790–800. doi:10.1109/TC.1977.1674917

Mechler, F., Reich, D., & Victor, J. (2002). Detection and discrimination of relative spatial phase by V1 neurons. *The Journal of Neuroscience, 22*, 6129–6157.

Mehrotra, R., & Grosky, W. (1989). Shape matching utilizing indexed hypothesis generation and testing. *IEEE Transactions on Robotics and Automation, 5*(1), 70–77. doi:10.1109/70.88019

Mehta, A. D., Ulbert, I., & Schroeder, C. E. (2000). Intermodal selective attention in monkeys, I: distribution and timing of effects across visual areas. *Cerebral Cortex, 10*(4), 343–358. doi:10.1093/cercor/10.4.343

Meister, M., & Berry, M. J. (1999). The neural code of the retina. *Neuron, 22*, 435–450. doi:10.1016/S0896-6273(00)80700-X

Mekuz, N., & Tsotsos, J. (2007). Hierarchical learning of dominant constellations for object class recognition. *Asian Conference on Computer Vision*, (pp. 492-501).

Melamed, I. D. (1997). *Measuring semantic entropy*. SIGLEX Workshop on Tagging Text with Lexical Semantics, Washington DC.

Meng, M., & Tong, F. (2004). Can attention selectively bias bistable perception? Differences between binocular rivalry and ambiguous figures. *Journal of Vision (Charlottesville, Va.), 4*, 539–551. doi:10.1167/4.7.2

Meriaudeau, F., Ferraton, M., Stolz, C., Bigué, L., & Morel, O. (2008). Polarization imaging for industrial inspection. In *SPIE Electronic Imaging - Machine Vision Applications in Industrial Inspection XIII, Vol. 6813*.

Merigan, W. H., & Pham, H. H. (1998). V4 lesions in macaques affect both single- and multiple-viewpoint shape discriminations. *Visual Neuroscience, 15*, 359–367. doi:10.1017/S0952523898152112

Meso, A., & Zanker, J. (2009). Perceiving motion transparency in the absence of component direction differences. *Vision Research, 49*, 2187–2200.

Mestre, D., Masson, G., & Stone, L. (2001). Spatial scale of motion segmentation from speed cues. *Vision Research, 41*, 2697–2713.

Mesulam, M. M. (1981). A cortical network for directed attention and unilateral neglect. *Annals of Neurology, 10*, 309–325. doi:10.1002/ana.410100402

Meur, O. L., Callet, P. L., Barba, D., Member, S., & Thoreau, D. (2006). A coherent computational approach to model the bottom-up visual attention. *IEEE Transactions on Pattern Analysis and Machine Intelligence, 28*(5), 802–817. doi:10.1109/TPAMI.2006.86

Meyers, E., Embark, H., Freiwald, W., Serre, T., Kreiman, G., & Poggio, T. (2010). *Examining high level neural representations of cluttered scenes*. Tech. Rep. MIT-CSAIL-TR-2010-034, Massachusetts Institute of Technology.

Milanese, R., Wechsler, H., Gill, S., Bost, J.-M., & Pun, T. (1994). Integration of bottom-up and top-down cues for visual attention using non-linear relaxation. *Proceedings of IEEE Conference on Computer Vision and Pattern Recognition* (pp. 781-785). IEEE Computer Society Press.

Miles, F. A. (1998). The neural processing of 3-D visual information: Evidence from eye movements. *The European Journal of Neuroscience, 10*, 811–822. doi:10.1046/j.1460-9568.1998.00112.x

Miller, E. K., Gochin, P. M., & Gross, C. G. (1993). Suppression of visual responses of neurons in inferior temporal cortex of the awake macaque by addition of a second stimulus. *Brain Research, 616*(1-2), 25–29. doi:10.1016/0006-8993(93)90187-R

Milner, A. D. (1992). Separate pathways for perception and action. *Trends in Neurosciences, 15*(1), 20–25. doi:10.1016/0166-2236(92)90344-8

Min, D., & Sohn, K. (2006). Edge-preserving simultaneous joint motion-disparity estimation. *Proceedings of the 18th International Conference on Pattern Recognition* (ICPR'06) Vol. 2, (pp. 74-77).

Missal, M., Vogels, R., Li, C. Y., & Orban, G. (1999). Shape interactions in macaque inferior temporal neurons. *Journal of Neurophysiology, 82*(1), 131–142.

Mitchell, J. F., Stoner, G. R., & Reynolds, J. H. (2004). Object-based attention determines dominance in binocular rivalry. *Nature, 429*, 410–413. doi:10.1038/nature02584

Miura, K., Sugita, Y., Matsuura, K., Inaba, N., Kawano, K., & Miles, F. A. (2008). The initial disparity vergence elicited with single and dual grating stimuli in monkeys: Evidence for disparity energy sensing and nonlinear interactions. *Journal of Neurophysiology, 100*(5), 2907–2918.

Miyazaki, D., Ammar, M., Kawakami, R., & Ikeuchi, K. (2009). Estimating sunlight polarization using a fish-eye lens. *IPSJ Transactions on Computer Vision and Applications, 1*, 288–300. doi:10.2197/ipsjtcva.1.288

Mok, D., Ro, A., Cadera, W., Crawford, J. D., & Vilis, T. (1990). Rotation of listing's plane during vergence. *Vision Research, 32*, 2055–2064.

Mokhtarian, F. (1995). Silhouette-based isolated object recognition through curvature scale space. *IEEE Transactions on Pattern Analysis and Machine Intelligence, 17*(5), 539–544. doi:10.1109/34.391387

Mokhtarian, F., & Mackworth, A. (1984). Scale-based description and recognition of planar curves and two-dimensional objects. *IEEE Transactions on Pattern Analysis and Machine Intelligence, 8*(1), 34–43. doi:10.1109/TPAMI.1986.4767750

Mole, C. (2009). Attention. *The Stanford encyclopedia of philosophy* (2009 ed., Vol. 37). doi:10.3928/00904481-20080101-02

Möller, R., Lambrinos, D., Pfiefer, R., Labhart, T., & Wehner, R. (1998). Modeling ant navigation with an autonomous agent. In *Proceedings of the Fifth International Conference on Simulation of Adaptive Behavior: From Animals to Animats.*

Monaco, J. P., Bovik, A. C., & Cormack, L. K. (2009). Active, foveated, uncalibrated stereovision. *International Journal of Computer Vision, 85*(2), 192–207.

Montagnini, A., Mamassian, P., Perrinet, L., Castet, E., & Masson, G. S. (2007)... *The Journal of Physiology, 101*, 64–77.

Moran, J., & Desimone, R. (1985). Selective attention gates visual processing in the extrastriate cortex. *Science, 229*(4715), 782–784. doi:10.1126/science.4023713

Morel, O., & Fofi, D. (2007). Calibration of catadioptric sensors by polarization imaging. In *IEEE International Conference on Robotics and Automation.*

Morel, O., Ferraton, M., Stolz, C., & Gorria, P. (2006). Active lighting applied to shape from polarization. In *IEEE International Conference on Image Processing* (pp. 2181-2184).

Morel, O., Seulin, R., & Fofi, D. (2007a). *Measurement of the three-dimensional mirror parameters by polarization imaging applied to catadioptric camera calibration.* In IEEE/SPIE 8th International Conference on Quality Control by Artificial Vision (QCAV'2007).

Morel, O., Seulin, R., & Fofi, D. (2007b). *Catadioptric camera calibration by polarization imaging.* In Iberian Conference on Pattern Recognition and Image Analysis.

Morel, O., Stolz, C., & Gorria, P. (2004a). *Polarization applied to 3D reconstruction of highly reflective metallic objects.* In OSAV.

Morel, O., Stolz, C., & Gorria, P. (2004b). Application of polarimetric imaging to 3D inspection of highly reflective metallic surface. In *SPIE Optics East - Two- and Three-Dimensionale Vision Systems for Inspection, Control, and Metrology II, Vol. 5606* (pp. 82-89).

Morel, O., Meriaudeau, F., Stolz, C., & Gorria, P. (2005). Polarization imaging applied to 3D reconstruction of specular metallic surfaces. In *SPIE Electronic Imaging* (*Vol. 5679*, pp. 178–186). Machine Vision Applications in Industrial Inspection XIII, Electronic Imaging. doi:10.1117/12.586815

Morel, O., Seulin, R., & Fofi, D. (2008). Measurement of three-dimensional mirror parameters by polarization imaging applied to catadioptric camera calibration. *Journal of Electronic Imaging, 17*(3). doi:10.1117/1.2958290

Morel, O., Stolz, C., & Gorria, P. (2006). Polarization imaging for 3D inspection of highly reflective metallic objects. *Optics and Spectroscopy*, *101*(1), 15–21. doi:10.1134/S0030400X06070034

Morel, O., Stolz, C., Meriaudeau, F., & Gorria, P. (2005). Three-dimensional inspection of highly-reflective metallic objects by polarization imaging. *Electronic Imaging Newsletter*, *15*(2), 4.

Morel, O., Stolz, C., Meriaudeau, F., & Gorria, P. (2006). Active lighting applied to 3D reconstruction of specular metallic surfaces by polarization imaging. *Applied Optics*, *45*(17), 4062–4068. doi:10.1364/AO.45.004062

Morgan, M. J., & Castet, E. (1997). The aperture problem in stereopsis. *Vision Research*, *37*, 2737–2744.

Morgan, M. J., & Fahle, M. (2000). Motion-stereo mechanisms sensitive to interocular phase. *Vision Research*, *40*, 1667–1675. doi:10.1016/S0042-6989(00)00016-X

Morgan, S. P., Khong, M. P., & Somekh, M. G. (1997). Effects of polarization state and scatterer concentration on optical imaging through scattering media. *Applied Optics*, *36*, 1560–1565. doi:10.1364/AO.36.001560

Morillas, C., Pelayo, F., Cobos, J. P., Prieto, A., & Romero, S. (2008). Bio-inspired image processing for vision aids. *BIOSIGNALS 2008 - Proceedings of the 1st International Conference on Bio-Inspired Systems and Signal Processing, 2,* 63-69.

Morillas, C., Romero, S., Martínez, A., Pelayo, F., & Fernandez, E. (2005). A computational tool to test neuromorphic encoding schemes for visual neuroprosthesis. *8th International Work-Conference on Artificial Neural Networks (IWANN 2005),* Barcelona, (pp. 510-517).

Morillas, C. A., Romero, S. F., Martinez, A., Pelayo, F. J., Ros, E., & Fernandez, E. (2007). A design framework to model retinas. *Bio Systems*, *87*(2-3), 156–163. doi:10.1016/j.biosystems.2006.09.009

Morillas, C., Romero, S., Martinez, A., Pelayo, F., Reyneri, L., Bongard, M., & Fernandez, E. (2007). A neuroengineering suite of computational tools for visual prostheses. *Neurocomputing*, *70*(16-18), 2817–2827. doi:10.1016/j.neucom.2006.04.017

Mortara, A., Vittoz, E. A., & Venier, P. (1995). A communication scheme for analog VLSI perceptive systems. *IEEE Journal of Solid-state Circuits*, *30*(6), 660–669. doi:10.1109/4.387069

Mota, C., Dorr, M., Stuke, I., & Barth, E. (2004). Categorization of transparent motion patterns using the projective plane. *Journal of Computer and Information Science*, *5*, 129–140.

Motter, B. (1994). Neural correlates of attentive selection for color or luminance in extrastriate area V4. *The Journal of Neuroscience*, *14*(4), 2178–2189.

Mountcastle, V. (1978). The unit model and the distributed system. In Edelman, G. M., & Mountcastle, V. B. (Eds.), *The mindful brain*. MIT Press.

Mozer, M. (1991). *The perception of multiple objects*. MIT Press.

Mozer, M. C., & Sitton, M. (1998). Computational modeling of spatial attention. In Pashler, H. (Ed.), *Attention* (pp. 341–393). London, UK: UCL Press.

MSRA Salient Object Database. (2007). Retrieved September 21, 2011, from http://research.microsoft.com / en-us/um/people/jiansun/SalientObject/salient object.htm

Mueller, T. J. (1990). A physiological model of binocular rivalry. *Visual Neuroscience*, *4*, 63–73. doi:10.1017/S0952523800002777

Mulligan, J. (1992). Motion transparency is restricted to two planes. *Investigative Ophthalmology & Visual Science*, *33*(Supplement), 1049.

Murphy, T., & Finkel, L. (2007). Shape representation by a network of V4-like cells. *Neural Networks*, *20*, 851–867. doi:10.1016/j.neunet.2007.06.004

Murray, J. D. (2003a). *Mathematical biology: Spatial models and biomedical applications. Interdisciplinary applied mathematics*. Springer Verlag.

Murray, J. D. (2003b). *Mathematical biology: An introduction* (pp. 1–551). Berlin, Germany: Springer Verlag.

Mutch, J., & Lowe, D. (2006). Multiclass object recognition with sparse, localized features. *IEEE Conference on Computer Vision and Pattern Recognition*, (pp. 11-18).

Nakayama, K., & Silverman, G. (1991). Serial and parallel processing of visual feature conjunctions. *Nature, 320*, 264–265. doi:10.1038/320264a0

Navalpakkam, V., & Itti, L. (2006). An integrated model of top-down and bottom-up attention for optimal object detection. *Proceedings IEEE Conference on Computer Vision and Pattern Recognition (CVPR)*, (pp. 2049-2056).

Navalpakkam, V, & Itti, Laurent. (2006). Top-down attention selection is fine grained. *Journal of Vision (Charlottesville, Va.), 6*(11), 4. doi:10.1167/6.11.4

Navalpakkam, V., Arbib, M., & Itti, L. (2005). Attention and scene understanding. In Itti, L., Rees, G., & Tsotsos, J. K. (Eds.), *Neurobiology of attention* (pp. 197–203). Academic Press. doi:10.1016/B978-012375731-9/50037-9

Navalpakkam, V., & Itti, L. (2005). Modeling the influence of task on attention. *Vision Research, 45*(2), 205–231. doi:10.1016/j.visres.2004.07.042

Navalpakkam, V., & Itti, L. (2005). Modeling the influence of task on attention. *Vision Research, 45*(2), 205–231. doi:10.1016/j.visres.2004.07.042

Nayar, S. K., Fang, X. S., & Boult, T. (1997). Separation of reflection components using color and polarization. *International Journal of Computer Vision, 21*, 163–186. doi:10.1023/A:1007937815113

Nestor, P., Klein, K., Pomplun, M., Mizkikiewicz, M., & McCarley, R. (2009). Gaze cueing of attention in schizophrenia: Individual differences in neuropsychological functioning and symptoms. *Journal of Clinical and Experimental Neuropsychology, 32*(3), 281–288. doi:10.1080/13803390902984472

Neumann, H., & Sepp, W. (1999). Recurrent V1-V2 interaction in early visual boundary processing. *Biological Cybernetics, 81*, 425–444. doi:10.1007/s004220050573

Neumann, O. (1987). Beyond capacity: A functional view of attention. Perspectives on perception and action. In Heuer, H., & Sanders, A. F. (Eds.), *Perspectives on perception and action* (pp. 361–394). Hillsdale, NJ: Lawrence Erlbaum Associates.

Niblack, W., & Wolf, E. (1964). Polarization modulation and demodulation of light. *Applied Optics, 3*, 277–277. doi:10.1364/AO.3.000277

Niku, S. B. (2001). *Introduction to robotics: Analysis, systems, applications*. Prentice Hall.

Nilsson, D.-E., & Warrant, E. J. (1999). Visual discrimination: Seeing the third quality of light. *Current Opinions in Biology, 9R535-R537*, 9, 535-537.

Nishimoto, S., Ishida, T., & Ohzawa, I. (2006). Receptive field properties of neurons in the early visual cortex revealed by local spectral reverse correlation. *The Journal of Neuroscience, 26*(12), 3269–3280.

Noë, A. (2004). *Action in perception*. Cambridge, MA: MIT Press.

Normann, R. A., & Branner, A. (1999). A multichannel, neural interface for the peripheral nervous system. *Proceedings of the 1999 IEEE International Conference on Systems, Man and Cybernetics, 4*, (pp. 370-375).

Normann, R. A., Greger, B. A., House, P., Romero, S. F., Pelayo, F., & Fernandez, E. (2009). Toward the development of a cortically based visual neuroprosthesis. *Journal of Neural Engineering, 6*(3), 035001. doi:10.1088/1741-2560/6/3/035001

Normann, R. A., Maynard, E., Guillory, K. S., & Warren, D. J. (1996, May). Cortical implants for the blind. *IEEE Spectrum*, 54–59. doi:10.1109/6.490057

Nothdurft, H.-C., Gallant, J. L., & van Essen, D. C. (1999). Response modulation by texture surround in primate area V1: Correlates of popout under anasthesia. *Visual Neuroscience, 16*, 15–34. doi:10.1017/S0952523899156189

Novales, F. I., & Hawryshyn, C. W. (1997). Is the use of underwater polarized light by fishes restricted to crepuscular time periods? *Vision Research, 37*, 975–989. doi:10.1016/S0042-6989(96)00236-2

Nover, H., Anderson, C. H., & DeAngelis, G. (2005). A logarithmic, scale-invariant representation of speed in macaque middle temporal area accounts for speed discrimination performance. *The Journal of Neuroscience, 25*, 10049–10060.

Nyquist, H. (2002). Certain topics in telegraph transmission theory. *Proceedings of the IEEE, 90*, 280–305.

Nystrom, M., & Holmqvist, K. (2008). Semantic override of low-level features in image viewing both initially and overall. *Journal of Eye Movement, 2*(2), 1–11.

O'Connor, D., Fukui, M., Pinsk, M., & Kastner, S. (2002). Attention modulates responses in the human lateral geniculate nucleus. *Nature Neuroscience*, *5*(11), 1203–1209. doi:10.1038/nn957

O'Regan, K., & Noë, A. (2001). A sensorimotor account of vision anvisual consciousness. *The Behavioral and Brain Sciences*, *24*(5), 883–917.

Ogle, K. N. (1940). Induced size effect with the eyes in asymmetric convergence. *Archives of Ophthalmology*, *23*, 1023–1028. doi:10.1001/archopht.1940.00860131147008

Ohzawa, I. (1998). Mechanisms of stereoscopic vision: the disparity energy model. *Current Opinion in Biology*, *8*, 509–515.

Ohzawa, I., DeAngelis, G. C., & Freeman, R. D. (1990). Stereoscopic depth discrimination in the visual cortex: Neurons ideally suited as disparity detectors. *Science*, *249*, 1037–1041.

Ohzawa, I., DeAngelis, G. C., & Freeman, R. D. (1997). Encoding of binocular disparity by complex cells in the cat's visual cortex. *Journal of Neurophysiology*, *77*, 2879–2909.

Okada, M., Nishina, S., & Kawato, M. (2003). The neural computation of the aperture problem: An iterative process. *Neurology Report*, *14*(4), 1767–1771.

Olshausen, B. A., & Field, D. J. (1997). Sparse coding with an overcomplete basis set: A strategy employed by V1? *Vision Research*, *37*, 3311–3325. doi:10.1016/S0042-6989(97)00169-7

Olshausen, B., Anderson, C., & Van Essen, D. (1993). A neurobiological model of visual attention and invariant pattern recognition based on dynamic routing of information. *The Journal of Neuroscience*, *13*(11), 4700–4719.

Olushen, B. A., & Field, D. J. (1996). Emergence of simple –cell receptive field properties by learning a sparse code for natural images. *Nature*, *381*, 607–609. doi:10.1038/381607a0

Ooi, T. L., & He, Z. J. (1999). Binocular rivalry and visual awareness. *Perception*, *28*, 551–574. doi:10.1068/p2923

Orabona, F., Metta, G., & Sandini, G. (2008). A proto-object based visual attention model. In Paletta, L. (Ed.), *Attention in cognitive systems. Theories and systems from an interdisciplinary viewpoint (WAPCV)* (pp. 198–215). Berlin, Germany: Springer. doi:10.1007/978-3-540-77343-6_13

Orban, G. A. (2008). Higher order visual processing in macaque extrastriate cortex. *Physiological Reviews*, *88*, 59–89. doi:10.1152/physrev.00008.2007

Orban, G. A., Kennedy, H., & Bullier, J. (1986). Velocity sensitivity and direction selectivity of neurons in areas Vl and V2 of the monkey: Influence of eccentricity. *Journal of Neurophysiology*, *56*(2), 462–480.

Orban, G., Kato, H., & Bishop, P. (1979a). Dimensions and properties of end-zone inhibitory areas of hypercomplex cells in cat striate cortex. *Journal of Neurophysiology*, *42*, 833–849.

Orban, G., Kato, H., & Bishop, P. (1979b). End-zone region in receptive fields of hypercomplex and other striate neurons in the cat. *Journal of Neurophysiology*, *42*, 818–832.

Osborne, L. C., Bialek, W., & Lisberger, S. G. (2004). Time course of information about motion direction in visual area MT of macaque monkeys. *The Journal of Neuroscience*, *24*(13), 3210–3222. doi:10.1523/JNEUROSCI.5305-03.2004

Ouerhani, N., Hügli, H., Burgi, P.-Y., & Rüdi, P.-F. (2002). A real time implementation of the saliency-based model of visual attention on a SIMD architecture. *Proceedings of the 24th DAGM Symposium on Pattern Recognition, Lecture Notes in Computer Science, 2449*, (pp. 282-289). Springer Verlag.

Ouerhani, N. (2003). *Visual attention: From bio-inspired modeling to real-time implementation*. Université de Neuchâtel.

Ouerhani, N., & Hugli, H. (2003). *A model of dynamic visual attention for object tracking in natural image sequences* (pp. 702–709). Lecture Notes in Computer ScienceSpringer. doi:10.1007/3-540-44868-3_89

Oyekoya, O., & Stentiford, F. W. M. (2004). Exploring human eye behaviour using a model of visual attention. *International Conference on Pattern Recognition,* Vol. 4, (pp. 945-948).

Pack, C. C., & Born, R. T. (2001). Temporal dynamics of a neural solution to the aperture problem in visual area MT of macaque brain. *Nature, 409,* 1040–1042. doi:10.1038/35059085

Pack, C. C., Born, R. T., & Livingstone, M. S. (2003). Two-dimensional substructure of stereo and motion interactions in macaque visual cortex. *Neuron, 37,* 525–535. doi:10.1016/S0896-6273(02)01187-X

Paisley, J., & Carin, L. (2009). Nonparametric factor analysis with beta process priors. In *Proceedings of the International Conference on Machine Learning.*

Palmer, D. (1999). *Vision science: Photons to phenomenology.* Cambridge, MA: MIT Press.

Palmer, S. E. (1999). *Vision science.* London, UK: MIT Press.

Pannasch, S., Helmert, J. R., Roth, K., Herbold, A.-K., & Walter, H. (2008). Visual fixation durations and saccade amplitudes: Shifting relationship in a variety of conditions. *Journal of Eye Movement Research, 2*(2), 1–19.

Parkhurst, D., Law, K., & Niebur, E. (2002). Modeling the role of salience in the allocation of overt visual attention. *Vision Research, 42,* 107–123. doi:10.1016/S0042-6989(01)00250-4

Park, S. J., An, K. H., & Lee, M. (2002). Saliency map model with adaptive masking based on independent component analysis. [Elsevier.]. *Neurocomputing, 49*(1), 417–422. doi:10.1016/S0925-2312(02)00637-9

Pashler, H. E. (1998). *The psychology of attention.* Cambridge, MA: MIT Press.

Pasupathy, A., & Connor, C. (1999). Responses to contour features in macaque area V4. *Journal of Neurophysiology, 82*(5), 2490–2502.

Pasupathy, A., & Connor, C. (2001). Shape representation in area V4: Position-specific tuning for boundary conformation. *Journal of Neurophysiology, 86*(5), 2505–2519.

Pasupathy, A., & Connor, C. (2002). Population coding of shape in area V4. *Nature Neuroscience, 5*(12), 1332–1338. doi:10.1038/nn972

Patterson, D. A., & Hennessy, J. L. (2005). *Computer organization and design: The hardware/software interface* (3rd ed.). Amsterdam, The Netherlands: Morgan Kaufmann.

Pavlidis, T. (1972). Segmentation of pictures and maps through functional approximation. *Computer Graphics and Image Processing, 1,* 360–372. doi:10.1016/0146-664X(72)90021-4

Peissig, J., & Tarr, M. (2007). Visual object recognition: Do we know more now than we did 20 years ago? *Annual Review of Psychology, 58,* 15–96. doi:10.1146/annurev.psych.58.102904.190114

Pelayo, F. J., Romero, S., Morillas, C. A., Martinez, A., Ros, E., & Fernandez, E. (2004). Translating image sequences into spike patterns for cortical neuro-stimulation. *Neurocomputing, 58-60,* 885–892. doi:10.1016/j.neucom.2004.01.142

Pelayo, F. J., Ros, E., Arreguit, X., & Prieto, A. (1997). VLSI implementation of a neural model using spikes. *Analog Integrated Circuits and Signal Processing, 13*(1-2), 111–121. doi:10.1023/A:1008240229616

Peng, Q., & Shi, B. E. (2010). The changing disparity energy model. *Vision Research, 50,* 181–192. doi:10.1016/j.visres.2009.11.012

Perreira Da Silva, M., Courboulay, V., Prigent, A., & Estraillier, P. (2010). Evaluation of preys / predators systems for visual attention simulation. In P. Richard & J. Braz (Eds.), *VISAPP 2010 - International Conference on Computer Vision Theory and Applications* (Vol. 2, pp. 275-282). Angers, France: INSTICC.

Perrone, J. A. (2004). A visual motion sensor based on the properties of V1 and MT neurons. *Vision Research, 44,* 1733–1755.

Persoon, E., & Fu, K. (1974). Shape discrimination using Fourier descriptors. *Second International Joint Conference on Pattern Recognition*, (pp. 126-130).

Peters, R. J., Iyer, A., Itti, L., & Koch, C. (2005). Components of bottom-up gaze allocation in natural images. *Vision Research*, *45*(8), 2397–2416. doi:10.1016/j.visres.2005.03.019

Phillips, J. B., & Waldvogel, J. A. (1988). Celestial polarized light patterns as a calibration reference for sun compass of homing pigeons. *Journal of Theoretical Biology*, *131*, 55–67. doi:10.1016/S0022-5193(88)80120-6

Pinto, N., Cox, D., & Dicarlo, J. (2008). Why is real-world visual object recognition hard? *PLoS Computational Biology*, *4*(1), 151–156. doi:10.1371/journal.pcbi.0040027

Pizlo, Z. (2001). Perception viewed as an inverse problem. *Vision Research*, *41*, 3145–3161. doi:10.1016/S0042-6989(01)00173-0

Poggio, G. F. (1995). Mechanism of stereopsis in monkey visual cortex. *Cerebral Cortex*, *5*, 193–204.

Poggio, T., Torre, V., & Koch, C. (1985). Computational vision and regularization theory. *Nature*, *317*, 314–319. doi:10.1038/317314a0

Pollard, S. B., & Frisby, J. P. (1990). Transparency and the uniqueness constraint in human and computer stereo vision. *Nature*, *347*, 553–556.

Polpitiya, A. D., & Ghosh, B. K. (2002, May). *Modelling and control of eye-movement with muscolotendon dynamics*. Paper presented at the meeting of the American Control Conference, Anchorage, AK.

Pomozi, I., Horváth, G., & Wehner, R. (2001). How the clear-sky angle of polarization pattern continues underneath clouds: Full-sky measurements and implications for animal orientation. *The Journal of Experimental Biology*, *204*, 2933–2942.

Pomplun, M. (2006). Saccadic selectivity in complex visual search display. *Vision Research*, *46*, 1886–1900. doi:10.1016/j.visres.2005.12.003

Pomplun, M., Carbone, E., Koesling, H., Sichelschmidt, L., & Ritter, H. (2006). Computational models of visual tagging. In Rickheit, G., & Wachsmuth, I. (Eds.), *Situated communication* (pp. 213–246). Berlin, Germany: Mouton de Gruyter.

Pomplun, M., Ritter, H., & Velichkovsky, B. M. (1996). Disambiguating complex visual information: Towards communication of personal views of a scene. *Perception*, *25*, 931–948. doi:10.1068/p250931

Ponce, C. R., Lomber, S. G., & Born, R. T. (2008). Integrating motion and depth via parallel pathways. *Nature Reviews. Neuroscience*, *11*, 216–223. doi:10.1038/nn2039

Portfors-Yeomans, C. V., & Regan, D. (1996). Cyclopean discrimination thresholds for the direction and speed of motion in depth. *Vision Research*, *36*, 3265–3279. doi:10.1016/0042-6989(96)00065-X

Posner, M. I. (1980). Orienting of attention. *The Quarterly Journal of Experimental Psychology*, *32*, 3–25. doi:10.1080/00335558008248231

Posner, M. I. (1987). Cognitive neuropsychology and the problem of selective attention. *Electroencephalography and Clinical Neurophysiology. Supplement*, *39*, 313–316.

Posner, M. I., & Petersen, S. E. (1990). The attention system of the human brain. *Annual Review of Neuroscience*, *13*, 25–42. doi:10.1146/annurev.ne.13.030190.000325

Posner, M. I., Rafal, R. D., Choate, L. S., & Vaughan, J. (1985). Inhibition of return: Neural basis and function. *Cognitive Neuropsychology*, *2*(3), 211–228. doi:10.1080/02643298508252866

Pouget, A., Dayan, P., & Zemel, R. (2003). Inference and computation with population codes. *Annual Review of Neuroscience*, *26*, 381–410. doi:10.1146/annurev.neuro.26.041002.131112

Pratt, W. K. (1969). *Laser communication systems*. New York, NY: Wiley.

Prazdny, K. (1985). Detection of binocular disparities. *Biological Cybernetics*, *52*, 93–99.

Priebe, J. N., Lisberger, S. G., & Movshon, J. A. (2006). Tuning for spatiotemporal frequency and speed in directionally selective neurons of macaque striate cortex. *The Journal of Neuroscience*, *26*(11), 2941–2950.

Prince, S. J. D., Cumming, B. G., & Parker, A. J. (2002). Range and mechanism of encoding of horizontal disparity in macaque V1. *Journal of Neurophysiology*, *87*, 209–221.

Pun, S., Chan, C., & Chen, L. (2005). A novel optical frequency shift keying transmitter based on polarization modulation. In *Optical Fiber Communication Conference. Technical Digest. OFC/NFOEC,* Vol. 3.

Qian, N., & Sejnowski, T. J. (1989). Learning to solve random-dot stereograms of dense and transparent surfaces with recurrent backpropagation. In *Proceedings of the 1988 Connectionist Models Summer School,* Morgan Kaufmann.

Qian, N. (1994). Computing stereo disparity and motion with known binocular cell properties. *Neural Computation, 6*(3), 390–404.

Qian, N., & Andersen, R. A. (1997). A physiological model for motion–stereo integration and a unified explanation of Pulfrich-like phenomena. *Vision Research, 37*(12), 1683–1698.

Qian, N., Andersen, R. A., & Adelson, E. (1994). Transparent motion perception as detection of unbalanced motion signals, III- Modeling. *The Journal of Neuroscience*, *14*, 7381–7392.

Qian, N., & Mikaelian, S. (2000). Relationship between phase and energy methods for disparity computation. *Neural Computation, 12*, 303–316.

Quattoni, A., & Torralba, A. B. (2009). Recognising indoor scenes. In *Proceedings of the 2009 IEEE Computer Society Conference on Computer Vision and Pattern Recognition* (pp. 413-420). Miami, FL: IEEE.

Raab, M., & Johnson, J. G. (2007). Expertise-based differences in search and option- generation strategies. *Journal of Experimental Psychology. Applied, 13*, 158–170. doi:10.1037/1076-898X.13.3.158

Raftery, A. E. (1995). Baysian model selection in social research. *Sociological Methodology, 25*, 111–163. doi:10.2307/271063

Raina, R., Battle, A., Lee, H., Packer, B., & Ng, A. Y. (2007). Self-taught learning: Transfer learning from unlabeled data. In *Proceedings of the International Conference on Machine Learning.*

Rambold, H. A., & Miles, F. (2008). A human vergence eye movements to oblique disparity stimuli: Evidence for an anisotropy favoring horizontal disparities. *Vision Research, 48*, 2006–2019.

Ramirez-Manzanares, A., Rivera, M., Kornprobst, P., & Lauze, F. (2006). *Multi-valued motion fields estimation for transparent sequences with a variational approach.* Rapport De Recherche Inria, number RR-5920.

Ramon y Cajal, S. (1888). Sobre las fibras nerviosas de la capa molecular del cerebelo. *Rev Trim Histol Norm Patol, 1*, 33–49.

Ramon y Cajal, S. (1894). The Croonian lecture: La fine structure des centres nerveux. *Royal Society of London Proceedings Series I, 55*, 444–468. doi:10.1098/rspl.1894.0063

Ramon y Cajal, S. (1904). Variaciones morfologicas, normales y patologicas del reticulo neurofibrilar. *Trab Lab Investig Biol Madrid, 3*, 9–15.

Rankin, A., & Matthies, L. (2008). Daytime mud detection for unmanned ground vehicle autonomous navigation. In *Proceedings of the 26th Army Science Conference.*

Ranzato, M., Poultney, C., Chopra, S., & Lecun, Y. (2006). Efficient learning of sparse representations with an energy-based model. In *Proceedings of the Neural Information Processing Systems.*

Rao, R. P. N., Zelinsky, G. J., Hayhoe, M. M., & Ballard, D. H. (2002). Eye movements in iconic visual search. *Vision Research, 42*, 1447–1463. doi:10.1016/S0042-6989(02)00040-8

Rao, R., & Ballard, D. (1997). Dynamic model of visual recognition predicts neural response properties in the visual cortex. *Neural Computation, 9*(4), 721–763. doi:10.1162/neco.1997.9.4.721

Rao, R., & Ballard, D. (1999). Predictive coding in the visual cortex: a functional interpretation of some extra-classical receptive-field effects. *Nature Neuroscience, 2*(1), 79–87. doi:10.1038/4580

Rapantzikos, K., & Tsapatsoulis, N. (2003). *On the implementation of visual attention architectures*. Tales of the Disappearing Computer Conference, Santorini.

Rapantzikos, K., Avrithis, Y., & Kollias, S. (2007). Spatio-temporal saliency for event detection and representation in the 3D wavelet domain: Potential in human action recognition. In N. Sebe & M. Worring (Eds.), *Proceedings of the 6th ACM International Conference on Image and Video Retrieval, CIVR 2007* (pp. 294-301). New York, USA: ACM.

Rashbass, C., & Westheimer, G. (1961). Disjunctive eye movements. *The Journal of Physiology*, *159*, 339–360.

Rauber, H.-J., & Treue, S. (1999). Revisiting motion repulsion: Evidence for a general phenomenon? *Vision Research*, *39*, 3187–3196.

Raudies, F., & Neumann, H. (2010). A model of neural mechanisms in monocular transparent motion perception. *The Journal of Physiology*, *104*, 71–83.

Read, J. C. A. (2002). A Bayesian approach to the stereo correspondence problem. *Neural Computation*, *14*, 1371–1392.

Read, J. C. A. (2002b). A Bayesian model of stereopsis depth and motion direction discrimination. *Biological Cybernetics*, *86*(2), 117–136. doi:10.1007/s004220100280

Read, J. C. A., & Cumming, B. G. (2004). Understanding the cortical specialization for horizontal disparity. *Neural Computation*, *16*(10), 1983–2020.

Read, J. C. A., & Cumming, B. G. (2005a). Effect of interocular delay on disparity-selective V1 neurons: Relationship to stereoacuity and the Pulfrich effect. *Journal of Neurophysics*, *94*, 1541–1553. doi:10.1152/jn.01177.2004

Read, J. C. A., & Cumming, B. G. (2006). Does depth perception require vertical disparity detectors? *Journal of Vision (Charlottesville, Va.)*, *6*(12), 1323–1355.

Read, J. C. A., Parker, A. J., & Cumming, B. G. (2002). A simple model accounts for the response of disparity-tuned V1 neurons to anti-correlated images. *Visual Neuroscience*, *19*, 735–753.

Read, J. C. A., Phillipson, G. P., & Glennerster, A. (2009). Latitude and longitude vertical disparities. *Journal of Vision (Charlottesville, Va.)*, *9*(13), 1–37.

Reeves, A., Lynch, D., Tran, M., & Grayem, R. (2010). Multiple planes in stereo-transparency. *Vision Research*, *10*(7), 375.

Regan, D., & Beverley, K. I. (1973). Some dynamic features of depth perception. *Vision Research*, *13*, 2369–2379. doi:10.1016/0042-6989(73)90236-8

Regan, D., Beverley, K. I., Cynader, M., & Lennie, P. (1979). Stereoscopic subsystems for position in depth and for motion in depth. *Proceedings of the Royal Society of London. Series B, Biological Sciences*, *42*, 485–501. doi:10.1098/rspb.1979.0042

Regan, D., & Gray, R. (2009). Binocular processing of motion: Some unresolved problems. *Spatial Vision*, *22*, 1–43. doi:10.1163/156856809786618501

Rensink, R. (1989). *A new proof of the NP-Completeness of visual match. Tech. Rep. TR 89-22*. Dept. of Computer Science, University of British Columbia.

Rensink, R. (2000). The dynamic representation of scenes. *Visual Cognition*, *7*(1-3), 17–42. doi:10.1080/135062800394667

Rensink, R. A. (2000). The dynamic representation of scenes. *Visual Cognition*, *7*, 17–42. doi:10.1080/135062800394667

Rensink, R. A., Regan, J. K. O., & Clark, J. J. (1997). To see or not to see: The need for attention to perceive changes in scenes. *Psychological Science*, *8*(5), 1–6. doi:10.1111/j.1467-9280.1997.tb00427.x

Reynolds, J. H., Chelazzi, L., & Desimone, R. (1999). Competitive mechanisms subserve attention in macaque areas V2 and V4. *The Journal of Neuroscience*, *19*(5), 1736–1753.

Richards, W., & Hoffman, D. D. (1984). *Codon constraints on closed 2D shapes*. MIT, AI lab.

Richards, W., Dawson, B., & Whittingham, D. (1988). *Encoding contour shape by curvature extrema*. Paper presented at the Natural Computations.

Riesenhuber, M., & Poggio, T. (1999). Hierarchical models of object recognition in cortex. *Nature Neuroscience, 2*, 1019–1025. doi:10.1038/14819

Riesenhuber, M., & Poggio, T. (1999a). Are cortical models really bound by the "binding problem"? *Neuron, 24*(1), 87–93. doi:10.1016/S0896-6273(00)80824-7

Riesenhuber, M., & Poggio, T. (2000). Models of object recognition. *Nature Neuroscience, 3*(Suppl), 1199–1204. doi:10.1038/81479

Riesenhuber, M., & Poggio, T. (2002). Neural mechanisms of object recognition. *Current Opinion in Neurobiology, 12*(2), 162–168. doi:10.1016/S0959-4388(02)00304-5

Ringach, D. (2002). Spatial structure and symmetry of simple-cell receptive fields in macaque primary visual cortex. *Journal of Neurophysiology, 88*, 455–463.

Rissanen, J. (1978). Modeling by shortest data description. *Automatica, 14*, 465–471. doi:10.1016/0005-1098(78)90005-5

Rizzo, J. F. III, Wyatt, J., Loewenstein, J., Kelly, S., & Shire, D. (2003). Methods and perceptual thresholds for short-term electrical stimulation of human retina with microelectrode arrays. *Investigative Ophthalmology & Visual Science, 44*(12), 5355–5361. doi:10.1167/iovs.02-0819

Rodman, H. R., & Albright, T. D. (1987). Coding of visual stimulus velocity in area MT of the macaque. *Vision Research, 27*(12), 2035–2048.

Rodríguez-Sánchez, A. (2010). *Intermediate visual representations for attentive recognition systems.* PhD, York University. Retrieved from http://www.cse.yorku.ca/tech reports/2010/?abstract=CSE-2010-06

Rodríguez-Sánchez, A., & Tsotsos, J. (2011). The importance of intermediate representations for the modeling of 2D shape detection: Endstopping and curvature tuned computations. *IEEE Conference on Computer Vision and Pattern Recognition (CVPR 2011)* (pp. 4321-4326).

Roe, A. W., Pallaqb, S. L., Kwon, Y. H., & Sur, M. (1992). Visual projections routed to the auditory pathway in ferrets: Receptive fields of visual neurons in primary auditory cortex. *The Journal of Neuroscience, 12*(g), 3651-3664

Rokers, B., Cormack, L. K., & Huk, A. C. (2008). Strong percepts of motion through depth without strong percepts of position in depth. *Journal of Vision (Charlottesville, Va.), 8*, 1–10. doi:10.1167/8.4.6

Rokers, B., Cormack, L. K., & Huk, A. C. (2009). Disparity- and velocity-based signals for three-dimensional motion perception in human MT+. *Nature Reviews. Neuroscience, 12*, 1050–1055. doi:10.1038/nn.2343

Rolls, E. T., & Deco, G. (2002). *Computational neuroscience of vision.* Oxford, UK: Oxford University Press.

Rolls, E. T., & Stringer, S. M. (2006). Invariant visual object recognition: a model, with lighting invariance. *The Journal of Physiology, 100*(1-3), 43–62. doi:doi:10.1016/j.jphysparis.2006.09.004

Rolls, E. T., & Tovee, M. J. (1995). The responses of single neurons in the temporal visual cortical areas of the macaque when more than one stimulus is present in the receptive field. *Experimental Brain Research, 103*(3), 409–420. doi:10.1007/BF00241500

Rolls, E., & Deco, G. (2002). *Computational neuroscience of vision.* Oxford.

Romero, S., Morillas, C., Cobos, J. P., Pelayo, F., Prieto, A., & Fernández, E. (2009). Computer aids for visual neuroprosthetic devices. *Communications in Computer and Information Science, 25*(2), 96–108. doi:10.1007/978-3-540-92219-3_7

Rosenblatt, F. (1962). *Principles of neurodynamics: Perceptrons and the theory of brain mechanisms.* Spartan Books.

Rossel, S. (1989). Polarization sensitivity in compound eyes. In Stavenga, D. G., & Hardie, R. C. (Eds.), *Facets of vision* (pp. 298–316). Berlin, Germany: Springer Verlag. doi:10.1007/978-3-642-74082-4_15

Rothenstein, A., & Tsotsos, J. K. (2011). Computational models of visual attention. *Scholarpedia, 6*(1), 6201. Retrieved March 15, 2012, from http://www.scholarpedia.org/article/Computational_models_of_visual_attention

Rothenstein, A. L., Zaharescu, A., & Tsotsos, J. K. (2005). In Paletta, L., Tsotsos, J. K., Rome, E., & Humphreys, G. (Eds.), *TarzaNN: A general purpose neural network simulator for visual attention modeling* (*Vol. 3368*, pp. 159–167). Lecture Notes in Computer ScienceSpringer Verlag. doi:10.1007/978-3-540-30572-9_12

Rothenstein, A., & Tsotsos, J. (2006). Attention links sensing to recognition. *Image & Vision Computing Journal. Special Issue on Cognitive Vision Systems, 26*, 114–126.

Rothenstein, A., & Tsotsos, J. K. (2008). Attention links sensing with perception. *Image & Vision Computing Journal. Special Issue on Cognitive Vision Systems, 26*(1), 114–126.

Rötting, M. (2001). *Parametersystematik der Augen- und Blickbewegungen. Für Arbeitswis-senschaftliche Untersuchungen*. Aachen, Germany: Shaker Verlag.

Rousselet, G., Fabre-Thorpe, M., & Thorpe, S. J. (2002). Parallel processing in high level categorization of natural images. *Nature Neuroscience, 5*, 629–630.

Rowe, M. P., Pugh, E. N., Tyo, J. S., & Engheta, N. (1995). Polarization-difference imaging: A biologically inspired technique for observation through scattering media. *Optics Letters, 20*, 608–610. doi:10.1364/OL.20.000608

Royden, C. S. (1997). Mathematical analysis of motion-opponent mechanisms used in the determination of heading and depth. *Journal of the Optical Society of America. A, Optics, Image Science, and Vision, 14*(9), 2128–2143.

Rumelhart, D., & Mcclelland, J. (1986). *Parallel distributed processing: Explorations in the microstructure of cognition: Foundations*. MIT Press.

Rushton, S. K., & Duke, P. A. (2007). The use of direction and distance information in the perception of approach trajectory. *Vision Research, 47*, 899–912. doi:10.1016/j.visres.2006.11.019

Rushton, S. K., & Warren, P. A. (2005). Moving observers, relative retinal motion, and the detection of object movement. *Current Biology, 15*(14), R542. doi:10.1016/j.cub.2005.07.020

Sabatini, S. P., Gastaldi, G., Solari, F., Pauwels, K., Van Hulle, M. M., & Diaz, J. (2010). A compact harmonic code for early vision based on anisotropic frequency channels. *Computer Vision and Image Understanding, 114*, 681–699.

Sabatini, S. P., & Solari, F. (2004). Emergence of motion-in-depth selectivity in the visual cortex through linear combination of binocular energy complex cells with different ocular dominance. *Neurocomputing, 58–60*, 865–872.

Sadato, N., Pascual-Leone, A., & Grafman, J. (1996). Activation of the primary visual cortex by Braille reading in blind subjects. *Nature, 380*, 526–528. doi:10.1038/380526a0

Saito, M., Sato, Y., Ikeuchi, K., & Kashiwagi, H. (1999b). Measurement of surface orientations of transparent objects using polarization in highlight. In *Proceedings of IEEE Conference on Computer Vision and Pattern Recognition*.

Saito, M., Sato, Y., Ikeuchi, K., & Kashiwagi, H. (1999a). Measurement of surface orientations of transparent objects using polarization in highlight. *Journal of the Optical Society of America, 16*(9), 2286–2293. doi:10.1364/JOSAA.16.002286

Salvucci, D., & Goldberg, J. (2000). Identifying fixations and saccades in eye tracking protocols. *Proceedings of the Symposium on Eye Tracking Research and Applications*, (pp. 71–78).

Sanada, T. M., & Ohzawa, I. (2006). Encoding of three-dimensional surface slant in cat visual areas 17 and 18. *Journal of Neurophysiology, 95*, 2768–2786.

Sandon, P. (1989). Simulating visual attention. *Journal of Cognitive Neuroscience, 2*(3), 213–231. doi:10.1162/jocn.1990.2.3.213

Sanger, T. D. (1988). Stereo disparity computation using Gabor filters. *Biological Cybernetics, 59*, 405–418.

Sanguineti, V., Giugliano, M., Grattarola, M., & Morasso, P. (2001). Neuro-engineering: From neural interfaces to biological computers. In Riva, R., & Davide, F. (Eds.), *Communications through virtual technology: Identity community and technology in the internet age* (pp. 233–246). Amsterdam, The Netherlands: IOS Press.

Santini, F., & Rucci, M. (2007). Active estimation of distance in a robotic system that replicates human eye movement. *Robotics and Autonomous Systems*, *55*(2), 107–121.

Saproo, S., & Serences, J. T. (2010). Spatial attention improves the quality of population codes in human visual cortex spatial attention improves the quality of population codes in human visual cortex. *Journal of Neurophysiology*, *104*, 885–895. doi:10.1152/jn.00369.2010

Sarafraz, A., Negahdaripour, S., & Schechner, Y. Y. (2009). Enhancing images in scattering media utilizing stereovision and polarization. In *Proceedings of IEEE Workshop on Applications of Computer Vision.*

Sarkar, M., Bello, D. S. S., Hoof, C. V., & Theuwissen, A. (2010b). Integrated polarization-analyzing CMOS image sensor for detecting incoming light ray direction. In *Sensors Applications Symposium, 2010 IEEE* (pp. 194-199).

Sarkar, M., Bello, D. S. S., Hoof, C. V., & Theuwissen, A. (2010a). Biologically inspired autonomous agent navigation using an integrated polarization analyzing CMOS image sensor. *Procedia Engineering*, *5*, 673–676. doi:10.1016/j.proeng.2010.09.199

Sarwal, A., Nett, J., & Simon, D. (2004). *Detection of small water-bodies*. Littleton, CO: PercepTek Robotics.

Sato, T. (1989). Interactions of visual stimuli in the receptive fields of inferior temporal neurons in awake macaques. *Experimental Brain Research*, *77*, 23–30. doi:10.1007/BF00250563

Schack, T. (2012). A method for measuring mental representation. IN G. Tenenbaum, R. C. Eklund, & A. Kamata (Eds.), *Handbook of measurement in sport,* (pp. 203-214). Human Kinetics.

Schack, T., & Essig, K. (2011). Perceptual motor skills and the cognitive architecture of action - Methods and perspectives in motor control research. In Columbus, A. M. (Ed.), *Advances in psychology research* (*Vol. 81*, pp. 35–73). New York, NY: Nova Science Publishers.

Schack, T., & Mechsner, F. (2006). Representation of motor skills in human long-term memory. *Neuroscience Letters*, *391*, 77–81. doi:10.1016/j.neulet.2005.10.009

Schack, T., & Ritter, H. (2009). The cognitive nature of action – functional links between cognitive psychology, movement science, and robotics. *Progress in Brain Research*, *174*, 231–251. doi:10.1016/S0079-6123(09)01319-3

Scharr, H., & Küsters, R. (2002). A linear model for simultaneous estimation of 3D motion and depth. *IEEE Workshop on Motion and Video Computing*, Orlando FL, (pp. 1-6).

Scharstein, D., & Pal, C. (2007). *Learning conditional random fields for stereo.* In IEEE Computer Society Conference on Computer Vision and Pattern Recognition (CVPR 2007).

Scharstein, D., & Szeliski, R. (2002). A taxonomy and evaluation of dense two-frame stereo correspondence algorithms. *International Journal of Computer Vision, 47*(1/2/3), 7-42.

Scharstein, D., & Szeliski, R. (2003). High-accuracy stereo depth maps using structured light. In *IEEE Computer Society Conference on Computer Vision and Pattern Recognition* (CVPR 2003), Vol. 1, (pp. 195-202).

Schechner, Y. Y., & Karpel, N. (2004). Clear underwater vision. In *IEEE Conference on Computer Vision and Pattern Recognition* (pp. 536 543).

Schechner, Y. Y., Narasimhan, S. G., & Nayar, S. K. (2001). Instant dehazing of images using polarization. In *Proceedings of IEEE Conference on Computer Vision and Pattern Recognition* (pp. 325-332).

Schechner, Y. Y., Narasimhan, S. G., & Nayar, S. K. (2008). Polarization-based vision through haze. In *Proceeding of ACM SIGGRAPH Asia,* Vol. 42.

Schechner, Y. Y., Shamir, J., & Kiryati, N. (1999). Polarization-based decorrelation of transparent layers: The inclination angle of an invisible surface. In *Proceedings of IEEE International Conference on Computer Vision* (pp. 814-819).

Schechner, Y. Y., & Karpel, N. (2005). Recovery of underwater visibility and structure by polarization analysis. *IEEE Journal of Oceanic Engineering, 30*, 631–636. doi:10.1109/JOE.2005.850871

Schechner, Y. Y., Narasimhan, S. G., & Nayar, S. K. (2003). Polarization-based vision through haze. *Applied Optics, 42*, 511–525. doi:10.1364/AO.42.000511

Schechner, Y. Y., Shamir, J., & Kiryati, N. (2000). Polarization and statistical analysis of scenes containing a semi-reflector. *Journal of the Optical Society of America. A, Optics, Image Science, and Vision, 17*, 276–284. doi:10.1364/JOSAA.17.000276

Schein, S., & Desimone, R. (1990). Spectral properties of V4 neurons in the macaque. *The Journal of Neuroscience, 10*(10), 3369–3389.

Schiller, P., Finlay, B., & Volman, S. (1976). Quantitative studies of single-cell properties in monkey striate cortex, I: Spatiotemporal organization of receptive fields. *Journal of Neurophysiology, 39*(6), 1288–1319.

Schmidt, E. M., Bak, M. J., Hambrecht, F. T., Kufta, C. V., O'Rourke, D. K., & Vallabhanath, P. (1996). Feasibility of a visual prosthesis for the blind based on intracortical microstimulation of the visual cortex. *Brain, 119*(Pt 2), 507–522. doi:10.1093/brain/119.2.507

Schmolke, A., & Mallot, H. A. (2002). Polarisation compass for robot navigation. In D. Polani, J. Kim, & T. Martinez (Eds.), *Fifth German Workshop on Artificial Life*.

Schneider, W., & Shiffrin, R. (1977). Controlled and automatic human information processing, I- Detection, search, and attention. *Psychological Review, 84*(1), 1–66. doi:10.1037/0033-295X.84.1.1

Schor, C. M., Maxwell, J. S., McCandless, J., & Graf, E. (2002). Adaptive control of vergence in humans. *Annals of the New York Academy of Sciences, 956*, 297–305.

Schreiber, K. M., Hillis, J. M., Filippini, H. R., Schor, C. M., & Banks, M. S. (2008). The surface of the empirical horopter. *Journal of Vision (Charlottesville, Va.), 8*(3), 1–20.

Schreiber, K. M., Tweed, D. B., & Schor, C. M. (2006). The extended horopter: Quantifying retinal correspondence across changes of 3d eye position. *Journal of Vision (Charlottesville, Va.), 6*, 64–74.

Schreiber, K., Crawford, J. D., Fetter, M., & Tweed, D. (2001). The motor side of depth vision. *Nature, 410*, 819–822.

Schuler, D. L., Lee, J. S., & Hoppel, K. W. (1993). Polarimetric SAR image signatures of the ocean and Gulf Stream features. *IEEE Transactions on Geoscience and Remote Sensing, 31*, 1210–1221. doi:10.1109/36.317442

Schwind, R. (1983). Zonation of the optical environment and zonation in the rhabdom structure within the eye of the backswimmer, Notonecta glauca. *Cell and Tissue Research, 232*, 53–63. doi:10.1007/BF00222373

Schwind, R. (1984). The plunge reaction of the backswimmer Notonecta glauca. *Journal of Comparative Physiology. A, Neuroethology, Sensory, Neural, and Behavioral Physiology, 155*, 319–321. doi:10.1007/BF00610585

Schwind, R. (1991). Polarization vision in water insects and insects living on a moist substrate. *Journal of Comparative Physiology. A, Neuroethology, Sensory, Neural, and Behavioral Physiology, 169*, 531–540. doi:10.1007/BF00193544

Sela, G., & Levine, M. D. (1997). Real-time attention for robotic vision. *Real-Time Imaging, 3*, 173–194. doi:10.1006/rtim.1996.0057

Semmlow, J. L., Hung, G. K., & Ciuffreda, K. J. (1986). Quantitative assessment of disparity vergence components. *Investigative Ophthalmology & Visual Science, 27*, 558–564.

Sereno, M. E., Trinath, T., Augath, M., & Logothetis, N. K. (2002). Three-dimensional shape representation in monkey cortex. *Neuron, 33*, 635–652.

Serrano-Pedraza, I., Phillipson, G. P., & Read, J. C. A. (2010). A specialization for vertical disparity discontinuities. *Journal of Vision (Charlottesville, Va.)*, *10*(3), 1–25.

Serrano-Pedraza, I., & Read, J. C. A. (2009). Stereo vision requires an explicit encoding of vertical disparity. *Journal of Vision (Charlottesville, Va.)*, *9*(4), 1–13.

Serre, T., Wolf, L., & Poggio, T. (2005). *Object recognition with features inspired by visual cortex*. IEEE Conference on Computer Vision and Pattern Recognition.

Serre, T., Oliva, A., & Poggio, T. (2006). A feedforward architecture accounts for rapid categorization. *Proceedings of the National Academy of Sciences of the United States of America*, *104*(15), 6424–6429. doi:10.1073/pnas.0700622104

Serre, T., Wolf, L., Bileschi, S., & Riesenhuber, M. (2007). Robust object recognition with cortex-like mechanisms. *IEEE Transactions on Pattern Analysis and Machine Intelligence*, *29*(3), 411–426. doi:10.1109/TPAMI.2007.56

Serre, T., Wolf, L., Bileschi, S., Riesenhuber, M., & Poggio, T. (2007). Object recognition with cortex-like mechanism. *IEEE Transactions on Pattern Analysis and Machine Intelligence*, *29*(3), 411–426. doi:10.1109/TPAMI.2007.56

Shabayek, A. E. R., Fofi, D., & Morel, O. (2009). *A novel non-central catadioptric auto-calibration approach*. In 9th Workshop on Omnidirectional Vision (OMNIVIS) in conjunction with International Conference on Computer Vision (ICCV).

Shabayek, A. E. R., Morel, O., & Fofi, D. (2010). *Auto-calibration and 3D reconstruction with non-central catadioptric sensors using polarization imaging*. In 10th Workshop on Omnidirectional Vision (OMNIVIS) in conjunction with Robotics Systems and Science RSS.

Shabayek, A. E. R., Morel, O., & Fofi, D. (2012a). *Polarization in the eye of a catadioptric sensor*. Unpublished work.

Shabayek, A. E. R., Morel, O., & Fofi, D. (2012b). *Polarization as seen by a catadioptric sensor: A simulation and calibration toolbox*. Unpublished work.

Shabayek, A. E. R. (2010). *Non-central catadioptric sensors auto-calibration*. LAP Lambert Academic Publishing.

Shabayek, A. E. R., Demonceaux, C., Morel, O., & Fofi, D. (2012). Vision based UAV attitude estimation: Progress and insights. *Journal of Intelligent & Robotic Systems*, *65*, 295–308. doi:10.1007/s10846-011-9588-y

Shahraray, B., & Anderson, D. J. (1989). Optimal estimation of contour properties by cross-validated regularization. *IEEE Transactions on Pattern Analysis and Machine Intelligence*, *11*, 600–610. doi:10.1109/34.24794

Shannon, C. E. (2001). A mathematical theory of communication. *SIGMOBILE Mobile Computer Communication Review*, *5*, 3–55. doi:10.1145/584091.584093

Shashar, N., Adessi, L., & Cronin, T. W. (1995). Polarization vision as a mechanism for detection of transparent objects. In Gulko, D., & Jokiel, P. L. (Eds.), *Ultraviolet radiation and coral reefs* (pp. 207–211).

Shashar, N., Hagan, R., Boal, J. G., & Hanlon, R. T. (2000). Cuttlefish use polarization sensitivity in predation on silvery fish. *Vision Research*, *40*, 71–75. doi:10.1016/S0042-6989(99)00158-3

Shashar, N., & Hanlon, R. (1997). Squids (Loligo pealii and Euprymna scolopes) can exhibit polarized light patterns produced by their skin. *The Biological Bulletin*, *193*, 207–208.

Shashar, N., & Hanlon, R., & Petz, de M. A. (1998). Polarization vision helps detect transparent prey. *Nature*, *393*, 222–223. doi:10.1038/30380

Shashar, N., Milbury, C., & Hanlon, R. (2002). Polarization vision in cephalopods: Neuroanatomical and behavioral features that illustrate aspects of form and function. *Marine and Freshwater Behaviour and Physiology*, *35*, 57–68. doi:10.1080/10236240290025617

Shashar, N., Sabbah, S., & Cronin, T. W. (2004). Transmission of linearly polarized light in seawater: Implications for polarization signaling. *The Journal of Experimental Biology*, *207*, 3619–3628. doi:10.1242/jeb.01187

Sheliga, B. M., & Miles, F. A. (2003). Perception can influence the vergence responses associated with open-loop gaze shifts in 3-d. *Journal of Vision (Charlottesville, Va.)*, *3*, 654–676.

Sheridan, H., Reingold, E. M., & Daneman, M. (2009). Using puns to study contextual influences on lexical ambiguity resolution: Evidence from eye movements. *Psychonomic Bulletin & Review*, *16*(5), 875–881. doi:10.3758/PBR.16.5.875

Shic, F., Chawarska, K., & Scassellati, B. (2008). The incomplete fixation measure. *Proceedings of the 2008 Symposium on Eye Tracking Research and Applications*, (pp. 111-114). Savannah, GA: ACM.

Shic, F., Chawarska, K., Bradshaw, J., & Scassellati, B. (2008) Autism, eye-tracking, entropy. In *Proceedings of the 7th IEEE International Conference on Development and Learning,* Monterrey, California, August 2008.

Shic, F., Jones, W., Klin, A., & Scassellati, B. (2006). *Swimming in the underlying stream: Computational models of gaze in a comparative behavioral analysis of autism*. 28th Annual Conference of the Cognitive Science Society, 2006.

Shic, F., & Scassellati, B. (2007). Pitfalls in the modeling of developmental systems. *International Journal of Humanoid Robotics*, *4*, 435–454. doi:10.1142/S0219843607001084

Shimojo, S., Silverman, G., & Nakayama, K. (1989). Occlusion and the solution to the aperture problem for motion. *Vision Research*, *29*, 619–626. doi:10.1016/0042-6989(89)90047-3

Shin, D., Lee, S., Kim, B., Park, Y., & Lim, S. (2008). Visual attention deficits contribute to impaired facial emotion recognition in boys with attention-deficit/hyperactivity disorder. *Neuropediatrics*, *39*(6), 323–327. doi:10.1055/s-0029-1202286

Shioiri, S., Saisho, H., & Yaguchi, H. (2000). Motion in depth based on inter-ocular velocity differences. *Vision Research*, *40*, 2565–2572. doi:10.1016/S0042-6989(00)00130-9

Shutov, A. M. (1993). Videopolarimeters. *Soviet Journal of Optical Technology*, *60*, 295–301.

Siddiqi, K., & Pizer, M. (2008). *Medial representations: Mathematics, algorithms and applications*.

Simoncelli, E. P., & Heeger, D. J. (1998). A model of neuronal responses in visual area MT. *Vision Research*, *38*, 743–761.

Smith, T. J., & Henderson, J. M. (2009). Facilitation of return during scene viewing. *Visual Cognition*, *17*, 1083–1108. doi:10.1080/13506280802678557

Snowden, R. J., Treue, S., Erikson, R. G., & Andersen, R. A. (1991). The response of area MT and V1 neurons to transparent motion. *The Journal of Neuroscience*, *11*, 2768–2785.

Solgi, M., & Weng, J. (2008, Nov). *Developmental stereo: Topographic iconic-abstract map from top-down connection.* In International Neural Network Society, Symposia Series New developments in Neural Networks, Auckland, New Zealand-Takemura, A., Inoue, Y., Kawano, K., Quaia, C., & Miles, F. A. (2001). Single-unit activity in cortical area MST associated with disparity vergence eye movements: Evidence for population coding. *Journal of Neurophysiology*, *85*, 2245–2266.

Spies, H., Jähne, B. J., & Barron, J.L. (2002). Range flow estimation. *Computer Vision Image Understanding (CVIU2002)*, *85*, 209-231.

Spillman, L., & Werner, J. S. (Eds.). (1987). *Visual perception: The neurophysiological foundations*. New York, NY: Academic Press.

Spitzer, H., & Hochstein, S. (1985). A complex-cell receptive-field model. *Journal of Neurophysiology*, *53*(5), 1266–1286.

Spratling, M. W., & Johnson, M. H. (2004). A feedback model of visual attention. *Journal of Cognitive Neuroscience*, *16*(2), 219–237. doi:10.1162/089892904322984526

Stafstrom, C. E., Schwindt, P. C., & Crill, W. E. (1984). Receptive firing in layer V neurons from cat neocortex in vitro. *Journal of Neurophysiology*, *2*, 264–277.

Stevenson, S. B., Comack, L. K., & Shorr, C. M. (1991). Depth attraction and repulsion in random dot stereograms. *Vision Research*, *31*, 805–813.

Stocker, A. A., & Simoncelli, E. P. (2006). Noise characteristics and prior expectations in human visual speed perception. *Nature Neuroscience*, *9*(4), 578–585. doi:10.1038/nn1669

Stringer, S. M., & Rolls, E. T. (2000). Position invariant recognition in the visual system with cluttered environments. *Neural Networks: The Official Journal of the International Neural Network Society*, *13*(3), 305–315. doi:10.1016/S0893-6080(00)00017-4

Studholme, C., Hill, D. L. G., & Hawkes, D. J. (1999). An overlap invariant entropy measure of 3D medical image alignment. *Pattern Recognition*, *32*, 71–86. doi:10.1016/S0031-3203(98)00091-0

Styles, E. A. (2006). *The psychology of attention* (2nd ed., p. 351). New York, NY: Psychology Press.

Subramaniam, N., & Hancock, E. (2010). Surface material segmentation using polarisation. *Lecture Notes in Computer Science*, *6256*, 115–124. doi:10.1007/978-3-642-15992-3_13

Suhai, B., & Horváth, G. (2004). How well does the Rayleigh model describe the E-vector distribution of skylight in clear and cloudy conditions? A full-sky polarimetric study. *Optical Society of America A*, *21*, 1669–1676. doi:10.1364/JOSAA.21.001669

Sun, Y., Fisher, R., Wang, F., & Gomes, H. (2008). A computer vision model for visual-object-based attention and eye movements. *Computer Vision and Image Understanding, 112*(2), 126-142. Elsevier Inc. doi:10.1016/j.cviu.2008.01.005

Sung, K., Wojtach, W. T., & Purves, D. (2009). An empirical explanation of aperture effects. *Proceedings of the National Academy of Sciences of the United States of America, 106*, 298–303. doi:10.1073/pnas.0811702106

Sun, Y., & Fisher, R. (2003). Object-based visual attention for computer vision. [Elsevier.]. *Artificial Intelligence*, *146*(1), 77–123. doi:10.1016/S0004-3702(02)00399-5

Suzuki, N., Hashimoto, N., Kashimori, Y., Zheng, M., & Kambara, T. (2004). A neural model of predictive recognition in form patway of visual cortex. *Bio Systems*, *76*, 33–42. doi:10.1016/j.biosystems.2004.05.004

Sweeney, A., Jiggins, C., & Johnsen, S. (2003). Insect communication: Polarized light as a butterfly mating signal. *Nature*, *423*, 31–32. doi:10.1038/423031a

Takemura, A., Kawano, K., Quaia, C., & Miles, F. A. (2006). Population coding of vergence eye movements in cortical area MST. In Harris, L., & Jenkin, M. (Eds.), *Levels of perception*.

Tanabe, S., & Cumming, B. G. (2008). Mechanisms underlying the transformation of disparity signals from V1 to V2 in the macaque. *The Journal of Neuroscience*, *28*(44), 11304–11314.

Tanaka, K. (1996a). Inferotemporal cortex and object vision. *Annual Review of Neuroscience*, *19*, 109–139. doi:10.1146/annurev.ne.19.030196.000545

Tanaka, K. (1996b). Representation of visual features of objects in the inferotemporal cortex. *Neural Networks*, *9*(8), 1459–1475. doi:10.1016/S0893-6080(96)00045-7

Tanaka, K., Saito, H., Fukada, Y., & Moriya, M. (1991). Coding visual images of objects in the inferotemporal cortex of the macaque monkey. *Journal of Neurophysiology*, *66*(1), 170–189.

Tang, C. H., & Rubin, M. D. (1972). Optimum polarization for rain cancellation. In *Proceedings of IEEE Antennas and Propagation Society International Symposium,* Vol. 10.

Tang, G., Peng, L., Baldwin, P. R., Mann, D. S., Jiang, W., Rees, I., & Ludtke, S. J. (2007). EMAN2: An extensible image processing suite for electron microscopy. *Journal of Structural Biology*, *157*, 38–46. doi:10.1016/j.jsb.2006.05.009

Tatler, B. W. (2007). The central fixation bias in scene viewing : Selecting an optimal viewing position independently of motor biases and image feature distributions. *Journal of Vision (Charlottesville, Va.)*, *7*, 1–17. doi:10.1167/7.14.4

Tatler, B. W., Baddeley, R. J., & Gilchrist, I. D. (2005). Visual correlates of fixation selection: Effects of scale and time. *Vision Research*, *45*(5), 643–659. doi:10.1016/j.visres.2004.09.017

Tatler, B. W., Baddeley, R. J., & Vincent, B. T. (2006). The long and the short of it: Spatial statistics at fixation vary with saccade amplitude and task. *Vision Research*, *46*, 1857–1862. doi:10.1016/j.visres.2005.12.005

Tatler, B. W., Hayhoe, M. M., Land, M. F., & Ballard, D. H. (2011). Eye guidance in natural vision: Reinterpreting salience. *Journal of Vision (Charlottesville, Va.)*, *11*(5), 1–23. doi:10.1167/11.5.5

Taylor, J. S. J., & Wolff, L. (2001). *Partial polarization signature results from the field testing of the SHallow water Real-time IMaging polarimeter (SHRIMP).* In OCEANS MTS/IEEE Conference and Exhibition.

Taylor, J. S. J., Davis, P., & Wolff, L. (2003). Underwater partial polarization signatures from the shallow water real-time imaging polarimeter (SHRIMP). In *SPIE Proceedings, Detection and Remediation Technologies for Mines and Minelike Targets VIII.*

Taylor, J. S. J., Davis, P., & Wolff, L. (2002). Underwater partial polarization signatures from the SHallow water Real-time IMaging Polarimeter (SHRIMP). In *OCEANS MTS*. IEEE. doi:10.1109/OCEANS.2002.1191863

Terrier, P., Devlaminck, V., & Charbois, J. M. (2008). Segmentation of rough surfaces using a polarization imaging system. *Optical Society of America*, *25*(2), 423–430. doi:10.1364/JOSAA.25.000423

Theeuwes, J., Atchley, P., & Kramer, A. F. (1986). Serial and parallel processing of visual feature conjunctions. *Nature*, *320*, 264–265. doi:10.1038/320264a0

Theeuwes, J., Atchley, P., & Kramer, A. F. (1998). Attentional control within 3-d space. *Journal of Experimental Psychology. Human Perception and Performance*, *24*(5), 1476–1485. doi:10.1037/0096-1523.24.5.1476

Theeuwes, J., & Pratt, J. (2003). Inhibition of return spreads across 3-d space. *Psychonomic Bulletin & Review*, *10*(3), 616–620. doi:10.3758/BF03196523

Theimer, W. M., & Mallot, H. A. (1994). Phase-based vergence control and depth reconstruction using active vision. *CVGIP. Image Understanding*, *60*(3), 343–358.

Thibaux, R., & Jordan. (2007). *Hierarchical beta processes and the Indian buffet process*. In International Conference on Artificial Intelligence and Statistics.

Thomas, O. M., Cumming, B. G., & Parker, A. J. (2002). A specialization for relative disparity in V2. *Nature Neuroscience*, *5*(5), 472–478.

Tibshirani, R. (1996). Regression shrinkage and selection via the lasso. *Journal of the Royal Statistical Society. Series B. Methodological*, *58*, 267–288.

Timofeeva, V. A. (1969). Plane of vibrations of polarized light in turbid media. *Izvestiya. Atmospheric and Oceanic Physics*, *5*, 603–607.

Tombu, M., & Tsotsos, J. K. (2008). Attending to orientation results in an inhibitory surround in orientation space. *Perception & Psychophysics*, *70*(1), 30–35. doi:10.3758/PP.70.1.30

Torralba, A., Castelhano, M. S., Oliva, A., & Henderson, J. M. (2006). Contextual guidance of eye movements and attention in real-world scenes: The role of global features in object search. *Psychological Review*, 113.

Toyoshima, H., Yamanoi, T., Yamazaki, T., & Ohnishi, S. (2005). Human recognition of symbols and words having the same meaning: An EEG and eye movement study. *Proceedings of 13th European Conference on Eye Movement*, PA-172.

Tramo, M. J., Loftus, W. C., Thomas, C. E., Green, R. L., Mott, L. A., & Gazzaniga, M. S. (1995). Surface area of human cerebral cortex and its gross morphological subdivisions: In vivo measurements in monozygotic twins suggest differential hemisphere effects of genetic factors. *Journal of Cognitive Neuroscience*, *7*(2), 292–302. doi:10.1162/jocn.1995.7.2.292

Treibitz, T., & Schechner, Y. Y. (2006). Instant 3descatter. In *Proc. IEEE Computer Vision and Pattern Recognition.*

Treibitz, T., & Schechner, Y. Y. (2009). Active polarization descattering. *IEEE Transactions on Pattern Analysis and Machine Intelligence*, *31*, 385–399. doi:10.1109/TPAMI.2008.85

Treisman, A. (1969). Strategies and models of selective attention. *Psychological Review*, *76*, 282–299. doi:10.1037/h0027242

Treisman, A. (1985). Preattentive processing in vision. *Computer Vision Graphics and Image Processing*, *31*(2), 156–177. doi:10.1016/S0734-189X(85)80004-9

Treisman, A., & Gelade, G. (1980). A feature integration theory of attention. *Cognitive Psychology, 12*, 97–136. doi:10.1016/0010-0285(80)90005-5

Treue, S., & Andersen, R. A. (1996). Neural responses to velocity gradients in macaque cortical area MT. *Visual Neuroscience, 13*, 797–804.

Treue, S., Andersen, R. A., Ando, H., & Hildreth, E. (1995). Structure-from-motion: Perceptual evidence for surface interpolation. *Vision Research, 35*(1), 139–148.

Treue, S., Hol, K., & Rauber, H.-J. (2000). Seeing multiple directions of motion - physiology and psychophysics. *Nature Neuroscience, 3*, 270–276.

Trucco, E., & Verri, A. (1998). *Introductory techniques for 3-D computer vision*. Prentice Hall.

Tsai, J. J., & Victor, J. D. (2003). Reading a population code: A multi-scale neural model for representing binocular disparity. *Vision Research, 43*, 445–466.

Tsang, E. K. C., & Shi, B. E. (2007). *Estimating disparity with confidence from energy neurons*. NIPS2007.

Tsang, E. K. C., & Shi, B. E. (2009). Disparity estimation by pooling evidence from energy neurons. *IEEE Transactions on Neural Networks, 20*(11), 1772–1782.

Tsapatsoulis, N., & Rapantzikos, K. (2006). Wavelet based estimation of saliency maps in visual attention algorithms. In Kollias, S. (Ed.), *Artificial neural networks* (pp. 538–547). Heidelberg, Germany: Springer. doi:10.1007/11840930_56

Tsapatsoulis, N., Rapantzikos, K., & Pattichis, C. S. (2007). An embedded saliency map estimator scheme: Application to video encoding. *International Journal of Neural Systems, 17*(4), 289–304. doi:10.1142/S0129065707001147

Tseng, P., Cameron, I., Munoz, D., & Itti, L. (2010). Differentiating patients from controls by gazing patterns. *Journal of Vision (Charlottesville, Va.), 10*(7), 277. doi:10.1167/10.7.277

Tsirlin, I., Allison, R. S., & Wilcox, L. M. (2008). Stereoscopic transparency: Constraints on the perception of multiple surfaces. *Journal of Vision (Charlottesville, Va.), 8*(5), 1–10.

Tsotsos, J. K. (1987). *A 'complexity level' analysis of vision*. In International Conference on Computer Vision: Human and Machine Vision Workshop, London, England.

Tsotsos, J. (1988). A complexity level analysis of immediate vision. *International Journal of Computer Vision, 2*, 303–320. doi:10.1007/BF00133569

Tsotsos, J. (2003). *Visual attention mechanisms: The selective tuning model*. Kluwer Academic.

Tsotsos, J. K. (1988). A 'complexity level' analysis of immediate vision. *International Journal of Computer Vision, 2*(1), 303–320. doi:10.1007/BF00133569

Tsotsos, J. K. (1990). Analyzing vision at the complexity level. *The Behavioral and Brain Sciences, 13*(3), 423–445. doi:10.1017/S0140525X00079577

Tsotsos, J. K. (2007). *A selective history of visual attention*. France: Les Houches.

Tsotsos, J. K. (2011). *A computational perspective on visual attention*. The MIT Press.

Tsotsos, J. K., Culhane, S. M., Kei Wai, W. Y., Lai, Y., Davis, N., & Nuflo, F. (1995). Modeling visual attention via selective tuning. [Elsevier.]. *Artificial Intelligence, 78*(1-2), 507–545. doi:10.1016/0004-3702(95)00025-9

Tsotsos, J. K., Itti, L., & Rees, G. (2005). A brief and selective history of attention. In Itti, L., Rees, G., & Tsotsos, J. K. (Eds.), *Neurobiology of attention*. Elsevier Press. doi:10.1016/B978-012375731-9/50003-3

Tsotsos, J. K., Liu, Y., Martinez-Trujillo, J., Pomplun, M., Simine, E., & Zhou, K. (2005). Attending to visual motion. *Computer Vision and Image Understanding, 100*(1-2), 3–40. doi:10.1016/j.cviu.2004.10.011

Tsotsos, J. K., Rodriguez-Sanchez, A.-J., Rothenstein, A. L., & Simine, E. (2008). The different stages of visual recognition need different attentional binding strategies. *Brain Research, 1225*, 119–132. doi:10.1016/j.brainres.2008.05.038

Tsotsos, J. K., & Rothenstein, A. (2011). Computation models of visual attention. *Scholarpedia, 6*(1), 6201. doi:10.4249/scholarpedia.6201

Tsotsos, J., Culhane, S., Wai, W., Lai, Y., Davis, N., & Nuflo, N. (1995). Modeling visual attention via selective tuning. *Artificial Intelligence*, *1-2*, 507–547. doi:10.1016/0004-3702(95)00025-9

Tsunoda, K., Yamane, Y., Nishizaki, M., & Tanifuji, M. (2001). Complex objects are represented in macaque inferotemporal cortex by the combination of feature columns. *Nature Neuroscience*, *4*, 832–838. doi:10.1038/90547

Tweed, D., & Vilis, T. (1990). Geometric relations of eye position and velocity vectors during saccades. *Vision Research*, *30*(1), 111–127.

Tyler, C. W. (1971). Stereoscopic depth movement: Two eyes less sensitive than one. *Science*, *174*, 958–961. doi:10.1126/science.174.4012.958

Tyo, J. S. (1998). Optimum linear combination strategy for an N-channel polarization-sensitive imaging or vision system. *Journal of Optical Society*, *15*, 359–366. doi:10.1364/JOSAA.15.000359

Tyo, J. S., Rowe, M. P., Pugh, E. N. Jr, & Engheta, N. (1996). Target detection in optically scattered media by polarization-difference imaging. *Applied Optics*, *35*, 1855–1870. doi:10.1364/AO.35.001855

Tzvetanov, T., Wirmer, A., & Folta, K. (2007). Orientation repulsion and attraction in alignment perception. *Vision Research*, *47*, 1693–1704.

Uehara, H., Seto, I., Ohtsuki, T., Sasase, I., & Mori, S. (1992). *Phase noise insensitive multilevel POLSK based on QAM mapping in coherent optical systems*. In Singapore ICCS/ISITA: Communications on the Move.

Uhr, L. (1972). Layered recognition cone networks that preprocess, classify, and describe. *IEEE Transactions on Computers*, *21*, 758–768. doi:10.1109/T-C.1972.223579

Ullman, S., & Yuille, A. (1989). Rigidity and smoothness of motion. In Ullman, S., & Richards, W. (Eds.), *Image understanding*. Norwood, NJ: Ablex Publishing Corporation.

Urban, F., Follet, B., Chamaret, C., Meur, O. L., & Baccino, T. (2011). Medium spatial frequencies: A strong predictor of salience. *Cognitive Computation*, *3*(1), 34–47. doi:10.1007/s12559-010-9086-8

Usher, K., Ridley, P., & Corke, P. (2001). *A camera as a polarized light compass: Preliminary experiments*. In Australian Conference on Robotics and Automation.

van der Heijden, a H., & Bem, S. (1997). Successive approximations to an adequate model of attention. *Consciousness and Cognition*, *6*(2-3), 413–428. doi:10.1006/ccog.1996.0284

van Ee, R., & Anderson, B. L. (2001). Motion direction, speed and orientation in binocular matching. *Nature*, *410*, 690–694. doi:10.1038/35070569

van Ee, R., & Schor, C. M. (2000). Unconstrained stereoscopic matching of lines. *Vision Research*, *40*, 151–162. doi:10.1016/S0042-6989(99)00174-1

Van Rullen, R., & Koch, C. (2005). Visual attention and visual awareness. In Celesia, G. (Ed.), *Disorders of visual processing* (*Vol. 5*, pp. 65–83). Elsevier.

Vanduffel, W., Tootell, R. B. H., & Orban, G. A. (2000). Attention-dependent suppression of metabolic activity in the early stages of the macaque visual system. *Cerebral Cortex*, *10*(2), 109–126. doi:10.1093/cercor/10.2.109

VanRullen, R. (2003). Visual saliency and spike timing in the ventral visual pathway. *The Journal of Physiology*, *97*(2-3), 365–377. doi:doi:10.1016/j.jphysparis.2003.09.010

VanRullen, R., Reddy, L., & Koch, C. (2004). Visual search and dual tasks reveal two distinct attentional resources. *Journal of Cognitive Neuroscience*, *16*(1), 4–14. doi:10.1162/089892904322755502

Vedula, S., Baker, S., Rander, P., Collins, R., & Kanade, T. (2005). Three-dimensional scene-flow. *IEEE Transactions on Pattern Analysis and Machine Intelligence*, 475–480. doi:10.1109/TPAMI.2005.63

Veraart, C., Wanet-Defalque, M. C., Gerard, B., Vanlierde, A., & Delbeke, J. (2003). Pattern recognition with the optic nerve visual prosthesis. *Artificial Organs*, *27*(11), 996–1004. doi:10.1046/j.1525-1594.2003.07305.x

Vetro, R., Ding, W., & Simovici, D. (2010). Mining for high complexity regions using entropy and box counting dimension quad-trees. In *Proceedings of the 9th IEEE International Conference on Cognitive Informatics*, Beijing, China.

Vickers, J. N. (2007). *Perception, cognition and decision training: The quiet eye in action*. Champaign, IL: Human Kinetics.

Victor, J. D. (1999). Temporal aspects of neural coding in the retina and lateral geniculate. *Network (Bristol, England)*, *10*(4), R1–R66. doi:10.1088/0954-898X/10/4/201

Viola, P., & Jones, M. (2002). Robust real-time object detection. *International Journal of Computer Vision*, *57*(2), 137–154. doi:10.1023/B:VISI.0000013087.49260.fb

Viswanathan, L., & Mingolla, E. (2002). Dynamics of attention in depth: Evidence from multi-element tracking. *Perception*, *31*, 1415–1437. doi:10.1068/p3432

Vitay, J., Rougier, N. P., & Alexandre, F. (2005). A distributed model of spatial visual attention. *Biomimetic Neural Learning for Intelligent Robots Conference* (pp. 54-72). Springer.

Volterra, V. (1928). Variations and fluctuations of the number of individuals in animal species living together. *ICES Journal of Marine Science*, *3*(1), 3–51. doi:10.1093/icesjms/3.1.3

von der Heydt, R., Peterhans, E., & Baumgartner, G. (1984). Illusory contours and cortical neuron responses. *Science*, *224*(4654), 1260–1262. doi:10.1126/science.6539501

von der Malsburg, C. (1973). Self-organization of orientation sensitive cells in the striate cortex. *Kybernetik*, *14*(2), 85–100. doi:10.1007/BF00288907

von Helmholtz, H. (1962). In Southall, J. P. (Ed.), *Helmholtz's treatise on physiological optics* (*Vol. 1*, pp. 312–313). New York, NY: Dover. (Original work published 1910)

Wallach, H. (1935). Über visuell wahrgenommene Bewegungsrichtung. *Psychologische Forschung*, *20*, 325–380. doi:10.1007/BF02409790

Wallis, G., & Rolls, E. (1997). Invariant face and object recognition in the visual system. *Progress in Neurobiology*, *51*(2), 167–194. doi:10.1016/S0301-0082(96)00054-8

Walther, D. (2006). *Interactions of visual attention and object recognition: Computational modeling, algorithms, and psychophysics*. Ph.D. thesis, California Institute of Technology.

Walther, D., Itti, L., Riesenhuber, M., Poggio, T., & Koch, C. (2002). Attentional selection for object recognition - A gentle way. *Proceedings Biologically Motivated Computer Vision, LNCS*, *2525*, 472–479. doi:10.1007/3-540-36181-2_47

Walther, D., & Koch, C. (2006). Modeling attention to salient proto-objects. *Neural Networks*, *19*, 1395–1407. doi:10.1016/j.neunet.2006.10.001

Wang, G., Zhang, Y., & Fei-Fei, L. (2006). Using dependent regions for object categorization in a generative framework. *IEEE Conference on Computer Vision and Pattern Recognition*, (pp. 1597-1604).

Wang, H., & Lages, M. (2011). *A biologically-inspired Bayesian model of 3D velocity estimation*. AVA Meeting, Cardiff.

Wang, X., Kinh, T., & Grimson, E. (2006). Learning semantic scene models by trajectory analysis. *Computer Vision – ECCV 2006. Lecture Notes in Computer Science*, *3956*, 110–123. doi:10.1007/11744078_9

Wang, Y., & Shi, B. E. (2009). Autonomous development of vergence control driven by disparity energy neuron populations. *Neural Computation*, *22*, 1–22.

Warren, D. J., Fernandez, E., & Normann, R. A. (2001). High-resolution two-dimensional spatial mapping of cat striate cortex using a 100-microelectrode array. *Neuroscience*, *105*(1), 19–31. doi:10.1016/S0306-4522(01)00174-9

Watanabe, O. (2008). A neural model for stereo transparency with the population of the disparity energy models. *Neurocomputing*, *71*, 3158–3167.

Watanabe, O., & Kikuchi, M. (2005). Nonlinearity of the population activity to transparent motion. *Neural Networks*, *18*, 15–22.

Waterman, T. H. (1981). Polarization sensitivity. In Autrum, H. (Ed.), *Handbook of sensory physiology* (pp. 281–463). Berlin, Germany: Springer Verlag.

Watt, S. J., Akeley, K., & Banks, M. S. (2005). Focus cues affect perceived depth. *Journal of Vision (Charlottesville, Va.)*, *5*(10), 834–862. doi:10.1167/5.10.7

Wayland, S., & Taplin, J. E. (1985). Feature-processing deficits following brain injury, part I - Overselectivity in recognition memory for compound stimuli. *Brain and Cognition*, *4*, 338–355. doi:10.1016/0278-2626(85)90026-0

Webster, M., & Ungerleider, L. (1998). Neuroanatomy of visual attention. In Parasuraman, R. (Ed.), *The attentive brain*. MIT Press.

Wehner, R. (1987). Matched filters'-Neural models of the external world. *Journal of Comparative Physiology. A, Neuroethology, Sensory, Neural, and Behavioral Physiology*, *161*, 511–531. doi:10.1007/BF00603659

Wehner, R. (2001). Polarization vision a uniform sensory capacity? *The Journal of Experimental Biology*, *204*, 2589–2596.

Weidemann, A., Fournier, G. R., Forand, L., & Mathieu, P. (2005). In harbor underwater threat detection/ identification using active imaging. In *Proceedings of SPIE, Photonics for Port and Harbor Security, Vol. 5780* (pp. 59-70).

Weigelt, M., & Schack, T. (2007). Selektive Effekte unbewusster Handlungsbahnung beim Beobachter anderer Fußballspieler. In *Abstract-Band, Congress of the DVS-Committee Soccer in the Sport Center* Kamen-Kaiserau (pp. 9-10).

Weigelt, M., Bosbach, S., Schack, T., & Kunde, W. (2006). Wenn wir anderen Menschen beim Handeln zusehen, interpretieren wir gleichzeitig auch deren Intention. In Raab, M., Arnold, A., & Gärtner, K. (Eds.), *Zukunft der Sportspiele: Fördern, fordern, forschen* (pp. 49–52). Flensburg, Germany: University Press.

Weinshall, D. (1989). Perception of multiple transparent planes in stereo vision. *Nature*, *341*, 737–739.

Weiss, Y., & Fleet, D. J. (2001). Probabilistic models of the brain: perception and neural function. In Rao, R. P. N., Olshausen, B., & Lewicki, M. S. (Eds.), *Velocity likelihoods in biological and machine vision* (pp. 81–100). Cambridge, MA: MIT Press.

Weiss, Y., Simoncelli, E. P., & Adelson, E. H. (2002). Motion illusions as optimal percepts. *Nature Reviews. Neuroscience*, *5*, 598–604. doi:10.1038/nn0602-858

Welchman, A. E., Lam, J. M., & Bülthoff, H. H. (2008). Bayesian motion estimation accounts for a surprising bias in 3D vision. *Proceedings of the National Academy of Sciences of the United States of America*, *105*, 12087–12092. doi:10.1073/pnas.0804378105

Welchman, A. E., Tuck, V. L., & Harris, J. M. (2004). Human observers are biased in judging the angular approach of a projectile. *Vision Research*, *44*, 2027–2042. doi:10.1016/j.visres.2004.03.014

Westheimer, G. (1986). Spatial interaction in the domain of disparity signals in human stereoscopic vision. *The Journal of Physiology*, *370*, 619–629.

Williams, A. M., & Ward, P. (2007). Perceptual-cognitive expertise in sport: Exploring new horizons. In Tenenbaum, G., & Eklund, R. C. (Eds.), *Handbook of sport psychology* (pp. 203–223). Hoboken, NJ: John Wiley & Sons.

Wilson, H. R. (1999). *Spikes, decisions and actions*. Oxford University Press.

Wilson, H. R. (1999). *Spikes, decisions, and actions: The dynamical foundations of neuroscience*. Oxford University Press.

Wilson, H. R., Blake, R., & Lee, S. (2001). Dynamics of travelling waves in visual perception. *Nature*, *412*, 907–910. doi:10.1038/35091066

Wilson, H. R., Ferrera, V. P., & Yo, C. (1992). A psychophysically motivated model for two-dimensional motion perception. *Visual Neuroscience*, *9*(1), 79–97. doi:10.1017/S0952523800006386

Wilson, R. A., & Keil, F. C. (Eds.). (1999). *The MIT encyclopedia of the cognitive sciences (MITECS)*. London, UK: MIT Press.

Wischnewski, M., Belardinelli, A., Schneider, W. X., & Steil, J. J. (2010). Where to look next? Combining static and dynamic proto-objects in a TVA-based model of visual attention. *Cognitive Computation*, *2*, 326–343. doi:10.1007/s12559-010-9080-1

Witelson, S. F., Glezer, I. I., & Kigar, D. L. (1995). Women have greater density of neurons in posterior temporal cortex. *The Journal of Neuroscience*, *15*, 3418–3428.

Wolfe, J. (1998). Visual search in attention. In Pashler, H. (Ed.), *Attention* (pp. 13–74). London, UK: University College London Press.

Wolfe, J. M. (1998). Visual search. In Pashler, H. (Ed.), *Attention*. Taylor & Francis.

Wolfe, J. M., & Horowitz, T. S. (2004). What attributes guide the deployment of visual attention and how do they do it? *Nature Reviews. Neuroscience*, *5*(6), 495–501. doi:10.1038/nrn1411

Wolfe, J., & Cave, R. (1989). Guided search: An alternative to feature integration theory for visual search. *Journal of Experimental Psychology. Human Perception and Performance*, *15*, 419–443. doi:10.1037/0096-1523.15.3.419

Wolff, L. B. (1989). Using polarization to separate reflection components. In *Proceedings of IEEE Conference on Computer Vision and Pattern Recognition* (pp. 363-369).

Wolff, L. B. (1995). Applications of polarization camera technology. *IEEE Expert*, *10*(5), 30–38. doi:10.1109/64.464928

Wolff, L. B. (1997). Polarization vision: A new sensory approach to image understanding. *Image and Vision Computing*, *15*, 81–93. doi:10.1016/S0262-8856(96)01123-7

Wolff, L. B., & Andreou, A. G. (1995). Polarization camera sensors. *Image and Vision Computing*, *13*, 497–510. doi:10.1016/0262-8856(95)94383-B

Wolff, L., Mancini, T., Pouliquen, P., & Andreou, A. (1997). Liquid crystal polarization camera. *IEEE Transactions on Robotics and Automation*, *13*(2), 195–203. doi:10.1109/70.563642

Wooding, D. S. (2002). Eye movements of large populations: II. Deriving regions of interest, coverage, and similarity using fixation maps. *Behavior Research Methods, Instruments, & Computers*, *34*, 518–528. doi:10.3758/BF03195481

Wu, L., Gao, J., Fan, Z., & Xie, Z. (2010). How to get navigation information within patches of sky as insects do? A primitive orientation by skylight polarization maps. In *2nd International Conference on Signal Processing Systems*.

Xie, B., Xiang, Z., Pan, H., & Liu, J. (2007). Polarization-based water hazards detection for autonomous off-road navigation. In *IEEE/RSJ International Conference on Intelligent Robots and Systems*.

Yamada, M., Ueda, K., Horiba, I., & Sugie, N. (2001). Discrimination of the road condition toward understanding of vehicle driving environments. *IEEE Transactions on Intelligent Transportation Systems*, *2*(1), 26–31. doi:10.1109/6979.911083

Yamanoi, T., Toyoshima, H., & Yamazaki, T. (2005). Spatio-temporal dipole modeling of EEGs during perception of straight movements. *Proceedings of 13th European Conference on Eye Movement*, PA-178.

Yanai, K., & Barnard, K. (2005). Image region entropy: A measure of "Visualness" in web images associated with one concept. *Proceedings of ACM Multimedia*, Singapore.

Yang, D. S., FitzGibbon, E. J., & Miles, F. A. (2003). Short-latency disparity vergence eye movements in humans: Sensitivity to simulated orthogonal tropias. *Vision Research*, *43*(3).

Yedidia, J. S., Freeman, W. T., & Weiss, Y. (2003). Understanding belief propagation and its generalizations. In Lakemeyer, G., & Nebel, B. (Eds.), *Exploring artificial intelligence in the new millennium* (pp. 239–269). San Francisco, CA: Morgan Kaufmann Publishers.

Yemelyanov, K. M., Lin, S.-S., Luis, W. Q., Pugh, J. E. N., & Engheta, N. (2003). Bio-inspired display of polarization information using selected visual cues. In *Proceedings of SPIE - The International Society for Optical Engineering, 5158*.

Yemelyanov, K. M., Lo, M. A., Pugh, J. E. N., & Engheta, N. (2003). Display of polarization information by coherently moving dots. *Optics Express*, *11*, 1577–1584. doi:10.1364/OE.11.001577

Yeong, L. S., Ngau, C. W. H., Ang, L.-M., & Seng, K. P. (2009). Efficient processing of a rainfall simulation watershed on a FPGA-based architecture with fast access to neighbourhood pixels. *EURASIP Journal on Embedded Systems*, *7*(4).

Zanker, J. (2005). A computational analysis of separating motion signals in transparent random dot kinematograms. *Spatial Vision*, *18*, 431–445.

Zeki, S. (1983). Colour coding in the cerebral cortex: the responses of wavelength-selective and colour-coded cells in monkey visual cortex to changes in wavelength composition. *Neuroscience*, *9*(4), 767–781. doi:10.1016/0306-4522(83)90266-X

Zhang, H., Berg, A., Marie, M., & Malik, J. (2006). SVM-KNN: Discriminative nearest neighbor classification for visual category recognition. *IEEE Conference on Computer Vision and Pattern Recognition*, (pp. 2126-2136).

Zhang, Z. Y., Cheng, H. F., Chen, Z. H., & Zheng, W. W. (2009a). Analysis of polarimetric characteristics of camouflage targets. In *Proceedings of SPIE 4th International Symposium on Advanced Optical Manufacturing and Testing Technologies: Optical Test and Measurement Technology and Equipment, Vol. 7283*.

Zhang, Z. Y., Cheng, H. F., Chen, Z. H., & Zheng, W. W. (2009b). Analysis of polarimetric scattering for backgrounds and camouflage materials. In *Proceedings of SPIE International Symposium on Photoelectronic Detection and Imaging: Advances in Infrared Imaging and Applications, Vol. 7383*.

Zhao, Y., Pan, Q., & Zhang, H. (2006). Object detection by fusion spectral and polarimetric imagery. In *Proceedings of SPIE, Vol. 6031*.

Zhao, K., Chu, J., Wang, T., & Zhang, Q. (2009). A novel angle algorithm of polarization sensor for navigation. *IEEE Transactions on Instrumentation and Measurement*, *58*, 2791–2796. doi:10.1109/TIM.2009.2016299

Zhao, Q., & Koch, C. (2011). Learning a saliency map using fixated locations in natural scenes. *Journal of Vision (Charlottesville, Va.)*, *11*(3), 1–15. doi:10.1167/11.3.9

Zhao, Y.-Q., Gong, P., & Pan, Q. (2008). Object detection by Spectropolarimeteric imagery fusion. *IEEE Transactions on Geoscience and Remote Sensing*, *46*, 3337–3345. doi:10.1109/TGRS.2008.920467

Zhao, Y., Zhang, L., Zhang, D., & Pan, Q. (2009). Object separation by polarimetric and spectral imagery fusion. *Computer Vision and Image Understanding*, *113*, 855–866. doi:10.1016/j.cviu.2009.03.002

Zheng, W., Li, J., Si, Z., Lin, F., & Zhang, B. (2006). Using high-level semantic features in video retrieval. In Sundaram, H., Naphade, M. R., Smith, J. R., & Rui, Y. (Eds.), *Image and video retrieval* (pp. 370–379). Tempe, AZ: Springer. doi:10.1007/11788034_38

Zoccolan, D., Cox, D. D., & DiCarlo, J. J. (2005). Multiple object response normalization in monkey inferotemporal cortex. *The Journal of Neuroscience*, *25*(36), 8150–8164. doi:10.1523/JNEUROSCI.2058-05.2005

Zrenner, E., Gekeler, F., Gabel, V. P., Graf, H. G., Graf, M., Guenther, E., & Weiss, S. (2001). Subretinal microphotodiode array as replacement for degenerated photoreceptors? *Der Ophthalmologe*, *98*(4), 357–363. doi:10.1007/s003470170141

About the Contributors

Marc Pomplun is a Professor of Computer Science at the University of Massachusetts Boston. In 1998, he received a Ph.D. in Computer Science (Dr. rer. nat.) from Bielefeld University in Germany and the University's "Best Dissertation in 1998" award. He subsequently conducted research as a post-doctoral fellow in the Department of Psychology at the University of Toronto and as a research scientist at the Centre for Vision Research, York University, Canada. In 2002, he joined the University of Massachusetts Boston, where he founded the Visual Attention Laboratory and initiated the Talks in Cognitive Science (TICS) colloquium series. His research focuses on human vision, particularly visual attention, and how insight into biological vision can be applied to the fields of computer vision and human-computer interaction. In 2007, he received the Outstanding Achievement Award for Scholarship from the College of Science and Mathematics. By the time of his promotion to Professor in 2012, he had made more than 160 contributions to scientific journals and conferences and obtained research funding as a PI and Co-PI from the National Institutes of Health, the National Science Foundation, and the US Department of Education.

Junichi Suzuki is an Associate Professor of Computer Science at the University of Massachusetts, Boston. He received a Ph.D. in Computer Science from Keio University, Japan, in 2001. He was a post-doctoral research fellow at the University of California, Irvine (UCI) from 2001 to 2004. Before joining UCI, he was with Object Management Group Japan, Inc., as Technical Director. His research interests include biologically-inspired computing, autonomous adaptive distributed systems, sustainable networking, molecular communication, model-driven software/performance engineering and multiobjective optimization. In these areas, he has authored two books, edited five journal special issues, and published one industrial standard specification and 120+ papers in international journals and conferences. He received nine best paper awards and two best poster awards at major conferences such as IEEE SPECTS 2008 and IEEE SCC 2007. He serves on the editorial boards for six international journals including Elsevier *Nano Communication Networks Journal*. He has chaired or co-chaired 15 international conferences such as BodyNets 2012, BIONETICS 2010 and ICSOC 2009. He has served on the steering committee of five conferences as well as the program committee of 100+ conferences such as IEEE CEC, ACM GECCO, IEEE ICTAI, IEEE SECON, IEEE AINA, ACM/IEEE BIOSIGNALS, and IEEE ICCCN.

* * *

Li-Minn Ang is currently a Research Fellow in School of Engineering, Edith Cowan University, Australia. He was an Associate Professor at the University of Nottingham Malaysia Campus. He received his Bachelor and PhD degrees from Edith Cowan University in 1996 and 2001, respectively. His research interests are in the fields of visual processing, intelligent processing techniques, hardware architectures, and reconfigurable computing.

Neil Bruce completed a Double Honours Bachelor's degree in Computer Science and Mathematics at the University of Guelph. Following this, he was a member of the Vision and Image Processing lab in the Department of System Design Engineering at the University of Waterloo. He then joined the Centre for Vision Research at York University as a member of the Computer Science and Engineering Department where he completed his Ph.D. Following Postdoctoral fellowships at York University and INRIA in Sophia Antipolis, France, he recently joined the Faculty of Computer Science at the University of Manitoba as an Assistant Professor. He is most recognized for his work in modeling visual salience and the prediction of fixational eye movement behavior in humans.

Andrea Canessa received his Master Degree in Bioengineering (curriculum "Neuroengineering") at the University of Genoa in 2007. In 2011 he obtained his Ph.D. in Bioengineering at the University of Genoa. Since 2007 he is with the Physical Structure of Perception and Computation (PSPC) Group in the Department of Biophysical and Electronic Engineering (DIBE) of the University of Genoa. His research interests include neuromorphic models inspired by visual cortex processing, eye movements and their influences on depth perception, and bioinspired active visual systems.

Manuela Chessa is a Postodoctoral Research scientist at the University of Genoa, Italy. She received her MSc in Bioengineering from the University of Genoa in 2005, and the Ph.D. in Bioengineering from University of Genoa in 2009. She has been working in the PSPC Lab since 2005, and her research interests are focused on the study of biological and artificial vision systems, on the development of bioinspired models for the estimation of optic flow and disparity, on the study of the interplay existing between vision and motion control in the peripersonal space, and on the development of virtual and augmented reality system for the study of the perception of tridimensionality.

Vincent Courboulay received the Master's degree in Engineering from the University of Orleans, 1999. He did his PhD in Image Processing in the Computer Science Department of the L3I, laboratory of image interaction and computer science, La Rochelle, France. He is currently an Associate Professor in the L3I. His research interests include image processing, visual attention, and biologically plausible vision models; he is also interested in extraction of information.

Begoña del Pino received the Ph.D. degree in Computer Science from the University of Granada, Granada, Spain, in 1999. She is currently an Associate Professor with the Department of Architecture and Computer Technology, University of Granada. Her main research interests include visual rehabilitation, bioinspired processing schemes based on spiking neurons, high-performance computer vision, and embedded systems on reconfigurable devices.

Curtis Deutsch directs the Psychobiology Program at the Eunice Kennedy Shriver Center, and co-directs the NIH P30 Intellectual and Developmental Disability Statistics and Informatics Core at the Center. He is trained as geneticist and psychologist, and his research focuses on the development of biologically-interpretable phenotypes for molecular genetic studies, with an emphasis on childhood neuropsychiatric disorders, including autism, and major psychoses.

Abd El Rahman Shabayek is a Researcher at Le2i CNRS UMR 6306, University of Burgundy, France, with a permanent teaching position in the Faculty of Computers and Informatics, Computer Science department, Suez Canal University, Egypt. He was awarded a full grant from the EU to obtain his MSc within Erasmus Mundus Vision and Robotics VIBOT program. His PhD is about combining omnidirectional sensors with polarization vision for robot navigation. His research interests include catadioptric vision, polarization vision, bioinspired robotics, and autonomous robotics.

Kai Essig graduated 1998 in Computer Science and Chemistry (M.Sc.) at Bielefeld University, Germany. He joined the Neuroinformatics Group at Bielefeld University (Germany) in 1998 and received a Ph.D. in Computer Science in 2007, working on a vision-based image retrieval system. His fields of research include eye tracking, visual perception, image processing, computer vision, and eye-hand coordination. From 2008 on he joined the Neurocognition and Action-Biomechanics Group at the Faculty of Psychology and Sport Sciences at Bielefeld University. He is currently a postdoctoral researcher at the Excellence Cluster "Cognitive Interaction Technology" (CITEC) doing research on the influence of movement expertise on visual perception during the observation and/or interaction with objects and ongoing events in the environment and the implementation of (multi-modal) software solutions in the field of eye-tracking.

David Fofi is currently a Professor at the University of Burgundy, Head of the Computer Vision Department of the Le2i UMR CNRS 6306 and Coordinator of the Erasmus Mundus Masters in Vision and Robotics (VIBOT). He received a MSc degree in Image and Signal Processing of the University of Cergy-Pontoise / ENSEA in 1997 and a PhD in Computer Vision from the University of Picardie Jules Verne in 2001. He has been awarded a research fellowship from the SnT (University of Luxembourg) since 2012. His research interest includes multiple- view geometry, catadioptric vision, projector- camera systems and structured light. He participated and leaded several French and European projects in the field of computer vision (Erasmus Mundus, CNRS, ANR, PHC, etc.). Since 1998, he published more than 20 papers in international peer-reviewed journals, 2 patents and more than 50 conference papers.

Agostino Gibaldi received his degree in Biomedical Engineering at the University of Genoa, Italy, in 2007. In 2011 he obtained his Ph.D. in Electronic Engineering, Information Technology, Robotics, and Telecommunications at the Physical Structure of Perception and Computation (PSPC) Group. Actually he is working in the same group as a PostDoc. His research interests concerns the study and development of neuromorphic models for active vision systems. In particular they involve cortical models of V1, MT, and MST areas in relation to the perception-action loop for the control of vergence eye movements, the estimation of disparity, eye tracking and analysis of eye movement, the autonomous learning of active behaviors, and the optic flow analysis for navigation.

Nurit Haspel received her BSc, MSc, and PhD from Tel Aviv University in Israel. She later did a 2 year postdoctoral work at the Department of Computer Science at Rice University in Houston, TX and in 2009 she joined the department of Computer Science at UMass Boston as an Assistant Professor. Her research area is structural bioinformatics - the application of computational methods to solving key biological problems. Specifically, she develops and applies computational algorithms based on concepts taken from computational geometry, graph theory, and robotics to model the structure, function, and dynamics of proteins and biomolecular interactions.

Isao Hayashi is a Professor of Department of Informatics, Kansai University. After developing Neuro-fuzzy Systems as a staff researcher in the Sharp Corporation and Matsushita Electric Industrial (Panasonic) Co. Ltd, he received PhD of Engineering from Osaka Prefecture University in 1991, and he was a Professor of Department of Management Information of Hannan University. He moved to the Department of Informatics of Kansai University in 2004. He was a Secretary of International Fuzzy Systems Association (IFSA), a Chair of Kansai Chapter of Japan Society for Fuzzy Theory and Intelligent Informatics (SOFT), and a Chair of the Technical Group on Brain and Perception in SOFT. He is an Editorial Member of *International Journal of Hybrid Intelligent Systems* and *Journal of Advanced Computational Intelligence and Intelligent Informatics* (JACIII). His main researches are on visual models, neural networks, fuzzy systems, neuro-fuzzy systems, and brain-computer interface.

Suzanne Heron obtained her BSc in Psychology at Glasgow University, UK. Currently she is in the final year of her Ph.D. at the School of Psychology, Glasgow University, UK.

Shubha Kadambe obtained her PhD EE from the Univ. of Rhode Island in May 1991. Currently she is a Senior Principal Systems Engineer at the Communications Systems and Applications group in the Advanced Technology Center, Communication Navigation and Systems department of Rockwell Collins. Prior to joining Rockwell she was a program officer at Office of Naval Research (ONR) where she managed a "Signal/Image processing and understanding" program. Dr. Kadambe has successfully executed several funded efforts from various funding agencies such as DARPA, OSD, and Navy while she held research positions at AT&T Bell laboratories (Murray Hill, NJ), Atlantic Aerospace Electronics Corporation (Greenbelt, MD), and HRL Laboratories LLC. (Malibu CA). She also held a visiting research associate position at the Mathematics department, University of MD, College Park where she conducted research in the area of "bio inspired intelligent algorithms." She has extensively worked in the areas of advanced communications, situation awareness, electronic warfare, radar, sonar, speech, time-frequency representations, advanced signal and image processing, and bio-medical signal processing. She has over 20 years of experience in developing advanced technologies in these areas. She has 23 US patents (9 issued and 14 under review), over eighty technical papers, one video tutorial, six invited chapters, and one monogram to her credit. Her biography has been included in Who's-Who in America, Who's-Who of American Women and Who's Who Worldwide. She has served as an Associate Editor for *IEEE Transactions on Signal Processing* and as a member of technical committee of several international conferences. She has also chaired several technical sessions in various international conferences. She is a senior member of IEEE and an active participant of IEEE activities. She was an Adjunct Professor at the University of Maryland Baltimore campus (UMBC). She has taught graduate and undergraduate courses at UCLA, UMBC, California Institute of Technology, and University of Southern California.

Martin Lages holds a Dipl.Psych. and a Ph.D. in Psychology from the University of Heidelberg, Germany. In 1998 he obtained a D.Phil. in Experimental Psychology at the University of Oxford, UK. From 1997-99 he worked as a Postdoctoral Fellow at the Max Planck Institute for Human Development in Berlin. Since 1999 he is a Lecturer in Psychology at Glasgow University, UK.

Antonio Martínez-Álvarez was born in Granada, Spain in 1976. He received the M.S. and Ph.D. degree in Electronics Engineering by the University of Granada, Spain, in 2002 and 2006, respectively. From 2002-2006 he joined the Department of Computer Architecture and Technology at the University of Granada, Spain. He is currently an Associate Professor with the Department of Computer Technology, University of Alicante, Spain. His main research interests deal with methods and tools for dependable design of digital integrated circuits and FPGAs, high-performance image-processing architectures and embedded systems based on reconfigurable devices. He is also interested in neuroengineering and neuroprosthesis devices. Currently he is working in the design and development of the SHE (Software Hardening Environment).

Olivier Morel received the M.Sc. degree in Computer Vision and Image Processing in the University of Burgundy, in 2002. In November 2005, he received the Ph.D. degree in Computer Vision from the University of Burgundy. Since September 2007, he works as an Associate-Professor in the Vision Department of the Le2i Lab. His main research interests are polarization imaging, 3D vision, catadioptric vision and applications of these technics to robotics.

Christian Morillas received the B.Sc. In Computer Science in 2002, the M.Sc. in Computer Engineering degree in 2004, with Hardware Design major, and the Ph.D. degree in 2006, all from the University of Granada, Spain. He is currently an Associate Professor at the Department of Computer Architecture and Technology of the same university. His research interest lies in hardware architectures and embedded systems for image processing, specially aimed at low-vision aids and visual neuroprostheses.

Heiko Neumann studied Computer Science at the Technical University of Berlin and received a Doctoral degree in Computer Science At the University of Hamburg in 1988. He received the Habilitation degree in 1995. Since 1995, he is appointed as a full Professor in the Department of Neural Information Processing at Ulm University. He spent several research sabbaticals at the Center for Adaptive Systems at Boston University. He is co-Founder and co-Director of the Competence Center of Perception and Interactive Technologies (PIT) at Ulm University. His research interests include neural modeling in computational and cognitive neuroscience, biologically inspired computational vision, and various aspects of the mechanisms underlying visual perception.

Christopher Wing Hong Ngau received his Bachelor degree from the University of Nottingham in 2008. He is currently pursuing his PhD at the University of Nottingham Malaysia Campus. His research interests are in the fields of visual processing, hardware architectures, reconfigurable computing, and wireless sensor network.

Francisco Pelayo received the B.Sc. degree in Physics in 1982, the M.Sc. degree in Electronics in 1983, and the Ph.D. degree in 1989, all from the University of Granada, Spain. He is currently a full Professor at the Department of Computer Architecture and Technology (http://atc.ugr.es) of the same University. He has worked in the areas of VLSI design and test, artificial neural networks and fuzzy systems. His current research interest lies in the fields of hardware and HW–SW design of bioinspired processing and control systems, robotics, and neuroengineering.

Matthieu Perreira Da Silva is Associate Professor in the IVC team of the IRRCyN Lab. He received a M.Sc in Image Processing in 2001 and a Ph.D. in Computer Science and applications in 2010, both from the University of La Rochelle, France. From 2001 to 2006 he worked as a R&D engineer in a private company dealing with biometric identification. From 2006 to mid 2011, he was successively engineer, Ph.D. student, and Teaching Assistant at the University of La Rochelle. His research interests include human perception, visual attention, human computer interaction, artificial curiosity, autonomous machine learning, image processing, and computer vision.

Florian Raudies studied Computer Science as a major and Electrical Engineering as a minor subject at the Ulm University in Germany, earning a Diploma (equivalent to a Master's) degree in 2006. He then received a scholarship from the Graduate Program in "Mathematical Analysis of Evolution, Information, and Complexity" at the University of Ulm and graduated with a doctoral degree in 2010. In March 2010 he joined the Center of Excellence for Learning in Education, Science and Technology (CELEST) at Boston University as a Postdoctoral Associate. In March 2012 he was appointed a Research Assistant Professor in the recently funded Center for Computational Neuroscience and Neural Technology (CompNet) at Boston University. His research focuses on the development of biologically inspired models of motion processing for visual navigation.

Helge Ritter is head of the Neuroinformatics Group at the Faculty of Technology, Bielefeld University. His main interests are principles of neural computation and intelligent systems, in particular cognitive robots with "manual intelligence." In 1999, Helge Ritter was awarded the SEL Alcatel Research Prize and in 2001 the Leibniz Prize of the German Research Foundation DFG. He is co-founder and Director of the Bielefeld Cognitive Robotics Laboratory (CoR-Lab) and coordinator of the Bielefeld Excellence Cluster "Cognitive Interaction Technology" (CITEC).

Antonio J. Rodríguez-Sánchez is currently a senior research fellow in the Department of Computer Science at the University of Innsbruck, Austria. Born in Santiago de Compostela (La Coruña, Spain), he completed his Ph.D. at York University, Toronto, Canada under the supervision of Prof. John Tsotsos on the subject of modeling attention and intermediate areas of the visual cortex. Currently, he is part of the Intelligent and Interactive Systems group under the supervision of Prof. Justus Piater, and his main interests are Computer Vision and Computational Neuroscience. He has been involved in important Computational Neuroscience projects such as NeoVision2 and currently works on EU projects about Robotics and Computer Vision.

Samuel Romero (born 1974) received his Computer Engineering degree from the University of Granada in 1998. After a one year stay at the University of California, Santa Barbara (UCSB), he joined as a fellow the Spanish National Institute of Aerospace Technology (INTA), working on real time control of an experiment for the International Space Station. He joined the research team of the project CORTIVIS in 2001, to develop a cortical neuro-prosthesis for the blind at the University of Granada. He received his PhD degree on Computer Engineering in 2006, and a Master's Degree in Neuroscience in 2007. His research lines and interests include neuroengineering, brain-machine interfacing, and rehabilitation engineering. He currently works as an Associate Professor at the Dept. of Computer Architecture and Technology of the University of Granada (Spain).

Albert L. Rothenstein received an Electronics and Telecommunications Engineering degree from IPTVT, Romania in 1989, an M.Sc. in Computer Science from the University of Toronto in 2002, and a PhD in Computer Science from York University, Toronto, Canada. He is currently a post-doctoral fellow at York University, Toronto, Canada.

Silvio P. Sabatini received the Laurea degree in Electronics Engineering and the Ph.D. in Computer Science from the University of Genoa in 1992 and 1996. He is currently Associate Professor of Bioengineering at the Department of Informatics, Bioengineering, Robotics and Systems of the University of Genoa. In 1995 he promoted the creation of the "Physical Structure of Perception and Computation" (PSPC) Lab to develop models that capture the "physicalist" nature of the information processing occurring in the visual cortex, to understand the signal processing strategies adopted by the brain, and to build novel algorithms and architectures for artificial perception machines. His research interests relate to visual coding and multidimensional signal representation, early-cognitive models for visually-guided behavior, and robot vision. He is author of more than 100 papers in peer-reviewed journals, book chapters, and international conference proceedings.

Thomas Schack is the head of the Neurocognition and Action – Research Group at Bielefeld University (Germany). Dr. Schack's main research interest concerns the basic building blocks and the cognitive architecture of motor action of manual action and complex movements. Especially he is interested in research topics like mental movement representation, mental imagery, the neurocognitive basis of motor control, and cognitive robotics. He received many excellence certificates in the field of cognitive motor control research for instance the Bernstein-Scientific Award in 1996 and the TOYOTA-Scientific Award in 2002. Since 2007 he is a Principal Investigator and Head of the Graduate School in the Center of Excellence "Cognitive Interaction Technology," and he is a Principal Investigator in the Research Institute for Cognition and Robotics (CoR-Lab)at Bielefeld University. Since 2009 he is a managing council member of the International Society of Sportpsychology (ISSP). An important component in Thomas Schack's research laboratories (Cognition and Action-Labs: COALA) is the combination of experimental and modelling methods from psychology, biomechanics, cognitive science and robotics to learn about the cognitive construction and principles of human actions.

Kah Phooi Seng is currently a Professor at Sunway University Malaysia. She was an Associate Professor at the University of Nottingham Malaysia Campus. She received her Bachelor and PhD degrees from the University of Tasmania in 1997 and 2001, respectively. Her research interests are in the fields of intelligent visual processing, biometrics and multi-biometrics, artificial intelligence, and signal processing.

Fabio Solari received the Laurea degree in Electronic Engineering in 1995 and the Ph.D. in Computer Science in 1999 at the University of Genoa, Italy. Since 2005 he has been appointed as Assistant Professor of Computer Science at the University of Genoa. His research activity concerns the study of visual perception with the aim to develop computational models of cortical vision processing, to devise novel bio-inspired computer vision algorithms, and to design virtual reality environments for ecological visual stimulations. In particular, his research interests are related to neuromorphic architectures of visual cortex, space-variant visual processing, motion and depth estimation and interpretation, active vision systems, and augmented reality systems for the visuo-motor coordination in the peripersonal space.

Oleg Strogan received his Master degree in the program "Intellectual systems of control" at the National University of "Kyiv-Mohyla Academy" in Kyiv, Ukraine in 2005. He also did a specialist degree qualification work on the "Exploration of differential schemes in modeling and forecasting of substance transmission." From 2005 to 2009 he was a Research Assistant in the research programs of CCM (Centro de Ciências Matemáticas), University of Madeira, and of the NEMO project, where he implemented and tested communication models and algorithms for numerical computations, visual data representation and data processing. Since January 2010 he is a member of the Neurocognition and Action-Biomechanics Group at the Faculty of Psychology and Sport Sciences at Bielefeld University, Germany. He is currently a programmer at the Excellence Cluster "Cognitive Interaction Technology" (CITEC) implementing a hierarchical clustering method for measuring mental representation structures in long-term memory and on complex movement studies in classical ballet and golf.

Hisashi Toyoshima joined Japan Technical Software Corporation (JTS). He completed the Doctoral Course of Graduate School of Engineering, Hokkai-Gakuen University in 2006. He is developing computer software at JTS and researching at Hokkai-Gakuen University.

John Tsotsos is Distinguished Research Professor of Vision Science at York University and hold the Canada Research Chair in Computational Vision. He received York's Inaugural President's Research Excellence Award, is also a Fellow of the Royal Society of Canada, has been a Fellow of the Canadian Institute of Advanced Research and received several other awards. Born in Windsor, Ontario, he holds a doctoral degree from Computer Science at the University of Toronto where he is cross-appointed in Computer Science and Ophthalmology and Vision Sciences. His research spans computer science, psychology and neuroscience and is focused on visual attention and visual object recognition in both man and robots as well as mobile robotics and assistive technology.

Hongfang Wang obtained her BEng degree in Polymer Material Science and Engineering from Xi'an Jiaotong University, China, and her MSc degree in Informatics from University of Edinburgh, UK. In 2008 she obtained her PhD degree in Computer Science from University of York, UK. Before she started her MSc study in Edinburgh, she worked for six years as a Computer Software Engineer in China. Since 2007, she worked as a postdoctoral researcher in the School of Psychology and the Institute of Neuroscience and Psychology, University of Glasgow, UK.

Takahiro Yamanoi is a Professor of Department of Life Science and Technology, Faculty of Engineering, Hokkai-Gakuen University. He had graduated from the Doctoral Course of Graduated School of Engineering, Hokkaido University in 1979. Soon he had joined the Faculty of Engineering, Hokkaido University as a Research Assistant. During this period in 1984-1985, he obtained a scholarship from the Ministry of Education of France, and stated at Laboratory GRAI, the University of Bordeaux I in France as a visiting researcher. After returned to Hokkaido University, he moved to the Faculty of Engineering of Hokkai-Gakuen University as an Associate Professor in 1987, and then he became a Professor in 1989. During this period in 1999-2000, he stayed at Faculty of Medicine, Aix-Marseille University II in France as a visiting Professor. He was a director of Administration of Hokkai-Gakuen University from 2002 to 2006 and a Dean of Faculty of Engineering from 2009-2012. His main researches are on spatiotemporal activities in the human brain, brain computer interface, and analytic hierarchy process.

Index

I

K

L

M

N

O

P

Q

R

S

T

V